REFERENCE GUIDE TO UNITED STATES MILITARY HISTORY 1815–1865

[V.2]

CHARLES REGINALD SHRADER
General Editor

Facts On File

REFERENCE GUIDE TO UNITED STATES MILITARY HISTORY 1815–1865

Facts On File, Inc.
460 Park Avenue South
New York NY 100016
USA

Library of Congress Cataloging-in-Publication Data
Reference guide to United States military history.
Includes bibliographical references (v. 1, p. 265–268) and index.
Contents: v. [1]. 1607–1815 — v. [2]. 1815–1865.
1. United States—History, Military—To 1900.
I. Shrader, Charles R.
E181.R34 1991 973 90-25673
ISBN 0-8160-1836-7 (v. 1)
ISBN 0-8160-1837-5 (v. 2)

A British CIP catalogue record for this book is available from the British Library.

Composition and Manufacturing by the Maple-Vail Book Manufacturing Group
Printed in the United States of America

10 9 8 7 6 5 4 3 2 1

This book is printed on acid-free paper.

Contents

Text Chapter Authors

Chapter 1	Charles R. Shrader Lieutenant Colonel (Ret.), U.S. Army
Chapters 2, 3 & 4	Tommy R. Young II, Ph. D. Deputy Command Historian Air Force Communications Command
Chapter 5	Michael A. Hughes, Ph.D.
Chapters 6 & 7	William G. Robertson, Ph.D. Combat Studies Institute U.S. Army Command and General Staff College

List of Contributors

Ted Alexander
Antietam National Battlefield

Robert K. Angwin
Captain, U.S. Air Force
U.S. Air Force Academy

Louise A. Arnold-Friend
U.S. Army Military History Institute

Daniel T. Bailey
University of Wisconsin—Madison

Robert H. Berlin, Ph.D.
Combat Studies Institute
U.S. Army Command and General Staff College

M. Guy Bishop, Ph.D.
Seaver Center for Western History Research
Natural History Museum of Los Angeles County

Alan C. Cate
Captain, U.S. Army
U.S. Military Academy

Jeffrey S. Cohen
U.S. Air Force Academy

Leo J. Daugherty III
Ohio State University

James Sanders Day
Captain, U.S. Army
U.S. Military Academy

George B. Eaton
Captain, U.S. Army
U.S. Military Academy

Uzal W. Ent
Brigadier General (Ret.), PNG

Peter R. Faber
Major, U.S. Air Force
Yale University

Louis D. F. Frasche
Colonel (Ret.), U.S. Army

Russel A. Hart
Ohio State University

Jonathan M. House
Major, U.S. Army

Michael A. Hughes, Ph.D.

Richard F. Kehrberg
University of Wisconsin—Madison

Roger D. Launius, Ph.D.
Chief Historian
National Aeronautics and Space Administration

Stephen J. Lofgren
U.S. Army Center of Military History

Ed Martin
Captain, U.S. Air Force
U.S. Air Force Academy

Kevin McKedy
Captain, U.S. Army
U.S. Military Academy

Richard B. Meixsel
Ohio State University

Tamara Moser Melia, Ph.D.
Naval Historical Center

Deborah L. Mesplay
Southern Illinois University

Ralph P. Millsap, Jr.
Captain, U.S. Air Force
U.S. Air Force Academy

Thomas C. Mulligan
Ohio State University

Matthew Oyos
Ohio State University

Mark Pitcavage
Ohio State University

Carol Reardon, Ph.D.
University of Georgia

Michael J. Reed
U.S. Air Force Academy

William G. Robertson, Ph.D.
Combat Studies Institute
U.S. Army Command & General Staff College

Charles R. Shrader
Lieutenant Colonel (Ret.), U.S. Army

Lynn L. Sims, Ph.D.
Army Historian
Fort Lee, Virginia

Christine L. Stevens

Carol E. Stokes
Command Historian
U.S. Army Signal Center

Thomas W. Sweeney
Colonel, U.S. Army
Director U.S. Army Military History Institute

Anne Cipriano Venzon, Ph.D.

Steve R. Waddell
Texas A&M University

Grant H. Walker
Major, U.S. Army
Senior Instructor, U.S. Naval Academy

R. John Warsinske
2nd Lieutenant, U.S. Army Reserve

Joseph W. A. Whitehorne
Lieutenant Colonel (Ret.), U.S. Army
Lord Fairfax Community College

Karen S. Wilhelm
Captain, U.S. Air Force
U.S. Air Force Academy

Tommy R. Young II, Ph.D.
Deputy Command Historian
Air Force Communications Command

Photographic Services
by Jim Enos, Carlisle,
Pennsylvania

Introduction

The 50 years from 1815 to 1865 comprise an era of significant growth and development for the United States, an era in which fundamental national values, attitudes, and institutions took clear form. National attention was focused on westward expansion, industrialization, and the great issues of slavery and states rights. Contemporaneously, the military and naval forces of the United States grew and matured. In military terms, the era can be divided into four periods: 1815–45, the so-called Thirty Years Peace; 1846–48, the Mexican War; 1848–60; and 1861–65, the Civil War. Each of these periods was characterized by distinctive military threats, organizational structures, doctrines, and technology.

Although the threat of invasion by any of the major European powers all but disappeared after 1815, the United States found that a return to the naive, unarmed state that existed before 1812 was not possible. The period between the War of 1812 and the Mexican War is often called the Thirty Years Peace, but the military forces of the United States, principally the army, undertook three major campaigns—the First Seminole War (1817–19), the Black Hawk War (1832), and the Second Seminole War (1835–42)—and countless lesser engagements against small, but widespread and persistent, Indian uprisings east of the Mississippi River. At the same time, the small U.S. Navy patrolled and occasionally fought to protect the nation's growing commerce on the high seas, particularly in the Mediterranean and the Caribbean. The most important technological developments in this period were the percussion cap for firearms and steam propulsion for naval vessels. However, the lack of any identifiable major external threat inhibited major organizational or doctrinal change in the armed forces.

The Mexican War (1846–48) posed new challenges for the military and naval forces of the United States. Although Mexico posed only a minor threat to the United States, the diplomatic conflict between the two countries provoked a strong U.S. reaction. Faced with its first overseas war, the United States evolved new and larger organizations within its army and navy and developed new doctrine to deal with the problems of a fairly sophisticated foe. Incorporated into the U.S. military agenda were overseas lines of communications, amphibious operations, and such technological innovations as mobile artillery, railroads, telegraph service, and steamships.

The 13 years (1848–60) between the end of the Mexican War and the start of the Civil War saw few external changes in U.S. military and naval affairs. The maintenance of civil order and the policing of Indians on the expanding frontiers and the protection of U.S. seaborne commerce were the main tasks at hand. However, territorial expansion in the wake of the war with Mexico added new dimensions to the challenges faced by both the army and the navy, and the impact of continuing technological development was especially profound. In particular, the navy had to cope with the advent of the steel ship, the screw propeller, and the ironclad as well as a new generation of naval guns. For the army, the technological innovations were fewer but nonetheless significant, particularly the transition from smoothbore to rifling in both small arms and artillery. For the most part, however, military organization and doctrine remained in 1860 much the same as they had been in 1848.

All of this changed, of course, with the coming of the Civil War in 1861. The threat posed by Southern armed defense of states rights, the right of secession, and slavery was of an entirely different nature and magnitude from what had gone before. Mass armies and vast theaters of war required significant changes in both the organization of military forces and the doctrines governing their employment. The war also spurred the application of modern technology to war, not only in the form of new weapons but also in such fields as communications, industrial production, transportation, and medicine. These developments, too, precipitated further changes in organization and doctrine—changes that laid the foundations for the U.S. armed forces of the early 20th century.

In large part, the history of the United States is a history of military establishment—the story of military leaders and the forces they have commanded in peace and war. The *Reference Guide to United States Military History* seeks to provide a fresh perspective on this important story. As with each of the other four chronologically organized volumes of the *Reference Guide,* this volume comprises a thorough examination of the role of the military and its leaders in American life during a given period. Introduced by a short description of the organization, equipment, and doctrine of the military forces of the United States and those of its allies and opponents, the narrative portion of the volume includes an extended discussion of the course of events and the development of U.S. military institutions from 1815 to 1865. The seven narrative chapters are supplemented by biographical profiles of the military and naval leaders of the period, detailed descriptions of the principal battles and events, and discussions of special topics. The text of the volume is enhanced by maps and illustrations depicting the nation's military leaders, military life, battles, and other events. This survey of U.S. history as viewed through the perspective of military activities provides a unique reference work for school and library use and should appeal to a variety of readers.

Obviously, every detail of the military history of the United States cannot be addressed even in a five-volume series. The editors of the *Reference Guide to United States Military History* have selected for emphasis those aspects that seem to be most important for understanding the course of U.S. military history and the role of the military in American society. Special attention is given to such key issues as the role of armed forces in a democratic society and their optimal size, nature, and functions. Similarly emphasized are the themes of citizen (militia) forces versus professional (standing) forces, competition among the various elements of the U.S. military establishment for resources and prestige, and ways in which U.S. attitudes toward such matters have differed in time of peace and in time of crisis. The attitudes toward soldiers, sailors, and their leaders displayed by U.S. political leaders and ordinary citizens is another important consideration of the *Reference Guide.* Throughout the five volumes, special care has been taken to highlight the independent nature of the U.S. soldier and sailor and the conditions under which he or she was required to operate. The unique solutions devised to coordinate military strategy, the organization of forces, and the use of technology to meet perceived threats are also investigated in some depth. The adaptation of technology to military ends also occupies an especially important place, in view of a consistent U.S. preference for substituting technology for manpower. Another prominent theme is the perpetual and characteristic failure of the United States to prepare adequately for war in time of peace. By repeatedly returning to these themes, the editors hope to give focus to the series and better explain the course and importance of military affairs in U.S. history.

Those who have contributed to this as well as the other volumes of the *Reference Guide to United States Military History* are among the best young scholars of U.S. military, naval, and air-power history. Some are military officers; others are civilian historians in government service, professors in colleges and universities, or independent scholars from across the nation. The editors have worked diligently to make this volume as complete, accurate, and readable as possible. However, errors of fact and interpretation are inevitable in any work of this magnitude. Readers are therefore encouraged to bring any misinformation to the attention of the editors for correction in subsequent editions.

Charles R. Shrader, Ph.D.
General Editor
Reference Guide to United States Military History

PART I

The Organization of American Armed Forces and Their History

1

The Organization of Military Forces: 1815–1865

At last free of significant outside threats, the youthful United States began a long period of national growth and development after 1815. Americans rejected both involvement in world affairs and the consequent need for large standing military forces. These preferences were reinforced by a strain of antimilitarism that found strong support in the Jacksonian era of democratic individualism. Nevertheless, the armed forces of the United States made great progress during the period 1815–65. Basic institutions of command and control as well as functional, tactical, and administrative organizations were established. The rapidly changing technology of the period was adopted to military ends. At the end of the period, all of the nation's institutions—military, political, social, economic, and spiritual—were tested by the fires of a great civil war, and they emerged refined and strengthened.

DEFENSE POLICY

The threat of conquest by European military power was ended effectively with the conclusion of the War of 1812. The long-distance deployment of sufficient strength to overcome even weak U.S. resistance proved all but impossible for even major European powers such as Britain, France, or Spain. Although the United States faced minor disagreements with the British and the challenge of the crumbling of the Spanish empire in the Americas, the only significant external threat was posed by Mexico. The annexation of Texas by the United States in 1845 sparked the long-expected open warfare of 1846. Although a decisive U.S. victory over Mexico ended any real possibility of a major Mexican riposte, the military forces of the United States would be required to keep a careful watch on the border well into the 20th century.

Internal Threats

Internal disturbances proved more troublesome. The encroachment of the expanding white population on Indian groups precipitated frequent small-scale conflicts. By mid-century, the settlements east of the Mississippi River were secure, but discord with native Americans continued along an increasingly well-defined line of settlement on the Western plains. The subjugation of the mounted Plains Indians would require the remainder of the century. By far the most serious threat to the continued existence of the United States in the 19th century emerged rather suddenly in 1861. The secession of the Southern states and the consequent war to restore the Union, although anticipated, could not be acted upon in advance. The gravity of the threat was recognized quickly, however, and the danger was decisively eliminated after four long years of terrible internal strife.

STRATEGIES

U.S. military strategy for most of the period 1815–65 was essentially defensive. The small regular army was designed to keep the peace by guarding the borders, suppressing civil disorder, and preventing Indian attacks. In the unlikely event of a major crisis such as invasion by a foreign power, the regular army would hold the line until a citizen (militia) army could be formed. In theory, the militia, or nation-in-arms, would constitute the principal protection for the territory and sovereignty of the United States. The navy was designed to protect U.S. citizens and U.S. commercial enterprises aboard. In a major crisis, the navy would assist in the protection of U.S. coasts and harbors, but the army would play the key role in coastal defense, the ships of the navy being reserved for raiding the enemy's sea lines of communication rather than directly confronting its main battle fleet. Accordingly, there seemed to be little need throughout the period for either a large standing army or a large fleet in being.

Public Attitudes

Before 1861, U.S. citizens and their elected representatives gave little thought to the doings of the army or the navy and usually considered them in a negative light if at all. The military services were generally viewed as citadels of decidedly undemocratic hierarchy and privilege inconsistent with the American self-image of rugged individualism and equality. The lack of any demonstrable threat to the survival of the nation and the focus of attention on developing the new lands of the West resulted in long periods of neglect for U.S. military forces interspersed with provisory bursts of interest and activity when threats were suddenly perceived.

The distaste for large standing forces was manifest in persistent congressional attempts to limit the size of the army and the navy, often below levels necessary for them to perform their internal security and minimal external defense tasks efficiently. Attitudes began to shift somewhat in the 1840s as the idea of "Manifest Destiny" began to take hold. The successful performance of both services in the war with Mexico and in the annexation of extensive additional territories brought some recognition of the necessity for an adequate defense force. However, sectional conflict during the 1850s held down military appropriations and limited the growth of the army and navy. It was only with the coming of the Civil War that military affairs became a national preoccupation in both the North and the South, and soldiers, particularly those who were efficient and effective, achieved public acclaim and support. The large numbers of men on both sides who donned uniforms between 1861 and 1865 served to place military affairs in a prominent and permanent place in the national consciousness.

Budget Levels

Public expenditures on defense and the consequent size of forces maintained reflect the prevailing perception of threat and the costs of the period's technology. From 1816 to 1861, there was a slow but steady increase in the amounts included in the U.S. federal budget for the maintenance of the army and the navy. During that period total federal expenditures amounted to $1,510,650,000, of which $854,941,000 (or about 56.6 percent of the total) was dedicated to national security: $469,858,000 for the army (including $39,143,900 for forts, arsenals, and armories), $306,531,000 for the navy, and $78,552,000 for veterans' compensation and pensions. As might be expected, federal expenditures on the army and navy increased substantially in time of war. The Mexican War (1846–48) cost $118,500,000 ($100,000,000 in direct expenses, $15,000,000 to Mexico as compensation for California and New Mexico, and $3,500,000 in damage claims against Mexico assumed by the United States). The army budget escalated from $22,989,000 in 1861 to $1,031,323,361 in 1865. In the same period, navy expenditures rose from $12,421,000 to $122,617,434. The U.S. War Department expenditures for the entire Civil War totaled some $2,739,000,000 while navy expenditures were approximately $327,000,000.

LAND FORCES

The tasks assigned to the army between 1815 and 1865 were mainly defensive and oriented toward the maintenance of internal security as the nation expanded westward. The first priority was the coastal defense of the United States, and considerable money and effort were invested in erecting and manning a system of coastal fortification. The Rivers and Harbors Act of 1824 put the army's Corps of Engineers in control of the nation's seaports and inland waterways, a mission it still performs today. Yet the army's most pressing task was to facilitate the westward expansion of Euro-American settlement by controlling the native Indian groups. And as the territorial area of the United States increased, so did the responsibilities of the army, which not only played a major role in maintaining public order, but also explored and surveyed the newly acquired territories. Two major conflicts during the period required the army to perform more purely military missions: the defeat of Mexico and the subsequent occupation and military government of Mexican territory and the preservation of the Union by defeat of the armed rebellion of the Confederate states.

Size

Realistically, the United States had no need for a large army for most of the 19th century. A small standing force to deal with the Indians, control the borders, and preserve a semblance of military expertise was sufficient. Although its authorized strength grew slowly from 1815 to 1865, the U.S. Army remained quite small and expanded only temporarily to meet the demands of major campaigns against the Indians, the war with Mexico, and, of course, the four years of the Civil War.

In 1821, the authorized strength of the army was set at 6,183 officers and men. It remained near that figure for many years, with the actual strength always considerably less. When the conflict with the Seminole escalated in 1836, Congress increased the authorized strength. By 1840, the actual strength of the regular army had grown to 789 officers and 11,541 enlisted men. After 1842, the authorized strength declined to approximately 8,600, but with the outbreak of open hostility with Mexico in 1846, Congress doubled the strength of the regular army and authorized Pres. James K. Polk to call for volunteers. Altogether, a total of 104,000 men (60,000 volunteers, 12,000 militia, and 32,000 regulars) were raised for the war, but the total under arms at any one time did not exceed 50,000. By 1848, the strength of the regular army had reached 2,865 officers and 44,454 men but was soon reduced to a peacetime strength of some 9,878 officers and men. In the 1850s, with the addition of considerable territory in the West and increased westward migration, additional mobile forces were needed to control the hostile Plains Indians. The authorized strength of the army was expanded, and by Jan. 1, 1861, the regular army of the United States numbered 1,098 officers and 15,304 men.

The Civil War saw tremendous increases in the number of men under arms. The distribution of population in 1861 heavily favored the North. The free white population of the North was nearly 19,000,000, while that of the South was only about 5,500,000 (plus approximately 3,500,000 slaves). The South had about 1,140,000 white males of military age (15–40 years old) to the North's 4,000,000. The South got maximum strength in the field early in the war then saw it drain away. The military forces of the Confederate states numbered some 500,000 at the end of 1862 but declined to only 230,000 men present for duty at the end of 1863. By the end of 1864, only 100,000 Confederate soldiers were present for duty. By contrast, the Union army experienced a steady buildup. In the four months from the fall of Fort Sumter to Aug. 3, 1861, the U.S. Army grew 27 times its original strength. By the end of the war in 1865, the Union had more than 1,000,000 men in the field. Overall, the United States mobilized some 1,556,000 men (2,900,000 total enlistments) while the Confederacy fielded an aggregate total strength of about 1,000,000 men.

Stationing

The concentration of the army into larger units (brigades, divisions, corps, and armies) for such major undertakings as the Second Seminole War (1835–42), the Mexican War, and the Civil War was only temporary. The reality for most of the period was the dispersion of individual companies and sometimes even smaller units at many small, isolated, and often temporary forts scattered along the eastern seaboard, the Gulf Coast, the Great Lakes, and the advancing western frontier. After 1848, small units were also stationed on the West Coast. In the 1850s, about four-fifths of the army was stationed on the frontier, engaged in constant operations against the Indians. On Jan. 1, 1861, the U.S. Army comprised 198 companies. Of these, 183 were scattered at 79 posts along the western frontiers from Texas to Minnesota and from Puget Sound to southern California. The remaining 15 companies manned posts along the Atlantic coast and the Canadian border and at 23 arsenals.

Commanders in Chief, U.S. Armed Forces, 1809–1865

Name	*Dates of Service*
James Madison	March 1809-March 1817
James Monroe	March 1817-March 1825
John Quincy Adams	March 1825-March 1829
Andrew Jackson	March 1829-March 1837
Martin Van Buren	March 1837-March 1841
William Henry Harrison	March 1841-April 1841
John Tyler	April 1841-March 1845
James Knox Polk	March 1845-March 1849
Zachary Taylor	March 1849-July 1850
Millard Fillmore	July 1850-March 1853
Franklin Pierce	March 1853-March 1857
James Buchanan	March 1857-March 1861
Abraham Lincoln	March 1861-April 1865

Command and Control

The fundamental issue of civilian control of the military was already decided by 1815. In accordance with the U.S. Constitution, the president stood at the top of the organizational pyramid as the commander in chief. Directly under the president was the secretary of war, who administered the army and directed its operations with the assistance of a number of civilian clerks. The major unresolved issue of higher command and control in the early 19th century centered around the role of the senior uniformed officer of the army. In the immediate aftermath of the War of 1812, two major generals were authorized, one to command each of the two territorial (administrative) divisions into which the army was divided. Yet in March 1821, Congress prescribed that there should be only one major general. The perceived need for a senior professional military adviser led Sec. of War John C. Calhoun to install Maj. Gen. Jacob Brown as commanding general of the army. Congress determined that the commanding general of the army could hold office until retirement and would supervise army expenditures and oversee efficiency, discipline, and conduct. The question of the relationship between the secretary of war and the commanding general was left unresolved. It remained unclear whether the commanding general was merely an adviser to the secretary of war or whether he exercised genuine command of the army.

From July 5, 1841, until shortly after the beginning of the Civil War, the commanding general was Bvt. Lt. Gen. Winfield Scott. Scott frequently contended for supremacy with various secretaries of war, removing his headquarters to New York when dissatisfied with the incumbent civilian

Gen. Henry W. Halleck was promoted to general in chief of the U.S. Army in 1862, after commanding the Department of the Missouri and the Department of the Mississippi. (U.S. Army Military History Institute)

leadership. In the early 1850s, Sec. of War Jefferson Davis, himself a strong-willed individual, gave special attention to clarifying the relationships among the president, the secretary of war, and the commanding general. In 1855, the commanding general was redesignated as general in chief and stripped of command and control over the administration and supply of the army, responsibilities that reverted to the secretary of war. The secretary now looked to the staff bureau chiefs, especially the adjutant general, for assistance.

The aged and infirm Scott retired on Nov. 1, 1861, and was replaced by Maj. Gen. George B. McClellan, who was in turn replaced by Maj. Gen. Henry W. Halleck in July 1862. In 1864, the general in chief temporarily regained command and unlimited authority over the army. In February 1864, Congress revived the rank of lieutenant general; in March, Ulysses S. Grant was promoted and made general in chief. Grant reported to Sec. of War Edwin M. Stanton and Pres. Abraham Lincoln on the broad aspects of strategic plans and logistical as well as personnel requirements. He had a small staff of his own to plan the conduct of operations and assist him in controlling the 17 different field commands and 500,000 men under his direction. Grant communicated directly with Maj. Gen. George G. Meade, commander of the Army of the Potomac, with whose headquarters his own were located. He communicated with the other army commanders through Halleck, who remained in Washington to act as chief of staff and who worked well with Grant. The system so laboriously constructed during the Civil War was dismantled in 1865, and there was a return to the earlier, problematic general-in-chief system. The issues surrounding supreme command over the army thus remained undecided until the Root reforms of the early 20th century.

Secretaries of War, 1814–1867

Name	*Dates of Service*
James Monroe	September 1814-March 1815
William H. Crawford	August 1815-October 1816
John C. Calhoun	October 1817-March 1825
Majees Barbour	March 1825-May 1828
Peter B. Porter	May 1828-March 1829
John H. Eaton	March 1829-June 1831
Lewis Cass	August 1831-October 1836
Benjamin F. Butler	October 1836-March 1837
Joel R. Poinsett	March 1837-March 1841
John Bell	March 1841-September 1841
John C. Spencer	October 1841-March 1843
James M. Porter	March 1843-January 1844
William Wilkins	February 1844-March 1845
William L. Marcy	March 1845-March 1849
George W. Crawford	March 1849-July 1850
Charles M. Conrad	August 1850-March 1853
Jefferson Davis	March 1853-March 1857
John B. Floyd	March 1857-December 1860
Joseph Holt	January 1861-March 1861
Simon Cameron	March 1861-January 1862
Edwin M. Stanton	January 1862-August 1867

Staff

The basic outline for the staff system of the U.S. Army was established early in the 19th century. In 1815, provision was made for a number of staff departments to operate independently under the direction of the secretary of war. By May 1846, the staff of the army included three general officers and nine staff departments (adjutant general, inspector general, quartermaster, subsistence, medical, pay, ordnance, the Corps of Engineers, and the Corps of Topographical Engineers) with 259 officers and 17 military storekeepers. In 1861, Congress provided for an assistant secretary of war and authorized additional staff department personnel. The judge advocate general was given bureau status on July 17, 1862, and the Corps of Topographical Engineers was merged with the Corps of Engineers on Mar. 3, 1863. On the same date, the separate Signal Corps was established. A provost marshal general's department was also created to manage the draft.

The heads of staff departments, or bureau chiefs as they were sometimes known, reported directly to the secretary of war and were responsible for various aspects of the army's administration. For example, the logistical support of the army was entrusted to the heads of the four "supply" departments: the quartermaster general, responsible for clothing and equipment, forage, animals, transportation, and housing; the commissary general of subsistence, responsible for rations; the chief of ordnance, responsible for weapons, ammunition, and miscellaneous related equipment including accoutrements; and the surgeon general, responsible for medical supplies and for evacuation, treatment, and hospitalization of the wounded.

Although usually augmented in time of war, the staff departments remained seriously undermanned throughout the period, both at their headquarters and in the field. Before the Civil War, the staff departments had very few officers and noncommissioned officers in the field with troop units. The officers of the various supply departments, for example, were to be found almost exclusively in staff positions in Washington, at the permanent depots, or at the headquarters of the several geographical departments into which the army was organized. The small number of staff department officers meant that at lower levels (regiment, brigade, and even division) the various functions were often performed by officers drawn from the line. Although there were a few trained staff officers and noncommissioned officers, specialized units did not exist, and for the most part the army relied on hired civilians or line soldiers to perform essential support tasks.

Many of the administrative and supply bureaus developed high professional standards and proficiency due to the long tenure of the chiefs of some departments (some of whom served from the end of the War of 1812 up to the Civil War). Yet several issues retarded the full development of an integrated support system for the army. The uncertain division of authority and responsibility between the secretary of war and the commanding general of the army placed the bureau chiefs in the enviable position of maintaining their own independence by playing one superior against the other. The two most difficult problems were maintaining effective central planning and coordination among the bureaus and delegating authority between "staff" and "line" (that is, establishing the subordination of the officers of the staff departments to the chief of their department rather than to the field commander whom they served). As was the case with the relationship of the secretary of war and the commanding general of the army, these issues would not be solved until the Root reforms of the early 20th century.

Administrative Structure

Between 1815 and 1865, the U.S. Army was organized into a varying number of geographical "departments," several of which might be grouped into a territorial "division" (not to be confused with a tactical division). The military department was the basic organizational unit for administrative and logistical purposes, and the commander of each department dealt directly with the secretary of war, the commanding general of the army, and the bureau chiefs in Washington. At the end of the War of 1812, two divisions were created: the Northern Division (with four departments) and the Southern Division (with five departments). In 1821, the Northern and Southern divisions were replaced by the Eastern and Western departments. These were replaced in turn in 1842 by nine smaller geographical departments, which, after the Mexican War, were grouped into three divisions: East, West, and Pacific. By 1861, there were six independent departments: East, West, Texas, New Mexico, Utah, and Pacific. The system of geographically oriented administrative divisions/departments was retained during the Civil War and continued to play a role in the administrative and logistical support of the armies in the field. The number of departments increased, the boundaries changed, and it was not unusual to group several geographical departments under a military "division" headquarters. Frequently, commanders such as Grant and William T. Sherman simultaneously held command of both field armies and one or more of the geographical divisions/departments.

Senior Officers* of the U.S. Army, 1815–1869

Name	*Dates of Service*
Maj. Gen. Jacob Brown	June 1815-February 1828
Maj. Gen. Alexander Macomb	February 1828-June 1841
Maj. Gen. Winfield Scott[1]	July 1841-November 1861
Maj. Gen. George B. McClellan	November 1861-March 1862
Maj. Gen. Henry W. Halleck	July 1862-March 1864
Lt. Gen. Ulysses S. Grant[2]	March 1864-March 1869

*designated as commanding general of the army, 1821–1855; general in chief, 1855–1865.

[1]brevet lieutenant general from Mar. 29, 1847

[2]general from July 25, 1866

Tactical Organization

Regiments and companies (sometimes designated batteries in artillery units and troops in cavalry units) were the basic tactical building blocks throughout the period. The internal structure of regiments and companies as well as the number of officers, noncommissioned officers, and enlisted men authorized for each type of company or regiment fluctuated significantly until the Civil War, when more or less standard organizations were prescribed. It should be kept in mind, however, that few units ever had present for duty the authorized number of officers and men. Detached service, recruiting shortfalls, desertions, and, in time of war, casualties served to keep the actual duty strength of all army units well below their authorized strength throughout the period.

The size of the company varied widely between 1815 and 1865. Typically, the number of privates was increased in time of war and then reduced when peace came. The number of privates in an infantry company, for example, ranged from 42 (in 1821 and 1848) to 100 (in 1846). Although the actual number of officers and men present for duty at any given time varied greatly, the "standard" Union infantry company in the Civil War was authorized 1 captain, 1 first lieutenant, 1 second lieutenant, 1 first sergeant, 4 sergeants, 8 corporals, 2 musicians, 1 wagoner, and 82 privates. Confederate infantry companies were similarly organized. As the war wore on, it was more common on both sides to find companies of 35–40 men. Civil War cavalry companies, or troops, were authorized 60 privates (Confederate) or 72 privates (Union). Each Union artillery battery of six guns at full war strength was authorized 1 captain, 3 lieutenants, 150 men, and 88 horses. Horse artillery batteries, usually attached to each calvary brigade, had the same number of guns, officers, and men but had 140 horses since all cannoneers were mounted.

Throughout the period, the allocation of 10 companies per regiment remained fairly stable but the number of regiments of various types changed frequently. The reorganization of the army in March 1815 provided for an army composed of 8 infantry regiments, 1 rifle regiment, 1 regiment of light artillery, and an 8–battalion corps of artillery to man permanent fortifications. In 1821, the 8th Infantry was eliminated, the 6th Infantry and the Rifle Regiment were merged, and the Light Artillery Regiment, the Corps of Artillery, and the Ordnance Corps were consolidated into four artillery regiments each with 8 foot or garrison companies and 1 light company. The foot artillery remained essentially infantry through the Civil War. The provision for one company of light artillery in each regiment remained a dead letter until 1838 when Sec. of War Joel B. Poinsett approved the formation of light artillery companies complete with the necessary horses, field guns, and ammunition wagons.

In May 1833, the battalion of mounted rangers raised for the Black Hawk War was added to the regular army as the Regiment of Dragoons to protect the overland routes to the West. Another regiment of dragoons was added in 1836. In 1838, Congress added an eleventh company to each regiment of artillery and the 8th Infantry was reactivated. At the beginning of the war with Mexico, in May 1846, a regiment of mounted riflemen and a company of sappers, miners, and pontoniers were added to the existing 8 regiments of infantry, 2 regiments of dragoons, and 4 regiments of artillery. In February 1847, Congress voted an additional 9 regiments of regular infantry and another regiment of dragoons. In March 1847, each artillery regiment was increased by 2 additional companies and 2 companies per regiment were designated as light artillery.

At the end of the Mexican War, the regular army formations created during the war were disbanded, but the Regiment of Mounted Rifles and the 2 companies added to each artillery regiment were retained. On the recommendation of Secretary of War Davis, 4 new regiments were authorized in March 1855. The 1st and 2d cavalries were formed as were 2 new infantry regiments, the 9th and 10th, both armed with the new percussion-rifled musket. Thus, at the beginning of the Civil War, the regular army of the United States consisted of 4 artillery regiments, 5 mounted regiments, and 10 infantry regiments plus the staff bureaus and the Corps of Engineers. In July 1861, President Lincoln ordered the creation of 9 new regular infantry regiments (the 11th–19th infantries), 1 additional artillery regiment (the 5th Artillery organized entirely with light field batteries), and 1 new cavalry regiment (the 6th Cavalry). The older mounted units were redesignated: the 1st and 2d dragoons became the 1st and 2d cavalries, respectively. The Regiment of Mounted Riflemen became the 3d Cavalry and the old 1st and 2d cavalries were redesignated the 4th and 5th cavalries, respectively.

In addition to the increased regular force, the Union army was also augmented by newly raised volunteer forces. Overall, during the Civil War, the United States raised 2,144 infantry regiments, 61 heavy artillery regiments, 272 cavalry regiments, and 13 engineer regiments plus 9 light infantry battalions, 432 artillery batteries, and a large number of signalmen and other supporting troops. Included in the total were the 1st and 2d regiments of sharpshooters, U.S. Volunteers, and the Invalid Corps, U.S. Volunteers (later redesignated the Veteran Reserve Corps). (These were national volunteer units as opposed to state volunteers.) In addition, the United States raised a national volunteer force of U.S. Colored Troops totaling 186,017 men in 120 regiments of infantry, 12 of heavy artillery, 1 of light artillery, and 7 of cavalry.

The regular army of the Confederacy was nominally organized with 6 infantry regiments, 1 cavalry regiment, 1 corps of artillery and ordnance, and 4 staff bureaus. Many regular Confederate units are mentioned in the records, but it appears that only 1 battery of artillery and 12 cavalry and 7 infantry regiments were actually formed. Like the Union army, the Confederate army relied on state volunteer units for the majority of its combat power. The Confederates organized 642 infantry regiments, 137 cavalry regiments, 16 artillery regiments, and 227 batteries of artillery.

The size of the standard Civil War regiment was fixed by the War Department in May 1861. Each "old" regular and "new" volunteer infantry regiment was to have 10 companies and 1 regimental staff consisting of 1 colonel, 1 lieutenant colonel, 1 major, 1 adjutant, 1 quartermaster, 1 surgeon, 2 assistant surgeons, 1 chaplain, 1 sergeant major, 1 quartermaster sergeant, 1 commissary sergeant, 1 hospital steward, 2 principal musicians, and a band of 24 men. These were so-called 1-battalion regiments with a minimum strength of 869 and a maximum strength of 1,049. The 9 "new" regular-army infantry regiments were organized with 3 battalions of 8 100-man companies each and were also authorized 3 additional majors, 1 for each battalion. These 3 battalion regiments were never recruited to full strength, and after the Civil War they were reorganized as single-battalion regiments. The Civil War cavalry regiment typically had 10 companies or troops, and most Union cavalry regiments had a squadron organization. Two troops constituted a squadron. Battalions commanded by a major were constituted of a varying number of squadrons, usually 2. Three battalions made up a regiment commanded by a colonel.

The organization of the army into tactical units larger in size than the regiment was undertaken only during times of major conflict. The regular, volunteer, and militia units of the Mexican War were organized into 3 field armies under Gens. Scott, Zachary Taylor, and Stephen W. Kearny. A brigade and division structure was put into effect, and Scott's army in Mexico in 1847 had divisions of approximately 6,600 men in 3 brigades plus an artillery battery. The brigade and division structures disappeared after the Mexican War and were not revived until 1861. However, there was no firmly fixed structure for higher units on either side in the Civil War. Brigades in the Union army were really flexible "task forces" with 2–6 (usually 4) regiments, or about 800–1,700 men, commanded by a brigadier general. A division commanded by a major general might have 3,000–7,000 men in 3–4 brigades. The corresponding Confederate units were usually larger. Confederate brigades usually had 1,400–2,000 men, and divisions had 6,000–14,000. An exception was Ambrose P. Hill's light division, which had 7 brigades and 17,000 men.

In the spring of 1862, Lincoln directed that the Army of the Potomac be organized into 4 corps and in July of the same year, Congress decreed the corps organization for the army generally. The Confederates adopted a corps organization in November. Commanded by a major general, the Union corps usually consisted of 12,000–14,000 men in 3 divisions (about 45 regiments of infantry and 9 batteries of artillery). Confederate corps had 24,000–28,000 men and were commanded by lieutenant generals. Corps and divisions were combined arms teams having their own field artillery batteries. The Confederates allocated 1 artillery battalion to each division. Until 1863, Union artillery was parceled out to divisions, but from July 1863, the artillery was usually controlled by the corps, with 1 battery assigned to each of the corps' 9 brigades. Corps often had limited cavalry assets as well. Early in the war, some Union infantry divisions had attached cavalry; later, Union cavalry was organized into cavalry brigades, divisions, and corps similar to those of the Confederate army.

Civil War field armies were composed of a varying number of corps plus army artillery, cavalry, engineer, and signal units. For example, the Army of the Potomac in May 1864 had 3 infantry corps of approximately 25,000 men each and 1 cavalry corps of approximately 12,000 men, in addition to proportionate numbers of supporting troops.

Reserve Forces

Until the War of 1812, the national military establishment depended upon the state militias to provide the bulk of the military manpower in time of invasion or other serious external threat. However, during the period 1815–65, the effectiveness of the militia underwent a serious deterioration. Little attempt was made to insure its viability as a military force or its integration with the regular army. This was at least partly due to the low esteem of the militia in the eyes of regular-army officers who felt the War of 1812 had been won by the regulars despite the debacles of the militiamen. After 1815, public indifference and the apathy of state authorities blocked even the feeble efforts made by the federal government to improve the militia. As a result, in the early 1820s, Secretary of War Calhoun finally repudiated the militia tradition and devised a plan by which the small regular army could be expanded in time of crisis. Calhoun's "expansible army" plan provided for a small, professional peacetime army supported by an efficient staff. This army would form the basis for mobilization of a total force that would grow by stages from 6,000 to 11,000 and then to 19,000 men. Although Calhoun's plan was rejected by Congress, the underlying assumption (namely, reliance on expansion of the regular army by volunteers in time of war) was to remain at the foundation of U.S. military policy up to World War I.

By the 1830s, in those areas where the militia tradition was still maintained, voluntary militia units had replaced mandatory formations. The militia was called out in 1846, and its term of service was extended from the usual 90 days to 6 months. However, the low state of its training and equipment as well as public opposition to the deployment of militia outside the United States made its effective use all but impossible. In its place, Congress authorized the president in May 1846 to call up a maximum of 50,000 volunteers to serve for 1 year or the duration of the war, at the president's option. The volunteers were given some training, but at the end of 12 months, they were mustered out of service and new units had to be raised. The 12-month term proved far too short for either effective training or deployment. Nevertheless, a total of 73,532 men served in units other than those of the regular army during the Mexican War. Volunteers contributed significantly to the defeat of the Mexicans, just as they had earlier assisted in the defeat of the Indian tribes east of the Mississippi.

Although there were still 3,000,000 men on the militia rolls in 1861, the militia was all but dead as an effective institution. The militia call of April 15 was a dismal failure, but when Lincoln called for 75,000 volunteers for the regular army, nearly 100,000 men answered. Although the strength of the small regular army was greatly increased, it was still insufficient to handle the task of subduing the

Southern rebellion. On July 22, 1861, Lincoln signed an authorization for the enlistment of an additional 500,000 volunteers for three years. Three days later, the term of service was changed to extend "for the duration of the war." The initial public enthusiasm for enlistment soon died down, and when Lincoln asked for another 300,000 volunteers on July 2, 1862, only 85,000 responded. Subsequently, the Union army had to utilize conscription to fill its ranks. The Confederates also initially attempted to use the militia system of the Southern states to meet their manpower requirements but found that, except for local defense, they had to rely on volunteer units raised by the individual Confederate states.

Officers

The period from 1815 to 1865 was one in which the officer corps of the U.S. Army became a skilled professional body with high standards of performance and conduct. Initially, most officers of the regular army were drawn from the urban areas of the eastern seaboard. By the 1950s, however, the army drew its officers from all sections of the country. Southerners were particularly attracted to a military career, but in 1861, 313 officers (29 percent of the total officer corps) resigned their commissions and offered their services to the Confederacy. Even in the best of times, the retention of junior officers was no easy task. Pay was low, and prospects for advancement were dismal under a seniority system in which attrition was slow due to the absence of any retirement system. That so many competent men chose a military career despite these drawbacks is remarkable.

Through this period, the principal source of trained professional officers was the U.S. Military Academy at West Point, New York, reorganized by Bvt. Maj. Sylvanus Thayer in 1817. By the 1840s, West Point produced about

By the time that the Civil War broke out, both the Union and the Confederacy had many able officers to call upon. Here, Union officers under Philip H. Sheridan (front, right) *gather to discuss war strategy.* (U.S. Army Military History Institute)

Freed slaves were recruited for the Union Army's black regiments, which were led by white officers. Here, enlisted men of Company E of the 4th U.S. Colored Troops are shown. (National Archives)

45 graduates per year. By 1845, there were approximately 500 graduates of the academy on active duty (about 70 percent of the total officer corps). Another 500 occupied important civilian positions contributing to national growth and development. At the same time, there was an attempt to create a more democratic officer corps. In 1837, experiments were undertaken to commission a few officers from the ranks. When the 8th Infantry was raised in 1838, its entire officer complement was composed of officers drawn from civilian life.

Most of the practical military training of regular officers was gained from service-related experience, but in April 1824, Calhoun established the first U.S. postgraduate military school, the Artillery School of Practice at Fortress Monroe, Virginia. In 1827, the Infantry School of Practice was established at Jefferson Barracks, Missouri; the Cavalry School of Practice was later established at Carlisle Barracks in Pennsylvania. These schools served to disseminate at least basic knowledge of tactical and administrative skills throughout the officer corps. However, all attempts to improve the quality of the officer corps were hindered by the dispersion of the army in small detachments and by the frequent absence of officers from their units. In 1836, for example, about one-third of the officer corps (183 officers) was on detached service with the staff departments, engaged in recruiting duty, special missions, or activities at departmental headquarters.

While West Point and the schools of practice produced a corps of competent, trained junior officers, the majority of the senior officers of the army throughout this period were still seriously undereducated in their profession. Some, such as Scott and Taylor, more than made up in natural ability and experience for their lack of formal education. Yet political reality also meant that in times of mobilization, a sizeable proportion of the army's senior leadership would be comprised of civilians with far less military experience or talent. For example, 4 out of the 5 major generals commanding in September 1861 had been appointed from civilian life, and 24 of the 71 brigadier generals had no previous military experience. While officers of the regular army were appointed by the president, regimental commanders of the volunteer forces were appointed by state governors, and company officers in the volunteer units were often elected by the men. Thus, the quality and experience of the large Civil War officer corps was quite uneven. Although many "citizen soldiers" proved to have the qualities necessary for superior wartime leadership, many were inadequate to their tasks. The price for teaching the less capable or less experienced officers their duties was all too often paid in the blood of their soldiers.

Enlisted Men

Despite the fact that the overall size of the army was kept quite small through most of the period, the army had to struggle to recruit up to authorized levels and to maintain the discipline of the enlisted men. Low pay, isolated and hazardous posts, little training, poor rations, disease, and drunkenness all served to make desertion a major problem. Some improvements in pay and living conditions were made in the late 1820s and early 1830s, but the opening of new territories and the economic opportunities they offered led to a worsening of the already bad desertion problem in the years after the Mexican War.

The majority of army enlistees during the period were recent immigrants or residents of the urban areas of the eastern seaboard where economic opportunities were limited. Many were of Irish or German descent. Despite the poor conditions of military service, many such men sought service in the army as a means to a better life. The quality of such recruits was rarely high, but most served loyally

Black soldiers defend the Union at Dutch Gap, Virginia. (U.S. Army Military History Institute)

and effectively. At the beginning of the Civil War, only 26 of some 15,000 enlisted men went over to the Confederate cause.

Until the Civil War, black Americans were not regularly enlisted in the U.S. Army. However, the demand for manpower and changing political attitudes led to their use as soldiers in the Union army, in segregated units of the Corps d'Afrique, the U.S. Colored Troops, and in state units such as the famous 54th Massachusetts Volunteer Infantry. Perhaps as many as 180,000 black Americans served in the Union army, 65 percent of whom were from the South. The Civil war also saw the formal employment of women to supplement the army. A corps of female nurses was given semiofficial sanction, and, for the first time, female clerks were employed in the various offices of the staff departments in Washington, notably in the Quartermaster Department. The first 3 women copyists were hired by the quartermaster general in 1862. By the end of 1864, there were 29 female clerks in the department.

Conscription

Until the Civil War, military service was almost entirely voluntary. But faced with severe manpower shortages, the Confederate states were the first to move to conscription. Three conscription acts passed between April 1862 and February 1864 provided for the enrollment of able-bodied white males between the ages of 17 and 50, with certain important exceptions. The maintenance of the institution of slavery and fears of slave insurrection required that the Confederacy exempt many able-bodied white males who might otherwise have been available for military service, in order to prevent potential internal disruption. Indeed, despite critical manpower shortages and a slave population of some 3,500,000 men, the Confederacy long resisted the enrollment of slaves for military purposes, although they were occasionally "rented" or "loaned" to the government by their owners for labor tasks. As the South's manpower position grew even more critical, the Third Conscription Act of Feb. 17, 1864, did authorize the enlistment of free blacks and even slaves in labor units. Finally, as a last gasp, an act of Mar. 30, 1865, authorized the use of slaves as soldiers.

By 1863, the North was also feeling the effect of depleted military manpower. On Mar. 3, 1863, Congress passed an act "for enrolling and calling out the national forces and for other purposes." The Enrollment Act was the first national draft law and called for the conscription of all male citizens and declarant aliens between the ages of 20 and 45. Certain categories of persons were exempted: the physically or mentally unfit, felons, men with specified types of dependents, the vice president, federal judges, the heads of federal executive departments, and state governors. The Enrollment Act was extremely unpopular and led to many abuses, particularly of the provision permitting the hiring of substitutes for military service. The draft was particularly unpopular in urban areas. Following the Battle of Gettysburg (July 1863), serious draft riots broke out in New York City. Although only about 6 percent of the 2,666,999 men raised by the North in the Civil War were conscripts, the Enrollment Act of 1863 did establish the principle that all U.S. citizens owed a military obligation to their nation and that the federal government could compel such service directly, without the intervention of the states.

Tactical Doctrine

From the War of 1812 until well into the Civil War, tactical doctrine did not keep pace with the rapidly changing technology of war. U.S. tactical doctrine, based on the writings of Baron Henri Jomini, continued to emphasize Napoleonic massed columns of infantry and massed artillery firepower. Revised army regulations codifying Napoleonic precepts were issued under the direction of General Scott in 1820–21 and remained in force essentially unaltered until after the Mexican War. Jomini's work also formed the basis for tactical discussions and drill manuals produced by such U.S. tacticians as Dennis H. Mahan and Halleck.

There were, in fact, some small modifications to "pure" Napoleonic tactics before the Civil War. In the War with Mexico, frontal assaults and shallow envelopments were the principal tactical methods, and infantry moved in column and deployed into lines three ranks deep for defense and attack. However, more use was made of turning movements, and field guns of increased mobility were used to provide close artillery support. Attack by rushes of small groups rather than one continuously advancing "dressed" line was also practiced to a limited extent. Amphibious operations involving assault landings were also introduced. Following the Mexican War, Secretary of War Davis prescribed new light infantry tactics to incorporate the lessons of the Mexican War and to adapt doctrine to new weapons such as the rifled musket and mobile field battery. The deployed line of infantry was reduced from three to two ranks with an interval of about two feet between men and less than three feet between the first and second rank. Increased emphasis was placed on the use of skirmishers in advance of the main line. The fact that infantry formations armed with the rifled musket could tear an attack to pieces before it could close with the defenders was recognized and reflected in *Hardee's Rifle and Light Infantry Tactics,* the new tactical manual issued in 1855. Yet the full import of the new weapons would not be fully understood until after the Civil War was well underway.

The Civil War began with both sides employing tactical formations and methods little different from those used by George Washington or Napoleon, but by 1863, the war had entered a new phase. The effects of long-range rifled firearms and massed mobile artillery were much better understood, and the revised infantry manual of 1863 reflected the new conditions. By 1864, defenders almost always constructed light field fortifications to protect against rifle and artillery fire, and increased use was made of skirmishers to drive in the enemy outposts and cover the approach of the attacking force. Attacks started in close order, but the troops often scattered for cover and concealment and advanced by short rushes supported by fire from nearby units. The futility of frontal assault on prepared positions led to increased emphasis on envelopment and flanking attacks.

Infantry was the basic arm in Civil War armies. Infantry forces were the easiest to recruit and train and could be used on all kinds of terrain. Infantrymen relied on the massed firepower of their rifled muskets. Volume of fire was achieved by deploying infantry in close-order linear

During the Civil War, mobile artillery, such as gunboats on rivers, were important support for land troops. Pictured above is the gunboat Cairo. (U.S. Army Military History Institute)

By 1864, to protect against long-range rifle fire, mobile artillery, and massed attacks, trenches and field fortifications were used increasingly, as shown at the siege of Vicksburg. (U.S. Army Military History Institute)

formations, which provided maximum firepower to the front but left the flanks vulnerable. A trained infantryman, carrying a basic load of 60 rounds, could deliver accurate aimed fire at a rate of about two rounds per minute. The rifled musket could be used to good effect against infantry in line at ranges greater than 400 yards, and a defending force could get off several volleys before an attacker advancing at the quickstep could close. The key development in the evolution of infantry formations was the change from column to line and back again. Infantry usually marched in column (8–20 men deep) for speed and better control but attacked and defended in a line of two ranks, or occasionally in "open order"—that is, an irregular single line. A regiment in the attack might occupy a front of about 300 yards with one company advanced to the front as skirmishers. A deployed brigade occupied a front of about 1,500 yards. A division usually attacked in a column of brigades with 150–300 yards between brigades.

Civil War field artillery sustained troops in the attack, facilitated movements and opposed those of the enemy, and destroyed enemy forces and the obstacles or defenses that protected them. Guns were interspersed with the infantry, which relied on them for protection against enemy infantry and cavalry. Often, the guns were advanced 50–100 yards in front or placed on the flanks of the infantry formation. Civil War guns were direct fire weapons—that is, the gunner had to be able to see the target to deliver accurate fire. The selection of favorable positions and rapid movement were the keys to effective support of the infantry, particularly since the artillery had to cease fire when its own infantry closed with the enemy in order to avoid causing casualties among friendly troops.

Civil War cavalry performed reconnaissance, protected columns on the march, provided local security of headquarters and other key points, and acted as military police to control movements, guard prisoners, and apprehend stragglers. Cavalry drill and tactics were similar to those of infantry, with column and line being the principal tactical formations. Cavalrymen armed with sabers, pistols, and breechloading carbines were really dragoons who rode to battle but dismounted to fight. The rifled musket made the direct attack of entrenched infantry by cavalry all but impossible. Despite their claims to the contrary, cavalrymen were usually just auxiliaries on the Civil War battlefield.

NAVAL AND MARINE FORCES

From 1815 to 1865, the principal mission of the U.S. Navy was to protect and promote the maritime commerce of the United States. This was accomplished primarily by the protection of U.S. citizens and property on the high seas and in foreign ports, the suppression of piracy, and the transportation and protection of U.S. diplomats. From the 1830s, the navy was also called upon to suppress the African slave trade. In time of war, the navy took on the additional missions of blockading, commerce raiding, and assisting the army in coastal defense, amphibious operations, and riverine operations. Throughout the period, the navy was also active in exploration, hydrographic survey, and other scientific activities. The U.S. Marine Corps provided sentinels and brig guards aboard ships of the navy and at navy yards ashore. Marines serving aboard navy ships also provided emergency gun crews and landing-party infantry when required.

Personnel

From 1815 until the Civil War, the navy remained quite small due to domestic political opposition to large standing military forces that might involve the United States in foreign adventures. However, the navy and Marine Corps did increase temporarily in time of crisis, and there was a slow but steady growth in both the number of men and number of ships until the Civil War brought a major expansion.

In 1816, the navy numbered 5,540 officers and men on active duty. The total fell during the early 1820s to a low point of fewer than 4,000, but the diplomatic crisis with Great Britain (1837–41) brought a substantial, if temporary, increase in naval personnel. From 1844 to 1857, the authorized number of seamen was fixed by Congress at 7,500. During the Mexican War, the navy increased to 1,141 officers and 10,097 men but soon returned to prewar levels. The number of authorized seamen was increased to 8,500 in 1857. Like the army, the navy expanded rapidly during the Civil War. By 1865, the navy had grown to 6,759 officers and 51,537 men. The Confederate navy was considerably smaller and probably never exceeded 5,000 officers and men.

The size of the Marine Corps remained proportionate to the size of the navy over the period. In 1817, Congress authorized a marine corps of 50 officers and 938 men. At first, the number of marines was tied to the number of ships in service, but in 1825, the so-called Bainbridge scale, which authorized 1 marine for each gun of the navy, was adopted. In 1834, the Marine Corps underwent a

U.S. Marines stand at attention at the Washington Navy Yard in 1864. (U.S. Army Military History Institute)

thorough reorganization, and by Jan. 1, 1861, the Marine Corps had 63 officers and 1,829 men present for duty. On July 25, 1861, the authorization was increased to 93 officers and 3,074 men. By April 1865, the corps had reached its maximum strength of 87 officers and 3,775 men. In contrast, the Confederate marine corps had 46 officers and seldom more than 600 men.

Ships

The navy was relatively more successful in adding new ships than in obtaining the personnel to man them. The first serious U.S. naval building program was instituted in 1816, but by November 1823, the active navy still had only 1 line-of-battle ship, 1 44-gun frigate, 1 36-gun frigate, 12 sloops of 30 guns or less, and 15 minor vessels. Ten vessels were under construction. The keel for the navy's first steam vessel was laid in 1836, and in 1839, Congress authorized 3 more steam warships. In the early 1840s, Sec. of the Navy Abel P. Upshur favored the expansion of steam propulsion and iron ships as well as a "ratio system" by which the U.S. Navy would have a strength at least one-half that of the strongest naval power in the world. By 1860, a total of 38 steam warships had been added to the navy inventory.

In 1846, the United States acquired the entire Texas navy by terms of the annexation treaty, but no major expansion of the U.S. Navy took place before or during the war with Mexico. Manifest Destiny in the 1850s, however, brought renewed interest in a stronger navy. In 1853, the navy list included 10 ships of the line (3 in commission, 3 in inactive status, and 4 under construction), 13 50-gun sailing frigates (most of them inactive), 6 steam frigates, 24 sailing sloops and brigs, and 1 schooner. In the six years before the Civil War, the navy was provided with 18 reasonably modern and effective steam screw ships largely through the efforts of southern officials. Ironically, these vessels would prove effective against the Confederacy. The strength of the Union navy in April 1861 was about 90 ships, of which only 42 were in commission. In the first six months of the Civil War, 100 warships were added, and by December 1864, the U.S. Navy reached a strength of 671 vessels (113 screw steamers, 52 paddle steamers, 71 ironclads, 323 steamers of other than warship types, and 112 sailing vessels of all types) carrying 4,610 guns. In addition, there was the so-called stone fleet of 78 vessels sunk as obstacles to navigation. The small Confederate navy had fewer than 150 vessels, including 7 commerce-raiding "cruisers."

Stationing

For both administrative and strategic purposes, the navy established various semipermanent squadrons or "stations" that were named for the geographical area in which they were located. The Mediterranean Squadron was established in 1815, the Pacific and the East Indian (including China) squadrons in 1817, the West Indian Squadron in 1822, and the Brazilian Squadron in 1826. The Home (or North Atlantic) Squadron was established in 1837 and absorbed the West Indian Squadron in 1841. In 1853, the African Squadron was added. During the Civil War, the waters surrounding the Confederate States were divided for patrol and blockade purposes into six divisions (the North Atlantic, South Atlantic, East Gulf, and West Gulf blockade squadrons and the Potomac and Mississippi flotillas), and a squadron under the command of a flag officer or rear admiral was assigned to each.

U.S. Secretaries of the Navy, 1815–1869

Name	*Dates of Service*
Benjamin W. Crowninshield	January 1815-September 1818
Smith Thompson	January 1819-August 1823
Samuel L. Southard	September 1823-March 1829
John Branch	March 1829-May 1831
Levi Woodbury	May 1831-June 1834
Mahlon Dickerson	July 1834-June 1838
James K. Paulding	July 1838-March 1841
George E. Badger	March 1841-September 1841
Abel P. Upshur	October 1841-July 1843
David Henshaw	July 1843-February 1844
Thomas W. Gilmer	February 1844*
John Y. Mason	March 1844-March 1845
George Bancroft	March 1845-September 1846
John Y. Mason	September 1846-March 1849
William B. Preston	March 1849-July 1850
William A. Graham	August 1850-July 1852
John P. Kennedy	July 1852-March 1853
James C. Dobbin	March 1853-March 1857
Isaac Toucey	March 1857-March 1861
Gideon Welles	March 1861-March 1869

*Feb. 19, 1844-Feb. 28, 1944

Higher Level Command

Until 1815, the secretary of the navy administered the navy directly with the assistance of a few clerks. On Feb. 5, 1815, Congress authorized a three-man board of naval commissioners to oversee the matériel of the navy and to advise the secretary of the navy on all matters. The board was responsible for certain administrative tasks and the design, procurement, and construction of naval vessels, but the secretary of the navy retained responsibility for policy, strategy, operations, and personnel. Commodore John Rodgers dominated the board until 1837. The commissioners were intent on preserving the navy's coast defense and commerce raiding missions but opposed the introduction of steam power, iron ships, and the new Paixhans shell guns, often against the inclinations of the president and the secretary of the navy.

Secretary of the Navy Upshur took office on Oct. 11, 1841, and set out to reform the navy with the aid of his political allies. In 1842, the Board of Naval Commissioners was abolished and was replaced by six independent, functional bureaus (Yards and Docks; Construction, Repair and Equipment; Provisions and Stores; Ordnance; Hydrography; and Medicine and Surgery). The chief of each bureau was chosen by and reported directly to the secretary of the navy. However, the naval act of Aug. 31, 1842, had no provisions for organizing the chiefs of the bureaus into a collective body vested with corporate functions. In July 1862, the six bureaus were reorganized into eight new ones (Yards and Docks, Equipment and Recruiting, Navigation, Ordnance, Construction and Repair, Steam Engineering, Provisions and Clothing, and Medicine and Surgery). The chiefs of each were designated to serve terms of four years.

Until 1861, there was no settled policy regarding who should act for the secretary of the navy in his absence. Sometimes the chief clerk or one of the bureau chiefs performed that duty; even the secretary of war was known on occasion to assume the responsibilities of his naval colleague. In 1861, the post of assistant secretary of the navy was authorized. Gustavus Vasa Fox, who occupied that position during the Civil War, became the virtual chief of naval operations for the Union navy.

Naval Organization

The basic administrative and tactical unit of the U.S. Navy in the period 1815–65 was the individual vessel. The captain of a naval vessel was responsible for all aspects of his vessel's operation and maintenance, administrative as well as tactical. Warships could and did act independently but were often grouped into squadrons, flotillas, or fleets, with the number and types of vessels being determined by the mission, available forces, distance from home port, and other such factors. On land, the commanders of navy yards exercised wide administrative powers over their activities, sometimes independent of the desires of the Navy Department in Washington or any other higher authority. At the beginning of the Civil War, the principal navy yards were at Boston, New York, Norfolk, Pensacola, and Mare Island (California). Secondary yards were located at Portsmouth (New Hampshire), Philadelphia, and Washington (which specialized in ordnance manufacturing and testing).

The marines were organized administratively and tactically in much the same way as the army. Indeed, for a time the marines operated in accordance with army rather than navy regulations. Considerable operational confusion arose from the marines' dual chain of command. One chain of command and administration led up to the colonel commandant of the corps in Washington. Yet, marines aboard ship were also subject to the commands of the captain of the vessel, and when ashore often fell under the control of the commander of the navy yard to which they were assigned. In extraordinary cases, they might even be subordinate to an army officer when part of a joint land force. The various commandants of the Marine Corps, therefore, struggled throughout the period to gain clear and exclusive control over their marines wherever they served.

Commandants of the U.S. Marine Corps, 1804–1876

Name	*Dates of Service*
Franklin Wharton	March 1804-September 1818
Anthony Gale	March 1819-October 1820
Archibald Henderson	October 1820-January 1859
John Harris	January 1859-May 1864
Jacob Zeilin	June 1864-October 1876

Reserve and Regular Forces

For all practical purposes, there were no reserve naval forces from 1815 to 1861. A few states continued to maintain naval militias, but these were moribund. The U.S. merchant marine was considered a possible source of naval officers and seamen in time of crisis, but no overt steps were taken to formalize a naval reserve system. Only the small Coast Guard was available to augment the navy in time of war. Some 500 coastguardsmen served in the Mexican War, and 2,409 served in the Civil War. However, the Civil War renewed interest in reserve naval forces, and Massachusetts proposed the raising of a Massachusetts volunteer navy. It was never formed, but the U.S. Naval Volunteer Corps was created, and about 7,500 volunteer officers were employed. By 1865, there were 2,060 line officers, 1,805 engineers, 370 paymasters, and 245 surgeons in the volunteer naval forces.

Officers

Throughout the period, the navy struggled to improve the selection, training, and discipline of naval officers. As might be expected, most naval officers were drawn from the eastern coastal areas of the United States, but only a very few were drawn from the merchant service until the Civil War. Before the Mexican War, the most important factor in the selection of midshipmen (the "entry" naval officer rank) was personal and political influence. Experience, aptitude for naval service, and schooling of any kind were not required. Indiscipline, particularly an exaggerated sense of "honor" and the dueling to which it often led, was a serious impediment to improvement in the image of the naval officer. Dueling, which had cost the navy the services of such heroes as Stephen Decatur, was finally prohibited in 1857.

The training early naval officers received was "on-the-job" and often sketchy at best. The founding of the U.S. Naval Academy at Annapolis, Maryland, in 1845 was a major step toward an educated, well-prepared professional naval officer corps. In 1850, the course at the Naval Academy was extended to four years and came to include academic as well as technical subjects. A further step forward came with the introduction in 1864 of examinations for promotion below the rank of commodore.

The two most pressing officer personnel issues for the navy were the naval officer rank structure and the problem of superannuated or incompetent officers. The prevailing view until the Civil War was that the title of admiral was unsuitable for the navy of a democratic nation. Beginning in the late 1850s, captains with additional responsibilities were permitted to use the title of flag officer (which also distinguished them from steamboat skippers and army captains). The naval act of July 16, 1862, finally resolved the question of higher grades for naval officers by specifying the various grades and determining the number of officers who would be authorized in each grade. In December 1864, the rank of vice admiral was created for David G. Farragut. Regarding the question of retirement, the disposition of superannuated officers was facilitated with the passage on Aug. 3, 1861, of an act providing for a naval retired list. Officers could be placed on the retired list in the event of their incapacitation or retire voluntarily after 40 years of service. On Dec. 21, 1861, retirement at age 62 and after 45 years service was provided.

Selection, training, and discipline of marine officers were similar to that of naval officers throughout the period. Yet the marines were even more prone, if possible, to internal dissension, frequent dueling, and appointment or assignment by influence than naval officers. Commandants such as Archibald Henderson strove mightily to overcome such impediments to the creation of an effective marine corps. A few marine officers attended West Point, and each year after 1845, a few graduates of the Naval Academy were commissioned as marine officers.

At the beginning of the Civil War, some 322 navy and 20 marine officers "went South," but almost no enlisted men of either service left to serve the Confederacy. The several officer grades of the Confederate navy, except for the very lowest, were filled by former U.S. Navy officers.

Enlisted Men

Between 1815 and 1865, desertion, drunkenness, and chronic insubordination among U.S. naval crews were common and the navy had severe difficulty in recruiting the authorized number of seamen and marines. Additional disciplinary problems were caused by the persistent antagonism between seamen and the marines serving aboard ship. Gradual reforms during the period improved conditions somewhat. Sec. of the Navy Samuel L. Southard built a naval hospital and improved medical service, instituted a naval criminal code, and promoted other reforms. Flogging was abolished in 1850, much to the disapproval of many officers and some of the "old salts." The rum ration was eliminated in 1861 but had little effect on carousing ashore. From the 1830s, a few officers, such as Comdr. Andrew H. Foote, promoted temperance and religion among the crews of U.S. naval vessels with varying degrees of success.

The sources of enlisted personnel for the navy throughout the period were much the same as for the army, with immigrants and men from the eastern seaboard predominating. African-Americans were often found aboard U.S. naval vessels, and perhaps as many as 29,000 served in the Union navy during the Civil War. Ordinarily, crews enlisted for only a three-year voyage, and there was no permanent corps of seamen until one was created by Pres. Franklin Pierce and Sec. of the Navy John P. Kennedy in 1852. Training, such as it was, was of the on-the-job variety, although periodic attempts were made to institute more formal systems. In 1837, Congress established a naval apprentice system with school ships at the principal navy yards. This program lasted until 1843. A new system was adopted in 1855 but soon collapsed, although the concept of training ships was revived in 1857. Many naval vessels had a schoolmaster aboard to provide rudimentary education for crewmen.

Tactical Doctrine

Naval tactics in 1865 were much the same as they had been in 1815; the changes were technical rather than doctrinal. Rifling and other improvements in naval ordnance improved the accuracy of naval gunfire and made decisive engagement possible at greater ranges. The shell gun spelled doom for the wooden sailing ship so vulnerable to fire. The transition to steam power and the screw propeller largely eliminated the wind as a major factor in naval tactics. Riverine warfare came into its own on both sides in the Civil War, and Confederate naval tactics emphasized the extensive use of mines ("torpedoes") and ramming by ironclad vessels. The techniques of amphibious warfare were first worked out during the Mexican War. The landings at Veracruz in March 1847 comprised the first large-scale amphibious operation for the U.S. Navy and included all the elements of later amphibious campaigns: landing craft, assault waves, floating depots, and naval gunfire support. The drill and tactics of marines ashore were essentially the same as that used by the army.

WEAPONS TECHNOLOGY

Between 1815 and 1865, newer, more reliable, and more efficient weapons, on both land and sea, brought significant changes in tactics, but direct-fire artillery and hand-held firearms continued to dominate the battlefield. New methods of communication and transport also greatly influenced the nature of warfare at the strategic level during the period. At the tactical level, however, communication and movement did not progress much beyond those of the 18th century, and progress in the healing arts did not keep up with advances in the means of destruction. Not only the weapons themselves but also the processes by which they were produced significantly improved in the first half of the 19th century. Eli Whitney introduced the concept of interchangeable parts and assembly-line production in 1800, and throughout the 19th century, there were steady and cumulative improvements in iron and steel manufacturing essential to weapons production. Eliphalet Remington II improved techniques of barrel making, and at mid-century, Thomas J. Rodman developed a method for producing lighter and stronger guns by casting them hollow and chilling the inside first. During the Civil War, techniques of mass production were adapted to meet the needs of huge armies requiring massive amounts of weapons, ammunition, and other matériel. Federal arsenals alone produced 7,892 pieces of artillery and some 4,000,000 stand of small arms, while federal artillery fired some 5,000,000 rounds during the course of the war, about 4 rounds per gun per day.

Infantry Weapons

Two technological developments, the percussion cap and the cylindroconoidal bullet, greatly increased the reliability, range, and accuracy of infantry weapons. The percussion cap, invented by Joshua Shaw of Philadelphia in 1814, was in general use by the 1820s. It reduced misfires and facilitated development of breechloaders and repeating guns. After 1820, the U.S. Army began conversion of flintlocks to percussion, but the process took some time. Mexican War volunteer units were armed mostly with the new percussion weapons, but the regulars still carried flintlocks little different from those used in the war of 1812. Eventually, the Model 1841 caplock became the standard infantry shoulder weapon. After 1842, U.S. arsenals ceased to produce flintlocks altogether.

The cylindroconoidal bullet with a hollow base that expanded to catch the rifling grooves, invented in 1823 by Captain Norton of the British army but usually known as the Minié ball (after the French officer who promoted its use), made possible the manufacture of an accurate, dependable muzzle-loading rifle at least as quick to load as the smoothbore musket. Production of muskets was stopped in U.S. arsenals in 1855, and many of the older smoothbore weapons were converted. Although many state troops were still armed with the smoothbore musket at the beginning of the Civil War, the regulars, and ultimately all the volunteers as well, carried the Model 1855 (or slightly improved Model 1861) .58-caliber Springfield rifled musket with 18-inch socket bayonet. Using the Minié ball, paper cartridge, and improved percussion cap, the Springfield's maximum range was 1,000–2,000 yards and its effective range of 200–500 yards (versus 50–75 for the smoothbore) made possible fairly rapid fire. Consequently, a unit armed with the new rifled musket could tear an attack to pieces before it could close with the defenders, a fact that led to new tactics favoring open formations, indirect (flanking) attacks, and greater use of cover and concealment. The new rifled musket thus strengthened the defensive and almost abolished cavalry as an important "shock" element on the battlefield.

The new percussion-cap technology led to the perfection of the Colt revolver in 1835, the first practical repeating firearm. A few were used in the Second Seminole War, but the real test for the Colt came during the Mexican War, and it was subsequently improved in various ways. The metallic cartridge was invented in 1856, but was not produced in significant numbers until after 1861. The metallic cartridge made the breechloading repeating rifle possible, although further advances in metallurgy and methods of accurate measurement were needed before a practical production model could be developed. The first really satisfactory breechloader was the single-shot Sharps carbine perfected by Christian Sharps at Harpers Ferry in 1859. The U.S. Army conducted tests of the available models of repeating breechloaders before the Civil War, but the decision was made not to produce and issue them in large numbers due to the problems of retooling at the arsenals in wartime. The Sharps was used in the Civil War, notably by Hiram Berdan's U.S. Sharpshooters, and a few repeating rifles were also used in the Civil War, the 7-shot, rimfire, .52-caliber Spencer carbine being perhaps the most famous. The Spencer increased the rate of fire of an individual rifleman to 16 shots per minute and played an important role in several Civil War battles, notably around Atlanta, Georgia, and at Franklin, Tennessee.

Artillery

Improvements in both field and coast artillery weapons lagged somewhat behind those for small arms until the Mexican War. The chief innovation before 1846 was the introduction of an improved carriage for the light field piece, which permitted the development of light, mobile horse artillery, a characteristic of both the Mexican War and the Civil War. The Model 1841 bronze 6-pounder, muzzle-loading cannon of Mexican War fame was still in use during the Civil War. It had a maximum range of 1,523 yards. Design improvements in the 1850s reduced the weight and increased the reliability of the bronze cannon. Perhaps the most important new artillery weapon introduced in the aftermath of the Mexican War was the 12-pounder, smoothbore brass "Napoleon," developed for the light artillery batteries and introduced in 1857. It had an effective range of 800–1,000 yards and could fire a 12-pound cast-iron shot nearly a mile. The 12-pounder Napoleon was the favorite gun of both sides during the Civil War. It was preferred by artillerymen over rifled cannon because it was easier to clean, it was much more effective at short range when firing canister against enemy infantry, and its trajectory was such that it could fire on reverse slopes.

There were four main areas of improvements in artillery weapons during the 19th century: rifling, breechloading, interior ballistics, and recoil mechanisms. Of these four innovations, only rifling was perfected before 1865. The development of an elongated expanding projectile (similar in principle to the Minié ball) improved both accuracy and effectiveness and permitted the outstanding 19th-century development in artillery technology—the rifled cannon—with both increased accuracy and almost double its effective range. In 1851, Capt. Robert P. Parrott developed a rifled cannon with cast-iron bands reinforcing the breech and using percussion and time fuses. The 10-pounder Parrott had a range of 1,900 yards. Parrotts ranged in size up to an enormous 300-pounder and were adapted for naval as well as field use. However, rifled artillery pieces such as the Parrott were not extensively used until the Civil War. The lightest and strongest of the Civil War rifled cannon was the 3-inch ordnance rifle, which had an effective range of 1,830 yards and a maximum range of 4,000 yards, but these were mostly wasted due to the lack of adequate indirect fire control techniques. One advantage of the rifled gun was that its ammunition could be fitted with an impact (percussion) fuse. Although no effective breechloading cannon were used in any significant numbers during the Civil War, there were several other improvements and innovations in artillery weapons. The first true machine gun, the Gatling gun, invented by Dr. Richard J. Gatling in 1862, could fire approximately 550 rounds per minute but was not adopted as a standard weapon until after 1865. Railway artillery was also introduced during the Civil War.

Civil War artillery had a rate of fire of about two rounds per minute using a variety of types of ammunition. Round shot consisted of a solid cast-iron ball and was used against distant, fixed targets, particularly obstacles and fortifications or troops in column. Spherical case shot consisted of a hollow cast-iron ball filled with lead balls and a small black-powder charge. It was fused and burst at a predetermined interval after being fired. It was used primarily against troops at ranges of 300–1,300 yards. Canister consisted of 27 balls packed in sawdust and enclosed in a

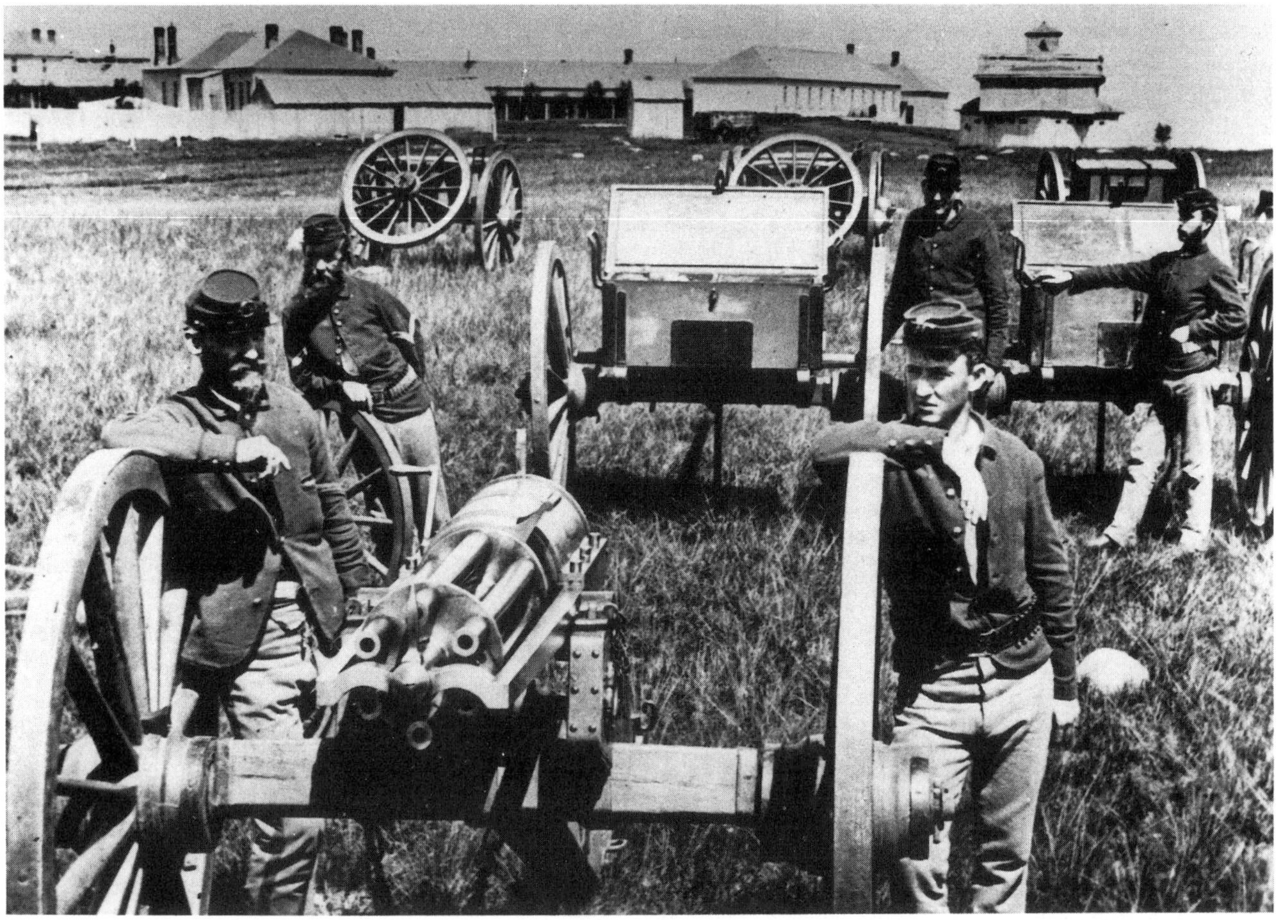

The Gatling gun, patented in 1861, was equipped with 6 barrels that revolved, firing as many as 550 rounds per minute. (Matthew Forney Steele Collection, Military History Institute)

Mortars mounted on railway flatcars, such as the Union's "Dictator" above, could be moved by rail from battle to battle. (U.S. Army Military History Institute)

tin can. It was employed against troops at close range, less than 400 yards. Some varieties of exploding shell were also used against cavalry, artillery, and infantry in the open or in trenches at ranges of up to 1,300 yards.

Naval Training

The first half of the 19th century was a period of tremendous innovation in naval technology. The change from sail to steam was made, the screw propeller was introduced, iron armor and iron ship construction were employed, and bigger guns and the armor plating to defend against them were built.

Steam propulsion was resisted for a long time and did tie the navy to its supplies of fuel, but the change from sail to steam brought a revolution in naval technology, freeing ships from the vagaries of wind, tide, and current. The first steam warship, Robert Fulton's *Demologos,* was launched in 1814. Designed for the defense of New York harbor, it carried 30 long 32-pounder guns but was relatively immobile and never saw active service. The navy's first really operational steam vessel, the *Fulton II,* was laid down in 1836; the following year, construction was started on the 120-gun USS *Pennsylvania,* the largest sail battleship ever built. In 1839, Congress authorized three wooden paddle-steamer "frigates" with 2 10-inch and 8 8-inch shell guns. The USS *Mississippi,* for example, had a weight of 1,693 tons, a maximum speed of 9.5 knots, a 620-ton fuel capacity, and a crew of 260. The development of the screw propeller to replace the paddle wheel increased speed and maneuverability and reduced the space required for the driving mechanism. The first screw-propeller warship, the USS *Princeton,* was launched in 1843. By the Civil War, about half of the navy's vessels were steam-powered.

Second in importance only to the change to steam was the introduction of armor plating and steel ship construction. Iron armor was the only answer to the incendiary shell gun. The U.S. Navy's first ironclad warship, the *Stevens Battery,* was authorized in 1842. The first engagement of ironclad vessels, the fight between the CSS *Virginia* (formerly the USS *Merrimac*) and the USS *Monitor* in Hampton Roads, Virginia, on Mar. 9, 1862, ushered in the era of armored ships. But iron construction, rather than iron plating, was the most significant innovation. It permitted vessels of greater size and strength to be developed, made compartmentalization possible, and provided a better platform for larger guns and heavier armor. The first iron ship of the U.S. Navy, the 570-ton side-wheeler USS *Michigan,* was launched on Lake Erie in December 1843.

Advances were also made in naval armaments, which brought ships heavier and more accurate guns. The shell gun, developed by French artillery officer Henri J. Paixhans in 1822 permitted the construction of guns of larger caliber without additional weight penalties. The Dahlgren "soda bottle" gun, invented by Lt. John A. B. Dahlgren in 1850, was the first scientifically designed naval cannon in the United States. The thickness of the metal along its bore was varied to conform to the changes in internal pressures when the gun was fired. Dahlgren's modification of the Paixhans shell gun made it safe in calibers up to 11 inches. Heavier, rifled guns using explosive shells increased the range and firepower of naval vessels. Moreover, wooden ships proved extremely vulnerable to the fires caused

The Union ironclad Monitor (foreground), *and the Confederate ironclad* Virginia (*formerly the USS* Merrimac), *battle off the coast of Virginia, Mar. 9, 1862.* (Library of Congress)

The Confederate submarine CSS H. L. Hunley, *which required eight men to hand-crank the propeller, sank a Union blockade ship near Charleston in 1864, but sank itself in the attack.* (U.S. Army Military History Institute)

Photographer Mathew Brady, who documented the Union forces in the Civil War, brought his photographic equipment, including a portable darkroom, to the field. (U.S. Army Military History Institute)

by the exploding shells. Among other naval innovations were the revolving turret, better position-finding methods, and the submarine. On Feb. 17, 1864, the CSS *H. Hunley* sank the USS *Housatonic,* the first effective use of a true submarine. Throughout the period, advances in naval technology were matched by advances in seacoast fortification design and armament, thus provoking an arms race of sorts.

Communications and Observation

For most of the 19th century, battlefield communications remained limited by line of sight and range of sound, but the overall control of armies in the field was improved dramatically by widespread use of the telegraph. The electrical telegraph, perfected by Samuel F. B. Morse in 1836, was used extensively for military purposes for the first time during the Mexican War. By the time of the Civil War, it had been improved and had become the common method of long-distance communication. For the most part, the importance of the telegraph as a means of military communication was restricted to the strategic or operational sphere. On the battlefield itself, the primary means of communication continued to be the age-old methods of the

Hot-air balloons, such as this one at Gaines Mill, Virginia, were used by the Union army to direct artillery and to gather information on enemy movements. (U.S. Army Military History Institute)

messenger on horse or foot, voice, music (bugle and drum), and visual signals. However, some newer methods of battlefield communication were introduced. Wigwag and torch signaling (ancient methods to be sure) were used extensively as was the heliograph. The perfection of insulated field wire led to some attempts to lay and use telegraphic wire on the battlefield itself, and the portable electric transmitting set (the Beardslee magnetic electric machine, or "buzzer") saw some use.

By the Civil War, optical instruments were greatly improved over those available in 1815, and even the new technology of photography was used to a limited extent for military purposes. Perhaps the greatest improvement to battlefield surveillance and intelligence was the introduction of the military balloon during the Civil War. Balloons enabled commanders to chart enemy positions and track enemy movements despite intervening obstacles. Although balloons also were employed to direct the fire of artillery weapons, true indirect fire techniques were to be a later development.

Mobility

The railroad and steamboat greatly improved strategic mobility, but tactical mobility remained limited to the pace of the foot soldier and the horse throughout the period 1815–65. The first overland troop movements by railroad were made during the Mexican War, and by the time of the Civil War, railroad movements of both troops and supplies over long distances were the norm. But like the telegraph, the railroad was important almost exclusively at the strategic or operational level. At the tactical level even in 1865, the armies were dependent upon horse-drawn transportation. The standard six-mule army wagon in good condition could haul two tons on good roads in the best season of the year. The rate of march of wagon trains varied from 12 to 24 miles per day depending on road conditions. Since ideal conditions were seldom found, the maximums of two tons and 24 miles per day were seldom achieved. Perfected early in the 19th century, the steamboat, for both ocean and river, was also an important element in the movement and supply of the army throughout the period. Like the railroad, its impact was mostly at the strategic or operational level.

Medical

Greater effectiveness of weaponry brought with it greater and more drastic casualties. The medical technology of the 19th century did not accelerate as early or as rapidly as the technology of destruction. Some advances were made in surgical technique, anesthetics in the form of chloroform were introduced, and a few items were added to the pharmacopoeia during the period 1815–65. Yet equally significant was what was *not* yet done. Aseptic surgery remained in the future, as did a comprehensive understanding of communicable diseases such as typhoid, yellow fever, cholera, and typhus. Consequently, as late as 1865, despite more effective methods of battlefield evacuation devised by Union surgeon general Jonathan Letterman, more soldiers died from disease, shock, or secondary infection than from the direct effects of the improved weaponry.

CONCLUSION

By 1865, the military and naval forces of the United States had expanded and matured far beyond anything imaginable in 1815. Their basic structures and procedures were well-established and "modern" by the standards of the day. They had been tested around the world at sea; in small, mobile operations against the Indians; in an overseas campaign against Mexico; and in the full-scale continental conflict of the Civil War. Nevertheless, their evolution was not yet complete nor had military technology reached its apogee. The following half-century would bring even greater and more profound changes.

2

National Consolidation: 1815–1835

Even before the Treaty of Ghent was signed on Christmas Eve 1814, ending the War of 1812, the U.S. Congress began to restructure the defense establishment of the United States. The intention was to return the military establishment to a peacetime force, correct some of the problems that had appeared during the war, and meet the new challenges presented by the ever-changing situation on both the nation's frontier and in the world arena.

For many Americans, the early failures of the regular army (supplemented by the citizen soldiers) during the war were quickly forgotten in the flush of the war's favorable conclusion. The victories on the Niagara frontier and Maj. Gen. Andrew Jackson's victory at New Orleans were remembered and held up as examples of the ability of the United States to defend itself against the greatest military and economic power in the world (Great Britain). Indeed, many Americans had the mistaken impression that the United States had won a magnificent victory over the British. However, the terms of the Treaty of Ghent reflected the fact that the two nations had fought each other to a virtual draw. The war's inconclusive results only served to confuse the issue of what type of military policy the nation should follow in the years to come.

EARLY POSTWAR YEARS

Upon reflection it became clear that the stunning victories on the Niagara had been won by regulars, not by the citizen soldiers who were supposed to play such a significant part in the defense of the country. However, the Battle of New Orleans was fought largely by militia forces from the southern states—supplemented by regulars—and resolutely led by Jackson. Thus, public debate over the composition of the force that should be maintained to defend the nation continued. For many, it still seemed that a small regular establishment supplemented during wartime by the citizen soldiers of the militia was adequate to meet the nation's needs. However, many of the nation's leaders began to realize that a truly professional military force of sufficient size to defend the United States against an enemy was necessary until the citizen soldiers could be adequately trained. These leaders were convinced that this was the only way to avoid the disasters that had befallen the United States during the first year and a half of the war with England.

Congress initially agreed with the need for a professional force. Following the announcement of the signing of the Treaty of Ghent, Congress, meeting in a temporary location because the British had burned the Capitol, voted to maintain an army of 10,000 men. But problems at the War Department helped to dilute the postwar enthusiasm for strengthening the military establishment.

Following the burning of Washington, Sec. of War John Armstrong had been forced to resign. James Monroe served as secretary until March 1815, when he resigned for health reasons. The U.S. minister to France, William H. Crawford, was appointed by Pres. James Madison to replace Monroe but would not be in Washington until August. In the interim, Sec. of the Treasury Alexander J. Dallas assumed directorship of both the Treasury and War departments. As war secretary, Crawford energetically worked to correct a number of problems that the strain of the war had made evident. However, in the fall of 1816, Madison

A statue of Andrew Jackson in Jackson Square, New Orleans, commemorates the U.S. victory over the British here in 1815 at the end of the War of 1812. (Louisiana Tourist Development Commission)

asked Crawford to resign and become secretary of the treasury. For more than a year, while one politician after another declined to accept the position of secretary of war, Chief Clerk George Graham ran the affairs of the department. Finally, on Dec. 8, 1817, John C. Calhoun became the secretary of war. The new secretary was faced with a situation much different than he would have faced only a year earlier; there were proposals to reduce the size of the army, to eliminate the General Staff, and to close the Military Academy at West Point. His term coincided with a number of events that would eventually transform the U.S. military establishment into a professional force—small in size but professional nonetheless. Despite the problems he encountered, Calhoun would leave his indelible mark upon the nation's military establishment before his tenure was over in 1825.

Combined with Calhoun's intelligent and energetic direction of the War Department was the emergence of a new group of enthusiastic and highly competent officers thrust into prominence by the war with England. Such memorable officers as Jackson, Winfield Scott, Edmund P. Gaines, and Jacob Brown would provide the small regular army with the type of leadership necessary to mold it into an efficient force.

Thayer and West Point

As a part of the initial postwar outpouring of support, Congress appropriated nearly $140,000 to build new buildings and acquire books and scientific equipment for the Military Academy at West Point. In July 1817, President Monroe appointed Sylvanus Thayer to be superintendent of the academy, and during his 16-year tenure, Thayer trans-

James Monroe, fifth president of the United States, served as Pres. James Madison's secretary of war from 1814 to 1816. (Library of Congress)

formed West Point into a school that would produce not only well-qualified engineers but also the men who would become the leaders of a truly professional military force.

In order to fulfill the intent of the academy to provide the cadets a regular degree from an academic staff, Thayer established the Academic Board. The board consisted of the permanent members of the faculty and met with Thayer to provide direction to the academy by establishing a curriculum and setting requirements for graduation. The curriculum was expanded to include courses not strictly connected with engineering. In order to assist in evaluating the students and encourage them to study, Thayer instituted the practice of weekly progress reports for each cadet. Thayer also created the position of commandant of cadets to further the military training and discipline of the cadets. The cadets were organized into tactical units under cadet officers and were required to take part in three summer encampments at which they sharpened their military skills.

A statue of Sylvanus Thayer on the grounds of West Point proclaims Thayer the "Father of the Military Academy." (Library of Congress)

The Academic Building at West Point was long the focal point of cadet life. (U.S. Military Academy)

With the goals of publicizing the achievements at West Point and gaining much-needed public support, Thayer diligently cultivated the Board of Visitors. Established in 1815 and composed of officers, educators, and government officials from all around the country, the board visited West Point each year and prepared a detailed report that made recommendations both to the academy and to Congress. The board became permanent in 1819 and provided patronage from a body independent of the military establishment.

Thayer's efforts at West Point were aided and supported by the contributions of Dennis H. Mahan. Mahan arrived at the academy in 1820, graduated first in his class in 1824, served as an instructor for two years, and then was sent to France by Thayer for advanced study. Mahan returned to West Point in 1830 and remained there until his death in 1871. It was Mahan, as professor of civil and military engineering, who initiated strategic studies and promoted professionalism among the cadets. He insisted that military science was a specialized body of knowledge that required concentrated study, especially of military history, to understand its complexities.

Although it took a number of years before the young officers trained under the program developed by Thayer and Mahan assumed senior leadership positions in the regular army, the training at West Point eventually produced a new breed of officer. In addition, the graduates of West Point were the only trained engineers educated in the United States until Rensselaer Polytechnic Institute in Troy, New York, graduated its first engineers in 1835. In the period immediately following the War of 1812, the training of engineers was essential to the industrialization of the United States.

Naval Policy

On Feb. 27, 1815, Congress directed that the navy's gunboat flotilla be sold and that the armed boats on the Great Lakes be stripped of their weapons and put into dry dock. Soon afterward, Congress authorized a long-range program to build a peacetime navy in order to avoid military disasters like those that had occurred during the War of 1812. In 1816, the U.S. Navy received an appropriation of $1,000,000 a year for the next eight years to build 9 74-gun ships of the line, 12 44-gun frigates, and 3 coast-defense steam batteries. However, just as the enthusiasm for army appropriations had waned quickly, so did the support for naval appropriations. In 1821, the appropriation was cut in half, although Congress did extend the original deadline until 1827. The $500,000 appropriation was extended for six years in 1827 and then for six more years in 1833. The navy would eventually acquire all of the ships authorized

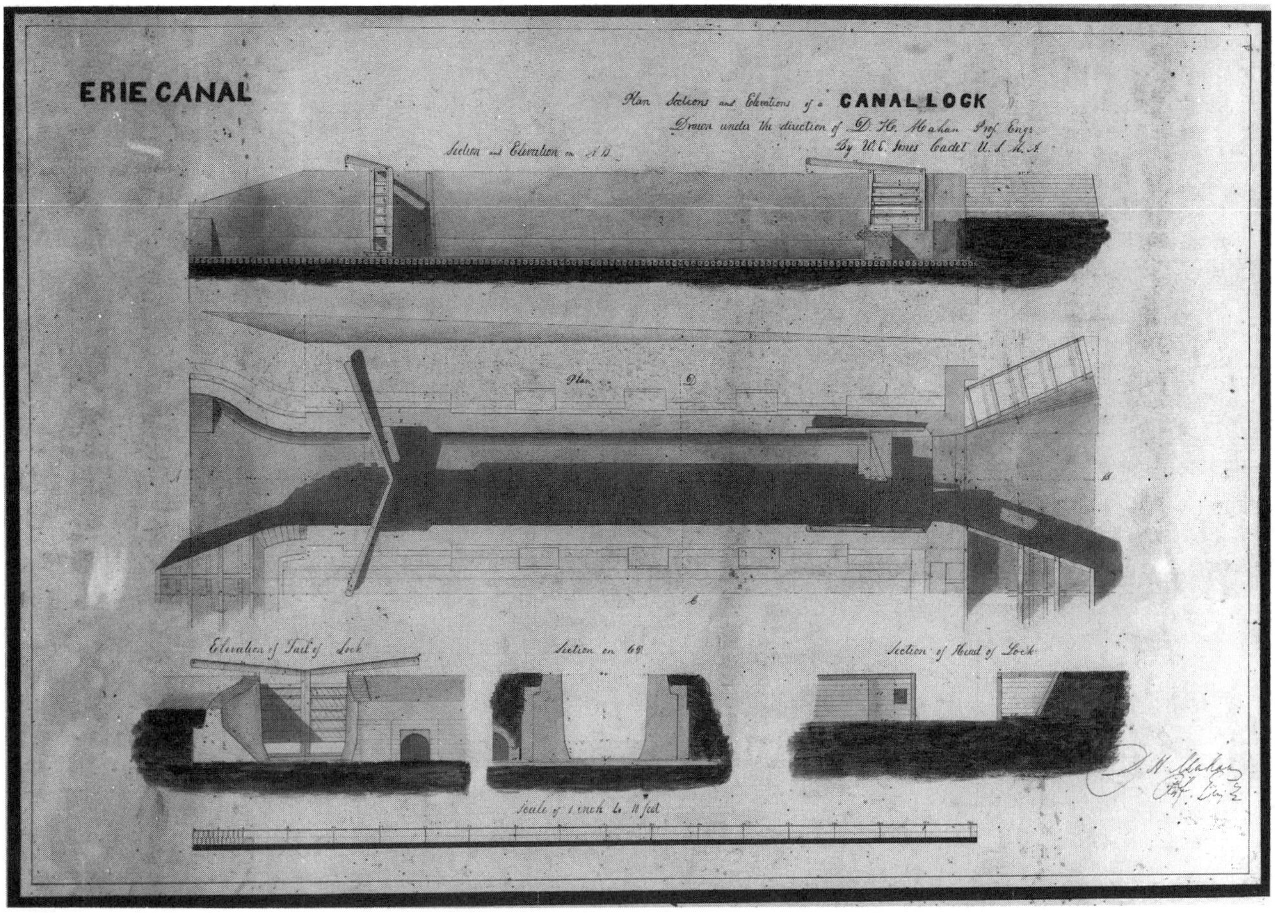

Under Professor Dennis H. Mahan, cadets at West Point mastered the complexities of engineering feats, such as a cadet's drawings of the lock system on the Erie Canal. (U.S. Military Academy)

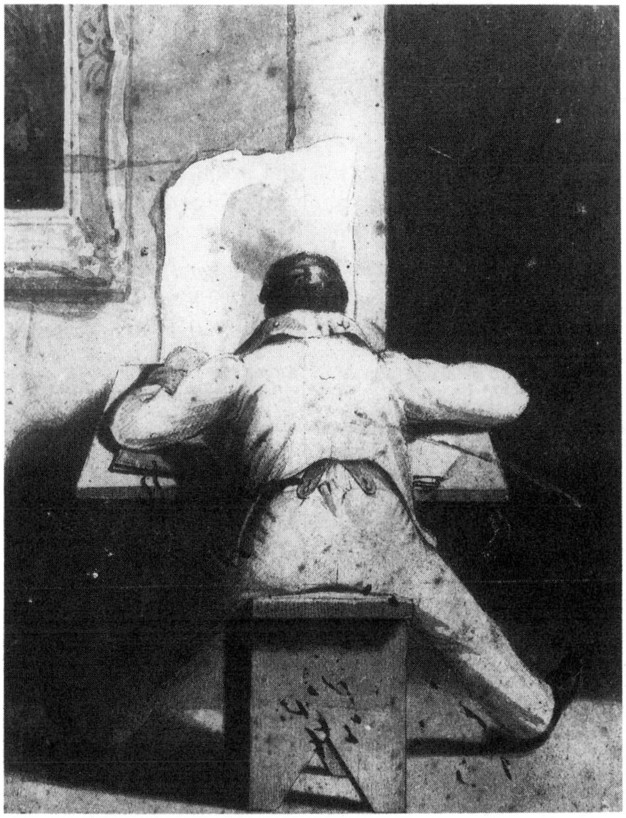

Thayer's restructuring of the curriculum at West Point assured the country of well-trained officers. Until 1835, the academy was the only U.S. institution that offered engineering courses; here, a cadet works at a drafting board. (U.S. Military Academy)

in 1816, but its primary reliance was on small warships rather than on the larger ones authorized by Congress in 1816.

During the War of 1812, the bey of Algiers and other North African rulers had renewed their raiding of U.S. shipping. The bey had expelled the American consul, declared war on the United States, and held U.S. citizens hostage, claiming that he was not receiving enough tribute from the United States. In response, on Mar. 3, 1815, Congress declared war on the bey. Capt. Stephen Decatur sailed from New York for the Mediterranean aboard the new, 74-gun ship of the line *Washington,* with nine other ships. Decatur's strong fleet passed into the Mediterranean in June and completely surprised the Algerian fleet. Decatur quickly captured the 44-gun frigate *Mashouda* and the 22-gun brig *Estido* before sailing into the Bay of Algiers and demanding that the bey make peace without further tribute. Initially refused, the demand was finally accepted when Decatur threatened to land a military force and seize the city. On June 30, a treaty was agreed upon whereby the bey agreed to cease his harassment of U.S. ships, give up his demand for tribute, and release the U.S. hostages without payment of ransom.

Decatur then took his fleet to Tunis, where, on July 26, he obtained a peace settlement as well as an indemnity of $46,000 for past offenses against U.S. shipping. On August 5, he imposed a similar settlement on the rulers of Tripoli. Decatur subsequently returned to the United States and served on the three-man Board of Navy Commissioners until he was killed in a duel on Mar. 22, 1820, by Capt. James Barron.

The Board of Navy Commissioners had been created by Congress in 1815 to assist the secretary of the navy in administering the various squadrons. The War of 1812 had clearly demonstrated that the secretary and his small staff were unable to manage the navy efficiently. The three captains who sat on the board, therefore, provided the type of technical assistance that the civilian secretary needed in order to fulfill the duties of his office. Yet at the same time, the secretary retained control of navy policy and thereby maintained civilian control of the department. The major problem with the board was its basic conservatism and reluctance to accept most of the technological innovations that would keep the U.S. Navy on an equal footing with the other navies of the world. In 1842, Congress replaced the board with five bureaus.

In general, the basic strategy employed by the U.S. Navy in the post–War of 1812 era was based on the use of small ships. The navy's mission was to protect the expanding U.S. commerce, and there was no great nation posing a maritime threat. Instead, it was pirates such as those in Algiers and Tripoli or privateers and commerce raiders who presented the navy its strongest challenge. Any attempt to capture these pirates with ships of the line was virtually impossible. Consequently, the navy decided to employ its ships in small squadrons that would patrol specific areas of the world. The first squadron was established in the Mediterranean, and others were established as the need arose: the Pacific Squadron in 1818; the South Atlantic Squadron in 1826; the East Indian Squadron in 1835; the Home Squadron in 1841; the African Squadron in 1843.

Military Command Structure

Secretaries of War Crawford and Calhoun took positive steps to strengthen the administration of the army. In 1813, the problems caused by the stress and strain of the war on the administrative system of the army had prompted Congress to establish an army general staff to assist with the department's wartime administration. The General Staff in actuality consisted of a number of autonomous bureau chiefs, including the adjutant general, the inspector general, the quartermaster general, and (later) the surgeon general and the commissary general of subsistence. Each of these bureau chiefs reported directly to the secretary of war. In 1816 and 1818, Congress passed additional acts to strengthen

John C. Calhoun became secretary of war in 1817 under Pres. James Monroe and was a strong advocate of reorganization of the U.S. Army. (Library of Congress)

the General Staff and to ensure that the secretary had sufficient access to professional advice.

However, the bureau system created new problems. The bureau chiefs, who occupied their positions for long periods, often came into conflict with secretaries of war, who, as political appointees, were unlikely to occupy their positions for extended periods of time. In addition, the bureau chiefs tended to guard their areas of specialization jealously, and the consequent lack of cooperation among the bureaus frequently thwarted efficient management of the War Department.

The creation of the General Staff with its various bureaus also created a continuing struggle for precedence between line and staff officers. Line officers felt that staff officers were not really their equals because the staff officers did not command troops and did not suffer the hardships that the line officers endured with the troops in the field. Staff officers, for their part, resented the attitudes of the line officers. Yet the problem of who commanded the staff officers when they were in the field was a serious one and frequently brought commanders into direct conflict with the bureau chiefs in Washington.

The question of who controlled staff officers when they were operating in one of the military districts had been raised before Calhoun came into office. Jackson had raised the question of the appropriate chain of command for staff officers in his division when he asked the War Department for an explanation of why Maj. Stephen H. Long of the Topographical Engineers had been ordered to Washington without Jackson having received a copy of the order. Chief clerk of the War Department and acting secretary of war Graham returned a sharp reply to the general, informing him that the War Department would continue to assign officers to special duties without consulting with him. Jackson, ever mindful of his position and ever ready to take exception to what he believed to be an affront to his station, took the case to President Monroe. Jackson argued against the policy that the War Department could move officers without the knowledge of the commander of the affected geographic region. When Monroe did not answer quickly enough to suit him, Jackson ordered officers in his division to ignore any War Department orders that did not pass through his headquarters.

This independent order received a prompt response from Monroe, who informed Jackson that all orders from the War Department were to be considered the orders of the president and, therefore, were to be executed. Jackson's original protest concerning the chain of command was quickly lost in the larger issue of the president's constitutional role as commander in chief. Despite Calhoun's efforts, the issue remained clouded and would cause further problems.

In 1818, Jackson court-martialed a deputy commissary who had disregarded an order from him. Secretary Calhoun canceled the court-martial but again left the issue unresolved. In yet another case, Jackson countermanded the order of the surgeon general to the assistant surgeon generals and post surgeons that they should submit their reports directly to Washington without sending them through Jackson's division headquarters. Consequently, Calhoun informed Jackson that he would have to change his policy. In a forceful letter, Calhoun made his point: If Jackson refused, Calhoun would take whatever actions were necessary to ensure that the orders of the government were carried out. Although Jackson relented, the questionable relationship between staff and line persisted, and it would periodically surface to create further problems throughout the rest of the century.

Calhoun took the opportunity to correct another serious problem in the administration of the army when Congress reduced the number of generals in the army to three (one major general and two brigadier generals) in 1821. Previously, the regular army lacked a supreme commander; the country was divided into departments whose commanders operated independently, although their actions were theoretically coordinated by the secretary of war. Calhoun decided that Major General Brown be brought to Washington to become the commanding general of the army. The two brigadiers, Scott and Gaines, would command the two

Pres. John Quincy Adams oversaw the 1828 controversy about the appointment of a supreme commander of the U.S. Army. (Library of Congress)

geographic departments. On the surface, it appeared that the changes should have eliminated many of the problems that had plagued the War Department. The secretary would receive technical advice from the bureau chiefs and direct the activities of the army through the commanding general. However, the reluctance of the bureau chiefs to cooperate and questions about the commanding general's authority caused continuing friction.

Another problem was the choice of Brown's successor. After Brown died on Feb. 24, 1828, Pres. John Quincy Adams and the secretary of war (first James Barbour and then Peter Porter) were in a difficult situation since the two department commanders, Scott and Gaines, detested each other. If either was named as commanding general, the other would view it as a personal insult and probably resign from the army. Much of the controversy between the two men centered around a question of rank, as both claimed to be the senior officer. Because their commissions as brigadier generals bore the same date, Gaines claimed alphabetical seniority. However, Scott's brevet as a major general antedated Gaines's brevet, so Scott claimed he was senior.

The solution finally reached by the War Department only created another problem. Alexander Macomb, who had been retained as a colonel in 1821, was promoted over both Scott and Gaines. In bitterness, Scott resigned his commission. The War Department was able to placate him enough to recall his letter of resignation, but for a long time, Scott had only the most formal relations with Macomb.

Calhoun's most lasting contribution as secretary of war was an idea rather than a substantial change in the administrative machinery of the War Department. The idea was for an expansible army. Calhoun was driven to the plan when Congress decided to cut the authorized size of the regular army to 6,000 men in 1820. The basic premise behind Calhoun's plan was that the nation had to rely on regulars to defend the nation rather than on a mobilized militia. Consequently, he proposed to build an army that would be capable of expanding during a national emergency without reducing its efficiency. In order to accomplish this feat, the peacetime force would maintain a full organization of companies and regiments that would be manned at full strength by staff and line officers. The disparity between the peacetime and wartime strengths was in the number of privates in the organization. Upon the outbreak of war, the new privates brought into the already existing companies would be trained by experienced officers. Calhoun said that an expansible regular army of 6,316 men could be expanded to 11,558 without the addition of a single officer. An even larger force of 19,035 men could be fielded by adding just 288 officers.

Calhoun contended that new recruits placed in existing units with trained officers and noncommissioned officers would be more easily trained and would become good soldiers more rapidly than they could under new officers and noncommissioned officers. Calhoun's idea was rejected by Congress in 1821 when the regular army was reduced to an authorized strength of 6,183. Some regiments were eliminated, and the number of officers was reduced.

THE WESTERN FRONTIER

The advance of the settlement line across the continent meant that the members of the regular army would have to face the challenge of maintaining peace between restless, ever-advancing settlers and various Indian peoples. The soldiers were continually called upon to advance into frontier areas, ahead of the settlers. To protect these settlers, the army had established a line of forts known as the military frontier in the 18th and early 19th centuries. In 1816, there were only three U.S. military posts west of the Mississippi River (Forts Claiborne, Osage, and Belle Fontaine). Yet in the 1820s, more than 60 percent of the army was stationed on the western frontier. The presence of soldiers on the frontier helped maintain order and encouraged the Euro-American settlement of the region. The ever-expanding nature of the army's responsibilities on the frontier was indicated by the growing number of posts the troops were called upon to occupy. In the first years of Pres. Thomas Jefferson's administration (1801–09), there had been 27 posts. When Calhoun became secretary of war in 1817, there were 73 garrisons.

The ideal location for a frontier post was on a river, preferably on a bluff or hill in the "V" formed by the junction of two rivers. The river furnished protection against attack on at least one side and ensured a continuous supply of water. The river was also a ready-made highway that could be used for the transportation of both men and supplies. The army used every available method of river transportation, including the new steamboats, during the 19th century.

There were various classifications of military garrisons used by the U.S. Army. A dwelling place with permanent wooden structures and various conveniences was called a "cantonment." Usually it lacked extensive defenses and was occupied for only one or two seasons. The dwelling place and high-walled defense position of troops was called a fort. This type of facility was characteristic of the region east of the Great Plains where timber was plentiful. When the army moved onto the Great Plains and such building supplies were not readily available, army garrisons were commonly made of adobe and were more properly called posts.

The soldiers stationed at a certain post were responsible for its construction. As they continued to occupy the post, they made improvements and slowly converted the fort into a structure of brick and stone. Indeed, the army possessed something that the pioneer family could never hope for, the use of large numbers of men in a coordinated operation directed toward a common goal. Between 1783 and 1846, U.S. Army troops constructed, either completely or in part, 148 forts, which were occupied for varying periods.

Administrative Changes

The regular army had been reduced even before the Treaty of Ghent was ratified, and on Mar. 3, 1815, Congress further reduced the size of the regular army to a maximum of 10,000 enlisted men. This force was to be composed entirely of infantry and artillery, the dragoons having been dropped from the army's table of organization. Since the military frontier was still in the woodlands east of the Mississippi River, dragoons were a relatively ineffective fighting force in dealing with the Indians. Another important consideration in eliminating the dragoons was the fact that cavalry was expensive to maintain, and Congress was concerned with cutting expenditures.

The War of 1812 had pointed out one glaring weakness in the army's supply system, that the contract system was inefficient and at times had left the army almost devoid of supplies. In April 1818, Congress abolished the contract system and made the commissary general, whose office was established by the same act, responsible for supplying the troops. The soldiers would no longer have to depend upon the whims of a civilian contractor who might or might not meet his obligations.

To aid the supply system, a policy was instituted in 1818 that required that the garrisons of permanent posts maintain their own vegetable gardens. The gardens were to supply the garrisons throughout the year. Vegetables that were grown beyond the needs of the garrison could be sold to the commissary at the post. Profits from the sales were to be distributed among the enlisted men at the post on payday. It was not long, however, before this system received severe criticism from inspecting officers, for it was found that the soldiers at many posts were spending more time tending their gardens than on their duties.

The War of 1812 had demonstrated that roads were needed to provide adequate transportation and communications, then lacking on the frontier. As a result, the army turned to its soldiers for the construction of roads. For this labor, the soldiers were usually paid an extra 15 cents per day. The roads were normally constructed between frontier posts in order to facilitate communications and the transportation of supplies. The roads were generally rough tracks cut through the forest, with the stumps of the trees cut to a height of six inches and left to rot away. Although primitive, the roads served their purposes.

The army's efforts to improve transportation were aided in the years after the War of 1812 by the Corps of Engineers (created in March of 1802) and the Topographical Engineers (authorized in May 1816 and placed in the Topographical Bureau of the Engineering Department by Secretary of War Calhoun in 1818). Major Roberdeau was placed in charge of the Topographical Bureau and presided over the collection of information submitted by the engineers.

In the following years, the Corps of Engineers and the Topographical Engineers made significant contributions to the improvement of inland transportation. In the first 10 years of its existence (1802–12), West Point produced only 71 graduates, and this was the only source of trained engineers in the United States. By 1824, the federal government was deeply involved in improving the nation's transportation system. The engineers were operating a professional training school, undertaking western explorations and mapping the nation, determining the extent of the nation's mineral resources, surveying rivers and harbors, and designating the courses of roads and canals.

With the General Survey Act of 1824, Congress intended to coordinate the projects undertaken to improve the transportation system. The president was given the authority to have surveys and plans prepared of the routes that he believed to be of national importance. The national government would then subscribe to stock in the companies undertaking these projects. To carry out the provisions of this act, President Monroe established the Board of Engineers for Internal Improvements. In 1828, the board reported that in 4 years it had surveyed 100 projects, including 34 canal routes, 18 roads, and 44 river and harbor projects. Despite this activity, during the 14 years the General Survey Act was in effect, the appropriations for the board were only $424,000.

Exploration and Survey

One of the most prominent members of the Topographical Engineers was Long, who received his commission as a second lieutenant in 1815. Long's first assignment took him to St. Louis, where he prepared plans for a new arsenal. He then proceeded to Lake Peoria and the Illinois River, where he examined sites for a military post. One side benefit of this trip was a map of the Illinois country that Long prepared in 1816. He gave special attention to the possible improvement of the rivers in the area and the most likely places for roads and canals.

In 1817, Lieutenant Long was ordered to make a topographical survey of the upper Mississippi River and the Wisconsin River, paying particular attention to the selection of sites for future military installations. He accomplished this mission and, after 75 days in the Northwest, Long was dispatched by the War Department to the Arkansas frontier. The purpose of the reconnaissance on the Arkansas River was to select a site for a fort on the river near the boundary of the Osage territory. Long selected a site and named the fort erected there Belle Point (the name was later changed to Fort Smith).

In 1818, Long received orders to conduct an expedition to the land between the Mississippi River and the Rocky Mountains. He was to survey several of the large rivers in the area—the Missouri, the Red, the Arkansas, and the Mississippi above the mouth of the Missouri—but the scope of this expedition was later limited to the Missouri, Red, and Arkansas rivers. In order to transport the members of his expedition on the western waters, Long oversaw the construction of a steamboat, the *Western Engineer*, at Pittsburgh.

Long's expedition spent nearly a year exploring the Great Plains, during the course of which it discovered Long's Peak. The report of the expedition helped to perpetuate the myth of the Great American Desert, and the accompanying cartography became the area's basic map for many years. In 1823, the War Department ordered Long to lead an expedition to the Red River of the North and then to the 49th parallel. At Pembina (in what is now the extreme northeast corner of North Dakota), Long ascertained the location of the parallel, which separates the United States and Canada, something that had not been done before because no one possessing the technical skill had traveled through that region.

The use of a steamboat in Long's 1819 expedition was emblematic of a new development in frontier settlement, and the army's use of steamboats demonstrated that they were a practical means of transportation. The *Western Engineer* was the first steamboat to make a successful appearance on western waters and was one of six steamboats that the army had operating on the western rivers in that year. In December 1818, the quartermaster general had let a contract for the construction of five steamboats, which were to be used to transport troops and provisions up the Mississippi. The steamboat became the primary mode of transportation on the western rivers until the railroad era.

Later in his career, Long, no longer making surveys for the Topographical Engineers but still a member of the Corps of Engineers, was assigned the duty of improving the western rivers, primarily the Mississippi, Ohio, Missouri, and Arkansas rivers. Long was ordered to survey routes for a canal around the Falls of the Ohio and to remove snags below the falls. On the Mississippi, he was to remove snags from the mouth of the Missouri. On the Missouri, he was to remove snags from the Mississippi to Fort Leavenworth. On the Arkansas, he was to remove snags and fallen trees. In the four years that he worked at this assignment, Long and his men removed more than 150,000 obstacles. This constant attention to the problems of navigation on the western rivers was a great aid to the nation's transportation network, and it was a job that no state could or would undertake at its own expense.

Early in 1816, the War Department began a survey to determine where new fortifications should be constructed and which of the existing fortifications should be improved and expanded. The secretary of war requested that the governors of the various states have their legislatures cede the land needed if they had not already done so. The construction of the new works was a logical result of the War of 1812, when many of the permanent fortifications had been found to be inadequate. By May, Congress had appropriated $838,000 for the construction of fortifications during 1816. The secretary of war informed Gen. Joseph G. Swift (chief engineer of the army) that the soldiers who worked on the fortifications were to receive an extra 15 cents per day and an additional ration of spirits. The payments were to be made at the end of each month and would enable the soldiers almost to double their monthly salary. The construction of the works was delayed because Congress had authorized President Madison to employ French engineer Gen. Simon Bernard, who had to confer with Swift before the work could begin.

The president had determined that the soldiers should be put to work on the frontier. They were to begin cutting a road from the Tennessee River to Mobile and New Orleans—a project "no less necessary to the discipline, health, and preservation of the troops, than useful to the public interest," according to the president. General Jackson was to select the best route for the road and assign the troops to the operation.

On Aug. 15, 1816, Jackson was authorized to requisition whatever tools his troops might need for opening the new road from Tennessee to Mobile. In September he was to have other troops begin working on the road from Columbia, Tennessee, to Madisonville, Louisiana. Congress had appropriated $10,000 to repair that road and the road from Georgia to Fort Stoddert. However, the secretary had decided that all of the funds should be expended on only one of the roads.

It was not until May 1817 that the soldiers began to work on the road. The road from Madisonville to Muscle Shoals on the Tennessee River was to be opened by troops under Lt. John Tarrant. The route they were to follow had been marked through the wilderness by Capt. Hugh Young, an assistant topographical engineer. The assistant adjutant general of the 8th Department issued detailed instructions to Tarrant to guide him in the work on the road: (1) the path was marked by a single blaze on the trees on the north and south sides; (2) the road was to be 35 feet wide; (3) all streams, except the Pearl and Tombigbee rivers, were to be bridged; (4) all bridges were to be above the high-water mark and framed; (5) causeways were to be built through swamp grounds and were to be high enough to allow passage in the wet season; (6) ditches were to be dug on each side of the causeway, 4-feet wide and 3-feet deep; (7) the width of the causeways was to be 27 feet; (8) at streams with firm sandy bottoms, the road was to be cut down to the water at the best fording place near the bridge.

FIRST SEMINOLE WAR

In 1817, Jackson suggested that Indians known to be a threat within U.S. territory be followed into Florida and attacked in their refuge. The idea of pursuing the Indians into Florida was not new. Gaines had been told earlier to "use sound discretion in the propriety of crossing the line and attacking them and breaking up their towns."

Jackson's activities in Spanish Florida during the spring and summer of 1817, beginning what became known as the First Seminole War, were extremely effective and brought an end to the Indian war. He soundly defeated the hostile forces in a number of small engagements, executed two Englishmen captured among the Indians, and, finally, captured two Spanish towns, St. Marks and Pensacola. He appointed one of his officers as the civil and military governor of Pensacola and established U.S. revenue laws there.

In 1818, while Jackson was pursuing the Indians through Florida, an incident occurred that tested the relations between civil and military authorities. A part of Jackson's force consisted of about 1,600 Creek warriors, under the leadership of Gen. William McIntosh, a Euro-Creek. While the Creek warriors were assisting Jackson, a company of Georgia militia attacked a Creek village and killed most of the inhabitants, mainly women, children, and old men, including McIntosh's uncle, Chief Howard. In addition, many of the young men serving with Jackson's army were from the village and had lost members of their families. The entire incident was a deplorable blunder on the part of the militia since they had attacked the wrong village.

Upon learning of the affair, Jackson ordered the arrest of the officer who had commanded the attacking troops, Capt. Obed Wright. Jackson feared that the friendly Indians would leave him and return home to protect their families. Jackson also feared that if Wright were not punished, the Indians might take some punitive action on their own. However, since Wright's militia company had not been sworn into federal service, it was responsible to the state rather than to federal authorities.

Wright was arrested by one of Jackson's officers and confined under military guard. Shortly after a civil court ordered his release, Wright was arrested again by order of Governor Rabun of Georgia. The governor intended to have him tried by a federal court. Both Jackson and Rabun felt that Wright should be punished, but they could not agree on the question of who should try him. In their attempt to bring the case to justice, the two men eventually lost patience with each other. Jackson informed the governor that no state official had the right to issue military orders while he (Jackson) was in the field with a military force. The governor considered Jackson's letter haughty and stated that he would continue to issue orders.

Both men submitted their views to President Monroe for his opinion. On June 2, 1818, Secretary of War Calhoun informed Jackson that the trial of Wright by a court-martial was preferable to a trial in the federal court. It was believed that a trial by a jury in federal court would be a mockery. The secretary suggested that all officers of the grade of captain who had accompanied Wright should also be arrested and tried. The following day, the governor of Georgia was told that "the defense of the Georgia frontier will be devised by the general commanding in that quarter." In August 1818, it was reported that Wright would be tried under an 1802 law against killing Indians. By the end of the month, Wright had broken his parole and fled from the United States.

The Southeast

The acquisition of the Floridas from Spain in 1819 under the Adams-Onis Treaty ended the First Seminole War and meant that the army's manpower would be spread in an even thinner line across the frontier. Long estimated the length of the frontier line in 1818 as 12,885 miles, and by the end of the same year, the secretary of war reported that

United States Acquisition of the Floridas, 1810–1819

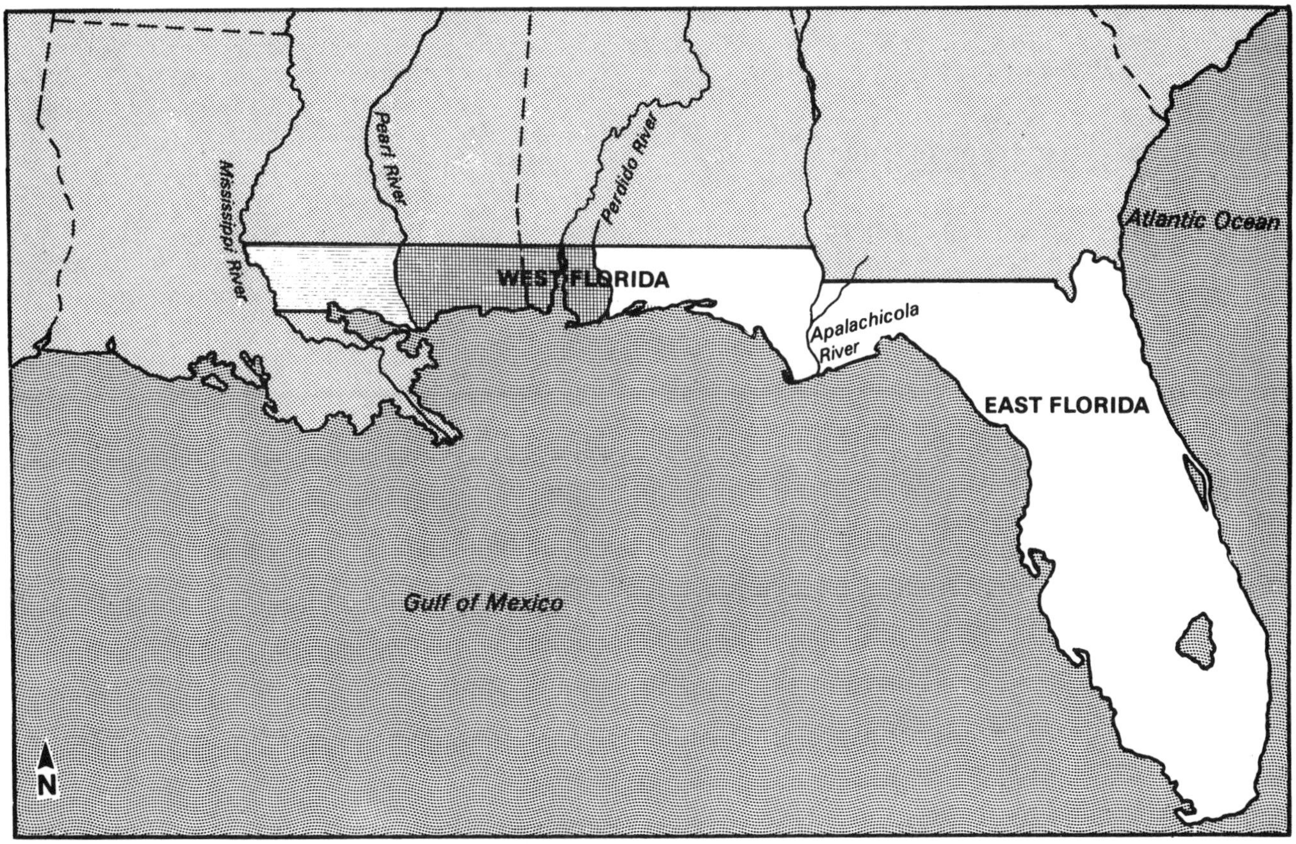

Seized 1810

Seized 1813

Aquired by Adams-Onis Treaty, 1819

there were 8,668 men in the army. The acquisition of the Floridas, therefore, caused a pause in the army's movements on the frontier, for, as in the case of past territorial occupations, the U.S. Army was forced to consider carefully the disposition of its limited force.

In February 1821, the Adams-Onis Treaty was finally ratified by the U.S. Senate and was proclaimed on February 22. Within a week, Congress adopted a new organization for the army. Despite the recommendation of Secretary of War Calhoun that his plan for an expansible force be adopted, Congress reduced the size of the army from 12,664 to 6,183 men. Twenty days after the reduction of the army, orders were issued to occupy Florida, an operation that would require that garrisons in other parts of the country be stripped of most of their troops. The troops from Mobile were to occupy Pensacola. Fort Gadsden was to be evacuated, and the troops were to march to St. Marks, while the troops from Amelia Island were to go to St. Augustine.

In the meantime, troops in the Alabama Territory were given the task of curtailing the illegal cutting of public timber. Reports indicated that a large quantity of cedar and other timber was being cut and floated down the Alabama and other rivers in the territory to the Gulf of Mexico. The soldiers were to patrol the public lands and prevent any further thefts. The names of the individuals found cutting the trees and any evidence collected were to be turned over to the district attorney.

The troops assigned to watch for the illegal cutting and shipping of timber had some success. Orders were issued to Lt. Col. William Trimble, commanding the 8th Department, to have a naval officer examine the cedar logs that had been confiscated at Mobile. Any logs that were found to be suitable for shipbuilding were to be turned over to the navy; the others were to be offered at a public sale, with proceeds going to the U.S. Treasury. The timber confiscation became the subject of some controversy. Capt. George Peters, who had seized a raft of logs, was taken to court by the men who claimed it was their property. The secretary of war ordered the district attorney for the area to defend the officer on behalf of the government, and this was the first in a long series of similar court cases.

On the eastern part of the Florida frontier, the troops were occupied throughout 1820 in preventing the illegal importation of slaves into the United States and apprehending runaways. The runaways were returned to their masters when they were identified and when the bills incurred during their detention were paid.

THE MONROE DOCTRINE

The Monroe Doctrine, as first enunciated by President Monroe in his annual message to Congress on Dec. 2, 1823, was prompted by a fear that the European powers were preparing to divide up among themselves the newly independent, former colonies of Spain. The president's message included four main points: (1) the American continents should no longer be considered as locations for future colonization by the European powers; (2) there existed in the Americas a political system that was different and separate from the political system of Europe; (3) the United States would consider any attempt on the part of the European powers to extend their political system to the Americas to be dangerous to the peace and safety of the United States; (4) the United States would not *(a)* interfere with existing European colonies in the New World, *(b)* interfere in the internal affairs of European nations, *(c)* take part in any European wars that had no direct relation to the United States.

Monroe's pronouncement drew little international attention at the time. If the European powers even considered it, they did so with contempt. The United States did not possess the military force necessary to enforce the doctrine. Its navy was not strong enough to prevent a European power from bringing a military force to the New World, and its army was not large enough to intervene against a European force in the former Spanish colonies. Only in later years would the Monroe Doctrine come to play an important part in U.S. defense policy.

The Southwest

As the military frontier moved steadily westward, events were taking place in the Southwest that would drastically alter the composition of the U.S. Army. U.S. merchants had discovered the lucrative Santa Fe trade and were sending caravans of heavily loaded wagons into Mexican territory in order to gain a share in the profits. In the autumn of 1828, however, a returning caravan was attacked by Indians and suffered loss of life and property.

The merchants requested that the government supply a military escort to protect the 1829 caravan. The government complied with the request by ordering four companies of the 6th Infantry to escort the wagons to the boundary with Mexico. The troops were transferred from Jefferson Barracks, Missouri, west to Cantonment Leavenworth, on the Missouri River, which would be their point of departure for Santa Fe, by the steamboat *Diana,* owned by the American Fur Company. To transport the escort's supplies, the army tried a method that had never been employed on the plains. To avoid the greater cost of horses and mules, the military wagons would be drawn by oxen. In the opinion of the army's higher eschelons, the oxen might be slower but they were edible.

The troops escorted the merchants to the Arkansas River, where they waited for the caravan to return from Santa Fe on the east bank of the river. It was during this period that the infantry discovered that they were no match for the mounted Indians of the Great Plains. The Plains Indians used hit-and-run tactics, and their swift ponies quickly placed them out of reach of the foot soldiers. Maj. Bennet Riley, the commander of the escort, reported upon his return to Fort Leavenworth that his troops had been unable to pursue the Indians when they were under attack.

In December 1831, Sen. Thomas Hart Benton introduced a bill in the U.S. Senate that authorized the raising of mounted volunteers for the defense of the frontier. The bill passed both houses by December 29, and President Jackson signed the bill into law on Jan. 18, 1832. The president was given the authority to raise six companies of one-year volunteers who were to furnish their own arms and mounts and be compensated at the rate of $1 per day. The Mounted Rangers proved to be less than satisfactory, and in December 1832, a bill was introduced to convert the rangers into a regiment of dragoons.

On Mar. 2, 1833, the new bill passed through Congress and was signed by the president. The bill authorized the discharge of the rangers and the enlistment of dragoons as a part of the regular army. The new regiment of dragoons was to be composed of 1,832 men and financed by sufficient appropriations. This organization was to be the 1st Dragoons, commanded by Col. Henry M. Dodge, previously an officer in the mounted volunteers, with Lt. Col. Stephen Watts Kearny as second in command. The intention, as the name "dragoon" implied, was for the men to ride only until it was time to fight, then they would dismount and fight on foot. The first year of the dragoons' existence would turn the survivors into seasoned veterans.

During the summer of 1833, the men of the 1st Dragoons began to arrive at Jefferson Barracks. The men arrived before their equipment, supplies, and, most important, their horses. In November, the Western Division headquarters decided to send those members of the 1st Dragoons who were organized and trained on a 500-mile march to Fort Gibson on the Arkansas River. Three companies of mounted troops and two dismounted companies began the long march, which most of the men survived to reach Fort Gibson. The march, through winter storms and uninhabited territory, turned the men into veteran cavalrymen in a short period.

The remaining five companies of the 1st Dragoons moved to Fort Gibson in the spring of 1834. Almost as soon as the entire regiment was assembled, Brig. Gen. Henry Leavenworth led them off on a mission that would complete their introduction to life on the Great Plains. The entire regiment, all mounted, would march more than 200 miles farther west from Fort Gibson. The purpose of the movement was to visit the Pawnee and Comanche villages, make treaties with the Indians, and conduct a general reconnaissance of the area. The veterans of the winter march now found themselves struggling through the blistering summer heat of the Great Plains. The heat and bad water took their toll on many of the men and their horses. Kearny and a number of men and horses that could not continue the march were left behind at the junction of the Little and Canadian rivers. By the time the rest of the dragoons reached the False Washita River, fewer than half were still able to travel. Leavenworth, unable to continue, stopped with the rest of the sick. However, he instructed Dodge to take the 200 men who were still physically able to ride and continue on to the Indian villages. Dodge was able to reach the Pawnee and Comanche and negotiate the treaties that the government wanted. Upon his return to Fort Gibson, the 1st Dragoons were no longer fit for duty, and rest and recuperation were needed before they could actively participate in any military operations.

The bill authorizing the dragoons had not been enacted in time to allow them to escort the 1833 caravan on the Santa Fe Trail; instead, a mixed command of a few members of the 6th Infantry and one company of mounted rangers had furnished protection for the merchants' wagons. However, the dragoons, after an absence of 18 years, were returned to the organizational framework of the army. The demand for mounted troops was to become greater and greater in the years to come as the army was called upon to deal with the Indians of the Great Plains.

Personnel Reforms and Problems

U.S. troops were required to render steadfast service in the face of countless hardships but could not hope to receive personal fame or material rewards. In these circumstances, men were reluctant to offer their services to the federal government without the incentive supplied by a national emergency, and many of those who enlisted were not of high caliber. This situation had existed since the American Revolution, but it was not until the late 1820s and the early 1830s that a concerted effort was made to improve the type of men who served in the ranks of the army. The reforms were directed at the enlisted men and had little effect on the officers. The first reform attempted was one designed to make the army more American.

The enlisted strength of the army in peaceful periods was drawn largely from the northeastern cities and at times consisted of a large number of immigrants. In fact, during the years 1821–23, approximately 25 percent of the men who entered the U.S. Army were foreign born. In 1825, however, the *General Regulations*—which in 1820 had stated that "all free male persons, above eighteen and under thirty-five" who were physically fit might enlist—were revised to read that "no foreigner shall be enlisted in the Army without special permission from general headquarters." The number of enlistments dropped in 1825 and 1826, and the restriction was removed on Aug. 13, 1828, when it was ordered that all residents of the United States could be accepted for service, without regard to place of birth.

Although the officers complained about the type of recruits that the army attracted, little or no improvement could be expected as long as no inducements could be offered to attract more favorable recruits. The term of service was long; the duties were arduous; the hazards were many; the chances to advance were limited; the pay was low; and the benefits to be derived from the service were few. Many Americans viewed the very existence of the army with suspicion. Faced with these uninviting prospects, most were reluctant to enlist. In addition, a large proportion of the enlistees deserted before their terms of service expired.

As a result, the actual strength of the army was rarely equal to that authorized by Congress. Even when the paper strength of the army was increased by congressional action to meet specific emergencies, such as the War of 1812, the number of men who entered the army fell short of the new quotas. In the early years, the disparity between real and authorized strength lay in the numbers of both officers and enlisted men on duty. After the War of 1812, when many officers chose to remain in the service and new vacancies in the officer corps were filled with graduates from the Military Academy, a deficiency resulted because the number of enlisted men was lower than authorized by law.

The condition of the U.S. economy also influenced the recruiting efforts of the army. During periods of prosperity, most men could find some type of employment that would pay them considerably more than they could receive for service in the army. Yet when periods of recession and depression set in, many found the prospect of steady military service to be inviting. As might be expected, a direct relationship also existed between the economic condition of the country and the rate of desertion from the army; that is, desertions rose during periods of prosperity and fell during periods of depression.

Economic conditions also influenced the differences between the actual and the authorized strength of the army. During the depression that lasted from 1816 through 1820, the number of army officers was higher than the authorized level in four of the five years. In the middle three years of the same period, the enlisted strength was not substantially below the legal limit and fluctuated only slightly. Economic factors alone cannot fully explain why men chose to join or leave the army, but it appears that they were important considerations.

The recruiting parties, therefore, faced not only the task of increasing the size of the army to its legal limit, but also of matching the rate at which men left the ranks, because of discharge, death, or desertion. The yearly losses from the ranks were such that it required a concerted effort to hold the strength at a constant level. Indeed, the high number of desertions were a constant drain upon the army's limited manpower. The War Department and the officers of the army were generally at a loss to explain why so many of the men who enlisted subsequently decided to desert. Most of those who ventured an opinion on the subject attributed the higher desertion rate to an 1812 act of Congress that prohibited flogging as a punishment for desertion.

On Jan. 25, 1830, Adj. Gen. Roger Jones reported on the 5,669 desertions since 1823. He noted that 1,340 recruits had deserted either from the mobilization point or before they joined their company. Another 2,796 had deserted during their first year, most of these during the first six months. Jones estimated that these 5,669 desertions represented a total loss of $471,263 to the government. The magnitude of the desertion problem is clearly illustrated by comparing the number of men who were either killed or wounded to the number of men who deserted. Between 1789 and 1846, the regular army was engaged in 168 actions in which 2,320 officers and men were killed and another 3,750 wounded. The 6,070 casualties suffered in combat by the regulars in 57 years was just slightly higher than the desertions reported for the short period from 1823 to 1829.

In his report to the U.S. Senate, Sec. of War John H. Eaton supported the conclusions of his officers. He added one factor that they had not considered: the limited opportunities for advancement open to enlisted men greatly influenced the level of recruits. Because of established practice, although not by law, the graduates of West Point had the exclusive privilege of becoming officers. The consequences of this system were that any hope of advancement based on loyal and meritorious service was futile. The enlisted man knew that no matter how diligently he worked and how proficient he became, he could not advance beyond the rank of sergeant. Eaton believed that if this practice were altered in some way, better recruits might be enlisted.

Secretary of War Eaton, Generals Macomb and Gaines, and Colonel Jones all agreed that some type of reform was necessary to improve the army. They also agreed on the essential areas that required attention: reducing the number of desertions, reducing the term of service from five years to either three or four years, making the punishments of military courts conform more closely to the nature of the crime committed in order to make them effective, increasing the pay of enlisted men to enable the army to compete more effectively with civilian employers, and, most important, discontinuing the ration of whiskey issued to the men and making additional efforts to curtail the intemperate habits of the soldiers. These reforms, recommended in 1830, were directed toward solving problems that had plagued the army and had hindered its operations since its early days. Although officials agreed in general as to what needed to be done, specific reforms would be difficult to achieve. Some problems could be eliminated simply by an order from the War Department, others required congressional action, and some virtually defied solution.

The Nullification Crisis

In bitter opposition to President Jackson's support of the tariffs of 1828 and 1832 and his advocacy of protectionism, a South Carolina convention met and adopted resolutions nullifying the tariff acts of 1828 and 1832 on Nov. 24, 1832. On November 27, the state legislature passed laws for the enforcement of the Nullification Ordinance. Provisions were included that authorized the raising of a military force and appropriations to buy weapons.

The political posturing continued until Jan. 16, 1833, when Jackson asked Congress to pass a law authorizing him to use military force, if necessary, to enforce the nation's revenue laws. At the same time that it was debating the Force Bill, Congress was debating a compromise tariff bill. Both pieces of legislation were passed by Congress, and the president signed them on March 2. As a result of the compromise tariff, the South Carolina legislature passed an ordinance rescinding the Nullification Ordinance on March 15. However, while the politicians were working out the compromise, the military establishment had been taking the actions necessary to prepare for any eventuality.

As the nullification crisis developed, the commander of the troops at Charleston, South Carolina, was cautioned to be alert to any attempt to seize the fortifications or other federal property in the city. On Oct. 29, 1832, the War Department ordered Maj. Julius Heileman to defend the fortifications against a possible attack by state militia forces. Early in November, two companies of artillery were dispatched from Fortress Monroe, Virginia, to reinforce the troops at Charleston. Commanding General Macomb instructed Heileman to inspect the ordnance stores in Charleston's arsenal and transfer any and all essential supplies to the fort in the harbor. The major was to keep the commanding general informed concerning conditions within the city and the state, specifically whether the people of South Carolina actually planned to resist federal authority. As a last precaution, he was to determine if any of his men were inclined to side with those who opposed the authority of the United States. If Heileman found any supporters of the nullification movement, they were to be transferred from Charleston.

On November 12, Macomb sent additional instructions to Heileman. If the authorities of South Carolina demanded that Heileman surrender the Citadel and the state weapons stored there, he was to comply with the request. The Citadel actually belonged to the city but was occupied by a company of artillerists. Heileman was cautioned to conduct all negotiations with the city and state officials in writing. He was to avoid any commitment about hostilities, but he was to defend himself if attacked.

On November 18, Sec. of War Lewis Cass ordered General Scott to Charleston. He was to inspect the fortifications and make any prudent repairs. He was also authorized to draw from other posts any additional troops that might be necessary in order to reinforce the garrisons in and around Charleston. The federal laws were to be enforced by the civil officials until the president decided otherwise.

In late November, Macomb informed Scott that four additional companies had been ordered to move from Fortress Monroe to Fort Moultrie and that all officers had been ordered to join their companies at Charleston. Col. James Bankhead was to assume command of the force gathering at Charleston. On December 7, another company of artillerists was ordered from Fortress Monroe to Charleston Harbor.

On Jan. 26, 1833, Cass ordered Scott to assume command of the forces gathering in South Carolina. The troops were to act only in self-defense against the citizens of the state. The secretary expressed concern for the security of the federal arsenal at Augusta, Georgia. He felt that Scott had acted wisely in ordering a company of troops from the Indian country to Augusta to reinforce the garrison. The arsenal was to be defended to the "last extremity" if it was attacked by the citizens. Col. David Twiggs, the arsenal commander, was to destroy the arms and ammunition rather than allow them to fall into the hands of South Carolinians.

While Congress considered the Force Bill and the compromise tariff, General Scott and his troops waited patiently to learn the outcome of the debates. On February 20, Cass told Scott that a settlement of the dispute by Congress was not certain and informed the general that until some definite decision was made, "the President relies upon you to pursue the same discrete and firm course you have heretofore taken." By mid-March, Macomb was able to inform Scott that if the situation in South Carolina had quieted sufficiently, he could begin to return the troops to their regular duties.

INDIAN REMOVALS

President Jackson's Indian policy centered around the emigration of the eastern tribes to lands west of the Mississippi River. In 1830, Congress made provisions for their removal; in 1834, it established a designated Indian territory in the Arkansas country. To manage relations with the Indians, the Bureau of Indian Affairs was established in 1836. Jackson followed a policy of extinguishing Indian land titles in the various states and then ordering the removal of the Indians. During his presidency, more than 90 treaties were concluded, with the Creek, Choctaw, and Chickasaw, among others. Only the Cherokee refused to cede their lands. Finally, on Dec. 29, 1835, the Cherokee relinquished all titles to their lands east of the Mississippi for $5,000,000 and land in the Indian territory.

The army had a number of duties connected with the Indian removals, most of which placed them squarely between the Indians and the white settlers. On more than one occasion, the troops found themselves on the side of the Indians opposing the whites and their elected representatives. The soldiers were responsible for seeing that the various treaties were enforced and that the legal provisions of the treaties and federal laws were observed. The troops were called upon to evict white settlers who had moved onto Indian lands before the Indians had formally given up their titles. The troops served as escorts for the Indians as they moved to the new Indian territory. In some cases, the troops were forced to protect the white settlers from Indians who were intent on carrying out retaliatory raids.

Black Hawk War

In cases when the Indians violently resisted removal from their homelands to lands west of the Mississippi, the army was called upon to subdue the tribes. In 1832, the troops of the regular army along with militia forces from Illinois participated in such an operation against the Sac and Fox Indians—a conflict that became known as the Black Hawk War. The problems with these Indians had begun in 1827 when the state of Illinois requested that the War Department have the tribes moved out of the state to an area west of the Mississippi River. While some of the Indians moved west of the river, one of their leaders, Black Hawk, refused to leave his village. When settlers began to move into the vicinity of Black Hawk's village, tensions rose and it appeared likely that fighting would soon erupt. Army regulars and Illinois militia were ordered to the village to prevent trouble, but when they arrived on the scene, they found that Black Hawk and his followers had crossed the

Mississippi into Iowa. Throughout the subsequent winter months, Black Hawk gathered assurances of support from other Indian tribes and was informed (mistakenly, as it turned out) that he could expect British support from Canada.

On Apr. 5, 1832, Black Hawk and approximately 1,800 men, women, and children recrossed the Mississippi River and entered their traditional territory in Illinois. Although they said that they planned no hostile actions, they were well armed and prepared to defend themselves. Officials again rushed troops to the area to prevent warfare. Gen. Henry Atkinson brought a force of 220 regulars from St. Louis, Missouri, to Fort Armstrong at Rock Island, Illinois, and Scott was ordered west from New York with additional troops. Governor Reynolds called out the Illinois militia, and eventually 1,700 volunteers were sent to the Rock River valley. Black Hawk never reached his former village. Instead, he continued up the Rock River in the hope of gaining support from the Winnebago and Pottawatomie. At the same time, Black Hawk refused Atkinson's demands that he surrender. However, when the Winnebago and Pottawatomie decided not to join his rebellion, Black Hawk chose to return to Rock Island and surrender to Atkinson.

On May 14, a small band of Sac who were attempting to surrender were fired upon by the Illinois militia. The resulting Battle of Stillman's Run proved to be an Indian victory, but it indicated that a peaceful settlement of the dispute was probably impossible. The Sac warriors fled north into Wisconsin where they hoped to cross the Mississippi and elude the large force that was pursuing them. After fighting a number of rearguard actions as well as the more significant Battle of Wisconsin Heights, Black Hawk and his followers reached the Mississippi River near the mouth of the Bad Axe River. Here, Black Hawk once more tried to surrender; again his offer was refused.

As the Indians attempted to cross the Mississippi, the regulars opened fire on them. Even more serious casualties were inflicted by the gunboat *Warrior* from Prairie du Chien, which caught the Indians in the middle of the river and repeatedly raked their rafts with fire from its six-pound gun. By the time the battle was over, most of the fleeing Sac were dead; those who reached the western side of the river were attacked by Sioux and either killed or captured. Black Hawk, however, survived the Battle of Bad Axe and was eventually allowed to surrender to officials in Wisconsin. He was later sent east to visit President Jackson and spent his later years in Iowa, where he died in 1838.

Although Scott had been ordered to Illinois with 1,000 infantrymen and artillerists from the East Coast, he did not arrive until five days after Bad Axe. He had only a small number of troops with him because Asiatic cholera had broken out aboard the transports as they crossed the Great Lakes. More than one-third of his force either died or was disabled by the sickness.

Second Seminole War

On Dec. 28, 1835, Capt. Francis L. Dade was leading an escort force for a supply column from Tampa Bay to Fort King. Dade's force consisted of a company of the 4th Infantry and one company each from the 2d and 3d artilleries. The men had nearly completed their 130-mile journey and had relaxed their march discipline as they neared Fort King. It was at this point that Seminole ambushed the force and killed 107 officers and men. Only two or three men of the escort force survived the attack. On the same day, near Fort King, Osceola, leader of the Seminole, and a band of warriors killed Wiley Thompson, the federal agent who was supposed to oversee the removal of the Seminole to Arkansas. Thus, with the massacre of Dade's force and the killing of Thompson, the Second Seminole War began. At the time, there were 536 officers and men of the regular army stationed in Florida under the command of Bvt. Brig. Gen. Duncan L. Clinch. There were fewer than 5,000 Indians in Florida, and of that number only about 1,200 were warriors.

The outbreak of the Second Seminole War presented President Jackson and Secretary of War Cass with an interesting dilemma. The country was divided into Eastern and Western departments; General Scott commanded the former while General Gaines commanded the latter. Although the war had begun in the Western Department, the president gave the command to Scott. Gaines was ordered to the western boundary of Louisiana to direct operations along the Texas border. Scott was then ordered to Florida to direct the war against the Seminole.

Scott, always the careful planner, stopped in both South Carolina and Georgia on his way to Florida. In both states he arranged for militia forces to be sent to Florida and set up a supply depot at Savannah. He arrived in Florida in late February 1836, but it was not until the first week in April that he would begin his campaign at Tampa. Before Scott could accomplish anything, however, the Seminole disappeared into the Everglades, a tactic they would employ successfully during most of the war.

Scott's problems in launching his operations were soon aggravated by the actions of his old adversary Gaines. Despite his orders, Gaines and a large force of Louisiana militia had arrived in Florida before Scott. Gaines used the provisions Scott had shipped to Florida for his campaign, fought an inconclusive battle with the Seminole, and then departed for New Orleans in March. Scott was furious, and the recriminations between the two generals caused the War Department to reprimand both for their conduct.

Scott also experienced logistical problems that were the result of a wholly inadequate transportation system and an almost complete lack of maps of the region. In addition, Scott managed to anger the citizens of not only Florida but also the people of the various states that had sent volunteers to serve with his force. Scott accused the people of Florida

The Seminole Wars, 1816–1858

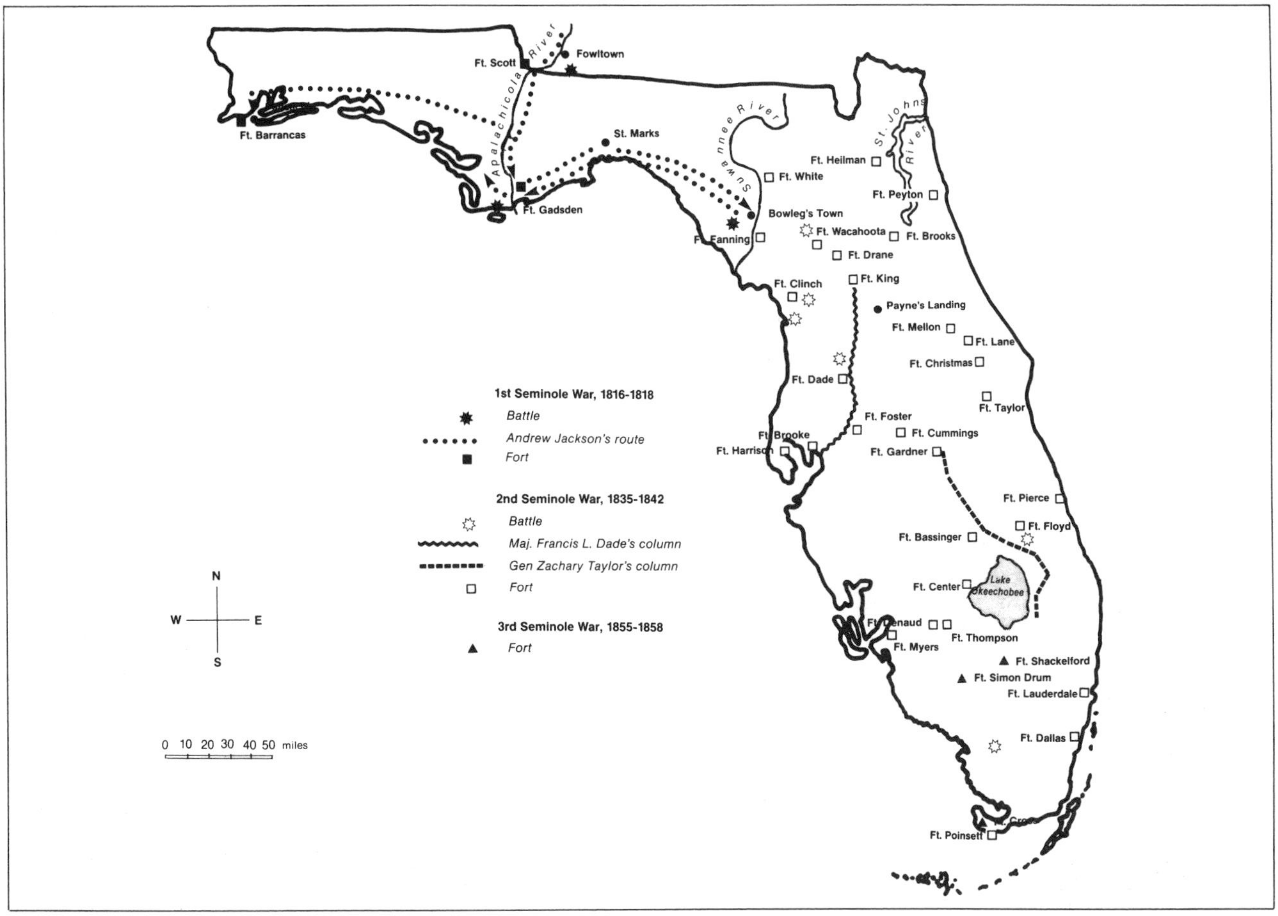

of being cowards and implied that the volunteers were not good soldiers and did not want to fight.

Because of his public relations problems, Scott was transferred to Georgia in May to assist in putting down a Creek uprising that was threatening to engulf Alabama, Georgia, and Florida in yet another Indian war. While in Georgia, Scott became involved in a serious controversy with Col. Thomas S. Jesup, who was commanding the regular troops in Alabama. The result was that Scott was ordered back to Washington to face an investigation of his conduct in Florida. Although he was absolved of any blame in the failure of the campaign, he was not returned to command in Florida. Instead, he was sent on a diplomatic mission to arbitrate conflicts between U.S. and Canadian settlers on the northern frontier.

Because of the shortage of army troops at the beginning of the Second Seminole War, Col. Archibald Henderson offered a regiment of marines for service in the conflict. Congress had passed a law on June 30, 1834, that had placed the Marine Corps under the direction of the secretary of the navy, but which also gave the president the authority to direct that the marines serve with the army if he believed that it was necessary. The same law enlarged the size of the corps and raised the rank of the commandant, Henderson, to the rank of colonel. President Jackson, who had once proposed the elimination of the corps, quickly accepted Henderson's offer. In less than two weeks, Henderson had collected and organized the regiment and was moving south to join the battle against the Seminole. In 1837, Henderson was acting brigade commander and participated with his regiment at the Battle of Hatchec-Lustec. Even though Henderson was ordered back to Washington to resume his duties as commandant, the marines remained in Florida to continue their operations with the army. In 1843, the Senate approved Henderson's promotion to brigadier general for his service as commander of the marines in Florida, Alabama, and Tennessee.

The overall command of the U.S. forces in the Second Seminole War was changed repeatedly. With Scott's departure, command in Florida fell to Jesup. From late 1836 until May 1838, Jesup won a number of decisive victories that led him to hope that the Seminole would realize that they were beaten. However, they continued to fight against all odds. In a move that demonstrated the unconventional nature of the war he was fighting, Jesup invited Chief Osceola to a conference under a flag of truce. When the

The American soldier of 1839, during the Second Seminole War. (U.S. Army Center of Military History)

Seminole arrived for the conference, they were taken captive. Jesup's disregard for military custom by violating the flag of truce outraged the people of the United States and Congress. It also proved to be counterproductive, as it merely made the Seminole fight even harder.

Col. Zachary Taylor replaced Jesup, and on Christmas Day 1837, he managed to bring the Seminole to the biggest battle of the war on the shore of Lake Okeechobee. Following the battle, the Seminole escaped into the swamps and reverted to guerrilla warfare. Taylor then proposed a strategy that might have been effective if it had been given enough time to work. Taylor's plan would have divided the entire region into sections, roughly 20-miles square, with a stockade in each section to protect the soldiers. The troops were to sweep through the sections on alternate days in an effort to search and destroy the hostile Indians. Taylor even employed bloodhounds at one point in an effort to track the Indians through the swamps. Taylor's strategy had two drawbacks: the use of bloodhounds again aroused public outrage, and the process of eliminating the Indians would be too time consuming.

The War Department was unwilling to invest the time necessary for Taylor's strategy to be effective. Consequently, hostilities were suspended and negotiations were tried again. When the negotiations failed and the hostilities resumed, Taylor asked to be relieved of his command. Col. Walker K. Armistead replaced Taylor and again tried to negotiate an end to the hostilities. When the negotiations failed, Armistead was replaced by Col. William J. Worth in May 1841. Worth brought a new strategy to the war. Rather than chase the elusive Indians through the swamps, he would destroy their homes and food supplies. The troops campaigned throughout the summer of 1841, thereby preventing the Indians from planting and raising their crops. In addition, villages and stores of food were destroyed whenever they were found. The Indians broke into small bands, and resistance simply faded away. By August 1842, the war was declared officially over.

The U.S. military establishment was clearly unprepared to fight a war such as the Seminole waged. Patterned after the British and European armies, the regular army was ill-prepared to fight an enemy that did not believe in fighting pitched battles. The Seminole were prepared to fight for as long as it took to break the will of their enemies. The strategy was almost successful, for not until Worth waged a devastating campaign against the entire Seminole people did their will to fight on against all odds fail.

The war had been costly. Almost 10,000 regulars and 30,000 short-term volunteers had seen service in Florida at various times. Close to 1,600 men had died either in combat or from disease. The war had cost the United States approximately $30,000,000.

An Era of Change

The two decades between the end of the War of 1812 and the beginning of the Second Seminole War had seen the beginning of some slow changes to the U.S. defense establishment. It was a period of transformation that would eventually bring about the emergence of a professional military force. The transition began earlier in the army than in the navy. The infusion of well-trained, highly professional young officers who graduated from West Point would eventually provide the leadership necessary to lead the army during a period of ever-expanding responsibilities. The navy, lacking a school for young officers during this period, was slower in beginning the transition toward professionalism. But by the end of the Florida war, the navy also had a cadre of officers that would help to change the force in the coming years.

The years of isolation, either at frontier posts or aboard ships at sea, gave officers and men the opportunity to hone their skills and learn their jobs. Despite the army's seeming inability to defeat the 1,200 Seminole warriors in Florida, the officers and men who participated in the campaigns gained invaluable experience. Although the military establishment would remain small in the coming years, it was being changed into a force capable of protecting the interests of the United States around the world.

3

Expansion and Reform: 1815–1846

During the period between the War of 1812 and the Mexican War (1846–48), the men of the U.S. armed forces continued to perform their duties at distant frontier posts and aboard ships sailing the seas of the world almost totally unaware of the forces that were transforming both the military and the society in which they lived.

TECHNICAL DEVELOPMENTS

In both the army and the navy, sweeping changes were taking place that would alter the way the nation planned its defense and eventually its perception of its place among the nations of the world. The technological changes of the era affected not only military hardware, but also the methods of transportation and communications vital to military operations. In the more strictly operational military areas, improvements in armaments, gunpowder, and guns and in the manufacturing of all types of military equipment would have a lasting impact on how the military would operate in the coming years.

Communications and Transportation

Prior to 1844, military communications had been no faster than the speed of a messenger, on foot or mounted. With the invention of the telegraph in 1844 by Samuel F. B. Morse, the potential existed for virtually instantaneous communication between military units and their commanders. But the telegraph was only one of a number of inventions that would eventually change military tactics and strategies. The beginning of efficient steamboat service, commercially introduced in 1807, freed waterborne transportation from the vagaries of wind and currents.

At the same time, the establishment of long-distance railroads provided transportation for men and supplies across the vast expanses of the interior United States. In most instances, poor weather did not hinder the operations of

Samuel F. B. Morse's invention of the telegraph in 1836 led to important advances in military communications. (Library of Congress)

Towns sprang up as the railroad advanced the frontier and army posts protected the settlers. (Library of Congress)

the railroads, whose main lines followed the advancing edge of settlement along the frontier. Eventually the railroads would solve many of the supply problems that the army had encountered on the frontier. The construction of railroads near the frontier posts encouraged the growth of civilian populations and the establishment of towns.

Frontier posts attracted settlers not only because they afforded protection against Indians, but also because they offered ready-made markets for surplus goods. The army depended upon the War Department and its quartermaster general for many of its supplies, but each post had its own commissary officer who purchased supplies for the garrison. The supplies purchased would be drawn from the vicinity of the fort; thus, not only did the fort offer a market for agricultural products, it was also a marketplace for skilled labor. The skills necessary to maintain the post and its men could not always be supplied by the army, and the settlers were ever ready to make up for any deficiency. Eighty-six towns arose on or near the sites of the 148 forts established between 1783 and 1846, an indication of the influence of the frontier post. As the army posts were erected on the Great Plains, they became way stations where wagon trains could stop to rest and repair their equipment under the watchful eye of the U.S. Army.

Firearms

Initially more important to the soldier in the field were the numerous inventions and innovations in personal armament. Over the first half of the 19th century, the basic weapon of the infantryman underwent a transformation that revolutionized warfare: the smoothbore musket gave way to the rifle, the flintlock was replaced by percussion caps, and muzzleloaders were slowly replaced by breechloading and repeating weapons.

The percussion cap, as perfected by Joshua Shaw, was made of copper and contained fulminate of mercury. The copper cap was placed on a cone, located where the flash pan had been, and when the hammer hit the cap, it exploded. The explosion was directed through a small hole into the barrel of the weapon where the main charge was ignited and the ball discharged.

No one seriously questioned the fact that rifles were vastly more accurate than the smoothbore muzzleloaders, but they were extremely difficult to load, especially with speed. When using a smoothbore muzzleloader, the soldier simply placed a wadding patch around the lead ball and rammed it home. There was no requirement for a tight fit. However, in a rifle, it was necessary for the ball actually to grip the rifling in order to apply the spin that gave the rifle its accuracy. In the early rifles, it was often necessary to ram the ball home using a hammer. Although the rifle was much more accurate, its slow rate of fire made it the weapon of choice only for hunters and a few elite military organizations. With the invention of a cylindroconoidal bullet by Capt. Claude E. Minié, a French army officer, the rapid loading of a rifle was possible. The new bullet, called the "minié ball," had a hollow base that expanded when the powder charge exploded, allowing the lead bullet to fill the rifling. Despite its obvious advantages, the U.S. Army would not adopt a percussion-cap, muzzleloading rifle until after the Mexican War. However, the new rifles were slowly making their way into the equipment of some of the state volunteer units. The rifles would prove their value by extending the effective range of the infantryman to almost 500 yards—a vast improvement over the 50–60-yard range of the old smoothbore weapon.

The development of an effective and reliable breechloading rifle would have to wait for the development of a metal cartridge. John H. Hall developed a breechloading rifle, but the weapon was far from perfect and posed almost as much of a risk of injury to the soldier firing it as to the enemy. The breech leaked, which allowed the gas intended to propel the bullet to escape and reduced the range and accuracy of the weapon. Even more dangerous for the individual firing the rifle, fire escaped along with the gas and blew into the rifleman's face. Hall's primary contribution came in the establishment, at Harpers Ferry Armory, of a mass-production facility for rifles. The system used precision machine tools to produce weapons with interchangeable parts. Although Eli Whitney had first publicized this system, it was Hall who implemented it.

Robert Fulton built (1814) the first steam warship, Fulton, *but military applications were delayed until the 1830s.* (Library of Congress)

Naval Technology

While technological changes were making their appearance in the army, similar innovations were being made in the navy. Iron hulls slowly replaced wood, and steam replaced wind as the main motive power. The first steam warship, the *Fulton,* had been constructed by Robert Fulton in 1814. Yet while commercial companies quickly adopted the concept of steam-powered vessels, the U.S. Navy was much slower to take advantage of the new technology.

Sec. of the Navy Mahlon Dickerson managed to authorize the construction of one steam warship, a second vessel named *Fulton,* in 1835. The ship, completed in 1837, was built under the supervision of Matthew C. Perry at the New York navy yard. The ship was never intended to be an oceangoing vessel, but was designed for harbor defense. Perry was the *Fulton*'s first commander, and for the next five years, he used the ship to demonstrate the advantages of steam-powered vessels. It was not until Congress forced Sec. of the Navy James K. Paulding to convene two special naval boards in 1839 that the construction of two oceangoing ships was authorized. In that year, Congress appropriated funds to construct three more steamships. Two of the ships, the *Mississippi* and the *Missouri,* were completed in 1842, using Perry's design. These two ships were constructed using the latest technological innovations yet the third ship never performed according to expectations.

One of the primary problems with the installation of steam engines in ships was the amount of room required for an engine of sufficient size to propel the vessel. Approximately one ton of machinery was required to provide one horsepower. Not only was the size of the engine a consideration, the early ships were equipped with side paddle wheels that seriously limited the number of guns that could be mounted on the ship. An additional problem created by the steam engines was the need for secure coaling facilities around the world. The space needed to carry coal reduced the area available for guns, crew members, and supplies. The navy was very much aware that the new steam-powered vessels were not nearly as self-sufficient as the old sailing vessels. A typical 19th-century cruise was two years or longer. During a cruise of the same length, steamships would require repair depots and extensive use of coaling stations in order to remain on patrol.

Matthew C. Perry commanded the second Fulton *steam warship (built 1835) and, believing steam-powered ships to be the future of the navy, urged the construction of more.* (U.S. Bureau of Ships—National Archives)

The new naval vessels would require overseas bases, and the United States had none.

In addition, the early steamships were highly vulnerable. Their exposed paddle wheels could be destroyed by a single well-placed shot. Although their wooden hulls were capable of withstanding a tremendous amount of punishment from solid shot, the development of exploding shells rendered them obsolete. These new shells would shatter the hull's wooden planks and set the ships on fire.

The difficulties presented by paddle wheels and wooden hulls would eventually be solved by advances in technology. The development of the screw propeller, placed below the water line at the ship's stern, eliminated the two main drawbacks associated with the paddle wheel: the propulsion system was no longer vulnerable to shell fire, and the sides of the ships were able to support more guns. The problem of wooden hulls was solved by iron plates and iron construction. In 1843, the *Michigan,* the first iron ship, was placed in service on the Great Lakes. The previous year, Congress had authorized the construction of a steam-powered, screw-propellered ironclad warship. However, the contract was never fulfilled, and France would launch the first seagoing ironclad in 1859.

The construction of ironclad ships presented the designers with a perplexing query: How much armor plating should be added to the sides of the ships? The issue was complicated by the fact that the same technology that allowed the manufacture of better armor plate also allowed for the construction of more powerful guns. The race to build ships with sufficient armor to protect them from existing guns while building better guns to penetrate the armor carried by the ships of potential enemies would continue into the 20th century. The first seagoing, iron-hulled ironclad was launched by the British in 1860.

Naval guns capable of firing shells, rather than shot, on a relatively flat trajectory, were developed by the French in the 1830s. By the end of the decade, both France and England had adopted the shell gun for their naval forces, and the United States quickly followed suit. The primary problem was the velocity of the shell being fired. Artillery pieces used by land forces had used shells for a number of years. However, they were designed for high trajectory and low velocity. Naval guns required flat trajectory and high velocity to be effective against other ships.

On Feb. 28, 1844, the explosion of a prototype cannon aboard the recently completed *Princeton* virtually ended much of the innovation that had been slowly transforming both the construction of naval vessels and their ordnance. Killed in the explosion were former secretary of the navy Abel P. Upshur and five other officials. The *Princeton* had been constructed using a screw propeller driven by engines mounted below the water line. The ship had been designed by Swedish naval engineer John Ericsson, with the assistance of Capt. Robert F. Stockton. Aboard the vessel were two experimental 12-inch guns, one designed by Ericsson and one by Stockton. The cannon that exploded had been built by Stockton based upon a design by Ericsson. However, the cannon—a 12-inch-diameter, wrought-iron gun reinforced with metal bands—was an inexact reproduction of Ericsson's design.

Following the explosion, recriminations between Ericsson and Stockton over responsibility for the explosion resulted in Ericsson's refusal to continue designing ships for the U.S. Navy until the Civil War. Advances in naval armament were also slowed following the *Princeton* disaster. Only John A. B. Dahlgren, who was assigned to the Washington navy yard in 1847 as an assistant inspector of ordnance in charge of rocket manufacture, would continue efforts to modernize the navy's heavy and light cannons.

Data Collection

In the 1830s, a number of young naval officers would make lasting contributions to U.S. maritime endeavors. Just as members of the army were compiling information about the territory of the United States, the navy was collecting vast quantities of information, not just about U.S. territorial waters, but about the world's oceans and continents as well.

One officer engaged in a lifelong quest for information was Charles Wilkes, a junior officer interested in scientific studies. In 1830, Wilkes became chief of the newly created Depot of Charts and Instruments in Washington. At his own expense, he built a small astronomical observatory on Capitol Hill in 1834. This small observatory formed the basis for what would eventually become the world-famous U.S. Naval Observatory. In 1842, after Wilkes had departed from the Depot of Charts and Instruments, Congress authorized the construction of a larger observatory with more adequate equipment and facilities.

Wilkes left his position in Washington in 1837 to head an expedition to explore and chart the South Seas. Although he was a junior lieutenant, Wilkes received the command after it had been declined by a number of more senior officers. The expedition, known as the South Seas Surveying and Exploring Expedition, consisted of a number of selected naval officers and civilian scientists. On Aug. 18, 1838, the party sailed from Norfolk, Virginia, aboard the sloops *Vincennes* and *Peacock,* the brigantine *Porpoise,* the schooners *Sea Gull* and *Flying Fish,* and the supply ship *Relief.*

Upon entering the Pacific Ocean by way of Cape Horn, the expedition began conducting a wide variety of scientific experiments and surveys. Tragically, the *Sea Gull* was lost with all hands while serving on detached duty. In early 1840, as the *Vincennes* slowly worked its way along the Antarctic ice barrier, Wilkes made a number of scientific observations and sightings that would identify the area as a continental landmass for the first time.

The expedition also surveyed the Fiji and Hawaiian islands. In Fiji, on the island of Malolo, two of the expedition's officers were killed by natives. In retaliation, Wilkes landed a military force and burned settlements across the entire island. The expedition reached Hawaii in 1840. There, the members of the party conducted a number of scientific observations. These included observations made from the rim of Kilauea's volcanic crater and from the top of Mauna Loa. The expedition departed Hawaii in 1841 and sailed to Puget Sound, where the expedition charted the sound and extensive areas of the northwest coast of North America. While surveying the mouth of the Columbia River, the *Peacock* grounded in the shallows and had to be abandoned. Upon the conclusion of its work on the Pacific coast, the expedition sailed west to the Philippines, Singapore, and then Cape Town on its way back to the United States. The ships entered New York Harbor on June 10, 1842.

Over the next two decades, Wilkes wrote *Narrative of the United States Exploring Expedition* (5 vols., 1844) and supervised the preparation of the expedition's scientific volumes. He personally wrote 3 of the 19 titles: *Meteorology* (1851), *Atlas of Charts* (2 vols., 1858), and *Hydrography* (1861). The information contained in the report was important not only to the navy but to commercial shipping interests and to the general scientific community.

While Wilkes was leading the South Seas expedition, Matthew F. Maury, another young naval officer, continued the valuable work of the Depot of Charts and Instruments. Maury had gained prominence in 1836 when he published *A New Theoretical and Practical Treatise on Navigation.* The book was the first scientific study on navigation written by an American naval officer and it won Maury worldwide recognition not only as an astronomer but also as a hydrographer. Consequently, Maury was assigned to the South Seas expedition as the official astronomer and hydrographer; however, his overriding personal dislike for Wilkes caused him to decline the assignment and spend the next two years surveying the harbors of the southeastern United States for the location of a proposed naval yard.

In 1842, at the age of 36, Maury was appointed superintendent of the Depot of Charts and Instruments. From this office, Maury embarked on a lifetime of work that would greatly benefit the maritime interests of all nations. In 1844, he added the administration of the newly completed naval observatory to his other duties. Maury's first contribution was a systematic study of atmospheric conditions. Based upon information contained in the log books prepared aboard all naval vessels, Maury published *The Wind and Current Chart of the North Atlantic* (1847) and *Explanations and Sailing Directions to Accompany the Wind and Current Charts* (1851).

In order to learn more about the world's oceans, Maury developed a set of charts and data forms that U.S. ship captains were required to fill in and submit to his office. Drawing upon the information supplied, Maury published charts of the Pacific and Indian oceans. In addition, he published rain charts, storm charts, and other charts of interest to captains of sailing vessels. Maury's contributions resulted in shorter sailing times and a less hazardous existence for all sailors. Both the navy and commercial U.S. maritime interests benefited by the reduction in sailing times and reduced transportation costs. By applying Maury's studies, the sailing time from New York to San Francisco, for example, could be cut by about 50 days.

In 1851, at Maury's suggestion, an international conference on oceanography was held. In addition to his work on oceanography, Maury took advantage of his access to the facilities of the Naval Observatory to conduct astronomical studies. In 1846, he published the first volume of American astronomical observations. In 1858, he published what he considered to be his most important study, *The Physical Geography of the Sea.*

Naval Personnel

Since the end of the War of 1812, overall naval policy in the United States had been driven in large measure by the international situation. During times of international tensions, Congress increased the strength of the navy, but when the tensions eased, Congress reduced the size of the force. From 1816 until 1837, a period of relative calm on the international scene, the strength of the navy fell from

5,540 men to about 4,000. When international tensions increased between 1837 and 1842, so did the strength of the navy, reaching 11,250 men in the latter year. But with the signing of the Webster-Ashburton Treaty in 1842 and the relaxation of tensions, Congress once again reduced the size of the navy. On June 17, 1844, Congress cut the strength of the navy to 7,500 seamen.

The composition of the navy was a matter of concern to the senior officers, to the secretary of the navy and to civilian proponents of a strong and effective naval force. The relative weakness of the navy, the long and arduous years of service required of recruits, and the low pay made enlistment in the navy far less attractive than employment on commercial ships. Consequently, there were a large number of foreigners serving in the U.S. Navy. On Mar. 2, 1937, Congress finally adopted a law that allowed the enlistment of boys between the ages of 13 and 18 for service until age 21. This idea, which had been advocated by various secretaries of the navy, would eventually increase the proportion of native-born seamen in the navy. The law established an apprenticeship system that would provide the young men an education in such subjects as reading, writing, arithmetic, navigation, and seamanship.

Naval officers could expect little in the way of reward during their careers beyond the satisfaction of having faithfully served their country. They could not expect rapid promotions; indeed, U.S. naval ranks were below those of officers holding comparable positions in the navies of other nations. Wilkes, for instance, was officially a lieutenant when he commanded the South Seas expedition. At the time, he argued that because of the importance of the command he should be promoted to the rank of captain. When the Navy Department and Pres. Martin Van Buren refused, Wilkes put on a captain's uniform and flew a squadron commodore's pennant from his flagship during the voyage. In essence, he promoted himself, a step few of his fellow officers would have dared take.

During the administration (1837–41) of Pres. Martin Van Buren (above), *Lt. Charles Wilkes explored and charted the South Seas.* (National Portrait Gallery)

The United States did not have the rank of admiral, despite the fact that the secretaries of the navy all had argued for the establishment of the rank. Opponents of the rank of admiral argued it had no place in a democracy since it was a carry-over from the aristocratic societies of Europe.

U.S. Naval Academy

Efforts to establish a naval academy encountered the same criticism as the efforts to establish the rank of admiral. In addition to the fears of elitism, many believed that practical nautical experience could be gained only through sea duty. Therefore a formal school such as a naval academy would do little to produce competent naval officers. Opponents also argued that the graduates of such an institution would form a special class within the navy and would eventually dominate all of the senior positions. Efforts to gain congressional approval for an academy began in 1815 and continued until the establishment of the naval school at Annapolis in 1845. Acceptance of the idea did not come easily. A bill authorizing such a school was defeated in Congress in 1827. Another bill, proposed in 1835, would have provided instruction in seamanship at West Point, but this act was also defeated.

With eventual congressional approval, however, Sec. of the Navy George Bancroft, who was temporarily acting as the secretary of war, transferred Fort Severn in Annapolis from the army to the navy. The secretary ordered a small instructional staff to report to Annapolis. He also directed that all midshipmen returning from sea duty should report to Annapolis. In 1850, the name of the institution officially became the U.S. Naval Academy.

The fundamental changes that Sylvanus Thayer and Dennis H. Mahan had instituted at the U.S. Military Academy during the 1820s and 1830s were beginning to shape a new type of army officer. The navy, because of its lack of an educational institution such as West Point until 1845, continued to use the apprentice-midshipman system for the training of its officers. Despite some obvious shortcomings in this system, a number of excellent officers joined the navy between the War of 1812 and the Mexican War. These young officers, through the long years of service required to earn positions of command and influence in the service, learned the complicated lessons necessary to command warships. The contributions made by these young officers would be felt in the years to come as their influence spread and their abilities were utilized. However, the U.S. Navy still lacked one of the basic prerequisites for a truly professional force: a formal system of education for its officer corps.

Advances in Military Education

In 1847, Dennis Hart Mahan, noting the lack of American textbooks on either military engineering or the history of warfare, published his own book. His work, with the cumbersome title *An Elementary Treatise on Advanced Guard, Outpost, and Detached Service of Troops, and the Manner of Posting and Handling them in the Presence of an Enemy. With a Historical Sketch of the Rise and Progress of Tactics, etc.,* was known to a generation of West Point cadets simply as *Outposts.* Mahan's book was the first American study of war. It relied upon the Napoleonic Wars, as interpreted by the Baron Antoine Henri de Jomini, to convey its lessons. Jomini's interpretation of Napoleon, as set forth in his *The Art of War,* stressed the use of speed and movement and the importance of strategic geographic locations; it also emphasized the importance of communications and supply lines. The year before Mahan published *Outposts,* one of his students, Henry W. Halleck, had written *Elements of Military Art and Science.* Although "Brains" Halleck's study was more original than Mahan's, it also was based on Jomini's interpretation of Napoleon.

The works of Mahan and Halleck were the beginning of strategic studies in the United States. The volumes provided the army's officers with a solid foundation upon which to begin building a knowledge and understanding of their profession. The two officers stressed the fact that military science was a highly specialized body of knowledge that could be mastered only through long years of diligent study, particularly the study of military history.

The creation of a truly professional officer corps required more than could be offered by West Point. Additional schooling was necessary to teach the young officers the specialized skills of the various branches of the service. Sec. of War John C. Calhoun had established the Artillery School of Practice at Fortress Monroe in 1824. In 1827, Sec. of War James Barbour directed the establishment of the Infantry School of Practice at Jefferson Barracks. Yet, by the middle of the next decade, the Artillery School was closed and the Infantry School was serving no useful purpose. Not until after the Civil War would the army establish the schools of the line necessary to continue the officers' education begun at West Point.

In addition to providing a basic education for its officers at West Point, the army attempted to provide all personnel with up-to-date manuals for the conduct of military operations. Following the War of 1812, a board of officers had revised William Duane's *Handbook for Infantry,* the first official tactical manual for the infantry. In 1822, Lt. Col.

Dennis Hart Mahan's Advanced Guard, Outpost, and Detachment Service of Troops, *better known as* Outposts, *was required reading at West Point.* (U.S. Military Academy)

Pierce Darrow published *Cavalry Tactics,* which integrated cavalry tactics with the infantry system. In 1826, Gen. Winfield Scott helped to prepare cavalry and artillery manuals that provided guidelines for the coordination of operations with the infantry. In 1829, Scott prepared a comprehensive statement of infantry tactical regulations. As new innovations made their appearance, the tactical manuals were revised and updated.

In addition to the publication of manuals by the army and the studies of military science by Mahan and Halleck, three journals appeared in the 1830s that furthered the growth of professionalism: *Military and Naval Magazine* (1833–36), *Army and Navy Chronicle* (1835–44), and *Military Magazine* (1839–42). These journals contained articles and letters on a wide variety of issues—ranging from tactics to pay—that were of concern to the entire military community. They also offered officers serving at the isolated frontier posts the opportunity to learn of the latest developments in their profession.

During the same period, Perry was responsible for establishing the Naval Lyceum at the New York navy yard. His intention was to educate the younger naval officers by drawing upon the experiences of older officers in the public discussion of problems and tactical situations. Perry was also a participant in the efforts to establish the *Naval Magazine,* the first professional naval journal published in the United States. However, despite the efforts of Perry and a few other dedicated naval officers, the journal ceased publication after only a few issues.

WEAPONS AND PERSONNEL

The term "ordnance," used in its broadest sense, includes all military weapons, their ammunition, and the equipment necessary to maintain the weapons. In the reorganization of the army following the Treaty of Ghent, an ordnance department was created and Col. Decius Wadsworth was appointed chief of ordnance with Lt. Col. George Bomford as his assistant. During Wadsworth's six-year tenure, the Ordnance Department tried to impose three guiding principles upon the manufacture of ordnance for the army: "Uniformity, Simplicity, and Solidarity." A major effort was made to standardize weapons. New arsenals were opened, and the armories at Springfield, Connecticut, and Harpers Ferry, Virginia, were placed under the supervision of the department. Measures were instituted to standardize the army's small arms and to provide a uniform system for their production.

Wadsworth wanted to standardize not only the army's small arms but also its artillery, and to that end, he tried to persuade the War Department to adopt a new system of field carriages. However, when the Ordnance Board, handpicked by Wadsworth, refused to adopt the new system and recommended in its place an entirely obsolete system, Wadsworth lost much of his influence and became disillusioned with the bureaucratic process.

In 1821, Wadsworth was unable to persuade Congress even to retain the Ordnance Corps when it reorganized the army. So in June 1821, he returned to his home in Connecticut, where he died a few months later. Following the reorganization and only a few months before Wadsworth's death, Bomford became the head of the Ordnance Department. Bomford followed the course set by Wadsworth in the effort to standardize army weapons. However, the task had been complicated by the reorganization of 1821. All of the ordnance officers had been commissioned in the artillery when the Ordnance Corps was abolished. The artillery officers were then detailed to work for the Ordnance Department for short periods. By the time they became thoroughly familiar with their duties and the technical aspects of the work of the Ordnance Department, they were returned to their artillery units to be replaced by new officers who had to repeat the learning process. The result was that the department fell behind in its work, and Congress finally reestablished the Ordnance Corps in 1832.

Bomford, promoted to colonel, was placed in charge of the new corps. The next few years were devoted to eliminating the backlog of work that had accumulated during the previous decade, while attempting to develop standards for the artillery and producing the equipment necessary to outfit the new regiment of dragoons. While supervising the overall activities of the Ordnance Corps, Bomford devoted much of his attention to the development of new and improved large-caliber guns for the nation's coastal fortifications. Bomford had implicit faith in the concept of large-caliber shell guns. He had developed a gun in 1811 that had quickly become obsolete, but working with the basic concept through the 1820s and 1830s, he was able to develop a new weapon by 1844. The new weapon, which chambered the shell like a howitzer but had a tube length more like a heavy gun, fired both shot and exploding shell. The gun was standardized in both 8- and 10-inch models and quickly replaced the old howitzers in the nation's coastal fortifications. The gun had a range of almost 5,000 yards.

The career of Alfred Mordecai illustrates the changing nature of warfare during the mid-19th century and the necessity of incorporating the rapidly growing mass of scientific information into the operations of the military establishment. During the reorganization of the army in 1832, Mordecai was appointed to the rank of captain in the Ordnance Corps. For more than 25 years he would devote his attention to improving the weapons available to the military forces of the United States.

Mordecai was a member of the Ordnance Board after its reestablishment in 1839 until he left the service on the eve of the Civil War. The original purpose of the board had been to provide a standard system for army ordnance. However, the board quickly expanded its function to include approval of new weapons and related equipment. The board directed extensive testing of new equipment in order to evaluate its effectiveness and design. In effect, the board became a very rudimentary research and development agency for the army.

Mordecai participated in the formulation of the first comprehensive system for the army's artillery. Its details were published in 1849 as *Artillery for the United States Land Service, as Devised and Arranged by the Ordnance Board.* In addition, Mordecai produced the first *Ordnance Manual* in 1841. Mordecai also conducted numerous experiments and tests of weapons and ammunition. The results of these tests were initially published in a *Report on Experiments on Gunpowder Made at Washington Arsenal, in 1843 and 1844* (1845). Mordecai published the results of additional tests and studies in a second volume, *Second Report of Experiments on Gunpowder, Made at Washington Arsenal, in 1845, 1847, and 1848* (1849). These two volumes were of particular value to the manufacturers of gunpowder and to the ordnance and artillery officers who were required to test and use the final product.

Personnel Reforms

While sweeping changes were taking place in the technology of warfare and in the intellectual preparation and pursuits of officers, change came more slowly to the everyday life of the men who made up the bulk of the military establishment. Problems that had been present within the military since the establishment of the United States were still prevalent in the 1820s and 1830s.

Whether they served at isolated frontier posts or aboard the small naval vessels, the servicemen of the United States endured harsh and in some cases brutal conditions. Pay was low, discipline inhumane, living conditions primitive, and rewards for faithful service virtually nonexistent. Officers and enlisted men alike shared the same hardships. For the enlisted men, desertion was commonplace; for officers, resignations were high. In 1830, more than 1,000 men deserted from the army. By 1847, only 597 West Point graduates (of a total of 1,330) who had been commissioned remained on active service. Deserters also plagued the navy, and naval officers also left the service in large numbers. Between 1799 and 1861, more than 25 percent of the court-martials in the navy were for drunkenness and desertion. There were occasional attempts to improve conditions, but few of them went to the root of the problem.

In 1842, the salary of an army second lieutenant was $25 a month plus four rations. It was not unusual for an individual in the army to serve 20–30 years to reach the rank of major. In the navy, 50-year-old lieutenants were the rule rather than the exception. There were two principal reasons for the slow promotions: the small size of both the army and the navy and the lack of a retirement system. Since promotions were based on a seniority system, if older officers did not retire, they served until they died or were forced to retire because of physical incapacity. In an effort to retain the services of West Point graduates, the army lengthened the terms of their obligations in 1838 to 4 years. Prior to that time, the obligation was only 1 year of service after graduation.

A number of reforms were tried to improve the life of the common soldier and sailor, but most of them failed. Critics held that two practices, common in both services, were responsible for most of the problems encountered in maintaining discipline among the men. The first was the practice of issuing a ration of spirits to each man each day. The extent of the ration is indicated by the fact that in 1830, the army issued 72,537 gallons of whiskey at a cost of $22,132. The army abolished the whiskey ration in 1830 and replaced it with a coffee and sugar ration or monetary payment.

The navy did not abolish its grog ration until 1862. Critics of the liquor ration attributed drunkenness among the soldiers and sailors to the ration, if not directly at least indirectly by encouraging the consumption of spirits. Supporters of the ration argued that the consumption of a small amount of liquor was beneficial to the health of the men and that such a small amount was hardly the cause of insobriety. Whatever the merits of the argument on either side, the elimination of the ration did little to improve the general lot of enlisted men.

The second area of reform addressed the issue of harsh discipline, particularly flogging. The army prohibited flogging in 1812 but restored its use in 1833 as a punishment for desertion. The navy abolished flogging in 1850. Despite the fact that the treatment of the men was more humane, officers complained that there was little or no improvement in discipline. In fact, they argued that many men preferred confinement to active duty. Considering the harsh and hazardous duties performed by soldiers and sailors, confinement in a cell was safer and less taxing than the day-to-day existence of those who faithfully performed their duties.

Disciplinary Measures

Authorized punishment in the U.S. armed forces included being confined in a small cage (or "black hole"), having an ear cropped, being marked with an indelible pen (or tattooed), standing in a barrel for long periods of time, marching with heavy weights in one's pack, wearing a ball and chain, and being bucked and gagged. This last punishment was particularly harsh and rendered the soldier silent and immobile. The soldier's arms were bound around his knees with a stick inserted between legs and arms—an especially painful form of punishment when applied for extended periods. Because of their isolation, some officers overstepped both the bounds of army regulations and civilized behavior. Such punishments as branding, the splitting of a man's nose, and the use of the whip for crimes other than desertion were reportedly imposed.

Flogging had been an accepted part of life in the U.S. Navy since its founding and was believed by most officers to be necessary to maintain discipline aboard warships. Instead of using the whip, Navy regulations called for the use of a cat-o'-nine-tails. The "cat" consisted of nine small, twisted cords, about 18 inches long, that were attached to a wooden handle. At the end of each cord was a bead of lead or a hard knot that helped keep the cords taut while the whip was being swung. Floggings were held as ceremonial affairs aboard ships and were considered useful examples to maintain the good behavior of the other sailors. The floggings were supervised by the ship's surgeon, who could stop the proceedings if he felt the sailor could not tolerate the prescribed number of lashes. Howevei, if the surgeon stopped the flogging, the sailor would receive the remaining lashes after his back had healed. The ship's marine detachment was drawn up with fixed bayonets during the flogging, to maintain order and to add to the ceremonial aspect of the punishment.

The marines found themselves in a strange position where flogging was concerned. When they served on land, the marines were bound by army regulations and, after 1812, therefore, could not be flogged. However, when serving at sea, the marines were governed by navy regulations and were subject to flogging as punishment for their crimes. Just as officers at frontier posts might sentence soldiers to types of punishment not included in the army's regulations, so, too, might the captains of ships on long sea voyages.

Pay and Promotion Reforms

Efforts to increase the pay of both officers and enlisted men did little to improve their general situations. Officers, especially those who had the benefit of a West Point education, could earn much more money in civilian life, where they would not have to tolerate all of the hardships of frontier duty. For the naval officer, life aboard commercial vessels would bring them higher pay and a higher standard of living than what could be realized in the navy. For the enlisted men, even increased military pay was still below the wages paid to civilian workers in the expanding U.S. economy of the 19th century.

The pay rates for enlisted members of the navy were set in 1820 and remained essentially unchanged until 1854. Pay for able seamen was $12 per month, for ordinary seamen $10, and for boys $7. Throughout the period, the increasing disparity between naval pay and the wage rates of the merchant service made it difficult to recruit good men. The conversion of the navy to steam power created an additional problem in the wage rates for sailors, since firemen and coal heavers were now needed to run the new ships. The pay rate in effect in 1847 authorized $30 a month for first-class firemen, $20 for second-class firemen, and $15 for coal heavers. The fact that this higher pay scale was in effect while the navy was still attempting to recruit ordinary sailors at the older pay rates was certain to create resentment and serious morale problems among the men. Although the bounty system was instituted in the hope of attracting more recruits, the amount of the bounty was never sufficient to make up the difference in pay. The monthly pay of a private in the army was $6 in 1833 and was increased to $8 by the time of the outbreak of the Mexican War. The army also used enlistment bonuses, but they were no more successful than the navy's. At a time when common laborers were paid as much as a dollar a day, the $8 a month paid to army privates was far below the norm.

Reform of the promotion system was discussed and debated by Congress and the members of the military, but little serious consideration was given to eliminating the principle of seniority or to establishing a retirement system. In 1837, the War Department sought to reward deserving enlisted men by promoting them into the ranks of the officer corps. While this experiment might have improved the morale of the enlisted men, it hurt the morale of the officer corps. In light of the already limited opportunity for promotions, none of the officers was anxious to increase the size of the officer corps.

Morale among officers was also affected by the development of new professional specialties. In the army, line officers who served with the operational troops at isolated frontier posts resented the more comfortable situation of those staff officers whose duties required them to serve in cities and more urbanized regions of the nation. In the navy, a rivalry developed between the old line officers and the engineers required to run and maintain the new ships. As was the case in the conflict between the line and staff officers of the army, the naval officers of the line considered the engineers to be something less than full-fledged officers. In the officer corps of both army and navy, where promotions were slow and officers served long, isolated tours, any situation that caused resentment could seriously affect morale and in some cases result in violence.

Second Seminole War Lessons

The Second Seminole War (1835–42) affected the military establishment in a number of ways, only a few of which were beneficial. More than 60,000 regulars and volunteers had served at one time or another during the seven years of conflict in Florida. The most positive result of this service was that many of the members of the army and a large number of men from the navy and marines gained combat experience against a resourceful and resolute enemy. This experience would serve both officers and men well when, in just a few short years, they would engage in a much larger war against the military forces of a foreign nation.

The major negative impact was that a nation of more than 17,000,000 people had fought a seven-year war with an Indian tribe that at no time numbered more than 1,200 warriors. Nonetheless, Congress reduced the army from 12,500 to 8,600 on Aug. 23, 1842, just nine days after the end of the war with the Seminole. In less than two years, the strength of the navy would be reduced from 12,000 to 7,500 men and boys. The end of the Second Seminole War and the relaxation of international tensions had convinced Congress that it could safely reduce the size of the peacetime military establishment.

Throughout the Second Seminole War, the army's frontier posts had been stripped of all but a few soldiers who served as caretakers while the rest of the garrisons served in Florida. In some cases, it was almost impossible for garrison commanders to maintain their patrols and continue to protect the frontier. It was fortunate for the frontier settlements that no serious hostilities with other Indian groups broke out during this period. At the conclusion of the war, troops returned to their garrisons as seasoned combat veterans, far better prepared to meet the demands of duty on the western frontier.

WESTERN FRONTIER

Despite mounting tensions on the Louisiana-Texas border, the small standing army could do little more than send a limited force to patrol the border and authorize the commander to call upon the states and territories for militia volunteers if he needed more troops to maintain the peace. The dragoons served as escorts on the Santa Fe Trail four times in the years between 1834 and 1845. Three of the escort missions, one in 1834 and two in 1843, were round-trip escorts, but the 1845 mission was only for the return trip. Col. Stephen W. Kearny accompanied the wagon train while the dragoons were returning from their expedition to South Pass. Prior to the Mexican War, the military escorts did not guard the Santa Fe Trail but only protected the individual wagon trains. After 1848, army posts were established along the trail to protect the wagons and travelers.

The infantry usually was assigned to garrison duty but occasionally was sent against the Indians as a mounted force after Congress sanctioned the infantry's use of mules in 1850. Although the results of this practice were often less than satisfactory, over the next 50 years, mule-mounted foot soldiers would be sent against Indians whenever an emergency arose and there was no properly constituted mounted troops. An alternative to mounted infantry was the use of mounted volunteers. These troops demonstrated the characteristic weaknesses of all militia troops: they had no organized training, they were poorly disciplined, and they enlisted for only short terms. However, until the government saw fit to supply large enough forces of regular army troops to suppress the Indians, the settler-volunteers would be used to fight in their own defense.

The Great Plains presented the army with a transport problem that was to raise costs to new highs, since the rivers were not deep enough to allow the use of normal river-going vessels. Because the army had to move its supplies by wagons, drawn by oxen or mules, the annual cost of transporting supplies increased from $130,000 in 1845 to more than $2,000,000 in 1851. Even more expensive was the cavalry. It was estimated that the annual cost of supplying an infantry regiment was $250,000–$300,000, but the cost for a regiment of cavalry was $500,000–$600,000. These figures represented the cost when the

The expeditions of John C. Frémont in the 1840s contributed greatly to knowledge of the western regions. (Library of Congress)

troops were on routine duty; when the cavalry took to the field, the cost jumped to $1,500,000, exclusive of the initial cost of mounts, arms, and the men's pay. One added cost of cavalry was the type of horse that the men rode. The horses purchased for the army were all eastern horses and had been grain-fed in order to attain the size necessary to carry men and their equipment. These large horses could not subsist without oats and barley; therefore, huge amounts of grain had to be transported to the cavalry post as well as into the field. Eventually, the expansion of the railroads would help to eliminate some of the problems posed by the difficulty of river transportation on the Great Plains.

Frémont Expeditions

The army continued its explorations and mapping expeditions in the 1840s. The most prominent leader of the decade was John C. Frémont, a young officer who owed his initial appointment to his father-in-law, Sen. Thomas Hart Benton. From June until October 1842, Frémont and his party explored the Wind River chain of the Rocky Mountains. Accompanying Frémont were two men who would also participate in his later expeditions: Kit Carson as scout, guide, and pathfinder and Charles Preuss as topographer.

Upon publication of Frémont's first report, Congress authorized a second and more extensive expedition. From May 1843 until July 1844, Frémont's party made a great swing through the West, exploring the region north of the Great Salt Lake, the Snake and Columbia river valleys, the Klamath Lake country (southern Oregon), eastern Nevada, and west through Kit Carson Pass in the Sierra Mountains to Sutter's Fort in California.

Kit Carson, who served as John C. Frémont's guide and scout in the 1840s, fought Indians in New Mexico during the Civil War. (U.S. Army Military History Institute)

After a short rest, the expedition set off to Los Angeles, where they picked up the Old Spanish Trail and started east. The party detoured and crossed southern Nevada and Utah. On July 1, 1844, the party reached Bent's Fort on the Arkansas River. Although Frémont's judgment might be questioned for some of his reckless acts, such as crossing the Sierras during midwinter, his second report firmly established his reputation as an explorer. His accomplishments were no less than those of his most noted predecessors, Meriwether Lewis, William Clark, Zebulon M. Pike, and Stephen H. Long.

In July 1845, Frémont began the third of his expeditions. Again crossing into California, where he moved up the Sacramento Valley to Oregon, he returned to California in time to become involved in the events of the California Bear Flag Rebellion and the Mexican War.

Naval Developments

Secretary of the Navy Paulding worked from 1838 until he left office in 1841 to expand the navy. By the time he stepped down, there were 26 ships commissioned in the navy and the department budget exceeded $5,000,000 a year. The most important function performed by the U.S. Navy during the 1830s and 1840s was the projection of U.S. power and influence around the world. Naval officers frequently acted as diplomats and smoothed the way for commercial interests. During China's Opium War (1839–42), the United States was a neutral power, but a naval squadron, commanded by Lawrence Kearny, was present to provide protection for U.S. merchants should it have been necessary. In 1844, the United States and China signed the Treaty of Wanghia, largely through the efforts of Kearny. The treaty opened five ports in China to U.S. merchants on a most-favored-nation basis. For the first time, U.S. commercial relations with China were protected by a treaty, an act that signified the entry of the United States into the economic race for markets in the Far East.

The navy was also engaged in a number of operations intended to protect U.S. lives and property. Throughout the period prior to the Civil War, the sailors and marines made landings in Asia, the Mediterranean, the Caribbean, South America, and the East African coast. Most of these

Many of the naval officers who served the Union during the Civil War had come up through the ranks during the 1830s and 1840s at a time when the U.S. Navy was projecting an image of power and influence around the world. (U.S. Army Military History Institute)

landings lasted for only a short period, and most were accomplished without bloodshed; however, there were exceptions. In 1832, Pres. Andrew Jackson ordered a naval force to Sumatra to protect U.S. interests following an attack on a merchant vessel. John Downes, the commander of the dispatched naval vessel, landed a force of marines and sailors, who destroyed the town of Quallah Buttoo and killed a number of the inhabitants. Also, Wilkes's force had carried out a retaliatory raid on Fiji.

The marines serving aboard naval vessels during this period were specially assigned to protect U.S. interests and lives. Marines accompanied the Wilkes expedition and made several landings on Fiji, Samoa, and the Gilbert Islands to subdue hostile inhabitants. In 1843, they landed on the West African coast several times to put an end to attacks on U.S. merchant shipping. In 1844, the marines landed in China to discourage threats against U.S. merchants during anti-American riots.

Other general naval activities included efforts to end the slave trade by patrolling the waters off of the African coast. In addition, the Mediterranean and West Indies squadrons mounted a continuing effort to eliminate pirates who preyed on U.S. merchantmen.

Manifest Destiny

The term "manifest destiny" was first used in the *United States Magazine and Democratic Review* in 1845 to further the movement to annex Texas. John L. O'Sullivan, editor of the *Review,* caught the expansionist spirit of the nation when he wrote that it is "our manifest destiny to overspread the continent allotted by Providence for the free development of our yearly multiplying millions." Although O'Sullivan had been advocating only the annexation of Texas, the expansionists soon adopted his words to support the acquisition of any new territory by the United States.

Those who advocated the doctrine of Manifest Destiny based their belief on several arguments. One was a firm conviction that the political institutions of the United States were far superior to those of its neighbors, and consequently it was inevitable that the superior institutions should reign supreme. Another argument was that the dramatic population growth of the United States since its founding made necessary the acquisition of more territory for homes, towns, and farms. Another factor was the inherent racist belief that the talents and energy of the people of the United States were superior to those of their native American, Mexican, and South American neighbors. When all these arguments were put forward together, the expansionists were able to present a powerful emotional appeal for territorial expansion.

Annexation of Oregon

The question of who "owned" the Oregon Territory became increasingly important in the 1830s and 1840s as settlers from the United States began to move into the area in growing numbers. Initially, there were four claimants to the territory; Spain, Russia, Great Britain, and the United States. Russia surrendered its claims south of 54 degrees and 40 minutes north latitude in separate treaties with Great Britain and the United States in the mid-1820s. Spain surrendered its claim to all lands north of 42 degrees north latitude to the United States in the Adams-Onís Treaty of 1819. The other two claimants, the United States and Great Britain, had agreed to the joint occupancy of Oregon in the Convention of 1818.

Great Britain's claim to Oregon was based on the discoveries made in the area by Sir Francis Drake, Capt. James Cook, and Capt. George Vancouver; the explorations and settlements by various British fur companies; and the 1790 Nootka Convention with Spain, which had recognized British rights in the area. The United States's claims were based on the discovery of the Columbia River by Capt. Robert Gray, the explorations by Lewis and Clark, the establishment of Astoria by the Pacific Fur Company, provisions contained in the Adams-Onís Treaty, and the presence of U.S. settlements in the area.

The large number of settlers in the Oregon Territory aroused the interest of the U.S. electorate, and Oregon became a political issue in the 1844 presidential campaign. James K. Polk used the slogan "Fifty-four Forty or Fight" (in reference to territorial aspirations in the Northwest—that is, to the 54 degrees and 40 minutes north latitude) during his successful campaign. Shortly after Polk became president, Congress authorized him to notify Great Britain of the termination of the Joint Occupation Treaty.

The settlement of the dispute was relatively simple. Great Britain's government, in the hands of a party that hoped to maintain peace, was unwilling to go to war with the United States over Oregon. Since the United States had initially put forth its maximum demands, it was actually willing to accept less than it had demanded. In June 1846, the two nations agreed to a settlement that extended the 49th parallel westward from the Rocky Mountains to the Pacific Ocean. The only deviation in the line was a slight southward alteration at Vancouver Island in order to leave it in the hands of the British.

California and Texas

After Mexico gained its independence from Spain in 1822, its relations with the United States slowly deteriorated until the two nations went to war in 1846. The basis of the deterioration in relations was territorial. Mexico possessed land that bordered the United States and which had previously been the subject of disputes between the United States and Spain. Once settlers from the United States began to establish themselves in Mexican territory, the potential for future dispute was clear.

In California, there were only a few U.S. settlers present before 1841. The overland settlement had started as early as 1826 when Jedediah Smith arrived in California. However, only about 300 settlers followed him to California in the next 15 years. But in 1841, the immigration of settlers to California dramatically increased.

The settlers entered a volatile political situation. Mexico's political control over California was weak. The governors dispatched from Mexico were often ignored or deposed by local factions. Even locally appointed governors frequently aroused the opposition of powerful local factions. The settlers from the United States quickly became involved in regional politics. Following the establishment of John Sutter's fort, known as New Helvetia, a virtually autonomous community of Anglo-American settlers arose and challenged the other factions for political powers. Whether a free and independent state of California would be established or whether the area would be annexed by the United States depended entirely upon the power of the Anglo-American settlers. Yet, open hostilities would erupt in California only after the United States and Mexico had gone to war.

Disputes concerning sovereignty over Texas had been frequent since the United States purchased Louisiana from France. Although the formal boundary dispute between the United States and Spain had been settled by the Adams-Onís Treaty of 1819, the movement of settlers from the United States into Texas made the situation far more complex. The migration to Texas of settlers from the United States began in 1821 when Moses Austin received a charter from the government of New Spain granting land for the settlement of 200 families. Before the settlers could arrive, however, both of the principal parties to the agreement changed. Austin died on June 10, 1821, and the independent state of Mexico subsequently replaced New Spain as the sovereign power. On August 12, Stephen F. Austin arrived in Texas to carry out his father's plans and, during the following year, traveled to Mexico City to have his land grants confirmed by the new government.

Indeed, the grants were renewed by each succeeding government during the revolutions in Mexico during the next two years. When the Republic of Mexico was established under the constitution of 1824, Texas was incorporated into one of the states in the Mexican republic. In 1825, Mexico enacted a colonization law that opened Texas to settlement. The obvious success of Austin's efforts attracted others from the United States who received charters or grants and brought in more and more settlers.

The political situation in Mexico produced a series of revolutions and governmental changes during the next five years. In 1830, the Mexican congress enacted a law that prohibited any further colonization of Texas by settlers from the United States. This action, combined with other laws that the earlier settlers viewed as violations of their rights and charters, caused them to petition the Mexican government for a redress of their grievances.

In 1834, when Austin went to Mexico City to present the resolutions and petitions of the settlers to the government, he was arrested and held in prison for eight months. As the Centralist government, headed by Gen. Antonio López de Santa Anna, attempted to assert its authority over the Texans, the situation steadily deteriorated. During the summer of 1835, the settlers clashed with the forces of the Mexican government. Then, in the fall, at a number of conventions held throughout Texas, the settlers denied the authority of the Mexican government, voted in favor of local self-government, and affirmed the right of Texas to secede from Mexico.

Texas and Independence

As the situation in Texas worsened, volunteers began to arrive from the United States to reinforce the settlers for the expected fight with the Mexican government. Santa Anna's reply to the demands of the Texans was the establishment of a unitary state that abolished all local rights. The general also raised an army of approximately 6,000 men to move against the Texans.

On Mar. 1, 1836, a convention met at Washington, Texas, and on the following day passed a declaration of independence and drew up a constitution based upon that of the United States. A provisional government was established, and Sam Houston was appointed to command the provisional army being raised to defend Texas from attack by the Mexican forces.

While the convention was meeting in Washington, Santa Anna's army was engaged in an effort to drive the Texans from the Alamo in San Antonio. Approximately 3,000 Mexican soldiers, personally led by Santa Anna, were held

Sam Houston commanded the provisional army of Texas that drove the Mexican army under General Santa Anna from Texas and won its independence. (Library of Congress)

"Davy" Crockett, immortalized in song and verse, died defending the Alamo. (Library of Congress)

at bay by 187 Texans and Americans led by William B. Travis. From February 23 until March 6, the Mexican commander hurled assault after assault against the old mission only to be driven back by the determined resistance of the defenders. Finally, the Mexicans stormed the Alamo and killed all of the defenders. Three weeks later, Santa Anna ordered the massacre of the 300 Texans (commanded by Capt. James Fannin) who had been captured by the second part of his army at Gollad.

The defense of the Alamo had delayed Santa Anna's advance and had given Houston the opportunity to escape the advancing Mexican army. During his retreat, Houston drew together a large force of Texas settlers. Halting his retreat, Houston quickly moved against the Mexican force camped near Galveston Bay.

On the morning of April 21, the Texans attacked the Mexican force on the western bank of the San Jacinto River. The Texans charged into battle with the cry "Remember the Alamo!" ringing through the still morning. The 1,200 Mexicans were quickly defeated and Santa Anna captured. Santa Anna then ordered his main army to leave Texas and promised to work for the recognition of Texas independence. However, the agreement signed by Santa Anna was repudiated by the Mexican congress.

Annexation of Texas

Despite the rejection of the Mexican congress, the Republic of Texas was a fact. The continued existence of the government and constitution agreed upon in March had been assured at the Battle of San Jacinto. However, despite the fact that Presidents John Quincy Adams and Andrew Jackson both had made diplomatic efforts to readjust the boundaries drawn by the Adams-Onís Treaty so that the entire area of Texas would be included in the United States, there was no rush by the United States to annex the newly independent republic.

Although the people of Texas voted overwhelmingly in favor of annexation to the United States in September 1836, Congress and President Van Buren declined to consider the offer in 1837. For the next five years, annexation was not considered again. There were a number of reasons why the annexation of Texas was not particularly popular in the United States. One was the possibility of arousing international complications, especially with English interests in the area and in light of the still unsettled Oregon question. Yet the biggest stumbling block to the annexation of Texas was the politically sensitive issue of slavery. The antislavery forces viewed proposals for the annexation of Texas as a ploy by proslavery forces to open vast new areas to the institution of slavery. It was no coincidence that President Jackson did not recognize the independence of the Republic of Texas until the last day of his administration, when the action could no longer damage him politically.

In April 1844, however, Pres. John Tyler introduced a measure into Congress that would have Texas annexed as a territory rather than a state. Although the Senate rejected this bill, the issue of Texas and the principle of Manifest Destiny became entangled in the 1844 presidential cam-

On his last day in office in 1845, President John Tyler started the proceedings that gave statehood to Texas and hastened the deterioration of relations with Mexico. (Library of Congress)

paign. Polk, the Democratic presidential candidate, pledged to "re-annex" Texas. This clever argument defused some of the political opposition since it argued that in annexing Texas, the United States would simply be regaining territory it had previously purchased from France and had temporarily surrendered to Spain with the signing of the Adams-Onís Treaty.

After Polk's victory in November, Congress authorized the president either to offer the Republic of Texas annexation as a state or to negotiate a new annexation treaty with Texas. The outgoing president, Tyler, feeling that the American people had spoken on the subject of annexation by electing Polk, decided to act on the first of the two alternatives. On the last day of February 1845, a joint resolution passed both houses of Congress, admitting Texas as a state without it first becoming a territory. The resolution also provided that, with the approval of Texas, four more states could be formed from its territory; that Texas would be required to pay its own public debt; and that the Missouri Compromise line would be extended west through the new state. The people of Texas accepted these terms, and on December 29, Texas was admitted to the United States. On Feb. 19, 1846, a state government was installed at Austin.

Preparations for War

The annexation of Texas hastened the break in relations between the United States and Mexico. In March 1845, Mexico recalled its diplomatic representative to Washington and began a buildup of its military forces to resist the annexation. Although the Mexicans had already rejected the claim that the southern boundary of Texas was the Rio Grande, the United States, prompted by Sec. of State James Buchanan, argued that the annexation of Texas had revived the U.S. territorial claims given up in 1819, and that the international boundary should be the Rio Grande.

While the question of Texas was debated in the political arena, the United States military establishment was slowly preparing to defend the nation's claims if called upon to do so. On Jan. 23, 1836, shortly after the Texas Revolt against Mexico, Maj. Gen. Edmund P. Gaines, commander of the Western Department, was ordered to the western Louisiana frontier by the War Department. By the summer of 1836, Gaines was given permission to cross the border between Louisiana and Texas in order to pursue and subdue Indian groups who were raiding white settlements. He was also given authority to call upon the militia from the surrounding territories if needed. Thus, while the United States was technically neutral in the dispute between Texas and Mexico, its military forces were operating in the disputed area.

For the next eight years, the U.S. Army simply observed events in Texas and waited for the Texas question to be settled politically. On Apr. 17, 1844, Brig. Gen. Zachary Taylor was ordered to Natchitoches, Louisiana, to establish a corps of observation. Initially, this force consisted of 7 companies of dragoons and 16 companies of infantry, but it continued to expand so as to be prepared to act immediately if needed.

By the end of May 1845, Taylor had collected 25 companies of infantry at his headquarters at Fort Jesup, Louisiana. On June 15, the War Department ordered Taylor to move his force, now grown to an "army of observation," to a point "on or near the Rio Grande." On July 26, Taylor and his force crossed the Texas border and moved to the south bank of the Nueces River near Corpus Christi, about 150 miles from the Rio Grande. By October, Taylor had gathered almost 4,000 regulars at Corpus Christi and had been granted authority to call upon the states for militia forces if he needed them to strengthen his force. Thus the stage was set for the opening of hostilities. Although President Polk had directed Taylor to avoid the appearance of hostile action against Mexico, the general had already been given command of approximately one-half of the regular army.

On Feb. 3, 1846, Taylor received instructions to move to a position on or near the left bank of the Rio Grande. Taylor moved into the disputed territory and placed his force in a position where a clash with the Mexican forces could be expected.

Readiness of U.S. Forces

The U.S. forces that stood arrayed against the military forces of Mexico were far different than those that had been a part of U.S. military establishment on the eve of previous conflicts. Although still small compared to the forces of many other nations, it was experienced and battle tested. The years of pursuing the Seminole through the swamps of Florida and the Plains Indians on the western frontier had given both the officers and men of the army valuable experience against determined enemies. The officers, both senior and junior, were prepared to lead the forces that were gathering on the Texas-Louisiana border. The infusion of young officers, trained at West Point and seasoned by their assignments on the frontier and in jobs that required the exercise of independent judgment, represented the beginning of a significant change in the army. The old officer corps composed of officers with little or no formal military training was giving way to an officer corps composed of men who had received a fundamental education in the basic principles of military operations. The combination of formal education and practical experience present in the officer corps would provide the army a quality of leadership that had not been available at the beginning of previous wars.

While the navy officer corps lacked the advantage of a formal military education such as that provided by West Point, the naval officer corps was also changing. The efforts of a number of naval officers had done much to help educate the young officers, and long years of service in junior positions aboard ships cruising the oceans of the world produced a number of highly capable officers.

The enlisted sailors and soldiers were also highly experienced. The long terms of enlistment and service aboard isolated ships and at distant frontier posts provided ample opportunity for the men to learn their professions. Although they were viewed by many citizens, as well as by many officers, as some of the least desirable members of society, large numbers of enlisted men served faithfully for many years in both the army and navy. It was this group of career military men that would form the nucleus of the force that would face and defeat the army of Mexico.

Just as the nature of regular army and navy was changing, so was the role of the militia. The traditional reliance upon the citizen soldier called into service in times of national emergency was no longer viewed as the best solution to military manpower problems. No longer would short-term militia forces be used as extensively as they had been in previous conflicts. The emphasis would be placed on volunteer units that would serve for at least a year and in many cases for the duration of the conflict. The elimination of short-term volunteers reduced the need to conclude campaigns before the expiration of militia enlistment. In addition, the longer terms of enlistment gave the volunteers the time necessary to receive the training to enable them to operate effectively with the regulars. While political appointments were still common among the officers corps of volunteer units, many of the appointees had previous military experience, either with the regular army or as volunteers in previous military campaigns.

4

The Mexican War: 1846–1848

In early 1846, Gen. Zachary Taylor was directed to move his force from the Nueces River to the left bank of the Rio Grande. Beginning his movement on March 8, he arrived at Point Isabel, soon after its burning by the Mexicans, on March 24. Gen. William J. Worth, Taylor's second in command, continued on to a location on the north bank of the Rio Grande opposite Matamoros, where the Mexicans had assembled almost 6,000 troops. For the next month, the two forces faced each other across the river. On April 12, Maj. Gen. Pedro de Ampudia, commander of the Mexican forces at Matamoros, warned Taylor that his forces were in Mexican territory and that he should move back to the Nueces at once. Taylor rejected the demand. At the same time, Taylor requested that U.S. naval forces move to blockade the mouth of the Rio Grande.

OPENING ENGAGEMENTS

On April 24, Maj. Gen. Mariano Arista replaced Ampudia and notified Taylor that he considered that hostilities had already begun between the two nations. On the same day, the Mexican commander sent a force of 1,600 cavalry under the command of Brig. Gen. Anastasio Torrejon across the Rio Grande. The following day, the Mexicans attacked a force of U.S. dragoons that were patrolling along the river. Capt. Seth Thornton, commander of the force, lost 11 men killed and 5 wounded; the remaining 47 were captured. When he learned of the attack, Taylor notified Washington that hostilities had begun. He called upon the governors of Louisiana and Texas for a total of 5,000 volunteers. While Taylor marched to the relief of his supply base at Point Isabel, the Mexicans crossed the Rio Grande and laid siege to Fort Texas, a U.S. construction opposite Matamoros.

News of the fighting along the Rio Grande reached Washington on May 9. On May 11, Pres. James K. Polk delivered his war message to Congress. Congress then passed an act declaring war on Mexico as well as an act that authorized the raising of 50,000 volunteers and the appropriation of $10,000,000 to finance the war.

Battle of Palo Alto

At the time of the outbreak of hostilities, the land forces of the United States consisted of eight regiments of infantry, four regiments of artillery, and two regiments of dragoons. Although the authorized strength was 8,613 men, the actual strength was only 7,365. The Mexican forces numbered about 32,000; however, the troops were not well trained or equipped and the Mexican officer corps, although consisting of a good proportion of high-ranking officers, was not of the highest quality. On the U.S. side, many of the junior officers were talented, well-trained West Point graduates, and the high-ranking U.S. officers were very experienced, having spent long years in the service of their nation. Yet the Mexicans had the advantage of fighting on familiar ground, and the vast distances gave them a great deal of mobility. The chief disadvantages faced by the U.S. forces were a lack of an adequate communications system and the great distances between the troops and their supply bases.

While news of the fighting on the Rio Grande was being transmitted to Washington, events were moving rapidly on the border. After constructing defensive works at Point Isabel, Taylor marched back to relieve the garrison of Fort Texas. On the road to Matamoros, Taylor and his force of 2,300 met a Mexican force of 6,000 at Palo Alto. Terrain favored cavalry, and the Mexican cavalry overwhelmed Taylor's dragoons. However, the U.S. artillery was far superior to that of the Mexicans, and the selection of emplacements for the guns during the battle by the young staff officers allowed Taylor to break up the advancing Mexican forces with canister and shot. Following an afternoon grass fire, which obscured the battlefield and caused the fighting to be suspended for more than an hour, the Mexican forces retreated from the field. Mexican casualties, most of them resulting from artillery fire, were about 300 killed and 380 wounded. U.S. casualties were 9 killed (including the commander of Taylor's flying artillery, Maj. Samuel Ringgold) and 47 wounded.

On May 9, Taylor, never a strategist and only an average tactician, moved against the Mexican position without waiting for reinforcements. Arista's force consisted of 5,700 men, while Taylor advanced against a strong defensive position with only 1,700 troops. Taylor's men reached a ravine called the Resaca de la Palma, which bordered the Mexican position. Because the dense underbrush prevented the effective use of the U.S. artillery, the battle was reduced almost exclusively to an infantry engagement. The Mexicans, still disorganized and demoralized from their defeat at Palo Alto, had little spirit left for the savage fighting at close quarters and finally fled toward Matamoros.

The U.S. pursuit of the fleeing Mexican army was halted at the Rio Grande. Although Taylor had requested pontoon equipment while he was still at Corpus Christi, the War Department had not managed to provide the equipment. For his part, Taylor had made no effort to obtain bridging material or boats locally. Consequently, the U.S. troops were forced to await the arrival of boats from Point Isabel before they could cross the Rio Grande. Meanwhile, the Mexican forces abandoned their positions at Matamoros and retired to rest and refit.

That same evening, the siege of Fort Texas was broken and the post was renamed Fort Brown in honor of the

The U.S. victory at Resaca de la Palma in 1846 was one of the first major battles of the Mexican War. (U.S. Army Military History Institute)

commanding officer. By May 18, Arista and his force had left Matamoros and Taylor crossed the Rio Grande to occupy the town. When news of Taylor's actions reached the United States, he became an instant hero and potential political rival to President Polk.

Naval Operations

The U.S. naval force operating in the Gulf of Mexico was the Home Squadron. Commodore David Conner, who had commanded the Squadron since 1843, was convinced that the problems between the United States and Mexico could be resolved peacefully. Yet when it became clear that a crisis was approaching, Conner, who was operating near Veracruz, rushed north to the Rio Grande with the bulk of his force. They arrived at the Rio Grande while the Battle of Palo Alto was in progress and assisted Taylor's troops across the river so that they could pursue the retreating Mexican army.

Conner immediately instituted a blockade of the Mexican Gulf coast. However, naval operations were initially limited because of a lack of the appropriate types of vessels and adequate supplies. Before the navy could take any offensive action against the Mexican coastal towns and defensive works, a sufficient number of small, shallow-draft boats would have to join the squadron. Despite these problems, Conner attempted several operations against the Mexicans. In August, he attacked the town of Alvarado but was forced to call off the attack because of a change in the weather. He again launched an attack on Alvarado in October but again was forced to withdraw when a part of his force was unable to cross the bar protecting the approaches to the city.

On October 23 and 24, Conner's second in command, Commodore Matthew C. Perry, managed to capture the town of Villahermosa on the Grijalva River. But Perry did not have a force large enough to enable him to retain possession of his prize. On November 14, Conner himself led a force that captured Tampico.

Winfield Scott, a master logician, served as general in chief of the army from 1841 until his retirement in 1861. (U.S. Army Military History Institute)

U.S. STRATEGY AND COMMAND

Just days after the declaration of war, the War Department ordered Col. Stephen W. Kearny, who was the commander of the dragoon regiment stationed at Fort Leavenworth, Kansas, to lead a force on a march to New Mexico. Kearny's force consisted of his regular troops and was to be supplemented by a group of Missouri volunteers. The force, known as the "Army of the West," was to occupy Santa Fe, the capital of New Mexico. At the same time, Conner was ordered to blockade Mexican ports on the Gulf of Mexico. In addition, Commodore John D. Sloat was directed to blockade the Mexican ports on the Pacific coast and seize and hold San Francisco Bay. On June 3, 1846, Kearny was sent additional instructions, authorizing him to capture California in concert with Sloat's naval forces.

Despite the fact that tensions and threats of hostilities had been present for months before the war began, no detailed plans had been drawn up for U.S. military operations against Mexico. In order to solve this problem, President Polk, Sec. of War William L. Marcy, and Cmd. Gen. Winfield Scott had held a meeting on May 14 to develop an overall plan to govern the conduct of the war. It was agreed that the first major effort would be against the thinly populated northern states of Mexico. Polk then faced a difficult decision concerning the supreme command of the forces operating against Mexico. Since 1841, the commanding general of the army had been Scott, and he seemed to be the most competent of the senior officers. Brigadier General Taylor, who was actually in command of the forces engaged in the fighting, was another choice. Less likely as a candidate was Maj. Gen. Edmund P. Gaines, who was the commander of the Western Department, in which Texas would have been located, but who had strained relations with Scott and who was known on occasion to disregard instructions from the War Department.

The president was reluctant to appoint either Scott or Taylor to the overall command, since both were members of the Whig party and both had presidential ambitions. Polk, a Democrat, did not want to create a military hero from the opposing political party if he could possibly avoid it. He even went so far as to propose reviving the position of lieutenant general, a rank that no one had held since George Washington, and appointing a member of his own party, probably Sen. Thomas Hart Benton, to the position. However, Congress refused to support the president, and Polk was eventually forced to conduct the war with generals whose political motives he did not always trust. The president's distrust was reciprocated by both Taylor and Scott, for the generals saw every logistical problem they encountered as an indication of the lack of support from the White House. Fortunately for the war effort, this political infighting had only a minimal effect on the conduct and eventual outcome of the war.

Although both Taylor and Scott were Whigs who harbored political aspirations and had been successful commanders, the two shared few other similarities. "Old Rough and Ready" Taylor cared little about military thought and strategic planning. He rarely wore a uniform and was an unlikely personality to serve as one of the senior officers of the U.S. Army. Taylor was so well-known for his administrative shortcomings that General Scott assigned one of the army's most brilliant and promising young officers, Capt. William W. S. Bliss (nicknamed "Perfect" by fellow officers) as Taylor's chief of staff. Bliss would try to keep Taylor's army functioning.

General Zachary ("Old Rough and Ready") Taylor, the 12th U.S. president (1849–50), was not concerned much with administration or the logistics of war strategy, but he was a great motivator and example to his troops during the Mexican War. (Library of Congress)

In sharp contrast, "Old Fuss and Feathers" Scott was thoroughly versed in military affairs and had written numerous tactical manuals. He was flamboyant and extremely fond of fancy uniforms. He was jealous of his position and station in the army, as his earlier feud with Gen. Alexander Macomb had demonstrated. He was also quick to take offense when he felt himself slighted or personally injured at the hand of fellow officers, as illustrated by his nearly 30-year conflict with General Gaines. Scott was a careful planner, preparing his forces meticulously before each encounter with the enemy. He paid particular attention to logistical concerns and details.

President Polk, despite his lack of military experience, fulfilled not only his constitutional role as commander in chief, but devoted his attention to all aspects of the war. The president maintained close contact with the various theaters and continually urged his field commanders on to a greater effort when they would have preferred to move more slowly and deliberately. Polk totally overshadowed his secretary of war. During the summer of 1847, for example, Polk assumed most of Secretary Marcy's duties when Marcy left the capital to avoid the sickly season and the oppressive heat. Polk asserted presidential control over the bureau chiefs, something Marcy was never able to accomplish. When the bureau chiefs resisted the instructions of the president, Polk made it abundantly clear to them that he was in charge of national defense policy and was in ultimate control of the War Department.

The President also took an active role in the preparation of the budget for the war effort. Since the time of Washington's administration, the Treasury Department traditionally collected the budget estimates from the various executive departments and submitted them to Congress. Polk stopped this practice, insisting that he personally review the estimates before they were submitted to Congress. During the subsequent review process, Polk met with the bureau chiefs and carefully studied all of the estimates to insure that they were necessary and valid. In this way, he was able to judge how the bureau chiefs were managing their operations. Although many of Polk's activities in the administration of the war effort would not be continued by his successors, his actions set the precedents for future presidential involvement in military affairs.

Organization and Manpower

Prior to the declaration of war against Mexico, the army of the United States consisted of 734 officers and 7,885 enlisted men. To raise the strength of the army, Congress voted to increase the enlisted strength of the companies from 64 to 100 privates. In addition, it approved the establishment of special companies of sappers, miners, and pontoniers along with the companies of mounted riflemen. This rather moderate increase in the regular army was to be supplemented by volunteer militia units. In February 1847, after nearly a year of fighting in Mexico and California, Congress further increased the regular army by adding nine new infantry regiments and one regiment of dragoons. Congress also changed the term of service, from a five-year enlistment period to enlistment for the duration of the war.

In March 1847, Congress added two companies to each artillery regiment. In light of the exceptional service the light artillery had rendered thus far in the war, two companies of each regiment, instead of only one, were to be organized as light artillery batteries. At the same time, the regular army was to be augmented by the enlistment of volunteer militia units. When Congress declared war on Mexico, it authorized the president to call upon the states for 50,000 men. These volunteers were to serve for 12 months or the duration of the war, depending upon the decision of the president. It was understood by the president and Congress that the 50,000 volunteers would be obtained by bringing volunteer companies, and even larger units, into the federal service. Initially, the president allowed the states to decide whether or not the volunteers would serve for 12 months or the duration of the war. Not surprisingly, the states selected the 12-month option, which caused a number of problems for the field commanders. In 1847, the 12-month option was dropped, and the volunteers were accepted only if they enlisted for the duration of the war.

In April 1846, even before hostilities began and Congress had approved the enlistment of volunteers from the states, Taylor had called upon the governors of Texas and Louisiana for three-month volunteers to supplement his small force. Taylor's immediate superior, General Gaines, had, on his own initiative, also called for volunteers to assist Taylor. By May, more than 8,000 of these men had been sent to join Taylor. Gaines was later court-martialed for this unauthorized action, relieved of his command, and eventually sent to New York to command the Department of the East. Gaines's action, which was a repetition of his actions at the beginning of the Second Seminole War, caused serious problems for Taylor. While the men poured into camp, their terms of enlistment were too short for them to serve any useful purpose, and most would be sent home before they saw any service. However, they had to be fed, housed, and transported, all of which strained a logistical system that was totally unprepared to deal with the situation.

Brig. Gen. Archibald Henderson, commandant of the Marine Corps, offered the services of the marines to President Polk at the beginning of the war. Just as a similar offer had been readily accepted at the beginning of the Second Seminole War, the president accepted the general's offer. However, the army made little use of the marines until the closing days of Scott's campaign against Mexico City. Their primary service was performed by small detachments serving with the naval forces.

DEVELOPMENTS IN MEXICO

Before the outbreak of hostilities, President Polk attempted to resolve the international crisis through a bit of intrigue and political maneuvering. In February 1846, Polk learned from an expatriate American, Col. A. J. Atocha, that Gen. Antonio López de Santa Anna, who was living in exile in Cuba, was willing to work with the United States to bring about a settlement of the differences between the two nations. In exchange for $30,000,000 the general promised to arrange for a Mexican agreement that the Rio Grande would be the southwest border of Texas and that the California border would run through San Francisco Bay. Polk decided to accept the offer in order to avert a war, and Santa Anna was allowed to pass through the U.S. naval forces blockading the Gulf Coast of Mexico. The decision was unfortunate. As soon as he arrived at Veracruz, Santa Anna denounced former President José Joaquín Herrera for attempting to negotiate a settlement with the United States. On August 6, Pres. Mariano Paredes y Arrillaga was deposed and Gen. Mariano Salas was installed as acting president of Mexico.

On September 19, Santa Anna rejected U.S. Sec. of State James Buchanan's efforts to negotiate a settlement and on September 28 left Mexico City with a force to oppose Taylor in northern Mexico. On December 6, the Mexican congress elected Santa Anna president and dashed any hopes for a quick end to the hostilities between the two nations.

Battle of Monterrey

By June 1846, the volunteers that Congress had authorized began to join Taylor's force on the Rio Grande. By August, Taylor's force had grown to about 15,000. Taylor's base camp was located at Camargo. The rapid increase in the size of the force, the extremely high summer temperatures, and a lack of proper field sanitation measures reduced the effective strength of Taylor's force by more than half. When he began his advance toward Monterrey, his force consisted of only 6,000 men, almost equally divided between regulars and volunteers, and was divided into four contingents, loosely called divisions. The regulars made up the 1st and 2d divisions, the volunteers made up a field division, and two regiments of mounted Texas volunteers were called the Texas Division. More than 1,500 of the men were mounted, including the 1st Mississippi Rifle Regiment under the command of Col. Jefferson Davis, a West Point graduate and newly elected U.S. senator.

The force that marched out of Camargo for Monterrey on August 19 was equipped with a mixture of weapons: the mounted troops with the newer percussion rifles, and the infantry with the older flintlock muskets. This mixture reflected the changing technology that would influence military affairs throughout the remainder of the century, while preserving the commander's preference. General Taylor was a firm believer and proponent of the bayonet and its effectiveness at close quarters.

On September 19, Taylor's army reached Monterrey, a city built in a pass in the Sierra Madres. The Mexicans, numbering about 7,000, had constructed elaborate defensive works that added to the already formidable position provided by the city's stone buildings and Citadel. The city was protected on the south by a river and on the north by the Citadel. In addition, there were stone forts all around the perimeter of the town, especially to the west on Independence and Federation hills.

After the Mexican defenses were thoroughly scouted by Taylor's engineers, the attack was launched on September 20. General Worth, in command of one of the regular divisions, supplemented by about 400 Texans, was sent to attack the western part of the town and to cut the road leading to Saltillo. Advancing along the Saltillo Road in a heavy rain and against stiff resistance, Worth's force managed to capture Federation Hill on September 21 and Independence Hill the following day. Although Worth had lost nearly 400 men killed and wounded, he controlled the western approaches to Monterrey.

Taylor was in command of the forces that began the assault on the eastern approaches to the city. They managed to break into the city on September 21, but the outcome of the battle was not decided for four days. In vicious house-to-house fighting, the U.S. soldiers slowly drove the Mexican defenders back into the center of the city. The end came for the defenders when Taylor brought a 10-inch mortar into position to shell the great plaza area of the city. Most of the Mexican troops had been driven into that part of the city, and the Mexican commander realized that his situation was hopeless. He agreed to surrender provided that his troops were allowed to retire from the city without opposition and that an eight-week armistice would be put into effect. Although the U.S. forces were obviously winning the battle, they were not in the best position to continue the fight. Because Taylor had lost almost a sixth of his force (800 killed or wounded), had expended a considerable amount of ammunition, had consumed a large quantity of supplies, and was operating at the end of a 125-mile supply route, he readily agreed to the Mexican conditions.

Political Suspicions

When word of the armistice reached Washington in mid-October 1846, President Polk disavowed the agreement. He accused Taylor of allowing the Mexican army to escape and ordered an end to the armistice. When the new orders reached Taylor, he notified the Mexicans that the armistice would end on November 13. Yet the summary order from the War Department also increased Taylor's suspicions concerning the political motivations of the president.

In response to the War Department's order to resume his advance, Taylor dispatched a force of 1,000 men to capture Saltillo. The city was at a major road junction about 70 miles southwest of Monterrey, controlling the only road to Mexico City from the north that was suitable for heavy guns and wagons and the east-west road from Victoria to Chihuahua. Victoria was the capital of the province of Tamaulipas, which contained Tampico, the second largest port on the Gulf of Mexico. While Taylor's forces were advancing on Saltillo, two other expeditions were underway in the area.

On November 17, the forces of the naval squadron operating in the Gulf of Mexico captured the port of Tampico. An expedition under the command of Gen. John E. Wool, which had left San Antonio in late October, captured the town of Parras on December 5. Wool's force had originally been sent to capture Chihuahua, but upon learning that the Mexicans had left that city, he moved to join Taylor at Saltillo, which had been occupied on November 16.

Taylor planned to establish a defensive position along a line through Victoria, Monterrey, Saltillo, and Parras. However, before he could consolidate his position, he learned of Polk's decision to curtail operations in northern Mexico and adopt Scott's strategy of launching an attack against Mexico City from Veracruz. In order to give Scott an army with which to invade Mexico, the War Department directed that much of the force Taylor had planned to use was to be taken out of his control and given to Scott.

Scott arrived in Mexico early in December and proceeded to dismember Taylor's force. He took most of the regulars, nearly 4,000, and an equal number of volunteers, leaving Taylor a force of less than 7,000. Scott ordered Taylor to evacuate Saltillo and withdraw to Monterrey, where he was to place his force on the defensive. Taylor was also directed to remain in communication with Scott concerning his activities. Taylor was certain that Polk wished to halt his successful campaign and thus his public popularity. He also believed that Scott was trying to use military glory to increase his own political position with the Whigs. Consequently, Taylor decided to disregard Scott's order to withdraw from Saltillo to Monterrey.

Battle of Buena Vista

On Feb. 5, 1847, Taylor began an advance from Saltillo toward Agua Nueva, 18 miles south. Taylor's force consisted of 4,600 men, most of them volunteers who were not fully trained and who lacked combat experience. At the same time, Santa Anna was gathering a force of nearly

20,000 men just 200 miles to the south at San Luis Potosí. Taylor believed that the force under Santa Anna would not be able to advance up the road through the desert terrain and that Santa Anna would use his large force to oppose the operations of Scott, which had been leaked to the press. However, Santa Anna's men had captured a copy of Scott's order to reduce the size of Taylor's army. Thus, Santa Anna, hoping for a quick victory against Taylor and then a fast march to oppose Scott, pushed his army across the rugged desert to La Encarnacion, 35 miles from Agua Nueva.

On the morning of February 21, Taylor was informed that a large Mexican army was advancing on his position. Besides initiating operations directly in his front, Santa Anna had dispatched a large cavalry force that was to circle to the east and then cut in behind the U.S. troops, blocking the road from Agua Nueva to Saltillo. Upon learning of the Mexican advance, Taylor ordered a withdrawal up the Saltillo Road to establish a better defensive position. Only about a mile from the hacienda of Buena Vista, Taylor's forces, under the careful direction of Wool, organized their defensive positions.

The terrain seemed to favor the U.S. forces. On the east, mountain spurs reached down to the road. The spurs were separated by a wide plain that was divided by two deep ravines. On the west side of the road, the ground was broken by a series of deep gullies behind which was a line of hills. The U.S. soldiers took up their main positions east of the road and arrayed their artillery on La Angostura, the highest of the spurs. To the west of the road, only a few U.S. troops were deployed because Wool believed that the gullies would afford adequate protection against a Mexican attack.

When Santa Anna arrived on the scene, he demanded that Taylor surrender—a demand Taylor emphatically rejected. After the refusal, the two forces spent the rest of the day probing for weaknesses and trying to gain a tactical advantage. The Mexicans managed to gain an advantage

Major Battles of the Mexican War, 1846–1848

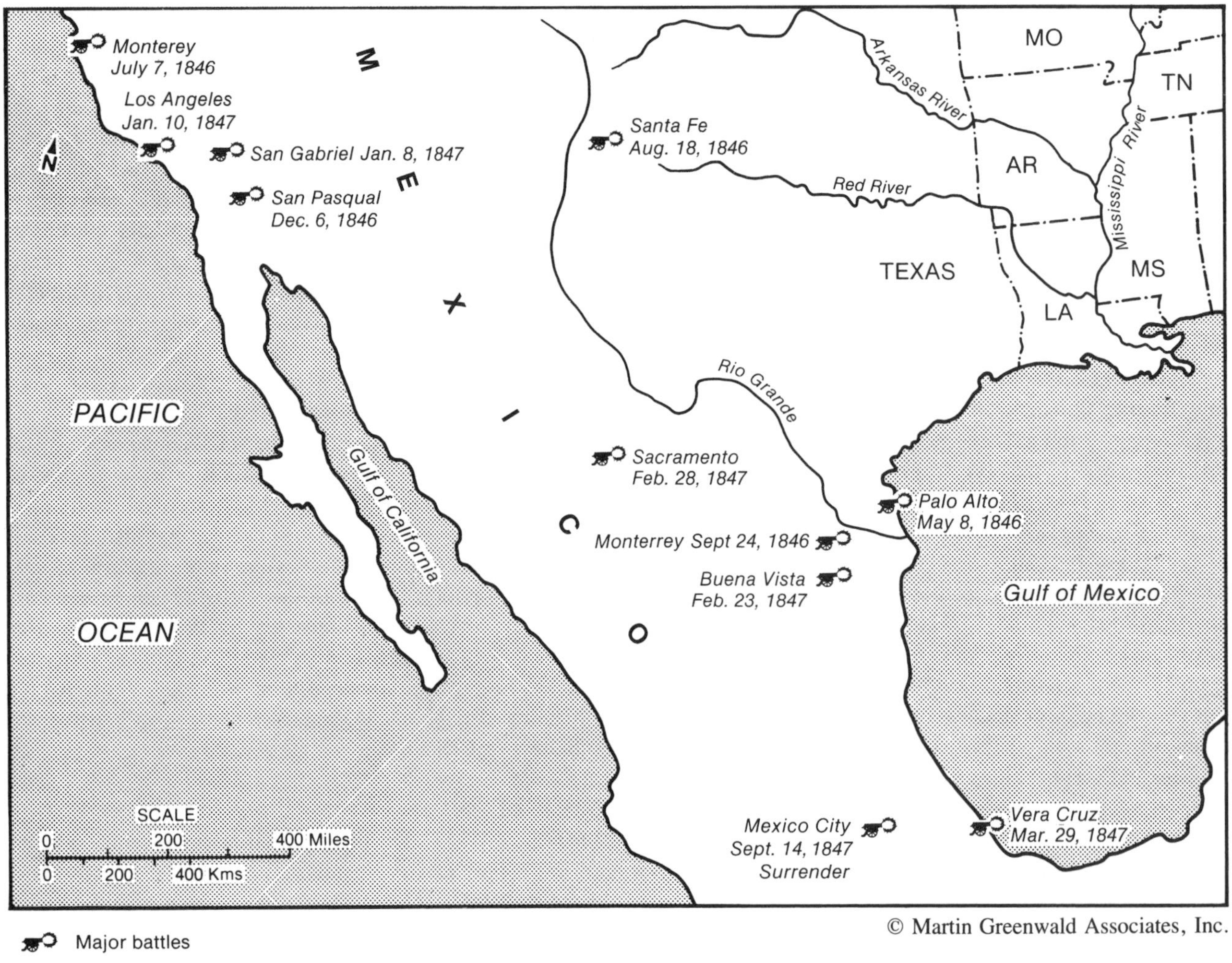

in the mountain spurs east of the road, but the U.S. troops moved out onto the plateau with both infantry and artillery. When it appeared that the Mexicans might be attempting an advance through the hills west of the road, Taylor sent a regiment of Kentucky volunteers and two guns from Maj. Braxton Bragg's battery onto the high hills, but the attack failed to materialize. As darkness fell, Taylor returned to Saltillo, while the troops settled in to get some rest before the next day's anticipated battle. The badly outnumbered U.S. troops were disturbed by the magnificent appearance of the Mexican army and its vastly superior size.

On February 23, with the initial maneuvering out of the way, the battle was joined in earnest. Initially, Santa Anna sent a division straight up the road toward La Angostura, but the Mexican advance was quickly stalled by U.S. artillery fire strongly supported by the infantry. The blunting of this attack ended the Mexican effort in the vicinity of the road. On the east, far from the road, the Mexicans launched their strongest effort. Two divisions supported by a strong battery moved against the southern ravine on the plateau. An Indiana regiment was the first to bear the brunt of the attack, and for more than 30 minutes they held up the Mexican advance. However, when ordered to retreat by their commander, they soon broke and ran. Their breaking spread to the regiments supporting them, and the retreat rapidly turned into a rout.

Fortunately for the U.S. troops, Taylor returned to the field from Saltillo with the Mississippi Rifles in time to stem the tide. The Mississippi troops, supported by some of the Indiana troops that Taylor managed to rally, threw themselves against the Mexican cavalry that was attempting to turn the U.S. position north of the plateau. At the same time, Bragg with his artillery and the Kentucky regiment moved from the hills to the west to join in the fight.

The U.S. troops seemed to be on the verge of victory when Santa Anna committed his reserves against the U.S. forces on the plateau. The fresh Mexican troops had been hiding in one of the deep ravines throughout the early hours of the battle. Divided into a right and left column, they moved against the weakened center right of the U.S. forces. The left column attacked three U.S. regiments and drove them back on the Saltillo Road. The right column threw itself against the center and slowly began to drive it from the field.

Just as it appeared that the battle was about to be won by the Mexicans, two batteries supported by the hard-riding Mississippi Rifles arrived on the scene from the north. The U.S. forces fell upon the Mexicans' right flank and rear and forced them back into the ravine. The Mexican column chasing the troops of the Illinois and Kentucky regiments up the road made the mistake of coming within range of the batteries emplaced on La Angostura. Working at a frantic pace, the U.S. gunners shattered the Mexican force and forced it to withdraw. That night, the battered Mexican force began its withdrawal toward San Luis Potosí. Santa Anna had lost 1,500–2,000 killed or wounded. Taylor had lost 264 killed, 456 wounded, and 23 missing.

Aftermath of Buena Vista

The U.S. victory at Buena Vista could be attributed to a number of factors, but most of the credit belonged to the U.S. artillery. The fast-moving batteries, moving across the battlefield to the point of greatest need with the speed of cavalry, had shattered the Mexican formations and broken the momentum of their assaults. In addition, the batteries that were able to deliver a murderous fire of canister and shot had served as rallying points for the hard-pressed infantrymen. Also, the conduct of the volunteers could hardly have been better. Although largely untrained in formal military operations, they fought with a tenacity that was worthy of the most highly trained veterans.

Along with the valor of the artillerists and the volunteers, the leadership of the U.S. forces was excellent. Colonel Davis, serving with his former father-in-law, General Taylor, and although wounded during the battle, continued to ride at the head of the Mississippi Rifles throughout the day. This was only one instance of the younger officers leading by example. Perhaps the best example was set by Taylor himself. Taylor often neglected intelligence reports and frequently misjudged his adversary's strength and intentions, but he understood how to motivate soldiers. He possessed a physical and moral courage far beyond that of most of his contemporaries. During the Battle of Buena Vista, Taylor sat astride his horse in full view of his own troops, as well as the enemy, with a total disregard for the bullets that whined about him and even ripped his coat. He encouraged, he rallied, and he inspired his men. For their part, the troops believed that with such a man in command, defeat was impossible.

Taylor would remain in command of the forces in northern Mexico for nine months after the Battle of Buena Vista. Then, at his own request, he was relieved of command. He returned to the United States a hero. General Wool then assumed command of the occupation forces in northern Mexico. Santa Anna left the northern theater and went to Mexico City, where he was sworn in as the president of Mexico on Mar. 21, 1847.

OPERATIONS IN THE WEST

During the summer of 1846, a month after leaving Fort Leavenworth, Colonel Kearny and the Army of the West, consisting of 1,700 men, arrived at Bent's Fort, at the junction of the Arkansas River and the Santa Fe Trail. On July 31, Kearny issued a proclamation to the people of

New Mexico stating that he was entering the province on their behalf. On August 1, he sent a letter to the governor warning him not to resist the advance of his force. The next day, he began his march to Santa Fe, which he subsequently captured without a fight.

Doniphan's Volunteers

One of the most remarkable expeditions in U.S. military history occurred during the operations of the Army of the West. It was carried out by the 1st Regiment of Missouri Volunteers, a force of mounted riflemen consisting of farmers, boys, unemployed workers, and German immigrants recruited from eight Missouri counties. They were commanded by Alexander W. Doniphan, who had enlisted in the force as a private and was elected colonel by the men of the unit. Doniphan whipped the 900 men of the regiment into a hardened fighting force on the five-week, 850-mile march from Fort Leavenworth to Santa Fe. After Kearny continued on with more than half the force to California, Doniphan was left with fewer than 900 men to complete the conquest of New Mexico, subdue the Indians in the territory, and then invade northern Mexico. All of this was to be accomplished while operating in complete isolation from the government and their supply base.

The Indians living in the territory were Ute, Navajo, and Zuni, all of whom had to be either persuaded or coerced into accepting the United States as the new governing agency for the territory. In their efforts to track down a portion of the Indians, some of the Missouri volunteers marched more than 1,000 miles. On Nov. 22, 1846, Doniphan signed a treaty of peace with the Navajo chiefs. This pact secured Doniphan's right flank and rear and freed him to move into Mexico.

On December 14, Doniphan left Valverde for El Paso—a march of 90 miles through barren and waterless country. On December 25, as the force emerged from the desert, a force of 1,200 Mexican dragoons attacked Doniphan's force at El Paso. The attackers vastly underestimated the fighting ability of their opponents. Toughened by their grueling march and displaying a spirit born of shared hardship, the volunteers broke the cavalry charge with seeming ease. The Mexicans lost some 50 killed and 150 wounded in the engagement; U.S. losses were 7 wounded.

After occupying El Paso, Doniphan again attempted to win the support of the local population before moving on to Chihuahua to meet the force commanded by General Wool. As had been the case before entering Mexico, the biggest threat was posed by the local Indian tribes, in this case the Apache. In attempting to subdue the Apache and bring a sense of security to the local population, Doniphan's troops spent valuable time and expended precious supplies before leaving for Chihuahua, 270 miles away.

Along the Sacramento River north of Chihuahua, the Mexicans made one last effort to stop the relentless advance of the men from Missouri. Doniphan's skillful use of his artillery broke the Mexican defensive position, and the defenders fled in the face of the U.S. attack. The U.S. force occupied Chihuahua with 2 U.S. and 300 Mexican fatalities.

Doniphan had instructions to assist Wool in operations to capture Chihuahua. However, unable to locate the general or his force, Doniphan finally received word from Taylor, who was still at Buena Vista, directing the Missouri volunteers to join him. Thus, the volunteers spent another three weeks marching through the desert to join the main U.S. army. By this time, the men's enlistments had expired, they had not been paid, and they were ragged, dirty, and exhausted—not surprisingly, most of them decided to go home rather than reenlist. Between June 1846 and April 1847, the men had marched more than 3,600 miles since leaving Fort Leavenworth. By March 1847, the northern provinces of Mexico were quiet and the U.S. hold on them was tight.

Bear Flag Revolt

By 1846, there were about 500 U.S. settlers living along the 500 miles of the California coast from Sonoma to San Diego. There were also 8,000–12,000 Mexicans and 24,000 Indians living in California. The local provincial government was weak, and the situation was made even worse by a power struggle between the provincial governor at Los Angeles, Pio Pico, and the military commandant at Monterrey, José Castro.

As early as October 1842, believing that the United States and Mexico were at war, Commodore Thomas Catesby Jones had landed a U.S. naval force at Monterey and seized the city. When he learned that relations between the two nations were normal, Jones took down the U.S. flag and returned control of the city to the Mexican officials. The United States repudiated Jones's actions, made reparations to Mexico, and apologized. However, on Oct. 17, 1845, President Polk assigned Thomas O. Larkin, the U.S. consul at Monterey, the secret mission of persuading the U.S. settlers in California to establish an independent state or even join the United States.

On Jan. 27, 1846, Capt. John C. Frémont, on his third surveying expedition, reached Monterey and made camp in the Salinas Valley. When General Castro warned him to leave, Frémont's men fortified a position on Gavilan Mountain and raised the U.S. flag. On March 9, faced by a superior Mexican force, Frémont began a slow withdrawal to the north. The U.S. forces stopped their movement at Lake Klamath on the Oregon border. At this point, the party was overtaken by marine lieutenant Archibald H. Gillespie, who brought Frémont new instructions. Although the precise contents of the instructions given to Frémont are open to question, he soon moved back into California and helped foment resistance to the Mexican authorities.

John C. Frémont and the Bear Flag Revolt, 1844–1845

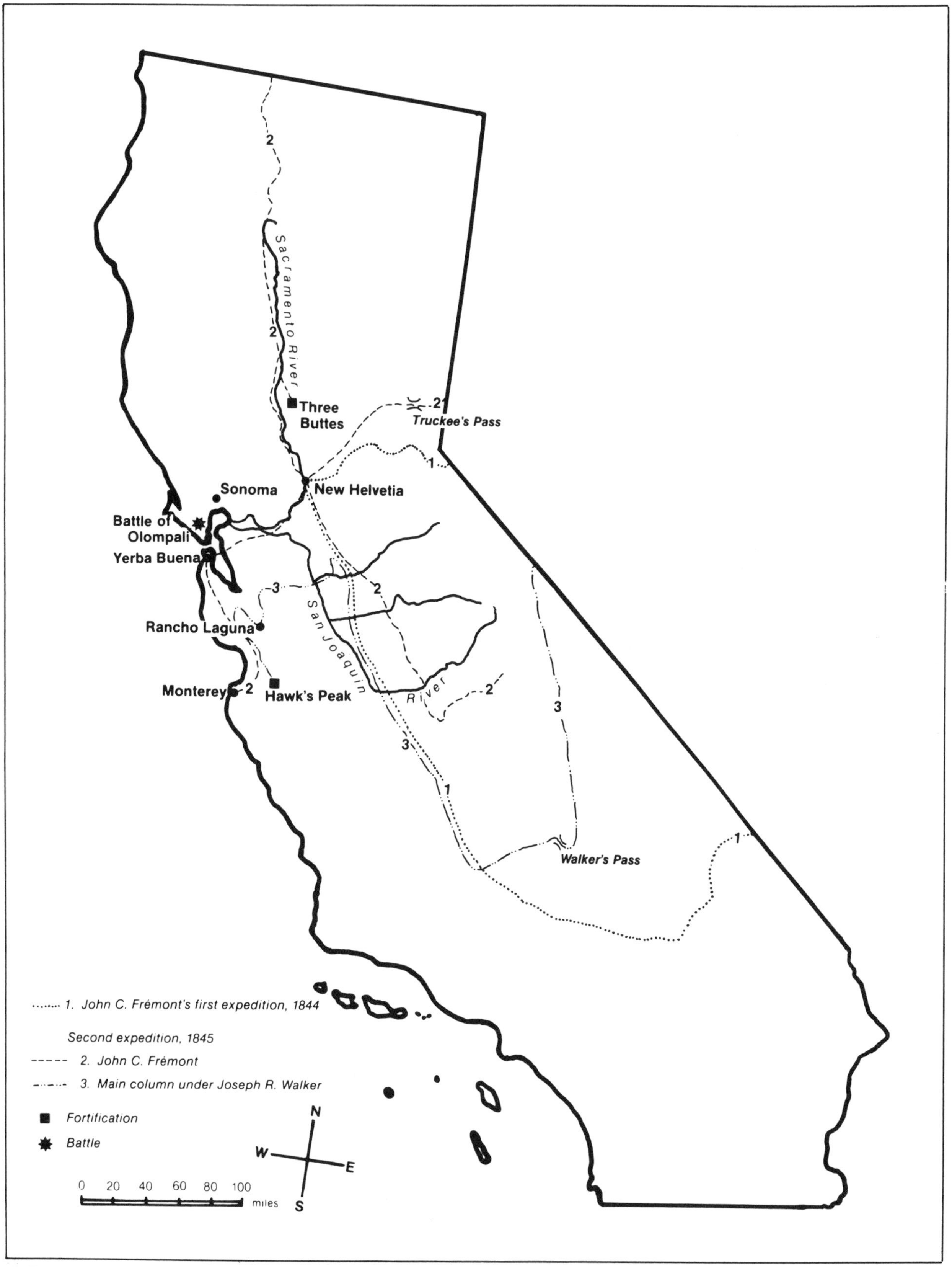

John C. Frémont, while surveying the California region for the United States, was instructed to lead U.S. troops during the conquest of California. (U.S. Army Military History Institute)

When news reached California that President Herrera had been deposed and Paredes had been installed in his place, the political conflict between Pico and Castro rapidly intensified. Pico called for a general convention to set California up as an independent state, while Castro pledged his support to Paredes and sent troops to Los Angeles to overawe Pico and his supporters. While Castro's force was marching to Los Angeles, a group of U.S. settlers attacked a part of the column on June 10. On June 14, another group of settlers seized Sonoma and declared their independence, raising a flag emblazoned with a grizzly bear facing a red star. On June 25, Frémont and his party arrived at Sonoma, and Frémont pledged his support to the independence movement. On July 5, the settlers chose Frémont to direct the affairs of the Republic of California.

Conquest of California

On July 2, Commodore Sloat, in command of the U.S. naval squadron operating in the Pacific, arrived at Monterey and sent a landing party ashore, raised the U.S. flag, and declared California to be a part of the United States. On July 9, the naval forces of Comdr. John B. Montgomery captured San Francisco and Lt. James W. Revere took Sonoma. A few days later, a party of sailors took possession of Sutter's Fort on the Sacramento River.

In the face of the Bear Flag Revolt, Castro and Pico put their differences aside and assembled a force at Los Angeles to resist the independence movement of the U.S. settlers. On July 23, Commodore Robert F. Stockton replaced Sloat, publicly condemned the Mexican resistance, and organized the California Battalion under Frémont's command. Naval forces under Stockton occupied Santa Barbara and captured Los Angeles on August 13. On August 17, after declaring that the United States had officially annexed California, Stockton established a new territorial government with himself as governor. Frémont was appointed military commandant of the northern district and Lieutenant Gillespie commandant of the southern district.

In late September 1846, Capt. José María Flores launched a revolt against U.S. authority and succeeded in driving the U.S. faction out of Los Angeles, Santa Barbara, San Diego, and several other areas. By the end of October, Flores was acting as governor and military commandant of all of California south of San Luis Obispo. On December 12, General Kearny arrived at San Diego from New Mexico. He joined forces with Stockton and, together with a force of 559 dragoons, sailors, marines, and volunteers, marched on Los Angeles. After two minor battles with the Mexicans, the force captured Los Angeles on Jan. 10, 1847. On January 13, the remnants of the Mexican forces signed the Treaty of Cahuenga.

As soon as the Mexican resistance in California was eliminated, a conflict arose between Kearny and Stockton. Both men thought that their instructions gave them the authority to organize the government of California. Stockton suspended Kearny from all command except over his small force of dragoons, and at the same time appointed Frémont governor. Despite the fact that Kearny warned Frémont that he was guilty of disobedience to orders from a superior officer, Frémont continued to perform as governor and to support Stockton.

On February 13, Kearny received new instructions from Washington that gave him explicit authority to organize the government of California. Yet even with the arrival of these new orders, Frémont still refused to obey Kearny's commands. The dispute continued until Kearny appointed Col. Richard B. Mason governor. Kearny, Stockton, and Frémont then left for Washington, where Kearny preferred charges of mutiny, disobedience, and prejudicial conduct against Frémont. A court-martial found Frémont guilty of all charges and directed his dismissal from the U.S. Army. President Polk upheld Frémont's conviction on all charges except for those of mutiny. Although Polk eventually remitted all penalties and directed his return to duty, Frémont resigned his commission and left the army.

THE MEXICAN THEATER

On Feb. 18, 1847, Scott arrived at Tampico from Washington and established his headquarters. The force he was to lead was supposed to number 20,000, but troops in that number were not available; in fact, Scott's force never numbered much more than 10,000 men. His orders were to capture Veracruz and then, operating from this base, to move along the national highway to Mexico City. The task presented Scott with several serious problems, since Veracruz was acknowledged to be the most powerful fortress in the Western Hemisphere. Its conquest would require the first large-scale amphibious operation in U.S. military history. As a first step, Scott would have to assemble enough water transportation to move his force to Veracruz. If he were successful in taking the city, he would have to secure the support of the Mexican population along his line of march from Veracruz to Mexico City if he was not to suffer from guerrilla raids against his lines of communications. He would also have to reach the highlands between Veracruz and Mexico City before the beginning of the yellow-fever season. Despite all of these problems, any one of which could have resulted in the failure of the expedition, Scott began his operations confidently.

Estimates concerning the supplies needed to support Scott's force varied widely. Quartermaster General Thomas S. Jesup estimated that a force of 25,000 men, moving from Veracruz to Mexico City, would require about 2,900,000 pounds of supplies. At least 9,300 wagons and 17,400 mules would be needed to move the supplies. Among the supplies were such items as 300,000 bushels of oats, 200,000 bushels of corn, 200,000 muleshoes, and 100,000 horseshoes. In addition, Jesup included 5,000 quills, 300 bottles of ink, and 1,000 pounds of tape, all necessary to account for all of the other items. Scott believed that much smaller quantities of supplies would be sufficient to support his force. He also felt that most of the pack animals could be obtained easily in Mexico, a point with which the president agreed. Polk was incensed at the prospect of transporting U.S. mules to a country famous for its pack animals. The president rebuked Jesup and insisted the affairs of the War Department be managed more efficiently. Polk criticisms notwithstanding, Jesup's supply estimates proved far more accurate than Scott's.

On February 19, Scott issued General Order No. 20, which established procedures for dealing with situations not specifically covered by the Articles of War. The order was intended to prevent a number of abuses committed by Taylor's volunteers against the Mexican people, and it was hoped that the order would help gain Mexican support once Scott began his advance on Mexico City. The order left local government, wherever militarily possible, in the hands of the local Mexican officials. In essence, General Order No. 20 established the first civil affairs administration of foreign territory occupied by U.S. military forces.

Scott established his assembly site at Lobos Island, about 50 miles south of Tampico. After his 13,660 troops, composed of 5,741 regulars and 7,919 volunteers, were assembled, the fleet under the command of Commodore Conner moved the force to the final assembly point, about 12 miles south of Veracruz. By March 5, the force was off the coast at Veracruz where they met the U.S. naval squadron that was blockading the city.

P. G. T. Beauregard, later a general in the Confederate Army, was a young officer under Gen. Robert Patterson during the Mexican War. (U.S. Army Military History Institute)

Conquest of Veracruz

Scott, Conner, Worth, Gen. David E. Twiggs, and Gen. Robert Patterson, along with several of Patterson's young engineers, Robert E. Lee, George G. Meade, and P. G. T. Beauregard, made a personal and dangerous reconnaissance of Veracruz's defenses in a small boat. A shell, fired by a Mexican battery located in the fortress of San Juan de Ulua, barely missed their boat. Nevertheless, based upon the results of his personal inspection and the strong recommendation of the naval officers, Scott decided against trying to take the city by a direct assault from the ships.

As a landing site, Scott and his staff selected a stretch of beach about three miles south of Veracruz. The site was beyond the range of the heavy guns of Veracruz and offered a broad beach upon which the surf boats that would bring the men ashore could operate. The boats that Scott used for his landing were the first U.S.–built amphibious craft. Designed by Lt. George M. Totten of the U.S. Navy, 141 of these boats were constructed at Philadelphia for the army's Quartermaster Department, at a cost of $795 each. In order to nest the boats aboard specially configured transports, the boats came in three sizes, ranging from 35 feet 9 inches to 40 feet. Each of the boats would carry 40 men in addition to an 8-man crew. The surf boats were double ended, broad beamed, flat bottomed, and well suited for use in an amphibious landing. One drawback was that they were built of light planks, which limited their useful-

The amphibious landing of Gen. Winfield Scott's troops on the beaches of Veracruz only took about four hours, but it was twenty days later before the troops captured the city. (U.S. Army Military History Institute)

ness as cargo lighters between supply ships and the beach. Also, they were not suited for the transportation of horses. Consequently, the horses were forced to jump overboard from the transports and then swim ashore.

In order to supplement the naval force supporting Scott's landing at Veracruz, Sec. of the Navy John Y. Mason temporarily sent the ship of the line *Ohio* to the Gulf rather than to the Pacific. He also dispatched three additional sloops of war to the Gulf. The navy also purchased four coastal schooners and converted them into bomb vessels, which were intended to help in the reduction of Fortress San Juan de Ulua. However, none of the naval reinforcements reached Veracruz before Scott's successful landing. The navy blamed the late arrival on bad weather. President Polk blamed the lateness on a lack of cooperation between the army and the navy.

Scott's force was organized into three divisions: two composed of regulars and commanded by Worth and Twiggs, and a third division composed of volunteers and commanded by Patterson. The initial landings would be made by Worth's division, followed by Patterson's and then finally Twiggs's force. The actual assault upon the beachhead was simple in concept. It was the execution of the plan that was filled with uncertainty. The shallow-draft steamers and gunboats were to form a line close to the shore and be prepared to shell any Mexican troops that might oppose the landing. Once the beaches were cleared, the surf boats would form a single line parallel to the beach and sweep in to deliver the troops to the landing area. The initial assault force would seize the beachhead, regroup, and then push inland. It would be supported by the shallow-draft boats standing offshore while the surf boats returned to the transports for more troops.

On March 9, the landing operation began, and within four hours, Scott's entire force of slightly more than 8,000 men had landed. The troops quickly moved inland to establish a beachhead large enough to take the supplies that would follow. The landing of artillery, supplies, and horses was slowed by a change in the weather, but by March 22, the troops had managed to emplace seven 10-inch mortars within a half a mile of Veracruz. The siege of Veracruz was opened that same day, after the Mexicans rejected an initial demand that they surrender.

Scott soon discovered that his mortars were not effective against the strong Mexican fortifications. He was therefore obliged to call upon the commander of the naval forces, Commodore Perry, for additional guns. The large naval guns soon broke through the city's walls, and on March 27, the city surrendered and was occupied two days later.

Battle of Cerro Gordo

Following the successful landing of the army, Perry relieved Commodore Conner. In the following months, he directed efforts by the naval forces to capture other Mexican coastal towns and actively encouraged a secessionist movement in Yucatan. Naval operations were, however, still hampered by some of the problems that Conner had faced early in the war. Although Lt. David P. Dixon failed in an initial attack on the Mexican town of Tabasco, he subsequently led a 70-man landing party that eventually captured the city's main fort. For his efforts in this action, he was given command of the war steamer *Spitfire*. Yet the navy simply did not have the manpower nor the vessels necessary to hold coastal towns for an extended period. The need to transport men and supplies to Scott's base at Veracruz was far more pressing. The invasion force needed all available manpower if it was to capture Mexico City.

The rapidly approaching yellow-fever season was another source of anxiety for Scott and his staff. Although they wanted to begin the 55-mile advance across the lowlands before the season was upon them, the collection of a sufficient number of wagons and pack mules delayed the movement from Veracruz until April 8. On that day, an advance element of about 2,600 men under the command of Twiggs left for the city of Jalapa, about 75 miles from Veracruz. Included in Twiggs's party were two artillery batteries, one of which consisted of 24-pounder guns, 8-inch howitzers, and 10-inch mortars. The other battery, officered and manned by members of the Ordnance Corps, was armed with rockets and mountain howitzers. The rockets were mainly Congreve, of the type used since before the War of 1812, but a limited number of new Hale rockets were to be field-tested during the campaign. These rockets were to be fired from troughs mounted on portable stands.

After advancing only a few miles, Twiggs's scouts detected the presence of Mexican forces at Plan del Pio, just below Cerro Gordo, where the national highway traversed a mountain pass. The scouts had encountered an advance party of Santa Anna's 12,000-man force, which was deployed on both sides of the national road. On the U.S. left, the Mexican guns were placed on the mountain spurs; farther down the road on the U.S. right, the guns were on a high hill. Santa Anna thus had complete command of the national road and was in a position to prevent the passage of Scott's guns and supply train.

On April 12, Twiggs managed to escape Santa Anna's trap when the Mexican guns opened fire prematurely. Temporarily withdrawing a short distance, Twiggs, who was unsophisticated as a tactician, planned a head-on attack for the following day. Fortunately for the U.S. forces, Patterson recovered sufficiently from an illness to assume command and cancel this potentially disastrous attack.

Scott arrived on the scene on April 14 and ordered a full reconnaissance of the area. The next day, Captain Lee discovered a narrow path that wound around the left flank of the Mexican position. On April 16, the engineers worked to make the path passable for men and guns. The plan of attack was easy enough to formulate but difficult to execute because of the hills and broken terrain. The U.S. troops were to use the path to flank the Mexican position and then cut the road behind Santa Anna's force. On April 17, Twiggs finally began his movement around the Mexican position. Because of confusion and overanxiousness, the plan was not completely executed and the opposing sides spent much of the day strengthening their positions. The U.S. soldiers hauled artillery pieces up the steep and rugged hills to support the attack to be launched the next day, while the Mexicans strengthened their positions in the sector where they expected the U.S. attack to be made.

As a young officer, Robert E. Lee distinguished himself throughout the Mexican War. (U.S. Military Academy)

The basic plan on April 18 was the same as it had been the previous day. However, this time the plan was executed almost flawlessly. Twiggs directed two brigades to bypass the hill named El Telegrafo and cut the road behind the Mexican camp. His third brigade was to assault El Telegrafo directly, supported by the guns that the troops had struggled to emplace the previous day. The assault on El Telegrafo carried the Mexican works and captured the Mexican guns on the hill. Capt. John B. Magruder quickly turned the captured guns on the fleeing Mexican soldiers. Twiggs diverted a part of his second brigade to attack along the reverse slope of the hill while the rest of the brigade assaulted the Mexican guns behind the hill. As the Mexicans rushed down the Jalapa Road, the third U.S. brigade burst out of the underbrush and overran the Mexican camp. The Mexican troops not killed or captured fled into the mountains, led by Santa Anna.

For the United States, the road to Mexico City, just 170 miles away, was now open. The magnitude of Scott's victory at Cerro Gordo was revealed by the casualty figures: although no figures exist for the number of Mexicans killed or wounded, those captured were recorded as 199 officers and 2,837 men. Lt. Col. Ethan A. Hitchcock, the army's inspector general, speculated that at least another 1,000 prisoners managed to escape. If Hitchcock was correct, nearly a third of the Mexican force was captured; if the number of killed and wounded were added, it is likely that no more than one-half of the Mexican army escaped. Scott's losses were 63 killed and 368 wounded out of approximately 8,500 men engaged.

March to Mexico City

While the troops rested at Jalapa, Scott contemplated his next move. The road to Mexico City lay open to him, but the extension of his thin supply line for another 170 miles was of obvious concern. The rapidly approaching warm weather and the necessity of moving his forces out of the Veracruz area before the onset of the yellow-fever season also played upon the general's mind. Equally worrisome was the continued shortage of supply transport. By the end of April, Scott suggested to the War Department that it might be wise to abandon his base at Veracruz and that his army could secure enough food by foraging the countryside.

A new problem had arisen since the Battle of Cerro Gordo. Incidents of guerrilla warfare directed primarily at

Scott's supply lines and isolated outposts had increased dramatically. The Mexicans' resort to guerrilla warfare was the result of several factors. The formation of a "light corps of the National Guard" was expressly intended to engage in hit-and-run raids against the invaders. Additionally, the governor of Veracruz and the legislature of the state of Mexico had called upon the citizens to begin a guerrilla campaign against U.S. troops.

Scott took immediate action to curtail the growth of the guerrilla warfare movement. The mayor or local leader (the *alcalde*) nearest the scene of a guerrilla attack was made responsible for apprehending the guilty parties. If the suspects were not promptly turned in to the U.S. occupation forces, the *alcalde* would be personally fined $300. As a result of this policy, the incidents decreased, but not entirely.

At the end of April 1847, yet another problem arose that seriously threatened Scott's position. The terms of the 12-month volunteers were rapidly expiring. Because the president and secretary of war had already decided to replace these regiments with six or eight new regiments of volunteers who had enlisted for the duration of the war, Scott decided to send the nonduration men home before the onset of the yellow-fever season. This was probably a wise decision on Scott's part, for as the time for the men's discharges approached, they would become more difficult to manage and control. Scott was well aware of the problems that Gen. Andrew Jackson had endured during the War of 1812 when his militia's terms had expired. Therefore, on June 6 and 7, the seven militia regiments started back to Veracruz. Scott's army now consisted of only 7,113 men.

Scott resumed his relentless advance toward Mexico City. He ordered Worth forward to seize Puebla. Yet as the U.S. troops prepared to advance, Santa Anna moved toward Puebla with a small force he had collected after the Battle of Cerro Gordo. Santa Anna arrived ahead of Worth, and his scouts soon discovered that Worth's supply train had become separated from the main U.S. force. The Mexican general hoped to defeat the two U.S. forces in detail. However, Worth discovered the attempt to bypass him and reinforced the supply train before Santa Anna's 3,000-man cavalry could attack. Once the Mexicans realized that the situation had changed, they quickly rejoined Santa Anna in Puebla and marched with him to Mexico City.

Worth and his men entered Puebla on May 15, and the rest of the army arrived a week later. It was at Puebla that Scott decided that it was essential to reinforce his army, even if it meant evacuating Jalapa and Perote. When the forces from these two cities joined Scott, the U.S. Army had effectively cut its communications with the coast and would have to live off of the country during the rest of its advance on Mexico City. But the army was still too small to mount an attack on Mexico City. On August 8, when reinforcements reached Scott, his force rose to 8,061 men fit for duty, with 2,235 on the sick list. Arriving soon afterward was a force commanded by Brig. Gen. Franklin Pierce, about 2,500 strong and including a marine battalion commanded by Col. Samuel E. Watson.

With reinforcements arriving to join him, Scott issued the order to proceed against the Mexican capital. On August 7, Twiggs's division had begun the advance from Puebla. The divisions of Worth, Gen. John A. Quitman, and Gen. Gideon J. Pillow followed at one-day intervals. A 3-mile-long wagon train carrying the expedition's supplies brought up the rear. The entire force numbered 10,738 officers and men. Despite the fact that Santa Anna had a force of more than 30,000 men in and around Mexico City, he made no move against the opposition. Twiggs's division arrived at Ayotla, about 15 miles from the capital, on August 11. Within the next 48 hours, the remaining divisions arrived and took up supporting positions.

Battle of Churubusco

The direct approach to Mexico City from the east was guarded by strong fortifications. Consequently, Scott decided upon a wide flanking maneuver to the south, which would allow him to assault the city from the west. The attackers would have to follow a narrow road that ran between two lakes and the mountains. The road passed by the edge of a 15-mile-wide lava bed, known as the Pedregal, before it swung north, passed over a bridge at Churubusco, and then passed through the western gates into the city.

The Pedregal was considered to be impassable, but Lee found a narrow path that led to the village of Contreras. Supported by Twiggs's division and some light artillery, a work party began efforts to improve the road. They soon came under heavy fire, and Pillow, after hauling his artillery to higher ground, opened an artillery duel with the Mexicans. However, the U.S. light artillery was no match for the 68-pounder howitzer and reinforcements brought to the scene by Santa Anna. On the morning of August 20, U.S. forces, using another route through the Pedregal discovered by the engineers, attacked the Mexicans from the rear while Pillow's force made a frontal assault. The battle lasted less than 20 minutes.

Scott ordered an immediate pursuit of the fleeing Mexicans, yet Santa Anna was able to rally his forces and made a stand at Churubusco. Santa Anna's position was strongly fortified, with the bridge strengthened and a stone church and convent converted into fortresses. The first U.S. soldiers to arrive at the bridge drew heavy fire from the defenders. The initial fighting was furious, but the fire from the Mexicans slackened as they gradually exhausted their ammunition. The defenders were soon driven from their positions, ending the battle. Santa Anna had lost more than

4,000 killed and wounded; Scott lost 155 killed and 876 wounded.

Conquest of Mexico City

After the Battle of Churubusco, Santa Anna sought to reopen peace negotiations with the United States. Scott responded with the offer of a truce, which was readily accepted. For two weeks, presidential envoy Nicholas P. Trist negotiated in vain with representatives of the Mexican government. On September 6, Scott called a halt to the talks and began preparations for the attack on Mexico City.

Overshadowing the Mexican capital was the castle of Chapultepec, which guarded the western approaches to the city. Yet Scott's primary concern was how to capture the Molino del Rey, a low group of stone buildings about 1,000 yards west of Chapultepec. The position was heavily fortified, and the defenders possessed interlocking fields of fire that would make any attack extremely difficult.

Scott selected Worth's division to make the assault. On September 8, the 3,500 men, supported by two 24-pound siege guns and two 6-pounders and a special force of 500 men who were to assault the western side of the buildings waited for the attack to begin. Worth began the assault after a light bombardment, because it was reported that the Mexicans had abandoned their positions. The reports, however, were wrong; the Mexicans had only moved closer to the buildings. When the assault force came within range, the Mexican guns opened fire and drove the U.S. troops back. The special assault force lost 11 of its 14 officers, and as it was reeling under the effects of the fire from the buildings, it was hit by a charge of the 3d Light Infantry. The force was completely broken.

It was on the right side that the battle was finally decided. There, in a series of disorganized battles typical of small-unit actions, the U.S. troops managed to force their way into the buildings. Fighting from room to room, they finally managed to clear the building. Supporting units stopped Mexican reinforcements from arriving from Chapultepec. In two hours of fierce fighting, Worth lost a quarter of his command. Scott ordered the buildings destroyed, and by midday, the troops had withdrawn to their starting positions.

Scott still faced a difficult decision: which route would be best for the main assault on the city. The U.S. positions were connected to the southern gates of the city by three causeways, each a little more than 1,000 yards long. The Acapulco Road crossed one causeway to the San Antonio Garita, a second ran from Pedregal to the Garita de Belen at the southwest corner of the city, and a third carried the San Angel Road to the Nino Perdido Garita. On the west, two more causeways ran to the castle of Chapultepec.

On September 11, Scott and his commanders held a conference to determine which route to choose. On the following day, U.S. soldiers demonstrated as a diversion. In addition, a number of guns were brought into service, and fire was opened against the city. On the morning of September 13, the assault began at about 5:30, covered by artillery fire. The force that would capture the castle and force its way into the city was commanded by Quitman.

At the beginning of the war, Quitman had offered his services to President Polk, but not until a number of prominent politicians, including Sen. John C. Calhoun, spoke to the president was he commissioned as a brigadier general of volunteers. He served with distinction under Taylor at the Battle of Monterrey. After Scott began assembling his force, Quitman was ordered to join the expedition against Mexico City.

On September 13, Quitman's division charged straight up the steep hill and captured the fortress of Chapultepec by 9:30 A.M. After capturing the fortress, Quitman ordered his men to attack down the causeway leading to the Belen Gate. Although the attack along the causeway was only to be a feint, Quitman and his men forced their way across the causeway and, after some of the hardest fighting of the war, managed to reach the gate by 6:00 P.M. Because of the danger of entering the city after dark, the U.S. troops spent the night outside the city's walls. U.S. casualties on this first day were 130 killed, 703 wounded, and 29 missing.

The next morning, Quitman and his division resumed the attack. They fought their way into the city, where they raised the U.S. flag. (Despite Scott's anger with Quitman's rash action on the causeway, he later appointed Quitman to the position of civil and military governor of the city.) Santa Anna's force withdrew from the city to Guadalupe Hidalgo. A delegation from the city arrived at Scott's headquarters to surrender the city to the invading army.

DIPLOMACY AND PEACE

Upon learning of the fall of Veracruz, President Polk, with the support and advice of his cabinet, had decided to try to negotiate a peace treaty before Scott began his advance upon Mexico City. To conduct the negotiations, Polk selected Trist, chief clerk of the State Department. Trist's secret instructions, issued on Apr. 15, 1847, contained essentially the same terms as those offered to Santa Anna before he left Cuba. The only differences were that Trist was authorized to negotiate for Lower California and the right to cross the Isthmus of Tehuantepec. Although Trist's mission was supposed to be secret, it became common knowledge within a week after his departure from Washington on April 16.

On May 6, Trist, who had traveled to Mexico under an alias, arrived at Veracruz. Although Trist was empowered by the president to negotiate an end to hostilities, he immediately came into conflict with Scott. The general

United States Acquisitions from Mexico, 1848

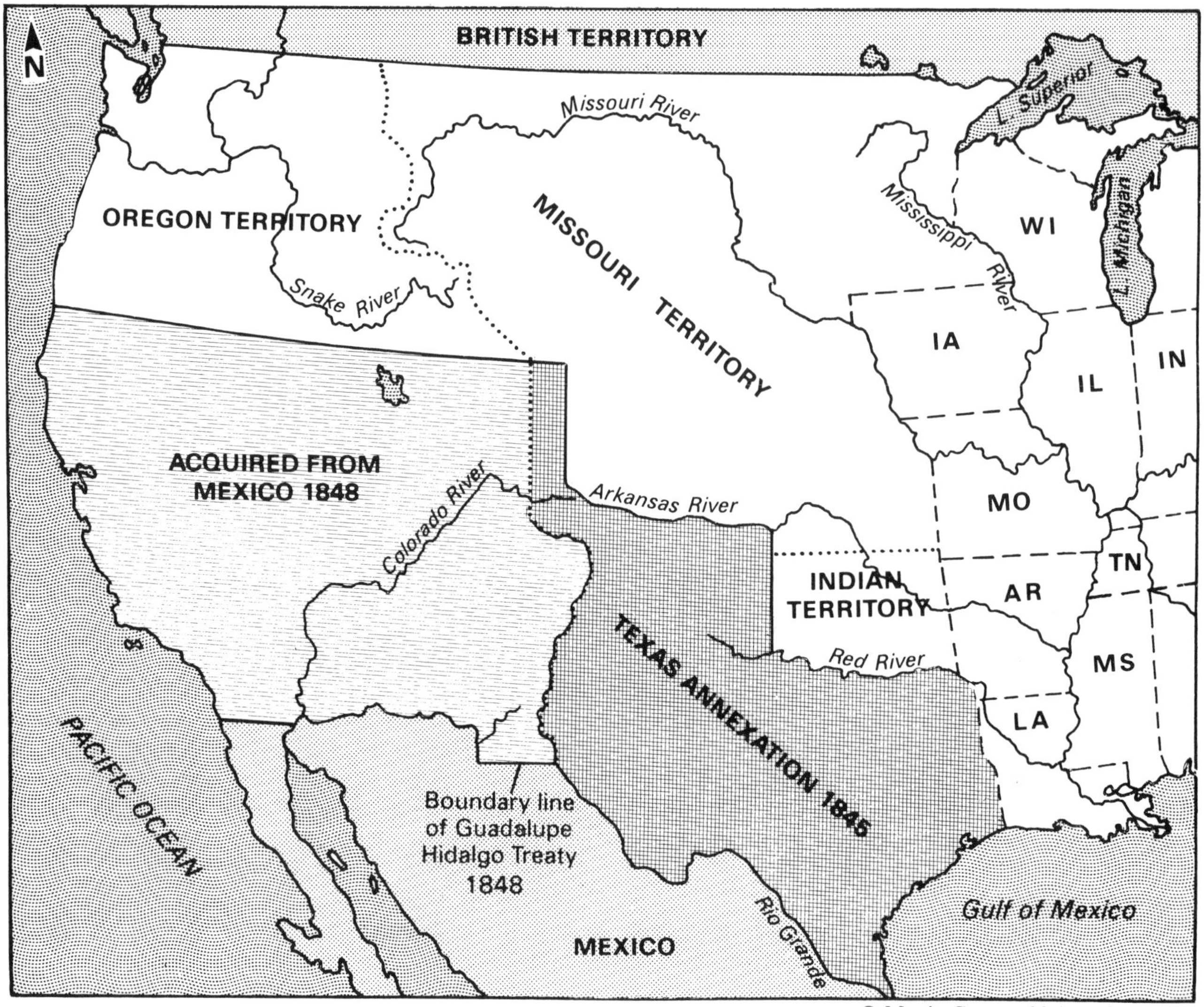

Texas Annexation, 1845 — Acquired from Mexico, 1848

believed that his authority as military commander gave him exclusive authority over any questions concerning an armistice. Consequently, he would not allow Trist to usurp his prerogatives. A particularly angry exchange of letters between the two men only served to widen the gap between them. It took the efforts of the British officials in Mexico to resolve the issue and restore a working relationship between the two men. Scott arranged an armistice, but negotiations between Trist and the Mexican officials failed, and Scott began his movement on the Mexican capital. Trist, hopeful of fulfilling his mission, accompanied Scott's army on its march on Mexico City.

Between August 27 and September 6, while Scott's army waited outside Mexico City, Trist again attempted to negotiate an end to the war. However, following the capture of Mexico City, Santa Anna renounced the presidency on September 16. On October 7, he was deposed as the head of the Mexican army and subsequently fled the country. The political turmoil caused by the capture of the capital, the abdication of the president, and the loss of the army's commander threw the Mexican government into a state of chaos for nearly two months. During this period of uncertainty, Trist received instructions recalling him to Washington.

On November 11, Pedro Maria Anaya was elected interim president of Mexico. On November 22, the new government informed Trist that it was ready to negotiate a peace settlement. However, Trist notified the Mexican government that he had been recalled and had no authority to act on behalf of the United States. Because the Anaya government had not received notification of the recall and insisted on negotiating with Trist, the U.S. commissioner decided to ignore his recall order and open peace talks with the Mexicans.

On Jan. 2, 1848, the talks between the representatives of the two governments began in Guadalupe Hidalgo. The terms of the treaty negotiated by the two sides gave the United States virtually everything it had hoped to gain from Mexico. The Mexican government abandoned all claims to Texas above the Rio Grande and ceded New Mexico and California to the United States. This newly acquired territory added 1,193,061 square miles to the United States.

In return for the territorial cession, the United States agreed to pay Mexico $15,000,000 and assume the responsibility for paying the claims of U.S. citizens against the Mexican government. The boundary between the two countries was fixed at the Rio Grande, then westward and northward along the Gila and Colorado rivers, and then along a line between Upper and Lower California to the Pacific Ocean. The U.S. Senate ratified the Treaty of Guadalupe Hidalgo on March 10, and the Mexican Congress ratified it on May 25.

In anticipation of the ratification of the treaty, an armistice had been declared on February 29. The last military action was fought at Todos Santos in Lower California on March 30. U.S. troops evacuated the Mexican capital on June 12, and the last U.S. soldiers left Veracruz on August 2. The cost of the war to the United States had been 1,721 killed or dead of wounds, 11,155 dead of disease, and 4,102 wounded. The expenditures to support the military operations had amounted to $97,500,000.

U.S. Military Status

The U.S. military establishment that emerged from the Mexican War was much different from those that had weathered earlier conflicts. The decisive U.S. victory in the Mexican War was won primarily by regulars supported by long-term volunteers. In both the American Revolution and the War of 1812, serious questions had been raised concerning whether the United States had actually won the wars or simply managed to outlast England. However, the resounding defeat in Mexico of a numerically superior military force operating on its home soil left little doubt that the United States was the strongest force in the Western Hemisphere and was also a force that the great powers of Europe might have to contend with on the international stage.

The performance of both the army and navy had been far superior to their performances in previous conflicts. There were many problems during the war, but none of them were serious enough to hinder the overall war effort. Considering the fact that the United States was projecting a large military force onto foreign soil for the first time in its history, and given the long distances involved, the difficulties and problems encountered were not unexpected.

The senior army officers had learned the skills of their profession during long years of service. Generals Scott and Taylor had both entered the army in 1808; General Wool had been commissioned in the militia in 1807 and received his regular army commission in 1812; General Twiggs had been commissioned in 1812; General Patterson had served during the War of 1812, left the service in 1815, and was commissioned a major general of volunteers when the Mexican War began. The two senior naval officers, Commodores Conner and Perry, had both entered the navy in 1810. Although not educated as officers in the same sense as their young subordinates, their long years of service had given them the experience necessary to conduct the war effort successfully.

The senior officers were supported by a remarkable group of young officers educated at West Point. In little more than 12 years, these men would lead Civil War armies that would dwarf those of Taylor and Scott. During the Mexican War, these officers contributed much to the eventual victory of the United States. Their ability, knowledge, and understanding of the military arts, especially engineering and artillery, were major factors in the superb performance of the U.S. Army in Mexico.

The soldiers fought well. Their years of service on the frontier had provided them with the necessary training and experience. In addition, the hard life of the frontier had toughened them and prepared them for the hardships encountered during the campaigning in Mexico. The regulars were well supported in most cases by the volunteers. The year-long enlistments, and then enlistments for the duration of the war, provided ample time to transform the citizen soldiers into seasoned veterans. Units such as the 1st Missouri Volunteers would have been a credit to any military organization.

The overall direction of the war effort was closely supervised by President Polk. He vastly expanded the role of the chief executive in the administration of the military affairs of the nation. The victory in Mexico was in no small part the result of his close attention to the details of the war effort. The president worked to correct a number of the problems encountered in the wartime administration of the government, but as soon as the crisis passed and peace returned, many of the lessons learned were quickly forgotten.

The military forces that returned to peacetime duties with the conclusion of the Mexican War were faced with new challenges. The regular army would be called upon to protect a vastly expanded frontier. Although its men were seasoned combat veterans, the officers and soldiers would face the challenge of subduing the Indians of the Great Plains—a far different challenge than facing the armies of another nation state. The navy would, at the same time, return to its efforts to protect the commerce of the nation—a commerce that would continue to grow and require more and more effort on the part of the navy.

5

From the Mexican War to the Civil War: 1848–1861

Few wars in history have been more successful than the Mexican War in accomplishing a nation's military objectives, yet so disastrous in worsening that nation's internal political divisions. Between 1848 and 1861, the U.S. military faced few external enemies but was constantly occupied in the newly acquired territories keeping the peace among such factions as Mexicans, Mormons, proslavery and antislavery emigrants, and Indians. The army was also called upon to survey routes by which the regions of the now-continental United States might be tied together, but the leaders who selected the routes were motivated by unabashed sectional prejudices. Eventually, the regional hostility led to the Civil War, in which such opponents as Ulysses S. Grant and Robert E. Lee, and George H. Thomas and Braxton Bragg, utilized the experience they had gained in the Mexican War to fight fellow Americans rather than foreign enemies.

THE WESTERN FRONTIER

By the end of the 1840s, the settlement of disputes over Oregon (1846) and the discovery of gold (1848) in California created a secure territorial hold on the far Pacific West. At the same time, the secure possession of Texas (annexed in 1845) and the expansion of the agricultural frontier toward the 98th meridian continued the nation's push toward the Great Plains. During these years, the army took on a new, western character as it became committed to the exploration and protection of the vast expanse between the Mississippi River and the Pacific coast.

The increase in the military's territorial responsibility, however, was not met by a corresponding increase in the size of its forces. At the end of the Mexican War, the army reverted to a peacetime strength of fewer than 10,000 men, the number authorized following the War of 1812. A significant number of these troops were committed to manning coastal and border posts and forts and were not available for frontier service. Congress authorized only two modest increases in the army's size during the next decade. In 1850, upon the recommendation of Sec. of War George W. Crawford and Gen. in Chief Winfield Scott, the authorized strength of companies serving on the frontier was raised. Thereafter each might possess 74 privates, which eventually raised the army's authorized size to around 13,000 men.

The army's first priority after the Mexican War was exploration. The government still knew very little about the far reaches of the Louisiana Purchase when it acquired the additional unmapped realms of Texas, the Oregon country, and the Mexican cession. Many emigrant leaders knew more about the Great Plains and its trails than did the military officers assigned to protect them. The important tasks of exploration and discovery were assigned to the 36 officers of the Corps of Topographical Engineers, who took on four herculean missions prior to 1861. Completing surveys of the Mexican and Canadian boundaries, they determined the best courses for the central overland trails, conducted feasibility studies for transcontinental railroad routes, and laid out routes connecting the main settlements of the newly acquired Southwest territories.

The border established with Mexico in the Treaty of Guadalupe-Hidalgo was based on vague, and occasionally completely erroneous, geographical assumptions. Boundary commissioner John Bartlett and surveyor Lt. William H. Emory and their Mexican counterparts labored to delineate a discernible boundary from Brownsville on the Rio Grande to San Diego on the Pacific. Emory believed that to secure a good railroad route, the United States should exercise its option to purchase land south of the Gila River, an aim satisfied by the Gadsden Purchase, surveyed in 1854–55. On the Canadian border, Lt. John G. Parke worked with the British Royal Engineers to define the boundary through the forests of the Pacific Northwest.

At the insistence of the senators from Illinois, Missouri, and Arkansas, the army also explored and rerouted central continental emigration routes. In 1849–50, Capt. Howard Stansbury searched for a location for a fort to assist emigrants preparing for the crossing of the West's arid basin country and for a route to connect the Mormon settlements in Utah with the Oregon Trail. In the process, Stansbury surveyed the entire basin of the Great Salt Lake, found a direct route to it from the east via Bridger's and Cheyenne passes, and proved that the Rocky Mountains were not an impenetrable barrier. Portions of Stansbury's trail were later used by the Pony Express, Overland Stage, and Union Pacific Railroad. In the same years, Capt. Randolph B. Marcy and Lt. James H. Simpson, an engineer, escorted a party of gold seekers from Fort Smith west along the Arkansas and Canadian rivers. Their explorations established both the "Marcy Route" or California Road (as opposed to the California Trail), which became the shortest route to California, and a trail from Fort Smith to El Paso.

The most spectacular engineering feats of the pre–Civil War era were the four Pacific railroad route surveys ordered by Jefferson Davis, Pres. James Buchanan's secretary of war from 1853. Davis clearly wanted to see a route chosen that would benefit his native South, which he genuinely believed was the region best situated to further the nation's "manifest destiny." Not surprisingly, the points of origin of the other three surveys were influenced by powerful representatives of rival regions. The northern survey, above the 47th parallel, was carried out by Isaac I. Stevens, who was seconded by George B. McClellan, then a young engineer. Stevens's survey began at St. Paul on the Mississippi and sought to connect the Great Lakes with the Pacific. The difficult central survey was directed by John W. Gunnison, who sought to find suitable passes through the Utah ranges of the Rockies southeast of Great Salt Lake. Amiel Weeks Whipple led a survey along the 35th parallel through the Indian Territory (Oklahoma), Texas panhandle, and New Mexico Territory. A belated southwestern survey, the one favored by Davis, was based in part on Emory's suggestion that a railroad route be located south of the Gila River. This last survey was unique in that it was simultaneously conducted eastward from California by Parke and eastward from its midpoint on the Rio Grande by John B. Pope.

All of the surveys seemed star-crossed. To Stevens's chagrin, McClellan reported the Cascade Mountains impassable. Gunnison's advance party was massacred by Paiute, and no especially promising passes were located by those who followed. Whipple initially overcalculated by more than $50,000,000 the cost of a railroad using his route, while Parke knew of no suitable pass over the Sierra Nevadas. Yet, each survey leader claimed that his route was feasible, leading to a congressional deadlock over railroad appropriations until the Civil War. However, routes for some future military roads were discovered and general knowledge of the West's geography, ethnography, and natural history was greatly expanded.

Other significant army explorations, which built on the work of Texas Rangers, were undertaken to connect San Antonio and other Texas settlements with the settlements of the upper Rio Grande. In 1849, an upper route was established north of the Edwards Plateau and a lower route south of the plateau. The lower route was improved to become the San Antonio–El Paso military road. Both trails were used by gold seekers, settlers, stagecoaches, and, eventually, continental railroads.

Western Forts

By the Civil War, 90 percent of the army's personnel was assigned to chains of forts in the trans-Mississippi West. Before the Mexican War, a line of eight western forts (founded 1817–42) had been laid out during the establishment of the supposed "Permanent Indian Frontier." In the 1840s, however, prospector and emigrant traffic across the Great Plains made the "permanent frontier" a fiction. The only original forts that remained particularly active were Fort Leavenworth, Kansas, a headquarters and supply base for newer forts, and the forts needed to maintain the peace among the concentrated tribes of the Indian Territory.

As westward traffic and consequent friction with the Indians increased, a new series of bases was established along the principal trails across the Department of the West. The most important posts were Forts Laramie (1849) and Kearny (1849) on the Oregon-California Trail, Forts Union (1851) and Larned (1859) on the Santa Fe Trail, and Fort Riley (1853) on the Smoky Hill between them. The far end of the Oregon Trail lay in the Department of the Pacific and was guarded by Fort Dalles (1850) and the post eventually known as Vancouver Barracks (begun in 1849) in what later became Washington. Additional forts, such as Fort Walla Walla (1856), were constructed during conflicts with the northwestern tribes.

Four chains of forts were established in the Department of Texas, two of them running north to south from the Red River to the Rio Grande along the expanding Texas frontier. The first chain (1849) proved somewhat ineffective as it was largely garrisoned with infantry. The second chain (early 1850s), farther west and parallel to the Great Comanche War Trail, included the 2d Cavalry's Fort Belknap (1851), a particularly active post. Another line of forts, including the strategically located Fort Duncan (1849), was placed down the Rio Grande to the Gulf of Mexico. The fourth line of Texas forts ran along the San Antonio–El Paso Road, with Fort Davis (1849) the largest and most important along it. The frontier in the rest of the desert and mountain Southwest, in the departments of New Mexico and California, was a scattered pattern of villages, mines, and ranches interspersed throughout Apache and Navajo lands. Forts Defiance (1851) and Craig (1854) were important early posts for dealing with these two tribes.

In contrast to the familiar cinematic portrayals of palisaded fortifications, most frontier posts were open clusters of barracks, offices, and stables organized around a rectangular parade ground. Constructed virtually overnight by the soldiers of raw timber, sod, or adobe, they usually provided primitive accommodations. Eventually, the structures of some of the longer-lived forts would be replaced piecemeal by new ones of sawed lumber, stone, or brick.

Many of the soldiers serving in the West were immigrants or Easterners escaping poverty, ill fortune, or the law. The skilled tradesmen among them supplemented their low pay by working as barbers, saddlers, carpenters, or masons. Military campaigning was minimal, leaving a life of tedious drill, guard duty, and fatigue duty that was only rarely punctuated by moments of excitement or terror in the field. Sanitation was frequently poor, and, as would be true during the Civil War, disease took far more lives than did combat.

Indian Campaigns

There were at least 11 significant Indian wars, uprisings, or military campaigns between 1848 and 1861. In the late 1830s, many such battles had taken place in the Republic of Texas. There, the Texas Rangers had been established largely to curb the raids of the Comanche and allied Kiowa. Yet the U.S. Army became inextricably involved in warfare with the tribes in the 1840s. With the annexation of Texas, the United States assumed responsibility for the protection of the former republic and also inherited the Mexican government's difficulties with the Apache and Navajo in the territory of New Mexico. The most costly war of the 1840s, however, took place in what is now Washington and involved the militia. In 1843, a small group of Cayuse massacred the inhabitants of Whitman Mission, having mistaken a measles epidemic for poisoning by the missionaries. The Oregon territorial militia, by making war on the wrong bands and tribes, expanded the conflict until they were in danger of unifying all the major northwestern tribes against the settlers. At that point, the disbanding of the militia led to the end of the Cayuse War.

With the dramatic influx of U.S. settlers into the West during the 1850s, military activity increased. In 1857 alone, there were 37 army operations or expeditions during which combat occurred. The steady westward traffic on the Oregon Trail created the setting for the army's first armed confrontations with the tribes of the northern and central plains. The overlanders' arrival as permanent settlers and miners in the Oregon country and California created great resentment among the tribes of the Northwest and the Sierra Nevadas. At the same time, the opening of gold fields in Colorado led to the first armed confrontations with several southern plains and mountains tribes.

The conflicts in Oregon, Washington, and northern California in the 1850s usually stemmed from land disputes. One such war largely resulted from the ambitions of Oregon territorial governor Isaac I. Stevens, an aggressive man who cowed some northwestern chiefs into ceding large areas of tribal land at a council in 1855. By 1856, Chief Yamiakin of the Yakima tribe of eastern Washington, the most powerful of the Columbia River basin chiefs, became exasperated at Stevens's premature opening of his land to settlement, the continued traffic of prospectors across his land to a gold field at Colville, and the restriction of his people to a de facto reservation. Settlers began to realize that an uprising was underway after four separate massacres had occurred. As in the Cayuse War, area militia managed to push some nonbelligerents into taking its side. Yamiakin managed to secure his own allies from the Walla Walla, Umatilla, and Cayuse. At one point, the sloop *Decatur* was called upon to bombard Yakima and other tribesmen besieging Seattle, making the Yakima War one of the few Indian conflicts in which the navy saw action.

In the spring of 1856, Gen. John Wool, commander of the Department of the Pacific, dispatched two columns, largely drawn from the new 9th infantry, to the field. The column bound for the Yakima homeland was largely unable to bring its opponents to battle. However, Stevens's militia overcame a group of 300 Walla Walla, Cayuse, and Umatilla in July. Tribal resistance was reduced by the regular and volunteer forces, but the war ended inconclusively. Forts Simcoe and Walla Walla were then constructed because of the need for continued army vigilance. Because of his concern for justice to the Indians and his failure to prosecute the war with the aggressiveness Governor Stevens desired, Wool was removed and replaced by the more politically sensitive Newman S. Clarke.

The Yakima War coincided with a war in the Rogue River valley of southern Oregon. A brief war had been won and a peace negotiated near Lower Table Rock in 1853. The commander of nearby Fort Lane, Capt. Andrew J. Smith, managed to prevent a second war until 1855. In that year, Rogue River and other Indians disturbed by intrusions on the Table Rock Reservation began to leave, and conflict resulted. Fearing the brutality of the local militia, Smith gave sanctuary to some male tribesmen at the fort, but before the women and children could be relocated, area militia struck and slaughtered 23 people at their old camp. War resulted, with the reluctant Smith forced to take sides against the Indians. The nine-month conflict was largely a militia effort, assisted by Smith's 1st

Dragoons, against the Rogue River and allied Shasta and Umpqua tribes.

Distracted in the meantime by the Yakima War, Wool was unable to send infantry until the spring of 1856. The decisive battle of the war occurred on May 27, 1856, after the major Rogue River chiefs promised to surrender to Smith at Big Meadows on the Rogue. The chiefs intended instead to annihilate Smith's 50 dragoons and 30 infantrymen. Smith, warned by Indian allies, took a position on a defensible hilltop. As the chiefs prepared for a last charge, a fresh company of regulars arrived, catching the warriors in a cross fire. The tribes involved in the Rogue River War were then removed to the Siletz Reservation, and portions of southern Oregon and northern California were almost depopulated of their original inhabitants.

By 1858, Yamiakin was again distressed by a fresh stream of miners crossing his lands en route to Colville. He argued that the native peoples of the Northwest were at a crisis point, but it was tribes farther up the Columbia River who acted, fearing a military invasion of their territory. In May, Maj. Edward J. Steptoe and 164 men detoured from another expedition in order to impress the Palouse with a show of force and to reassure the miners. On May 18, approximately 1,000 Palouse, Spokane, and Coeur d'Alene warriors attacked Steptoe's forces, driving them to a knoll. That night, Steptoe and his men escaped and made an 85-mile forced march to safety among friendly Nez Percé. In response, columns of regular infantry were dispatched from Forts Simcoe and Walla Walla to scour both sides of the Columbia Valley. Col. George Wright's 600 men, mostly from the 1st Dragoons and 9th Infantry, met and defeated an equal force of allied warriors in the Battle of Four Lakes on September 1. The battle was one of the military's first tests of a new long-range arm, the 1855 rifle-musket. On September 5, Wright again defeated the tribes in a running battle across 25 miles of the Great Spokane Plain. In the aftermath of these successful Spokane War battles, Wright aggressively pursued the war leaders and ended serious resistance to Anglo settlement in much of Oregon and Washington.

Treaty Negotiations

Many of the army's problems in the 1850s were caused by important shifts in the government's Indian policies. In 1849, the Indian Bureau was transferred from the War Department to the newly created Department of the Interior. This frequently made the army responsible for providing military solutions for problems created by civilian officials, who were variously motivated by ignorance, idealism, personal gain, or political ambition. At the same time, the pressing need to guarantee safe passage on the overland trails led to a subtle change in the status of the plains tribes. Officially, all recognized tribes were "domestic dependent nations," with passage rights to be obtained by signed treaties. In exchange, tribal leaders received gifts at the negotiations, and the tribes were promised subsidies to be allotted at centrally located agencies at specified times. The most important such treaties, at least temporarily, were the treaties of Forts Laramie and Atkinson. The former was negotiated with the principal tribes of the northern and central plains in 1851, the latter with the Comanche and Kiowa of the southern plains in 1853. These treaties required that the Indians not only permit transit across tribal lands but also withdraw from the vicinity of the trails. This marked the beginnings of an evolving policy of concentration of the tribes. Concentration would lead, in turn, to the hated reservation system.

Ironically, the peace treaties themselves would create discord because of the different cultural perspectives of the Anglos and the Indians. The tribal leaders, who had no concept of land ownership, often assumed that they were agreeing simply to permit shared land use, not granting exclusive rights. U.S. peace commissioners generally failed to recognize that the chiefs, who ruled by consensus, could not effectively commit all of their people to an agreement against their wills. Then, too, decades-old native traditions of gaining horses, goods, and honor through raiding could not be overcome in a few days of negotiations. Matters were not helped when the government cheated on treaty conditions, as when the payment period for annuities for the Treaty of Fort Laramie was arbitrarily reduced from 50 to 10 years. It was the army's job to escort and protect the peace commissioners and agents, enforce the treaties, and combat the traditional patterns of raiding.

Great Plains and Southwest

The 35-year period of hostilities between U.S. forces and the tribes of the central and northern plains began with an unnecessary tragedy near Fort Laramie. On Aug. 18, 1854, an ox belonging to a Mormon settler was butchered by a Miniconjou Sioux who was a guest at a large Sioux encampment east of the fort. After the military rejected an offer to compensate the settler for the ox, a confrontation with Sioux led by Conquering Bear followed. After some shots were fired, Conquering Bear managed to control the situation temporarily, until the Americans fired a volley. The Sioux then attacked, pursued, and wiped out the detachment of Lt. John L. Grattan.

In response to the "massacre," the army launched a punitive campaign by a mixed force of 600 men from Fort Kearny under Col. William S. Harney. On Sept. 3, 1855, Harney's force arrived at Blue Water Creek, a tributary of the Platte River. There, scouts discovered the village of Little Thunder, leader of the band of Sioux who had killed Grattan, together with some northern Cheyenne lodges. The chief remained strangely complacent about the approach of Harney's soldiers until it was too late. Members of the 2d Dragoons circled the village and attacked on the south side, while soldiers of the 6th and 10th infantries attacked on the north. Although most of the inhabitants managed to escape, 80 warriors and 70 women and children were killed. Harney, having lost 4 dead and 7 wounded, then proceeded north through the heart of Sioux country but was unable to bring other Sioux bands to battle. The Sioux would avoid further armed conflict for almost a decade.

Until the early 1850s, the Cheyenne had been, to the Anglos, one of the most amiable tribes of the Great Plains. In the mid-1850s, however, Cheyenne warfare with the Pawnee encouraged some of the young men to conduct raids on U.S. settlers as well. A consequent retaliatory raid by troops from Fort Kearny in 1856 only seemed to provoke the tribe further. As a result, three columns under Col. Edwin V. Sumner swept the Cheyenne country between the Platte and Arkansas rivers in the summer of 1857. On July 29, Sumner, with 300 men of the 2d Dragoons and the young 1st Cavalry, found perhaps the same number of Cheyenne awaiting them on the Solomon Fork in Kansas Territory. The warriors were confident, believing that some recently acquired "medicine" made them immune from bullets. But when Sumner ordered a saber charge, the Cheyenne were demoralized and fled in what became a seven-mile running battle. Sumner destroyed their abandoned camp and seized the Cheyenne's treaty annuity. Only nine warriors were killed, but the battle had such an impact that the tribe would not go to war again until 1863.

Other expeditions of the 1850s were designed to discourage a much older tradition of raiding against Anglos by tribes of the southern Rocky Mountains and the Apache tribes of the Gila River watershed. In 1854, raids by the Jicarilla Apache on the Santa Fe Trail became intense. Eventually, a dragoon expedition led by Col. St. George Cooke and guided by Kit Carson routed Jicarilla in the mountains west of Fort Union. The expedition then successfully followed up with an operation south of the fort. Influenced by Jicarilla refugees and disturbed by expanding white settlement in Colorado, the Ute raided Hardscrabble (Pueblo) and a settlement in the San Luis Valley in late 1857. In March 1858, 500 troops of the 1st Dragoons, 2d Artillery, and territorial volunteers, all led by Col. Thomas T. Fauntleroy, began operating out of the San Luis Valley. On April 28, Fauntleroy struck a war party under Blanco, killed 40 members, and pursued the rest. A month later, a Jicarilla camp on the Purgatory River was destroyed. Ute and Jicarilla resistance collapsed. However, victories by southwestern garrisons over the Gila, Mogollon, and Coyotero Apache in the late 1850s failed to gain lasting results.

Expansion of the Army

The army was aided in its tasks, especially on the plains, by a second expansion in the 1850s. During the previous decade, the government had maintained a ratio in the

Jefferson Davis, secretary of war under President Buchanan, supported an expanded military and hoped that the transcontinental railroad route would benefit the South. (U.S. Army Military History Institute)

regular army of eight infantry regiments and four artillery regiments to only three mounted regiments. This ratio was in part due to the facts that the army formerly had been an eastern institution and that the forests of the East did not permit maximum use of cavalry. Perhaps more important, the parsimonious Congress was aware that a mounted regiment cost four or five times as much to maintain as an infantry regiment. But the preponderance of infantry meant that the majority of military contingents in the open West were capable of little more than a defensive role. Even the two dragoon regiments and the regiment of mounted riflemen were little more than mounted infantry.

When Jefferson Davis became secretary of war in 1853, he argued vigorously for a more adequate military, and for true horse soldiers in particular. Two years later, Congress grudgingly authorized the creation of two additional infantry regiments and the nation's first two "cavalry" regiments. This gave the army a ceiling of approximately 18,000 men. However, the pay was so low, the period of enlistment so long (five years), and the life so unattractive that the army rarely operated at above 80 percent of its authorized strength. At the outbreak of the Civil War, the army had 16,000 men to cover 7 western military departments embracing more than 2,500,000 square miles. However, the 1855 expansion gave the army the ability to garrison more of the West. More important, there were now troops capable of launching offensive operations against mounted native warriors. The 2d Cavalry, in particular, proved so effective a force that it would produce 12 Confederate and 4 Union general officers for the Civil War.

In 1855, the Comanche, the most aggressive and hostile of the plains tribes, and the allied Kiowa began to shift their raiding targets from Mexico to the United States. At the same time, many Texans were determined to drive even pacific reservation Cheyenne out of the state. By 1858, Gen. David E. Twiggs, commander of the Department of Texas, and Texas governor Harin R. Runnels had decided to join forces to combat the Comanche. Runnels began the offensive by ordering out five companies of Texas Rangers under Capt. John S. "Rip" Ford. Ford led his 100 rangers and 100 allied Indian warriors far north of the Red River into unexplored Comanche territory. On May 11, Ford and his men fought their way to a large village of Cheyenne raiders on a tributary stream of the Canadian River north of the Antelope Hills. In the day-long battle, Ford reportedly routed 300 warriors and killed 76. Prizes of war included an ancient suit of Spanish armor belonging to war leader Iron Jacket.

The Wichita Expedition was to be a major punitive expedition. Four companies of the 2d Cavalry and 135 Texas tribal auxiliaries under Capt. Earl Van Dorn took the field from Fort Belknap in mid-September 1858. Buffalo Hump, a Comanche war leader who had come north to make peace, notified the commander of Fort Arbuckle that he had no hostile intentions; unfortunately Van Dorn did not learn of this. On October 1, Van Dorn destroyed Buffalo Hump's encampment near Rush Springs in a pitched battle. Eighty-three Comanche were killed or fatally wounded, 120 lodges were destroyed, and 300 horses were captured; there were 5 U.S. fatalities, and Van Dorn was severely wounded.

A new season of campaigning began in late April 1859. This time, Van Dorn found that some of the Cheyenne had retired almost to the Arkansas River. On May 13, Van Dorn's advance forced a group of more than 90 Comanche into a brush-clogged ravine south of modern Dodge City, Kansas. The trapped Cheyenne fought savagely, seriously wounding future Confederate generals E. Kirby Smith and Fitzhugh Lee. Forty-nine Cheyenne were killed and 5 wounded in the battle called Crooked Creek or (erroneously) Nescatunga; 37 Cheyenne were taken alive.

The results of the 1858–59 Comanche expeditions were mixed. The Comanche divided into smaller bands after the battles, some of them fleeing to the Staked Plains of the Texas panhandle, where they found a stronghold from which to launch future raids. Many of the Comanche remaining in or near Texas, however, reduced their resistance, and Texas mobs would soon massacre some of Texas's friendly reservation tribesmen.

The longest of all the Indian Wars began with a single inflammatory incident in 1861. Cochise and his band of the Chiricahua Apache had for years been on relatively good terms with the United States, concentrating their raiding in Mexico instead. This changed during a February meeting in Apache Pass with George N. Bascom, an inexperienced young officer from Fort Buchanan. On an unproven suspicion, Bascom accused Cochise of stealing some stock from an area rancher and of kidnapping the man's son. Although Cochise escaped, six of his men were placed under arrest. Cochise later attempted to exchange several hostages for the six captured tribesmen, but Bascom refused until the boy was returned. Since Cochise apparently did not have the boy, negotiations broke down. Soon the dragoons were called in, and as the situation escalated, each side killed hostages. The Bascom Affair led to a conflict with the Apache that only ended with Geronimo's surrender 25 years later.

Other Interwar Developments

The army usually did well in its interwar encounters because its organization, morale, and firepower were superior to those of the Indians. In addition, the tribes did not present a united front against the swelling tide of white newcomers. Many tribesmen had never encountered U.S. forces in combat and did not know what to expect. Others, especially those on the plains, found the aggressiveness shown by such officers as Harney, Sumner, and Van Dorn a dramatic change from the passive behavior of the beleaguered infantry post commanders of the 1840s. Military operations in the West between the Mexican and Civil wars were generally successful; in the Northwest and California, some campaigns were decisive, at times verging on the genocidal. Most other campaigns resulted in at least temporary cease-fires. In the 1860s, the transfer of regular army units eastward to participate in the Civil War reduced pressure on some tribes. Yet, at the same time, the opening of mining sites in Arizona, Idaho, and Montana led to new disturbances. While relatively few conflicts occurred in the 1860s, the Sand Creek Massacre, committed by Colorado volunteers in 1864, would incite war with the Sioux, Cheyenne, and Arapaho. The most severe wars with the Indians, however, did not come until the 1870s.

In the conflicts in the West, the army began to benefit from improved weapons technology. For several years after the Mexican War, the infantry continued to use .54-caliber U.S. Model 1841 ("Mississippi") and .69-caliber Model 1842 ("Harpers Ferry") muskets. These smoothbore, muzzleloading, single-shot weapons were little changed from

Types of rifles used by U.S. infantrymen over the years. (George B. Jarrett Collection, Military History Institute)

the shoulder arms of the 17th century except for the conversion from the flintlock to the percussion primer system. By the late 1850s, however, many infantrymen were equipped with the .58-caliber Model 1855 rifle-musket. Cavalry regiments were met with a variety of light rifles before the War Department unofficially settled on the Sharp's carbine toward the end of the decade. As a breechloading weapon a foot shorter than most muskets, the Sharp's at last provided a weapon appropriate for modern cavalry operations. Most mounted troops were also armed with the revolutionary Colt revolver, either the army or the lighter navy model. The Colt was, like the Harpers Ferry muskets, among the first machine-made products constructed entirely of interchangeable parts. So, despite chronic budgetary problems, the army managed to keep abreast of advances in weaponry. Firepower was one of the few areas in which the U.S. military maintained a clear advantage over its Indian adversaries prior to the 1870s.

What was perhaps the army's most unusual operation in the interwar period was directed not against the Indians but against the Mormons, members of the Church of Jesus Christ of Latter Day Saints. During a period of anti-Mormon sentiment and exaggerated reports of the subversion of federal law in Utah, President Buchanan replaced Mormon leader Brigham Young as territorial governor. To uphold the law, and to enforce acceptance of a non-Morman governor, Buchanan dispatched 2,500 men under Col. Albert Sidney Johnston. Adverse weather and scorched earth tactics by the Mormons left the expedition stranded at Fort Bridger (Wyoming) until spring 1858. Young was convinced by that time that his people were in no danger, and the army simply made a symbolic march through Salt Lake City to demonstrate federal power. The Mormon Expedition, wrote Gen. D. S. Stanley, "was a very expensive and wasteful expedition and its only use was in the instruction the troops received in campaigning on the plains."

NAVAL OPERATIONS

The navy's greatest interwar accomplishment was more diplomatic than military in nature. Japan had been virtually closed to the outside world for two centuries, but the United States was anxious to establish relations with Japan in order to develop trade, acquire a coaling station, and secure protection for its shipwrecked nationals. To accomplish this mission, Pres. Millard Fillmore chose the dignified if pompous Matthew C. Perry. In July 1853, a squadron under Perry landed in Edo (Tokyo) Bay and delivered gifts and a letter for Emperor Komei from Fillmore. In February 1854, Perry rushed back (to forestall Russian designs) from the coast of China with a larger fleet of seven vessels. Resplendently uniformed, Perry stepped ashore with three bands and a party of 500 sailors and marines. Impressed with Perry's "face" and the U.S. show of strength, the Japanese agreed to the Treaty of Kanagawa. The overture later led to increasingly favorable trade conditions and formal diplomatic relations.

During the 1850s, the navy was becoming the most professional of the services. In 1851, the course of study for officers was expanded to four years and the school at Annapolis acquired its current name, the U.S. Naval Academy. Then, in mid-decade, the fleet was modernized. Thirty steam-powered vessels were purchased, half of these with the recently invented screw propeller. The new ships included 6 powerful frigates of the Merrimack class and 12 sloops of war.

Between the Mexican War and the Civil War, the Marine Corps was largely used to provide garrison troops for naval yards and stations on the Atlantic coast and the Great Lakes. However, the 1,400 marines were the U.S. servicemen most frequently under fire during this period. Their overseas duties included enforcing woodcutting rights for naval vessels, engaging pirates and mutineers, protecting U.S. commercial facilities, and generally "enforcing respect for the flag." In 1855, the marines coerced the king of the Fiji Islands into agreeing to pay reparations for the destruction of U.S. merchant property and for the reported killing of shipwrecked seamen. When the reparations were

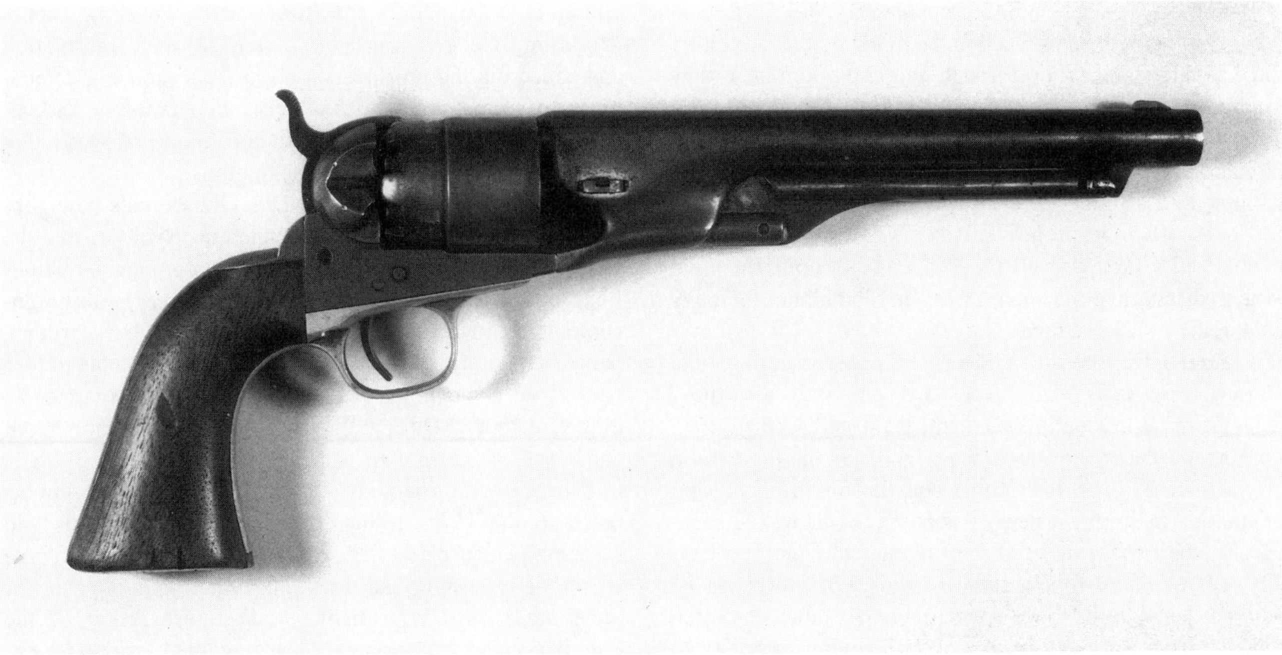

Revolvers, particularly the Colt, were favored by cavalrymen because of their close-range effectiveness and portability. (Library of Congress)

not forthcoming, the marines made several landings to burn Fijian villages.

In 1856, the marines became involved in one of the frequent U.S. operations in China. Believing that U.S. property might be endangered, after a U.S. launch was fired upon during tensions between the British and Chinese officials, U.S. Navy commodore James Armstrong began a bombardment of Canton's Barrier and Fiddler's forts prior to landing a force of approximately 290 sailors and marines. On November 20 and 21, U.S. forces captured the forts and repelled counterattacks from the approximately 5,000 Chinese defending the city.

During much of the 19th century, the United States invested more heavily in a passive coastal defense than in an active naval defense of the country. The coastal fortifications that the United States constructed in the 1840s and 1850s were part of the "third system" of such works. This system, initiated in 1817, was the country's first seacoast defense system designed by professional engineers as part of a systematic, comprehensive scheme. Extensive plans for the system were well matured by 1850, but a shortage of labor and appropriations tended to restrict construction to major harbors.

The simplest new constructions were secondary or auxiliary shore batteries, generally linear in plan with the guns in barbette (with the barrels protruding over a parapet). The most elaborate and expensive new fortifications were massive, vertically walled structures with tiers of gun casemates. The latter defenses were usually polygonal in plan, hexagonal in later cases, such as Fort Pulaski, Georgia, and Fort Sumter, South Carolina.

From 1829 the forts were often partially armed with muzzleloading, smoothbore 32- and 42-pounder (shot weight) cannon. After 1840, improved technology increased the capacity and reliability of seacoast artillery. Some of these versatile pieces trebled the range of a fort's armament to more than three miles. In the 1850s, ordnance officer Thomas J. Rodman devised a method for cooling and hardening the molten iron of a cast cannon barrel from the inside out. Rodman's tapered guns were able to handle the stress created when firing 15- or 20-inch-caliber projectiles at long range. Bottle-shaped Dahlgren gun tubes were developed using a concept similar to Rodman's. Rodman and Dahlgren guns would become important weapons in naval warfare and coastal defense during the Civil War.

SLAVERY ISSUE

Even as the nation grew territorially, slavery and the role of slavery in the southern economic and social system grew. The slave population increased by more than 23 percent between 1850 and 1860. Slave labor was established in Louisiana, southern Arkansas, and eastern Texas. Some historians have argued that by the time of the Civil War, slavery was losing its economic viability. It is true that in 1860 slavery was approaching its natural limitations in terms of expansion westward and that no more than one in four southern white families possessed slaves. But most white Southerners acquiesced in the holding of slaves either through indifference or through the aspiration that they might someday acquire slaves themselves. Evidence suggests that slavery still could have expanded with the exploitation of marginal land and with the need for industrial laborers in the South. Even though the importation of slaves had been officially prohibited since 1808, the government maintained a squadron off the African coast up to the Civil War to discourage the slave trade. In 1860 alone, the navy captured 12 slave runners.

Although by the late 1840s there was something of a national consensus that slavery was a morally disturbing legacy from a less enlightened era, the South seemed to be irrevocably dependent upon slave labor for the production of cash crops. As the North constituted an increasing population majority, it became apparent to many Southerners that the expansion of slavery numerically and territorially was essential to maintain a balance of power in the national legislature. Since southern social status was often linked to the acquisition of slaves, Southerners began to construct an increasingly elaborate defense of the institution and, implicitly, of themselves.

By the 1850s, the question of the status of slavery in the new territories required compromise over slavery if national unity were to be maintained. The Compromise of 1850, one of the most intricate balancing acts in U.S. political history, provided a temporary solution. However, violence during the settlement of Kansas under another compromise, the Kansas-Nebraska Act of 1854, was highly divisive. The act's principle of "popular sovereignty," self-determination over the question of slavery, invited confrontation by pro- and antislavery forces. About 5,000 prosouthern "border ruffians" from Missouri entered the territory. There the interventionists engineered the fraudulent election of a proslavery territorial legislature in 1855, while free-state colonists established a rival government. The stage was set for the crisis of "Bleeding Kansas" in 1856.

Bleeding Kansas

The first significant act of violence occurred on May 21 when border ruffians and proslavery settlers sacked and burned the town of Lawrence. Although only one person was killed, exaggerated accounts of the raid outraged many in the North. Abolitionist emigrant John Brown retaliated by hacking five proslavery settlers to death on the bank of Pottawatomie Creek. Territorial governor William Shannon, although a proslavery choice, ordered "all persons belonging to [unauthorized] military organization" to disband them. Despite this, a civil war was in progress by the time that around 250 proslavery men led by Gen. John W. Reid of the Missouri militia attacked the town of Osawatomie on August 30. Brown and some 30 free-state defenders were forced out, and the raiders pillaged the community. Shannon's successor, acting governor Daniel Woodson, declared Kansas in a state of open insurrection and called out the proslavery militia. Peacekeeping detachments of army regulars from Fort Leavenworth had attempted to keep the peace but had been rendered ineffective by a lack of direction from Washington.

When John W. Geary, Pres. Franklin Pierce's new gubernatorial appointee, arrived, he acted decisively to end the bloodshed. He sent antislavery military commander James Lane out of the territory, broke up proslavery militia encampments, and, utilizing a force of 300 U.S. troops, persuaded an army of perhaps 2,700 border ruffians to turn back from a movement against the town of Lawrence in mid-September. During the most intense 12 months of confrontation in Kansas, some 200 men had died.

The events in Bleeding Kansas were of lasting importance to the U.S. military. Thousands of Kansans and Missourians, in particular, gained a rough-and-ready type of military training, and several future Union generals, including Lane, James Blunt, and future Army of the Potomac corps commander Geary, gained command experience. So did several future Missouri State Guard and Confederate irregular officers, including William Quantrill. Most important, Bleeding Kansas foreshadowed and helped bring on the coming civil war. The tensions and resentments created in Kansas made the prospects of further national compromise much more unlikely.

EVE OF THE CIVIL WAR

Some historians have claimed that because of worsening sectional tension during the decade preceding the Civil War, there was a concerted effort by southern political leaders to weaken the army in order to prevent it from becoming an instrument of coercion. In fact, the opposite seems to be true. Believing that the pacification of the Southwest would permit the expansion of a southern agricultural empire, many of the most active supporters of an expanded army were Southerners such as Mississippi's Davis, Missouri's Benton, and Arkansas's Solon Borland.

As Americans fought Americans in Kansas, a ludicrous affair on the Canadian border almost led to war with Great Britain. The Oregon Treaty of 1846 had failed to specify which channel formed the boundary through the islands of Puget Sound. Rival regional officials generally maintained an uneasy truce in the islands until 1859. In that year, a U.S. squatter on San Juan Island killed a pig belonging to the powerful Hudson's Bay Company. During some subsequent confusion, the commander of the Department of Oregon sent in 461 troops while the governor of British Columbia prepared to call in 2,140 Royal Marines. Cooler heads fortunately prevailed, and an agreement was worked out in which each side would jointly garrison San Juan

Kansas and Nebraska Territories, 1854–1861

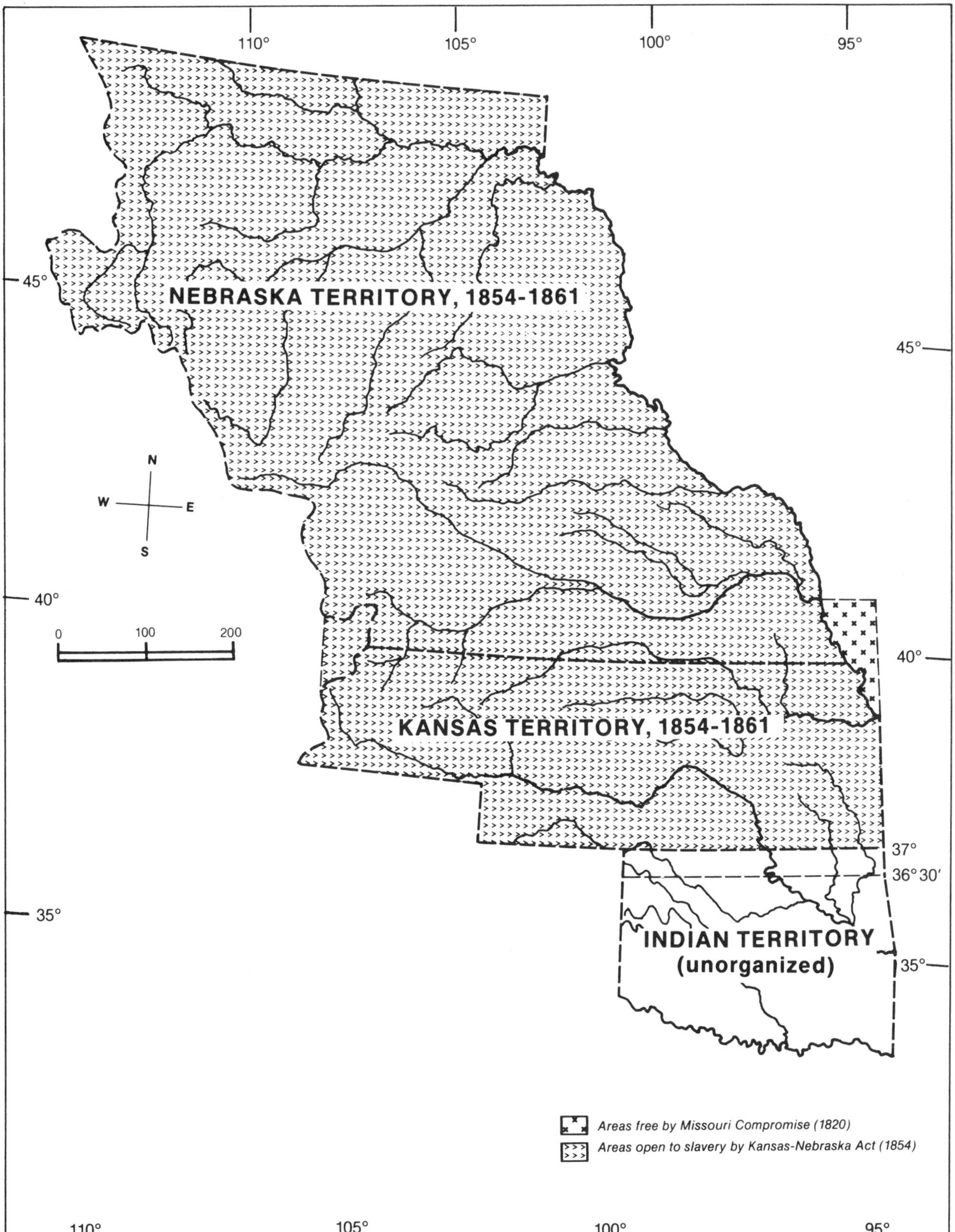

Abolitionist John Brown's raid on Harpers Ferry, Virginia, in 1859 was portrayed as a martyr's act in the northern press, but southerners saw him as a treasonous fanatic threatening the institution of slavery. (Library of Congress)

Island. For 13 years, the British garrison and the U.S. garrison (the latter at first commanded by Capt. George Pickett of later Gettysburg fame) spent their time gardening, rabbit hunting, and entertaining each other. The boundary dispute was arbitrated peacefully in 1872.

The most incendiary single act leading to civil war was John "Osawatomie" Brown's raid on the U.S. armory and arsenal at Harpers Ferry in western Virginia. Brown believed with fatal optimism that his "army" of 5 blacks and 14 whites could, through providing arms to the nation's slaves, initiate a decisive struggle to end slavery. He also hoped that the mountainous locale of Harpers Ferry would provide a secure base for operations in the initial phases of the campaign. During the evening of Oct. 16, 1859, Brown took the armory guard by surprise. However, Baltimore & Ohio Railroad employees and a local physician got word out of the town before Brown could escape. Local Virginia and Maryland militiamen, who recalled accounts of Nat Turner's bloody slave insurrection in Virginia in 1831, rushed to Harpers Ferry. Although Brown's group was forced to take refuge in the armory's engine house, the confused militia achieved little more than the rescue of some hostages. In the meantime, President Buchanan dispatched 90 U.S. Marines from the Washington navy yard. The marines, under the command of army colonel Robert E. Lee, successfully stormed the engine house and captured Brown and the surviving raiders. Brown was hanged on December 2 for treason against the state of Virginia.

The Harpers Ferry raid was probably even more important in U.S. military history than the troubles in Kansas. First, it was a major factor in the movement toward southern secession and, in turn, to war. Some alarmed Southerners began to question the wisdom of remaining in a Union that failed to take preemptive action against agitators such as Brown. Second, the perceived need to maintain forces to resist slave rebellion, and the demonstrated inefficiency of the Virginia companies, led to a determined reshaping of the southern militia. Southern leaders began to train and equip the previously green units into what would eventually form the core of the Confederate army. Other impacts were more subtle. Although the northern reaction to Brown's act was generally revulsion, the fact that the federal government had compliantly used troops to protect the interests of a slaveholding state did not go unnoticed. Just three years earlier, national Republicans had been defeated when they had tried to prohibit the use of federal troops (before Geary's arrival) to assist the proslavery legislature of Kansas.

Secession and Fort Sumter

The election of Republican presidential candidate Abraham Lincoln on Nov. 6, 1860, was the catalyst for southern secession. Northerners outraged by the atrocities in Kansas and by the sympathy shown toward the proslavery forces there by President Pierce had joined forces with Free-Soilers, abolitionists, nativists, and various reformers to found the Republican party in 1854. A schism between northern and southern Democrats over the issue of federal protection for slavery in the territories gave the new party victory in its second national election. The Republicans were outspoken in their opposition to the expansion of slavery into the trans-Mississippi West. However, they went on record affirming the right of each existing state to control "its own domestic institutions," including human bondage. Despite this, many Southerners saw the triumph of Lincoln and the Republicans as a revolutionary act representing only the first step toward the eventual elimination of slavery. At the least, Lincoln's election represented the ascent of a party whose positions called into question the honor and morality of southern slaveholders. Given their fears and resentments, many Southerners failed to see why they should remain in a country under a president elected with only 40 percent of the popular vote, who had not even been on the ballot of 10 southern states.

A number of important events took place before Lincoln's inauguration in March 1861. On Dec. 20, 1860, a special convention called by the South Carolina state legislature declared that "the union now subsisting between South Carolina and the other States, under the name of the 'United States of America,' is hereby dissolved." During the next four weeks, similar conventions in the six other states of the lower South committed their citizens to the "secession parade." The governors and militia leaders in Georgia, Alabama, and Louisiana were so eager to leave the Union that some federal forts and other installations in those states were seized even before the conventions could act. Although secession apparently had the approval of most of the lower South's white citizens, only Texas submitted the action to popular approval, and that after the fact (later Tennessee and Virginia would also engage in ex post facto referenda). The upper South, however, failed to follow suit, and secession was specifically rejected in the border states of Arkansas and Tennessee.

On Feb. 4, 1861, a convention of delegates from the seceding states met in Montgomery, Alabama, to form a new national government. Four days later, a constitution, differing from the U.S. Constitution only in its guarantees regarding slavery, was adopted and a "provisional" government was formed. On February 10, Jefferson Davis was elected president and Alexander H. Stephens was named

Secession of the Southern States, 1860–1861

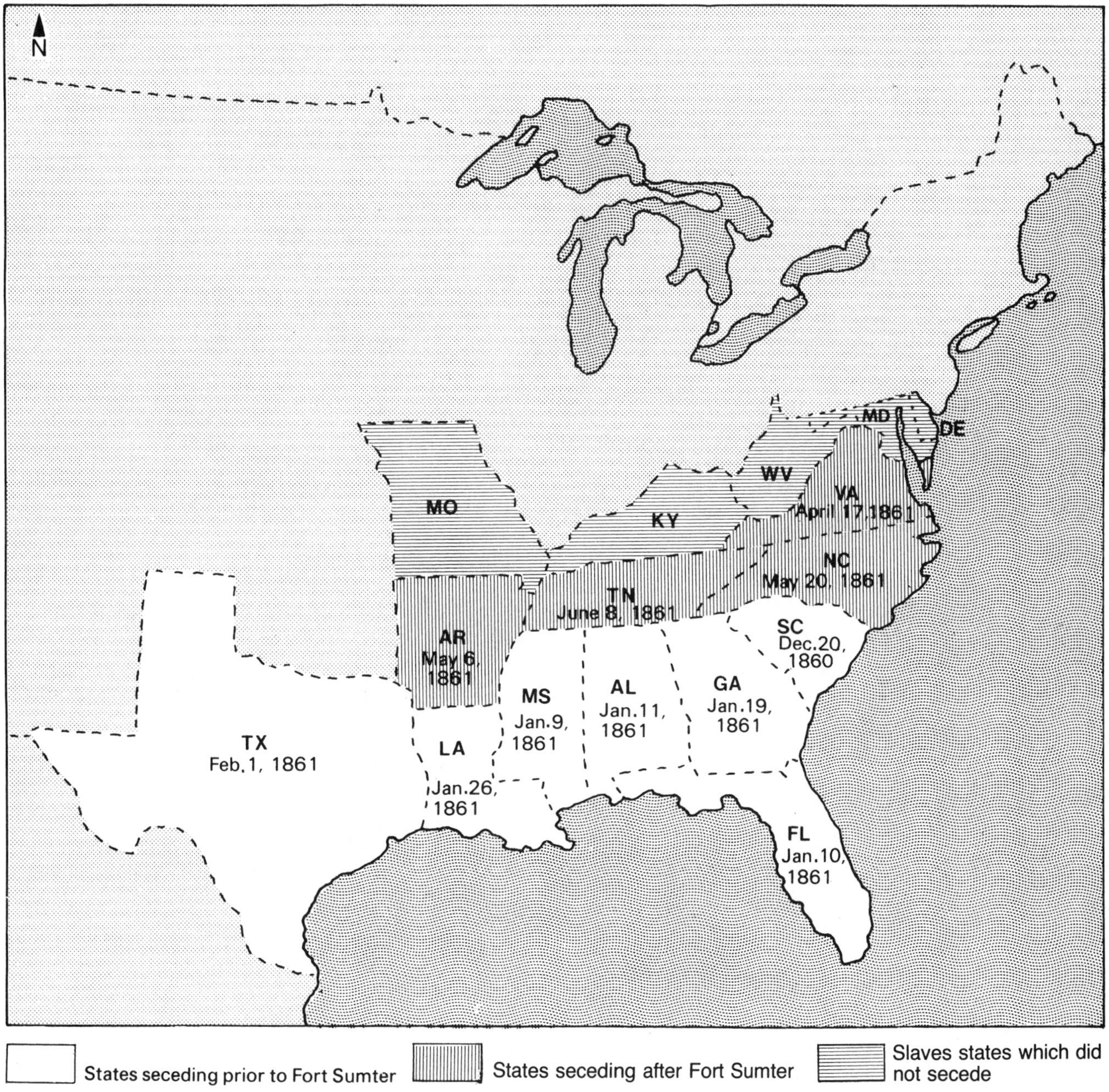

vice president of the fledgling Confederate States of America. Despite Davis's rigidity and failure to delegate responsibility, his experience, reputation, and patience probably made him the most suitable choice as president. In May 1861, after the secession of the upper South, the capital was moved to Richmond in an attempt to secure the dedication of Virginia, the most populous and developed Confederate state.

Claiming that federal properties reverted to the states on the dissolution of the Union, the Confederate states quickly seized post offices, depots, arsenals, and forts within their borders. Although opposed to secession and the seizures, outgoing President Buchanan generally seemed unwilling to fight to keep the installations. For the most part, Union post commanders surrendered without bloodshed or imprisonment when their situations became impossible. Only five forts in the lower South remained in Union hands, thanks to the personal initiative of four U.S. regular officers. In Florida, U.S. troops retained isolated Forts Jefferson and Taylor in the Florida Keys and Fort Pickens on Pensacola Bay. In South Carolina, Forts Moultrie and Sumter had not yet fallen.

On Dec. 26, 1860, Maj. Robert Anderson had moved the garrison of mainland Fort Moultrie to the unfinished Fort Sumter, located on an island near the mouth of Charleston Harbor. Anderson had hoped that this move would offer a more defensible position and, by removing his troops from contact with those of South Carolina, reduce the chances of bloodshed. South Carolinians, however, saw the transfer as a tactical move, an act of provocation. Although President Buchanan seemed unwilling to fight to recover the coastal forts already lost, he was determined to reinforce and resupply Anderson. South Carolina shore batteries, however, repulsed the *Star of the West,* a pri-

The surrender of Fort Sumter in Charleston harbor, South Carolina, ended the possibility of compromise between North and South. (U.S. Army Military History Institute)

vately owned supply vessel hired by the federal government in a vain effort to minimize the chance of confrontation. The resolution of the deadlock over Fort Sumter was therefore left to Lincoln to resolve.

At the time of Lincoln's inauguration in March, Fort Sumter was the most important U.S. installation remaining in the Confederacy. It was also an increasingly important symbol of both North and South. As long as the United States held the fort, it could claim sovereignty over the seceded states, and as long as the federals held the fort that controlled the South's most important seaport, the Confederacy would be hard-pressed to argue its legitimacy. Lincoln was, for the time being, quite willing to maintain the status quo at Charleston in hopes that the seceded states would reconsider their radical action. Anderson, however, would have to be resupplied or would have to evacuate, which might be taken as a validation of Confederate claims. Lincoln chose to take what he hoped would be a decisive but conciliatory approach: he would send supplies, not reinforcements, and would notify Gov. Francis Pickens in advance of his intent. If unsuccessful, this approach would place the blame for starting a war upon the Confederates.

On learning of Lincoln's plans from Pickens, Davis held a cabinet meeting to determine how to respond. Most of those present agreed that Anderson should be coerced or bombarded out of Fort Sumter before reprovisioning enabled him to remain there indefinitely. In addition, it was obvious that the rest of the South would not join the Confederacy unless a crisis forced them to make a commitment. Confederate Secretary of War Leroy P. Walker wired harbor commander P. G. T. Beauregard to demand once again that Anderson surrender the fort. Anderson refused, and hours later, at 4:30 A.M. on Apr. 12, 1861, the Confederates began a 36-hour bombardment. With resupply now impossible, and unwilling to suffer casualties in a futile defense of the undermanned fort, Anderson surrendered on April 14.

The war that began at Charleston Harbor had numerous causes. Many Southerners felt compelled to fight for independence through the fear of growing economic and political vassalage to the North. Similarly, many of them believed that they were taking steps to preserve their regional and social identities, their personal rights, or the rights of their states. Very few Northerners, for their part, conceived of the hostilities only as a struggle to end slavery. But the fact remained that slavery was a pervasive element in every apprehension, grievance, and misunderstanding that led to the war. Unfree labor was integral to the southern way of life to be protected; slaves were implicitly the personal property to be preserved; and the statutory protection of slavery was one of the perceived rights of each southern state to be defended at any cost. While the South's stated reason for fighting was to preserve its independence, many southern leaders said bluntly that the most vital reason for seeking independence was to continue subjugation of blacks.

National Mobilization

As it existed, the regular army of the United States could not conceivably coerce the Confederate States back into the Union. It possessed only 16,000 officers and men, and fewer than a tenth of them were stationed east of the Mississippi during the secession crisis. Of the 198 line companies of mid-1860, 183 were scattered among 79 different posts in 6 western military departments. For these reasons, Lincoln declared on Apr. 15, 1861, that the seceded states were in insurrection, and he asked the governors of the Union states to recruit a quota of militiamen. In this way, he hoped to acquire 75,000 men for a three-month term, the maximum time they could be called upon for national service. The request was so successful that around 100,000 militia became available, so many that the president was forced to ask the governors to hold some units back.

Later, on May 3, Lincoln proclaimed a vast expansion of the army, anticipating that Congress would approve the action when it reconvened in July. The action established 40 volunteer regiments, to contain more than 42,000 men, serving for three years or the duration of the war. Congress, in special session, approved the raising of 500,000 volunteers and began consistently to authorize new regiments rather than restore old ones. This was done in part because of the need for additional troops and in part because the governors preferred forming new regiments in order to grant new commissions as political patronage. The regular army was increased by 10 (later 11) regiments, 8 of them infantry. This congressional action would have increased the regular army by more than 22,780 men, but because of the less strenuous requirements for volunteer service, there were not enough recruits to meet the new authorization level. Unlike the volunteer regiments, however, the new regular regiments were more likely to be kept up to strength. The president also called for an increase in the size of the navy by 18,000 men for one- to three-year terms. The Marine Corps was authorized to recruit almost 1,800 more officers and men, which would have far more than doubled the prewar corps. However, there were never more than 3,900 marines during the war.

Lincoln's April call for militia forced the states of the upper South to commit themselves to secession, neutrality, or cooperation in the war against the Confederacy. The last course was adopted by none of the unseceded southern states. Virginia, Arkansas, Tennessee, and North Carolina felt compelled to join the Confederacy. The so-called "Five Civilized Tribes" and the Caddo and Wichita tribes also allied themselves with the Confederacy, although half or more of the Muskogee (Creek) and Cherokee eventually sided with the Union. Among the border states, Kentucky officially proclaimed neutrality. And the ambiguous positions of Missouri, Delaware, and Maryland, although the three states rejected secession, suggested they were de facto neutrals. The Confederacy thus had 11 member states, although entreaties were soon made to Kentucky, Missouri, and Maryland. The Missouri legislature probably had a legitimate quorum in October when it adopted an ordinance of secession after being driven from the capital. But Missouri, like the other border states, would produce far more Union than Confederate recruits.

In response to the outbreak of hostilities and the rapid expansion of the Confederacy, Lincoln took decisive action. On April 19, he declared a blockade of Confederate ports. As this could be merely a "paper" blockade for the present, the United States could only hope that the British and French would not press the issue of its legality (only an enforceable blockade was traditionally recognizable). Fortunately for Lincoln, the British were ready to accept the situation in exchange for a future diplomatic quid pro quo. And the Confederacy did not protest the declaration as aggressively as it might have, since a blockade gave the South international standing as a belligerent. On April 27, Lincoln extended the blockade to Virginia and North Carolina.

On the day the blockade was declared, the District of Columbia itself appeared to be cut off by hostile forces. The 6th Massachusetts Regiment, traveling to Washington in response to Lincoln's call for militia, reached the seething city of Baltimore on April 19. While the regiment was in transit between different railroad company depots (inconsistent track gauges and the lack of Union depots would complicate troop transfers throughout the Civil War), the troops were confronted by a pro-Confederate mob. Although both the details of the incident and the casualty numbers are unclear, it appears that 4 soldiers and 9–12 civilians were killed in an exchange of gunfire. Subsequently, angry Marylanders burned railroad tracks and cut telegraph lines from Pennsylvania, isolating Washington from the North. Ben Butler, commander of the Massachusetts militia, occupied Baltimore on May 13 and fortified Federal Hill, which commanded the harborfront and the depots.

On May 24, Lincoln's troops invaded Virginia, ending Davis's hopes that the Confederacy might simply be "let alone." Concerned for the security of Washington, the federals seized Alexandria and Arlington Heights, the latter named for Robert E. Lee's mansion. Construction was immediately begun upon a ring of forts around Washington that would eventually form the most extensive system of earthen fortifications on the continent. Although virtually forgotten, the capture of Alexandria was the U.S. Navy's first operation in the war. The crew of the sloop of war *Pawnee* restored the U.S. flag to the custom house there.

Confederate brigadier general Nathan G. Evans did, however, manage to retain much of the high ground on the Virginia shore of the Potomac and established artillery batteries. It seemed for a while as if Washington might be denied river access to the North, but the real purpose of the artillery was to repel amphibious operations. Despite bombardment from Union ships on the Potomac, these batteries were not evacuated until they were outflanked by land forces in 1862.

STRATEGIC OBJECTIVES

Following the outbreak of war, the aged and infirm General in Chief Scott was one of the few individuals to possess a clear, although overly optimistic, strategic vision. In the first week of May, Scott made three recommendations. First, he suggested that a major army be formed to operate in northern Virginia, both to defend Washington and to tie down a corresponding Confederate army. Second, he advised that the blockade be maintained. And third, he proposed a joint army-navy drive down the Mississippi River to deprive the South of commerce and split the western Confederacy. These actions, said the general, would "envelop the insurgent States and bring them to terms." Journalists derisively labeled Scott's concept for cordoning and strangling the Confederacy the "Anaconda Plan." Although the federals could do little more than carry out reconnaissances on the Mississippi in 1861, by the beginning of 1862, the idea of reopening the Mississippi would not only take root but be expanded to the notion of conquering the Tennessee River as well.

Additional strategic objectives were soon adopted, officially or unofficially. So many politicians conceived of victory in terms of political and territorial targets that the conquest of Richmond, a scant 100 miles from Washington, was of necessity an early goal. The threat to the Union posed by the potential loss of the border states also necessitated that they be secured immediately, even if force was required. The strategic objective of the South was simply to survive militarily until the civilian population of the North lost its determination to prosecute the war. Since the South was a confederacy of fiercely sovereign states, the Confederate government was required, at least in theory, to defend all territory equally rather than to set defensive priorities. Confederate policies were, in fact, dictated by the Confederacy's material weaknesses. First of all, the underdeveloped South would have to seek aggressively diplomatic recognition in order to acquire European armaments. Col. Josiah Gorgas, head of the Confederate Bureau of Ordnance, had discovered that his new country possessed only 159,000 small arms and about 1,000 cannons of various varieties. As a result, as many as 200,000 potential recruits were turned away in 1861 because they could not be equipped. Until 1863, by which time Gorgas had established several new armories and foundries, 90 percent of the Confederacy's weapons were procured by capture or by clandestine import rather than being manufactured in the South.

In an effort to apply economic pressure to secure diplomatic recognition, the Confederacy initially embargoed its cotton instead of placing it on deposit in Europe, as it had done before the war. However, this policy backfired as some British factories had a backlog of fiber and since there were alternative sources of cotton from Asia. In consequence, the Confederacy was forced to encourage the activity of private blockade-runners. The South also resorted to licensing commercial raiders to weaken the Union's maritime forces (authorized May 3). The United States never succeeded in convincing the European powers that the Confederate privateers should be treated as pirates.

Most of the North's advantages were obvious from the outset. The population of the 25 northern states and territories was 19,128,000, compared to a population of 12,315,000 in the 11 southern states. Eventually the Union would retain or recruit approximately 2,100,000 soldiers, sailors, and marines (including almost 179,000 blacks and more than 54,000 whites from Confederate states, excluding West Virginia). The disparity in the eligible military population between North and South was even greater, as 3,954,000 of the total southern population were slaves. In addition, many southern highlanders in the Appalachian and Ozark mountains were either neutral or pro-Union, and the Confederacy's alliances with Indians were often subject to sudden shifts in intertribal politics. Despite these handicaps, the South accomplished the astonishing feat of enlisting 750,000–800,000 men. However, this total included a number of conscripts and lukewarm volunteers who later fought for the Union. In fact, counting these men, West Virginians, and blacks, well over a fourth of the soldiers enlisted from Confederate domain fought under the U.S. flag.

The North also boasted formidable industrial and transportation facilities. The North possessed around 110,000 manufacturing facilities to the South's 18,000. Ironically, the magnitude of slavery in the South had discouraged other kinds of capital investments. The Union could utilize 21,970 miles of railroad track to the Confederacy's 9,280 and had a far larger merchant marine. And even though the South was an agricultural region, it was not adequately prepared to feed its armies when the war began. For example, although the South was far more suited to raise wheat than the North, it produced a crop in 1860 worth less than a quarter of that raised in the North.

The Union also had the benefit of an established central government, postal, and fiscal administration. The North saved all but a few naval vessels. In addition, in a frequently overlooked advantage, the federal government possessed most of the navigation charts, maps, and fortification and base plans of the old Union. While the latter fact was not used to full advantage in 1861, it would prove significant in the reduction of such positions as Fort Pulaski, outside Savannah, in 1862.

On the other hand, the Confederacy had the potential to win its independence by simply surviving until the North lost its will. The United States would have to launch extensive and costly offensives to reincorporate the South. This meant that the South would be fighting a largely defensive war, which would be less costly in men and matériel. In addition, the Confederacy would possess the advantage in morale of defending its native soil against an aggressor. (Yet the oft-purported Confederate advantage of possessing interior lines of communication was probably decisive only as long as the Confederacy's railroad system could be efficiently maintained. Physical deterioration and Union advances would seriously impair the use of the rails, at least west of the Appalacians, by the spring of 1862.) Finally, the South had the advantage of possessing a higher percentage of able officers at the outset and a more prevalent tradition of military training and experience.

Leadership and Command

Most Confederate officers commanding a brigade or above, and many in regimental command, had previous military experience with the militia in the Mexican War, or in the U.S. regular army. Of the 824 West Point graduates on active duty with the army in 1860, 184 resigned their commissions or were dismissed to serve the Confederacy. Of the approximately 900 graduates in civilian life, 114 returned to the army to serve the United States, 99 to serve the Confederate States. Surprisingly, almost a fourth of the West Pointers (both active and retired) who sided with the South were northern-born or appointed from free states. Equally surprising, almost half of the active-duty West Point graduates from slave states remained in Union service, most notably George Thomas. Of the total 1,080 active officers, 286 sided with the Confederacy. A smaller percentage of active-duty naval officers, 237 out of 1,457, chose to serve the Confederacy. Only 38 active officers left the U.S. Marine Corps. However, some wondered about the loyalty of elderly marine commandant Col. John Harris, who had replaced Brig. Gen. Archibald Henderson in 1859.

The South possessed the advantage of being able to distribute experienced officers to train and leaven volunteer units. Lincoln was criticized for not doing the same with his active-duty officers, but he was not free to dismantle the current command structure. Regular officers had to be retained at their posts in the West until volunteer units

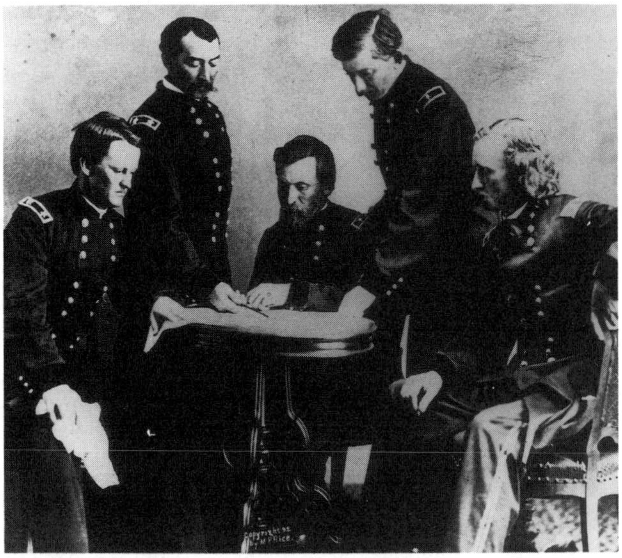

The Union army benefited from its many West Point–trained officers, including (left to right) *Wesley Merritt, Philip Sheridan, George Crook, James Forsyth, and George A. Custer.* (U.S. Military Academy)

could arrive there, and stripping away experienced officers would have adversely affected the morale of the regulars. General Scott argued that keeping the professional regiments intact was the only way to ensure that a few reliable regiments would be available for combat. Few anticipated that it would be a long war, and until 1862, regular officers without War Department exemptions lost their commissions if they transferred to the volunteer units. Fortunately for the North, good opportunities for promotion among the volunteers attracted a number of West Point graduates back from civilian life, including Ulysses S. Grant and William T. Sherman. Unfortunately, although Lincoln generally favored militarily experienced appointees, he selected some inferior brigade and division commanders solely on the basis of the political support they could bring his administration and the war effort. Davis, by contrast, never gave an untried volunteer officer higher than a brigade command. As for the lower levels of federal command, the soldiers of a volunteer company generally elected their own officers, and the state governors selected majors and colonels.

Both the United States and the Confederacy had serious problems during the first half of the war because of a lack of staff coordination. A departmental commander might or might not also be the commander of one of the expeditionary forces campaigning in his department. If he was, he generally had separate staffs, one for headquarters and one for the field operations. Also, departmental commanders were dependent on their president and chief of staff for strategic direction, and their war department for logistical support. These conflicts in administration and jurisdiction frequently created confusion.

In addition, the opposing war departments were initially completely overwhelmed by their responsibilities. On assuming office, U.S. Sec. of War Simon Cameron had a staff consisting only of two clerks. Matters were scarcely helped by the fact that Cameron was conspicuously larcenous (it was remarked that the only thing Cameron would not steal was a red-hot stove). Yet he could not be brought to resign until he was appointed minister to Russia in January 1862. In the Confederacy, Davis hindered efficiency by frequently assuming the responsibilities of Secretary of War Walker himself. When Walker resigned in September, Davis took the controversial step of appointing his inexperienced friend Judah P. Benjamin to head the South's war department.

As for the common soldiers, the majority of the Confederate recruits came from farms, as did almost half of the Union recruits. However, reflecting the different economic bases, almost a fourth of the U.S. volunteers were classified as mechanics and more than a fourth of its troops were foreign born, particularly from Germany and Ireland. More southern troops were experienced in horsemanship, which helps explain why the Confederacy had a larger proportion of cavalry regiments than did the Union. Southerners probably also had relatively more experience with firearms than

Simon Cameron, secretary of war during the early years of the Civil War, was ill-equipped for the job and was forced to resign in 1862. (U.S. Army Military History Institute)

The 12-pounder Napoleons, the 20-pounder Parrotts in the rear, and the 13-inch mortar (right) *were primarily used for siege warfare.* (U.S. Army Military History Institute)

their Union counterparts. On the other hand, the South's poverty and the lack of exposure to urban disease concentrations left more Confederates susceptible to fatal illnesses. Almost all of the common soldiers of the opposing armies were between the ages of 18 and 45. Yet the average age of a Union enlistee, 26, suggests that the struggle was not the "boys' war" often supposed.

Through the various levels of military organization, most soldiers probably identified most closely with the company in 1861. The recruiting area for a volunteer company might vary from five or six counties in the trans-Mississippi West to a single ward in the urban Northeast. Early in the war, a company frequently could be recruited with little more effort than word of mouth promotion and the exhibition of some posters. Typically, on the appointed day for mustering in, the men would mass in the square of a population center, elect their officers, and be given an oath of allegiance to the state or nation. The next 12–36 hours might then be taken up with preparing the company roll and with attending speeches, church services, and a flag presentation by local women. A short march, often made festive by civilian well-wishing and food offering, would then take the company to a rural training camp.

A volunteer regiment was composed of 5 squadrons of 2 companies each or of 12 cavalry companies. A U.S. regular regiment contained 2–4 battalions of 8 companies each. While a regiment might, in theory, contain more than 1,000 men, Union regiments in 1861 probably averaged around 700 men, Confederate regiments around 600 men. While most northern states had a policy of creating new regiments rather than replacing old ones, the Confederacy made some efforts to replace regimental losses and late in the war often resorted to consolidating depleted units. A brigade was composed of 2–6 (often 4) regiments. Early in the war, artillery batteries might be distributed among the brigades rather than be concentrated, especially in the Confederacy. A Union division would often be composed of 3 brigades, a Confederate division of 4. A corps consisted of 2 divisions and an army, frequently, of 2 or 3 corps. Both sides were handicapped at the outset by the fact that very few officers had experience with a command larger than a regiment. Confederate armies were generally named for the states or areas that were their primary defensive priorities, while Union armies were named for the principal waterways in their areas of operation. The Confederacy tended to make a commander's rank commensurate with the level of command. For example, while a Union volunteer brigade might be commanded by a colonel, a Confederate brigade frequently would be commanded by a brigadier general.

Armaments

The Civil War was largely fought with muzzleloading, mass-produced, single-shot rifle-muskets. Of all the wounds received during the war, more than 90 percent would be inflicted by the .58–.71-inch conical Minié-style bullets fired by such weapons. The two most common types were the U.S. Springfield (due to the abandonment of the Harpers Ferry Armory) and, particularly in the Confederacy, the imported British Enfield. However, the models 1842 Harpers Ferry musket and 1855 rifle-musket were still common in 1861. Good rifle-muskets had an effective range of 500–700 yards, a fact seldom considered in tactical planning before 1863. But only 8 percent of the federals' shoulder arms were rifled when the war began. Almost half of these had been converted to percussion arms from flintlocks. The

United States had to purchase 100,000 rifled muskets from Europe in July. During 1861, only around a third of the Union forces in the eastern theater and a fifth of the Confederates in that theater were equipped with first-rate arms. In the more poorly equipped western armies, perhaps two-fifths of the Union forces and half of the Confederate forces were still armed with smoothbore muskets late in 1861. Many of the latter troops were initially self-equipped with shotguns and hunting rifles.

Cavalry forces in 1861 were even more ill equipped. U.S. regulars had the single-shot horse pistols of the 1840s and 1850s, but there were few weapons available yet for the volunteer cavalry regiments. The situation was partially relieved by hastily purchasing 20,000 sabers and 10,000 revolvers overseas. Confederate cavalrymen often served initially with shotguns and a miscellany of pistols.

The workhorses of Civil War field artillery were smoothbore bronze 6- and 12-pounder field guns. About 70 percent of the Confederate artillery at First Bull Run consisted of such 6 pounders, although the South avidly sought more 12 pounders. The popular type of 12 pounder called the "Napoleon" could fire a 12.3-pound shot an effective range of 1,600 yards, but it served most effectively when it was used to fire exploding or fragmenting projectiles within 400 yards. Eventually, two of the most common pieces of rifled field artillery, especially in Union armies, would be the 3-inch (10-pounder) Parrot gun and the more desirable 3-inch ordnance gun. In 1861, however, the Union armies were still largely dependent on various 6- and 12-pounder rifled guns such as the 6-pounder rifle and the James rifle.

Rodman and Dahlgren smoothbore cannon were among the more common type of naval artillery, although the U.S. Navy, like the U.S. Army, also introduced Parrot guns. Such naval smoothbores had a range of more than 1,400 yards but were most effectively used against forts and ironclad vessels at less than 600 yards. Smaller craft might use 30-pounder smoothbores. On the western waterways, the federals would, by early 1862, utilize mortar boats, which fired high-trajectory 8–13-inch mortars against forts.

EARLY NAVAL OPERATIONS

The United States faced tremendous handicaps in its decision to establish a naval blockade, even though not all of the Confederate shore had to be cordoned, as the blockade was a "commercial" blockade rather than a more stringent "military" blockade. Yet, along the 3,500 miles of southern

Confederate boats, unsuccessful at running the Union blockade, lie in ruins at Sullivan's Island, South Carolina. (U.S. Army Military History Institute)

The Onondaga, *a Union ironclad gunboat, patrolled the James River in Virginia during the Civil War.* (National Archives)

coastline there were almost 200 inlets, bays, and harbors in which enemy merchantmen might lurk. The Union navy possessed no ironclad ships at the outset of the war, and only 42 of the navy's 84 available wooden ships were seen fit to be in commission. Furthermore, only 4 commissioned ships and 207 sailors were in continental waters when the blockade was declared.

To make matters worse, the United States suffered a severe blow with the evacuation of the Gosport (Norfolk) navy yard, at the great harbor of Hampton Roads. Without authorization, yard commandant Charles S. McCauley decided to destroy the facility on April 20 lest the newly seceded state of Virginia seize it. The sailors and the yard's marines did their best to deprive the South of an important base. Inexperience and haste, however, prevented the wrecking crews from destroying hundreds of cannon and thousands of arms, adequately damaging the ships' ways and dry dock, and completely burning several vessels before they sank. One result would be the Confederacy's construction, beginning in July, of the ironclad ram *Virginia,* utilizing the hull of the scuttled frigate *Merrimac*. However, the North retained the citadel of Fortress Monroe on the north side of Hampton Roads as a base for future land operations.

Despite the navy's difficulties, the blockade acquired some teeth rather quickly. By July, the federals had captured at least one ship off each of the South's nine major ports. However, the development of specialized blockade-runners by the Confederate merchant marine kept some southern ports in operation until late 1864.

The eventual expansion of the U.S. Navy was in large part due to the labors of the Union's secretary of the navy, the competent and energetic Gideon Welles. Welles was aided by his capable assistant, Gustavus Fox. The two men cautiously but effectively oversaw the introduction of new technology to the navy. In August 1861, the newly created Ironclad Board approved the acquisition of 7 casemated ironclad gunboats from James Eads of St. Louis. These boats would form the backbone of the western river fleet. In October, in response to reports of the massive armored ship being constructed by the Confederates at Norfolk, the navy authorized construction of the ironclad *Monitor*. The acquisition of more standard craft was also pressed. By December, the navy had purchased 136 vessels, ranging from clippers to tugboats, repaired 34, and had 52 under construction (mostly gunboats). The navy by then had 264 ships and boats. Flag Officer Silas Stringham's Atlantic Blockading Squadron had 22 of these vessels. Flag Officer William Mervine's Gulf Blockading Squadron was operating with 21.

The Confederacy's secretary of the navy, Stephen R. Mallory, had been the chairman of the prewar Senate Naval Affairs Committee. He would prove to be an even more vigorous and innovative leader than Welles. Mallory's hands were somewhat tied until the secession of Virginia, since only two northern vessels had been seized up to that time and the captured navy yard at Pensacola, Florida, was suitable only for repair work. Acquisition of the Norfolk navy yard and access to Richmond's Tredega Iron Works proved to be invaluable, as was the continuing purchase of ships from abroad. By the end of 1861, the Confederate navy had 35 vessels, 22 of them steam powered. However, most were small and lightly armed. The South's shipbuilding efforts were remarkable given the shortage of resources and facilities. One noteworthy accomplishment in 1861 was the launching of the ironclad ram *Manassas,* converted from a tugboat. On October 12, the *Manassas* became the first ironclad in history to engage an enemy warship and, in so doing, briefly lifted the blockade at the mouth of the Mississippi River.

STRUGGLE FOR VIRGINIA

The first significant land fighting of the Civil War took place in the mountainous region of Virginia. Four important transportation routes crossed western Virginia, providing Washington's only direct access to Kentucky and to the Union states north of the Ohio River. At the same time,

The Campaigns in Northern Virginia

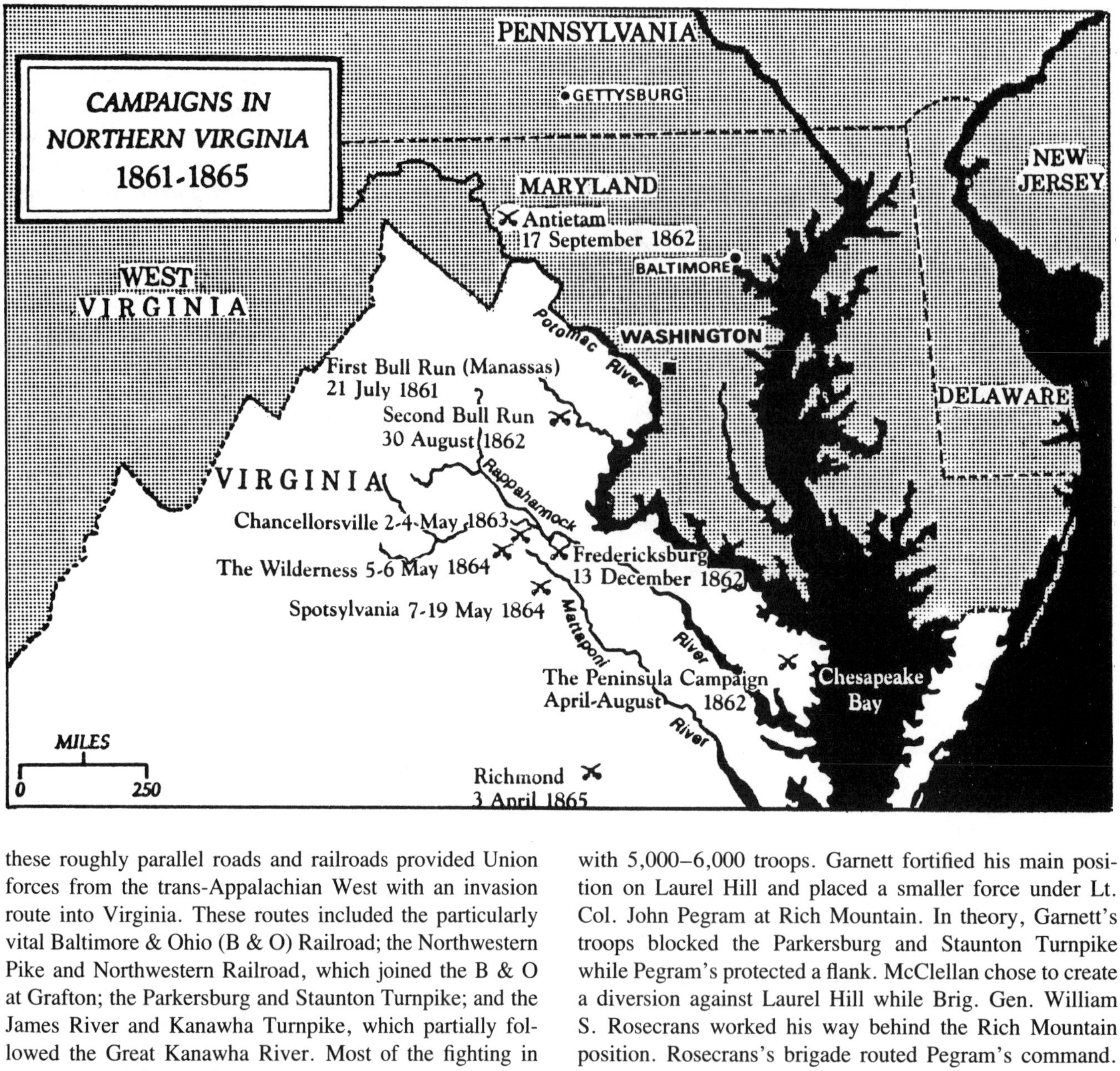

these roughly parallel roads and railroads provided Union forces from the trans-Appalachian West with an invasion route into Virginia. These routes included the particularly vital Baltimore & Ohio (B & O) Railroad; the Northwestern Pike and Northwestern Railroad, which joined the B & O at Grafton; the Parkersburg and Staunton Turnpike; and the James River and Kanawha Turnpike, which partially followed the Great Kanawha River. Most of the fighting in western Virginia would center on control of these routes.

McClellan was assigned to command the federal Department of the Ohio on May 14, 1861. On receiving assurances from Unionist western Virginians that his operations would be considered a relief rather than an invasion, McClellan began to concentrate 20,000 men in Virginia towns along the Ohio River. In the meantime, Lee, commanding Virginia's troops, ordered Col. George Porterfield to Grafton to recruit and to operate against the B & O. Threatened by McClellan's maneuvers, Porterfield retreated to Philipi. Porterfield's command was chased away on June 3 in the first land action of the war.

Lee responded to the setback in the mountains by sending Brig. Gen. Robert S. Garnett to the crossroads of Beverly with 5,000–6,000 troops. Garnett fortified his main position on Laurel Hill and placed a smaller force under Lt. Col. John Pegram at Rich Mountain. In theory, Garnett's troops blocked the Parkersburg and Staunton Turnpike while Pegram's protected a flank. McClellan chose to create a diversion against Laurel Hill while Brig. Gen. William S. Rosecrans worked his way behind the Rich Mountain position. Rosecrans's brigade routed Pegram's command. Garnett learned of this disaster and fell back from Laurel Hill to join Pegram. However, because of poor communication, Pegram and Garnett then resorted to separate attempts to escape the federals. Most of Pegram's command was cut off and forced to surrender. Garnett was killed in a rearguard action at Corrick's Ford on July 13, becoming the first general to die in the war. These small battles were important in encouraging the eventual secession of northwestern Virginia (as West Virginia) from Confederate Virginia and in promoting McClellan's career.

Garnett's surviving troops were consolidated with fresh troops to form the grandiosely named Army of the Northwest under William W. Loring. The so-called Army of the Kanawha under John Floyd was formed in similar fashion.

Meanwhile, McClellan's acting successor, Rosecrans, supervised a north-south defensive perimeter. Ten thousand federal troops now under Joseph J. Reynolds had been advanced on the turnpike to Staunton as far as Huttonsville and Cheat Mountain. To the south, Jacob D. Cox's federal brigade, 3,000 strong, had pushed forward on the Kanawha Pike to Gauley Bridge. An additional Union 7,000 troops were stationed around Sutton on a turnpike connecting Reynolds's and Cox's positions.

Lee (now commanding the Department of Northwestern Virginia) had arrived in western Virginia the first week of August to provide strategic direction. His first priority was to recover the Parkersburg and Staunton Turnpike, then strike the B & O Railroad. However, camp diseases and constant rain made the task difficult. Lee devised a plan for using part of Loring's command to envelop an Indiana regiment on Cheat Mountain summit. Lee meanwhile led the rest of the 15,000 area troops to flank the mountain and Huttonsville via the Huttonsville-Huntersville Pike. On September 12, the federals on Cheat Mountain summit were cut off and those on the Huttonsville Pike were driven back to Elkwater. The next day, however, the colonel assigned to administer the coup de grâce on the mountain held back from attacking a mere 300 federals, whom he mistakenly believed to number 4,000. Also, Lee's aide-de-camp, John A. Washington, was killed while trying to find a route past Elkwater. Lee's first campaign thus ended ignominiously.

Lee hoped to regain the Kanawha Valley, but this aim was complicated by quarrels between Floyd and his erstwhile subordinate and rival Henry A. Wise. In August, Floyd crossed the Gauley River at Carnifex Ferry with 2,000–2,600 men. He then routed a federal encampment and severed communications between the Kanawha and federal headquarters on the Staunton Pike. Yet Floyd failed both to exploit his situation and to heed Wise's warnings about the danger of having a river at his back. And because of transportation difficulties and obstinancy, Wise was slow to bring up the troops he had facing Gauley Bridge. Rosecrans responded by leading the 7,000 federal troops near Sutton to attack Floyd. The superior but largely inexperienced Union force was unable to dislodge Floyd's men from the fortifications of Camp Gauley in a day of spirited fighting on September 10. Before Rosecrans's force could take advantage of rest and daylight the next day, Floyd miraculously extricated his men and destroyed Carnifex Ferry.

Floyd's, Wise's, and Loring's commands were subsequently transferred or broken up. Lee was exiled for a time to the Department of South Carolina, Georgia, and Florida. Few other generals in 1861 had the audacity to attempt such a complicated maneuver, yet the western Virginia campaigns were such thorough Union victories that northern control of the region would not be seriously contested again until the fall of 1862. Eventually, the desire of the people of northwestern Virginia themselves, rather than force of arms, brought West Virginia into the Union as a new state in 1863.

First Battle of Bull Run

Between the war's opening action in western Virginia and Lee's subsequent offensive there, the greatest battle of 1861 took place just 26 miles from Washington. After retreating from Arlington Heights, the Confederates established a defensive position near the important rail junction at Manassas. The 21,000 troops under Beauregard who were encamped there were astride the best route to Richmond. The tantalizing proximity of the Confederate capital, only 100 miles from Washington, and an approaching session of the Confederate Congress created tremendous public pressure for a Union advance "on to Richmond." General Scott argued vigorously that more time was needed to train and equip the raw volunteers pouring into Washington, but Lincoln said of the opposing Confederates, "they are green also."

Because of Scott's infirmities, Irvin McDowell commanded the Union expeditionary army of 39,000 men. To prevent Beauregard from being reinforced, McDowell ordered Robert Patterson's army of 18,000 troops to continue pressing Joseph E. Johnston's small army of 11,000 men in the Shenandoah Valley. As McDowell's troops approached Bull Run, he discovered that the Confederates had taken a strong position behind the creek in response to his advance. He was accordingly forced to modify his plans. McDowell's new scheme was for a main force to move northwest to Sudley Springs Ford on July 21, cross and roll up the Confederate left flank, and cut the Manassas Gap Railroad to keep Johnston from the field.

As the federals descended from the ford, brigade after Confederate brigade was shifted to hold a line on Matthews Hill. When the sheer weight of Union numbers became too great, the Confederates fell back and rallied on Henry House Hill. Unfortunately for (and unknown to) McDowell, Patterson had utterly failed in his assignment. Johnston had managed to get two-fifths of his army to the battlefield in time despite overtaking the Manassas Gap Railroad. This was the first strategic use of a railroad in wartime. Johnston, now the superior officer on the field, left Beauregard to oversee the battle line while Johnston directed the arriving troops into the fray.

In the late afternoon, the exhausted federal right began to fall back. Beauregard ordered a general advance, and the Union line fell into retreat. Although the retreat quickly turned into a rout, the tired and disorganized Confederates were unable to follow up their victory. McDowell's army had suffered 2,898 casualties. Johnston and Beauregard lost 1,982 men of their 32,000. For the second of three times in 1861 (with Rich Mountain and Wilson's Creek), green troops proved incapable of completing complicated

The damage at Blackburn's Ford is examined in the aftermath of a skirmish in which Union troops were repulsed by James Longstreet's Confederate forces at the beginning of the First Battle of Bull Run. (U.S. Army Military History Institute)

flanking and converging maneuvers. The day after the battle, the unfortunate McDowell was demoted, to be replaced by McClellan, who, on July 27, took command of the Division of the Potomac, which included all troops in the vicinity of Washington. By August, these forces would be sufficiently trained, organized, and heartened to form the great Army of the Potomac.

The Potomac front remained quiet for most of the rest of 1861. The exception to this lull took place on October 21, when Union brigadier general Charles P. Stone instructed Col. Edward D. Baker to withdraw or reinforce an endangered detachment on the south side of the river at Ball's Bluff. Baker launched a thoroughly inept reconnaissance at the 70-foot height and was ambushed. The fiasco cost the federals 951 casualties, including Baker; the Confederates lost 149. In response to this disaster, Radical Republicans formed the meddlesome Joint Congressional Committee on the Conduct of the War. Stone was subsequently arrested as a scapegoat for the defeat at Ball's Bluff.

ACTION IN THE WEST

In terms of territory gained, the most far-reaching campaigns of 1861 took place in Missouri. Both sides had good reason to covet the state. Lincoln hoped that Missouri would provide him political supporters and a buffer for Union Illinois. Confederate leaders hoped that Missouri would join the now-ended secession parade. Missouri was also the greatest potential source of men and matériel in the trans-Mississippi West. In addition, the country's three greatest rivers traversed the state.

The secessionist desires of Gov. Claiborne Jackson were first frustrated on May 10, when the commander of the U.S. arsenal in St. Louis, Capt. Nathaniel Lyon, seized the governor's militia camp at Camp Jackson using Unionist home guards. While Lyon was marching the prisoners into town, however, a riot broke out. The resulting civilian deaths drove many Missourians to the southern cause and led to the formation of the Missouri State Guard under Sterling Price. After a hostile meeting with Jackson and Price, Lyon led his force up the Missouri and took the state capital at Jefferson City on June 15. Two days later, Lyon and 1,700 troops thoroughly scattered 1,000 raw militia with Jackson at Booneville. Jackson and a handful of loyalists then fled to the southwest.

By mid-July, Lyon and 6,000 volunteers and regulars were encamped at Springfield. He had advanced so far south that exiled governor Price and Arkansas officials agreed to place Price's 5,000 state guardsmen and N. Bart Pearce's 5,000 Arkansas state troops under the command of Confederate general Ben McCulloch. On July 31, McCulloch led his temporary army of 12,000–13,000 men northeast to attack Lyon's forces. Lyon moved out and routed McCulloch's lead elements but pulled back on realizing he was now outnumbered. McCulloch followed and encamped in the valley of Wilson's Creek, 12 miles from Springfield. Lyon decided to carry out a preemptive attack with his smaller force in order to secure a safe withdrawal.

Lyon's plans were for a surprise pincer movement at dawn on August 10. Col. Franz Sigel would attack from the south with 1,200 men while Lyon led 4,200 men from the north. Sigel's flanking attack swept through several Texas cavalry encampments. But Sigel's men had not yet made contact with Lyon's approaching force when McCulloch's Confederates successfully counterattacked, aided by federal confusion over a blue-clad Louisiana regiment. Lyon's wing was initially successful as well, quickly taking the crest of Bloody Hill. Lyon's soldiers held the hill for five hours against three counterattacks by Price's men. At

Brig. Gen. Irvin McDowell, commander of Union troops at the First Battle of Bull Run (1861), was relieved of his command, but was promoted to the rank of major general the following year. (U.S. Army Military History Institute)

last, however, the death of Lyon and the exhaustion of men and ammunition proved decisive, and the federals withdrew. While the amateur soldiers had merely fought credibly at Bull Run, they had fought with fanatical ferocity at Wilson's Creek. This may in part be explained by the lingering animosities of participants from "Bleeding Kansas" days. For its size, Wilson's Creek was the bloodiest battle of 1861. The federals lost 1,317 men, the southern army 1,222. A fourth of the combatants on Bloody Hill had fallen.

McCulloch's victory immediately encouraged a Confederate alliance with Missouri, although the exiled remnant legislature did not pass an ordinance of secession until October. Governor Price, without Confederate or Arkansas assistance, advanced to lay siege to the Missouri River port of Lexington. His victory there on September 20 gained him needed arms, dollars, and thousands of recruits. However, Price was unable to supply his forces so far north, and he retreated on learning of a planned autumn advance by Union commander John C. Frémont.

The secessionist Missourians had lost heavily in men and ammunition at Wilson's Creek. Lyon's sacrifice had purchased time for the establishment of a Unionist state government and the reorganization of troops in the Union Western Department. Frémont was removed in November because of his vacillation, his failure to back Lyon in the field, and his political errors. On November 9, Henry W. Halleck was assigned to command the new Department of Missouri.

The official neutrality of another border state, Kentucky, left Union and Confederate leaders on tenterhooks until August. Both sides needed the state as a buffer and for control of the Ohio River. Yet neither side was willing to risk driving Kentucky to the enemy by being the first to send troops into the state. Finally, Leonidas K. Polk, head of Confederate Department No. 2, decided that it was vital that his troops seize the commanding bluffs at Hickman and Columbus on the Mississippi. Grant, of the District of Southeast Missouri, had been waiting for such a move. On September 6, he landed troops at the important port of Paducah, Kentucky, on the Ohio River. This forestalled a further Confederate advance on the Ohio and safeguarded his base at Cairo, at the confluence of the Ohio and Mississippi rivers. By letting the Confederates make the first move, Grant ensured that the Kentucky legislature would turn against the Confederacy.

Two months later, Grant launched another army-navy operation. With the intention of creating demonstrations on the Mississippi, Grant landed at Belmont, Missouri. His aim was apparently to destroy the observation camp of the Confederate fortress across the river at Columbus and to intimidate Confederate forces in southeast Missouri. Although Grant's men took the camp, the Confederates regrouped and were reinforced by steamer by Polk. The federals narrowly escaped on their transports, with Grant

Union Capt. Nathaniel Lyon was wounded twice before he was killed during the Union's surprise attack on the larger Confederate forces at Wilson's Creek. (U.S. Army Military History Institute)

losing almost a fifth of his 3,100 men. But even though Grant's expedition was a near disaster, he had now twice demonstrated the kind of initiative that would be decisive later in the war.

NAVAL SUCCESS

The Union's categorical successes in 1861 were in coastal operations. The navy's only supply and coaling bases in the South were at Hampton Roads and Key West. By July, it was apparent that most ships enforcing the blockade were spending almost as much time in travel to and from these bases as they were on sentinel duty. As a result, the Blockade Board, headed by Flag Officer Samuel F. Du Pont, recommended that a harbor be secured in each of four blockading zones.

The first target was Hatteras Inlet, which gave access to Pamlico Sound through North Carolina's Outer Banks. The inlet was defended by Forts Hatteras and Clark. Stringham's blockade squadron provided seven warships and two transports while Butler commanded a hastily assembled landing and garrison force of 900 soldiers. On August 27, the federal landing boats were capsized by rough surf. Yet the Union warships pummeled Fort Clark, armed only with short-range and outdated 32 pounders, until it was evacuated. The next day, Fort Hatteras was bombarded into surrender. Shifts in the channel at the inlet later made the use of Pamlico Sound unfeasible, but the victory deprived the Confederacy of 670 men and 35 cannon and gave the North a needed boost in morale after the defeat at Bull Run.

Captain Du Pont himself was in charge of capturing his board's second target, Port Royal Sound in South Carolina. This bay was admirably situated between Charleston and Savannah, and it was hoped that an initial victory might be followed up by a move up the Broad River to sever the important Savannah & Charleston Railroad. It took Du Pont two months to assemble the 30 ships he felt he needed. The army's contingent of 13,000 troops was commanded by Thomas W. Sherman.

On November 7, Du Pont led a column of nine warships plus a flanking column of coastal vessels into the sound to bombard Fort Beauregard on the north side of the inlet.

The defenses of Port Royal Sound were better equipped and constructed than those at Hatteras Inlet, although not all the guns at Fort Beauregard had been emplaced. Yet it again proved hard for the Confederate defenders to strike moving steam-powered ships, and the U.S. fleet had 123 guns to the 43 guns and howitzers in the forts. Inside the sound, Du Pont turned the column back to strike Fort Walker on Hilton Head Island on the south. At night, as the larger vessels continued the bombardment, Forts Walker and Beauregard were abandoned. When Lee arrived in South Carolina shortly thereafter, he was so impressed with the Union fleet's firepower that he recommended moving all lower Atlantic coastal defense inland, out of range of the federals' ships. Although Port Royal Sound became an important base for the blockade, the mobile defense forces devised by Lee helped discourage a further Union operation against the Charleston & Savannah Railroad.

The U.S. Navy's one fiasco was diplomatic rather than military. On November 8, the captain of the U.S.S. *San Jacinto* halted the British packet *Trent* in the Bahamas without authorization and seized Confederate commissioners James M. Mason and John Slidell on their way to carry out diplomatic missions in London and Paris. The initial British reaction was serious, but both London and Washington were soon seeking ways to end the confrontation without losing face. When Mason and Slidell were released, the *Trent* Affair blew over.

During the fall of 1861, Confederate marines were engaged for one of the few times in the war. The Confederate States Marine Corps was established on March 16 as a virtual copy of its Union counterpart, with Col. Lloyd J. Beall as its commander. Although authorized to enlist 988 troops, it probably never mustered more than 600–650 men. On September 14, these marines drove off a raiding party that had destroyed a privateer at Pensacola, and on the evening of October 8–9, they ransacked a federal regiment's encampment on Pensacola Bay.

STATUS OF THE WAR

By the end of 1861, many Confederates still believed that there was cause for optimism. Their young nation had been indisputably victorious in the greatest battle of the year, although luck had played no small role in the outcome at Bull Run. At least 9 out of 10 blockade-runners were still getting through to southern ports. In the South, both public and military morale was high. While the Confederacy was to enjoy probably its best chance of victory in 1862, there were some important setbacks and adverse developments in 1861. Few Southerners realized that the northern populace and its leaders were now resolved rather than discouraged. Few could yet see that the trans-Mississippi was being lost and that the federals were making the upper Appalachians a military as well as a geographical barrier dividing the Confederacy. Few realized the significance of the Union's virtually unchallenged naval superiority. However, the most significant development of 1861 was not the gain or loss of territory by either side but the initiation and hardening of more than 785,000 mostly green, naive, but determined men on both sides into two of the most effective national armies in the world. Neither side could yet see that the only sure path to victory lay in the destruction or immobilization of the opposing army, not in the holding or gaining of territory.

6

The Civil War: 1862–1863

As the year 1862 opened, both the Union and the Confederacy struggled to train and equip the vast numbers of men who had volunteered to serve their respective causes. Only after the troops had been organized into regiments, and regiments collected into higher formations, and those formations properly armed and equipped could the question of their employment be addressed. For the North, there was no question but that federal armies must take the initiative; only in this way could the seceding states be returned to the Union. Yet taking the initiative meant devising an offensive strategy that would be implemented over an area almost as large as western Europe. In contrast, the South, which argued that it only wanted to be left in peace, rejected an offensive strategy for both philosophical and practical reasons. Simply standing on the defensive on their own territory satisfied most Southerners, although any opportunity to counterattack invading armies could not be overlooked. In sum, the South could win its independence by simply holding what it already controlled, while the Northern objective of restoring the Union required massive offensive action and even more massive logistical preparation.

Major geographical features such as the Appalachian Mountains and the Mississippi River divided the arena of conflict into two major theaters of operation. By 1862, these theaters were quite well-defined: the eastern theater stretched from the Atlantic coast to the Appalachians; the western theater covered the much larger area between the Appalachians and the Mississippi. A secondary theater, the trans-Mississippi, encompassed the land between that great river and the Rocky Mountains, but operations there were considered to be peripheral by all except the region's inhabitants. Operations would also be conducted along both the Atlantic and Gulf coasts of the South, but these efforts were also considered peripheral to the main efforts of the belligerents. Within each of the theaters, both the Union and Confederacy established several territorial commands, designated as departments. These departments nominally had fixed boundaries, but those boundaries could be, and frequently were, redrawn to reflect changing situations. In fact, departments were reorganized with dismaying frequency, as department commanders gained or lost influence, territory changed hands, or greater organizational efficiency was required. Department commanders, both Union and Confederate, usually controlled all forces within their departments and customarily led them in the field. Thus the war would eventually consist of a series of operations conducted within the ever-changing departmental structure of the belligerents.

EASTERN THEATER: 1862

At the beginning of 1862, the Union's hopes lay in the person of Maj. Gen. George B. McClellan, who had replaced Winfield Scott as general in chief. Although nominally commanding all federal armies, McClellan spent most of his time with the Army of the Potomac, which was considered to be the Union's premier fighting force. Personally organized and trained by McClellan, the Army of the Potomac waited in its camps just south of Washington for the word to move "on to Richmond," as the press and public demanded. As the spring campaigning season approached, Northern public opinion became more and more impatient for a forward movement. McClellan, however, counselled delay because he believed his force to be insufficiently strong to guarantee the defeat of the Confederate armies facing him. Although total Union strength in the eastern theater exceeded 150,000 men, McClellan estimated his opponents to have nearly 120,000 troops, hardly

Major Battles of the Civil War, 1861–1863

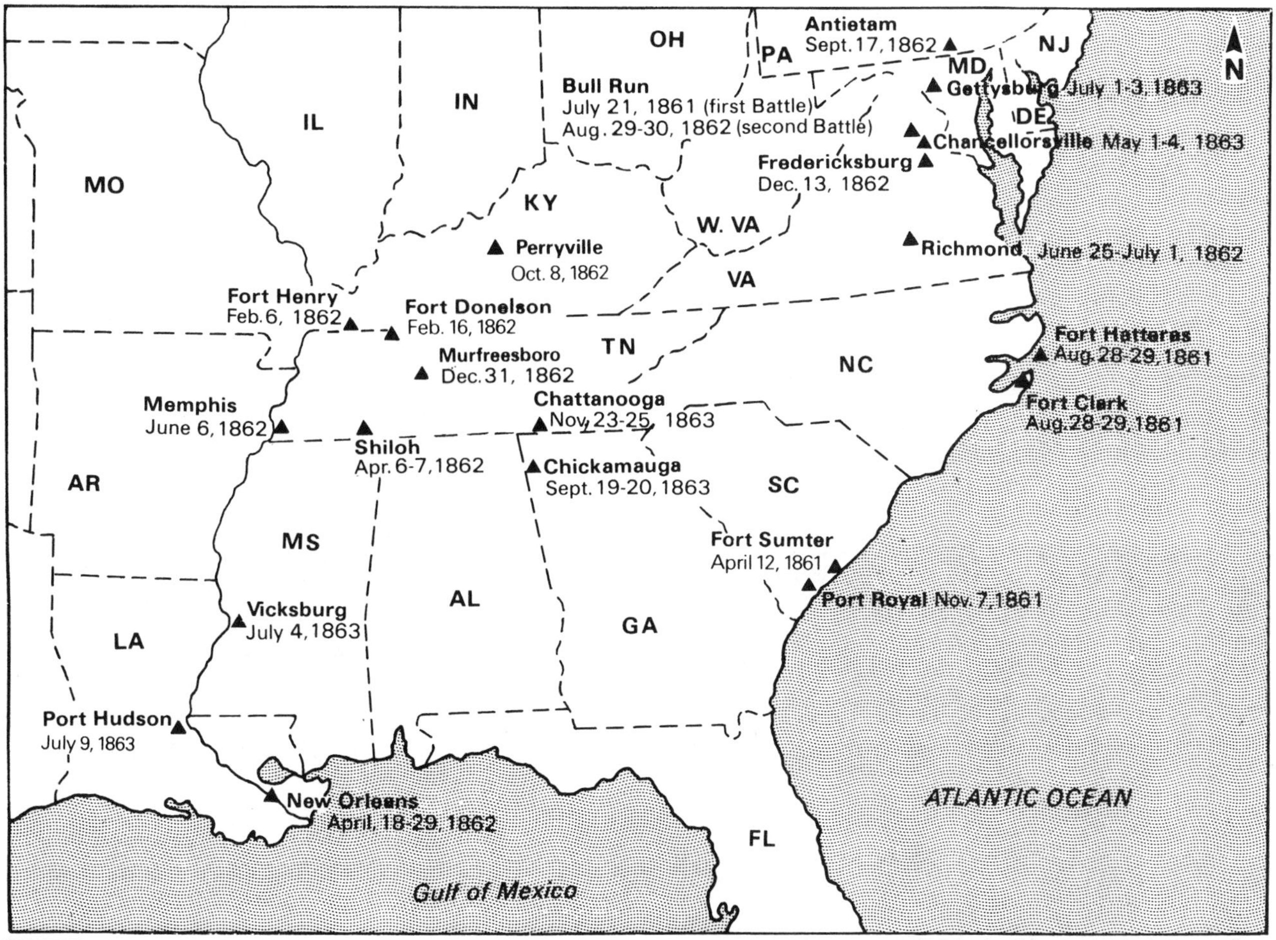

▲ Major Battles

a ratio likely to secure victory. In reality, however, the Confederate army facing McClellan from its fortifications around Manassas Junction, Virginia, actually numbered fewer than 50,000 men of all ranks. Commanded by Gen. Joseph E. Johnston, this Confederate army could hardly have been sanguine about its own prospects as it watched the federal numbers swell.

As January and February passed with no hint of movement by the Army of the Potomac, Pres. Abraham Lincoln attempted to force the issue by decreeing a general advance by all federal forces on George Washington's birthday, February 22. Nothing came of this bizarre approach to war-making by calendar and in terms of territorial gains, but McClellan apparently concluded that he must act, if only to forestall more civilian interference in purely military affairs. Gradually, a federal plan of campaign for the eastern theater began to emerge. In McClellan's view, two options presented themselves for the Army of the Potomac. On the one hand, he could make a conventional advance overland toward Manassas and ultimately toward Richmond, just under 100 miles to the south. In addition to protecting Washington, this option would meet Confederate strength face to face. Alternatively, McClellan could use the Union navy to transport the Army of the Potomac down the river to Chesapeake Bay and to a landing either on the lower Rappahannock River or to Fortress Monroe on the Virginia Peninsula. This option was seductive: it would simultaneously rest the troops and outflank Confederate strength. It would, however, incur some risk by greatly reducing the federal forces immediately south of Washington.

After due consideration but without civilian advice, McClellan settled on the waterborne option. He proposed to land the Army of the Potomac at Urbanna, Virginia, at the mouth of the Rappahannock River just 45 miles east of Richmond. When Lincoln heard of the plan, he objected vigorously. If the Confederates were as strong as McClellan postulated, Lincoln argued, they could easily seize Washington in McClellan's absence; if they were not so strong, there was no need to run the risk of exposing the federal capital. Although McClellan really had no answer to Lincoln's logic, he persisted in pushing for the Urbanna plan. Lincoln, as yet unsure of himself and his own military judgment, finally accepted McClellan's proposal, but with one caveat: McClellan must leave behind a force sufficient to protect the federal capital from a direct Confederate thrust. To guarantee that McClellan would not be distracted by events in other theaters, Lincoln relieved McClellan of his title of general in chief on Mar. 11, 1862. The Union war effort would now be coordinated by Lincoln himself and his new secretary of war, Edwin M. Stanton.

On March 19, just a day after McClellan's Urbanna plan was to be implemented, Johnston suddenly withdrew his army from Manassas, eventually halting it south of the Rappahannock near Fredericksburg, Virginia. Johnston's new position meant that he was no farther from Richmond than McClellan would be at Urbanna. Even worse for the federals, from Fredericksburg, Johnston could strike the Army of the Potomac in flank if it moved directly toward the Confederate capital. Disappointed, McClellan pushed his army forward and occupied the abandoned Confederate camps around Manassas. Although evidence found there indicated that Johnston had been heavily outnumbered, McClellan continued to believe that the Confederates facing him numbered nearly 100,000 men. So thinking, McClellan looked again at the waterborne option as a way to avoid facing this threat frontally. He concluded that while Urbanna no longer was useful as a landing site, Fortress Monroe was still acceptable. From a base at this Union stronghold on the tip of the peninsula between the James and York rivers, the Army of the Potomac could advance toward Richmond from the southeast.

Gen. Joseph E. Johnston maneuvered the Confederate army from Manassas, where it had been victorious at the First and Second Battles of Bull Run, to the area of Fredericksburg, Virginia, where he felt he would have a better chance of defending Richmond, the Confederate capital. (U.S. Army Military History Institute)

General George McClellan, shown in Washington with his wife, succeeded Winfield Scott as general in chief of the Union forces in November 1861. (Library of Congress)

Again, Lincoln approved McClellan's plan, but this time with two more conditions. First, the *Merrimac,* rebuilt and rechristened the CSS *Virginia,* an ironclad warship at Norfolk, Virginia, would have to be neutralized. After sinking two powerful wooden federal warships in Hampton Roads on March 8, the *Merrimac* had been fought to a draw by the USS *Monitor,* a Union ironclad of revolutionary design. McClellan and the navy would have to see that the *Merrimac* remained neutralized. Lincoln's second condition was more difficult to fulfill. Lincoln and Stanton had become concerned about the possibility of offensive movements by small Confederate forces in the Shenandoah Valley of Virginia. This rich agricultural region was not only a major supplier of food to the Confederacy, but its southwest-northeast orientation made it an ideal conduit for Confederate forces to use in threatening Washington. Defending the northern end of the valley was Maj. Gen. Nathaniel P. Banks with 23,000 men. Having been left behind by McClellan to protect Washington, Banks had subsequently been ordered to disperse a smaller Confederate force facing him and then return to the vicinity of the federal capital. Initially successful in pushing Confederates under Maj. Gen. Thomas J. "Stonewall" Jackson southward, Banks in late March prepared to withdraw toward Washington, having met Lincoln's second requirement.

Suddenly, on March 23, Jackson struck Banks's rear guard at Kernstown, near Winchester, Virginia. Although tactically defeated, Jackson made such a bold showing that Lincoln and Stanton became alarmed, fearing that the Confederates were preparing a larger thrust northward. Not only did they order Banks to return to the valley, they sent additional troops from McClellan's army to the area. When McClellan announced that he was leaving 75,000 troops behind to defend Washington, Lincoln and Stanton could find only 50,000, including Banks's force. Angered by McClellan's apparent disregard of their wishes, Lincoln and Stanton detained one of McClellan's corps, under Maj. Gen. Irvin McDowell, at Manassas. From there McDowell could reinforce either Banks or McClellan as the developing situation required. In a further insult to McClellan, Lincoln and Stanton decreed that Banks and McDowell would be independent of the Army of the Potomac. Although he still had more than 100,000 men under his command, McClellan bitterly protested these decisions. Thus on the eve of its first great effort in the East in 1862, the federal high command was in serious disarray, with inexperienced civilian leaders at odds with an angry army commander.

Peninsular Campaign

By April 4, McClellan had landed 90,000 troops at Fortress Monroe, with another 15,000 en route. He began his advance the same day, but was immediately confronted by a line of fortifications stretching across the Peninsula from the vicinity of Yorktown. To McClellan and his officers, this line appeared very strong, with many heavy cannon and perhaps a garrison of 50,000 men. Facing such a formidable obstacle, McClellan called upon Lincoln for more troops and ordered siege guns to be brought forward. In reality, the Confederate works were manned by only 15,000 men under Maj. Gen. John B. Magruder. Known in the prewar army as "Prince John" because of a fondness for the theatrical, Magruder used the same skills to make his meager force appear much larger than it was. By April 11, his force had indeed grown to 23,000 but was still overwhelmingly outnumbered by the federals, who had initiated an advance by regular siege tactics. A few days later, Magruder breathed more easily with the arrival of Johnston's army from the Rappahannock. The combined Confederate forces in the Yorktown line now numbered approximately 60,000 men.

Watching the federals dig their way ever closer to his works, Johnston became concerned that his flanks could be turned via either the James River or York River. Granted permission to retreat by Pres. Jefferson Davis if the situation warranted, Johnston elected to abandon his position on the night of May 3, two days before McClellan's grand

Maj. Gen. George B. McClellan (center) *and other Union generals.* (U.S. Army Military History Institute)

Virginia Campaigns, 1861–1863

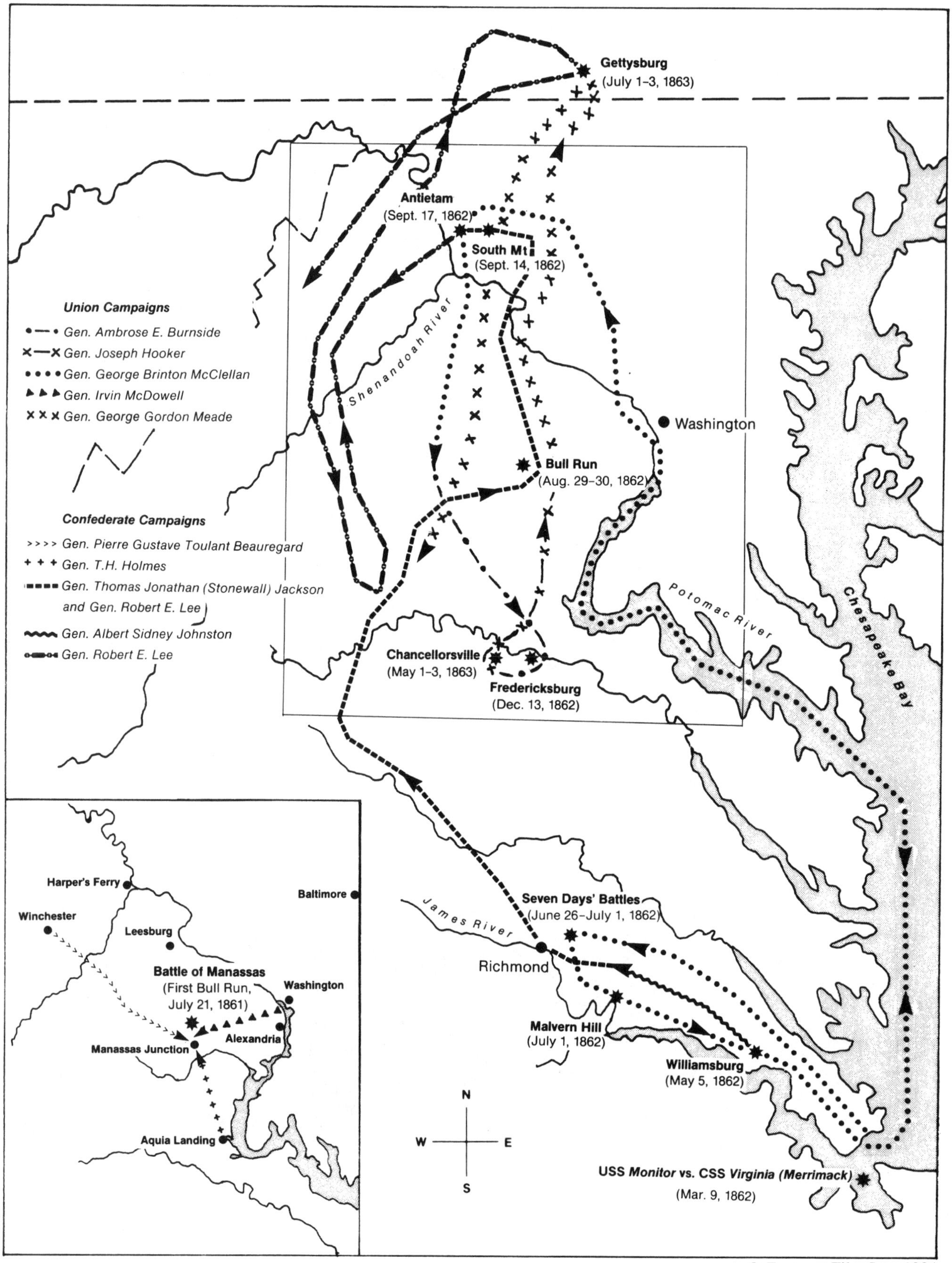
Gettysburg
(July 1-3, 1863)
Antietam
(Sept. 17, 1862)
South Mt
(Sept. 14, 1862)
Shenandoah River
Washington
Bull Run
(Aug. 29-30, 1862)
Union Campaigns
Gen. Ambrose E. Burnside
Gen. Joseph Hooker
Gen. George Brinton McClellan
Gen. Irvin McDowell
Gen. George Gordon Meade
Confederate Campaigns
Gen. Pierre Gustave Toulant Beauregard
Gen. T.H. Holmes
Gen. Thomas Jonathan (Stonewall) Jackson and Gen. Robert E. Lee
Gen. Albert Sidney Johnston
Gen. Robert E. Lee
Potomac River
Chesapeake Bay
Chancellorsville
(May 1-3, 1863)
Fredericksburg
(Dec. 13, 1862)
Harper's Ferry
Baltimore
Winchester
Leesburg
Battle of Manassas
(First Bull Run, July 21, 1861)
Washington
Alexandria
Manassas Junction
Aquia Landing
Seven Days' Battles
(June 26-July 1, 1862)
James River
Richmond
Malvern Hill
(July 1, 1862)
Williamsburg
(May 5, 1862)
N
W
E
S
USS Monitor vs. CSS Virginia (Merrimack)
(Mar. 9, 1862)

bombardment was to open. Upon discovering Johnston's departure, McClellan initially pursued vigorously. A bitter rearguard action fought by Maj. Gen. James Longstreet at Williamsburg on May 5 slowed the federal advance somewhat, and an attempt to use the York to outflank the retreating Confederates was blocked near West Point two days later. Thereafter, McClellan slowed the pace of the pursuit, reaching the vicinity of Richmond on May 25. Expecting McDowell's corps to join him overland from the north, he deployed three corps north of the Chickahominy River to facilitate that junction. South of the river, which split the Peninsula, he left only two corps. Even though he believed that Confederate strength now approached 200,000 and rising water in the Chickahominy threatened to separate the two halves of his own army, McClellan took no further action. Instead, he called loudly for additional troops.

Contrary to McClellan's estimate, Johnston had only 63,000 men shielding Richmond, although the large garrison of Norfolk had evacuated that city and was marching northward to join him. Because of its deep draft, the *Virginia* was unable to follow the army up the James, and it was destroyed by its crew. Thus the federal navy now controlled all of the York and most of the James. With his enemy at the gates of Richmond, Johnston resolved to mount an attack. Leaving Magruder to demonstrate north of the Chickahominy against McClellan's strength, Johnston attempted to fall upon one of the remaining federal corps south of the river and crush it. Unfortunately for Johnston, the resulting Battle of Fair Oaks (or Seven Pines) was badly mismanaged. Worse, Johnston was seriously wounded and forced to leave the field on the first day. His successor, Maj. Gen. Gustavus W. Smith, fared little better, as the federals reinforced their troops south of the Chickahominy and held the Confederates to no gain. Unsatisfied with Smith's performance, Davis sent his military adviser, Gen. Robert E. Lee, to assume command of the Confederate army defending Richmond. Renaming the force the Army of Northern Virginia, Lee began to study the possibility of offensive action. Fearing a repeat of Seven Pines, McClellan now shifted the bulk of his army south of the Chickahominy.

While the main armies were still around Yorktown, Banks attempted once again to secure the Shenandoah Valley for the Union cause. Assisting him was a smaller federal force under Maj. Gen. John C. Frémont, which was moving slowly eastward out of the Allegheny Mountains toward the valley. Between them was Jackson, who had been given command of scattered forces totaling 17,000 men. Rather than wait passively for the federals to concentrate against him, Jackson boldly took the initiative. Leaving part of his force under Maj. Gen. Richard S. Ewell to watch the lethargic Banks, Jackson raced westward and soundly defeated Frémont's advance at the Battle of McDowell on May 8. He then marched rapidly northward to deal with Banks. On May 23, Jackson overran a federal outpost at Front Royal, and two days later, he caught Banks's main body at Winchester, sending the federals fleeing north of the Potomac River.

Stonewall Jackson's celebrated Shenandoah Valley Campaign in the spring of 1862 brought a string of Confederate victories and tied up large numbers of Union troops. (National Archives)

Greatly distressed, Lincoln and Stanton denied McDowell's corps to McClellan and attempted to orchestrate a concentration to trap the impudent Confederates before they could withdraw southward. Jackson nimbly escaped the ponderous trap by rapid marching, while his pursuers were hindered by a lack of both aggressiveness and unity of command. Jackson halted his withdrawal on June 7 and in the twin battles of Cross Keys and Port Republic again defeated his assailants in detail. The chastened federals now withdrew northward down the valley. Jackson watched them go, all the while preparing to move eastward to join Lee at Richmond. His lightning Valley Campaign would soon come to be one of the most famous in military history. With little more than 17,000 men, he had occupied the attention of 70,000 federals for six weeks. During that time, he had marched 400 miles, fought 5 battles, and defeated 4 federal commanders. In fact, only one of McDowell's divisions ever got to the Army of the Potomac.

Lee Assumes Command

While Jackson was thrashing the hapless federal commanders in the Shenandoah Valley, Lee prepared to take the offensive. To maximize his limited numbers, he constructed an extensive belt of fortifications shielding Richmond on the east. To discover McClellan's dispositions, he sent a cavalry force under Brig. Gen. Jeb Stuart on a ride completely around the federal army. To gain strength, he called Jackson and Ewell from the valley. Since only one corps of the Army of the Potomac was north of the Chickahominy, Lee elected to strike his first blow there. His battle plan called for Magruder to employ his theatrical skills in a demonstration south of the Chickahominy while Jackson joined Lee's main body on the north bank. Timed to begin on June 26, the resulting Battle of Mechanicsville (or Beaver Dam Creek) began inauspiciously with Jackson's failure to arrive and a bloody repulse for Lee's troops. During the night, the federal corps withdrew to Gaines's Mill, where Lee again assaulted them. This time, the Confederates won the field, at great cost, but the federal corps successfully escaped across the Chickahominy.

Shaken by events north of the river, McClellan chose to transfer his base from White House on a tributary of the York to Harrison's Landing on the James. Placing the ponderous Army of the Potomac in motion, McClellan moved southward, followed by Lee. Fighting inconclusive actions at Savage's Station, White Oak Swamp, and Glendale, McClellan successfully extricated his massive army from the clutches of Lee's smaller force. As passive as they were, McClellan's men worked together as a team, while Lee found that his more individualistic subordinates would require much practice before they became a coherent fighting machine. On July 1, Lee found the federals in a strong position on Malvern Hill, not far from the James River. Ever aggressive, he ordered an attack, which was defeated with ease by massed federal artillery. On the following day, the federals withdrew to a fortified camp at Harrison's Landing. There Lee was content to leave them in peace. Known as the Seven Days' Campaign, this series of battles cost the Confederates far more casualties than it cost their opponents, but in the end, McClellan's army was driven from the outskirts of Richmond to the shelter of the federal navy.

While the main armies watched each other southeast of Richmond, the Lincoln administration attempted to rectify the command confusion in northern Virginia that had contributed so greatly to Jackson's success in the valley. On June 26, Maj. Gen. John Pope, fresh from minor victories in the western theater, was given command of the combined forces of Banks, McDowell, and Franz Sigel, Frémont's successor. However, Pope quickly alienated his 47,000 troops by comparing them unfavorably with Westerners. His mission was to cover Washington, hold the northern end of the Shenandoah Valley, and threaten Richmond from the north, thereby relieving pressure on McClellan's Army of the Potomac. In July, both Pope and McClellan were subordinated to Maj. Gen. Henry W. Halleck, who arrived from the western theater to be general in chief. Halleck's first task was to rule on McClellan's request for 30,000 additional troops. He sent 20,000, but McClellan, believing Lee had 200,000, next asked for 40,000. On August 3, Lincoln ordered McClellan and the Army of the Potomac back to Washington, from which they were expected to mount a conventional overland campaign against Richmond. McClellan's failure on the Peninsula thus discredited the waterborne thrust against Richmond for two years.

Aware than his 70,000 men were outnumbered two to one by the combined armies of Pope and McClellan, Lee boldly split his forces by sending Jackson with 24,000 troops northward to Gordonsville to watch Pope's Army of Virginia. In an attempt to catch part of Pope's army in an isolated position, Jackson attacked Banks's corps at Cedar Mountain on August 9. Banks was defeated, but only after a surprisingly strong fight. Pope now concentrated his army, forcing Jackson to withdraw. Gambling successfully that McClellan would remain quiescent, Lee took the majority of his army north to join Jackson. When the two Confederate forces met, Lee had approximately 55,000 men organized into two corps under Jackson and Longstreet. Pope's command by this time had approximately the same strength. Suddenly losing his bluster, Pope began to withdraw northward. McClellan meanwhile began to transfer his army slowly by water to northern Virginia. Lee learned of this transfer on August 24 and resolved to strike Pope before the Army of the Potomac could reinforce him.

Second Battle of Bull Run

Bold in the extreme, Lee's plan called for Longstreet's corps to hold Pope's attention on the Rappahannock while Jackson circled behind him to threaten his communications. Longstreet then was to move north, following Jackson's route, and the two Confederate corps would unite in Pope's rear. Having begun his march on August 25, Jackson burst into Pope's supply base at Manassas Junction two days later. Burning what he could not carry off, Jackson then disappeared northward. As Lee had anticipated, Pope focused on trapping Jackson and raced northward to Manassas Junction, which was deserted. On the evening of August 28, Jackson revealed himself by attacking one of Pope's divisions west of Manassas. Believing that Jackson was ripe for destruction, Pope concentrated his army for a battle while Jackson took a strong defensive position and awaited the federal assault. On August 29, the Army of Virginia battered itself senseless against Jackson's position, while elements of the army of the Potomac dawdled nearby. That night, Longstreet's corps secretly arrived. On August 30, Pope resumed his attacks but was quickly driven from the

General McClellan once again controlled the Union's Army of the Potomac after General Pope's defeat at the Second Battle of Bull Run in August 1862. (U.S. Army Military History Institute)

field by a massive Confederate counterattack. During the ensuing federal retreat, Jackson again struck part of Pope's army at Chantilly, but without decisive results.

For both combatants, the Second Battle of Bull Run (Manassas) had far-reaching results. Safe within the Washington defenses, Pope railed that McClellan and the Army of the Potomac had not supported him loyally. Although there was some merit in this argument, the bombastic Pope found little sympathy in the federal capital, and he was soon transferred to Minnesota to fight Indians. With no other successor in sight, the Lincoln administration dissolved Pope's command into the Army of the Potomac and left McClellan in charge. Meanwhile, the Confederates contemplated their recent success. In three months, Lee had moved the war from the outskirts of Richmond to the outskirts of Washington. A naturally aggressive commander, Lee believed the Army of Northern Virginia needed to maintain the initiative it had gained at such cost. Again he began to contemplate an offensive. Unlike Virginia, whose northern reaches had been devastated by contending armies, the North was untouched by the hand of war. An offensive beyond the Potomac River would relieve the pressure on Virginia, depress Northern morale, and possibly bring foreign intervention on the side of the Confederacy. Although his army numbered only 55,000 to McClellan's 97,000, Lee resolved to cross the Potomac into the enemy's country. Once there, he could cut key east-west railroads and threaten Washington, Baltimore, and Philadelphia.

SHIFT OF MOMENTUM

On September 4, the Army of Northern Virginia crossed the Potomac into Maryland. To secure his line of communication back into Virginia, Lee had to neutralize the federal garrison at Harpers Ferry, which lay astride it. He therefore daringly divided his small army into several parts. Jackson, with most of his corps, approached Harpers Ferry from the west, while two of Longstreet's divisions moved on the town from the north and one came in from the east. The remainder of Longstreet's corps moved northward to Boonsboro with the army's trains, while Jackson's remaining division acted as rear guard at the South Mountain pass. Lee himself moved with Longstreet. The dangers of scattering his units in the face of the massive Army of the Potomac were real, but Lee was willing to take the risk, believing that McClellan would be slow to react.

Battle of Antietam

When Harpers Ferry easily came under siege, the Confederate gamble seemed to be succeeding. However, an error in staff work and great good fortune on the part of the federals placed a copy of Lee's movement order in McClellan's hands on September 13. True to form, McClellan waited a day before acting. In bloody but minor actions at Turner's and Crampton's gaps, he brushed aside Lee's rear guard on September 14 but pressed no further. On the next day, Lee decided to cancel his invasion of the North and began to concentrate the widely separated parts of his army. The same day, Harpers Ferry fell to Jackson with booty of 11,000 prisoners and 73 cannon. Learning that Jackson was now en route to join him, Lee elected to stand at Sharpsburg, Maryland. With only 20,000 troops momentarily at hand and the unbridged Potomac River behind him, Lee gambled that McClellan would remain cautious. The gamble succeeded as McClellan spent an entire day slowly moving troops into position along Antietam Creek, behind which the Confederates waited. McClellan finally struck a blow on September 17, but it was struck piecemeal and haltingly. Lee's lines bent and occasionally broke, but the federals never applied enough sustained pressure to finish the job. When part of Jackson's force arrived in late afternoon, the Confederate line stabilized and McClellan pushed no further. On the following day, both armies remained in place without fighting, and that night Lee retreated across the Potomac unmolested.

The Battle of Antietam (or Sharpsburg) was a tactical victory for Lee because he had held his own against a force

General McClellan's Union troops had to cross Middle Bridge over Antietam Creek to attack General Lee's Confederate forces, which were between the creek and the Potomac River. (National Archives)

twice his size. Strategically, however, McClellan could claim success because Lee's invasion of the North had been hurled back. Both sides had suffered heavily, the combined casualty total of more than 25,000 men making it the single bloodiest day of the war. While not the total victory Lincoln had hoped for, Antietam was enough of a federal success for him to issue the preliminary Emancipation Proclamation, freeing slaves remaining under Confederate jurisdiction. Heretofore up for grabs, the moral high ground now belonged to the Union, making European intervention increasingly unlikely. Lee had saved his army to fight another day, but his cause had suffered a grievous defeat.

Astoundingly, McClellan continued to believe that Lee's army outnumbered him, and he remained north of the Potomac for one month before gingerly seeking the Confederates. Meanwhile, the Army of Northern Virginia recuperated around Winchester, Virginia, its numbers gradually growing to nearly 90,000. When McClellan finally entered Virginia on October 26, Lee again divided his army, leaving Jackson in the valley and sending Longstreet east of the mountains. McClellan tentatively moved between the two Confederate concentrations in early November but halted there. His patience exhausted, Lincoln relieved McClellan for the last time on November 7. McClellan's replacement was Maj. Gen. Ambrose E. Burnside, chosen because he was neither a troublesome personality nor excessively political. Believing himself unfit for the task, Burnside unsuccessfully tried to refuse the command. The Army of the Potomac, which had always loved McClellan, deeply regretted his departure.

Battle of Fredericksburg

Burnside's new offensive plan consisted simply of resuming the direct overland approach to Richmond. He proposed to establish a base on the Potomac just north of Fredericksburg, then across the Rappahannock and drive southward along the railroad to the Confederate capital. Burnside's leading elements reached the river across from Fredericks-

Some of the fallen lie in a field near Dunker Church at Sharpsburg after the Battle of Antietam, where more men were killed than on any other day during the Civil War. (Library of Congress)

President Lincoln visits with General McClellan (left center) *and other Union officers at Antietam after the Union victory.* (Library of Congress)

The initial lack of Union pontoon boats needed to cross the Rappahannock River at Fredericksburg afforded the Confederate army time to mass in Fredericksburg and repulse the Union attack. (U.S. Army Military History Institute)

A makeshift hospital served the wounded at Fredericksburg. (Library of Congress)

burg on November 17 but found no pontoons available with which to cross. Three days later, Longstreet arrived on the south bank and began to fortify the heights overlooking the river. By the time the pontoons appeared in early December, Lee had brought Jackson from the valley and the Confederates were concentrated in Burnside's front. On December 11, Burnside's men bridged the Rappahannock. After consolidating south of the stream, the Army of the Potomac assaulted the Confederate positions behind the town. The result was disastrous for the federals, who were repulsed with massive casualties. On December 15, the Army of the Potomac retreated across the river under cover of its artillery. Seeing no opportunity to counterattack, the Army of Northern Virginia let the federals depart in peace. The year 1862 thus ended with federal troops in the eastern theater farther from Richmond than they had been six months previously.

Maj. Gen. Ambrose Burnside's poor leadership at the Battle of Fredericksburg in December 1862 cost him the command of the Army of the Potomac. (U.S. Army Military History Institute)

WESTERN THEATER: 1862

As in the east, Union forces in the western theater felt obliged to assume the offensive as early as possible. After several reorganizations in 1861, the front-line federal departments in this theater were Halleck's Department of Missouri and Maj. Gen. Don Carlos Buell's Department of the Ohio. Together, these two commanders faced the problem of how best to crack the defensive line established earlier by Confederate general Albert Sidney Johnston. Unlike the divided federals, Johnston's unified command stretched from the bluffs on the Mississippi River at Columbus, Kentucky, all the way eastward to the mountain stronghold of Cumberland Gap. On the left of Johnston's line, Maj. Gen. Leonidas Polk commanded 12,000 troops at Columbus, closing navigation on the Mississippi with powerful batteries in elevated positions. Eastward, just below the Kentucky line in Tennessee, Forts Henry and Donelson similarly closed the Tennessee and Cumberland rivers. These two positions were manned by Brig. Gen. Lloyd Tilghman and 5,000 men. Still further eastward, Johnston himself personally superintended the bulk of his forces, 22,000 men around Bowling Green, Kentucky. On the far right flank, Brig. Gen. Felix Zollicoffer defended Cumberland Gap in the Appalachian chain with another 5,000 troops. It was this line that Halleck and Buell were charged to break.

Buell was first off the mark, beginning a tentative advance toward Cumberland Gap in January 1862. Asking Halleck to demonstrate against the other end of the Confederate line, he sent Brig. Gen. George H. Thomas with 6,000 men into southeastern Kentucky. Zollicoffer had unwisely taken an advanced position north of the Cumberland River, and when Maj. Gen. George Crittenden arrived to assume command, he decided that it was too late to withdraw in the face of Thomas's advance. In the Battle of Logan Cross Roads (or Mill Springs), Zollicoffer was killed, Crittenden was discredited, and the Confederates were driven from the field. Bad weather and terrible road conditions were used as an excuse to halt the federal advance at this point, but in reality, Buell's caution was the deciding factor.

At the other end of the Confederate line, more impressive results came from an offensive by Brig. Gen. Ulysses S. Grant, Halleck's most energetic subordinate. Grant proposed and Halleck approved a combined operation against Forts Henry and Donelson. If these positions were taken, not only would Johnston's defense line be broken, but Union naval vessels would be able to penetrate deeply into Tennessee and northern Alabama. On January 30, when news arrived that Confederate reinforcements were on their way to Johnston, Halleck authorized Grant to proceed. Grant's 15,000 men, convoyed up the Tennessee River by Flag Officer Andrew H. Foote's river ironclads and wooden gunboats, landed just north of Fort Henry in early February. Aware that the poorly sited fort was virtually untenable, Tilghman sent most of the garrison overland to Fort Donelson and contested the position with only a small number of artillerymen. On February 6, Foote's ironclads bombarded the garrison into submission before Grant's infantrymen could reach the works. The Tennessee River was now open to Union naval penetration as far as Muscle Shoals, Alabama.

While wooden gunboats probed up the Tennessee, burning railroad bridges and other lucrative targets, Grant and Foote took the bulk of their forces to the Cumberland River to invest Fort Donelson. In response, Johnston began to evacuate his position in Kentucky and sent 12,000 men under Brig. Gen. John Floyd to reinforce Fort Donelson. Donelson's commander, Brig. Gen. Gideon Pillow, chose not to harass Grant's advance, which appeared outside the fort on February 12. The Confederate reinforcements arrived on the next day, and Floyd assumed command. On

Tennessee Campaigns, January 1862–January 1863

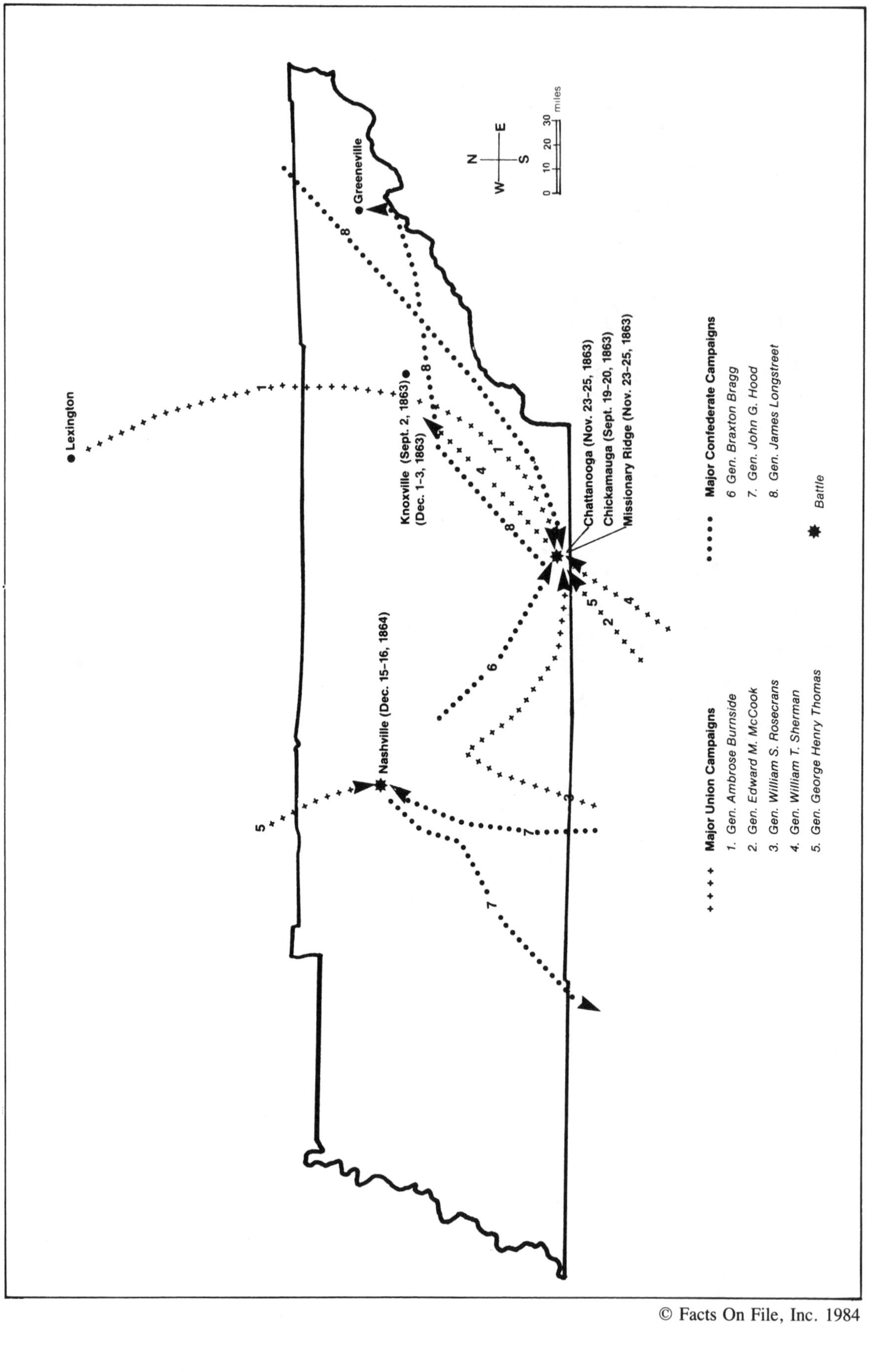

February 14, Foote's gunboats attacked the fort but were repulsed at significant cost, including Foote, who was wounded. By that night, Grant's strength had grown to 25,000 men while Floyd commanded only 15,000. Unsure of himself, Floyd called a council of war. Although Johnston desired Floyd to resist as long as possible to permit him to concentrate his forces, the beleaguered commander and his subordinates elected to break out of Grant's encirclement. In bitterly cold weather on February 15, the Confederates successfully opened a hole in the federal line but at the last minute lost their nerve and withdrew into the works. Floyd and Pillow then escaped upriver on steamboats with but a few troops, leaving Brig. Gen. Simon B. Buckner to capitulate unconditionally to Grant on February 16.

Although small affairs compared with battles soon to follow, the falls of Forts Henry and Donelson had significant consequences. Johnston's defense line in Kentucky was untenable with its left center pierced, and he was forced to evacuate that state. Following behind Johnston, Buell's army entered Nashville, the first Confederate state capital to fall—a serious blow to the Confederacy's war-making potential in the western theater. Twelve days after the loss of Fort Donelson, Polk evacuated the fortifications at Columbus and marched southward toward Memphis, Tennessee. The Confederacy's most advanced post on the Mississippi now was a complex of defenses 30 miles south of Columbus at Island No. 10 and New Madrid, Missouri. In the center of Johnston's department, there was no natural barrier upon which the Confederates could stand, so Johnston withdrew south of Nashville. Fortunately for Johnston, federal command disarray now gave him time to consider a counterstroke. Not only did Buell halt his pursuit at Nashville, but Halleck briefly relieved Grant of command for an apparent breach of protocol. Thus the victorious federal armies marked time while the shaken Confederates regrouped.

Primarily because of Grant's and Foote's victories, Halleck was perceived as the rising star in the western theater. At the same time, he was maneuvering himself to become sole commander in the theater. Fearful of Halleck's growing prestige, General in Chief McClellan resisted such an arrangement until he himself was deposed from supreme command. Thereafter, Lincoln placed Halleck in charge of both his own and Buell's forces. Momentarily, the string of federal victories continued, when another of Halleck's subordinates, Brigadier General Pope, successfully forced the Confederates to evacuate New Madrid, Missouri, on the Mississippi River. In a masterful example of army-navy cooperation, Pope next encircled the Confederate garrison of Island No. 10, forcing the surrender of 7,000 Confederate troops on April 8. This brilliant small campaign not only enhanced Halleck's reputation for military genius, it also brought Pope to the attention of the Lincoln administration, which soon called him to a larger command in the eastern theater.

Shiloh Campaign

While Pope completed his operations around Island No. 10, Halleck began to devise a new plan for the employment of Grant's and Buell's armies. A firm believer in the principle of concentration, Halleck proposed to combine the two armies and lead them in an offensive against the railroad junction of Corinth, Mississippi. At this small town, just a few miles below the Tennessee border, one of the Confederacy's two main east-west rail links was crossed by a north-south line from Columbus, Kentucky, to Mobile, Alabama. In Halleck's mind, Corinth was a decisive point and one that the Confederacy could hardly surrender without a fight. Relying upon the navy for mobility, Grant was able to advance quickly up the Tennessee River to within a few miles of Corinth, but Buell, who was marching overland from Nashville, required longer to effect the concentration. When one of Grant's subordinates, William T. Sherman, discovered an excellent campsite on the west bank of the Tennessee only 21 miles from Corinth, Grant chose to wait there for the arrival of Buell and Halleck. By early April, Grant's 42,000 troops had established pleasant camps in the woods near Pittsburg Landing, many of them around a rustic meeting house called Shiloh Church.

Although he had meekly withdrawn from Kentucky and much of Tennessee, A. S. Johnston remained an aggressive commander. As he continued his withdrawal toward Mississippi, Johnston learned of a major Confederate effort to reinforce him. From the vicinity of Memphis came Polk with the troops that had garrisoned Columbus; from Mobile came Gen. Braxton Bragg with all the units that could be spared from coastal defense; and from the eastern theater came Gen. P. G. T. Beauregard, who began to organize the reinforcements into a small army at Corinth. When Johnston arrived at Corinth with his own contingent in late March, the combined Confederate forces numbered approximately 50,000 men. Together, Johnston and Beauregard devised a plan to attack Grant at Pittsburg Landing before Buell could arrive. On April 3, Johnston led 42,000 troops north from Corinth. Bad roads and poor staff work hindered their march and prevented the Confederates from being ready to attack until the morning of April 6. Amazingly, Grant's army was unaware of their presence.

Usually called the Battle of Shiloh, but also known as the Battle of Pittsburg Landing, the conflict that resulted from Johnston's attack quickly lost all semblance of order. Apparently, Johnston had desired to separate the federal troops from their transports at the landing, but the initial direction of his attack and the inevitable mixing of successive attacking formations caused the battle to develop simply into a series of frontal assaults. While urging his men forward, Johnston received a mortal wound, and

Beauregard assumed command. At the end of the day, Grant's army had been compressed into a tight mass around the landing, but it had been neither crushed nor separated from the river. That night, large numbers of Buell's troops arrived to relieve Grant's exhausted men. On April 7, Buell's army and part of Grant's went on the offensive, forcing the equally exhausted Confederates to relinquish their hard-won gains. As so often was the case, the victors believed themselves to be in no condition for meaningful pursuit, and the Confederates withdrew unchallenged to Corinth.

Operations Under Halleck

For the North, Shiloh had many implications. Although he had been badly surprised, Grant was able to retain his command because Lincoln credited him with the Union victory. Similarly surprised, Sherman also escaped the battle with his reputation enhanced, especially in Grant's eyes. The large number of casualties, more than 23,000 in total, made it clear to both sides that the war would be long and costly. Angered that the battle had been fought and won without his permission or presence, Halleck soon arrived to command the united federal army in person. Corinth remained the federal goal, but Halleck believed the army must be reorganized first. Unable to remove Grant, Halleck eased him out of authority by making him second in command, then giving him nothing to do. By the end of April, Halleck had collected approximately 100,000 troops, which he organized into three columns under Thomas, Buell, and Pope. On April 30, he initiated the advance on Corinth.

Corinth was heavily fortified by Beauregard's army before Halleck's ponderous force reached the vicinity of the town. Believing that near-disaster had occurred at Shiloh because Grant had not fortified his position, Halleck insisted that his units entrench every night. While this procedure was prudent, it also ensured that the federal army would not close on Corinth for almost a month. By the time he reached Corinth, Halleck's army had grown to 120,000 men. Inside Corinth, Beauregard, too, was being reinforced, eventually to a total of 70,000 men. On Beauregard's orders, the Confederates made a great show of preparing to stand and fight, but in reality they were withdrawing supplies and preparing to evacuate the city. On the night of May 29–30, Beauregard's army departed Corinth secretly, retreating 45 miles to the vicinity of Tupelo, Mississippi. Although skillfully accomplished, the retreat displeased President Davis. Seeking an excuse to remove Beauregard from command, Davis found what he needed when Beauregard took unauthorized sick leave. Firing Beauregard, he replaced him with Bragg.

Following a pattern already well established in both major theaters, Halleck made only a short, ineffective pursuit of the retreating Confederates. With Bragg's army in disarray and momentarily out of reach, Halleck had several offensive options. He could advance southwestward toward Vicksburg, Mississippi, and thereby further open the Mississippi River to Union commerce. Similarly, he could turn eastward and advance toward Chattanooga, Tennessee, a gateway to both East Tennessee's loyalist population and north Georgia. The Confederacy would have been hard-pressed to counter either of these courses of action effectively, but Halleck apparently failed to grasp the possibilities open to him. Instead of boldly seizing the initiative, he proceeded to disperse the large force he had collected. On June 10, he dispatched Buell and 31,000 men toward Chattanooga with orders to rebuild the Memphis & Charleston Railroad as they went. Memphis having fallen to the federals after a brief naval battle on June 7, Halleck ordered Grant to establish garrisons in the Corinth-Memphis area. Finally, on June 11, Halleck received orders to return to Washington to be general in chief of the armies of the Union. His departure meant that Grant and Buell were once more independent commanders. It also meant that for the next year, the western theater would contain two major federal armies fighting separate campaigns with little reference to each other.

Tennessee and Kentucky Campaigns

Following his orders from Halleck, Buell began his slow advance toward Chattanooga along the railroad. Gradually reinforced to more than 50,000 men by transfers from Grant's forces, Buell quickly found himself hampered by guerrilla activity in his rear. By the end of June, he had reached Decatur, Alabama, halfway to his goal. There he dallied for two weeks before Confederate raiders further delayed his progress until mid-August with raids on his rear. Meanwhile, Bragg had not remained idle. Believing that a Confederate advance from Tupelo was impossible, Bragg decided to operate against Buell's army instead. Leaving Maj. Gens. Sterling Price and Earl Van Dorn with 16,000 men each to watch Grant in northern Mississippi, Bragg shifted 35,000 men by rail from Tupelo to Chattanooga via Mobile, Alabama. Bragg's army did not leave Tupelo until July 21, but he still arrived in Chattanooga well in advance of Buell's army. In Tennessee, Bragg proposed to unite with a smaller army under Maj. Gen. E. Kirby Smith in an invasion of Kentucky. If the lethargic Buell could be defeated, the combined Confederate army might turn on Grant. Kentucky itself might be brought into the Confederacy and provide thousands of new recruits for the Confederate cause.

The movements culminating in the Confederate invasion of Kentucky began on August 14 when Smith advanced from Knoxville, Tennessee, toward Lexington, Kentucky. On August 30, he easily defeated a small, inexperienced federal command at Richmond, Kentucky. Meanwhile, Bragg had departed Chattanooga on August 28 with 30,000 men. By mid-September, he had reached Mumfordville, Kentucky, astride Buell's supply line to Louisville. Buell, who had been nearing Chattanooga when Bragg seized the initiative, now felt compelled to make a series of hasty retreats. Although his 46,000 men significantly outnumbered Bragg's command, Buell fell back first to Nashville, then to Bowling Green, Kentucky. He could have struck Bragg several times en route, but feared to do so even though he was continually being reinforced from Grant's command. Although Buell was afraid to use them offensively, Buell's numbers did make Bragg cautious. Rather than remain on Buell's supply line and thereby force a decisive clash, Bragg in mid-September marched eastward, nearer to Smith. Together, the two Confederate armies could have matched Buell's strength, but Smith remained just beyond Bragg's reach near Lexington. Rather than follow Bragg toward Smith, Buell entered the safety of the defenses of Louisville.

Although he had saved his army and the city of Louisville, Buell had performed abysmally in the view of the Lincoln administration, which tried to replace him with Thomas. When Thomas refused the command, Lincoln and Halleck reluctantly retained Buell. The Confederates, meanwhile, inaugurated a Confederate governor in the Kentucky state capitol at Frankfort and searched fruitlessly for the thousands of recruits alleged to be eager to join the Confederate army. By early October, with his reasons for remaining in Kentucky dissipating, Bragg seemed unsure how to proceed. Buell now moved out of Louisville in search of the Confederates. While looking for water, parts of Buell's and Bragg's armies collided near Perryville, Kentucky, on October 8. Not yet concentrated, the Confederates were outnumbered two to one, but most of the battle was over before Buell was aware of the fight. As a result, the battle ended in a draw. Realizing his danger, Bragg quickly concentrated his own and Smith's scattered forces. He did not, however, attempt to regain the initiative, deciding instead to retreat to Tennessee via Cumberland Gap.

Bragg's withdrawal eventually carried him back to Chattanooga, from whence he advanced northward up the railroad to Murfreesboro. Instead of following the Confederates, Buell decided to return directly southward to Nashville. Angered by Buell's dilatory movements and his refusal to liberate the loyal Unionists in East Tennessee, Lincoln finally relieved him on October 23. Buell had served loyally and had shown talent as an organizer, but his lack of any sense of urgency in movement or a desire to close with his opponent caused his downfall. Buell's replacement was Maj. Gen. William S. Rosecrans, who was brought eastward from Grant's command. In early November, Rosecrans reoccupied Nashville with an army of 47,000 men. From there, he watched Bragg 35 miles southeast at Murfreesboro with 38,000 troops. Later that month, Bragg merged Smith's command with his own, naming both the Army of Tennessee.

Deadlock in the West

On November 24, Davis announced a new organizational scheme for the major Confederate forces operating in the western theater. Earlier in the year, there had been only one major command in the area, but when the federals split their massive army around Corinth into Grant's and Buell's separate forces, the Confederacy was forced to counter that move with a split of its own. By taking the war into Kentucky and, ultimately, Tennessee, Bragg had removed from Mississippi the largest deployable body of Confederate troops in the theater. Left behind was a variety of units with the mission of defending northern Mississippi as well as the city of Vicksburg on the Mississippi River in the south. These units were commanded by Lt. Gen. John C. Pemberton. Thus Davis found himself with two major commands in the western theater: that of Mississippi and that of Tennessee. Depending upon the timing of federal offensive thrusts, those major commands might assist one another through transfers of assets on a temporary basis. To determine which army most needed support and to facilitate such transfers, Davis appointed J. E. Johnston to a superdepartmental command. Thus Bragg remained in command at Murfreesboro, but Johnston technically stood above him in the Confederate command structure.

On the Union side, in the meantime, command conflicts continued. Under heavy pressure from Lincoln and Halleck and with Buell's example before him, Rosecrans still refused to be stampeded into an advance before his command was rested and refitted. Now renamed the Army of the Cumberland, Rosecrans's army finally began its advance on December 26. Four days later, his advance elements met the Army of Tennessee just west of Murfreesboro. Although both commanders planned to attack on December 31, Bragg struck first and thus shaped the Battle of Stones River (or Murfreesboro). By the end of the day, the federal right had been crushed and driven back three miles, leaving Rosecrans with only a tenuous hold on the road back to Nashville. With no available reserves, Bragg was unable to complete the destruction of the Army of the Cumberland and the fighting closed without decision. On Jan. 1, 1863, the armies remained in place watching each other. When a final Confederate attack on the following day ended in a bloody repulse, Bragg ceased offensive efforts. For still another day, the armies remained in place, but that night, Bragg ordered his men to leave the field. Tactically a draw, Stones River was a strategic victory for the Union. The Army of Tennessee withdrew a few miles to the southeast, while the Army of the Cumberland held its ground at Murfreesboro.

Although the moves and countermoves set in motion by Bragg's invasion of Kentucky had monopolized the news

Ulysses S. Grant's Mississippi campaigns in 1862–63 played a vital role in Union successes in the West. (Library of Congress)

from the western theater in the second half of 1862, events of even greater importance were beginning to unfold in the Mississippi Valley. Upon the departure of Halleck and Buell, Grant had been left to hold the Memphis-Corinth area with approximately 45,000 troops. For a time, Grant's mission was purely defensive, but he was unwilling to remain passive for long. Facing him in northern Mississippi were two small Confederate armies under Price and Van Dorn. According to Bragg's plan, Price was to lead his command northward in support of the Kentucky invasion. As he attempted to do so, he was struck by Grant's subordinate Rosecrans at Iuka, Mississippi, on September 19. Price and his army escaped destruction, but the plan to join Bragg was permanently shelved. The two Confederate forces now united under the leadership of Van Dorn and in early October advanced upon the Union garrison of Corinth. Again Rosecrans was the federal commander, and again the Confederates were defeated but escaped. On the strength of his showing at Iuka and Corinth, Rosecrans departed at the end of the month to replace Buell in central Tennessee.

Grant on the Mississippi

As the Confederate threat to Kentucky faded, additional troops began to flow back into Grant's department in western Tennessee, and he began to contemplate taking the offensive. Initially, he sought guidance from Halleck but was disappointed to find that Halleck would commit himself to no specific course of action. The general in chief finally gave Grant permission to make his own plans, which Grant was quite willing to do. For an objective, Grant chose the city of Vicksburg, Mississippi, which blocked federal penetration down the Mississippi River from its position on commanding bluffs overlooking a hairpin turn in the river channel. Vicksburg had first been visited on May 25 by a federal naval squadron moving upriver from New Orleans, itself captured a month earlier. The town had refused a demand to surrender, and the lack of a significant land component had rendered the squadron impotent in the face of Confederate intransigence. In late June, naval squadrons had gathered off Vicksburg from both upriver and downriver, but again lack of a sizeable land force caused a repeat of May's failure. Having become suddenly aware of the city's vulnerability, the Confederates acted quickly to fortify the bluffs and augment the city's small garrison. Now Grant would find the city a difficult target, indeed.

The first problem Grant faced in regard to Vicksburg was how to approach the city. Just below Memphis, the line of bluffs so well utilized by Confederate engineers north of that point departed from the east bank of the Mississippi for several hundred miles. The bluff line again approached the great river at Vicksburg, where heavy batteries were mounted to close the river with plunging fire. From Memphis to Vicksburg, the land on both sides of the Mississippi was low and swampy. East of the river, the land was especially fertile and also especially difficult to negotiate for much of the year. Crisscrossed by innumerable bayous and channels that occasionally coalesced into significant rivers such as the Yazoo, this inhospitable area was known as the Mississippi Delta. Clearly, the conventional way to approach Vicksburg was to advance southward on the high ground east of the Delta, cut its railroad communication with the rest of the Confederacy, and attack the city from the rear. Such was Grant's initial plan.

While Grant's command had been on the defensive, Confederate forces in northern Mississippi had been in serious disarray, but by the time Grant was ready to begin his advance, much of that disarray had been rectified. Because of personality differences, the Price-Van Dorn team had proven to be unworkable. Davis's solution at first had been to let Price return to the trans-Mississippi theater, send Van Dorn into Tennessee to join Bragg, and bring Pemberton to Mississippi to command all troops in the state. When Van Dorn proved unable to leave Mississippi and it was discovered that he outranked Pemberton, Davis promoted the latter to lieutenant general. On October 14, Pemberton assumed command of the Department of Mississippi and Eastern Louisiana, with orders to defend the entire area. Most of his available troops, approximately

24,000, were in northern Mississippi under Van Dorn, but his two most important fixed positions were the river fortifications and 4,500-man garrisons at Vicksburg and at Port Hudson, Louisiana, 100 miles to the south. As long as those two positions denied the federal navy free passage on the Mississippi, that 100-mile stretch of terrain served as the Confederacy's doorway to the resources of Texas and western Louisiana.

Grant opened his campaign against Vicksburg on November 2 with an advance southward from Tennessee along the line of the Mississippi Central Railroad toward Jackson. Under Pemberton's orders, Van Dorn began a series of withdrawals that by early December had carried the Confederates south to Grenada, Mississippi. Requests to adjacent department commanders for assistance were initially unavailing, and represented one of the reasons Davis established Johnston as overseer of Bragg's and Pemberton's armies. At this point, Grant momentarily slowed his advance, unwittingly providing the Confederates an opportunity to seize the initiative. When a subordinate proposed a cavalry raid against Grant's advanced supply base at Holly Springs, Mississippi, Pemberton readily approved the project. Under Van Dorn's command, the raiders broke into the base on December 20 and destroyed it. This raid, plus similar activity by more Confederate cavalry in Tennessee, made Grant's logistical situation untenable, and he began to withdraw northward.

Coinciding with Grant's overland advance toward Vicksburg's rear was a strike at the city from the delta. This expedition had its genesis in politics at the highest levels. One of the most politically prominent but least professional of the senior Union commanders in the western theater was Maj. Gen. John A. McClernand, a Democrat from Illinois who supported the war policies of the Lincoln administration. Believing that the war potential of the upper Midwest had not been fully tapped, McClernand in October had offered to raise an army in that region to take Vicksburg if he could have command. Without Grant's knowledge, even though McClernand would be operating within his department, Lincoln and Stanton approved the scheme on October 21. Soon, thousands of troops raised by McClernand began to gather in Memphis. McClernand, however, was not initially with them, having paused to get married in Illinois. Learning of McClernand's plan and his momentary absence, Grant asked Halleck for authority over the units, and it was readily granted. Grant then sent his trusted subordinate Sherman to Memphis to organize McClernand's command and lead it to Vicksburg without its commander.

Conceived in haste and poorly prepared, Sherman's expedition of 32,000 men sailed downriver in mid-December. Its destination was the line of bluffs a few miles north of Vicksburg where the Yazoo River provided easy access to the high ground. Pemberton learned of the expedition's approach on December 24 and began to transfer troops to Vicksburg from northern Mississippi. A division was already en route to Pemberton from Bragg, but it had not arrived. Thus, at the time of Sherman's landing, only 6,000 Confederate troops were available to counter the federal thrust. Sherman's troops landed unopposed on December 26 but did not hasten to cross the flooded lowlands toward the high ground. By the time the federals began their advance in earnest, Confederate numbers had doubled. Eventually, Sherman's main force reached flooded Chickasaw Bayou, which lay at the foot of the bluffs, and behind which the Confederate defenders were posted. A full-scale assault failed on December 28, and with each succeeding day, more Confederates arrived to man the works. Conceding defeat, Sherman withdrew to the mouth of the Yazoo, where he found an irate McClernand ready to reclaim his command. Coupled with Grant's withdrawal from northern Mississippi, Sherman's repulse signaled the failure of the Union's first concerted effort against Vicksburg.

At the end of the year, when the opposing commanders in the western theater toted up their gains and losses, the balance sheet decisively favored neither side. In terms of territory, the Union had gained all of western Tennessee and most of the central part of the state, including the capital city of Nashville. These losses, while grievous to the Confederacy, did not seem mortal to the Davis administration. The Confederate banner had been carried northward into Kentucky, but it had not remained there, nor had thousands of recruits flocked to its cause. Nevertheless, transit of the Mississippi River was denied to the Union and contact with the vast territory west of the river remained unbroken. Major Confederate armies still remained in the field ready to contest any further federal advance. In terms of organization, moreover, the Union troops in this theater lost their supreme commander when Halleck went east, while the Confederacy had in theory at least centralized command in the person of J. E. Johnston. The coming year was expected by both sides to be the year of decision.

EASTERN THEATER: 1863

The events of the previous year, especially McClellan's failure during the Peninsular Campaign and Jackson's masterful use of the Shenandoah Valley to play on Washington's fears, had reduced the strategic options open to federal commanders in the eastern theater. The Confederate capital of Richmond remained the goal of operations, yet that goal could only be approached by having the Army of the Potomac stand between Washington and Lee's Army of Northern Virginia. The new year found Burnside still in command of the Army of the Potomac, which faced the Confederates across the Rappahannock River near Fredericksburg. After his fiasco there in December 1862, Burnside was under instructions from Lincoln to make no movement without first informing the government. Nevertheless, on January 20, Burnside initiated an offensive movement that entailed a crossing of the Rappahannock west of Fredericksburg. Unfortunately beginning at the same time that a heavy storm struck the area, the advance quickly became stalled in a sea of mud and water. Eventually canceled, this "Mud March" was unfairly blamed on Burnside, and the hapless commander became the target of renewed criticism.

The Army of the Potomac, long riddled with factions that could agree on nothing but opposition to the commanding general, now boiled with intrigue. One of the loudest carpers was Maj. Gen. Joseph Hooker, who had assembled a coterie of equally vocal supporters. His patience at an end, Burnside, in late January, drafted an order dismissing Hooker and three of his friends from the army. He presented this order to Lincoln, along with an alternate proposal that he be relieved from command of the Army of the Potomac. Lincoln accepted the latter option, transferring Burnside temporarily to the western theater. Well aware that Hooker had intrigued against Burnside and had made derogatory remarks about him, Lincoln nevertheless appointed the outspoken general as Burnside's replacement. For all his faults, Hooker had the reputation of being a fighter, and Lincoln had had his fill of temporizers and procrastinators.

Gen. Joseph Hooker, nicknamed "Fighting Joe," took command of the Army of the Potomac after the Battle of Fredericksburg, but was relieved of command after his hesitation at Chancellorsville caused a Union defeat. (Library of Congress)

Hooker moved quickly to place his own stamp on the Army of the Potomac. Whereas Burnside had consolidated the army's corps into "grand divisions," Hooker abolished the new formations and returned the individual corps to prominence. He also united the scattered federal cavalry units into a corps for the first time. By the end of April, the Army of the Potomac was in its best shape ever, with 122,000 infantry, 12,000 cavalry, and 400 guns. Once the roads dried, Hooker proposed to begin operations much as Burnside had abortively attempted in January. According to the plan, Maj. Gen. John Sedgwick with two corps would cross the Rappahannock just downstream of Fredericksburg to attract the Confederates' attention. In the meantime, Hooker would lead five corps upstream to crossings of the Rappahannock well above the town. Once across the river, Hooker would circle south and east to get behind Lee's left and force him to abandon the heights above Fredericksburg. In support of the infantry advance, the federal cavalry would penetrate deeply into the Confederate rear to sever Lee's communications with Richmond. Hooker's route south of the Rappahannock passed through a large tract of second-growth woodland called the Wilderness, but he anticipated clearing the region before encountering significant numbers of Confederates.

In contrast to the Army of the Potomac, Lee's Army of Northern Virginia could not muster nearly so strong a force. Believing that the federals would be slow to begin their spring campaign, Lee had sent Longstreet with two divisions into southern Virginia to gather provisions. As winter turned to spring, Longstreet gathered additional troops south of Richmond and advanced upon the federal garrison at Suffolk, Virginia. Neither he nor Lee anticipated seizing the heavily fortified town, but simply driving the federals within their fortifications would permit Confederate commissary officers to reap a harvest of provisions from the surrounding countryside. The state of Confederate supplies in Virginia rendered this excursion attractive, but the risk of a federal advance before Longstreet could rejoin the Army of Northern Virginia was ever present. Longstreet moved promptly, laying a halfhearted siege against Suffolk on April 11, but he was still in southern Virginia when May arrived. As a result, Lee faced Hooker's massive army with only 53,000 infantry, 6,500 cavalry, and 228 guns.

Delayed for two weeks by bad weather, Hooker finally began to advance in late April. On April 27, Maj. Gen. George Stoneman took his cavalry south on the deep penetration raid that was an integral part of the plan. The raid, however, accomplished nothing except to leave Hooker blind to Confederate countermoves. The federal infantry left its camps on April 28, and on the following day, both Sedgwick's diversionary force and Hooker's main body began to cross the Rappahannock. Warned of Hooker's

A graduate of West Point, Confederate Gen. James Longstreet served as a key subordinate of Robert E. Lee through most of the war. (National Archives)

every move by his efficient cavalry under Stuart, Lee boldly decided to meet Hooker with the troops at hand rather than surrender the line of the Rappahannock. Sending a single division westward to retard the advance of Hooker's flanking force, Lee prepared to follow with the bulk of his army. On April 30, the division encountered Hooker's leading elements just leaving the Wilderness and began to delay them as Lee had planned. Leaving 10,000 men under Maj. Gen. Jubal Early to hold the Fredericksburg line, Lee marched westward with the remainder of his force.

Battle of Chancellorsville

On the verge of exiting the Wilderness successfully, Hooker, on May 1, suddenly lost his nerve and established defensive positions around a crossroads known as Chancellorsville. Fixing Hooker's attention with 17,000 troops, Lee sent Jackson with 26,000 on a long flank march to the federal right. In late afternoon on May 2, Jackson crushed the federal flank but in the hour of victory inadvertently was mortally wounded by his own men. Replacing Jackson, cavalryman Stuart continued the attack the following day. At the same time, Sedgwick routed Early's small command from the Fredericksburg heights and drove westward, a move that threatened to catch Lee's forces between the two halves of the federal army. Dazed by a blow to the head and already psychologically defeated, Hooker instead resolved to withdraw his army across the Rappahannock. Sensing that Hooker was beaten, Lee detached troops to halt Sedgwick while Stuart nudged more than twice his number of federals toward the river. Sedgwick crossed the Rappahannock on May 4, and Hooker followed with the remainder of the Army of the Potomac a day later. The Battle of Chancellorsville was Lee's masterpiece, but the cost of victory was high. Jackson would prove to be irreplaceable.

Lee's stunning victory at Chancellorsville ignited a wide-ranging debate on strategy within the Confederate high command. In the eastern theater, Hooker had been soundly thrashed, and if he followed normal patterns, he would not mount another offensive for some time. In the western theater, however, the Confederate situation was far less satisfactory. In Mississippi, Grant had successfully crossed to the east bank of the Mississippi and was maneuvering toward Vicksburg's rear. In central Tennessee, Rosecrans's Army of the Cumberland was showing signs of increased activity, forecasting a strong advance toward Chattanooga. Elsewhere, the federal naval blockade was beginning to pinch, and thousands of Confederate troops were tied down watching several coastal enclaves seized by the federals the previous year. Clearly, the Army of Northern Virginia needed to take action to relieve the pressure elsewhere, but the nature of that action remained debatable.

Lee Moves North

Lee argued that he could best assist other Confederate armies by again undertaking an open-ended invasion of the North. As in 1862, his troops could live off the abundant resources of the northern countryside, while war-ravaged northern Virginia was permitted to recover. Such an invasion might force the federals to withdraw troops from both Grant and Rosecrans, giving Johnston, Pemberton, and Bragg some relief. Further, a successful campaign in the North might improve the Confederacy's diplomatic position in Europe and at the same time lower Northern morale. Tempting as this strategy was, it was opposed by Longstreet, by now returned from Suffolk, and several influential members of the Confederate Congress. This group favored containing Hooker and the Army of the Potomac with as few troops as possible, while Lee took one corps west to join Bragg in crushing Rosecrans in central Tennessee. In turn, a victory there would force Grant to release his hold on Vicksburg and perhaps return Tennessee and Kentucky to the Southern cause. After lengthy discussions, President Davis, on June 16, approved Lee's plan for an invasion of

Maryland and Pennsylvania, momentarily quieting the critics.

In preparation for the advance, Lee organized his army's structure. For some time, Lee had operated with two large infantry corps under Jackson and Longstreet. Now that Jackson was dead, no successor of his stature was immediately apparent. Lee therefore divided his infantry and artillery into three corps under Longstreet and two newly promoted subordinates of Jackson, Lt. Gens. Richard S. Ewell and Ambrose P. Hill. Stuart retained command of the enlarged cavalry corps. When the reorganization was completed and troops were detached to secure Richmond, Lee had available approximately 76,000 troops and 272 guns. Even before Davis's final approval of the invasion, Lee prepared to resume the offensive. His preparations were momentarily stalled on June 9 when Maj. Gen. Alfred Pleasonton, the aggressive new cavalry leader of the Army of the Potomac, struck Stuart's cavalry corps at Brandy Station, Virginia. The resulting action quickly developed into the largest cavalry battle ever conducted in the Western Hemisphere. Eventually, Stuart chased the federals away, but they carried with them a new sense of self-assurance, and, even more important, some captured documents indicating that Lee's army was planning to move to the northwest soon.

The Confederate advance finally began on June 13, with Ewell's corps in the lead. Two days later, Ewell smashed the federal garrison at Winchester in the Shenandoah Valley, while cavalry units entered Maryland and Pennsylvania. As the main body of Lee's army gradually moved northward down the Shenandoah Valley, screened by Stuart's cavalry operating east of the Blue Ridge Mountains, Hooker followed cautiously with the Army of the Potomac. When Lee's intentions became clear, Hooker boldly proposed a quick strike toward Richmond, but Lincoln and Halleck rejected the idea in favor of keeping the federal army between Lee and Washington. On June 24, Lee's infantry corps were concentrated around Chambersburg, Pennsylvania, and Hagerstown, Maryland, while Hooker's army, although moving northward, was still in Virginia. Although the Army of the Potomac numbered more than 100,000 men, Hooker complained that he was outnumbered and continually asked for reinforcements. Three days later, the Army of Northern Virginia began to spread itself over southern Pennsylvania, while Hooker remained in Maryland, between Frederick and Hagerstown.

Battle of Gettysburg

As the two armies moved northward, Lincoln and Halleck became concerned that Hooker was losing his grip on the situation. When Hooker asked to evacuate the garrison at Harpers Ferry, Halleck refused, preferring instead to keep the post occupied as a threat to Lee's communications. In response, Hooker rashly offered his resignation as commander of the Army of the Potomac. Although possibly a bluff to gain greater freedom of action, Hooker's resignation was quickly accepted by Lincoln, who gave the command to Maj. Gen. George G. Meade, one of Hooker's corps commanders. Meade's mission was to find and fight Lee's army, while at the same time covering Washington and Baltimore. He soon learned that Stuart's cavalry was between the army of the Potomac and the capital. After screening the Confederate infantry movement to the Potomac, Stuart had been given permission to move northward by any route he chose, with the expectation that he would eventually rejoin Ewell's corps in Pennsylvania. Believing that the best but most daring way northward lay east of the Army of the Potomac, Stuart set out to regain the reputation tarnished by the fight at Brandy Station. Along the way, he caused some damage to Meade's logistics, but he was completely out of touch with Lee. Virtually without eyes, Lee's army remained scattered from Chambersburg to the Susquehanna River.

Lacking clear information on the location of his opponent, Lee ordered his army to concentrate in the Cashtown-Gettysburg area of Pennsylvania. Once concentrated, he could take a defensive stance if Meade moved against him, or he could threaten Meade's flank, if the Army of the Potomac moved against his line of communications. Slightly better informed about Lee's position, Meade probed gently northward while he tried to get a grip on his new command. Hoping to fight a defensive battle, he selected a tentative position along Pipe Creek in Maryland but was forced to advance beyond it when the Confederates did not accommodate his designs. On June 30, a Confederate brigade from Hill's corps entering Gettysburg met federal outposts and retired. This small event caused Hill to return to Gettysburg on July 1 in force. Northwest of the town, Hill's leading elements met strong resistance from Brig. Gen. John Buford's federal cavalrymen, and the battle was joined.

The Battle of Gettysburg, which resulted from the chance meeting of Hill's and Buford's troops, came to be the most famous battle of the war. On July 1, Hill's corps, then Ewell's, hastily concentrated north of the town, while federal infantry arriving from the south replaced Buford's cavalry. By nightfall, the attacking Confederates drove the federals through the town to a series of hills and ridges on its southern and eastern outskirts. On the second day, both sides continued to concentrate their scattered forces until Lee launched a massive attack on both federal flanks late in the day. Eventually halted after gaining some ground, the Confederates completed their concentration during the night. Finally, on July 3, Lee sent approximately 12,000 men forward in a desperate attempt to crack Meade's center. Known as Pickett's Charge, this assault failed disastrously. Thereafter, Lee assumed a defensive stance, which he continued the following day. To Lee's relief,

The Battle of Gettysburg

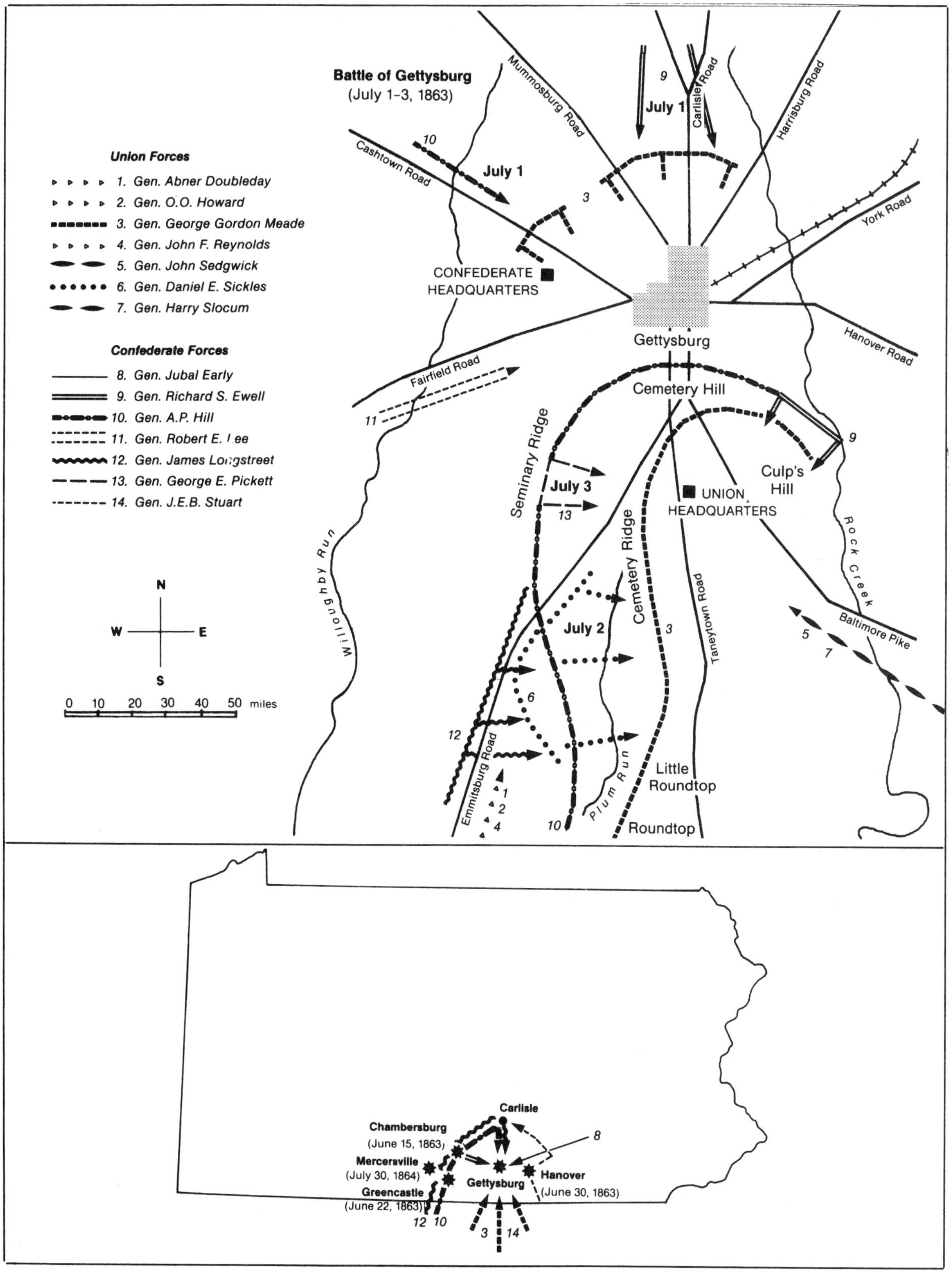

Battle of Gettysburg
(July 1-3, 1863)
Union Forces
1. Gen. Abner Doubleday
2. Gen. O.O. Howard
3. Gen. George Gordon Meade
4. Gen. John F. Reynolds
5. Gen. John Sedgwick
6. Gen. Daniel E. Sickles
7. Gen. Harry Slocum
Confederate Forces
8. Gen. Jubal Early
9. Gen. Richard S. Ewell
10. Gen. A.P. Hill
11. Gen. Robert E. Lee
12. Gen. James Longstreet
13. Gen. George E. Pickett
14. Gen. J.E.B. Stuart
N
W
E
S
0 10 20 30 40 50 miles
Mummosburg Road
Carlisle Road
Harrisburg Road
Cashtown Road
York Road
July 1
CONFEDERATE HEADQUARTERS
Gettysburg
Hanover Road
Fairfield Road
Cemetery Hill
Seminary Ridge
July 3
Culp's Hill
UNION HEADQUARTERS
Rock Creek
Willoughby Run
Cemetery Ridge
Taneytown Road
July 2
Baltimore Pike
Emmitsburg Road
Plum Run
Little Roundtop
Roundtop
Carlisle
Chambersburg
(June 15, 1863)
Mercersville
(July 30, 1864)
Greencastle
(June 22, 1863)
Gettysburg
Hanover
(June 30, 1863)

Meade also chose to remain inactive. That night, the Army of Northern Virginia began the long trek back to Virginia, with Meade following cautiously behind. When the rain-swollen Potomac forced a delay in Lee's crossing, Meade again missed an opportunity to strike a blow. On July 14, Lee successfully completed his escape to Virginia.

Aftermath of Gettysburg

The massive casualties suffered by both armies at Gettysburg caused Lee and Meade to proceed cautiously as the summer faded into fall. By mid-September the armies warily faced each other in the triangle of land between the Rappahannock and Rapidan rivers in north-central Virginia. Suddenly, events in the western theater caused a transfer of troops from both the Army of Northern Virginia and the Army of the Potomac. Rosecrans's long awaited advance against Bragg in late summer had caused the latter to face serious defeat around Chattanooga, Tennessee, unless reinforcements arrived quickly. Bragg's needs coincided perfectly with James Longstreet's desires, and on September 9, Davis authorized the temporary transfer of Longstreet's corps to Tennessee. With the aid of those troops, Bragg won a victory over Rosecrans at Chickamauga Creek in northern Georgia on September 20 and drove the Army of the Cumberland back into Chattanooga. Now it was the Union's turn to reinforce the western theater, and Meade received orders to send two corps from the Army of the Potomac to join the relief effort around the Tennessee city.

After all of the troop reductions had been completed, Lee was left with only 50,000 men to face Meade with 90,000. Ever one to seize the initiative, Lee responded with an advance in early October. Over the next few weeks, Lee and Meade maneuvered over a 40-mile expanse of territory with no decisive results. Except for a small but bloody Confederate repulse at Bristoe Station, there was little fighting. Eventually, the Confederate advance ended, and the process was reversed when Meade took the offensive in November. Finding Lee strongly entrenched behind Mine Run, Meade probed for a time, then called off the campaign on December 1. The two armies then went into winter quarters. Thus at the end of 1863, except for horrendous increases in the casualty lists, the situation in the eastern theater remained stalemated. Lee's second invasion of the North had been hurled back, but still another federal commander of the Army of the Potomac found himself no nearer to Richmond at the end of the year than at the beginning.

WESTERN THEATER: 1863

By the end of 1862, Grant had concluded that the overland route to Vicksburg was impractical. Any federal army moving by that route would have to be supplied by a long vulnerable rail line stretching southward from Columbus, Kentucky. Raids by Confederate cavalry could not be prevented, making the advancing army's supply line always subject to interdiction. With this fact in mind, Grant turned to the Mississippi River route, where the federal navy could guarantee a secure line of communications almost to Vicksburg itself. Further, as long as Grant remained inland, McClernand would command the army contingent on the river by right of seniority. Grant thus moved his headquarters to Memphis, Tennessee, on January 10. Only a two-day boat ride from Vicksburg, Memphis was a good place from which to supervise McClernand and make plans for a renewed advance against Vicksburg. Learning of Grant's arrival, McClernand angrily sent word to Lincoln that he and Grant could not both command the forces operating against Vicksburg. Moving downriver to the federal base at Milliken's Bend on January 30, Grant quietly assumed command, leaving McClernand to wait for Lincoln's reply, which never came.

Vicksburg Campaign

Grant found the federal army at Milliken's Bend to consist of 36,000 troops organized into three corps under Maj. Gens. McClernand, Sherman, and James B. McPherson. In simple terms, Grant's problem was how to move his army from the swamps along the Mississippi River onto the high ground in the vicinity of Vicksburg. North of the city, the vast delta region was a flooded morass, laced with small streams and bayous. Access through that region to the dry ground a few miles north of Vicksburg was blocked by heavy fortifications on the Yazoo River around Snyder's Bluff. Sherman had tried that route in December 1862 without success. South of Vicksburg, the high ground ran along the Mississippi's east bank, but reaching it involved a long journey through the swamps west of the river and naval assistance in crossing the stream. In turn, naval assistance could only be gained if vessels ran the gauntlet of fire along Vicksburg's waterfront. Clearly, Grant would have to master the inhospitable terrain before he could challenge Vicksburg's defenders.

The exact date on which Grant decided upon his final plan is uncertain. He may have selected the southern route as early as February 2, but he made no effort to implement it until much later. At any rate, he was unwilling to have his army remain idle in its flooded camps on the west bank of the Mississippi just a few miles upstream of its objective. To keep the troops busy while he waited for the weather to improve and the water to go down, Grant implemented several schemes over the next several weeks to place troops on the same high ground as the Confederates. The first effort consisted of digging a canal through the point of land opposite Vicksburg, thus bypassing the bend in the river on which the city sat. Begun in 1862, this project was never really viable, and the Confederates soon erected new batteries facing its projected exit. Second, some of Grant's troops cut the Mississippi levee far above Vicksburg at Lake Providence, creating a 400-mile channel back to the river 100 miles below Vicksburg. This project, too, proved unworkable. Third, another federal working party cut the Mississippi levee at Yazoo Pass 325 miles above Vicksburg to provide access to the Yazoo River and its bluffs north of the city. This circuitous route of 700 water miles showed some prospect of success until the expedition abruptly faced a small fortification known as Fort Pemberton. Unable to outflank the work and incapable of reducing it, the expedition stalled in mid-March. Fourth, a subsidiary operation up Steele's Bayou to relieve pressure on the Yazoo Pass contingent resulted in the Confederates nearly trapping several of the navy's ironclads.

By the end of March, all of Grant's alternatives to a southern approach to Vicksburg had failed. Disregarding the slanders and charges of incompetence that were published about him daily in Northern newspapers, Grant calmly set in motion his last, best plan as April began. Against the advice of everyone except McClernand, Grant ordered the bulk of his army to march southward through the flooded lowlands west of the river to a landing appropriately named Hard Times. The movement took an entire month to execute. To facilitate surprise, Grant implemented several diversionary movements while McClernand and McPherson marched their corps south. Sherman momentarily remained behind to demonstrate near the old battlefield of Chickasaw Bayou. In mid-April, Col. Benjamin Grierson raided southward from La Grange, Tennessee, through the entire length of Mississippi with a small cavalry force. Grierson's men wreaked havoc on railroads in the state, especially the east-west line connecting Vicksburg with the remainder of the Confederacy, before he rejoined federal forces at Baton Rouge, Louisiana. About the same time, Commodore David D. Porter took both ironclads and transports on a fiery night passage of the Vicksburg batteries.

From his headquarters at Jackson, Mississippi, Pemberton commanded nearly 60,000 troops, defending not only Vicksburg but northern Mississippi and Port Hudson, Louisiana, as well. Noting Grant's failures earlier in the year, Pemberton momentarily assumed that the federals would continue to operate against Vicksburg from the north. In early April, even as Grant's leading elements marched southward beyond the river, Pemberton concluded that Grant was detaching troops to send to Rosecrans in Tennessee, and he correspondingly began to transfer units to Bragg. Better intelligence caused him to change his mind in mid-April and recall the detachments, when suddenly Grierson's raid distracted him and seriously clouded his judgment. The raid, coupled with Sherman's demonstration at Chickasaw Bayou, caused Pemberton to lose track of what Grant's main body was doing. Therefore, he was not prepared to react when Grant suddenly appeared downstream of Vicksburg and joined Porter's squadron.

Denied his preferred landing site at Grand Gulf by Maj. Gen. John S. Bowen's garrison, Grant simply continued moving southward on the west bank of the river. Porter's gunboats then passed the Grand Gulf batteries, loaded Grant's troops, and put them ashore at Bruinsburg on April 30. Racing south from Grand Gulf, Bowen established a blocking position west of Port Gibson, Mississippi, where McClernand struck him on May 1. Heavily outnumbered, Bowen delayed the federals for most of a day, then safely extracted his small command. Rushing to Vicksburg from Jackson, Pemberton struggled to concentrate his scattered forces south of Vicksburg. Grant, meanwhile, seized Grand Gulf, moved a few miles inland, and paused for Sherman to join the main army. When Sherman arrived, Grant resumed his offensive on May 7, marching to the northeast. His goal was the railroad linking Vicksburg and Jackson, which he planned to reach near Edwards Station. To ease his logistical problems, Grant ordered his troops to forage widely in the countryside. Although he later claimed to have abandoned his supply line, in fact, Grant sustained himself throughout the campaign by a shuttle of wagons bringing hardtack and ammunition from the river.

When McPherson's corps encountered an aggressive Confederate brigade at Raymond on May 12, Grant turned eastward to deal with a new Confederate force concentrating near Jackson under J. E. Johnston. Believing the situation hopeless, Johnston evacuated Jackson and sent word for Pemberton to march eastward to join him. While Grant defeated Johnston's rear guard and entered Jackson, Pemberton was wracked by indecision. Fearful that his field force of 23,000 men would be cut off from Vicksburg if he moved farther east, Pemberton eventually decided to lunge southward toward Grant's line of communication. Begun on May 15, the Confederate thrust quickly collapsed because of poor staff work, bad weather, and dissension among the generals. In contrast, Grant methodically left Sherman to finish the destruction of Jackson and marched on Pemberton's position with his remaining two corps. The two armies collided at Champion Hill, just east of Edwards Station, on May 16, and after a hard fight, the federals drove Pemberton from the field. On the next day, the Confederate rear guard was routed at Big Black River, and Pemberton's dispirited army withdrew into the defenses of Vicksburg.

Siege of Vicksburg

Pursuing rapidly to the gates of Vicksburg, Grant, on May 19, attempted to carry the works by storm but was repulsed. Three days later, he ordered a deliberate attack by all three corps, but it also failed. Having seen for himself the strength of the defensive works, Grant began a siege. The federal base was transferred to Snyder's Bluff on the Yazoo

The Battle of Vicksburg, May 23–July 4, 1863

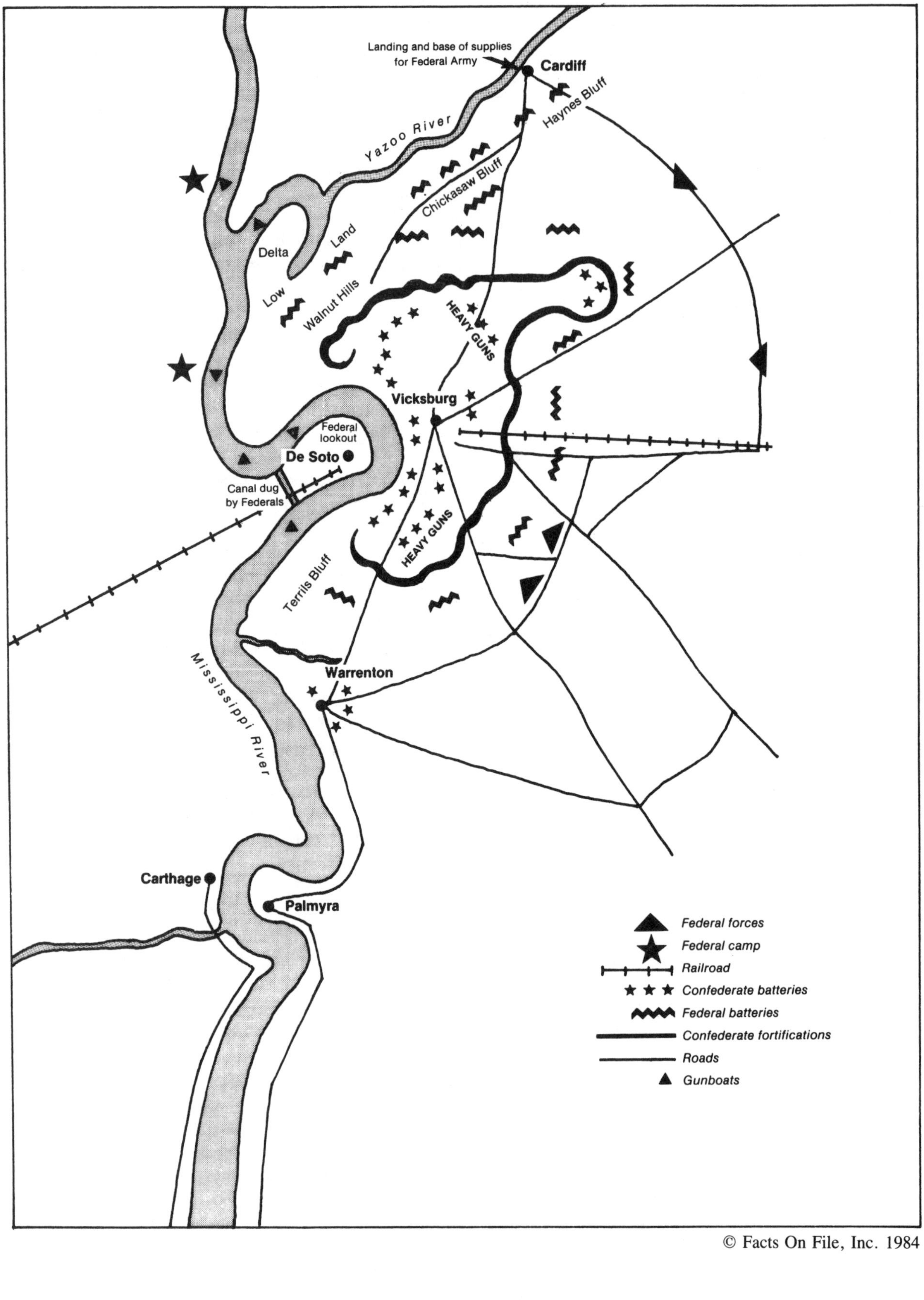
Landing and base of supplies for Federal Army
Cardiff
Haynes Bluff
Yazoo River
Chickasaw Bluff
Delta
Land
Low
Walnut Hills
HEAVY GUNS
Vicksburg
Federal lookout
De Soto
Canal dug by Federals
HEAVY GUNS
Terrils Bluff
Warrenton
Mississippi River
Carthage
Palmyra
Federal forces
Federal camp
Railroad
Confederate batteries
Federal batteries
Confederate fortifications
Roads
Gunboats

River, and reinforcements began to arrive daily. Inside the city, Pemberton could only husband his food and ammunition and hope for relief from the outside. As Johnston slowly gathered an army east of the Big Black River, Grant detached Sherman from the siege lines to block his approach. At the fortifications, the federals tried no more massive assaults, relying upon mining operations instead. By the end of June, Grant's besiegers had grown to 71,000 men, while Pemberton's 30,000 defenders grew weaker daily. Eventually, Johnston gathered 31,000 troops beyond the Big Black, but he never felt strong enough to intervene. At last, with no prospect of meaningful relief, Pemberton surrendered to Grant on July 4. When Port Hudson surrendered to a small federal army under Banks on July 9, the last Confederate bastion on the Mississippi River had fallen.

Union Achievements

Grant's dramatic success at Vicksburg and Meade's hard-won victory at Gettysburg in early July completely overshadowed an equally brilliant campaign by Rosecrans in central Tennessee. Having spent the previous six months encamped at Murfreesboro resting and refitting, Rosecrans's Army of the Cumberland finally began its advance on June 23. Meanwhile, Bragg had detached several units from the Army of Tennessee to assist Pemberton and Johnston in Mississippi. His remaining force occupied fortified camps at Tullahoma and Shelbyville with outposts defending a range of hills several miles to the northeast. In a masterful campaign of maneuver, Rosecrans feinted to Bragg's left, then deftly outflanked his right, causing the Confederates to withdraw hastily. Conducted in a series of torrential rainstorms, the federal offensive forced Bragg to evacuate most of Tennessee in only nine days and at a cost of fewer than 600 federal casualties. By July 4, Bragg had crossed the Tennessee River, halting around the railroad center of Chattanooga. Momentarily content, Rosecrans rested near Tullahoma for six weeks before resuming the offensive.

After Vicksburg, Grant proposed to move on Mobile, Alabama, while Rosecrans pursued Bragg, but Halleck vetoed the plan. Instead, just as in 1862, Grant was ordered to disperse his army on peripheral missions in Louisiana, Missouri, and Arkansas. When Rosecrans again advanced on August 16, he received no assistance from Grant's command. Rosecrans was promised aid from a small army under Burnside that was moving into eastern Tennessee from Kentucky. Burnside's goal was Knoxville, Tennessee, while Rosecrans focused upon Chattanooga. In two weeks, Rosecrans's Army of the Cumberland crossed the first range of mountains and reached the Tennessee River. Pausing only briefly to implement a deception plan, Rosecrans crossed the Tennessee at four places at the end of August. A few days later, as he began a wide-front advance to outflank Bragg's army at Chattanooga, Burnside's Army of the Ohio entered Knoxville. Fearing that he would be cut off from his railroad line to Atlanta, Georgia, Bragg evacuated Chattanooga without a fight on September 8, and elements of the Army of the Cumberland entered the city on the next day.

The serious threat to Bragg's army finally forced the Davis administration into action. Reinforcements were sent to the Army of Tennessee from Johnston's army in Mississippi, from eastern Tennessee, and from the Army of Northern Virginia. On the day that the federals entered Chattanooga, two divisions of James Longstreet's corps left Virginia to join Bragg via a roundabout rail route. Even before Longstreet's men arrived, Bragg decided to strike a counterblow. Believing that the Confederates were in wild retreat toward Atlanta, Rosecrans made no effort to concentrate his three scattered corps as they continued their pursuit through the mountains. On September 10, Bragg counterattacked, attempting to defeat part of Thomas's corps in detail. Foiled by indecisive subordinate leadership, Bragg tried on September 13 to catch another detached part of Rosecrans's army, Maj. Gen. Thomas L. Crittenden's corps. This effort also failed, primarily because of faulty intelligence. Disgusted with his commanders, Bragg decided to await the arrival of Longstreet's reinforcements. At last perceiving his danger, Rosecrans now scrambled to unite his army and withdraw it to Chattanooga.

Battle of Chickamauga

Learning that Longstreet was near, Bragg resolved to strike the federals before they could escape. A planned flanking movement launched north of Rosecrans's positions on September 18 ended in an engagement on the following day when Rosecrans inadvertently repositioned Thomas's corps into the path of the Confederates. The resulting battle along Chickamauga Creek lasted two days. Only half of Longstreet's men arrived in time to participate in the fight, giving Bragg approximately 65,000 men to Rosecrans's 62,000.

The first day ended in a bloody stalemate, and a coordinated Confederate attack on September 20 initially fared no better. When Rosecrans mistakenly pulled a division from his line to close a nonexistent gap, three Confederate divisions swept through the hole, routing the right wing of the federal army. Although Rosecrans and two corps commanders deserted the field, Thomas and two-thirds of the army stood firm. Anchoring his right on the high ground of Snodgrass Hill, Thomas held his position until dark with the assistance of some reserves who marched to the sound of the guns. That evening, he withdrew to Rossville, Georgia. After waiting there for a day, the Army of the Cumberland fell back into Chattanooga. This time, the Confederates were slow to pursue a beaten foe.

Tennessee Campaigns, February 1863–December 1864

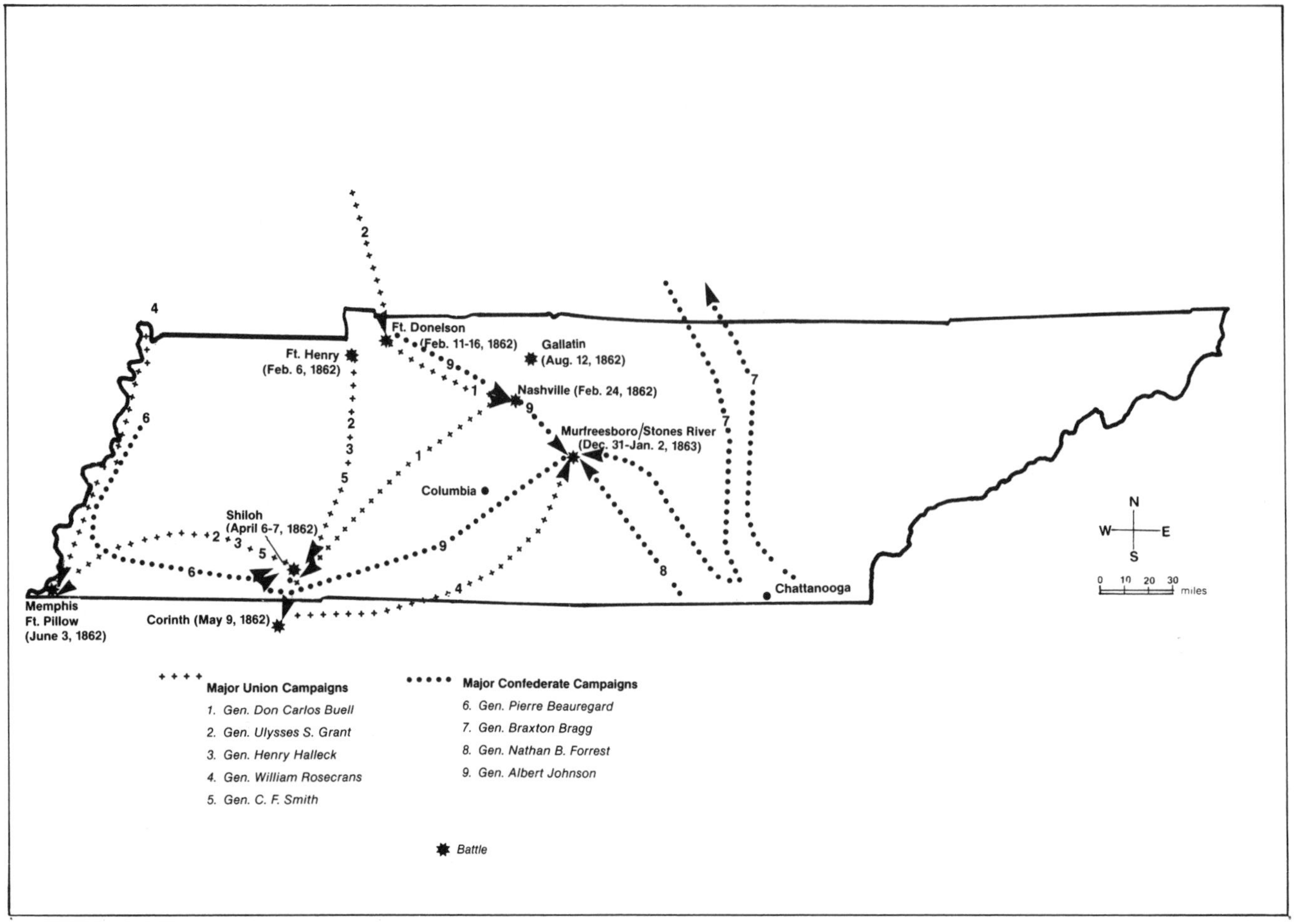

Chattanooga Campaign

After several days, the Army of Tennessee approached Chattanooga and began a siege. Because of the configuration of the Tennessee River and the surrounding mountains, the Confederates were able to interdict every route to Chattanooga except one, a 60-mile detour over Walden's Ridge to the federal base at Bridgeport, Alabama. The Army of the Cumberland could neither retreat over the route nor be satisfactorily supplied by it. Unwilling to see Rosecrans's army starve, the Lincoln administration rapidly mobilized support from other armies. As already described, two corps commanded by Hooker rushed west by rail from the Army of the Potomac. Another large contingent rapidly moved east from Vicksburg under Sherman. Most important of all, Grant received command of all troops in the western theater on October 17. Believing that Rosecrans's nerve was shot, Grant relieved him and elevated Thomas to lead the Army of the Cumberland. On October 23, Grant himself visited Chattanooga.

Grant's first task was to open a secure supply line to the besieged army. In late October, a combined thrust by some of Thomas's troops from Chattanooga and Hooker's from the west opened the "Cracker Line" to Bridgeport. When a weak effort by Longstreet to interrupt the federal line failed, Bragg lost patience with his contentious subordinate. Long plagued by dissension among his senior generals, Bragg had already relieved three commanders for poor conduct in the Chickamauga Campaign. Now he seized upon the opportunity to rid himself of Longstreet, offering him the chance to take his command north to drive Burnside from Knoxville. Longstreet's departure with 20,000 men left Bragg with 40,000 to continue the siege of Chattanooga. Meanwhile, Grant bided his time until Sherman arrived with several divisions from the Vicksburg army. By November 23, Sherman was in position, giving Grant 61,000 men in and around the city.

On November 24, Grant ordered Hooker to capture Lookout Mountain, a critical piece of terrain overlooking the city. Hooker easily accomplished his mission in the poetically named "Battle above the Clouds." Bragg then concentrated his army atop Missionary Ridge, which also rose above Chattanooga. Grant's plan next called for a double envelopment of the Confederate position by Sherman and Hooker while Thomas's Army of the Cumberland fixed Bragg's attention on his center. When the enveloping columns failed to make headway, Grant ordered Thomas to relieve pressure on the others by seizing the foot of Missionary Ridge. Eager to erase the stigma of Chickamauga, the Army of the Cumberland took its assigned objective; then, without further orders, it continued to the top of the ridge. Cracking Bragg's line in the center, Thomas's troops drove the Confederates from Missionary Ridge in disarray. Bragg's army fled into the mountains beyond Ringgold, Georgia, where an effective rearguard action halted federal pursuit.

Rather than continue the campaign into the mountains, Grant elected to halt most of his command in Chattanooga for the winter. He did send a relief expedition under Sherman toward Knoxville, where Longstreet had laid siege to the hapless Burnside and the Army of the Ohio. No better at sieges than Bragg and equally maladroit in his relationships with subordinates, Longstreet, on December 4, withdrew into the mountains of eastern Tennessee before Sherman could arrive. His departure ended major campaigning in the western theater for the remainder of 1863.

Unlike the stalemate in the eastern theater at year's end, the Union cause had reason for celebration in the West. On the Mississippi River front, the Confederacy had been lopped into two parts, never to be reassembled, and Northern commerce could once more flow unfettered to the Gulf of Mexico. Equally important to the prosecution of the war, the position won by Grant's army at Chattanooga in November represented an excellent starting point for a federal drive through the Appalachian barrier into the heart of the Confederacy.

7

The Civil War: 1864–1865

In January 1864, after two and one half years of war, after thousands of deaths and the expenditure of millions of dollars, few people in the North or South could see the end of the conflict. For much of the North, with its far larger population base and vast resources, the situation on the homefront remained business as usual, although the high casualty lists often reminded the citizens of the price required to restore the Union. In contrast, the South expended a far greater proportion of its meager resources for the war effort, but even there, some people managed to avoid doing their parts for the cause of independence. For both belligerents, the flush of patriotism so evident in 1861 no longer served to keep the ranks full, and conscription, by necessity, had been introduced by 1863. Willingness to suffer for a cause still motivated many soldiers on both sides, but few of the conscripts showed the same spirit as the volunteers of 1861. With the three-years enlistment of many Northern regiments about to expire, various inducements were offered to prevent the federal armies from withering away, and enough men succumbed to the pressure to ensure that a hard core of Union veterans would remain to finish the job. Confederates, who enlisted for the duration of the conflict, were offered no such rewards, but their government managed to find enough good men to continue the fight a while longer.

No longer able to mount a credible offensive punch, Confederate armies in both the eastern and western theaters could only hope to parry the Union's blows until war weariness in the North led either to recognition of Southern independence or some kind of negotiated settlement. Such prospects were not totally implausible because 1864 was an election year in the North, and, except for military achievements along the Mississippi River and in Tennessee, the Lincoln administration had little to show for the vast sums of treasure and soldiers' blood so far expended. Union commanders needed to continue to show positive results on the battlefield to improve Lincoln's chances for reelection and suppress the clamor of those willing to settle for less than complete restoration of the Union. Many federal generals had proven unequal to that task, and the foremost of them, George B. McClellan, would win the Democratic party's nomination for president and oppose Abraham Lincoln in the fall elections. Well aware that he needed victories in 1864, Lincoln, therefore, turned to the man who had given him victories in the western theater, Ulysses S. Grant.

Early in January 1864, Lincoln requested Grant to comment on possible strategies for Union forces in the eastern theater. Seemingly a simple request for information, this communication was actually Lincoln's final test of the man he had decided should lead all the armies of the Union. Called to Washington, Grant was promoted to the new rank of lieutenant general on March 12 and made general in chief, replacing Maj. Gen. Henry W. Halleck, who now became Grant's chief of staff. Grant was given the responsibility for formulating a strategy that would bring the war to a successful conclusion for the North in the shortest possible time. While Grant's earlier tactical thinking had been quite innovative, upon reaching Washington, he became quite conventional in his strategic formulations. In final form, his basic ideas were quite simple: First, the principle of concentration must be rigidly observed. No longer could the Union afford to scatter troops widely through areas of only marginal importance to the main effort; now, its units must be consolidated into a few powerful striking forces. Second, there must be close coordination among those striking forces in order to extend Confederate armies beyond their breaking points. In short, Union power would be both concentrated and coordinated, and the Confederacy would be overwhelmed.

Major Battles of the Civil War, 1864–1865

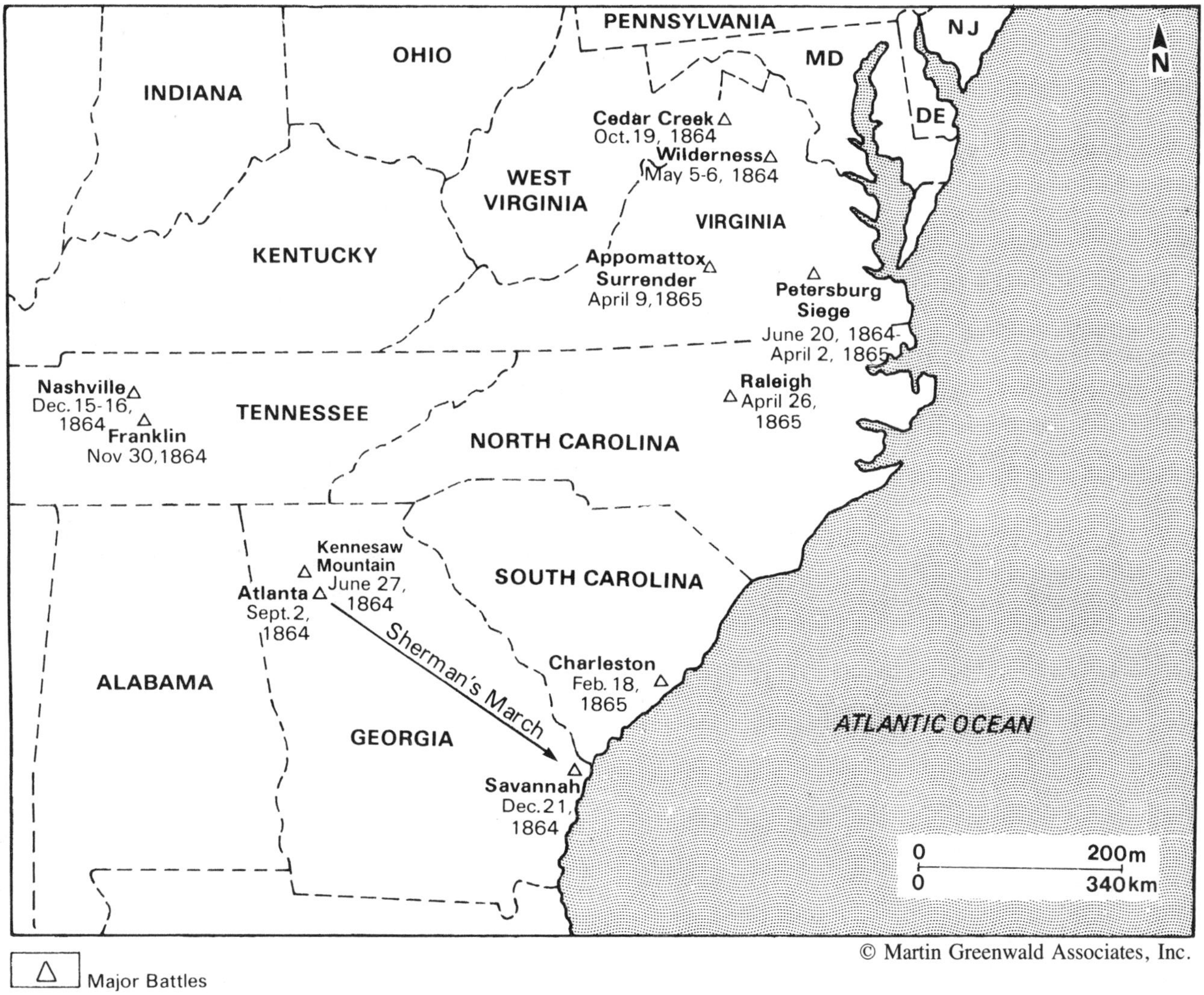

In specific terms, Grant proposed that there be two major concentrations of power, one in each major theater. In the eastern theater, George G. Meade's Army of the Potomac, reinforced by Ambrose Burnside's corps, would mount a drive overland toward Richmond along the route so often trod by failed federal commanders. Grant himself would travel with Meade's army. In the western theater, Maj. Gen. William T. Sherman would operate from Chattanooga toward Atlanta, with the combined Armies of the Tennessee, the Cumberland, and the Ohio. Supporting these two major drives were three subsidiary offensives. From Fortress Monroe, Maj. Gen. Benjamin F. Butler would lead the Army of the James up its namesake river to Richmond's back door. In the Shenandoah Valley, Maj. Gen. Franz Sigel would deny that region's produce to the Confederacy and prevent the valley from being used as an invasion corridor against Washington. Finally, Maj. Gen. Nathaniel P. Banks was to attempt to take Mobile, Alabama, with a small army. Of the three smaller operations, Grant considered Butler's to be the most significant, representing the left wing of his grand coalition, while Meade represented the center and Sherman the right. All five operations, major and minor, were to begin on receipt of a common signal from Grant, which would be given some time in early May.

EASTERN THEATER: 1864

When he joined the Army of the Potomac, Grant found it to be in good condition. The command consisted of three infantry corps under Maj. Gens. Winfield S. Hancock, Gouverneur K. Warren, and John Sedgwick; one cavalry corps under Maj. Gen. Philip H. Sheridan; and Major General Burnside's infantry corps, which was loosely associated with the army but not technically a part of it.

Counting Burnside's troops, the army numbered approximately 119,000 men. Major General Meade, the victor of Gettysburg, still commanded the army, although his relationship to Grant was as yet unclear. None of the officers was certain if Grant would really command the army, making Meade simply a conduit for orders, or if he would content himself with the strategic direction of the war, leaving Meade to be the commander of the Army of the Potomac. Grant was known to generals and privates alike only by the reputation he had won in the western theater. While that reputation was good, John Pope's had also been good before he faced Robert E. Lee and the Army of Northern Virginia.

Grant's plan required Meade's army to seek out the Army of Northern Virginia and destroy it by any means possible. The best way to accomplish the task was to disrupt Lee's communications with Richmond. If that could be done, Grant reasoned that Lee would be forced to respond with a fight, which Grant believed he could win. If the armies maneuvered, Grant anticipated always moving to Lee's right or eastern flank. Such a movement would ease the federal logistic burden by keeping the Army of the Potomac always within reach of a succession of supply bases established on Virginia's coastal rivers and protected by the navy. Aiding Grant's movements as he approached the Confederate capital would be the Army of the James under Butler, which was to seize a base as far up the James River as possible, then operate against Richmond from the south while the Army of the Potomac approached it from the north. Grant apparently believed he could easily defeat Lee or outmaneuver him, because he planned to unite Meade's army with Butler's outside Richmond within 10 days of the opening of the campaign.

Maj. Gen. George Meade, commander of the Army of the Potomac and the victor at Gettysburg, became subordinate to Grant, who was brought east to become the Union's general in chief. (National Archives)

Pres. Abraham Lincoln, up for reelection in 1864, needed Union victories to ensure his political victory over former chief of the Army of the Potomac, George B. McClellan, the Democratic party's presidential candidate. (U.S. Army Military History Institute)

Battle of the Wilderness

On May 4, the Army of the Potomac left its winter camps and crossed the Rapidan River, inaugurating the spring campaign. Lee's army lay to the west, beyond the tangled second-growth forest known as the Wilderness, where Union general Joseph Hooker had come to grief one year earlier. Grant hoped to move rapidly enough to pass through the Wilderness before Lee could react to the threat to his right flank. Unfortunately for the federals, even after rigorous clearing of the forest trails, the wagon train accompanying the army was too large and cumbersome to pass through the Wilderness in one day. Consequently, Hancock's and Warren's corps halted in the Wilderness to protect the passage of the train. This delay gave Lee the opportunity he needed to strike the Army of the Potomac in the Wilderness, where its numerical advantage in both men and guns would be negated. Lee himself had only 64,000 men, and when Grant's advance was reported, they were widely scattered. Nevertheless, Lee ordered the Army of Northern Virginia into action before the opportunity to fight in the constricted environment of the Wilderness was lost. Lt. Gen. Richard S. Ewell's corps led the way, followed closely by Lt. Gen. Ambrose P. Hill's. Now returned from East Tennessee, Lt. Gen. James Longstreet's corps lay farthest from the point of conflict and was unable to arrive for some time.

When Ewell's infantrymen stumbled onto some of Warren's troops early on the morning of May 5, the senior commanders on both sides had no idea of their enemy's dispositions. Yet they continued to move units forward into the forest to develop the situation. While Ewell battled Warren, Hill approached Hancock but was restrained by Lee, who wanted to await the arrival of Longstreet. In turn, Hancock attacked Hill but was repulsed. Both armies now proceeded to entrench in the woods, which had caught fire in places. By now aware that he was engaged in a major battle, Grant mounted a series of attacks on May 6 that threatened to break Hill's line, but the fortuitous arrival of Longstreet prevented a Confederate defeat. Lee now threw Longstreet's corps around the federal left flank in a successful attack on Hancock. At a critical moment, Longstreet was wounded by his own men in a manner reminiscent of Jackson's fate nearby in 1863, and the Confederate assault ground to a halt. On the following day, both armies rested and attempted to evacuate the wounded from the burning woods. All wondered what Grant would do now. Losses on both sides had been appalling, and previously, such battles had required a long pause for the armies to rejuvenate themselves.

Grant did not believe that such a breathing spell was warranted following the Battle of the Wilderness. Seeing no profit in a resumption of frontal attacks on Lee's entrenchments, however, Grant ordered Meade to put his troops in motion on the night of May 7 in a southeasterly direction toward Spotsylvania Courthouse. Lee anticipated Grant's decision, believing that the federals would push southward to more open territory beyond the Confederate right flank. To counter the federal move, Lee ordered Maj. Gen. Richard H. Anderson, who had replaced the wounded Longstreet, to pull his corps out of line and, after a brief rest, march southward to block the federal approach to Spotsylvania. When he reached his assigned rest area, Anderson discovered that the woods were on fire, so he began the march early. This simple decision ensured that Anderson would reach Spotsylvania Courthouse before Warren's corps. On May 8, Warren encountered Anderson's men blocking the road northwest of the village, and another clash between the armies was set in motion.

Grant's Offensive

By this stage of the war, troops had learned the virtues of entrenching, and they proceeded to do so whenever they halted for more than a few minutes. After the initial federal probing attacks failed to gain ground, both armies began to throw up defensive works and bring forward reinforcements. This process continued on May 9, and by the end of the day, the Confederate line was almost four miles long. Shaped by diverse circumstances, including location of the initial clashes and the roll of the terrain, the Confederate line traced a crooked, inverted V enclosing Spotsylvania Courthouse. From behind that line, Lee's 56,000 troops faced Grant's 101,000. The apex of the salient in the middle of the line, the most unsatisfactory and vulnerable portion of the defenses, was occupied by Ewell's corps. During a day of otherwise desultory firing by pickets, Sedgwick, one of Meade's corps commanders, was killed by a Confederate sharpshooter. He was replaced by Maj. Gen. Horatio G. Wright.

On May 10, the Army of the Potomac resumed its attacks. All but one of the assaults were conventional in their tactical formations and failed to penetrate the Confederate works. The exception was an attack on the west face of the salient now coming to be known as the "Mule Shoe." Led by Col. Emory Upton, that attack was conducted in a column of short, heavy lines instead of the long, thin lines then in vogue. Upton's men broke Ewell's lines, but when promised supporting units did not arrive, the federals were ejected from their gains. Nevertheless, the new tactical form showed enough promise to be tried on a larger scale two days later by Hancock's corps. Aided by a fog and the ill-timed withdrawal of some Confederate artillery, Hancock's attack on May 12 cracked the salient just as Upton had done earlier, gaining two Confederate generals and several thousand prisoners. Lee counterattacked vigorously, driving the federals back to the line of works at the apex of the Mule Shoe. There, the combatants traded blows literally at arms length for the remainder of the day. This fight for the "Bloody Angle" was perhaps unique in the war for its prolonged intensity. Ultimately, Lee's counterattack permitted the construction of a new defense line behind the salient, to which his troops withdrew after dark.

For the next several days, each side probed for weaknesses and extended its lines. Gradually, Grant transferred most of his forces to his left flank, extending his trenches slowly in that direction. Lee countered with extensions of his own works to meet the federals. After a federal attack on May 18 and a Confederate counterattack on the next day were repulsed with no gain, both commanders clearly saw that little more could be accomplished at Spotsylvania.

Forced by circumstances to remain on the defensive, Lee was content to repulse federal assaults, but Grant needed to show progress to maintain morale and to justify his growing casualty lists. On the night of May 20, Grant

Confederate cavalry leader Jeb Stuart's colorful career ended with his death at Yellow Tavern in May 1864 while opposing Philip Sheridan's Union cavalry. (Library of Congress)

ordered Hancock's corps to leave the trenches and resume the march to the southeast. When the remainder of the Army of the Potomac gave indications of preparing to follow Hancock, Lee started his own forces south, thus ending the Battle of Spotsylvania Courthouse. During the period that the two main armies had contended at that location, their respective cavalry commanders, Sheridan and Maj. Gen. Jeb Stuart, had conducted a running battle almost to Richmond. Sheridan's thrust was unable to penetrate the Richmond defenses, but during its course, Stuart was mortally wounded at Yellow Tavern on May 11.

Unwilling to leave Hancock unsupported for long, Grant soon joined him with the remainder of the federal army and continued southward. Using more direct roads, Lee once more got in front of Grant at the North Anna River, where he took up defensive positions behind the stream on May 22. The Army of the Potomac arrived on the following day and probed Lee's defenses until May 26 without finding an opening. Cleverly, Lee had again drawn a defensive line in an inverted V, but this time the apex of the V rested on the North Anna. Any federal movement from one flank to another would require crossing the river twice, while the Confederates labored under no such handicap. At this point, Lee's health momentarily failed, preventing a Confederate counterstroke before Grant realized that the North Anna was no place for him to fight a battle. As a result, Grant resumed his crablike motion to the southeast, while Lee followed him on the inside track.

Cold Harbor

This time, Grant marched only a few miles before again encountering the Army of Northern Virginia along Totopotomoy Creek northeast of Richmond. Grant probed Lee's defenses for several day's but found no openings worth an assault. Using Sheridan's cavalry as a spearhead, Grant once more marched southeastward, toward a crossroads known as Old Cold Harbor. The advance guards of the two armies met on June 1, inaugurating the Battle of Cold Harbor. Armed with breechloading, repeating carbines, Sheridan's troopers held their own against Anderson's infantrymen but were unable to drive back the Confederates. As the remainder of the two armies appeared and extended the hasty entrenchments already begun by the first arrivals, the battle lines solidified. To replenish their heavy losses, both armies now received reinforcements from unexpected sources, because the two subsidiary federal campaigns in the eastern theater had failed to achieve their objectives.

The first of these failed federal offensives was that of Sigel in the Shenandoah Valley. As commander of the Department of West Virginia, Sigel was ordered by Grant to demonstrate against Confederate forces in southwestern Virginia and the Shenandoah Valley, preventing them from reinforcing Lee's army. Subordinates successfully raided into southwestern Virginia, cutting the Virginia & Tennessee Railroad, while Sigel advanced southward up the valley from Winchester with 6,500 men. He was met at the small village of New Market by Maj. Gen. John C. Breckinridge with 5,000 men, including the 247-man student body of the Virginia Military Institute. On May 15, while Grant was stalled at Spotsylvania, Breckinridge attacked the federals and routed them. As Sigel's troops streamed northward in retreat, their commander was relieved on May 19. Breckinridge, meanwhile, left the valley to join the Army of Northern Virginia with 2,500 men.

Initially, Butler's secondary campaign in the lower James River valley showed prospects of success. Convoyed upriver from Fortress Monroe by the navy, Butler landed the Army of the James on May 5 at Bermuda Hundred, a peninsula bounded by the James and Appomattox rivers just 16 miles south of Richmond. As Butler understood his mission, he was first to seize a secure base south of Richmond, then advance slowly toward the city, breaking Confederate supply lines and diverting reinforcements from the Army of Northern Virginia. If all went well, Butler's and Meade's armies would meet somewhere near Richmond approximately 10 days after the campaign began. Unfortunately for the federals, Butler's view of the mission did not quite

Virginia Campaigns, 1864–1865

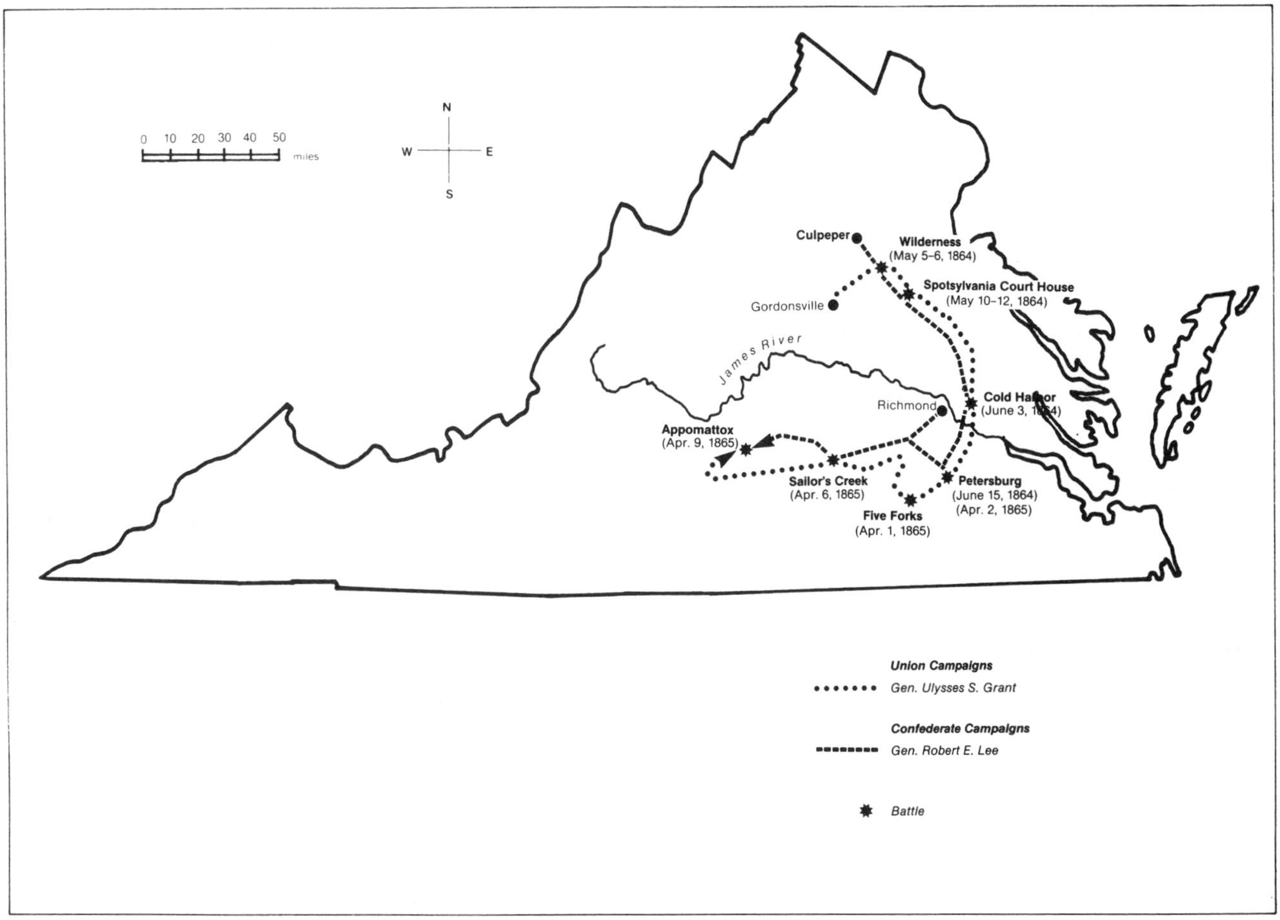

correspond with Grant's, although the two officers had held face-to-face discussions on the subject. Grant agreed that a base must be secured, but he placed greater emphasis on an early advance upon Richmond than did Butler. Grant verbally noted the importance of Petersburg, but he clearly specified Richmond as Butler's goal. Because Butler was inexperienced in field command, Grant gave him two professional soldiers as corps commanders, Maj. Gens. William F. Smith and Quincy A. Gillmore. The strength of the Army of the James was slightly more than 40,000 men.

In the meantime, Pres. Jefferson Davis's departmental system made the defense of Richmond's southern flank a cooperative effort between Maj. Gen. Robert Ransom's Department of Richmond and Gen. P. G. T. Beauregard's Department of North Carolina and Southern Virginia. Ransom guarded the area immediately around Richmond, while Beauregard controlled the territory south of Petersburg. Neither commander was clearly responsible for the 30-square-mile Bermuda Hundred peninsula between the two cities. Ransom's small garrison included numerous militia formations, while Beauregard had approximately 13,500 men scattered throughout North Carolina and southern Virginia. Watching the federal force at Hampton Roads growing daily, Beauregard begged the Davis administration for reinforcements throughout April and early May. The pleas were either rejected or disregarded, with all reinforcements going to Lee's army instead. Troops continually passed through Beauregard's department from the south en route to the Army of Northern Virginia, but Beauregard was forbidden to interfere with their passage.

Landing at the seam of the two Confederate departments, Butler pushed inland for several miles to a point where the peninsula narrowed, an ideal place for establishing a defensive line. While some troops constructed fortifications, Butler sent several expeditions a few miles westward to break the Richmond & Petersburg Railroad, critical to Richmond's and Lee's supply situation. When these expeditions were blocked by troops Beauregard commandeered from the reinforcement stream, Butler paused to wait for Grant. Upon receiving false information that Grant's army was nearing Richmond, Butler moved north on May 12 with a little more than 18,000 troops, leaving the remainder of his force to garrison the Bermuda Hundred enclave. After capturing an outer defense line, Butler halted in front of an even more formidable line of works near Drewry's Bluff to await Grant's arrival. Beauregard, meanwhile, had amassed a striking force of 17,500 men. On the morning of May 16, Beauregard's troops struck the right flank of the Army of the James in a thick fog and crushed it, but Butler was able to extricate his army and return it safely to Bermuda Hundred. Beauregard closely followed the retreating Army of the James to its fortifications and soon constructed a similar line across the peninsula.

Contrary to Grant's view that the Army of the James was "bottled up," Butler still had offensive options. His best chance of success lay in exploiting his foothold at City Point south of the Appomattox River to mount a new drive on the railroad center of Petersburg. He was preparing to implement just such an offensive with Smith's corps on May 29 when Grant ordered Smith's men to join the Army of the Potomac in the vicinity of Cold Harbor. Influenced by his staff, Grant had decided that Butler's command was not serving any purpose commensurate with its strength and that most of Butler's troops should join Meade's army. Instead of attacking Petersburg with an excellent chance of success, Smith's troops boarded transports that took them down the James, then up the York and Pamunkey rivers to White House, from whence they marched overland to Cold Harbor. Even before Smith's departure, Lee had begun to strip Beauregard's command of troops to replace his own horrendous losses. Thus, the Bermuda Hundred front momentarily lapsed into inactivity.

Smith's corps landed on May 31, but poorly written orders kept him from joining Grant until the following day. Grant now had approximately 100,000 men to throw against Lee's 40,000. Willing briefly to abandon his flanking marches to Lee's right, Grant decided instead to launch a frontal attack to penetrate Lee's front and drive the Army of Northern Virginia into the Chickahominy River. Early on the morning of June 3, Hancock's, Wright's, and Smith's corps advanced to the attack. The Confederate position had not been reconnoitered, nor had other elementary precautions been taken. The result was a slaughter of the three federal corps and utter failure to achieve a breakthrough in the face of the defensive firepower of Lee's heavily entrenched veterans. Nevertheless, the assaulting force refused to abandon the few yards of ground it had won at such great cost and entrenched within hailing distance of the Confederate lines. Heavy skirmishing and even heavier digging now occupied both armies until June 12, but there were no more massive assaults by either side.

The month of almost continuous fighting from the Wilderness to Cold Harbor represented a new development in the military history of the Civil War. Previously, armies in both theaters had maneuvered for some time, then fought a battle, and finally separated for a period of rest and recuperation before the next encounter. In contrast, Grant's overland campaign was marked by close contact between the combatants for an extended period of time. Casualties in the series of engagements, both large and small, had been extremely high. By the middle of June, Grant had lost 55,000 men, almost the same number with which Lee had begun the campaign. Lee himself had suffered losses of 40,000 men. In terms of results, Grant was still unable to sever Lee's line of communications or destroy the Army of Northern Virginia. In fact, the Army of the Potomac was not yet as near to Richmond as it had been under McClellan two years before. Yet Lee could take little comfort in his success. The quintessential offensive-minded general, Lee could mount no more sweeping campaigns of maneuver in the face of Grant's tenacity. Nor could Lee's army continue to take such continual pounding. Grant's losses could be and were replaced, while Lee's could be only partially renewed. In a campaign of attrition, Lee must inevitably lose; it would only be a question of time.

Lee's Countermoves

Well aware of the odds against him, Lee nevertheless was unwilling to await his fate passively. Because the federal troops in the Shenandoah Valley were again on the offensive, this time under Maj. Gen. David Hunter, Lee had been forced to detach Breckinridge's division to counter them. On June 5, Hunter had defeated Confederate forces at Piedmont, Virginia, and had occupied the city of Staunton. A few days later, he continued his advance to Lexington, where he burned the Virginia Military Institute. When Breckinridge reached the valley, he found Hunter too strong for him to face alone, and he appealed for reinforcements. Seeing in Breckinridge's plea a much larger opportunity, Lee determined to send Lt. Gen. Jubal A. Early, who had replaced Ewell, and his corps to the valley. Lee hoped that Early's and Breckinridge's combined forces could defeat Hunter, then reprise Stonewall Jackson's campaign down the valley. By threatening Washington from the valley, Jackson had diverted large numbers of federal troops from a drive on Richmond. Perhaps Early could do the same thing and reverse an even more threatening situation than in 1862. On June 12, Early and 13,000 veterans quietly left their trenches and headed west.

On the very day that Lee detached Early, Grant also acted to break the stalemate around Cold Harbor. In a bolder move than previously attempted, he decided to march rapidly southward to the James River, cross it on a pontoon bridge, and strike toward the railroad center of Petersburg. To work successfully, the plan required that Lee be completely fooled as to Grant's intentions. If Lee discovered the movement while it was in progress, the Army of the Potomac could be caught astride either the Chickahominy or the James, with disastrous consequences. On the night of June 12, the movement began with Hancock's and Wright's corps falling back a short distance to a more easily defensible line while Smith's corps returned to its transports at White House. Meanwhile, Warren's corps swung southward beyond Lee's right in what ap-

Lt. Gen. Ulysses S. Grant (seated, left) *meets with his staff at City Point, Virginia, a major Union staging area, in June 1864.* (Library of Congress)

peared to be Grant's normal flanking movement. Once Warren was in place, the remainder of the Army of the Potomac left its trenches and passed behind Warren en route to the James River.

Upon learning of Warren's advance, Lee concluded that the federals simply were making another short left hook to outflank his trenches. Taking the bait, Lee responded by moving the Army of Northern Virginia southward to the vicinity of Malvern Hill, where he confronted Warren on June 13. Believing that he faced the entire Army of the Potomac, Lee waited for Grant's attack. Meanwhile, the bulk of Grant's army continued its march toward the James. Once Lee was fixed in place, Warren abandoned his trenches and marched to join the remainder of Grant's army. To prevent Lee from discovering the ruse until it was too late, federal cavalrymen occupied Warren's works as long as possible. On June 14, while Smith's transports docked at Bermuda Hundred with his corps and other transports ferried Hancock's corps across the James, Grant's engineers accomplished a great bridge-building feat. Built by 450 men in eight hours, the bridge was 2,100 feet long, accommodated a 4-foot tidal rise, and contained a swing-span to permit the passage of transports. On June 15, Burnside's and Warren's corps began to cross the James on the bridge. Although Lee remained badly fooled about Grant's location, Beauregard at Bermuda Hundred had a much clearer picture of the federal activity, and he began to call loudly for reinforcements.

Grant's plan called for Smith's and Hancock's corps to assault Petersburg's defenses early on June 15. Believing that the operation would be a simple one, Grant elected to remain in the rear handling correspondence while Meade directed the attack. Meade, however, had grown accustomed to Grant's close supervision of every move he made, and he was, to a degree, unequal to the task. To complicate matters, Smith took an engineer's approach to field operations instead of an infantryman's and delayed for much of the day making a reconnaissance of the Confederate defense line. At the same time, Hancock's corps was hindered by poor maps, badly phrased orders, and Hancock's illness. At Petersburg, Beauregard had only 2,400 men, with the closest reinforcements being an additional 5,000 at Bermuda Hundred. Smith's corps alone numbered 16,000 men, and Hancock's nearly as many. Yet Smith spent the day in surveying the Confederate positions from afar and did not begin his assault until nearly nightfall. The federals easily penetrated the Confederate line and secured a long section of it, but Smith and Hancock decided that the lateness of the hour precluded further action on that day.

The federal delay on the evening of June 15 had far-reaching consequences. With defeat imminent, Beauregard boldly abandoned the Bermuda Hundred lines and moved the troops into a hastily constructed line nearer Petersburg. For the next two days, Grant's army hammered at Petersburg's defenders. The Confederates were forced to give ground on each day, but every night, they managed to cobble another defensive line. Finally, on June 18, Lee and the Army of Northern Virginia began to arrive at Petersburg and relieve Beauregard's beleaguered troops. En route, Lee's men also regained the Confederate defense line at Bermuda Hundred, which had been gingerly occupied by Butler's Army of the James. Tardy though it was, Lee's arrival at Petersburg meant that the federal opportunity to end the stalemate had passed momentarily, and trench warfare would begin again. For Beauregard and Butler, the arrival of the principal armies and their commanders meant that their days of independent command were also at an end, and both secondary armies were eventually subsumed into Lee's and Grant's commands.

Battle of Petersburg

Petersburg had become the target for Grant's operations because of its strategic importance to the Confederacy's railroad network in the eastern theater. At the beginning of the war, four railroads funneled into Petersburg and joined into a single line running northward to Richmond. By 1864, only two of those four lines had any importance, but they were vital to the movement of supplies to both the Confederate capital and the Army of Northern Virginia. Most important of all was the Petersburg Railroad, which ran due south to the town of Weldon, North Carolina. From Weldon, another line continued southward to the Confederacy's last remaining port of any significance, Wilmington, North Carolina. If Petersburg could be taken or the railroads around it severed, Richmond would have only one other tenuous link to the states south of Virginia. Thus, the battles that developed around Petersburg had railroads as their points of contention. Such was the case on June 22 when Grant sent two corps with cavalry support toward the railroad to Weldon. Violently counterattacked over several days by Hill's corps in the Battle of the Jerusalem Plank Road, the federals were stopped short of the railroad but did manage to extend their trenches some distance to the west.

On July 9, Grant ordered siege operations to begin against Petersburg. Already begun was an innovative attempt to tunnel under the Confederate lines in Burnside's sector and destroy them with a massive explosive charge. When completed in great secrecy on July 23, the tunnel was a minor engineering marvel, 511 feet in length with two lateral powder chambers holding 8,000 pounds of black powder. By the time the mine exploded early on July 30, Lee had only 18,000 troops in the Petersburg sector because

Union siege artillery is manned at Fort Brady during the siege of Petersburg. (National Archives)

City Point served as headquarters for General Grant and his Union troops during the siege of Petersburg, 1864–1865. (A. J. Russell Collection, Military History Institute)

of a federal diversion north of the James River. The explosion blew a great hole in the Confederate line, killing many troops and frightening others away from the area. The assault division failed miserably, however, to execute its assigned tasks. By the time other federal divisions were committed, Confederate reinforcements had arrived and counterattacked with great ferocity, eventually regaining the mine crater itself. Afterward, Grant recognized that a great opportunity to end the siege had been lost, primarily because of leadership failures. Although no more culpable than others, Burnside was among the officers relieved of command for their performance. Grant himself bore some responsibility, if only because he had not utilized all his men.

Toward Stalemate

For the remainder of the year, Grant continued to extend his lines in two directions, westward beyond Petersburg and north of the James River around Richmond. The first of these limited offensives finally cut the Petersburg Railroad south of the city on August 18. As before, the Confederates strongly counterattacked for several days, but the federal grip on the railroad could not be shaken. Confederate supplies coming up the railroad from Wilmington now had to be unloaded south of the federal lines and hauled laboriously by wagon around the federal flank into Petersburg. In an effort to make this process even more difficult, Grant sent Hancock's corps southward to destroy more of the railroad. Hancock was caught and soundly thrashed by a surprise Confederate counterattack at Reams Station on August 25. In late September, Grant again extended his lines. North of the James River, federal troops broke into Richmond's outer defense line and could not be ejected. At the same time, 20,000 federals gained an additional three miles of territory west of Petersburg, threatening its final railroad connection with the south, the South Side Railroad. Grant's final effort in 1864 to tighten his hold in Petersburg came on October 27, when two federal corps unsuccessfully attempted to cut the Boydton Plank Road.

Clearly, Grant would have to wait until Lee's army was appreciably weakened by the winter and events elsewhere in the Confederacy before he could expect a major success. The long campaign had sapped both armies of stamina and initiative. Thousands of experienced veterans had been lost along the way from the Wilderness to Petersburg. Many competent combat leaders were no longer available to inspire the rank and file to charge boldly forward in the face of killing fire. The folly of attacking well-entrenched defenders had been so well demonstrated that even the most obtuse commander could see the result. With the quality of both armies far lower than it had been earlier in the conflict, both Grant and Lee had fewer options in how they employed their troops. Backed by the industrial and demographic resources of the North, Grant could afford to play a waiting game more readily than Lee. Thus, Grant's 110,000 troops settled comfortably into their winter quarters, while a newly constructed railroad kept them well supplied from their base at City Point. In Petersburg, Lee's situation was far different, not quite hopeless but hardly cheerful.

As winter came to the lines around Petersburg and Richmond, Lee was disheartened to learn that his diversion in the Shenandoah Valley had failed. It had begun well in June when Early's corps had been shifted from the Cold Harbor lines to deal with Hunter's depredations in the valley. Early had easily defeated Hunter at Lynchburg, Virginia, and scattered Hunter's command back into the mountains. He had then attempted to emulate Jackson's exploits of 1862 by advancing northward down the valley to threaten Washington. Crossing into Maryland in early July, Early had defeated a scratch federal force at the Battle of Monocacy on July 9 and had continued his advance to the outskirts of Washington itself. Initially manned by reserves, the powerful Washington fortifications were in some danger of being penetrated until part of Wright's corps from the Army of the Potomac arrived to stabilize the situation. Too weak to seize the federal capital, Early gradually withdrew to Winchester, Virginia, in the valley. From there, he dispatched raids northward, during one of which Chambersburg, Pennsylvania, was burned in response to Hunter's depredations in Virginia.

Sheridan's Valley Campaign

To remove the Shenandoah Valley from Confederate control once and for all, Grant sent Sheridan to Washington in early August with instructions to unite all federal forces in the area and defeat Early. Sheridan was given 48,000 men, while Early's force initially numbered only 19,000, although Lee later increased it by an additional 6,000. Sheridan moved cautiously for a time but in late September vigorously attacked Early's command. On September 19, the federals defeated Early at the Battle of Opequon Creek, and again three days later at Fishers Hill. With his army in disarray, Early withdrew southward, while behind him,

General Philip Sheridan's 1864 campaign in the Shenandoah Valley broke Confederate resistance in this strategically important area and decimated Jubal Early's forces. (U.S. Military Academy)

Sheridan devastated the valley. In a last desperate effort to reverse the tide of federal success, Early turned and attacked Sheridan's army at Cedar Creek on October 19 while its commander was momentarily absent. Initially successful, Early's command proved unable to complete its victory. When Sheridan returned, he rallied his army and drove Early from the field. This defeat crushed Early's force and broke the back of Confederate resistance in the Shenandoah Valley. In December, the battered remnants of Early's corps returned to Lee at Petersburg, while Early himself remained in the valley with only 1,000 men. Early had proved to be no Jackson, and Lee's gamble had failed.

WESTERN THEATER: 1864

While the situation in the eastern theater in 1863 had been stalemated, such had not been the case in the western theater, where Union armies had opened the Mississippi River and driven Confederate forces from eastern Tennessee. The victorious concentration of federal troops wintering around Chattanooga, Tennessee, was especially well placed to drive through the Appalachian Mountains into Georgia when the spring campaign of 1864 opened. Southeast of Chattanooga, the Western & Atlantic Railroad broke through the mountain barrier then traversed more open country all the way to Atlanta. Atlanta itself was a significant railroad hub and manufacturing center supporting the Confederate war effort. If the railroad could be used to sustain the federal advance, a federal army striking south and east of Chattanooga would find few terrain barriers of significance between it and Atlanta. Once at Atlanta, a federal army would have many offensive options from which to choose, because the South's remaining industrial and agricultural heartland would be open to it. Clearly, the federal army at Chattanooga was poised to play a major role in the Union's strategic planning for 1864. Now that Grant had gone east to command all federal armies, Sherman commanded the Chattanooga concentration. Sherman would receive no assistance from Banks, however, who had already begun an expedition to northwestern Louisiana that would fail dismally in mid-May.

Johnston's Command

Facing Sherman's 99,000 men was a new Confederate commander. Following the disastrous Confederate defeat at Missionary Ridge in late November 1863, Braxton Bragg had asked to be relieved of command of the Army of Tennessee. On December 16, Davis granted Bragg's request, eventually bringing him to Richmond as his military adviser. Several officers were considered as Bragg's replacement, among them Longstreet, Beauregard, and Joseph E. Johnston. For one reason or another, Davis disliked them all, but he needed a commander and was forced to make a choice. That choice was Johnston, who took command on December 27.

Johnston's orders were to reorganize, refit, and recruit the Army of Tennessee and prepare it for offensive operations. Davis, Bragg, and Longstreet all seemed to believe that with a little work, Johnston's army would be able to enter Tennessee once more and regain what had long been lost. An extreme realist, Johnston knew that such proposals were fanciful. He therefore contented himself with rebuilding the Army of Tennessee and preparing it for defensive operations. By spring 1864, he was able to gather a force of approximately 60,000 troops. Most of them awaited Sherman's approach from the vicinity of Rocky Face Ridge, west of Dalton, Georgia.

Sherman's Operations

Sherman's mission was to attack Johnston's force, defeat or destroy it, and drive it as far southward as he could, destroying Confederate resources along the way. He divided his command into three components, the Army of the Cumberland under Maj. Gen. George H. Thomas, the Army of the Tennessee under Maj. Gen. James B. McPherson, and the Army of the Ohio under Maj. Gen. John M. Schofield. Although called armies, in reality the components of Sherman's command were nothing of the sort. Only the largest component, the Army of the Cumberland, was big enough to be called an army; the others, especially the Army of the Ohio, were little more than corps. These components had been gathered from all over the western theater and carried with them much intangible historical and political baggage. Therefore, the old designations were retained. In fact, Sherman actually commanded an augmented Army of the Cumberland, because the logistical and technical elements that supported his army had been constructed chiefly by Rosecrans during the previous year. The combined command reunited the two major federal armies in the western theater, which had been separate since 1862 except for the rescue operation at Chattanooga in November 1863.

Beginning his offensive in early May 1864 in accordance with Grant's timetable, Sherman confronted Johnston's defenses near Dalton at Rocky Face Ridge on May 7. Observation and preliminary skirmishing disclosed that the Confederate position was too strong to overcome by frontal assault. Rather than batter his way forward, Sherman ordered Thomas to fix Johnston's army frontally, while Schofield threatened Johnston's right flank and McPherson moved southward to Snake Creek Gap in the mountain wall. While McPherson marched, the remainder of Sherman's forces continued their demonstrations. By the afternoon of May 9, McPherson had passed through the gap and was in sight of the railroad at Resaca, Georgia. Vigorously opposed by a small force of defenders, McPherson lost his nerve and cautiously withdrew to the mouth of the gap, where he entrenched. Although he had not broken Johnston's line of communications, McPherson represented a threat to Johnston's rear that could not be ignored. Therefore, the Army of Tennessee evacuated the Rocky Face line on the evening of May 12 and marched south to Resaca.

Arriving at Resaca on May 13, Johnston found there a large reinforcement under Lt. Gen. Leonidas Polk, fresh from Mississippi. Polk's appearance gave Johnston three infantry corps, under Lt. Gens. William J. Hardee, John B. Hood, and Polk. While Hardee and Hood occupied defensive positions adjoining Polk's corps, Sherman's forces gradually moved into position at Resaca facing them. Throughout May 14, Sherman hammered first one section of Johnston's line then the other, but to little avail. A Confederate counterattack also gained less ground than its proponents had hoped. Even as he attacked Johnston frontally, Sherman sent other units to the southwest, looking for a way to flank Johnston out of the Resaca position. Eventually, a crossing of the Oostenaula River at Lay's Ferry provided just such an opportunity, and Sherman

Georgia Campaign, 1864

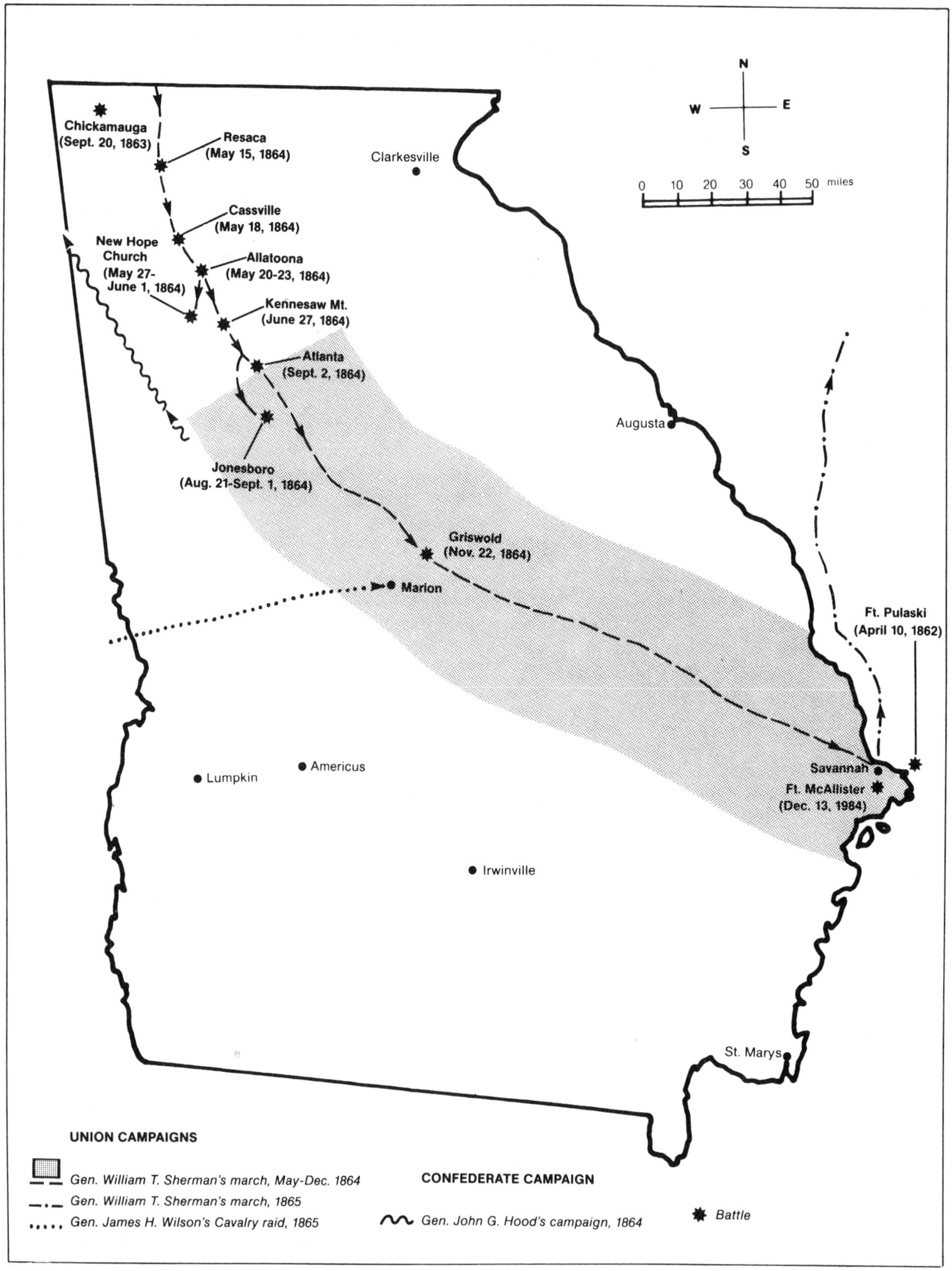
N
W
E
S
0 10 20 30 40 50 miles
Chickamauga (Sept. 20, 1863)
Resaca (May 15, 1864)
Clarkesville
Cassville (May 18, 1864)
New Hope Church (May 27-June 1, 1864)
Allatoona (May 20-23, 1864)
Kennesaw Mt. (June 27, 1864)
Atlanta (Sept. 2, 1864)
Jonesboro (Aug. 21-Sept. 1, 1864)
Augusta
Griswold (Nov. 22, 1864)
Marion
Ft. Pulaski (April 10, 1862)
Savannah
Ft. McAllister (Dec. 13, 1984)
Lumpkin
Americus
Irwinville
St. Marys
UNION CAMPAIGNS
Gen. William T. Sherman's march, May-Dec. 1864
Gen. William T. Sherman's march, 1865
Gen. James H. Wilson's Cavalry raid, 1865
CONFEDERATE CAMPAIGN
Gen. John G. Hood's campaign, 1864
Battle

pushed a small force across the stream. Upon receiving confirmation of the crossing on May 15, Johnston again withdrew to avoid being surrounded.

As Johnston marched southward, he discovered that the terrain initially was less promising for defense than he had hoped. Neither Calhoun nor Adairsville offered any opportunity for Johnston to secure his flanks on unassailable ground and face Sherman with any prospects of success. Therefore, the Army of Tennessee continued its retreat. Below Adairsville, however, the railroad and the principal wagon road diverged, providing Johnston with an opportunity for a counterstroke. Sending Hardee and the army's wagon trains along the railroad toward Kingston, Johnston led Hood's and Polk's troops along the more easterly wagon road toward Cassville. Because Sherman was following Johnston on a wide front, his columns were widely separated. Farthest to the east was Schofield's Army of the Ohio. Noticing the heavy tracks made by the Confederate wagons, Thomas's force, Sherman's largest component, followed them toward Kingston as Johnston had hoped. As Schofield approached the trap at Cassville, however, a dispute arose between Hood and Johnston, causing the Confederates to withdraw slightly behind the town. The delay caused the federals to recognize their dangerous position, and Sherman quickly concentrated his army. When Hood and Polk reported that their line was untenable, Johnston then resumed his withdrawal on the night of May 19.

With his army at its peak strength of 70,000 men, Johnston had lost a unique opportunity at Cassville to strike Sherman's forces. On May 20, he again halted his retreat and took up defensive positions covering the railroad at Allatoona Pass. While not as formidable as the line at Rocky Face Ridge, Johnston's new position was strong enough to dissuade Sherman from attacking it frontally. Sherman now paused for three days to restock his supplies and devise a new plan. Heretofore, Sherman had followed the line of the Western & Atlantic Railroad, which his efficient engineers were rapidly reconstructing behind him. Now he elected to swing westward away from the railroad in an effort to outflank the Allatoona position. Although the terrain to the west was rougher and he would have to be supplied solely by wagons, Sherman believed he could again force Johnston to evacuate the strong Allatoona position without a fight.

With McPherson's Army of the Tennessee leading, Sherman plunged westward into a broken, heavily wooded area little removed from wilderness. Johnston's scouts detected the movement, and Johnston quickly sent his own army westward to counter the federal thrust. En route to his initial goal of the town of Dallas, Sherman heard of Confederate infantry units nearby at New Hope Church. Doubting that Johnston's men could be so near, he ordered an attack on May 25. The information proved true, and Hood's corps dealt Sherman's advance guard a bloody setback. Both armies now concentrated and entrenched. On May 27, Sherman attempted to turn the Confederate right at Pickett's Mill. When the federals found not a flank but the front of a new Confederate line, they attacked anyway. The result was a disastrous repulse. Seeing that his outflanking maneuver had failed to be decisive, Sherman resolved to return to the railroad. As the federals extended their lines eastward, Johnston thought he saw an opening and launched a reconnaissance in force toward the federal right around Dallas. In a tragedy of errors equaled only by the federal mistakes at Pickett's Mill on the previous day, the Confederates were similarly repulsed.

Reaching the railroad again at Acworth on June 3, Sherman halted to rest his battle-worn army. Sherman's campaign thus far had gained 60 miles of territory without the necessity of fighting a full-scale battle, but Johnston's army remained intact. On June 10, the federals resumed their offensive, probing Johnston's position, which stretched for several miles along the tops of several small mountains. Rather than make a major frontal assault, Sherman gradually forced Johnston back by a series of small advances that rendered portions of the Confederate works untenable. In the skirmishing for one of these mountain positions, Polk was killed by a federal shell on June 14. Each time the federals gained a few yards of ground, Johnston fell back to a new line of works. The Confederates were trading space for time, and both sides knew it. On the night of June 18, Johnston gave up a bit more space and fell back to the most advantageous position he had held since Rocky Face Ridge in May. Anchored in the center by Kennesaw Mountain and its foothills, the line stretched for approximately 6 miles.

ATLANTA CAMPAIGN

During the Confederate withdrawal, Sherman was convinced that Johnston was in retreat to the Chattahoochee River some miles nearer Atlanta. Greatly disappointed when he learned the truth, Sherman once more began to probe for weak spots, but none were found. The bad weather, which had plagued the armies for weeks, continued to make the hauling of supplies difficult near the railroad and impossible far from it. For these reasons, Sherman weakened his resolve to avoid frontal attacks, and he ordered Johnston's position to be assaulted on June 27. Thomas's Army of the Cumberland was selected for the main effort, while McPherson's Army of the Tennessee received instructions to mount a diversionary attack to assist Thomas. Carried out with greater bravery then judgment, the attack was repulsed at great cost to the federals. The few yards of terrain gained were quickly fortified, however, and the Confederates proved unable to drive the federals from their new positions.

Reverting to his flanking maneuvers once more, Sherman forced some troops around the left of Johnston's Kennesaw Mountain line by July 2, forcing the Confederates out of their defensive positions that night. The ease with which this maneuver had been accomplished clearly showed that the slaughter at Kennesaw Mountain had been needless. On July 4, Johnston occupied another strong position in front of the Chattahoochee River, with both of his flanks resting on the stream. For a few days, Sherman confronted Johnston while he gradually extended troops to left and right. On July 9, Schofield forced a crossing of the Chattahoochee upstream from the Army of Tennessee's positions, forcing Johnston to withdraw to the east bank of the river. With Sherman across the Chattahoochee, Johnston could not stand there, so he fell back to Peach Tree Creek, the last significant barrier short of the Atlanta fortifications. This withdrawal was Johnston's last because Jefferson Davis relieved him of command on July 17. Johnston had traded space for time masterfully, and had preserved the Army of Tennessee in the process, but in the end, Sherman had reached Atlanta. Seeking a more aggressive commander, Davis chose Hood to replace Johnston.

The new commander of the Army of Tennessee was a physical wreck, having lost the use of an arm at Gettysburg and having had a leg amputated at Chickamauga, yet his aggressive spirit remained indomitable. Less evident was

General William T. Sherman's 1864 advance through Georgia split the South and introduced new concepts of total war. (Library of Congress)

Union Gen. William T. Sherman, on the outskirts of Atlanta, patiently directed the six-month campaign that resulted in the evacuation of the city by the Confederates. (Library of Congress)

his intellect, another quality needed by a successful commander. When Sherman crossed Peach Tree Creek on a wide front, Hood counterattacked hastily on July 20 with Thomas's Army of the Cumberland as the intended target. The attack showed boldness but little skill, and after it was repulsed, Hood withdrew into the circle of fortifications surrounding Atlanta. Once again misjudging a tactical retrograde for a precipitate retreat, Sherman did not concentrate his forces quickly enough. On July 22, Hood struck again, this time east of the city against the Army of the Tennessee. The attack was initially successful, killing McPherson in the process, but Hood was late in committing reserves, and the attack petered out in stalemate without benefit to the Confederates. Following a technique so often used by Grant at Petersburg, Sherman suddenly reversed himself and transferred the Army of the Tennessee from his left to his right in an effort to cut Atlanta's railroad connections. Now commanded by Maj. Gen. Oliver O. Howard, the Army of the Tennessee was struck by Hood west of Atlanta in the Battle of Ezra Church. As before, the federals hastily entrenched and successfully defended themselves.

Hood had now fought more battles in eight days than Johnston had in eight weeks, but had nothing to show for it except long casualty lists. Hood's surviving infantry numbered no more than 37,000 men to Sherman's 85,000, but Sherman had learned to be cautious and now slowed the tempo of operations.

Capture of Atlanta

In August, while federal artillery pounded Atlanta, first Hood, then Sherman, sent cavalry forces to raid the opposing army's communications. Although the Confederates got the better of the exchange, neither raid was decisive. On August 26, Sherman again mounted an offensive. Partially withdrawing from Confederate view to deceive Hood, Sherman sent virtually all of his force in a long, looping swing to the west and south. The goal was to cut the two railroads that entered Atlanta from the south. By August 31, the railroads were severed and a hasty counterattack at Jonesboro by two of Hood's corps had failed. With his supply lines in enemy hands, Hood had no alternative but to evacuate Atlanta, which he did on the evening of September 1. Sherman's forces entered Atlanta on the following day. They had gained the city, but had failed to destroy Hood's army.

After leaving Atlanta, Hood concentrated south of the city at Lovejoy's Station. After a brief pursuit, Sherman confronted him there, but finding the Confederate position too strong to justify an attack, he returned to Atlanta. For the next several weeks, the two armies warily watched each other while their commanders debated what to do next. Although he had gained the prize of Atlanta, Sherman was uncertain how to proceed. His supply line was a series of single-track railroads stretching all the way back to Tennessee and Kentucky, highly vulnerable to interdiction

In 1864 the Confederacy's president, Jefferson Davis, met with his generals and changed commanders in an unsuccessful effort to devise a plan to stop Sherman's advance through Georgia. (Library of Congress)

by either cavalry or infantry. If he resumed the advance beyond Atlanta without destroying it, the city would require a large garrison. To destroy Atlanta after it had fallen into his hands without resistance was contrary to accepted rules of war. Yet Sherman concluded that he had no other choice. After declaring Atlanta to be purely a military base, Sherman required all civilians to evacuate the city. The Confederates were outraged at this cruel action, but Sherman responded that war itself was cruelty. With Atlanta neutralized, Sherman began to look toward the coast, especially the city of Savannah. He also sought prior approval from Grant, in case an advance to the sea became desirable.

On September 21, Hood moved southwest of Atlanta to Palmetto, Georgia. There he met President Davis to devise a new Confederate strategy. Sherman's long line of communications was clearly his most vulnerable point. If Hood could maneuver behind Atlanta and sever that line, Sherman would have to come out of Atlanta and fight to regain his communications. Sherman was already beginning to detach significant numbers of troops to protect the railroad back to Chattanooga from cavalry raids, and an advance by Hood's infantry no doubt would accelerate the process. Therefore, on September 29, the Army of Tennessee crossed the Chattahoochee River on its way north. By October 5, Hood's 40,000 troops had reached the vicinity of Dallas after breaking the railroad north of Atlanta. A detachment sent to destroy the small federal garrison at Allatoona failed in its mission as Sherman rushed reinforcements northward. Hood then swung to the northwest, threatening the federal garrisons at Rome and Resaca before continuing on to Dalton and Tunnel Hill. Sherman followed to Resaca with 55,000 men on October 13.

Sherman's March to the Sea

By mid-October, both commanders were ready to adopt new strategies. Hood could continue destroying the railroad, only to see it rebuilt virtually overnight by Sherman's efficient engineers. Sherman could continue chasing Hood, but the more lightly equipped Confederates could use their greater mobility to remain just beyond his grasp. When Hood doubled back toward the southwest and entered northern Alabama, Sherman followed, but his heart was not in the chase. Late in September, Sherman had sent Thomas back to Nashville to orchestrate the defense of Tennessee and the railroad. He now reasoned that Thomas was probably strong enough to handle Hood's small army, freeing his own troops for other missions. When Halleck indicated that Grant might not oppose Sherman's movement through Georgia to the coast, Sherman began to work out the details of the daring project. Leaving Hood in his rear and casting loose from his supply line was a bold gamble, but Sherman embraced it readily. Compared with Sherman's plan, Hood's new formulation was positively fantastic. He proposed marching rapidly into Tennessee, defeating Thomas, then continuing northward into Kentucky, his home state. If Sherman followed and defeated him, Hood believed that he could retreat through Cumberland Gap into Virginia and eventually join Lee's army.

Of the two plans, Hood's received approval first. Since September 28, Beauregard had held Johnston's old title as supreme commander in the western theater, and on October 21, he reluctantly gave Hood permission for the Tennessee expedition. Five days later, the Army of Tennessee had reached Decatur, Alabama, and was poised to cross the Tennessee River en route to Nashville. Sherman, meanwhile, had finally decided to follow Hood no further, leaving him to be dealt with by Thomas. Sending Thomas reinforcements from several sources, including his own army, Sherman ordered the bulk of his force back to Atlanta. En route, he received word that Grant had approved his plan to march across Georgia to Savannah. Trusting Thomas's capacity to handle the situation in Tennessee, Sherman turned his back on Hood for the last time. By November 10, Sherman's force had reached Atlanta, where it began preparations for its march. Unnecessary matériel was sent north, the railroad and telegraph line were cut, and only the best men and matériel were selected for the journey. When the winnowing process was done, Sherman's mobile column consisted of 62,000 men, 64 guns, and around 3,000 wheeled vehicles. After putting Atlanta to the torch, the army marched away from the ruins on November 15, out of touch with the rest of the country.

While Sherman marched, Hood waited in northern Alabama for bad weather and swollen rivers to abate. At last, on November 19, his army crossed the Tennessee River and entered Tennessee. Thomas had not yet concentrated his forces, which remained scattered far and wide over the central part of the state. Having been joined by a large contingent of Confederate cavalry under Maj. Gen. Nathan B. Forrest, Hood's army now numbered approximately 39,000 men. In its immediate vicinity and blocking its path was Schofield with 30,000 troops. As Hood advanced, Schofield gradually withdrew, trying to buy time for Thomas to gather a larger force at Nashville. Delaying too long around Columbia, Tennessee, Schofield was nearly trapped when Confederate forces briefly interdicted his withdrawal route at Spring Hill on November 29. In a rage over the missed opportunity, which may have been of his own making, Hood pushed his army northward after the retreating federals. On November 30, he caught them in defensive positions south of the Harpeth River at Franklin. Rather than permit Schofield to escape again, Hood rashly threw most of his army against the federal defenses. The attack gained some initial success but was halted by a well-timed federal counterattack. Finally, during the night, Schofield resumed his retreat.

Grievously weakened by the massive casualties his army had suffered at Franklin, Hood pushed on to the outskirts of Nashville. There he found Thomas and Schofield within the heavy entrenchments covering the city. Without sufficient strength to force his way into Nashville, Hood waited outside, seemingly at a loss as to how to proceed. Meanwhile, Thomas continued to gather strength until he outnumbered Hood 49,000 to 23,000. Thomas wished not only to defeat Hood but to destroy his army once and for all. Therefore, the federals delayed for two weeks, waiting for more men, more cavalry horses, and for the freezing weather to improve. During this period, the Lincoln administration and especially Grant grew impatient with Thomas's lack of action. Grant was on the verge of relieving Thomas when the weather cleared, and Thomas struck Hood's shivering army a mighty blow on December 15. On the following day, Thomas attacked again, enveloping Hood on both flanks and completing the destruction of his army. The Army of Tennessee now virtually disintegrated and fled southward into Alabama. More vigorous than normal, the federal pursuit nevertheless was unable to prevent the Confederates from recrossing the Tennessee River.

Sherman's March to the Sea cut a swath of destruction through Georgia and produced "bummers," soldiers who foraged for supplies for the troops in any way they could—much to the outrage of the Confederacy's citizens. (U.S. Army Military History Institute)

Hood's decision to campaign northward into Tennessee meant that Sherman would have essentially no opposition as he advanced across Georgia. Dividing his army into a right wing under Howard and a left wing under Maj. Gen. Henry W. Slocum, each of which moved on multiple routes, Sherman traced a 50-mile-wide swath across Georgia. Hardee attempted to coordinate the Confederate response from Savannah, but his situation was hopeless from the beginning. Sherman was therefore free to operate in the Georgia hinterland as he pleased. Because he was unable to occupy the area he secured, he saw no reason to leave any part of the economic or transportation infrastructure intact. Also, because he had cut himself off from any supply line back to friendly territory, he expected to live off the land for much of his sustenance. To acquire that sustenance, each regiment employed far-ranging foraging parties, seizing what they needed and destroying the rest. Gradually, some of the foragers turned into "bummers," men who perpetually straggled from the main columns and perpetrated outrages on the civilian populace. Although most of the army was remarkably well-disciplined, the notoriety gained by the "bummers" has stained the memory of Sherman's "March to the Sea."

On December 10, Sherman reached the outskirts of Savannah, which was defended by Hardee with about 15,000 troops. Before beginning a siege of the city, Sherman moved to open communication with naval vessels off the coast by reducing Fort McAllister near the mouth of the Ogeechee River. On December 13, the fort was successfully stormed and the connection with the navy was made. Sherman then began desultory siege operations against Savannah and finally mounted an even more halfhearted attempt to encircle Hardee's garrison. Hardee nimbly escaped the trap, evacuating Savannah on December 21 and withdrawing northward. Sherman then entered the city and dispatched a famous message offering Savannah to President Lincoln as a Christmas present.

As the year ended, Sherman's victorious army lay safely around Savannah, well-supplied by sea, preparing to move wherever Grant directed with the new year. The remnants of Hood's army, meanwhile, gathered far away around Tupelo, Mississippi, were bypassed by events. Hood was relieved of command at his own request in January 1865, but by then it was too late. Just as at the end of 1863, the federal armies in the western theater stood poised on the verge of further victories at the end of 1864. Ironically, Davis's midyear search for a more aggressive commander to reverse the South's fortunes in that theater had done much to make the federal success possible.

EASTERN THEATER: 1865

The year 1865 opened in the east with Grant's army still encircling the southern and eastern approaches to Petersburg and Richmond, while Lee's much smaller army huddled behind its massive earthen fortifications. Marking time before improvements in the weather permitted the resumption of active operations at Petersburg, Grant, in early January, sent a large expedition to seize the Confederacy's one remaining seaport of significance, Wilmington, North Carolina. An earlier expedition led by Butler had returned to Virginia in failure the preceding month, leading to Butler's being relieved of command. Grant subsequently sent Maj. Gen. Alfred H. Terry on the same mission. With the assistance of the navy, Terry's troops stormed Fort Fisher, Wilmington's primary defense, on January 15. This federal victory closed the last major source of external support to Lee's Army of Northern Virginia. Three weeks later, Grant further diminished Lee's room to maneuver by sending another expedition westward toward Lee's right flank at Petersburg. While not decisive, the resulting Battle of Hatcher's Run on February 5–7 permitted the federals to extend their lines two miles farther to the west, stretching Lee's dwindling force accordingly.

On January 23, Davis elevated Lee to the command of all remaining Confederate forces, but the Confederacy's poor military position and collapsing internal communications system rendered the title virtually meaningless. Lee continued simply to direct the operations of his beloved Army of Northern Virginia. By March, the situation facing that army was so desperate that Lee believed it was necessary to risk taking the offensive. Careful study of the federal lines indicated that the best place for an assault lay around a work named Fort Stedman, where Confederate lines approached within a few yards of the federal trenches. If Lee's men could break through the federal cordon at Fort Stedman and move toward Grant's main supply base at City Point, Grant would probably have to shorten his lines. At worst, Confederate success would relax Grant's grip on Petersburg; at best, Lee might be able to detach some units to assist Confederate forces fighting in North Carolina. Led by Maj. Gen. John B. Gordon, the Confederate attack on March 25 was initially successful, opening a one-mile hole in the federal lines. This breach was soon closed, however, when massive federal reinforcements reached the scene. Before the end of the day, the remnants of Gordon's assaulting force was back within their own works. Lee's last offensive of the war had failed.

Sensing that the Fort Stedman attack had been Lee's last gasp, Grant on March 29 again ordered a large expedition to march westward beyond his left flank. Spearheaded by the cavalry corps of Sheridan, the expedition was given muscle by two infantry corps under Warren and Maj. Gen. Andrew A. Humphreys. By March 31, the infantry had extended the federal position another four miles westward, while Sheridan pushed farther still to Dinwiddie Courthouse. Lee responded by sending Maj. Gen. George E. Pickett with a mixed infantry-cavalry force of 10,000 men to repulse the federal thrust. Striking Sheridan's cavalry, Pickett drove it back several miles. He then withdrew his own force to a road junction known as Five Forks and hastily entrenched. A three-mile gap lay between Pickett's left and the main Confederate line. Calling Warren's infantry to his support, Sheridan, on April 1, penetrated that gap and decisively crushed Pickett's command. Pickett's defeat meant that the South Side Railroad, Petersburg's last connection to the south, was within federal reach.

The Union's capture of Fort Fisher, the key to the defense of Wilmington, North Carolina, in January 1865, opened the final offensive against the Confederacy. (Library of Congress)

By the time Union forces entered Petersburg, Virginia, on Apr. 3, 1865, much of the city had been reduced to rubble. (Library of Congress)

Hemmed in by federal units, Robert E. Lee surrendered to Grant at Appomattox on April 9, 1865. (Library of Congress)

Both sides recognized the importance of the Battle of Five Forks. With 125,000 federal troops to Lee's force of fewer than 60,000, Grant quickly moved to exploit Sheridan's victory. On April 2, he ordered an advance along his entire front. The greatest gains occurred in Wright's sector, midway in the federal line. Wright's men penetrated the Confederate defenses and exploited to both left and right, killing Hill in the process. As the day progressed, federal units swept eastward toward Petersburg itself. A sacrificial rearguard defense by the garrisons of two detached works west of the city bought enough time for the defenders to hold the federals back until nightfall. Under the cover of darkness, Lee evacuated the defensive lines around Petersburg and Richmond. While Davis and the Confederate government fled by train toward Danville, Virginia, the Army of Northern Virginia marched westward toward Amelia Courthouse. On the morning of April 3, federal troops entered both Petersburg and the capital of the Confederacy for the first time in four years.

Lee's Surrender

As his army marched westward, Lee saw clearly that his only remaining hope was to evade his pursuers and somehow join Johnston's forces operating in North Carolina. By this time, his command numbered no more than 30,000 troops of all descriptions. Crossing the Appomattox River, by April 5, Lee had concentrated most of his forces at Amelia Courthouse, where he had hoped to find rations. The rations were not there, but Sheridan's cavalry and infantry team soon arrived a few miles to the southwest, blocking Lee's route to North Carolina. Wearily, the Confederates turned westward toward another crossing of the Appomattox at Farmville. Although most of Lee's army reached Farmville safely, the pursuing federals caught his rear guard at Sayler's Creek and destroyed it on April 6. Lee continued westward toward Lynchburg, but on April 8, he was brought to bay by federal cavalry that had gained his front near Appomattox Courthouse. On the following day, when he attempted to brush the cavalry aside, Lee discovered federal infantry behind them. With other federal infantry crowding his rear, Lee had no choice but to seek terms of surrender from Grant. The capitulation of Lee and the Army of Northern Virginia on Apr. 9, 1865, ended the Civil War in the eastern theater.

WESTERN THEATER: 1865

Sherman, who had been lying quietly at Savannah, Georgia, when 1865 arrived, prepared for the coming spring campaign, in which he was to advance northward into the Carolinas, squeezing the Confederacy's remaining military forces between his own army and Grant's forces in Virginia. To assist Sherman's progress, Schofield came from Tennessee to lead a force of 30,000 men inland from Wilmington, North Carolina. Schofield's mission was to open a new supply line for Sherman running inland from the Atlantic coast to the vicinity of Goldsboro, North Carolina.

Delayed by bad weather, Sherman began his advance on February 1, and a few days later, Schofield advanced northward from Fort Fisher toward Wilmington. His troops took Wilmington on February 22, but Schofield soon found that New Bern, North Carolina, a long-held federal enclave to the north, would make a better base. While Schofield transferred his operations to New Bern, Sherman plunged into South Carolina. Confronting him was an impromptu Confederate force consisting of remnants of Hood's Army of Tennessee, Hardee's command, and local militia. All told, Beauregard could oppose Sherman's 60,000 men with only 22,500 of his own.

Feinting both westward toward Augusta, Georgia, and eastward toward Charleston, South Carolina, Sherman advanced on a wide front. Unable to discern Sherman's actual target, the Confederates attempted a cordon defense that

A preliminary surrender agreement between Sherman and the Confederacy's Joseph Johnston on Apr. 18, 1865, at Durham Station, North Carolina, led to a final surrender of the Army of Tennessee on April 26. (U.S. Army Military History Institute)

proved to be weak everywhere. Leaving Augusta and Charleston on his flanks, Sherman headed for Columbia, the state capital, which he reached on February 16. Just as he had pillaged the heart of central Georgia the previous year, Sherman destroyed both government and private property in South Carolina with a vengeance. Before Sherman left Columbia, a fire of suspect origin destroyed half of the city on February 17. Confederate forces evacuated Charleston on the same day.

Confederate Resistance

On February 23, at Lee's urging, Davis appointed Johnston once more to command all the troops facing Sherman. Beauregard, Bragg, and a host of other Confederate generals with their shrunken commands now came under Johnston's direction. While Bragg watched Schofield's federals advancing from New Bern, Hardee's troops gathered at Cheraw, South Carolina, and the Army of Tennessee concentrated at Chester, South Carolina. None of these commands alone was strong enough to do more than observe the progress of the federals in their front.

Realizing that he must concentrate his scattered forces if Sherman were to be halted, Johnston ordered that all Confederate units gather around Fayetteville, North Carolina. Hindered only by bad weather, Sherman appeared outside that town on March 12. Instead of meeting the

Gen. Robert E. Lee and his son, Maj. Gen. George Washington Custis, with Col. Walter Taylor in Richmond shortly after Lee's surrender of the Army of Northern Virginia at Appomattox Courthouse. (Library of Congress)

united Confederate force, Sherman found only Hardee's small command, which quickly withdrew out of reach. Johnston's concentration had been delayed by weather, decrepit Southern railroads, and the need to use part of the Army of Tennessee in an unsuccessful effort to halt Schofield's advance at Kinston. From Fayetteville, Sherman had two significant options. He could march directly on Raleigh, capital of the state, or he could swing eastward to link with Schofield at Goldsboro. Advised by Lee to strike Sherman before he could adopt either course, Johnston resolved to counterattack. When Sherman resumed the advance from Fayetteville in his customary wide-front style, Johnston struck Slocum's left wing at Bentonville on March 19. When his assault was repelled, Johnston withdrew slightly and entrenched. Just as Sherman prepared to crush his army on March 21, Johnston withdrew again, this time toward Raleigh. Two days later, Sherman's and Schofield's armies united at Goldsboro, making a combined force of 80,000 men.

End of the War

While Johnston took position at Smithfield, southeast of Raleigh, Sherman paused to visit Grant and Lincoln at City Point, Virginia. Upon his return to North Carolina, he resumed his advance about the time Lee surrendered at Appomattox Courthouse. In the face of the renewed federal offensive, Johnston again gave ground, evacuating Raleigh and halting near Durham Station. Sherman followed quickly, occupying Raleigh on April 13. Johnston now asked for a truce, which resulted in the offer and acceptance of very broad terms of surrender on April 18. When these terms were rejected by the federal government, Grant suggested that further negotiations be conducted on the basis of the slightly more restrictive agreement reached between himself and Lee. Johnston accepted the revised offer, and his command laid down its arms on Apr. 26, 1865.

Although Confederate units in the hinterland from the coastal plain to the trans-Mississippi would continue to surrender piecemeal until May 26, Lee's surrender of the Army of Northern Virginia at Appomattox Courthouse on April 9 and Johnston's surrender of the Army of Tennessee and its associated units at Durham Station on April 26 meant that the Civil War was finally over. The Union had indeed been restored, and the scourge of slavery had been abolished, but the cost had been high: nearly $10,000,000,000 (in 1865 dollars) and 622,511 lives.

PART II

Biographies

ADAMS, John Quincy (1767–1848)

Sixth president of the United States (1825–29), Adams was born in Braintree (now Quincy), Massachusetts. Previously minister to the Netherlands and Russia, and having led the U.S. commission to negotiate an end to the War of 1812, he became Pres. James Monroe's secretary of state (1817–25) and negotiated the cession of Florida from Spain in 1819 (the Adams-Onís Treaty). In 1822, Adams informed Russia that "the American continents are no longer subjects for any new European colonial establishments"; the following year, he assisted in writing the Monroe Doctrine.

Elected president in 1824, he encountered an opposition Congress and was not reelected. He returned to Washington in 1831 as representative from Massachusetts (1831–48). Acting independently, Adams upheld the right of petition (vindicated with the 1844 repeal of the "gag" rule) and strongly opposed the annexation of Texas.

He was among the best qualified of any secretary of state, but Adams's aversion to party politics hurt his presidency. His independent nature, strong intellect, and moral integrity, however, served him and the nation well during his congressional career.

Stephen J. Lofgren

ALEXANDER, EDWARD PORTER (1835–1910)

U.S. military engineer and Confederate general, Alexander was born in Washington, Georgia. After graduating third in his class at West Point (1857), he was commissioned an engineer and assigned an instructorship at the U.S. Military Academy. He participated in the Utah Expedition, against the Mormons, and conducted a number of ordnance experiments for the War Department.

In 1859, Alexander assisted Albert Myer, founder of the Army Signal Corps, in testing Myer's military signaling system. When Georgia seceded from the Union, Alexander resigned his commission for a captaincy in the engineers of the Confederate army. He served, successively, as the chief of General Beauregard's signal service at the First Battle of Bull Run, chief of ordnance of the Army of Northern Virginia, and chief of artillery under General Longstreet. An outstanding artilleryman, Alexander was one of three Confederate officers to attain the rank of brigadier general of artillery.

Bibliography: Gallager, Gary W., *Fighting for the Confederacy: The Personal Recollections of General Edward Porter Alexander* (Univ. of North Carolina Press, 1989).

Carol E. Stokes

ALLEN, HENRY WATKINS (1820–1866)

Confederate military leader and administrator, Allen was born in Prince Edward County, Virginia. He volunteered for the Confederate army at the beginning of the Civil War and saw early action. Commanding a regiment at Shiloh (April 1862), he was wounded in the face and at Baton Rouge (August 1862) sustained serious leg injuries. He became governor of Louisiana in 1864 and, before his resignation on June 2, 1865, was responsible for administrating the Louisiana region out of the economic crises of war and for advocating the judicious surrender that averted needless devastation to his state. Allen lived the last year of his life in Mexico, where he published an English-language newspaper.

Bibliography: Cassidy, Vincent H., and Amos E. Simpson, *Henry Watkins Allen of Louisiana* (Louisiana State Univ. Press, 1964); Spencer, James, *Civil War Generals* (Greenwood Press, 1986).

Capt. Karen S. Wilhelm

AMPUDIA, PEDRO DE (1805–c. 1846)

Mexican military leader, Ampudia was born in Havana, Cuba, and arrived in Mexico in 1821. He joined the rebel army during the fight for Mexican independence (1821), rose steadily in rank, and by 1846 was a major general commanding the Army of the North. Ampudia despised Texans and was noted for his cruelty toward them. Citizens of the northern district feared and distrusted him.

In September 1846, as U.S. forces pushed south, General Ampudia received orders to keep his 10,000 troops at Saltillo (north of Mexico City) and await the arrival of a new commander. Believing Saltillo to be impregnable, Ampudia disobeyed the command and moved his forces to Monterrey. His plan of defense centered on holding strong defensive positions in the city's suburbs at El Diablo, Fort Teneria, and the Citadel.

As U.S. forces led by Gen. Zachary Taylor advanced on Monterrey, Taylor's scouts warned of Ampudia's stout defenses surrounding the city. Taylor's men carefully skirted El Diablo and prepared to storm Monterrey. As the Americans charged, Mexican morale disintegrated, and Ampudia's army fled in panic. Following this rout, Gen. Antonio López de Santa Anna replaced Ampudia as commander of the Army of the North. Little is known of his subsequent life.

Bibliography: Bauer, K. Jack, *The Mexican War 1846–1848* (Macmillan Co., 1974); Connor, Seymour V., and Odie B. Faulk, *North America Divided: The Mexican War 1846–1848* (Oxford Univ. Press, 1971).

M. Guy Bishop

ANDERSON, JOSEPH REID (1813–1892)

Confederate general, Anderson was born in Fincastle, Virginia. He graduated fourth in the 1836 West Point class, but resigned his commission in 1837 to be a civil engineer for Virginia. From 1841 to 1861, he headed the Richmond firm Joseph R. Anderson & Co., owners of Tredegar Iron Works.

He supported secession and received ammunition and arms contracts. In 1861 he was appointed brigadier general in command of forces at Wilmington, North Carolina. He fought well in the Peninsular Campaign, being wounded at Frayser's Farm June 30, 1862. He left the army in July 1862 to manage his iron works. Anderson was chief supplier of ammunition and also produced cannons, railroad rails, and armament for the ironclad ship *Virginia* (*Merrimac*). After the war, he helped rebuild industry, especially in Richmond.

Lynn L. Sims

ARISTA, MARIANO (1802–1855)

Mexican military leader and president, Arista was born in San Luis Potosí. In 1820–21, he fought for the forces loyal to Spain during the Mexican Revolution. Although he had fought with Antonio López de Santa Anna, when that ambitious general came to power, Arista was forced into exile, spending some time in Cincinnati. By the late 1830s, he had returned to Mexico and reentered the military.

At the outbreak of the Mexican War in 1846, Arista commanded the Mexican forces around the Rio Grande. He is best known as the Mexican commander who lost to Zachary Taylor's forces at the Battle of Palo Alto (May 8, 1846). He followed that defeat with the unsuccessful defense of Matamoros.

Between 1848 and 1851, Arista served as Mexican president José Herrera's minister of war. He succeeded Herrera to the presidency in 1851 but was deposed two years later and went into exile in Lisbon, Portugal. It was there that Arista fell off a boat and drowned.

Bibliography: Bauer, K. Jack, *The Mexican War, 1846–1848* (Macmillan Co., 1974); Ramirez, Jose Fernando, *Mexico During the War with the United States* (Univ. of Missouri Press, 1950).

Roger D. Launius

ARMISTEAD, LEWIS ADDISON (1817–1863)

U.S. soldier and Confederate general, Armistead was born in New Bern, North Carolina. Dismissed from West Point after a cadet prank, Armistead became a second lieutenant in the 6th Infantry in 1839. He won brevets in the Mexican War for gallantry at Contreras, Churubusco, and Monterrey in Mexico. After resigning his captaincy in May 1861, he became colonel of the 57th Virginia Infantry in the Confederate service. Promoted to brigadier general in April 1862, he led his brigade of Virginia troops with distinction at Fair Oaks and in the Seven Days' Battles, especially at Malvern Hill. During the Battle of Gettysburg, on July 3, 1863, he fell mortally wounded inside Union lines on Cemetery Ridge near the deepest penetration of "Pickett's Charge." His death two days later came amid allegations that he had disavowed allegiance to the Southern cause.

Carol Reardon

ATKINSON, HENRY (1782–1842)

U.S. frontiersman and Indian fighter. In 1819 he commanded the Yellowstone Expedition, intended as a show of force to Indians and British at the mouth of the Yellowstone River (northwestern Wyoming). The unsuccessful expedition led to the building of Fort Atkinson near Council Bluffs (southwestern Iowa) in 1821, above which Atkinson thereafter favored establishing a permanent military post. In 1825, he commanded a successful expedition to the upper Missouri River to make Indian treaties. He selected the site north of St. Louis for Jefferson Barracks, where he subsequently lived, and sent Colonel Henry Leavenworth to establish a fort on the Kansas frontier. In 1827, Atkinson quelled an uprising among the Winnebago. He commanded troops in the 1832 Black Hawk War, including the August 2 fighting at Bad Axe. Atkinson's last significant assignment on the frontier was supervising the removal of Indians from Wisconsin in 1840.

Stephen J. Lofgren

BAINBRIDGE, WILLIAM (1774–1833)

U.S. naval leader, Bainbridge was born in Princeton, New Jersey. Perhaps better known for the several disasters that plagued his early career than for his fine victory as captain of the USS *Constitution* over the HMS *Java* on Dec. 29, 1812, he was in fact more often the victim of a dogmatic and inflexible personality than his nickname "Hard-Luck Bill" implies.

Bainbridge took great pride in being awarded prestigious squadron commands in 1815 and 1820 and later served as president of the Board of Navy Commissioners for several years. Still, upon his death, he was remembered chiefly for having surrendered the frigate *Philadelphia* to Tripolitan gunboats in 1803 and for his active role in arranging the infamous 1820 duel that cost the life of his archrival, Stephen Decatur.

Bibliography: Symonds, Craig L., "William S. Bainbridge: Bad Luck or Fatal Flaw?" *Command Under Sail*, ed. by William C. Bradford (Naval Inst. Press, 1985).

Maj. Grant H. Walker

BANCROFT, GEORGE (1800–1891)

U.S. historian and secretary of the navy, Bancroft was born in Worcester, Massachusetts. After graduating from Harvard in 1817, he received a Ph.D. from the University of Gottingen in 1820, possibly the first American to obtain a German doctorate. From 1823 to 1831, Bancroft ran a successful school for boys but then turned his attention to politics.

In the 1844 Democratic convention, James K. Polk obtained the presidential nomination with Bancroft's aid and rewarded Bancroft by appointing him secretary of the navy in 1845. Bancroft shared Polk's expansionist views, but as war with Mexico loomed, Bancroft feared congressional opposition and British hostility and was the last cabinet member to hold out against a declaration of war.

While Bancroft did not play an activist role in the war, he nonetheless left a lasting mark on the navy. He outlawed "casual" flogging of sailors and attempted unsuccessfully to force promotion boards to consider merit as well as seniority in officer promotions. In June 1845, while also serving as acting secretary of war, Bancroft, with the approval of Sec. of War William Marcy, transferred the army's Fort Severn at Annapolis, Maryland, to the navy for use as a school for midshipmen; it was renamed the Naval Academy in 1850.

Bancroft served as ambassador to Great Britain (1846–49) and ambassador to Prussia (1867–73). His highly acclaimed 10-volume *History of the United States from the Discovery of the American Continent* was among the many fine works that earned him the sobriquet "father of American history."

Richard B. Meixsel

BANKS, NATHANIEL PRENTISS (1816–1894)

U.S. political and military figure, Banks was born in Waltham, Massachusetts. He rose to a position of prominence in Democratic party politics, defected to the Republicans, and became governor of Massachusetts (1858–61). Banks was appointed a major general of volunteers by President Lincoln in 1861. Assigned to command federal forces in the Shenandoah Valley, he established a memorable, if unenviable, military reputation as the Union general consistently outmarched and outfought by Confederate Maj. Gen. Thomas "Stonewall" Jackson. Despite a force of some 17,000 Union troops, Banks was decisively defeated at Winchester on May 25, 1862. He hastily retreated northward, abandoning a good deal of supplies and many wagons to the Confederates. Banks later commanded the vanguard of Maj. Gen. John Pope's Army of Virginia at Cedar Mountain, where he again was bested by Jackson on Aug. 9, 1862.

Banks's political influence was sufficient to overcome severe criticism of his failures, and he was chosen to replace Benjamin Butler as the Union commander of the Department of the Gulf. There his primary mission was to advance north from New Orleans to cooperate with Maj. Gen. Ulysses S. Grant in gaining federal control of the Mississippi River. Banks was distracted by a peripheral effort up the Red River toward Shreveport, Louisiana, and it was only with the greatest difficulty that Grant was able to secure his cooperation in the main task at hand. Following the fall of Vicksburg to Grant's forces on July 3, 1863, Banks's 15,000-man army finally took Port Hudson, Louisiana, on July 7, thereby cutting the Confederacy in half. Once again, Banks's political influence enabled him to avoid the consequences of his military ineptitude that had caused heavy Union casualties at Port Hudson. Subsequently, Banks was instructed to cooperate with Rear Adm. David Farragut's naval forces in an amphibious operation against Mobile, Alabama, as part of Grant's overall strategy in 1864. Again, Banks frittered away his resources on peripheral tasks, and he was finally removed from command for failure to carry out his assigned strategic mission. Following the Civil War, Banks returned to Massachusetts. He served a number of terms in the U.S. House of Representatives (1853–57, 1865–73, 1875–79, 1889–91) and was the speaker of the House in 1856–57.

Bibliography: Faust, Patricia L., *Historical Times Illustrated Encyclopedia of the Civil War* (Harper & Row, 1986); Hattaway, Herman, and Archer Jones, *How the North Won: A Military History of the Civil War* (Univ. of Illinois Press, 1983); Matloff, Maurice, *American Military History* (Office of the Chief of Military History, U.S. Army, 1969).

Lt. Col. (Ret.) Charles R. Shrader

BARBOUR, JAMES (1775–1842)

U.S. politician and statesman, Barbour was born in Barboursville, Virginia. He was governor of Virginia (1812–15), a U.S. senator (1815–25), and chairman of the Military Affairs and Foreign Relations committees. As John Quincy Adams's secretary of war (1825–28), he established the short-lived Infantry School of Practice at Jefferson Barracks, his intention being to concentrate scattered infantry units for tactical drills. Barbour briefly served as minister to Great Britain (1828–29). Upon his return, he suffered politically from his association with the waning National Republicans (later the Whigs) and the Adams presidency, which had been lost to Democrat Andrew Jackson in 1828. Barbour presided over the 1838 Whig convention, which nominated William Henry Harrison and John Tyler.

Stephen J. Lofgren

BARTON, CLARISSA HARLOWE (CLARA) (1821–1912)

Founder of the American Red Cross, Barton was born in Oxford, Massachusetts. From the late 1830s until 1854, she enjoyed a successful career as a schoolteacher. In 1854, she became a clerk for the federal government (possibly the first woman to do so). Upon the outbreak of the Civil War in 1861, Barton became involved in relief work. She passed through many battle lines to distribute medical supplies and food. In 1869, she retired to Europe, where she soon was immersed in the work of the International

Red Cross during the Franco-Prussian War. Barton returned to the United States in 1873, where she actively sought, and ultimately achieved in 1882, U.S. ratification of the Geneva Treaty. She served as the first president of the American Red Cross from 1882 until 1904, when she reluctantly resigned.

Bibliography: Barton, Clara, *The Story of My Life* (Journal Pub. Co., 1907); Barton, William E., *The Life of Clara Barton* (Houghton Mifflin, 1922); Pryor, Elizabeth Brown, *Clara Barton: Professional Angel* (Univ. of Pennsylvania Press, 1987).

Deborah Mesplay

BEAUREGARD, PIERRE GUSTAVE TOUTANT (1818–1893)

U.S. military leader and Confederate general, Beauregard was born in St. Bernard Parish, Louisiana. After graduating second in his West Point class (1838), he was commissioned and spent the next eight years in engineering assignments along the coasts of the Atlantic and the Gulf of Mexico. His experience served him well as a staff engineer (1846–47) with Gen. Winfield Scott during the Mexican War. He emerged from the war a brevet major, a rank earned for wounds and gallantry.

Between the Mexican conflict and the Civil War, Beauregard resided mostly in his home state, engaging in a variety of engineering activities. He supervised the construction of forts on the lower Mississippi River, as well as the New Orleans Custom House. Although Beauregard campaigned unsuccessfully for mayor of New Orleans (1858), his political connections led to his appointment as superintendent of West Point (1861). Because of his outspoken sympathy for the Southern cause, however, his tenure lasted only four days.

In early March 1861, he resigned from the U.S. Army and was appointed a brigadier general in the Army of the Confederacy. As commander of forces in and about Charleston, South Carolina, Beauregard achieved instant fame. His command of the attack on Fort Sumter gave the South its first real victory and made him the "Hero of Sumter."

In his next assignment, as commander of the main Confederate force of Virginia, Beauregard was promoted to full general after achieving, with Gen. Joseph E. Johnston, victory at the First Battle of Bull Run. Ever the politico, Beauregard fell into disfavor with Confederate president Jefferson Davis, who transferred him to the western theater.

As second-in-command to Gen. Albert S. Johnston, Beauregard planned the Confederate attack (April 1962) on the Union army commanded by Ulysses S. Grant at Shiloh, Tennessee, and assumed command of the Confederate forces after Johnston was killed in battle. In spite of Beauregard's successful retreat from Shiloh and evacuation of Corinth, Mississippi, Davis relieved him from command for failing to secure permission to take leave from the army.

Beauregard returned to Charleston in 1863, as commander of the Department of South Carolina, Georgia, and Florida. He successfully defended the city against several Union assaults. In Beauregard's next assignment, as commander of the Department of North Carolina and Southern Virginia, he stymied Union forces on the Virginia peninsula and defended Petersburg pending the arrival of the army of Gen. Robert E. Lee. Beauregard spent the final days of the war in the Military Department of the West. He lived out the postwar years in New Orleans, active in business and political affairs.

Bibliography: Williams, T. Harry, *P. G. T. Beauregard: Napoleon in Gray* (Louisiana State Univ. Press, 1954).

Carol E. Stokes

BEE, BARNARD ELLIOTT (1824–1861)

U.S. soldier and Confederate general, Bee was born in Charleston, South Carolina, and graduated from West Point in 1845. After active service on the frontier and in the Mexican War, he resigned his captaincy in the 10th Infantry and became lieutenant colonel to the 1st South Carolina Regulars.

He took command of a brigade of Confederate army recruits at Manassas Junction in June 1861. Bee's brigade, and that of Col. Francis S. Bartow, absorbed the initial attack of the Union army at the First Battle of Bull Run, on July 21. Mortally wounded, Bee died the following day after derisively referring to Confederate Brig. Gen. Thomas J. Jackson as one who stood as a "stonewall," instead of coming to the support of Bee's and Bartow's brigades. Bee posthumously was awarded the rank of brigadier general by the Provisional Confederate Congress.

Bibliography: Freeman, Douglas S., *Lee's Lieutenants* (Scribner's, 1977).

Carol E. Stokes

BELL, JOHN (1797–1869)

U.S. politician and secretary of war, Bell was born near Nashville, Tennessee. He sat in the U.S. House of Representatives (1827–41), was appointed secretary of war (1841) by Pres. William Henry Harrison, and was a U.S. senator (1847–59). In 1860, Bell was the presidential nominee of the Constitutional Union party. The party's platform condemned sectional parties and supported "the Constitution of the Country, the Union of the States, and the enforcement of the laws." Bell had virtually no chance of winning the presidency. The best he and his party could hope for was to receive enough electoral votes to prevent a Republican victory by throwing the election into the House of Representatives. Bell's 39 electoral votes (from only Kentucky, Tennessee, and Virginia) were no deterrent to Republican Abraham Lincoln's victory.

M. Guy Bishop

BENJAMIN, JUDAH PHILIP (1811–1884)

U.S. lawyer and Confederate cabinet member, Benjamin was born on the island of St. Croix, British West Indies, and came to Charleston, South Carolina, as a young child. He entered Yale University at age 14 and later opened a successful law practice in New Orleans. Among his many political offices, he was senator from Louisiana (1853–61). When his state seceded in 1861, Benjamin served successively as attorney general (1861), secretary of war (1861–62), and secretary of state (1862–65) for the Confederacy. Despite Jefferson Davis's continuing support of him, Benjamin enjoyed little popularity among Confederates, due largely to his contention that slaves should be trained and armed as defenders of the Confederacy.

After the Civil War, he fled to England and began a lucrative career as a barrister. Benjamin was appointed queen's counsel in 1872. In 1883, he retired to Paris, where his wife had lived apart from him for many years.

Bibliography: Evans, Eli, *Judah P. Benjamin: The Jewish Confederate* (Free Press, 1987); Meade, Robert D., *Judah P. Benjamin: Confederate Statesman* (Oxford Univ. Press, 1943).

Roger D. Launius

BIDDLE, JAMES (1783–1848)

U.S. naval officer, Biddle was born in Philadelphia. He joined the U.S. Navy in 1800 and was captured by Barbary pirates in 1803 and imprisoned for 19 months. In the War of 1812, he was a lieutenant on the *Wasp* when it captured the *Frolic,* and later when the *Wasp* was taken by the British *Poictiers*. In 1813, Biddle commanded the *Hornet,* capturing the British brig *Penquin* on Mar. 23, 1815. In that same year, he was promoted to captain and awarded the Congressional Gold Medal. In 1817, he negotiated the handing over of British-held Oregon. In 1846, as commodore of the East India Squadron, he negotiated the first treaty between the United States and China.

Russell A. Hart

BLACK HAWK (c. 1767–1838)

Sac Indian chieftain, Black Hawk (Ma-ka-tae-mish-kia-kiak) was born near present-day Rock Island, Illinois. In 1829, the U.S. Government removed the Sac and Fox to Iowa. Black Hawk, a noted pro-British war chief, resisted removal until 1831 and, unhappy in Iowa, planned to return to Illinois. Encouraged by false hopes of support from other tribes and the British, he led his followers back in April 1832. Gen. Henry Atkinson immediately sent troops and demanded the band surrender. Black Hawk refused and fled. A bungled surrender attempt in May started a fighting retreat north and westward through Wisconsin. Black Hawk evaded his pursuers until he reached the Mississippi River near the mouth of the Bad Axe River in late July. There Atkinson's troops caught the Sac and Fox as they tried to cross the river and decimated them. Black Hawk surrendered after the fight and, following a brief imprisonment, returned to Iowa.

Bibliography: Black Hawk, *Life of Black Hawk: Ma-Ka-Tai-Me-She-Kia-Kiak,* ed. by Donald Jackson (Univ. of Illinois Press, 1964).

Richard F. Kehrberg

BONNEVILLE, BENJAMIN LOUIS EULALIE DE (1796–1878)

U.S. explorer and military leader, Bonneville was born in Paris, France, and raised in the United States. He graduated from West Point in 1815 and was posted to the frontier in 1821, where he became fascinated with the commercial fur trade in the West. In 1832 he was granted a two-year leave of absence from the army to explore and trap in the Rocky Mountains. Although he overstayed his absence, he returned to the army in 1836.

Bonneville was recognized for gallantry at Contreras and Churubusco during the Mexican War and, for his meritorious service, was brevetted a brigadier general at the close of the Civil War. His exploits were enlarged in Washington Irving's *The Adventures of Captain Bonneville* (1837).

2d Lt. R. John Warsinske

BRAGG, BRAXTON (1817–1876)

U.S. soldier and Confederate military leader, Bragg was born in Warren County, North Carolina, and graduated fifth from the West Point Class of 1837. Posted with the 3d Artillery, he was soon commissioned a captain and saw extensive action in Florida during the Seminole War. In 1838, Bragg was assigned to Gen. Winfield Scott's command, at that time posted near Chattanooga. Bragg soon took over command of Fort Cummins, a post he would hold for some time.

The Mexican War. During the Mexican War, Bragg was assigned to the forces commanded by Gen. Zachary Taylor and fought in the battles of Palo Alto and Resaca de la Palma. During the defense of Fort Brown, opposite Mariano Matamoros in May 1846, Bragg was commended for bravery under fire. Following the bombardment of Monterrey, he was cited for "conspicuous bravery." Likewise, during the Battle of Buena Vista, Bragg was complimented by his superior officers for personally leading an assault on an enemy position. After the war, Bragg accompanied Col. Albert Sidney Johnston on the latter's expedition to the Utah Territory. In January 1856, Bragg resigned his commission and retired to his Louisiana plantation.

The Civil War. At the outbreak of the Civil War, Bragg accepted a commission as a brigadier general in the Con-

Confederate Gen. Braxton Bragg was known for his organizational skills, but also for his harsh and sometimes brutal disciplinary measures, which often caused great animosity among his troops, and for his hesitancy on the field of battle. (Library of Congress)

federate army and was placed in command of Confederate forces in Pensacola, Florida. In September 1861, he was promoted to major general. In February 1862, he established headquarters at Mobile, Alabama. Bragg's 2d Division was ordered to join the army of General Johnston, which was then operating in the Trans-Mississippi Department, with Gen. P. G. T. Beauregard as commander in chief. Headquartered at Jackson, Bragg set about to organize and prepare his forces for the forthcoming fight. He established martial law, prohibited the sale of alcoholic beverages to his troops, and issued an order prohibiting the mistreatment of federal prisoners. While his administrative skills were excellent, Bragg's performance on the battlefield would be called into question.

Bragg's first major engagement was on Apr. 6, 1862, during the Battle of Shiloh, where he commanded the Confederates' center. Bragg's troops advanced toward the hastily entrenched Union forces approximately two miles before encountering their first heavy opposition. Fighting through layers of Union defenses, the Confederate forces became entangled with other units or were separated from their parent command. Writing his wife, Elise, of the first two days of battle, Bragg called Beauregard's overall plan for attacking Gen. Ulysses S. Grant's forces "muddled" and stated that the commander in chief "hesitated," thereby allowing the Union forces a chance to retreat. Likewise, Bragg has been faulted for ordering a costly bayonet charge in the face of heavy Union musket fire.

After Shiloh, Jefferson Davis appointed Bragg a full general, making him fifth-ranking officer in the Confederacy. With his promotion, Bragg's reputation throughout the South was enhanced favorably. Alabama's Gov. John G. Shorter and Congressman Jabez L. M. Curry praised Bragg's "brilliant performance at Shiloh . . . and his efforts to organize and train his army." Despite these acclamations, Bragg's reputation as a strict martinet, coupled with his inability to deal with his subordinates, caused severe morale problems among his troops. Bragg never granted furloughs and instead enforced temperance, maintenance of a strong training schedule, and severe punishments to offenders. He also enforced the newly enacted Conscription Act by refusing to allow the volunteers under his command to leave for home. Several newspapers criticized his "uncalled-for brutality, and unjust and improper treatment of volunteers." The Tennessee regiments in particular hated Bragg. In one case, an entire regiment of Tennessee volunteers refused to perform their duties. Bragg, wanting to make his point clear, surrounded the entire unit and gave them five minutes to resume their duties, or he would have them summarily executed for "mutiny." Those who deserted and later were caught were, without trial, executed by firing squads. Bragg was not necessarily as bloodthirsty as his detractors have claimed. Many contend that his harsh methods and insistence on prohibiting alcohol improved the overall health of his forces. In fact, Bragg's army became a model for further Confederate reorganization.

During the Battle of Corinth (April–June 1862), part of Bragg's corps supported Gen. Earl Van Dorn's attack against Gen. Henry Halleck's Union forces. Issuing a stirring proclamation to his troops, Bragg told them that by forcing the Union troops to retreat, the "portals to the entire Northwest would be open to them." Bragg's forces attacked the federals on time, but due to the failure of Van Dorn to force Gen. William Rosecrans out of his defensive positions at Corinth, Beauregard ordered a retreat.

After Corinth, Bragg and Gen. Kirby Smith proposed a two-pronged offensive aimed at securing Kentucky. On September 5, Bragg's forces entered the state and proceeded past Bowling Green, aiming for the capture of Munfordsville to demand its surrender. By September 17, Confederate forces were able to occupy the city. By October 4, both Bragg's and Smith's forces linked up at Frankfort, proclaiming that "Kentucky had been finally 'avenged'." Unwilling to concede Frankfort or Kentucky to the Confederacy, three powerful Union corps, commanded by Gen. Don Carlos Buell, recaptured Bardstown and advanced toward the Confederates at Perryville, hoping to force the Confederates into retreat. In some of the fiercest fighting that would take place on Kentucky soil, Buell attacked Bragg's forces from the rear with the intention of cutting off any Confederate retreat. Characteristic of his offensive-minded strategy, Bragg ordered his forces to charge the Union positions. As Bragg later recounted in his official report to President Davis, the fighting that proceeded was the "most severe and most desperately contested within [his] knowledge." Fighting outnumbered and underequipped, the Confederates desperately fought off repeated attacks that lasted all night. Casualties on both sides numbered approximately 6,500, including 2 Union and 3 Confederate brigadier generals. After the Battle of Perryville, Bragg's forces retreated back into Tennessee.

Bragg later directed Confederate forces at the battles of Chickamauga and Chattanooga, and his performance at both was dismal. During these engagements, Bragg's unpopularity with his fellow officers and enlisted men reached a climax, and his indecisiveness at critical moments revealed what most had known earlier: he was not capable of handling a major force in battle. After the failure at Chattanooga, Bragg was relieved of command and ordered to Richmond, where he served as President Davis's military adviser. When Gen. Robert E. Lee was appointed commander in chief of all Confederate forces, Bragg was appointed division commander in Gen. Joseph E. Johnston's Army of Tennessee.

As a field grade officer, Bragg's competence was never questioned, but his hesitancy and application of outmoded, Napoleonic-era tactics were his downfall. Yet, his talents as an organizer and strict disciplinarian turned raw volunteers into a highly effective fighting force. Had Davis recognized Bragg's "peculiar talent" (as Gen. Leonidas Polk wrote of Bragg), the coordination and overall fighting ability of Southern arms may have been dramatically improved.

Bibliography: McWhiney, Grady, *Braxton Bragg and Confederate Defeat; Vol. 1: Field Command* (Columbia Univ. Press, 1969); Snow, William Parker, *Southern Generals: Their Lives and Campaigns* (Charles B. Richardson, 1866); Williams, T. Harry, *The History of American Wars: From Colonial Times to World War I* (Knopf, 1981).

Leo J. Daugherty III

BRECKINRIDGE, JOHN CABELL (1821–75)

U.S. politician and Confederate secretary of war, Breckinridge was born near Lexington, Kentucky, and practiced law before entering politics. Having served in the U.S. House of Representatives (1851–55), he became James Buchanan's vice president (1857–61) and briefly a U.S. senator (1861). Breckinridge resigned his Senate seat and was appointed a Confederate brigadier general in November 1861. After commanding Kentucky troops at Shiloh, he led a division at Stones River, Vicksburg, and Chickamauga. He then commanded the Department of Southwest Tennessee until ordered to western Virginia in February 1864. There, he organized his forces and led them at Cold Harbor. He assisted in Gen. Jubal Early's raid on Washington and fought in the Third Battle of Winchester. In February 1865, Breckinridge was named Pres. Jefferson Davis's secretary of war. After Appomattox, he participated in surrender negotiations as adviser to Gen. Joseph E. Johnston. Soon after, Breckinridge fled the country, living in exile until his return to Kentucky in 1869.

Bibliography: Davis, William C., *Breckinridge: Statesman, Soldier, Symbol* (Louisiana State Univ. Press, 1974).

Lt. Col. (Ret.) Joseph W. A. Whitehorne

BROWN, JACOB JENNINGS (1775–1828)

U.S. military leader, Brown was born in Bucks County, Pennsylvania. He served with distinction in the War of 1812—particularly at Sacket's Harbor, Chippewa, and Lundy's Lane. He ended the war a major general and was given command of the northern division of the U.S. Army. By act of Congress, Brown formally became General of the Army in 1821. That same year, he suffered a stroke that permanently weakened his health. Until his death, Brown worked within the constraints of his ill-defined position in Washington, advising the administration on military matters and recommending such improvements as pay incentives for reenlistments, centralized unit training, and the establishment of schools of practice for the artillery and infantry.

Stephen J. Lofgren

BUCHANAN, FRANKLIN (1800–1874)

U.S. and Confederate naval officer, Buchanan was born in Baltimore, Maryland. Well known as a strict disciplinarian, a fine seaman, and an early proponent of steam power, he was selected as the first superintendent (1845–47) of the Naval Academy at Annapolis, an institute he helped found. He later saw action in the Mexican War and in 1852 departed with Matthew C. Perry on his historic voyage to Japan.

Siding with the South in the Civil War, Franklin (nicknamed "Old Buck") commanded the CSS *Virginia (Merrimac)* on the first day of the Battle of Hampton Roads (Mar. 8, 1862). He was promoted to admiral in August, and at the Battle of Mobile Bay (Aug. 5, 1864) he gained lasting fame by sailing the lone ironclad ram *Tennessee* into the midst of the 17-ship Union flotilla in a last-ditch quixotic charge. He was defeated and captured by Adm. David G. Farragut, but his heroics had earned him the label "the Nelson of the Confederacy."

Bibliography: Todorich, Charles M., "Franklin Buchanan: Symbol for Two Navies," *Captains of the Old*

Steam Navy, ed. by James C. Bradford (Naval Inst. Press, 1986).

Maj. Grant H. Walker

BUCHANAN, JAMES (1791–1868)

Fifteenth president of the United States (1857–61), Buchanan was born near Mercersburg, Pennsylvania, and practiced law before entering politics. After 10 years in the U.S. House of Representatives (1821–31), he served as minister to Russia (1832–34), U.S. senator (1834–45), secretary of state (1845–49), and minister to Great Britain (1853–56). As the Democrats' compromise candidate, he was elected president in 1856, amid the intensifying conflict over slavery that would predominate his presidency and eventually precipitate the Civil War.

Buchanan's objective clearly was to promote a peaceful reconciliation between the North and South, but his administration was ineffective due largely to the president's lack of personal and political consistency: Buchanan called slavery a moral wrong but opposed congressional interference; he vowed to save the Union but was decidedly sympathetic to proslavery interests; he denied any state's right to secede but denied the federal government's right to prevent secession. Throughout his term, Buchanan supported numerous measures of compromise, but by 1861, North-South tensions had escalated beyond negotiation and the Confederacy had been formed.

Stephen J. Lofgren

BUCKNER, SIMON BOLIVAR (1823–1914)

U.S. military officer and Confederate general, born near Munfordville, Kentucky, and graduated from West Point in 1844. After service in the Mexican War he resigned in 1855 to enter business. Although not a slave owner, Buckner's sympathies were with the South; he became a Confederate brigadier general in September 1861. On Feb. 16, 1862, he surrendered Fort Donelson to his West Point classmate and close friend Brig. Gen. Ulysses S. Grant, after his two seniors fled the battle. Exchanged and promoted to major general, Buckner commanded a division under Gen. Braxton Bragg during the latter's 1862 invasion of Kentucky. He was a corps commander at Chickamauga (1863) but broke with Bragg and joined those advocating Bragg's removal. Buckner later was promoted to lieutenant general in the Trans-Mississippi Department under Gen. Kirby Smith, where he surrendered after Appomattox. After the war, Buckner served as governor of Kentucky (1887–91) and ran unsuccessfully for vice president in 1896 on the Gold Democrat ticket.

Bibliography: Stickles, Arndt M., *Simon Bolivar Buckner: Borderland Knight* (Broadfoot Pub. Co., 1987).

T. C. Mulligan

BUELL, DON CARLOS (1818–1898)

U.S. military leader, Buell was born near Marietta, Ohio, and graduated from West Point in 1841. He served in the Seminole and Mexican wars, attaining the rank of brevet major in 1847. Appointed a brigadier general in May 1861, he helped organize Union troops around Washington and in November succeeded William T. Sherman as commanding general of the Department of the Ohio.

While Ulysses S. Grant advanced south along the Tennessee River, Buell occupied Bowling Green, Kentucky, and then Nashville, Tennessee, in February 1862. Promoted to major general in March, Buell led his forces to Shiloh, Tennessee, on April 6, 1862, in time to contribute to the Union victory. Buell's forces aided in the capture of Corinth, Mississippi, and then moved eastward toward Chattanooga, Tennessee. In July, Buell rushed northward to Louisville, Kentucky, to protect his supply lines threatened by Gen. Braxton Bragg's invasion of Kentucky. After much prodding, Buell moved south and engaged Bragg's force at Perryville, Kentucky, on October 8. The battle resulted in a draw. Bragg retreated southward to Tennessee, but Buell failed to pursue the retreating Confederate forces.

Buell was replaced by Gen. William S. Rosecrans, and a military commission began a seven-month investigation of Buell's conduct in Tennessee and Kentucky. No official report was ever issued. From May 1863, Buell awaited a new assignment; he resigned his commission on June 1, 1864. After the war, he served as president of the Green River Iron Company in Louisville, Kentucky.

Bibliography: McDonough, James, *Shiloh—In Hell Before Night* (Univ. of Tennessee Press, 1977).

Steve R. Waddell

BUFORD, JOHN (1826–1863)

U.S. military leader, Buford was born in Kentucky and graduated from West Point in 1848. He served with the cavalry on the frontier and during the Mormon War. In November 1861, he was assigned to the defenses of Washington. He was promoted in June 1862 to brigadier general in command of a cavalry brigade in Gen. John Pope's Army of Virginia. Buford did exceptionally well throughout the ill-fated Second Bull Run Campaign. He acted as army chief of cavalry at Antietam and Fredericksburg before returning to his brigade and participated in Gen. George Stoneman's raid on Richmond. Buford was promoted to major general in June 1863, and on July 1, he executed a brilliant defense of McPherson Ridge, west of Gettysburg. His men bought the time necessary for the federal army to deploy and bring on a decisive battle. Buford's constant hard campaigning resulted in a physical collapse; he died in December.

Bibliography: Hassler, Warren W., Jr., *Crisis at the Crossroads: The First Day at Gettysburg* (Univ. of Alabama Press, 1970).

Lt. Col. (Ret.) Joseph W. A. Whitehorne

BURNSIDE, AMBROSE EVERETT (1824–1881)

U.S. military leader, Burnside was born in Liberty, Indiana, and graduated from West Point in 1847. He was sent to the Southwest for service in the Mexican War. Burnside saw no active part in the war except as part of a detail that escorted a supply train through enemy country. He next served on the southwestern frontier, where he was wounded in a skirmish with the Apache in 1849. In 1851, he was promoted to first lieutenant.

During his time in Mexico and on the frontier, Burnside became interested in arms design. He noted numerous defects in the army's Hall breechloader and thought he could design a better weapon. In 1853, he resigned his commission to devote full attention to this endeavor. He moved to Bristol, Rhode Island, to manufacture his carbine. However, he lacked the political influence needed to get a government contract. The Panic of 1857 threw him into bankruptcy, and he was forced to assign his patent to creditors. The following year, he approached an acquaintance from West Point, George B. McClellan, about a job. McClellan, who was at the time chief engineer of the Illinois Central Railroad, got Burnside a job as a cashier in the company land office.

The Civil War. At the outbreak of the Civil War, Burnside held the rank of major general in the Rhode Island State Militia. In response to President Lincoln's call for volunteers, he organized and commanded the 1st Rhode Island Infantry Regiment. Burnside performed credibly in command of a brigade consisting of Rhode Island, New Hampshire, and New York regiments. In August 1861, he was promoted to brigadier general. In October, he organized a special division for operations against the North Carolina coast. What followed was one of Burnside's most successful wartime efforts. In combined operations with the Union navy, his force took Roanoke Island along with 2,500 Confederate prisoners on Feb. 8, 1862. He captured New Bern on March 14 and Beaufort on April 11. Forces were also sent to threaten other North Carolina cities as well as Norfolk and Suffolk, Virginia.

In July, Burnside and about 7,500 men from his command were sent to reinforce McClellan on the Peninsula. This became the nucleus of the IX Corps. While on the Peninsula, Burnside was offered command of the Army of the Potomac by Lincoln. He turned down the offer, arguing that his friend McClellan was the best man for the job and that he (Burnside) was not qualified for such a high command. Following the Union defeat at the Second Battle of Bull Run, he was again offered army command but refused.

At Antietam, McClellan placed Burnside in command of an entity known as his "right wing." This ambiguous command consisted of the I and IX Corps. However, the I Corps commander, Gen. Joseph Hooker, persuaded McClellan to detach his corps, leaving Burnside with only the IX Corps to operate on the Union left. This action and McClellan's failure to send Burnside reinforcements in his attacks against the Confederate right caused a serious rift between the two old friends.

When McClellan failed to pursue Gen. Robert E. Lee after Antietam, Lincoln relieved him of command and put a reluctant Burnside in his place. Burnside stalked Lee's army to Fredericksburg, where on December 13, the Army of the Potomac, hurled across open ground against well-entrenched Confederates, suffered nearly 13,000 casualties. Mortified by his losses, Burnside offered personally to lead the army against the enemy but was talked out of this suicidal gesture by his officers.

In January 1863, his army embarked on another failed effort against Lee known as the "Mud March." By now, Burnside's relations with many of his officers were severely strained, and he offered to resign. Instead, Lincoln assigned him to command the Department of the Ohio, where he supervised the arrest and trial of Copperhead Clement Vallandigham and led the defense of the region against Morgan's Raiders. In the fall of 1863, Burnside successfully defended Knoxville from Gen. James Longstreet's corps.

In May 1864, Burnside took command of the reorganized IX Corps in the Overland Campaign. He was accused of bungling the Union follow-up to the Petersburg mine assault (July 1864), an event that caused heavy Union casualties. Although the charges against him may not have been entirely fair—there were numerous problems at brigade, division, and army levels, plus last-minute political interference—Burnside was relieved of command and finally resigned on Apr. 15, 1865.

Postwar Career. Burnside retired to civilian life and was elected governor of Rhode Island (1866–69). In 1870, he went to Europe and served as an unofficial observer of the Franco-Prussian War and, on one occasion, as a go-between for the German and French governments. He returned to Rhode Island and was elected U.S. senator (1875–81). He is remembered for his distinctive style of whiskers, known then as "burnsides" and today as "sideburns."

Bibliography: Luvass, Jay, and Harold Nelson, *The U.S. Army War College Guide to the Battle of Antietam: The Maryland Campaign of 1862* (South Mountain Press, 1987); *Memorial Addresses on the Life and Character of Ambrose E. Burnside* (Washington, 1882); Sears, Stephen,

Landscape Turned Red: The Battle of Antietam (Ticknor and Fields, 1983); ———, *George B. McClellan: The Young Napoleon* (Ticknor and Fields, 1988).

Ted Alexander

BUTLER, BENJAMIN FRANKLIN (1818–1893)

U.S. attorney, politician, and military officer, Butler was born in Deerfield, New Hampshire. In 1860, he was elected as a delegate to the Democratic convention in Charleston, South Carolina, and voted for the nomination of Jefferson C. Davis from Mississippi. Likewise, he vigorously supported the nomination of John C. Breckinridge from Kentucky at the "rump" convention held in Baltimore, Maryland. Despite his apparent political ties to the South, when war broke out, Butler immediately offered his services to the Union.

The Civil War. Through political influence with Sec. of War Simon Cameron and the governor of Massachusetts, Butler secured a promotion to brigadier general of Massachusetts volunteers and took command of the 8th Regiment in April 1861. When his troops entered Baltimore by rail in May, prosecessionist forces attempted to block their train. Butler quickly took control of the city, enforcing a strict curfew and a suspension of civil liberties. On May 16, Butler became the first major general of U.S. volunteers.

Union Maj. Gen. Benjamin Franklin Butler, an attorney and politician in civilian life, was better at administrative duties than on the battlefield. (Library of Congress)

As a field commander, Butler was clearly underqualified, and one of the first engagements that exhibited his military incompetence followed his occupation of Fortress Monroe along the James River in Virginia. After an initial skirmish with Confederate forces, Butler's volunteers broke and ran, deserting the battlefield and leaving behind valuable equipment. This one incident almost cost Butler his commission. Soon afterward, however, Butler led a successful amphibious assault against the Confederate coastal areas along Cape Hatteras: In August 1861, Butler and a force of 900 soldiers occupied the forts guarding the entrance to Hatteras Inlet. The Union navy thus secured the base needed to establish a blockade against the Confederate ports of Wilmington and Charleston.

Butler led the land forces in the capture of New Orleans (May 1, 1862) and immediately became military governor. His administration of New Orleans was framed within a harsh civil code that aroused much criticism and protest throughout the South and among many Northerners as well. Issued on May 15, his "Woman Order" stated: ". . . when any female shall, by word . . . or movement . . . show contempt for any officer or soldier of the United States, she shall be . . . held liable to be treated as a woman of the town plying her avocation." When a citizen of New Orleans tore down a U.S. flag from a public building, Butler ordered his immediate execution. Such acts prompted outcries against the "barbarity" of the Union occupation of New Orleans and furthered English and French support of the Confederacy. Butler soon was dubbed "Beast" Butler, and a proclamation issued by Pres. Jefferson Davis branded him an outlaw to be "immediately executed if captured by hanging."

Amid widespread controversy, Butler continued his governorship of New Orleans and was regarded by many as an efficient and capable administrator. Butler also took steps to revive the city's economy, but these were tainted by numerous charges, never substantiated, of graft and corruption.

Butler was the first Union commander to raise his own regiments of black troops, something that no other Union commander had dared attempt—in light of Lincoln's known disapproval. Well aware of the president's sentiments, Butler raised his black troops without informing the War Department until it was an accomplished fact. In all, he formed three regiments of black infantry and two companies of black artillery. Butler was replaced as military governor by Gen. Nathaniel Banks in December 1862 and was given command of the Army of the James, which was comprised of two corps preparing for the assault on Richmond.

In May 1864, Butler's forces were transferred up the James River, landing 15 miles from the city limits of Richmond. Facing a Confederate force numbering only

5,000, Butler's 30,000-man force easily could have marched into the city. Here again, Butler's indecisiveness and lack of aggressiveness were brought to the fore as Gen. P. G. T. Beauregard, the Confederate general in charge of the city's defenses, was able to assemble a force nearly equaling that of Butler's and launch a furious counterattack that drove Butler's forces back across the narrow neck of land between the James and Appomattox rivers just north of Petersburg. Because of his political influence, however, Butler was able to avoid blame for this fiasco, although the War Department did assign Butler first to New York City then back home to Massachusetts to await further orders.

In October 1864, upon hearing about the plans to seize Fort Fisher near Wilmington, North Carolina, Butler successfully pressured the War Department for the top command. However, due to his inability to coordinate a successful assault, Butler's forces were forced to withdraw from the beachhead after Adm. David Porter's fleet had failed to silence the guns of Fort Fisher, thereby preventing Union troops from launching a direct frontal assault on the Confederate position. Instead, Butler ordered his forces to retire back to the James River, after which he finally was relieved of his command.

Postwar Career. After the war, Butler resumed his political life, serving in the U.S. House of Representatives (1867–75, 1877–79) and as governor of Massachusetts (1882–84). In 1884, the short-lived Anti-Monopoly and Greenback parties nominated Butler for the presidency.

Bibliography: Holzman, Robert S., *Stormy Ben Butler* (Macmillan Co., 1954); McPherson, James M., *Ordeal by Fire: The Civil War and Reconstruction* (Knopf, 1982); Reed, Rowena, *Combined Operations in the Civil War* (Naval Inst. Press, 1978).

Leo J. Daugherty III

BUTTERFIELD, DANIEL (1831–1901)

U.S. military leader, Butterfield was born in Utica, New York. He entered armed service in 1861 by way of the New York Militia and was colonel of the 15th New York at the First Battle of Bull Run. Promoted to brigadier general of volunteers, he commanded a brigade and was awarded (in 1892) the Medal of Honor for action at Gaines's Mill during the Peninsular Campaign (Mar.–July 1862). Rising to command a division and a corps, Butterfield became a major general but reverted to a division command after his lackluster performance in the Fredericksburg Campaign (Nov.–Dec. 1862). In January 1863, he became chief of staff of the Army of the Potomac. Wounded at Gettysburg, he recovered to command a division in the XX Corps at Chattanooga (Oct.–Nov. 1863).

After the war, Butterfield was chief of the recruiting service and commander of the 5th U.S. Infantry in the grade of colonel; he resigned in 1870 to return to private business. He was a bold fighter who won rapid promotion, but his abrasive personality and cronyism made him unpopular. He is credited with composing the bugle call "Taps" and instituting the army's system of corps badges. He died in Utica and is buried at the U.S. Military Academy.

Bibliography: Butterfield, Julia Lorrilard, *A Biographical Memorial of General Daniel Butterfield* (Grafton Press, 1904).

T. C. Mulligan

CALHOUN, JOHN CALDWELL (1782–1850)

U.S. secretary of war (1817–25) and vice president (1825–32), Calhoun was born near Abbeville, South Carolina. A graduate of Yale, he became a lawyer in South Carolina and in 1811 entered the House of Representatives, where he soon allied himself with the Warhawks. Calhoun maintained a lively interest in military affairs all through his public life, and in the War of 1812, he called for war "to avenge the wrongs, and vindicate the rights and honor of the Nation."

Offered the post of secretary of war by James Monroe after several others declined, Calhoun in 1817 took over a military establishment in disarray and deeply in debt. The U.S. army's poor performance in the War of 1812 convinced him that drastic reforms were needed to promote both efficiency and professionalism. Since food "sustains the immense machinery of war," he sought to improve rations, opposing only "the spirit part" that was issued regularly. He oversaw a reorganization of the army's pay and pension systems. He approved broad curricular reforms at West Point that greatly improved the quality of officer education. He backed the construction of a system of coastal defenses and frontier fortifications and established boards of experienced officers to examine the workings of each arm of the service and to suggest improvements; artillerymen especially appreciated his efforts to create "flying" artillery to accompany cavalry.

The size of the army and its efficient administration especially demanded Calhoun's attention. Despite fiscal concerns, he opposed a reduction in the legally mandated 10,000-man army, claiming that those who considered it "dangerous to our liberty" suffered more from "timidity than wisdom." As a compromise, he offered an expansible army plan that would allow a reduction in force in peacetime while retaining the capacity to expand quickly at the outset of war. Skeleton units, fully officered but with only partly filled enlisted ranks, could absorb recruits readily when needed. He believed firmly that no part of the army "requires more attention in peace than the general staff" and pushed for a larger and reorganized staff to promote the army's efficiency.

From 1828, when he first developed his theory of nullification, Calhoun was the foremost supporter of states' rights, a doctrine that became the philosophical basis of the Confederacy. In 1832, he resigned as Andrew Jackson's vice president to enter the Senate. He remained there until 1843, returned briefly to South Carolina, and then became secretary of state (1844–45). During his brief tenure, he supported the annexation of Texas, which would be open to slavery. He returned to the Senate in 1846 and served until his death.

In his later career, no longer fearing a foreign invasion, Calhoun supported reducing the army's size. He saw the navy now as "the right arm of defense." Opposing the use of force for national aggrandizement, he sought a peaceful solution to the Oregon question and disapproved of the Mexican War (1846–48). When Calhoun died in 1850, Gen. Nathan Towson spoke for many when he praised the South Carolinian's "master mind" for improving "all arms and all branches of the service."

Bibliography: Wilson, Clyde N., et al. (eds.), *The Papers of John C. Calhoun* (Univ. of South Carolina Press, 1959–); Wiltse, Charles M., *John C. Calhoun,* 3 vols. (Bobbs-Merrill, 1940–51).

Carol Reardon

CAMERON, SIMON (1799–1889)

U.S. political leader and secretary of war, born in Maytown, Pennsylvania. He entered the printing trade at age 17 and went on to become state printer. He was also appointed adjutant general of the Pennsylvania militia. As commissioner to the Winnebago, Cameron was accused of mishandling Indian claim funds.

Breaking with the Democrats over tariff policies and his own prospects for political advancement, Cameron joined the Whigs and won a seat in the U.S. Senate in 1845. In 1854, he joined the new Republican party, attracted by its free-soil and probusiness ideologies. In spite of a Democratic majority in the Pennsylvania state senate, Cameron's 1856 reelection to the U.S. Senate cemented his control of the Republican party in Pennsylvania. This remained his power base for the rest of his political career.

At the Republican national convention of 1860, Cameron held firm control of the Pennsylvania delegation. He negotiated a deal with Lincoln's campaign managers—without Lincoln's knowledge—trading the Pennsylvania votes for a cabinet post. Reluctantly, and with distaste, President Lincoln appointed Cameron secretary of war.

Secretary of War Cameron confronted the task of raising a huge national army, essentially from scratch, from within a polity that formerly had rejected such an institution on principle. His penchant for staffing the War Department with political cronies only furthered his reputation as a corrupt politician. (Historians have concluded that Cameron's friends were enriched by defense contracts, but no evidence shows that he profited personally.)

By January 1862, Lincoln eased him out of Washington with an appointment as minister to Russia. While at St. Petersburg, Cameron secured Russian support for the Union cause. Within a year, he was back in the United States, consolidating his control of Pennsylvania Republican politics. He continued to support the president and extended this support to Andrew Johnson after Lincoln's assassination.

Cameron's only rival for power in Pennsylvania was the strong-willed Gov. Andrew Curtin, with whom he had a protracted political struggle. By 1867, Cameron had clearly prevailed, winning a U.S. Senate seat in a direct contest with Curtin. He served in the Senate until 1877, when he managed to pass his seat to his son.

Bibliography: Bradley, Erwin Stanley, *Simon Cameron: Lincoln's Secretary of War, A Political Biography* (Univ. of Pennsylvania Press, 1966); Crippen, Lee L., *Simon Cameron: Ante-Bellum Years* (Mississippi Valley Press, 1942).

T. C. Mulligan

CARSON, CHRISTOPHER (KIT) (1809–1869)

U.S. scout and military officer, Carson was born in Madison County, Kentucky. In 1846, at the onset of the Mexican War, he served in California with Lt. Col. John C. Frémont. In August, Comdr. Robert F. Stockton, military governor of California, sent Carson east with dispatches regarding affairs on the West Coast. Carson met Gen. Stephen W. Kearny near Albuquerque. Learning of the conquest of California, Kearny prevailed upon Carson to guide his Army of the West back to California. Near Los Angeles, Andres Pico's Mexican forces, the Californios, ambushed Kearny at San Pasqual. Beseiged by Pico, Kearny sent Carson for a relief party. The arrival of more Americans caused the Californios to withdraw.

M. Guy Bishop

CASS, LEWIS (1782–1866)

U.S. military and political leader, Cass was born in Exeter, New Hampshire. He served in the War of 1812, attaining the rank of brigadier general. Appointed governor of the Michigan Territory (1813–31), he also served as President Jackson's secretary of war (1831–36) and the U.S. minister to France (1836–42). Twice elected to the Senate (1845; 1849), Cass aspired as many times to the presidency, losing the Democratic nomination to James K. Polk (1842) and the election to Whig Zachary Taylor (1848).

After Cass supported the Compromise of 1850, including the Fugitive Slave Law, and Stephen Douglas's doctrine of "popular sovereignty," Michigan's Republican legislature removed him from the Senate (1856). As President Buchanan's secretary of state (1857–60), Cass, who supported the Union and opposed slavery, resigned his office in 1960.

Bibliography: Woodford, Frank B., *Lewis Cass: The Last Jeffersonian* (Hippocrene Books, 1951).

Carol E. Stokes

CHAMBERLAIN, JOSHUA LAWRENCE (1828–1914)

U.S. educator and military officer, Chamberlain was born in Brewer, Maine, and graduated from Bowdoin College in 1852. At Bowdoin, he held professorships in rhetoric and oratory and in modern languages.

The Civil War. In 1862, Chamberlain took a leave of absence, ostensibly to study abroad. Instead, he joined the 20th Maine Regiment of Volunteers as lieutenant colonel. He fought at Antietam and Fredericksburg in late 1862 and was promoted to colonel in May 1863. At Gettysburg, Chamberlain's 20th Maine held the Union left on Little Round Top (July 2, 1863) against repeated assaults, finally breaking the Confederate attack with a furious bayonet charge. His inspiring leadership brought Chamberlain brigade command and the Congressional Medal of Honor (1893). He was wounded several times, almost fatally at Petersburg (June 1864), where Gen. Ulysses S. Grant promoted him on the spot to brigadier general, and a final time on the Quaker Road (March 1865), where he was brevetted major general. He fought conspicuously through Five Forks to Appomattox. There, Grant chose him to accept the formal surrender of Gen. Robert E. Lee's army. In a chivalrous gesture that enraged the Radical Republicans but was completely in character, Chamberlain rendered honors to his former enemies.

Joshua Lawrence Chamberlain, later a governor of Maine and president of his alma mater, Bowdoin College, was the officer chosen by General Grant to accept Confederate General Lee's surrender at Appomattox. (U.S. Army Military History Institute)

Postwar Career. Chamberlain was mustered out in 1866 and was elected governor of Maine (1866–71). He served as president of Bowdoin College (1871–83) and preserved the peace as major general of the Maine State Militia during election disputes (1878–79).

Bibliography: Chamberlain, Joshua Lawrence, *The Passing of the Armies* (Putnam's, 1915; reprint, Press of Morningside Bookshop, 1989); Powell, William H., *The Fifth Army Corps* (Putnam's, 1896); Pullen, John J., *The Twentieth Maine* (Lippincott, 1960; reprint, Press of Morningside Bookshop, 1983); Wallace, Willard M., *Soul of the Lion* (Nelson, 1960).

Col. (Ret.) Louis D. F. Frasché

CLARK, WILLIAM (1770–1838)

U.S. frontiersman and explorer, Clark was born in Caroline County, Virginia. He served with Gen. Anthony Wayne at the Battle of Fallen Timbers in 1794. Between 1803 and 1806, he and Meriwether Lewis led an expedition to the Northwest, proving the practicability of an overland route to the Pacific.

In 1813, Clark became governor of Missouri Territory, and during the War of 1812, he secured the frontier from British-incited Indian attack. When Missouri was admitted to the Union in 1822, Congress appointed Clark superintendent of Indian affairs. He is remembered as having been fair, humane, and honest in his dealings with the tribes.

Bibliography: Steffen, Jerome O., *William Clark: Jeffersonian Man on the Frontier* (Univ. of Oklahoma Press, 1977).

Roger D. Launius

COCHISE (1812?-1876)

Chief of the Chiricahua Apache, Cochise warred against the Mexicans in the 1850s alongside Chief Magnus Colarado of the Mimbrano Apache. In 1860, Cochise was falsely accused of kidnapping an American child. His subsequent capture by the U.S. Army resulted in his being arrested and wounded. Cochise escaped, but five of his followers were hanged.

After rallying his people, Cochise, with Magnus Colarado, ambushed Gen. James H. Carleton at the Apache Pass only to be dislodged at nightfall by howitzer fire. Cochise raided until September 1871, when the U.S. government guaranteed him the Chiricahua country. He returned to the warpath after the government reneged on its promise. He was again promised the territory shortly before his death, but this promise also was never honored.

Russell A. Hart

CODY, WILLIAM FREDERICK (BUFFALO BILL) (1846–1917)

U.S. scout and showman, Cody was born in Scott County, Iowa. When his father was killed by proslavers near Leavenworth, Kansas, young Cody became a teamster and Pony Express rider for Russell, Majors, and Waddell. He joined a gang of Jayhawkers in 1861, then scouted for the 9th Kansas Cavalry. In 1863, he enlisted in the 7th Kansas Cavalry and campaigned in Mississippi and Missouri. He mustered out as a private in 1865. Cody was a contract hunter for the Kansas Pacific Railroad, then served as chief of scouts with the 5th Cavalry (1868–72, 1876). In 1869, Cody met Ned Buntline (E. Z. C. Judson), whose fantastic dime novels helped make "Buffalo Bill" an international celebrity. Cody made and lost several fortunes during 30 years with his touring Wild West Show.

William Franklin Cody, known as Buffalo Bill, was a Union army scout at a young age and later toured the country with his Wild West show. (The Buffalo Bill Historical Center, Cody, Wyoming)

Bibliography: Burke, John, *Buffalo Bill, The Noblest Whiteskin* (Putnam's, 1973); Russell, Don, *The Lives and Legends of Buffalo Bill* (Univ. of Oklahoma Press, 1960).

Col. (Ret.) Louis D. F. Frasché

COLT, SAMUEL (1814–1862)

Inventor of the Colt revolver, Colt was born in Hartford, Connecticut. He went to sea at age 16, constructing a wooden prototype of his revolver on a voyage to Singapore. In 1836, he obtained a patent for this first practical, automatically revolving cylinder revolver. The U.S. Army ordered 1,000 Colt revolvers at the outbreak of the Mexican War (1846–48), which insured his success. In 1847 Colt established his own factory in Hartford. Colt also invented a submarine battery and experimented with a submarine telegraph cable in New York harbor in 1843.

Russell A. Hart

CRAWFORD, GEORGE W. (1798–1872)

Prominent Georgia Whig and U.S. secretary of war, Crawford was born in Columbia County, Georgia. As governor of Georgia (1843–47), he won much praise for revitalizing Georgia's economy in the aftermath of the Panic of 1837. He actively supported Zachary Taylor's race for the presidency in 1848. After several influential Whigs turned down the position of secretary of war, Taylor offered the post to Crawford. Fairly new to the art of politics in Washington, his influence was limited during his brief tenure (1849–50). His effectiveness was compromised further by his involvement in the Galphin claims, a highly controversial land case. Upon Taylor's death in July 1850, Crawford returned to private life, coming out of retirement only to chair Georgia's secession convention in 1861.

Carol Reardon

CRAWFORD, WILLIAM HARRIS (1772–1834)

U.S. legislator, secretary of war, and secretary of the treasury, Crawford was born in Nelson County, Virginia. He served in the U.S. Senate (1807–13) and in 1810 attacked Pres. James Madison for moving too slowly on military preparedness. Declining initially to serve as Madison's secretary of war, he accepted the post in 1815 before becoming secretary of the treasury (1816–25). Madison's successor, James Monroe, retained Crawford, who, consistent with his views on preparedness, worked to fund a system of coast defenses and supported the building of the National Road. In 1824, Crawford ran unsuccessfully for the presidency. He later publicized John C. Calhoun's alleged role in censuring Andrew Jackson's 1818 Florida incursion to help eliminate Calhoun as a rival before Crawford's planned political comeback, which failed.

Carol Reardon

CROCKETT, DAVID (DAVY) (1786–1836)

U.S. frontiersman, Crockett was born in Greene County, Tennessee. He served under Gen. Andrew Jackson during the Creek War (1813–14). He was elected to the state legislature in 1821 and again in 1832. He served in the House of Representatives as a Democrat for Tennessee from 1827 until 1831, when he broke with Jackson and the Democrats. Crockett returned to the House in 1833 as a Whig.

In January 1836, he led Tennessee volunteers to aid the Texan struggle for independence from Mexico. His heroic death at the famous Battle of the Alamo on Mar. 6, 1836, made him a legend.

Russell A. Hart

CROOK, GEORGE (1828–1890)

U.S. military leader and Indian fighter, Crook was born near Dayton, Ohio. He graduated from West Point in 1852 and served with the infantry on the frontier. Early in the Civil War, he was appointed colonel of the 36th Ohio Infantry and rose to command a brigade at Antietam. In 1863, he led a cavalry division in the Chickamauga Campaign. Assigned to West Virginia, Crook commanded a district, then the entire department. He commanded VIII Corps during the 1864 Valley Campaign, suffering a defeat at Kernstown before coming under Gen. Philip Sheridan at the Third Battle of Winchester, Fishers Hill, and Cedar Creek. Thereafter, he continued his department duties until captured by guerrillas in February 1865. Exchanged, he led the Army of the Potomac cavalry at Appomattox. Crook remained in the army after the war; his actions in the Northwest (1866–72), in the Sioux War (1876), and against the Apache (1882–85) made him the U.S. Army's preeminent Indian fighter. He was promoted to major general in 1888.

Bibliography: Schmitt, Martin F., ed., *General George Crook, His Autobiography* (Univ. of Oklahoma Press, 1946).

Lt. Col. (Ret.) J. W. A. Whitehorne

CURTIS, SAMUEL RYAN (1805–1866)

U.S. military leader, Curtis was born near Champlain, New York, and graduated from West Point in 1831. He resigned the following year to practice law and civil engineering in Ohio but returned to active service with Ohio troops in the Mexican War. Elected to Congress in 1856, Curtis resigned his seat in August 1861 to accept appointment as a brigadier general of U.S. volunteers. Commanding the Army of the Southwest, he led Union forces to a decisive victory at Pea Ridge, Arkansas (March 1862), and won promotion to major general. Curtis subsequently played a key role in countering Confederate attempts to gain control of the border states of Missouri and Kansas, commanding in turn the Departments of Missouri, Kansas, and the Northwest.

Lt. Col. (Ret.) Charles R. Shrader

CUSTER, GEORGE ARMSTRONG (1839–1876)

U.S. military officer, Custer was born in New Rumley, Ohio, and graduated from West Point in 1861. He served as a staff officer until July 1863, when he was promoted from captain to brigadier general and led a cavalry brigade at Gettysburg. On Oct. 2, 1864, he took over the 3d Cavalry Division, which played a prominent role in Sheridan's Shenandoah Valley Campaign. Custer led a decisive charge at Cedar Creek on October 19 and later that winter fought several skirmishes, notably at Lacey's Springs. In March 1865, he led the devastating attack against Gen. Jubal Early's remnants at Waynesboro, then fought at Appomattox. He remained in the army after the Civil War and was killed at the disastrous Battle of Little Big Horn on June 25, 1876.

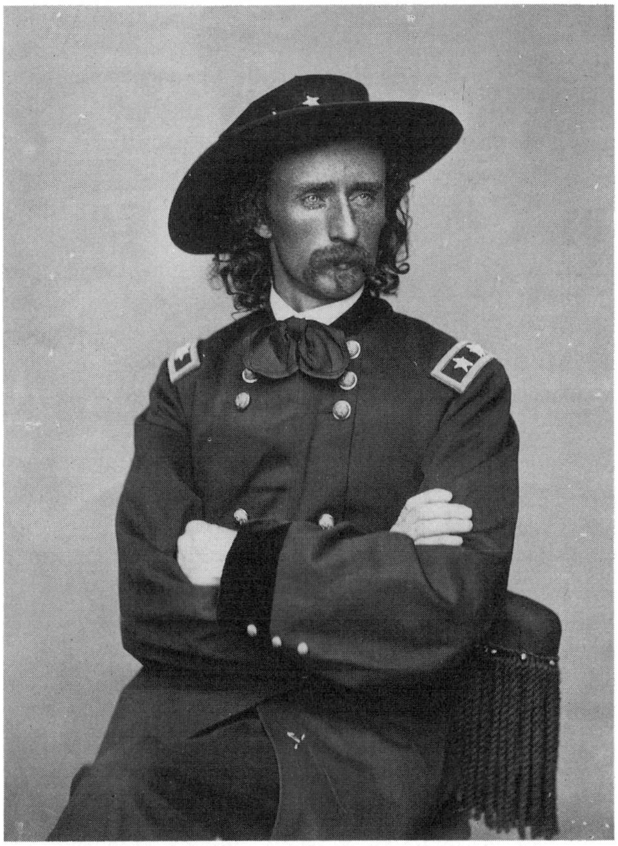

George Armstrong Custer, a brigadier general in the Union army while in his early twenties, served under Gen. Philip Sheridan. (Library of Congress)

Bibliography: Utley, Robert M., *Cavalier in Buckskin: George Armstrong Custer and the Military Frontier* (Univ. of Oklahoma Press, 1988).

Lt. Col. (Ret.) J. W. A. Whitehorne

DAHLGREN, JOHN ADOLPHUS BERNARD (1809–1870)

U.S. naval leader, Dahlgren was born in Philadelphia. He obtained a midshipman's warrant in 1824 and spent most of the next eight years at sea. Failing eyesight in the 1830s forced him to take an extended leave of absence from the navy until 1843. In 1847, he was assigned to the Washington navy yard, where he devised and developed a new gun. Nicknamed "soda-water bottle" for its characteristic shape, the Dahlgren gun revolutioned naval ordnance.

During the Civil War, Dahlgren was appointed chief of the Bureau of Ordnance (July 1862) and rear admiral (February 1863) in the Union navy. He took command of the South Atlantic Blockading Squadron in July 1863, leading Union naval operations at Charleston, South Carolina, for the remainder of the war.

Bibliography: Allison, David K., "John A. Dahlgren: Innovator in Uniform," *Captains of the Old Steam Navy,* ed. by James C. Bradford (Naval Inst. Press, 1986).

Maj. Grant H. Walker

DAVIS, JEFFERSON (1808–1889)

President of the Confederate States of America, Davis was born in Christian (now Todd) County, Kentucky. His family moved to Mississippi while he was a child, and he attended schools in both states prior to his appointment to West Point in 1824. Graduated in 1828, he served in the Black Hawk War (1832) before resigning his commission in 1835 to become a Mississippi planter. He soon became active in local Democratic politics and was elected to the U.S. House of Representatives in 1844.

When the Mexican War broke out in 1846, Davis left his seat to take command of a volunteer regiment, the "Mississippi Rifles," and distinguished himself in action at the battles of Monterrey (September 1846) and Buena Vista (February 1847). He returned home a hero and later in the year entered the U.S. Senate, where by 1850 he was a leading Southern spokesman in the gathering sectional crisis. A rising star in national politics, he served as secretary of war in the Pierce administration (1853–57). In 1857, he returned to the Senate, where he remained until he followed his state into secession in January 1861.

Due to his preeminence, a convention of the seceding states chose Davis as provisional president of the newly formed Confederate States of America in February 1861. Although he preferred a purely military command, he accepted this call to duty and was later elected, unopposed, to the regular six-year term provided for by the Confederate constitution.

Confederate President. Davis displayed many shortcomings as a war leader, especially in comparison with his Union counterpart, Abraham Lincoln. Davis insisted on personally directing the Confederate armed forces, which occasioned charges of meddling from subordinates and also pulled his attention away from critical matters on the home front. He largely ignored the problems associated with the mobilization and control of the civilian sector, or exacerbated them with inept policies. This resulted in severe economic hardship and deteriorating morale among the public, as well as great inefficiency in the war effort. Unlike Lincoln, the proud Davis was extremely sensitive to criticism; he feuded continually with other Confederate officials, his generals, and private citizens. This further eroded his support and drained his energies.

Nevertheless, while acknowledging his deficiencies, most historians also agree that Davis faced a nearly impossible task. In addition to confronting daunting military and economic odds, Davis's administration was plagued with serious internal political dissension. The Confederate Congress and press bitterly attacked his conduct of the war, and governors obstructed policies that infringed on the sovereignty of their states. Ultimately, the very ethos of the Confederacy frustrated him; he was unable to resolve the paradox that required him to exercise great national authority to preserve the cause of states' rights.

Davis fled Richmond as the war ended, and Union troops captured him near Irwinville, Georgia, in May 1865. Indicted for treason but never tried, he was imprisoned until May 1867. Following his release, he settled in Beauvoir, Mississippi, and wrote his memoirs. Increasingly venerated by Southerners in his last years, Davis died in New Orleans on Dec. 6, 1889, and was mourned throughout the South as a martyr to the "Lost Cause."

Bibliography: Eaton, Clement, *Jefferson Davis* (Free Press, 1977); Monroe, Haskell M., et al., eds., *The Papers of Jefferson Davis,* 5 vols. to date (Louisiana State Univ. Press, 1971–85); Potter, Davis M., "Jefferson Davis and the Political Factors in Confederate Defeat," *Why the North Won the Civil War,* ed. by David Donald (Louisiana State Univ. Press, 1960).

Capt. Alan Cate

DODGE, GRENVILLE MELLEN (1831–1916)

U.S. military leader, Dodge was born in Danvers, Massachusetts. He was a railroad builder and politician before becoming the 4th Iowa Infantry's colonel in 1861, at the outbreak of the Civil War. He quickly rose to command a brigade during the fighting in southern Missouri. Wounded at Pea Ridge, Arkansas, in March 1862, Dodge subsequently held a number of district commands under the Army of the Tennessee, where his duties centered around the construction and defense of Union rail and supply lines.

Union Maj. Gen. Grenville Mellen Dodge supervised the construction of railroads during and after the Civil War. (Union Pacific Railroad Museum Collection)

He took the field again at the head of a corps in October 1863, during the relief of Chattanooga. During the Atlanta Campaign (1864), Dodge, named major general of the U.S. volunteers, was severely wounded in the head. After a three-month convalescence, he took charge of the Department of Missouri and the bitter guerrilla war being fought there. He remained in Missouri until the war's end. After the war, Dodge's contributions to railroad development were significant: he was chief engineer of the Union Pacific Railroad (1866–70), played a major role in the Southwest rail system (1873–83), and built the railroad in Cuba (1899–1903).

Bibliography: Hirshson, Stanley P., *Grenville M. Dodge: Soldier, Politician, Railroad Pioneer* (Indiana Univ. Press, 1967).

Richard F. Kehrberg

DONIPHAN, ALEXANDER WILLIAM (1808–1887)

U.S. politician and military leader, Doniphan was born in Mason County, Kentucky. As a young man, he was admitted to the bars in both Kentucky and Ohio, but soon moved westward. He arrived in Missouri in 1830 and immediately achieved fame by serving as legal counsel for the Mormons of western Missouri. Doniphan then entered Missouri politics and held various offices.

In 1838, he became a brigadier general of the Missouri state militia, and when the United States entered the war with Mexico in 1846, he commanded the 1st Missouri Volunteers. Doniphan's Missourians made up nearly half of Stephen W. Kearny's 1,650-man Army of the West. This army departed Fort Leavenworth in June 1846 for the Southwest and by August had reached Santa Fe, where the Mexican government surrendered without a battle. While other parts of the army pushed on toward California, Doniphan's men remained in Santa Fe with orders to pacify or defeat hostile Indians and establish a government acceptable to Congress, and only then to push southward into Chihuahua, Mexico.

Doniphan quickly created a code of organic laws for the new territory and began actions to pacify the Indians of the region. In late 1846, he campaigned against the Navajo north of Santa Fe, hounding the Navajo and Zuni chieftains and their people until they were willing to meet at treaty tables. By December 1946, these efforts had brought at least a temporary peace among the southwestern Indians.

Doniphan's men then marched for El Paso and on Christmas Day camped near the city at El Brazito. They soon learned that a Mexican army was approaching, and by the time the Mexicans attacked, Doniphan's men had moved into defensive positions. After a short fight, the Mexicans had lost more than 40 killed and 150 wounded. Doniphan's casualties were 7 wounded.

A few days later, Doniphan's column marched into El Paso, where it rested before moving on to Chihuahua. On Feb. 28, 1847, Doniphan was nearing Chihuahua when he encountered a sizeable Mexican force of about 3,000 regular troops supported by another 1,000 ranchers and peasant farmers near the Sacramento River. The Missourians began a flanking action, which the Mexicans countered with a cavalry charge into Doniphan's center. Driven back by artillery, the tightly concentrated Mexican forces dispersed. Throughout this action, Doniphan sat serenely on his horse and at one point remarked sarcastically, "Well, they're giving us hell now boys." At a key moment, Doniphan ordered his troops to advance across the field. The battle secured the province for the United States.

Doniphan next joined Zachary Taylor's army at Buena Vista. Soon, with the 1st Missouri's enlistment expiring, Doniphan marched his force to Port Isabel, near Matamoros, where it sailed for New Orleans and then on to St. Louis, where the men were mustered out. In one year, Doniphan's men had traveled more than 3,500 miles by land and another 1,000 by water, fought two major battles in Mexico, established an Anglo-American-based democracy in New Mexico, pacified the southwestern Indians, and paved the way for the annexation of the territory that became New Mexico and Arizona.

After the Mexican War, Doniphan continued his business, legal, and political activities. His most significant political activity took place in 1860–61 when he worked to prevent Missouri's secession from the Union and as a delegate to the Washington Peace Conference.

Bibliography: Launius, Roger D., "Alexander W. Doniphan: Missouri's Forgotten Leader," *Missouri Folk Heroes of the Nineteenth Century,* ed. by Roger D. Launius and F. Mark McKiernan (Independence Press, 1989); Maynard, Gregory P., "Alexander V. Doniphan: Man of Justice," *Brigham Young University Studies* (Summer 1973).

Roger D. Launius

DOUBLEDAY, ABNER (1819–1893)

U.S. military leader, Doubleday was born in Ballston Spa, New York. He graduated from West Point in 1842 and fought in the Mexican War. He was present at Fort Sumter, at the opening of the Civil War, and is said to have aimed the first gun fired from the Union side. After Sumter's fall, he served in the Shenandoah Valley and was appointed brigadier general of the U.S. Volunteers in February 1862. In that same year, he commanded a brigade at the Second Battle of Bull Run and a division at Antietam and Fredericksburg. During the Gettysburg Campaign (1863), he assumed temporary command of I Corps when its commander, Gen. John F. Reynolds, was killed. Doubleday spent the remainder of the war on duty in Washington.

Abner Doubleday, mistakenly credited with inventing the game of baseball, is thought to have fired the first shot from a Union gun at Fort Sumter in 1861. (U.S. Military Academy)

He retired in 1873 and died at Mendham, New Jersey. His writings include *Reminiscences of Forts Sumter and Moultrie in 1860–61* (1876) and *Chancellorsville and Gettysburg* (1882). Doubleday is best known for the fiction, created long after his death, that he invented modern baseball.

Capt. Alan Cate

DU PONT, SAMUEL FRANCIS (1803–1865)

U.S. naval officer, Du Pont was born at Bergen Point, New Jersey, He obtained a midshipman's warrant in 1815 and spent much of the next three decades at sea in a variety of choice assignments. The 1850s were filled with shore duty, but the outbreak of the Civil War brought Du Pont, now a captain, back to sea in command of the Union's South Atlantic Blockade Squadron.

His successful seizure of Port Royal, South Carolina, in 1862 brought him great credit and promotion to rear admiral, but when he failed, against great odds, to capture Charleston the next year, he was personally blamed and asked to be relieved of command.

Bibliography: Bauer, K. Jack, "Samuel Francis Du Pont: Aristocratic Professional," *Captains of the Old Steam Navy,* ed. by James C. Bradford (Naval Inst. Press, 1986).

Maj. Grant H. Walker

EARLY, JUBAL ANDERSON (1816–1894)

Confederate military leader, Early was born in Franklin County, Virginia, and graduated from West Point in 1837. He fought in the Seminole War before resigning in 1838 to take up law and enter politics and later served briefly as a major during the Mexican War.

The Civil War. Although Early voted against secession, when Virginia did secede (April 1861), he immediately entered Confederate service as colonel of the 24th Virginia Infantry. Early was promoted to brigadier general in July after commanding a brigade at the First Battle of Bull Run. He was wounded at Williamsburg (May 1862) during the Peninsular Campaign but resumed command in time for the Second Battle of Bull Run and led a division at Antietam and Fredericksburg. Promoted to major general in April 1863, he continued at the head of his division at Gettysburg, the Wilderness, and Spotsylvania. Early assumed command of the II Corps in May 1864, fought with it at Cold Harbor, and took it to the Shenandoah Valley thereafter. He defeated Gen. David Hunter at Lynchburg in June, then took his force on a daring raid into Maryland to Fort Stevens on the edge of Washington, D.C. The forces he drew off from threatening Gen. Robert E. Lee at Petersburg on July

11 pressed him away from Washington back into the Shenandoah Valley. He defeated federal forces at Cool Spring, then again at Kernstown.

His renewed audacity resulted in a raid destroying Chambersburg, Pennsylvania, and led Maj. Gen. Ulysses S. Grant to appoint Maj. Gen. Philip H. Sheridan with a large force to destroy Early and the valley that sustained him. Federal forces overwhelmed Early in a series of battles in September and October culminating at Cedar Creek. There, Early enjoyed first success but ultimately was routed by Sheridan. The remnants of his force were eliminated at Waynesboro in March 1865, and Early held no position for the remainder of the war.

Postwar Career. At war's end, Early fled to Mexico and then Canada, where he wrote a memoir that posthumously was expanded into *Autobiographical Sketch and Narrative* (1912). Early returned to a law practice in Lynchburg in 1869 and became the longtime president of the Southern Historical Society, but he never vowed allegiance to the United States.

Legacy. A large, irascible man of intimidating wit, Early was known as a superb, aggressive brigade and division commander who showed a full understanding for close infantry and artillery coordination. He displayed greater hesitancy in corps command, tending to piecemeal commitments of his assets. He never showed much sympathy or understanding for cavalry. Despite contemporary criticism, most military analysts agree that Early's Shenandoah Valley performance met Lee's strategic objective by luring large forces away from Richmond-Petersburg with the greatest possible Confederate economy of force.

Bibliography: Bushong, Millard M., *Old Jube: A Biography of Jubal Early* (Carr Pub. Co., 1955).

Lt. Col. (Ret.) J. W. A. Whitehorne

EATON, JOHN HENRY (1790–1856)

U.S. politician and secretary of war, Eaton was born near Scotland Neck, North Carolina. His close association with Andrew Jackson led to prominence and a public career. He served in Jackson's Indian campaigns, published an uncritical biography of the general in 1817, and, as a U.S. senator from Tennessee (1818–29), defended Jackson's conduct in the Seminole Affair of 1818. When Jackson became president in 1829, Eaton was appointed secretary of war.

The most notable incident of Eaton's tenure was the dissolution of the Cabinet, an event precipitated by the failure of Washington society to accept his second wife, Peggy. He resigned in 1831, and Jackson rewarded his loyalty with the governorship of Florida and, later, with the ministry to Spain.

Matthew Oyos

ELLET, CHARLES, JR. (1810–1862)

U.S. civil engineer, Ellet was born in Bucks County, Pennsylvania. He was acclaimed for his work in waterway improvements, notably the suspension bridges over the Schuylkill in Pennsylvania (1842) and the Ohio in West Virginia (1849). In 1862, Ellet, a critic of Union military leadership in the Civil War, was made a colonel by Sec. of War Edwin M. Stanton, who gave Ellet the task of creating a ram fleet to clear the Mississippi River of Confederate vessels. On June 6, 1862, with his fleet of converted steamboats, Ellet helped rout a Confederate naval force at Memphis, an action that brought the surrender of the city. He died a few days later from a wound sustained in the battle.

Matthew Oyos

Union Col. Charles Ellet used converted steamboats for his ram fleet on the Mississippi River in 1862. (Harper's Weekly)

ERICSSON, JOHN (1803–1889)

Marine engineer, Ericsson was born in Värmland Province, Sweden. In 1826, he moved to England, where he introduced the screw propeller. In 1839, he settled in the United States and continued to be an innovator in naval engineering.

Ericsson is best known as the designer of the ironclad *Monitor* (1861), which defeated the Confederate ironclad *Virginia* in 1862. Driven by the Ericsson screw propeller and equipped with a revolving turret of mounted guns, the steam-powered *Monitor* revolutionized naval warfare. Ericsson generously turned over his unpatented plans to rival engineers, in order to provide the Union with an ironclad navy as rapidly as possible.

Bibliography: Hoehling, A. A., *Thunder At Hampton Roads* (Prentice-Hall, 1970); White, Ruth, *Yankee from Sweden: The Dream and the Reality in the Days of John Ericsson* (Henry Holt & Co., 1960).

Jonathan M. House

EWELL, RICHARD STODDERT (1817–1872)

U.S. soldier and Confederate general, Ewell was born in Washington, D.C., and spent his early life in Virginia. He graduated from West Point in 1840 and began what was a routine service career. He was commissioned in the 1st U.S. Dragoons, trained at the U.S. Cavalry School of Practice at Carlisle Barracks, and headed for frontier duty. He achieved some antebellum prominence, having been brevetted for gallantry in the Mexican War at the battles of Contreras and Churubusco and recognized for his service in the Southwest against the Apache in the late 1850s. He achieved the permanent rank of captain prior to the outbreak of the Civil War.

Although a Unionist at heart, Ewell resigned his commission in 1861. At first commissioned in Virginia's state forces, he became a colonel in the Confederate army and commanded the cavalry camp of instruction at Ashland, Virginia. Successive promotions and field commands ensued; he became brigadier general in 1861 and major general in 1862.

Ewell commanded a brigade at the First Battle of Bull Run, although he took no part in the fighting. He commanded a division under "Stonewall" Jackson in the Shenandoah Valley, Seven Days', and Second Bull Run battles. In August 1862, he lost a leg at the Battle of Groveton. A nine-month convalescence followed, and he returned to duty as lieutenant general in May 1863.

Ewell's return coincided with Gen. Robert E. Lee's reorganization of the Army of Northern Virginia following the death of Jackson at the Battle of Chancellorsville. Lee gave Ewell command of the army's II Corps, which led the Confederate invasion of Pennsylvania in June. Despite difficulties presented by riding with a wooden leg, Ewell performed well in the Gettysburg Campaign and through the next year until a fall from his horse at the Battle of Spotsylvania Court House (May 1864) incapacitated him from further field duty.

Toward war's end, he was given command of the defenses of Richmond, a post he held until his capture at the Battle of Sayler's Creek on Apr. 6, 1865. Ewell was imprisoned for four months at Fort Warren, Massachusetts. After his release, he retired to his farm near Spring Hill, Tennessee.

As a soldier, Ewell was known to his men, who gave him the unflattering nickname "Old Bald Head," as a resourceful and competent leader. He was often favorably compared to "Stonewall" Jackson, who had recommended him to Lee for corps command. Two of his wartime decisions have, however, clouded history's view of Ewell: He often is criticized for failing to attack Cemetery and Culp's hills on the evening of July 1, 1863, during the Battle of Gettysburg, a decision that many observers blame

Confederate Gen. Richard Ewell lost his leg in battle in 1862, but came back to command troops at Gettysburg. (U.S. Army Military History Institute)

for the Confederate loss of that battle. He also is frequently (and wrongfully) blamed for ordering Richmond burned after the evacuation of the capital in April 1865.

Bibliography: Hamlin, Percy G., *"Old Bald Head" and The Making of a Soldier: Letters of General R. S. Ewell* (Van Sickle Military Books, 1988).

Louise Arnold-Friend

FARRAGUT, DAVID GLASGOW (1801–1870)

U.S. naval officer, Farragut was born James Glasgow Farragut at Campbell's Station, near Knoxville, Tennessee. After moving his family to New Orleans, Farragut's father joined the U.S. Navy. His mother nursed the father of David Porter, commander of the local naval station, through his final illness, and upon her death in 1808, Porter informally adopted the young Farragut.

Early Career. With Porter's backing, Farragut, at age 9, was appointed midshipman by the secretary of the navy. Farragut served under Porter aboard the *Essex* in the Pacific during the War of 1812 and commanded the *Essex*'s prize vessel *Alexander Barclay* at age 12. After the defeat of the *Essex* by the British off Valparaiso in 1814, Farragut was taken prisoner, paroled, and exchanged, and returned to the United States. Porter commended him for his actions during the battle with the British, and Farragut took the name David Glasgow Farragut in 1814 in honor of David Porter.

Farragut spent the immediate postwar years on duty mainly in the Mediterranean on board the vessels *Independence, Washington,* and *Franklin* and spent nine months ashore at Tunis studying languages, literature, and mathematics. After eight years of routine sea duty, he rejoined Porter to fight West Indian piracy in the Gulf of Mexico, ultimately commanding his first naval vessel, the *Ferret.*

In 1823, Farragut settled in Norfolk, Virginia, and served several tours of duty on ship and ashore from that port for more than 30 years. Commissioned lieutenant in 1825, he served aboard the *Brandywine,* escorting the Marquis de Lafayette on his return to France, then did a tour of duty aboard the *Vandalia* in 1829–30. In the nullification crisis of 1832–33, Farragut was executive officer of the sloop *Nachez* and showed the U.S. flag at rebellious Charleston.

The Mexican War. In 1838, in command of the sloop *Erie* off Veracruz, Mexico, Farragut witnessed the French bombardment and capture of the Mexican castle of San Juan de Ulloa, then sought shore duty to care for his ailing wife, who died in 1840. After serving as executive officer of the *Delaware* in 1841, he was promoted to commander and given command of the sloop *Decatur*. When the possibility of war with Mexico loomed large in 1845, Farragut requested combat duty in the Gulf of Mexico, citing his familiarity with Spanish, the fortifications at Veracruz, and the Gulf waters. He did not, however, receive a significant assignment until January 1847, when he took command of the *Saratoga*. He quickly sailed to Veracruz only to find the castle already occupied by the U.S. Army. Disheartened at losing his opportunity for action, Farragut quarreled with his commanding officer over blockade duty and requested relief from his command.

David Glasgow Farragut in 1862 became the first naval officer to attain the newly created rank of admiral. (U.S. Army Military History Institute)

In subsequent years, Farragut was assigned primarily to shore duty. While on ordnance duty, he rewrote the navy's ordnance regulations and experimented with naval gun improvements. In 1854, he was sent to California to establish the Mare Island navy yard, where he was commissioned captain, the highest rank in the navy. After four years at Mare Island, he returned east and took command of the *Brooklyn* in 1859.

The Civil War. Farragut spent the secession winter of 1860–61 awaiting orders at his home in Norfolk. When Virginia seceded in April 1861, Farragut moved his family north and sought a Union naval command. His southern ties, however, aroused enough suspicion to keep him unemployed and on retiring board duty until late 1861.

When Northern strategists determined that the early capture of New Orleans was required to open the Mississippi River to Union occupation, they began looking for a naval officer capable of so difficult a task. As one of the few senior captains yet unassigned, Farragut gained early consideration. Among his most vocal champions in Washington was his adoptive brother David Dixon Porter, who had, for the moment, influence with both the Navy Department and the president. Assigned to command of the West Gulf Blockading Squadron in January 1862, Farragut was ordered to reduce the forts below New Orleans and to capture that city.

For two months, Farragut plotted strategy and collected his forces, wooden ships, and a flotilla of mortar boats and steamed toward New Orleans in his flagship *Hartford.* Forts Jackson and St. Philip defended the southern approach to the city and were backed by a Confederate naval flotilla. After the forts withstood his six-day bombardment, Farragut decided to change courses and run past the forts without reducing them. Under heavy Confederate fire from land and river, he led one of his three divisions of ships past the forts and defeated the Confederate flotilla, sinking 11 ships. On reaching New Orleans, Farragut took command of the city on April 25, provoking the surrender of the two forts and giving the Union a strategic base for operations against the South.

Farragut's daring victory during a period of Union reverses immediately earned him the thanks of the Union government and a position as the leading naval officer of his age, as well as a commission as the navy's first admiral, in July 1862. His subsequent cooperation with army forces and assiduous efforts to control Confederate ship traffic on the rivers and in the Gulf of Mexico enhanced Union victories on land and led to Union control of the Mississippi by July 1863.

As Union armies under Maj. Gens. Ulysses S. Grant and William T. Sherman began their coordinated assault on the Confederacy in 1864, Farragut finally gained long-sought permission to attempt to penetrate the naval defenses at Mobile Bay. Facing strong Confederate fortifications and staggered minefields in the channel approach to the bay, he assembled a fleet of 4 ironclads and 14 wooden ships lashed in pairs. After determining the extent and viability of the minefields, he gave orders for the advance into Mobile Bay to begin on the morning of Aug. 5, 1864.

From his position in the rigging of the *Hartford,* Farragut saw the ironclad *Tecumseh* turn east of a minefield buoy, contrary to orders, and detonate a recently planted mine. Warned of more mines (or "torpedoes") ahead, Farragut shouted, "Damn the Torpedoes!" and turned his ships west of the buoy where he knew that older, mostly inert mines lay. After leading his fleet through the minefields and past the forts, he methodically defeated the waiting Confederate flotilla, capturing the ironclad CSS *Tennessee.* On December 23, Farragut's heroism was rewarded with a promotion to vice admiral, a rank created just the day before. After the war, Farragut was appointed the navy's first full admiral (1866). In 1867–68, he commanded the European Squadron on a goodwill tour of the Mediterranean.

Bibliography: Farragut, Loyall, *Life of David Glasgow Farragut, The First Admiral of the United States Navy, Embodying His Journal and Letters* (Appleton, 1879); Hill, Jim Dan, *Sea Dogs of the Sixties: Farragut and Seven Contemporaries* (Univ. of Minnesota Press, 1935); Lewis, Charles Lee, *David Glasgow Farragut* (Naval Inst. Press, 1941–43); Mahan, Alfred Thayer, *Admiral Farragut* (Appleton, 1892); Still, William N., "David Glasgow Farragut: The Union's Nelson," *Captains of the Old Steam Navy,* ed. by James C. Bradford (Naval Inst. Press, 1986).

Tamara Moser Melia

FILLMORE, MILLARD (1800–1874)

Thirteenth president of the United States (1850–53), Fillmore was born in Locke, New York. After practicing law for several years in Buffalo, New York, he served as a Whig in the U.S. House of Representatives (1833–35, 1837–43). As an antislavery congressman, Fillmore opposed the annexation of Texas as a slave territory, supported John Quincy Adams's fight for the right to present abolitionist petitions in Congress, and favored prohibiting slave trade in the District of Columbia.

As Zachary Taylor's vice president (1849–50), Fillmore presided over the Senate debates on the Compromise of 1850. Upon President Taylor's death in July 1850, Fillmore succeeded to the presidency, whereupon his abolitionist support was undone by his advocacy of compromise measures and his endorsement of the Fugitive Slave Law. He subsequently had two highly unsuccessful bids for the presidency—as a Whig in 1852 and as a National American ("Know-Nothing") in 1856.

Christine L. Stevens

FLOYD, JOHN BUCHANAN (1806–1863)

U.S. secretary of war and Confederate general, Floyd was born in Montgomery County, Virginia, and served in the Virginia legislature and as governor of the state (1849–52). Appointed secretary of war in 1857 by Pres. James Buchanan, Floyd resigned on Dec. 29, 1860. Afterward there were allegations that he had tranferred arms and ammunition from northern armories to arsenals in the South.

Commissioned a brigadier general in the Confederate army in 1861, he fought at Cross Lanes and Carnifex Ferry, West Virginia. Ordered to Tennessee, Floyd fled Fort Donelson in February 1862 with a number of troops the night before its capture by Gen. Ulysses S. Grant. Censured by the Confederate government, he was removed from command on March 11. In May, he was appointed a major general of Virginia troops. He died that August.

Steve R. Waddell

FOOTE, ANDREW HULL (1806–1863)

U.S. naval officer, Foote was born in New Haven, Connecticut. He attended West Point for a few months in 1822 before accepting appointment as acting midshipman in the U.S. Navy. He subsequently served aboard ships of the West India, Pacific, Mediterranean, and East India squadrons before being assigned in 1840 as commandant of the U.S. Naval Asylum in Philadelphia. During the Mexican War he served as commandant of the Boston navy yard.

As first lieutenant of the frigate *Cumberland* in 1843, Foote convinced the 400 crewmen to give up their grog ration, and the *Cumberland* thus became the first "temperance ship" in the U.S. Navy. Noted for his religious fervor, Foote was instrumental in the ultimate abolition of both the grog ration and flogging throughout the navy. He also was active in efforts to suppress the African slave trade.

In 1856, Foote commanded the sloop *Portsmouth* and two smaller ships on the China station, assigned to protect U.S. interests at Whampoa, south of Canton. When the Chinese fired upon U.S. ships, Foote led a joint naval bombardment and land attack to punish the Chinese and destroy the so-called Barrier Forts (Nov. 16–20, 1856).

At the beginning of the Civil War, Foote commanded the Brooklyn navy yard. In June 1861, he was promoted to captain and replaced Comdr. John Rodgers, Jr., as commander of Union naval forces on the upper Mississippi. Permitted to use the title "flag officer" to distinguish himself from the many riverboat and army captains in the area, Foote prepared the available gunboats, including seven Eads ironclads, for cooperation with the army forces under Brig. Gen. Ulysses S. Grant in the movement down the Mississippi River that was to cut the Confederacy in two.

The first major engagement of the combined force came at Fort Henry on the Tennessee River on Feb. 6, 1862. Grant's forces were delayed, and Foote successfully attacked the works with his gunboats, gaining a victory that boosted sagging Union morale at a critical point. Grant and Foote then moved to take Fort Donelson on the Cumberland River. Plunging fire from the Confederate defenses forced Foote, himself seriously wounded, to withdraw his gunboats and leave the capture of Fort Donelson to Grant. In April 1862, Foote's flotilla, in cooperation with the army forces of Gen. John Pope, dashed past heavily fortified Confederate defenses and forced the surrender of Island No. 10 and New Madrid, opening the Mississippi as far south as Memphis.

His wounds and other ailments obliged Foote to relinquish command of the Mississippi Flotilla to Capt. Charles H. Davis in May 1862. He was promoted to rear admiral and, after a period of recuperation, became chief of the navy's Bureau of Equipment and Recruiting. In June 1863, Sec. of the Navy Gideon Welles named Foote to replace Adm. Samuel Francis Du Pont as commander of the South Atlantic Blockading Squadron. En route to take up his new command, Foote died in New York City.

Bibliography: Millett, Allan R., *Semper Fidelis: The History of the United States Marine Corps* (Macmillan Co., 1980); Spiller, Roger, J., ed., *Dictionary of American Military Biography,* vol. 1 (Greenwood Press, 1984).

Lt. Col. (Ret.) Charles R. Shrader

FORREST, NATHAN BEDFORD (1821–1877)

One of the finest Confederate cavalry officers, Forrest was born in Chapel Hill, Tennessee. With fewer than three months of formal schooling, he taught himself to write and speak clearly. At age 40, he was a millionaire from trading in land, livestock, and slaves.

Forrest enlisted as a Confederate private in 1861. At the request of the Tennessee governor, he was promoted to

Raider Nathan Bedford Forrest commanded the Confederate forces that captured Fort Pillow, Tennessee, in 1864 and was blamed for the "massacre" that followed. (U.S. Army Military History Institute)

lieutenant colonel and subsequently raised a regiment at his own expense. Forrest became an expert at maneuver and surprise. His philosophy was, "get there first with the most men." His superiors recognized his talent as a raider and used him to strike behind enemy lines. He had a keen sense of logistics, usually supplying his troops with captured Union matériel. He is probably best known for his raids on Gen. William T. Sherman's rear during Sherman's infamous drive to the sea.

Promoted to lieutenant general, Forrest was wounded four times, had 29 horses shot out from under him, and personally killed more than 30 men, most with his saber. Forrest finally was defeated at Selma, Alabama, on May 9, 1865.

Forrest returned to Memphis after the war. He was active in the Ku Klux Klan but left when the organization turned toward violence.

Bibliography: Henry, Robert S., *"First with the Most," Forrest* (Bobbs-Merrill, 1944); ———, *As They Saw Forrest: Some Recollections and Comments of Contemporaries* (McCowat-Mercer Press, 1956).

Capt. Robert K. Angwin

FOX, GUSTAVUS VASA (1821–1883)

U.S. naval officer, Fox was born in Saugas, Massachusetts. He embarked on a naval career in 1838 but resigned as a lieutenant after 18 years service. He returned to public life at the outbreak of the Civil War, with a plan for the relief of Fort Sumter in 1861. President Lincoln ordered him to implement the scheme, but Fox arrived after the fort's bombardment in April 1861 and was able only to evacuate the garrison. In August, he assumed the newly created post of assistant secretary of the navy. He served in this capacity until 1866, displaying an administrative ability that was indispensable to Union naval efforts. After the war, he led a diplomatic mission to Russia before returning to private business.

Matthew Oyos

FRÉMONT, JOHN CHARLES (1813–1890)

U.S. explorer (known as "The Pathfinder") and military officer, Frémont was born in Savannah, Georgia. He was commissioned second lieutenant in the U.S. Corps of Topographical Engineers in 1838 and joined French scientist Joseph N. Nicollet's two-year expedition to the upper Missouri and Mississippi rivers. Soon after their return, Frémont met expansionist Sen. Thomas Hart Benton of Missouri. Benton arranged for Frémont's 1841 expedition to the Iowa territory. In October 1841, Frémont married the senator's daughter Jessie, and thereafter Benton became Frémont's patron and protector.

Oregon and California Expeditions. In 1842, Frémont led an expedition to explore the Oregon Trail through the South Pass. On his return, and with his wife's assistance, Frémont produced a widely read report of his travels. In 1843, Frémont journeyed through Wyoming and Idaho to Oregon, from there up the Columbia River to Vancouver, then south to Nevada. That winter, he recklessly crossed the Sierra Nevada mountains into the Sacramento Valley and returned to St. Louis in June 1844. Frémont's vibrant account of his adventure provided considerable scientific and practical information about the Oregon Trail. Widely printed, the report made Frémont a national hero to a country intensely interested in the Oregon territory and spurred western emigration.

In 1845, while the threat of war with Mexico loomed, Frémont traveled to California on his third major expedition. Liberally interpreting his orders, as was his custom, he and his well-armed force participated in the 1846 Bear Flag revolt, and he and Comdr. Robert F. Stockton captured Los Angeles on August 13. Frémont became embroiled in a power struggle between Stockton, who appointed Frémont acting governor of California, and Gen. Stephen W. Kearny, Frémont's superior. Arrested by Kearny, and later found guilty of disobedience during a publicized court-martial in Washington (November 1847–January 1848), Frémont angrily resigned from the army.

In the winter of 1848–49, he led an expedition in search of a feasible rail route from the upper Rio Grande to California. He became one of California's first two senators (1850–51), and his national popularity and staunch antislavery stance led the new Republican party to nominate him for president in 1856. He lost to Democrat James Buchanan.

The Civil War. Appointed major general when the Civil War began, Frémont's political connections brought him command of the newly created Western Department. His lack of both experience and prudence proved costly: Contractors overcharged him for supplies, and his troops suffered defeats at Wilson's Creek and Lexington. On Aug. 30, 1861, he rashly declared Missouri rebels' property confiscated and their slaves emancipated; when he refused to retract his order, President Lincoln was forced to overrule and remove him. In March 1862, Frémont received command of the new Mountain Division but fared poorly against Gen. Thomas "Stonewall" Jackson during the latter's Shenandoah Valley Campaign that May. When Maj. Gen. John Pope was made his superior, Frémont resigned.

Postmilitary Career. In 1864, he was the Radical Republicans' presidential nominee, but, under pressure from other party factions, he withdrew in September. Frémont's railroad ventures brought him serious financial and legal troubles by the early 1870s, and after several years of poverty, he became territorial governor of Arizona (1878–83). Shortly before his death, Frémont was restored to his rank of major general and placed on the army retirement list.

Bibliography: Egan, Ferrol, *Frémont* (Univ. of Nevada Press, 1985); Frémont, John Charles, *Memoirs of My Life: A Retrospect of Fifty Years* (Belford, Clarke and Co.,

1887); Goetzmann, William H., *Army Exploration in the American West, 1803–1863* (Yale Univ Press, 1959; reprint, Univ. of Nebraska Press, 1979); Nevins, Allan, *Frémont: Pathmaker of the West* (D. Appleton-Century Co., 1939).

Stephen J. Lofgren

GADSDEN, JAMES (1788–1858)

U.S. diplomat and military officer, Gadsden was born in Charleston, South Carolina. He was commissioned into the Corps of Engineers in 1812, eventually serving as Andrew Jackson's inspector general and as a colonel in the Southern Division. He was appointed adjutant and inspector general of the army but resigned in 1821 when the Senate failed to confirm his appointment. He then became a planter in Florida, where he was active as U.S. representative in the Seminole removal and promoted internal improvements. He returned to Charleston in 1839 and served as a railroad executive. Gadsden advocated a southern rail route to California. To this end, as Pres. Franklin Pierce's minister to Mexico (1853–54), he negotiated the treaty that resulted in the 1853 purchase of what is now called the Gadsden Purchase—southern New Mexico and Arizona.

Bibliography: Clary, David A., and Joseph W. A. Whitehorne, *The Inspectors General of the U.S. Army, 1777–1903* (Center of Military History, 1987).

Lt. Col. (Ret.) J. W. A. Whitehorne

GAINES, EDMUND PENDLETON (1777–1849)

U.S. military officer, Gaines was born in Culpeper County, Virginia, and served most of his 51 years in the U.S. Army on the American frontier. He worked tirelessly to fulfill the U.S. doctrine of Manifest Destiny by promoting western expeditions, the construction of frontier forts and railroads, and the forced resettlement of Indians. However, while he commanded the army's western and eastern departments, General Gaines's penchant for military adventurism often proved troublesome. He pursued hostile Creek Indians into Spanish Florida, and thus helped instigate the First Seminole War. Early in the Second Seminole War, he mounted yet another unauthorized punitive expedition. In 1845–46, he disregarded orders and recruited more than 11,000 men to fight in the Mexican War. In the last case, the army court-martialed and acquitted Gaines for his actions.

Bibliography: Silver, James, *Edmund Pendleton Gaines: Frontier General* (Louisiana Univ. Press, 1949).

Maj. Peter Faber

GATLING, RICHARD (1818–1903)

Inventor of the early form of the machine gun that took his name, Gatling was born in Winton, North Carolina. As a youth, he helped his father perfect various mechanical inventions, notably a cottonseed sower. In 1838, he applied for a patent on a screw propeller but learned that John Ericsson's model had preceded his. By 1844, Gatling had perfected an automatic rice sower and wheat drill. When civil war became imminent in 1861, Gatling put aside agricultural inventions to concentrate on improving weaponry. On Nov. 4, 1862, he received a patent for his most famous invention—the rapid-fire, multibarrel, small-arm-caliber weapon since known as the "Gatling gun." The prototype could fire 250 shots per minute, but reloading was among the features that the Union army found awkward and impractical, and so it was rejected for combat use. In 1866, a greatly improved Gatling gun won the War Department's approval and was adopted by the U.S. Army. It was subsequently used extensively throughout the world.

Christine L. Stevens

GEARY, JOHN WHITE (1819–1873)

U.S. political leader and Civil War general, Geary was born in Mount Pleasant, Pennsylvania. During the Mexican War, he led the 2d Pennsylvania Infantry Regiment in the Mexico City Campaign. His civilian background lay in the legal profession and civil engineering. In 1849, he was chosen by Pres. James Polk to establish California's postal service. He was the first mayor of San Francisco (1850) and the governor of Kansas Territory (1856).

He began the Civil War as colonel of the 28th Pennsylvania Infantry and was promoted to brigadier general in 1862. Wounded at the Battle of Cedar Mountain, he returned to the Army of the Potomac to lead a division at Chancellorsville and Gettysburg before moving to the western theater with the XII Corps. There, he fought at Lookout Mountain and in the Atlanta Campaign. After Sherman's March to the Sea, he served as military governor of Savannah. He was brevetted major general in 1865. After the war, Geary served as Pennsylvania governor (1867–73).

Bibliography: Tinkcom, Harry, *John White Geary, Soldier-Statesman, 1819–1873* (Univ. of Pennsylvania Press, 1940).

Louise Arnold-Friend

GOLDSBOROUGH, LOUIS MALESHERBES (1805–1877)

U.S. naval commander, Goldsborough was born in Washington, D.C. He began active naval service as a midshipman in 1816. He had numerous domestic and foreign assignments and, following service in the Mexican War, explored California and Oregon. While superintendent of the U.S. Naval Academy (1853–57), he was promoted to captain (1855).

After the Civil War broke out, he received command of Union squadrons blockading the Atlantic coast. During the Peninsular Campaign, his mission was to support Gen. George McClellan's land forces. His fleet was unable to reduce Confederate positions along the James River, and Goldsborough asked to be relieved in September 1862, even though he had been promoted to rear admiral in July.

From then until his retirement in 1873, he worked in navy administration in Washington.

Maj. Grant H. Walker

GORDON, JOHN BROWN (1832–1904)

U.S. attorney and politician and Confederate military officer, Gordon was born in Upton County, Georgia, and studied law at the University of Georgia. In 1861, he recruited a company and joined the Confederacy's 6th Alabama. Gordon commanded his regiment on the Peninsula and fought brilliantly in Gen. Robert E. Lee's Maryland campaign (Antietam), where he was wounded five times. Promoted brigadier general (1862), Gordon distinguished himself at Chancellorsville, Gettysburg, and the Wilderness. His leadership of a division at Spotsylvania brought him promotion to major general (1864). At Petersburg, Lee gave Gordon command of II Corps. Save for Gen. James Longstreet, he was Lee's most trusted adviser by war's end.

After the war, Gordon became a prominent Georgia politician. He served as U.S. senator (1873–80, 1891–97) and governor of Georgia (1886–90) and was one of the New South's dominant voices for home rule and national reconciliation. A highly respected military figure, he was appointed commander in chief of the United Confederate Veterans.

Bibliography: Eckert, Ralph L., *John Brown Gordon: Soldier, Southerner, American* (University Microfilms, 1985); Gordon, John B., *Reminiscences of the Civil War* (Scribner's, 1903); Tankersley, Allen P., *John B. Gordon: A Study in Gallantry* (Whitehall Press, 1955).

Col. (Ret.) Louis D. F. Frasché

GORGAS, JOSIAH (1818–1883)

U.S. military officer and Confederate general and chief of ordnance, Gorgas was born in Dauphin County, Pennsylvania, and graduated from West Point in 1841 as an artillery officer. During the Mexican War, he headed the ordnance depot at Veracruz. In 1861, he resigned from the U.S. Army to side with the Confederacy. As one of the only professional ordnance officers in the South, he immediately became chief of ordnance. Gorgas (eventually a brigadier general) defied dire circumstances to provide the resource-poor South with adequate supplies of war matériel. He engineered European imports and virtually created a Confederate war industry, supplying the South's armies with guns and ammunition despite worsening production and distribution problems. Gorgas may be credited with much of the Confederacy's ability to field battleworthy armies.

Mark Pitcavage

GRANT, ULYSSES SIMPSON (1822–1885)

Eighteenth president of the United States (1869–77) and commander in chief of the Union army, Grant was born Hiram Ulysses Grant in Point Pleasant, Ohio. He entered West Point in 1839, under the appointment of a congressman who, having confused Grant's name with that of Grant's mother (maiden name Simpson), registered him as "Ulysses Simpson Grant," his accepted name from then on. Grant graduated in 1843 and was brevetted second lieutenant of infantry.

Gen. Ulysses S. Grant, commander of all U.S. armies during the latter part of the Civil War, later served as president for two terms (1869–77). (U.S. Military Academy)

Early Career. Grant served with the 4th U.S. Infantry at Jefferson Barracks, Missouri, and at New Orleans before joining at Corpus Christi with Gen. Zachary Taylor's army in 1846. During the Mexican War, although detailed much of the time as regimental quartermaster and commissary, Grant took part in the battles of Palo Alto, Resaca de la Palma (where he commanded his company in the absence of his captain), Monterrey, Chapultepec, and Mexico City. Having distinguished himself at Monterrey and Mexico City, he finished the war a brevet captain with citations for gallantry and meritorious conduct.

Among the many lessons of war on which Grant would rely in the Civil War were an appreciation of logistics and a sense of resourcefulness. Also, Taylor's humane treatment of surrendered Mexican troops taught him the value of magnanimity.

Between 1848 and 1852, Grant's 4th Infantry was stationed at a number of Great Lakes posts. In 1852, the regiment was sent to Oregon. Grant was detailed regimental quartermaster. In July 1853, he was promoted to full captain. Drinking was prevalent in this remote setting, and Grant's tolerance to whiskey was low. When heavy drinking led to negligence of duty, he was given the option of resigning or being court-martialed. In 1854, he resigned and returned to his wife (Julia Dent, sister of his West Point roommate) and children in Missouri. For two years, he was a wood hauler. He tried farming, but the Panic of 1857 nearly wiped him out. The next year, unseasonable cold destroyed his crop and illness incapacitated him for six months. In both investments and job opportunities, failure followed failure, and by 1860, Grant was almost destitute. By the time civil war was imminent, he was eager to return to the military.

The Civil War. Grant had lived in a slave state and despised abolitionists, but he was enraged when Virginia seceded from the Union. In June 1861, Illinois governor Richard Yates appointed him to command the 7th District Regiment, an unruly three-month outfit. Grant shaped up these undisciplined recruits (redesignated the 21st Illinois) in just three weeks, and the regiment reenlisted for the war.

In August, Grant was promoted to brigadier general and given control of southern Illinois and southeastern Missouri. In September, he occupied Paducah, Kentucky, strategically located at the mouth of the navigable Tennessee River. He then attacked Belmont, Missouri, but was driven away by Confederate reinforcements.

A minor incident in the same year showed Grant's stubborn determination to pursue what he considered the correct course. His persistence and strong will also characterized his actions as Union commander later in the war. Discovering that contractors and speculators were rigging government contracts and charging the army inflated prices for grain and forage, Grant canceled all contracts. In doing so, he ignored threats from an influential politician.

In February 1862, Grant captured Forts Henry and Donelson near the Tennessee-Kentucky border, earning him promotion to major general of volunteers and breaking the Confederate hold in the West. In April, Gen. Albert Sidney Johnston's army very nearly defeated Grant's troops at Shiloh. The timely arrival of Union reinforcements forced the Southerners to withdraw.

Grant's first attempts in late 1862 to take Vicksburg, a key Confederate fortress on the Mississippi, were repulsed. However, in the spring of 1863, in a brilliant campaign of speed and deception, he invested the city-fort, capturing it on July 4. The Vicksburg Campaign cost the South irreplaceable manpower and opened the way for Northern troops to slash deep into the Confederate heartland. In November, Grant won another major victory at Chattanooga, Tennessee. He was promoted to lieutenant general in March 1864 and given supreme command of all Union troops. With this came his unified strategy of applying pressure on the Confederacy all across its borders.

In the East, Grant traveled with the Army of the Potomac in the relentless pursuit of Gen. Robert E. Lee that led to the battles of the Wilderness, Spotsylvania, and Cold Harbor. The federal forces lost battles but drove on south as though ever victorious, forcing Lee into Richmond, Petersburg, and finally, Appomattox, where Lee surrendered. Among Grant's terms of surrender was the provision that Confederate officers and men who signed paroles and went home were "not to be disturbed by the United States authority so long as they observe their paroles and the laws in force where they reside." This statement saved many men from vengeful persecution, including Robert E. Lee.

The Presidency. After the war, Grant was promoted to the new rank of four-star general and retained command of the army. In the controversial move that preceded Pres. Andrew Johnson's impeachment trial, Sec. of War Edwin M. Stanton was replaced by Grant in 1867. In 1868, the Republican party ran Grant successfully for the presidency.

President Grant's intentions were essentially honest and for the public good. Nonetheless, his two terms were marked by numerous scandals and political failures, including Jay Gould's and Jim Fisk's attempt to corner the nation's gold supply; the aborted treaty that would have secured Santo Domingo for settlement by former slaves; the Crédit Mobilier affair (a construction company scandal); the corruptions of the secretary of war, the speaker of the House, and a member of Grant's personal staff; and the excesses of carpetbag governments in the South. Amid such dominating events, Grant waged an unsuccessful campaign to reform the wasteful, inefficient civil service system. He also struggled in vain to establish a fair reconstruction plan for the South.

Later Years. Upon leaving office, Grant went on a world tour lasting almost two and a half years. In 1880, an attempt to nominate him for president was unsuccessful. In 1884, his investments were wiped out, and he was bankrupt. He managed to recoup some finances through the commissioned writing of his military experiences. His immediate success as a writer inspired him to undertake his two-volume *Personal Memoirs of U. S. Grant* (1885–86). This work, written during Grant's agonizing affliction with throat cancer, generated financial security for his family and is considered a fine autobiography.

Bibliography: Catton, Bruce, *U. S. Grant and the American Military Tradition* (Little, Brown, 1954); Grant, Ulysses S., *Personal Memoirs of U. S. Grant,* 2 vols. (Webster & Co., 1885–86); Lewis, Lloyd, *Captain Sam Grant* (Little, Brown, 1950); McFeely, William S., *Grant: A Biography* (Norton, 1981); Williams, Kenneth P., *Lincoln Finds a General; Vol. 3: Grant's First Year in the West* (Macmillan Co., 1952.

Brig. Gen. (Ret.) Uzal W. Ent

GREENHOW, ROSE O'NEAL (1815?–1864)

A Confederate spy, Greenhow was born in Maryland and grew up in Washington, D.C. In 1835, Rose married Robert Greenhow and moved to San Francisco, where in 1854 Robert died in an accident. Rose returned to Washington. After the outbreak of the Civil War, she became involved in a Confederate spy ring. Her most valuable contribution was a series of messages warning the South of Northern troop movements leading to the First Battle of Bull Run. In August 1861, Greenhow was arrested, and although confined, she continued to transmit information; however, she never matched the Bull Run coup. In the spring of 1863, she was released and sent South. She was sent to Europe in August, as an unofficial agent of the Confederacy. The next year, while crossing the Atlantic, Greenhow's ship met a Union gunboat during a storm near Wilmington, North Carolina. She insisted on going ashore, and her small boat was overturned; weighed down with gold coins, she sank and drowned. Greenhow was buried with full military honors.

Deborah L. Mesplay

HALLECK, HENRY WAGER (1815–1872)

U.S. military engineer and adviser, Halleck was born in Westernville, New York. He graduated third in the West Point Class of 1839 and gained a commission as a second lieutenant in the Corps of Engineers.

Early Career. Before reporting to his first duty station, Halleck taught in the Military Academy's engineering department. Consequently, he adopted much of the professional and intellectual approach to officership espoused by West Point educators Dennis Mahan and Sylvanus Thayer. After a year on the faculty, Halleck became assistant to the Board of Engineers for Atlantic Coast Defenses. Based in New York City, he worked on the defenses of New York harbor from 1840 to 1846. During his tenure there, Halleck wrote a congressional publication entitled *Report on the Means of National Defence*. In 1845, he took a hiatus to tour the Vaubanian fortresses of France. Upon his return, Halleck presented a series of 12 lectures to the Lowell Institute of Boston, in which he blended his expertise in military engineering with the European literature on military policy, strategy, and tactics. Acclaimed as the first comprehensive study of the military art by an American, Halleck's work was published as *Elements of Military Art and Science* in 1846. Reflecting the influence of Henri Jomini, Thayer, and Mahan, the lectures included an historical perspective of and a moral apology for war combined with an evaluation of logistics, military education, and U.S. military policy.

The Mexican War. With the outbreak of the Mexican War (1846), Halleck received orders to the West Coast. During the seven-month voyage around Cape Horn, he translated Jomini's *Vie politique et militaire de Napoleon,* which was published in four volumes in 1864. Based in California, Halleck served as an aide-de-camp during naval and military operations on the Pacific coast, as lieutenant governor of Mazatlán after its capture, and as chief of staff during an expedition to Lower California. Brevetted to captain, Halleck also served as secretary of state for the military government while continuing work on coastal fortifications. In 1854 he resigned from the army and set up what became an influential law practice in San Francisco. He had widespread business investments and was active in the California militia.

The Civil War. As the Civil War gained intensity in the summer of 1861, Pres. Abraham Lincoln (at the suggestion of Gen. Winfield Scott) appointed Halleck to major general, regular army. In November, Halleck replaced John C. Frémont as commander of the Department of the Missouri. Challenged to "establish order out of chaos," Halleck reduced graft and corruption while promoting organization and administration. His threefold mission was to clean up the St. Louis headquarters, pacify militant Missouri, and prepare forces for a major advance down the Mississippi Valley.

Union successes at Forts Henry and Donelson (February 1862) brought Halleck further recognition although he had had no direct role in these successes. In March, the Department of the Mississippi was created to combine the Departments of Missouri, Ohio, and Kansas, and Halleck was appointed its commander. He directed the armies of Gens. Ulysses S. Grant and Don Carlos Buell at Shiloh, then took personal command of the units under Grant, Buell, and Gen. John Pope at Corinth, Mississippi. Halleck's cautious strategy led to slow, deliberate advances, but Corinth fell in June 1862. This operation, combined with other Union victories in the western theater, resulted in Halleck's promotion in July to general in chief of the U.S. Army.

As military adviser to the president and to the secretary of war, he carried out executive orders and coordinated communications between Union forces and the War Department. Reflecting his personal strengths and weaknesses, Halleck's headquarters became more administrative—working to recruit soldiers and to secure matériel—and less strategic in its emphasis. In his continual search for strategic direction in the Union war effort, Lincoln replaced Halleck with Grant in March 1864. Remaining in Washington until war's end as Grant's chief of staff, a demotion that he accepted without audible complaint, Halleck seemed to find his niche in the administrative requirements of the command.

Postwar Career. Upon Gen. Robert E. Lee's surrender at Appomattox (Apr. 9, 1865), Halleck assumed command of the Division of the James, responsible for the initial reconstruction of Virginia. After a dispute with Gen. William T. Sherman, he was transferred to the Division of the Pacific (1865–69). Halleck's last appointment was as commander of the Division of the South (1869–72).

An able organizer and administrator, "Old Brains" Halleck believed that the key to good leadership lay in the study of the principles and history of war. Greatly influenced by his professor and mentor, Dennis Hart Mahan, Halleck focused on professional study, flexible and pragmatic commanders, the spirit of the offensive, and fortifications. He advocated an expansible army, a professional officer corps, and a command and staff system. His organizational ability served him well in administrative matters, but his lack of strategic sense and his tendency to shun responsibility proved him inept as a field commander.

Bibliography: Ambrose, Stephen E., *Halleck: Lincoln's Chief of Staff* (Louisiana State Univ. Press, 1962); Cullum, George W., *Biographical Sketch of Major-General Henry W. Halleck of the United States Army* (A. G. Sherwood, 1880); Halleck, Henry Wager, *Elements of Military Art and Science* (Appleton, 1846); Sparks, David S., *Henry Wager Halleck* (Union College Press, 1962); Weigley, Russell F., *Towards an American Army* (Columbia Univ. Press, 1962).

Capt. James Sanders Day

HAMPTON, WADE (1818–1902)

U.S. political figure and Confederate general, Hampton was born in Charleston, South Carolina, the son of a wealthy planter and grandson of Gen. Wade Hampton, who served in the War of 1812. He graduated from South Carolina College in 1836 and, following his father's death, took over the administration of the family plantation, reputed to be the largest in the South. From 1852 to 1861, Hampton served in both the house and senate of the South Carolina legislature.

Although opposed to secession and lacking any formal military training, when South Carolina seceded from the Union, Hampton raised and equipped his own military formation, a regiment-sized unit including infantry, artillery, and cavalry companies known as Hampton's Legion. Hampton participated and was wounded in the First Battle of Bull Run (July 21, 1861), where his legion fought alongside Gen. Thomas "Stonewall" Jackson's brigade on Henry House Hill. He led a brigade of infantry during the Peninsular Campaign and was promoted to brigadier general in May 1862. He received his second wound at the Battle of Seven Pines (May 31, 1862). Assigned to the cavalry of the Army of Northern Virginia in July, Hampton was named Gen. Jeb Stuart's second in command in September 1862. He commanded a cavalry brigade during the subsequent campaigns in Maryland and Pennsylvania. Hampton's brigade distinguished itself in the June 1863 cavalry battles at Brandy Station and Upperville. He suffered his third wound during fighting at Gettysburg. In August 1863, Hampton was promoted to major general. Hampton fought in the Wilderness and, following Stuart's death in May 1864, took command of the Cavalry Corps.

At the start of the Civil War, Southern plantation owner Wade Hampton equipped Hampton's Legion, a regiment-sized unit, by selling his cotton crop to Europe. (U.S. Army Military History Institute)

At Trevilian Station, near Gordonsville, on June 11 and 12, Hampton's cavalry kept Gen. Robert E. Lee's supply line, the Virginia Central Railroad, open by fending off Gen. Philip H. Sheridan's Union cavalry. With both sides suffering 20 percent casualties, this battle ranks as one of the bloodiest cavalry actions of the war.

A similar effort to preserve Lee's supply line southwest of Petersburg failed at Reams's Station on August 25, 1864, when Hampton was unable to defeat Gen. Winfield S. Hancock's force, which destroyed a long stretch of the Weldon Railroad. Hampton aided in the defense of Petersburg throughout the remainder of 1864 and in 1865 was promoted to lieutenant general. He then joined Gen. Joseph E. Johnston in the Carolinas in the fight against Gen. William T. Sherman and the Union forces advancing from the south.

At the war's end, Hampton returned to South Carolina. He supported the moderate Reconstruction policy of Pres. Andrew Johnson and later opposed Radical Reconstruction. A leading Democrat, Hampton became governor of South Carolina in 1876. He resigned in 1879 to accept a seat in the U.S. Senate (1879–91). Hampton later served as U.S. railroad commissioner (1893–97).

Bibliography: Freeman, Douglas Southall, *Lee's Lieutenants: A Study in Command,* 3 vols. (Scribner's, 1942–44); Wellman, Manly Wade, *Giant in Gray: A Biography of Wade Hampton of South Carolina* (Scribner's, 1949).

Steve R. Waddell

HANCOCK, WINFIELD SCOTT (1824–1886)

U.S. military leader and politician, Hancock was born in Montgomery Square, Pennsylvania. He graduated from West Point in 1844 and was posted to Indian territory. He joined Gen. Winfield Scott's army in Mexico in 1847 and was brevetted first lieutenant for gallantry at Contreras and Churubusco. After the war, Hancock saw extensive field service as adjutant and quartermaster in the West and in Florida, experiences that enhanced his ability later to command large formations.

The Civil War. Still a captain in 1861, Hancock was rescued from obscurity by Gen. George McClellan, who promoted him to brigadier general of volunteers to command a brigade. Promoted to division command, he fought conspicuously in the suicidal assault on Fredericksburg and in covering the army's retreat from Chancellorsville, performances that earned him command of II Corps. At Gettysburg, when Gen. John F. Reynolds was killed (July 1, 1863), Gen. George G. Meade turned to Hancock as his best and most trusted commander to take control of the battle, even though two more-senior generals—Oliver O. Howard and Daniel E. Sickles—were on the field. Through force of leadership, Hancock stemmed the Union retreat and stabilized the lines on Culp's and Cemetery hills, then sent word to Meade that the army should stand at Gettysburg. In desperate fighting on July 2, Hancock led his own corps and III Corps to stop Gen. James Longstreet's assault on the Union left. On the next day, II Corps broke Gen. George E. Pickett's great charge and Hancock received a near-mortal wound.

In Grant's Virginia Campaign (May 1864–April 1865), he fought with customary brilliance in the Wilderness and at Spotsylvania; after Cold Harbor, he and his once-magnificent corps were worn out. Their performance before Petersburg was uneven, and Hancock suffered from his unhealed wound. Grant transferred him to raise an experimental corps, a project later canceled. Hancock ended the war commanding a military district.

Postwar Career. Hancock was promoted to regular major general in 1866 and briefly commanded the Department of the Missouri. As commander of the 5th Military District (1867–68), he issued a general order that restored primacy to civil courts and reversed Reconstruction policies, bringing the enmity of Grant and the favorable attention of the Democratic party. In 1868 and 1876, Hancock vied unsuccessfully for the party's presidential nomination. His restraint as commander, Division of the Atlantic, in suppressing the Great Strike of 1877 brought him greater prominence, and he was the landslide Democratic presidential candidate in 1880. He lost narrowly to Republican James A. Garfield, chiefly because party bickering cost him New York's electoral votes.

Bibliography: Jordan, David M., *Winfield Scott Hancock: A Soldier's Life* (Indiana Univ. Press, 1988); Junkin, Reverend D. X., and Frank A. Norton, *The Life of Winfield Scott Hancock: Personal, Military, and Political* (Appleton, 1880); The Military Service Institution of the United States, *Letters and Addresses . . . In Memory of Winfield Scott Hancock* (Putnam's, 1886); Walker, Francis A., *History of the Second Army Corps in the Army of the Potomac* (Scribner's, 1891); ———, *General Hancock* (Appleton, 1894).

Col. (Ret.) Louis D. F. Frasché

HARRISON, WILLIAM HENRY (1773–1841)

U.S. military leader and ninth president of the United States (1841), Harrison was born in Charles City County, Virginia. After gaining renown as an Indian fighter in the Battle of Fallen Timbers (1794), he was governor of the Indiana Territory (1801–13). His highly publicized defeat of the Shawnee leader Tecumseh at the Battle of Tippecanoe (1811) won Harrison national-hero status, and his victory at the Battle of the Thames (1813) secured his promotion to major general and his reputation as a military celebrity.

This fame was central to Harrison's political career and helped him attain seats in the U.S. House of Representatives (1816–19) and the Senate (1825–28). In 1840, as the Whig nominee, Harrison waged a spectacular presidential campaign based almost exclusively on his military experience and enhanced by a manipulative, hard-sell, public-image strategy. He won in a landslide over incumbent Martin Van Buren. On Apr. 4, 1841, exactly one month after his inauguration, Harrison became the first U.S. president to die in office.

Christine L. Stevens

HAUPT, HERMAN (1817–1905)

U.S. engineer and military leader, Haupt was born in Philadelphia. Upon graduation from West Point in 1835, he was made a brevet second lieutenant in the 3d Infantry Regiment.

Early Career. In September 1835, Haupt, enamored with the booming railroad industry, resigned from the army to become a draftsman. He was soon engaged in advanced design and engineering work and in the management of railroad construction. He led a project to construct rail lines to Gettysburg, where he taught architecture, mathematics,

Herman Haupt's background in engineering served the Union well during the Civil War when he was charged with construction of railroads and management of transportation for the army. (U.S. Army Military History Institute)

and civil engineering at Penn College. His *General Theory of Bridge Construction,* written in 1851, was adopted by the U.S. Military Academy and most engineering schools as the standard text on the subject.

Haupt helped to finish construction and to operate the main line of the Pennsylvania Railroad between Philadelphia and Pittsburgh, serving as its chief engineer (1853–56) and as a member of the board of directors. In 1856, he left the Pennsylvania to undertake the Hoosac Tunnel project in Massachusetts. The construction of this 4.5-mile railway tunnel was a monumental engineering project, one that would embroil Haupt in financial and political wrangling for the rest of his life. Planned to take 3 years to complete, the Hoosac Tunnel actually took 21, with cost overruns, political squabbles, and ruined reputations.

The Civil War. In April 1862, Haupt was appointed chief of construction and transportation on military railroads, his initial duty being to support Gen. Irvin McDowell's advance on Richmond. Haupt maintained an autonomy in his operations in the Department of the Rappahannock and later in the Army of Virginia despite the overall responsibilities of the quartermaster general for transportation and of Daniel McCallum for rail operations in general. Haupt organized rail operations, construction repair efforts, and devised a bridge kit system that allowed for the rapid establishment of rail lines hot on the heels of battle. He developed and trained a solid corps of operators and construction troops, allowing him to focus on advance planning and major organizational questions. He had made himself dispensable from current operations. His contribution in advance planning and in providing a well-functioning organization was instrumental at the Second Battle of Bull Run, Fredericksburg, and Gettysburg. His entanglements with the Hoosac project forced his resignation from the army in September 1863, and he returned to Massachusetts to save his name and personal financial assets.

Postwar Career. Besides a continuing involvement in the Hoosac Tunnel disputes, Haupt expanded his reputation in engineering and operations. For a short period after the war, he managed the southern rail lines that had been acquired by the Pennsylvania Railroad. He continued to develop new technology in the tunneling and mining industry. Haupt also built the first long-distance crude-oil pipeline. In 1882–83, he returned to railroading as the general manager of the Northern Pacific, the first of the northern transcontinental lines. Haupt continued to consult on engineering problems for the rest of his life.

Bibliography: Lord, Francis A., *Lincoln's Railroad Man: Herman Haupt* (Fairleigh Dickinson Univ. Press, 1969); Ward, James A., *That Man Haupt: A Biography of Herman Haupt* (Louisiana State Univ. Press, 1973); Weber, Thomas, *The Northern Railroads in the Civil War* (Columbia Univ. Press, 1952).

Thomas W. Sweeney

HEINTZELMAN, SAMUEL PETER (1805–1880)

U.S. military officer, Heintzelman was born in Manheim, Pennsylvania, and graduated from West Point in 1826. Routine garrison duty dominated his career, but he won a brevet promotion to major for gallantry in the Mexican War and another to lieutenant colonel in 1851 while fighting Indians in the Southwest.

Shortly after the Civil War began, Heintzelman became a Union brigadier general of volunteers. His heroic attempt to rally his division at the First Battle of Bull Run (1861) left him seriously wounded. Promoted to major general in May 1862, he took command of the III Corps in time for McClellan's Peninsular Campaign but failed to distinguish himself. Later that year, Heintzelman's poor performance at the Second Battle of Bull Run left him delegated to rear-area administrative commands for the rest of the war. He retired a major general in 1869.

Bibliography: Warner, Ezra J., *Generals in Blue: Lives of the Union Commanders* (Louisiana State Univ. Press, 1964).

Daniel T. Bailey

HENDERSON, ARCHIBALD (1783–1859)

U.S. marine commander, Henderson was born in Colchester, Virginia. He was appointed second lieutenant in the Marine Corps in 1806, and his first command was that of the marine guard in the sloop *Wasp* on a European cruise, April–October 1807. Appointed adjutant of the Marine Corps in 1809, he soon left that post to command marines at Charleston, South Carolina, aboard the frigate *President*, and at Charlestown (Boston) navy yard. During the War of 1812, Henderson commanded the marine detachment in the USS *Constitution* during the 1815 engagement of that vessel with the HMS *Cyane* and HMS *Levant*. Following the War of 1812, he commanded the marine barracks at Portsmouth, New Hampshire.

In 1817, Henderson took the unusual step of bringing charges against Marine Corps commandant Franklin Wharton for neglect of duty and dishonorable conduct. Wharton was acquitted but died in 1818, and Henderson served as acting commandant from Sept. 16, 1818, to Mar. 3, 1819, before assuming command of the marines at New Orleans. Following the dismissal of the corps' fourth commandant, Anthony Gale, in late 1820, Henderson became lieutenant colonel and commandant.

Under Henderson's direction, the Marine Corps established its usefulness and earned a permanent place in the U.S. defense establishment. As commandant, he acted forcefully to control the selection and assignment of officers and to improve the discipline, training, and economy of the corps. He also worked successfully to protect the marines against those, such as Pres. Andrew Jackson, who wished to disband the corps. During the Second Seminole War (1835–1842), Henderson offered the services of the marines to the army and personally led marines against the Creek and Seminole as a brigade commander, notably at the Battle of Hatchee-Lustee (Jan. 27, 1837), for which service he received brevet promotion to brigadier general in 1843. In addition to protecting the corps from detractors and reforming it internally, Henderson also oversaw the development of a doctrine of amphibious warfare in which marines were to play an important role in the 20th century.

Henderson died in office at Washington, D.C., having completed nearly 53 years of active service and more than 38 years as Marine Corps commandant. He generally is recognized as "the father of the United States Marine Corps."

Bibliography: Millett, Allan R., *Semper Fidelis: The History of the United States Marine Corps* (Macmillan Co., 1980); Parker, William D., *A Concise History of the United States Marine Corps, 1775–1969* (Historical Div., U.S. Marine Corps Hdqrs., 1970); Spiller, Roger J., ed., *Dictionary of American Military Biography,* vol. 2 (Greenwood Press, 1984).

Lt. Col. (Ret.) Charles R. Shrader

HILL, AMBROSE POWELL (1825–1865)

U.S. soldier and Confederate military leader, Hill was born in Culpeper County, Virginia, and graduated from West Point in 1847. He served late in the Mexican War as an artillery captain and also fought in the Seminole Wars in Florida and on the Texas frontier. From 1855 to the time he resigned his commission to join the Confederate army in March 1861, Hill was a captain assigned to the office of the superintendent of the U.S. Coast Survey.

He received an appointment as a colonel in the Confederacy's 13th Virginia Volunteers and participated in the First Battle of Bull Run. In February 1862, he was promoted to brigadier general and three months later to major general commanding a division. Hill did well in the Peninsular Campaign from Williamsburg (May) through the Seven Days' Battles (June–July). His division, known as "Hill's Light Division" for its swiftness of marching, was probably the best in Gen. Robert E. Lee's army at this

Known for his aggressiveness, the Confederacy's Gen. A. P. Hill led "Hill's Light Division" during 1862 before being promoted to a corps command in 1863. (U.S. Army Military History Institute)

time. He quarreled with Gen. James Longstreet almost to the point of dueling, but Lee intervened and transferred Hill's unit to Gen. Thomas "Stonewall" Jackson's corps. He and Jackson also quarreled, and Jackson arrested him but later restored his command.

Hill was at Sharpsburg, Second Bull Run, Antietam, and Fredericksburg. At Chancellorsville, he held the mortally wounded Jackson in his arms until called away and wounded himself. In May 1863, he rose to lieutenant general and was given command of the newly created III Corps. As a corps commander at Gettysburg, Hill was adequate, not outstanding. In October, he failed to make a reconnaissance at Bristoe Station, and instead of attacking the fleeing enemy, Hill was flanked and lost two brigades. After a period of sickness, he resumed command of his III Corps in May 1864. On June 18, Hill placed his troops in the Petersburg trenches protecting the city. He fought at Globe Tavern and Reams's Station in August although not fully recovered from his illness. When the Union troops broke through the Petersburg defenses on Apr. 2, 1865, Hill, just returned from another sick leave, rode to the front to find his men and was fatally shot by Union infantry.

Bibliography: Hessler, William W., *A. P. Hill, Lee's Forgotten General* (Univ. of North Carolina Press, 1957).

Lynn L. Sims

HILL, DANIEL HARVEY (1821–1889)

U.S. educator and army officer and Confederate general, Hill was born in York District, South Carolina, and graduated from West Point in 1842. He served on the frontier and in the Mexican War, where he received two brevets for service in the Mexico City campaign. He resigned his commission in 1849 to teach mathematics at Washington College (Washington and Lee University; 1849–54) and Davidson College (1854–59). From 1859 to 1861 he was superintendent of the North Carolina Military Institute.

During the Civil War, Hill briefly served as colonel of the 1st North Carolina Infantry Regiment, leading it at the Battle of Big Bethel Church (June 10, 1861). He was appointed brigadier general that same day and major general seven months later. He served the first two years of the war in the eastern theater, fighting in the Peninsular Campaign and at the battles of Second Bull Run, South Mountain, and Antietam.

Hill was appointed lieutenant general in 1863, a rank to which he never was confirmed. Soon he was transferred to the Army of Tennessee and largely was responsible for the Confederate defeat of Maj. Gen. William Rosecrans at Chickamauga. After the battle, he was highly critical of the performance of his commander, Gen. Braxton Bragg, much as he had been of Gen. Robert E. Lee during the Seven Days' Battles (of the Peninsular Campaign). Shortly thereafter, Hill was relieved of command, and for the duration of the war he commanded troops only twice, in 1865, briefly at Petersburg and as a major general at Bentonville.

After the war, Hill returned to the education field, serving as president of Arkansas Industrial University (University of Arkansas; 1877–84) and Middle Georgia Military and Industrial College (Georgia Military Academy; 1885–89). He edited two publications, *The Land We Love* and *The Southern Home,* and devoted much time to writing defenses of his wartime actions.

Bibliography: Bridges, Leonard H., *Lee's Maverick General: Daniel Harvey Hill* (McGraw-Hill, 1961).

Louise Arnold-Friend

HITCHCOCK, ETHAN ALLEN (1798–1870)

U.S. military officer, Hitchcock, the grandson of Revolutionary War hero Ethan Allen, was born in Vergennes, Vermont, and graduated from West Point in 1817. He fought in the Second Seminole War and earned two brevets in the Mexican War. Returning to West Point as an instructor and appointed as commandant in 1829, he criticized Andrew Jackson's interference in military academy matters. Hitchcock was heavily involved in many facets of Indian affairs, and he revealed so much government fraud in its dealings with the Cherokee that the War Department suppressed his report. His resignation as infantry colonel in 1855 followed indirectly from his breaking up of a filibustering expedition.

A deeply intellectual abolitionist, Hitchcock twice was offered the governorship of Liberia. During the Civil War, he became a Union commissioner for exchange of prisoners of war. He left an insightful autobiography, *Fifty Years in Camp and Field*, published by his descendants in 1907.

Carol Reardon

HOLT, JOSEPH (1807–1894)

U.S. political leader and judge advocate general, Holt was born in Breckinridge County, Kentucky, and became a well-known lawyer. Pres. James Buchanan selected him commissioner of patents (1857), postmaster general (1859–61), and secretary of war (1861). Holt was a firm advocate of the Union as Southern secession commenced. His strong unionism and work in preserving Kentucky for the North won him his commission as the first judge advocate general of the U.S. Army (1862–75). As judge advocate general, Holt expanded the power of military commissions to try civilians and prosecuted the Lincoln-assassination conspirators. He also conducted the case that led to the conviction of Henry Wirz, Confederate commandant of Andersonville Prison and the only Civil War participant to be executed for war crimes.

Matthew Oyos

John Bell Hood, despite a crippled arm and then the loss of a leg in 1862, served the Confederacy throughout the Civil War, strapped to his saddle. (Library of Congress)

HOOD, JOHN BELL (1831–1879)

U.S. soldier and Confederate military leader, Hood was born in Owingsville, Kentucky, and graduated from West Point in 1853. He was commissioned a brevet second lieutenant of infantry and served on the California frontier before successfully lobbying for a transfer to the newly organized 2d U.S. Cavalry. Hood reported to this unit in 1855 and joined a number of future Civil War luminaries that included Albert Sidney Johnston, Robert E. Lee, George Thomas, and Kirby Smith. During the winter of 1855–56, the 2d Cavalry deployed to Texas, where it patrolled the frontier and protected settlers against Indians.

The Civil War. Hood resigned his commission in April 1861, eager to support the Southern cause. When his native Kentucky failed to secede, he entered Confederate service from Texas. Upon reporting to Richmond, he was detailed to instruct cavalry units assembling at Yorktown. Experienced officers being at a premium, he rapidly attained the rank of major and won early praise in leading some troopers in a skirmish with the federals in July 1861. In October, he became colonel of the 4th Texas Infantry, which combined with other Texas units in Virginia to form the Texas Brigade—destined shortly to achieve greater renown as Hood's Texas Brigade.

Hood's rise to fame, like that of so many others in the Army of Northern Virginia, and indeed the army's itself, began in the spring of 1862. In March, Hood was promoted to brigadier general and given command of the Texas Brigade. He led this unit through the Peninsular Campaign (March–July) and particularly distinguished himself at Gaines's Mill during the Seven Days' Battles. Here a bold assault by his Texans carried the day, earning Hood a lasting reputation as a superb fighter and the affection of General Lee. Shortly thereafter, he rose to the command of the division that included his old brigade. He fought his division well at the Second Battle of Bull Run and at Antietam, where his men played a crucial role in saving Lee's left flank by blunting the initial Union thrust in the savage fighting around Dunkard Church in the battle's early stage.

Hood advanced to the rank of major general, and his division was assigned to Gen. James Longstreet's corps in the reorganization of Lee's army that followed Antietam. Hood saw little further action until Gettysburg (July 1863), where he was badly wounded. Despite a permanently crippled left arm, Hood was back at the head of his division when Longstreet's corps was temporarily attached to Gen. Braxton Bragg's Army of Tennessee in September 1863. Hood acted as a corps commander under Longstreet, who directed a wing of Bragg's army, at Chickamauga on September 20. While urging his forces on through a gap in the Union line, Hood sustained another wound that resulted in the amputation of his right leg.

In February 1864, he was promoted to lieutenant general and assigned a corps command in the Army of Tennessee, now headed by Gen. Joseph Johnston. In the campaign that followed, the cautious Johnston withdrew from north Georgia to the outskirts of Atlanta in the face of Sherman's advance without engaging him in decisive battle. This led an exasperated Pres. Jefferson Davis to replace him with Hood, who had a well-established record as an aggressive fighter, on July 17, 1864. The Army of Tennessee had long been riven with internal disputes over command, and both during and after the war, supporters of Johnston and enemies of Davis accused Hood of intriguing against his superior, a charge accepted by many historians.

In any event, within a week and a half of taking command, Hood conducted three costly attacks that at least succeeded in halting the steady federal advance on Atlanta. Nevertheless, by late August, Sherman succeeded in cutting Atlanta's sole remaining rail line to the south. Hood's effort to reopen it was easily repulsed, forcing him to evacuate the city on September 1. Hood then resolved to attack Sherman's tenuous supply line north of Atlanta leading back to Chattanooga. The federals pursued him for most of October and eventually drove his army into Alabama, before Sherman tired of the game and began his famous march to the sea. At this point, Hood launched a forlorn and ultimately disastrous campaign into Tennessee. In late 1864, powerful Union forces under Gen. George Thomas smashed Hood's worn army at the battles of Franklin and Nashville, and the battered remnants withdrew to the south and west. Hood was relieved of command at Tupelo, Mississippi, in January 1865. Shortly thereafter, he began to engage in recriminations that would continue for the rest of his life over his generalship with the Army of Tennessee.

Postwar Years and Legacy. After surrendering to Union forces at Natchez, Mississippi, on May 31, 1865, Hood settled in New Orleans and earned a living as a merchant and in the insurance business. In 1879, yellow fever claimed the lives of Hood, his wife, and a daughter. Hood's memoirs, *Advance and Retreat,* justifying his role in the war in the west and refuting charges made by Johnston, were published posthumously in 1881. The historical consensus, far removed from the emotions of contemporaries, holds that the "gallant Hood"—the youngest of the Confederacy's army commanders—was indeed a superb combat leader at the regimental, brigade, and divisional levels, but that he was out of his depth when commanding larger formations. This view maintains that he lacked both the ability and inclination to plan in sufficient detail and adequately supervise subordinates. Thus, these historians echo the judgment of Lee in 1864 in assessing Hood as a possible army commander: "Hood is a bold fighter. I am doubtful as to other qualities necessary."

Bibliography: Connelly, Thomas L., *Autumn of Glory: The Army of Tennessee, 1862–1865* (Louisiana State Univ. Press, 1971); Dyer, John P., *The Gallant Hood* (Bobbs-Merrill, 1950); McMurry, Richard M., *John Bell Hood and The War for Southern Independence* (Univ. Press of Kentucky, 1982).

Capt. Alan Cate

HOOKER, JOSEPH (1814–1879)

U.S. military leader, Hooker was born in Hadley, Massachusetts, and graduated from West Point in 1837. He saw action in the Second Seminole War and on the frontier. In the Mexican War, he served as a staff officer in northern Mexico and on Gen. Winfield Scott's Mexico City expedition, earning three brevets for gallantry. Hooker resigned in 1853 to farm in California but remained active as a civil engineer and in the militia.

The Civil War. He returned to the service in May 1861 as a brigadier general of Union volunteers, first commanding a brigade in the defense of Washington. Although able, he demonstrated blatant personal ambition and considerable disloyalty to his superiors. Assigned to lead a division, he deployed with it to the Peninsula, where in May 1862 he earned the nickname "Fighting Joe" and was promoted to major general of volunteers. He was involved in all the Peninsula battles and saw hard fighting at Second Bull Run and Chantilly. In September 1862, he fought at South Mountain and was wounded while a corps commander at Antietam but returned to fight at Fredericksburg in December. Following this federal defeat, Hooker successfully used his political connections to be named commander of the Army of the Potomac. He showed considerable administrative ability, doing much to restore the army's morale and logistics system. He skillfully maneuvered his forces against Gen. Robert E. Lee but then hesitated and was defeated at Chancellorsville in May 1863. He was relieved of army command shortly thereafter and sent west to command a corps in Tennessee and later Georgia. He fought at Missionary Ridge and was brevetted for gallantry at the Battle of Lookout Mountain (November 1863). Hooker then served in the first phase of Gen. William T. Sherman's Georgia Campaign but asked to be relieved in July 1864 when a junior officer was appointed to command over him.

Postwar Years and Legacy. Hooker served thereafter in command of various departments until retiring in October 1868 because of a stroke. He lived quietly in Garden City, New York, until his death in October 1879. His requirement that journalists sign their articles when reporting on his commands is said to be the origin of the byline in American newspapers.

Joseph Hooker earned the name "Fighting Joe" when he continued to lead his Union troops at Williamsburg in 1862 on foot after his horse had been shot. (U.S. Army Military History Institute)

Bibliography: Stackpole, Edward J., *Chancellorsville: Lee's Greatest Battle* (Stackpole Co., 1958).

Lt. Col. (Ret.) J. W. A. Whitehorne

HOUSTON, SAMUEL (1793–1863)

U.S. soldier and politician, Houston was born near Lexington, Virginia. He moved to Tennessee in 1807 and during the next 10 years worked as a store clerk, lived among the Cherokee, and served under Andrew Jackson during the War of 1812. Following military service, he studied law, won election to the U.S. House of Representatives (1823–27), and served as governor of Tennessee (1827–29).

President Jackson sent Houston to Texas in 1832 to negotiate a treaty with the Indians. With the outbreak of the war for Texan independence in 1835, Houston became commander in chief of the Texas army. On Apr. 21, 1836, he routed Santa Anna at San Jacinto, securing the independence of Texas from Mexico that had been declared seven weeks earlier.

Houston was the first president of the Republic of Texas (1836–38, 1841–44), and after statehood was achieved, he was elected U.S. senator (1846–59). He became governor of Texas in 1859 but was ousted by the Confederacy in 1861 because he advocated preservation of the Union.

M. Guy Bishop

HOWARD, OLIVER OTIS (1830–1909)

U.S. military leader and educator, Howard was born in Leeds, Maine, and graduated from West Point in 1854. At the outbreak of the Civil War, he became colonel of the 3d Maine and commanded a brigade at the First Battle of Bull Run. He lost an arm at the Battle of Fair Oaks (May 1862) but obtained command of the Union XI Corps upon promotion to major general in January 1863.

The corps fought poorly at Chancellorsville and Gettysburg but impressed Gen. William T. Sherman in the Atlanta Campaign after transferring to the western theater in September 1863. Sherman chose Howard to lead the Army of the Tennessee in the March to the Sea and in the Carolinas Campaign.

Howard's piety and effort to foster a religious attitude among his men gained him a national reputation as a "Christian soldier." After the war, President Lincoln chose him to head the Freedmen's Bureau (1865–74). He founded Howard University in Washington, D.C., for black students, in 1869 and served as its president until 1874. Howard retired from the army in 1894 after holding several regional commands, fighting the Nez Percé, and serving as superintendent of West Point (1880–82).

Richard B. Meixsel

Despite the loss of an arm at Fair Oaks early in the Civil War, Union Gen. Oliver O. Howard went on to command the Army of the Tennessee in Sherman's March to the Sea and in the Carolinas. (U.S. Army Military History Institute)

HULL, ISAAC (1773–1843)

U.S. naval officer, Hull was born in Shelton, Connecticut. He was appointed a lieutenant in the navy in 1798 and gained increasing fame as a skillful, just, and courageous seaman in the Quasi War, the Tripolitan Wars, and the War of 1812. His triumph over the British frigate *Guerrière* in 1812 while captain of the *Constitution* brought him immediate and lasting fame.

Hull spent much of his career ashore commanding the navy yards at Boston (1815–23) and Washington (1829–35). Exonerated of charges of misconduct while at Boston, he returned to sea in the mid-1820s for a three-year cruise as commodore of the Pacific Squadron. In 1838, although ill, he accepted command of the Mediterranean Squadron for financial reasons, serving at sea until a year before his death.

Bibliography: Maloney, Linda M., "Isaac Hull: Bulwark of the Sailing Navy," *Command Under Sail*, ed. by James C. Bradford (Naval Inst. Press, 1985).

Maj. Grant H. Walker

HUNT, HENRY JACKSON (1819–1889)

U.S. military leader, Hunt was born in Detroit, Michigan, and graduated from West Point in 1839. Commissioned in the artillery, he served on the northern frontier and along the East Coast. Twice wounded and brevetted to captain and major for meritorious conduct during the Mexican War, Hunt participated in the siege of Veracruz and in the campaign to capture Mexico City. He then served on the Indian frontier until 1856, when he was appointed to revise light artillery tactics. His board's report, submitted after three years of study and adopted by the War Department in 1860, laid the groundwork for artillery, infantry, and cavalry tactics in the Civil War.

As chief of artillery for the Army of the Potomac from the Peninsular Campaign of 1862 until Gen. Robert E. Lee's surrender at Appomattox in 1865, Hunt played a key role in Union campaigns. His batteries broke the Confederate pursuit at the First Battle of Bull Run, averted complete disaster at Chancellorsville, and decimated Pickett's Charge at Gettysburg. He also distinguished himself in the battles of Antietam, Fredericksburg, and the Wilderness, and in the siege of Petersburg. Although he received brevets to brigadier general and major general for gallantry on the field of battle, Hunt retained the permanent rank of colonel due to limitations in the U.S. Army table of organization.

Bibliography: Longacre, Edward G., *The Man Behind the Guns* (A. S. Barnes, 1977).

Capt. James Sanders Day

INGALLS, RUFUS (1818–1893)

U.S. military leader, Ingalls was born in Denmark, Maine, and graduated from West Point in 1843. In 1848, following Mexican War service with mounted troops, he transferred to the Quartermaster Department, serving on the West Coast and with the Steptoe transcontinental expedition (1854–55).

In July 1862, Ingalls was named chief quartermaster of the Army of the Potomac. Taking charge of the army's enormous, disorganized trains on the Peninsula, he restructured them into an efficient logistical tool. He devised a system for marking baggage and general supply wagons and instituted other measures to insure effective logistical movements that would not interfere with tactical maneuvers. In June 1864, he became chief quartermaster of all the Union armies operating against Richmond. A confidant of General Grant, he built and operated the great Union supply depot at City Point, Virginia, and rose to the rank of brevet major general.

After 1865, Ingalls served in various responsible positions until named quartermaster general in 1882. One of the first quartermasters general to have been "raised in the Department," he oversaw its return to a peacetime routine focused on supply of a small, scattered frontier army. He retired from active service in July 1883. A man of considerable ambition, drive, and professional competence, Ingalls was perhaps the most competent field quartermaster of the Civil War on either side.

Bibliography: Risch, Erna, "Quartermaster Generals of the Past [Rucker, Ingalls, Holabird]," *The Quartermaster Review* (May–June, 1953); ———*Quartermaster Support of the Army: A History of the Corps, 1775–1939* (Office of the Quartermaster General, Washington, 1962); Shrader, Charles R., "Field Logistics in the Civil War," *The U.S. Army War College Guide to the Battle of Antietam: The Maryland Campaign of 1862,* ed. by Jay Luvaas and Harold W. Nelson (South Mountain Press, 1987).

Lt. Col. (Ret.) Charles R. Shrader

JACKSON, ANDREW (1767–1845)

Military leader and seventh president of the United States (1829–37), Jackson was born in the Waxhaw settlement in South Carolina. He fought with his state's militia in the Revolutionary War and by the mid-1780s was a lawyer in what became Tennessee. His reputation as a military leader was established during the War of 1812, in which he achieved major victories at Horseshoe Bend, Mobile Bay, and Pensacola in 1814. By this time, he had been promoted to major general. He became a national hero with his defeat of the British at the Battle of New Orleans in 1815.

Jackson's reputation was further enhanced by his campaign against the Seminole along the Georgia border in 1818. Driving them southward, Jackson pursued them into Florida and took Pensacola from the Spanish. Following the capture of Pensacola, Jackson created an international incident by executing two British traders, Alexander Arbuthnot and Robert Ambrister, who stood accused of aiding the enemy. After the U.S. purchase of Florida from Spain in 1819, Jackson briefly served in 1821 as its territorial governor.

In 1824, Jackson narrowly lost the presidential election to John Quincy Adams, but defeated him four years later. As a frontiersman of humble origin and an expansionist determined to open up new territories, Jackson came to represent a new democratic spirit of optimism for workers and farmers, particularly in the South and West. His first term, however, was marked by controversy—the most significant issue being the opposition of the New England and Middle Atlantic states to the protective tariff. Jackson resolved the matter by securing congressional approval to use federal troops to enforce state compliance with federal laws. Also, in 1830, Jackson ordered the forcible removal of the Cherokee, Choctaw, and Chickasaw Indians from the Southeast to new lands across the Mississippi. Jackson's second term was dominated by his opposition to the Second Bank of the United States and other economic issues.

Jackson retired in 1837 to Hermitage, his estate near Nashville. His victories in the War of 1812, his shaping of federal policy toward the Indians, and his aggressive nationalism laid the foundations for the future shape of the country.

Bibliography: Remini, Robert, *Andrew Jackson and the Course of American Empire, 1767–1821* (Harper & Row, 1977); Schlesinger, Arthur M., Jr., *The Age of Jackson* (Little, Brown, 1945).

M. Guy Bishop

Confederate Gen. Thomas "Stonewall" Jackson earned his nickname by standing steadfast, like a stonewall, against the Union army at the First Battle of Bull Run in 1861. (Library of Congress)

JACKSON, THOMAS JONATHAN "STONEWALL" (1824–1863)

U.S. soldier and Confederate military leader, Jackson was born in Clarksburg, Virginia (now West Virginia), and entered West Point in 1842. Ill-prepared for the school's academic demands, he followed an exacting study regimen and graduated in 1846 with an impressively improved scholastic standing.

Early Career. Jackson was commissioned in the artillery. During the Mexican War, he won a succession of brevets to the rank of major, distinguishing himself at Veracruz, Cerro Gordo, and Chapultepec. After the war, he served at Fort Columbus in New York (1848–49). He then was posted to Fort Hamilton in New York until 1851 and, finally, to Florida. He resigned from the army in February 1852 to become professor of artillery tactics and natural philosophy at the Virginia Military Institute (VMI) in Lexington, Virginia.

Jackson was a stiff and formal teacher whose strict compliance with rules and regulations frequently earned him the ridicule of his cadets. He never bowed to such criticism and in fact became increasingly pious and uncompromising during his 10 years in Lexington. This was also a period of deepening religious conviction for Jackson, a zealous Presbyterian. In 1854, he was widowed after 14 months of marriage; he remarried in 1857.

A cadet artillery detachment, with Jackson in charge, was sent from VMI to Charles Town, Virginia, for the hanging of insurrectionist John Brown on Dec. 2, 1859. Jackson did not support secession, but he believed that the South should fight for its rights. As a result, when Virginia seceded in April 1861, he chose to go with his state. When the VMI corps of cadets left for war on April 21, Jackson commanded it.

The Civil War. Jackson was appointed colonel in Virginia's forces on April 27 and was sent to Harpers Ferry. His command soon was superseded by Brig. Gen. Albert Sidney Johnston, and Jackson was himself promoted to brigadier general in June. His sobriquet "Stonewall" was earned on July 21 at the First Battle of Bull Run when Brig. Gen. Barnard E. Bee, in rallying his routed Confederate troops, reputedly shouted: "There is Jackson standing like a stone wall."

In October, Jackson was promoted to major general in the Provisional Army of the Confederate States and in November was given command of the Shenandoah District. Leading a force that rarely numbered more than 15,000, he waged his famous Shenandoah Valley Campaign (May–June 1862), an operation considered among the most brilliant in military history. Equally successful in maneuver and in battle, his command tied down some 60,000 troops, which were vital for the federal drive toward Richmond, Virginia, the Confederate capital.

In late June, Jackson and his command were recalled to join the main Army of Northern Virginia. However, their arrival was delayed by Jackson's own physical exhaustion and his unfamiliarity with the new area of operations. As a result, his troops failed to attack Union positions at White Oak Swamp on June 30. This failure was one of the factors that disrupted Gen. Robert E. Lee's plan to envelop the federal position.

Jackson was again given a detached command. On August 18, he fought an inconclusive battle with the federals, then was ordered to rejoin the Army of Northern Virginia. The timely arrival of his troops on the battlefield on August 30 helped Lee win the Second Battle of Bull Run. In September, Lee's army marched north. Jackson, with five divisions, was ordered to capture Harpers Ferry. He accomplished this on September 15, then rejoined Lee at Sharpsburg. In the battle that followed, Jackson firmly held the left wing of the Confederate position against heavy and persistent Union assaults. In October, Jackson was promoted to lieutenant general and given command of the Army of Northern Virginia's II Corps, which fought with distinction at the Battle of Federicksburg.

In late April 1863, the Union and Confederate armies met in Virginia's Wilderness. On May 1, the federals were driven back into a strong defensive position near Chancellorsville. The next day, Jackson led a great turning movement against the Union right flank and rear. Early that evening, while returning from reconnaissance, he was seriously wounded when his men fired into what they believed to be advancing Union troops. After his left arm was amputated, he was moved to Guiney's Station, Virginia, where he died of pneumonia on May 10. He was interred at Lexington, Virginia.

The tall, wiry Jackson was remembered as a brave, aggressive, disciplined, energetic, and determined leader. His command's ability to march long distances in a short period of time had earned it the nickname "Jackson's Foot Cavalry." In spite of his hard-driving battle leadership, "Stonewall" Jackson had devoted great attention to the needs of his men and had been very popular with them. Lee was unable to replace this unique and valuable man, and the efficiency of the Army of Northern Virginia was damaged irreparably by his loss.

Bibliography: Bowers, John, *Stonewall Jackson: Portrait of a Soldier* (Morrow, 1989); Davis, Burke, *They Called Him Stonewall: A Life of Lt. General T. J. Jackson, C.S.A.* (Rinehart, 1954); Douglas, Henry Kyd, *I Rode with Stonewall* (Univ. of North Carolina Press, 1940); Freeman, Douglas Southall, *Lee's Lieutenants: A Study in Command,* vols. 1 & 2 (Scribner's, 1950); Vandiver, Frank E., *Mighty Stonewall* (McGraw-Hill, 1957).

Brig. Gen. (Ret.) Uzal W. Ent

JESUP, THOMAS SIDNEY (1788–1860)

Known as the "father of the Quartermaster Corps" of the U.S. Army, Jesup was born in Berkeley County, Virginia, the son of a Revolutionary War officer. He received his own commission as a second lieutenant in 1808 and served with distinction in the War of 1812. He fought in the battles of Chippewa, Niagara, and Lundy's Lane and was brevetted to colonel.

As part of the military reform required after the war, Sec. of War John C. Calhoun nominated Jesup to be the quartermaster general. On May 8, 1818, Jesup took up his appointment in the grade of brigadier general. Calhoun was determined to reform the army and eliminate the waste and abuse that had occurred in supplying the troops in the War of 1812, and as quartermaster general, Jesup would be the man to disburse the largest share of the army's budget. Jesup immediately issued regulations to guide the operation of his department. There were two central principles of his office: to ensure an ample and sufficient system of supply and to enforce strict accountability over money and supplies. As time went on and Jesup's strong control over his department became evident, many additional functions were transferred to his agency. These included, first, the distribution of clothing and equipment and, later, the purchase of those items as well. In his 42 years as quartermaster general, the longest served by a bureau chief, Jesup built a strong, functional, and accountable department.

The Seminole Wars. In May 1836, Pres. Andrew Jackson sent Jesup south on detached duty to command troops in the Seminole Campaign. He had been advanced to the rank of major general in 1828 and was now one of the most senior officers in the army. His handling of military operations and his capture of the chief Osceola, under a flag of truce, sparked controversy in Congress. Jesup nevertheless continued to press the Indians, believing it to be his military duty and leaving politics out of the campaign plan. He was severely wounded but stayed with his troops in the field, not returning to his post as quartermaster general until 1839.

The Mexican War. With the dispatch of U.S. soldiers to Texas and the outbreak of war with Mexico (1846), Jesup and the Quartermaster Department faced the great challenges of distance, slow communication, and poorly formulated tactical plans on which to base support requirements. In the midst of the squabbles between Gen. Zachary Taylor and Sec. of War William L. Marcy, Jesup himself went to the field to assess the condition of support for the army. Some of the people charged with conducting supply operations were recent political appointees and lacked both the military and business experience demanded by the situation. Jesup used this experience to extract from Congress additional officer spaces for his department. He also called for formal training in supply matter for soldiers, but this recommendation would languish until the 20th century.

Bibliography: Kieffer, Chester L., *Maligned General: The Biography of Thomas Sidney Jesup* (Presidio Press, 1979); Risch, Erna, *Quartermaster Support of the Army* (Center of Military History, 1989).

Thomas W. Sweeney

JOHNSON, ANDREW (1808–1875)

Seventeenth president of the United States (1865–69), Johnson was born in Raleigh, North Carolina. A tailor by profession, he was a self-educated man. Soon after moving to Greeneville, Tennessee, Johnson became engaged in politics. He was an alderman (1828–30), mayor of Greeneville (1830–33), and member of the state legislature (1835–43). He then served in the U.S. House of Representatives (1843–53), as governor of Tennessee (1853–57), and in the U.S. Senate (1857–62).

Johnson distinguished himself as the only Southern senator to support the Union during the Civil War. In 1862, President Lincoln appointed him military governor of the seceded state of Tennessee. In 1864, he was Lincoln's running mate on the Union-Republican ticket. Upon Lincoln's assassination in 1865, Johnson succeeded to the presidency. Upholding the plans set forth by Lincoln, he tried to implement Reconstruction policies based on mercy and leniency to the South. Radical Republicans in Congress, however, passed in 1867 their own harsher Reconstruction program, as well as the Tenure of Office Act, which limited presidential power. Johnson challenged the act, and the Radical Republicans instituted impeachment proceedings against him. He was acquitted by one vote and finished out his term as president.

Bibliography: Castel, Albert, *The Presidency of Andrew Johnson* (Univ. Press of Kansas, 1979); Trefousse, Hans L., *Andrew Johnson: A Biography* (Norton, 1989).

M. Guy Bishop

JOHNSTON, ALBERT SIDNEY (1803–1862)

U.S. and Confederate military leader, Johnston was born in Washington, Kentucky, and graduated from West Point in 1826. Johnston's early military experiences were varied. In 1832, he participated in the Black Hawk War as adjutant to the commander. In 1834, Johnston resigned his commission and two years later moved to the new Republic of Texas, where he was named senior brigadier general of the Texan army. He became the Texan secretary of war in 1838, resigned in 1840, and, when the Mexican War arose in 1846, raised a regiment of Texas volunteers and commanded it until his men's enlistments expired. Thereafter he served with other units, distinguishing himself at the Battle of Monterrey (September 1846).

In 1849, Pres. Zachary Taylor appointed Johnston to a regular commission in the U.S. Army and assigned him as paymaster of troops on the Texas frontier. By 1855, Johnston had attained the rank of colonel and was given command of the newly formed 2d Cavalry Regiment. Serving in this unit of distinction were more than a dozen future Civil War generals, including Robert E. Lee.

During his military career, Albert Sidney Johnston commanded the Texas army, the Utah Expedition, the Department of the Pacific, and the Western Division of the Confederate army before falling at Shiloh in 1862. (U.S. Army Military History Institute)

The Utah Expedition. In 1857, Pres. James Buchanan sent new officials to Utah Territory, and subsequent reports to Washington declared the Mormons in rebellion against the government. To counter the situation, Buchanan sent a military expedition to Utah to quell the Mormons and install the appointed territorial governor, Alfred Cumming. Departing in July 1857, 2,500 troops marched from Fort Leavenworth, Kansas, to Utah, at first under the command of Gen. William S. Harney, but within one month, Johnston was named as his replacement.

During the two-year period that Johnston headed this expedition, negotiations were conducted, eventually leading to a peaceful settlement of the controversy and the installation of federal appointees to office in Utah. His success in handling this crisis led to Johnston's promotion to brevet brigadier general and his appointment in 1860 to command the Department of the Pacific.

The Civil War. Johnston commanded the Pacific Department at the time of the secession of the lower South in the winter of 1860–61, and it led to a difficult career choice. Since his strongest loyalties rested with Texas, Johnston resigned his commission when Texas seceded, although he was never an advocate of secession. In June 1861, he and a company of other Southerners marched cross-country to offer military service to the Confederacy. As one of the foremost officers in the army, Johnston was appointed by a personal friend, Pres. Jefferson Davis, as a general in the Confederate army with command of the Western Division.

Johnston immediately set about to defend the western part of the Confederacy, developing a line of defenses from the Appalachians to what would become Oklahoma. Outnumbered and outgunned, the army's first real test came in the battles of Forts Henry and Donelson, both of which fell to Union forces in February 1862. The defeats prompted a Southern outcry against Johnston, but Davis defended his general as the South's best commander. In April, Johnston gathered many of his troops around Corinth, Mississippi, from which he attacked Union forces under Gen. Ulysses S. Grant near the Shiloh church in Tennessee. Nearly successful in crushing the federals on April 6, the first day of the Battle of Shiloh, Johnston was fatally wounded, and his second in command, Gen. P. G. T. Beauregard, halted the attack until the next morning. This gave Grant time to reorganize his forces and bring in reinforcements. The next day, Union troops drove the Confederates back to Corinth.

Legacy. Since Johnston was killed so early in the Civil War, it is difficult to assess his abilities as a commander of large numbers of troops. He demonstrated caution early in the war, but showed tactical brilliance while commanding at Shiloh. The effect of his death has been a point of controversy ever since. J. F. C. Fuller, a British analyst, called Johnston a "brave but stupid" man, but many historians have assigned Johnston a place somewhere in the middle, neither brilliant nor stupid in his command decisions. One conclusion is appropriate: Johnston was a capable military officer, was successful in every position of command he held, and, at least in his handling of Shiloh, showed real ability to lead a large army to victory. Had he survived, Johnston might have been able to develop his leadership skills more fully and been a source of great strength to the Confederacy.

Bibliography: Connelly, Thomas H., *Army of the Heartland: The Army of Tennessee, 1861–1862* (Louisiana State Univ. Press, 1967); Hafen, LeRoy R., and Ann W. Hafen, *The Utah Expedition, 1857–1858* (Clark, 1958); McDonough, James Lee, *Shiloh: In Hell Before Night* (Univ. of Tennessee Press, 1977); Roland, Charles P., *Albert Sidney Johnston: Soldier of Three Republics* (Univ. of Texas Press, 1964).

Roger D. Launius

JOHNSTON, JOSEPH EGGLESTON (1807–1891)

U.S. and Confederate military leader, Johnston was born in Prince Edward County, Virginia, and graduated from West Point in 1829. He served with distinction during the Mexican War, in which he was wounded five times. Johnston was promoted to lieutenant colonel in 1855 and brigadier general in 1860. He served as quartermaster general of the U.S. Army during 1860–61. Then, following the secession of Virginia, Johnston resigned his U.S. commission and accepted appointment as brigadier general in the Confederate army (May 1861).

At the First Battle of Bull Run (July 21, 1861), he played an instrumental role in turning back the Union forces. With 12,000 men, he defeated an army half again as large led by Gen. Robert Patterson, a veteran of the War of 1812. In firm control of their troops, Johnston and Gen. P. G. T. Beauregard launched a successful counterattack against the advancing federal forces of Gen. Irvin McDowell. Johnston soon received a commission as general. He was wounded while leading Confederate troops at the Battle of Seven Pines (Fair Oaks). In late May 1862, Union troops under Gen. George B. McClellan moved ponderously toward Richmond. Taking advantage of a tremendous storm on May 30–31, Johnston hurled his army against the Union forces.

His bold plan might have succeeded in destroying McClellan's army, but Gen. James Longstreet's division took a wrong road and failed to support Johnston. While the Battle of Seven Pines had no important strategic consequences, it did have a profound impact upon Confederate military leadership. Johnston, who had been the ranking Confederate officer, was wounded in the battle. His replacement was Gen. Robert E. Lee, who never relinquished command of the Army of Northern Virginia.

Although he was blamed by Confederate president Jefferson Davis for almost losing Richmond, failing to defend Vicksburg, and allowing the fall of Atlanta, Gen. Joseph Johnston was popular with his troops because of his concern for their welfare. (Library of Congress)

Many of his peers considered Johnston one of the South's premier generals. Yet, Confederate president Jefferson Davis bore a strong dislike for Johnston. Devastating Southern casualties and an apparent lack of decisive leadership at the Battle of Chickamauga (September 1863) led the Confederate high command to call for the replacement of Gen. Braxton Bragg. While both Johnston and Beauregard were capable of assuming the command, Davis chose to retain Bragg.

At last, following the disastrous Confederate defeat at Chattanooga in November, Davis reluctantly appointed Johnston commander of the Army of Tennessee. In 1864, Union general Ulysses S. Grant directed Gen. William T. Sherman to move his army against Johnston's forces. Sherman's army numbered 100,000, while Johnston commanded fewer than 65,000 men. Sherman was to break up the Confederates and open the way to Atlanta.

Johnston's army was entrenched in northern Georgia about 25 miles south of Chattanooga. In early May 1864, Union forces led by Gen. James G. McPherson broke through Johnston's thinly defended lines near Resaca, Georgia, forcing Johnston to fall back. For three days, the armies skirmished while each side probed for an opening.

Johnston's slow retreat paused at Cassville, where he turned to fight. Johnston planned a counterattack that he later had to scrap as the number of Union forces increased. As the Yankees pushed slowly forward, Johnston's army withdrew toward Kenesaw Mountain, north of Marietta, Georgia. The Confederates were entrenched along a 7-mile front blocking the way to Atlanta. On June 27, Sherman launched an all-out attack against Johnston. The Confederate army repelled this assault, but Sherman soon managed to flank Johnston's army, causing the latter to withdraw on July 9–10. The way to Atlanta now opened to Sherman.

Southern criticism of Johnston rose to a crescendo, and the hostility between Davis and Johnston now peaked. In Davis's view, Johnston's gamble at Seven Pines in 1862 had nearly led to the capture of Richmond. As the Confederate president saw it, only the gallantry of Lee had prevented defeat at that time. Further, Davis believed that Johnston's 1863 failure to relieve the defenders of Vicksburg had led to the fall of that city. Now Johnston had fallen back, opening the door to Atlanta. Davis and his cabinet unanimously recommended Johnston's removal from command. On July 17, the Confederate secretary of war informed Johnston: "As you have failed to arrest the advance of the enemy to the vicinity of Atlanta, far into the interior of Georgia . . . you are hereby relieved of command." This action was highly controversial. Johnston was popular with his troops for his efforts to minimize casualties. Sherman later observed that the Confederacy "rendered us most valuable service" by removing Johnston. Yet, political and military circumstances prohibited Davis from doing otherwise.

After capturing Atlanta, Sherman marched toward North Carolina hoping to catch Lee in a pincer movement between Grant's forces and his own. Lee beseeched the Confederate congress to reinstate Johnston so that the latter could cut off Sherman. This was a forlorn hope, however, since Johnston could muster only 22,000 men to face Sherman's 60,000. Johnston attempted to strike Sherman at Bentonville (near Raleigh), but the surprised Yankees dug in and held their ground. Johnston's effort to save Lee had collapsed.

Bibliography: Connelly, Thomas L., *Autumn of Glory: The Army of Tennessee, 1862–1865* (Louisiana State Univ. Press, 1971); McPherson, James M., *Ordeal by Fire: The Civil War and Reconstruction* (Knopf, 1982).

M. Guy Bishop

KEARNY, PHILIP (1814–1862)

U.S. military officer, Kearny (nephew of Gen. Stephen W. Kearny) was born in New York City and graduated from Columbia Law School in 1833. Commissioned into the 1st Dragoons in 1837, he earned the Legion of Honor in North Africa with the French in 1839 while attending the Saumur Cavalry School. He served as an aide to the General of the Army (1840–46) and led a cavalry company in the campaign against Mexico City, where he lost an arm at Churubusco. He resigned in 1851 and returned to France, where, in 1859, he earned a second Legion of Honor fighting against Austria.

Kearny returned to the United States at the outbreak of the Civil War and was commissioned a Union brigadier general (May 1861). He first led the Jersey Brigade, then in April 1862 commanded a division in the Army of the Potomac. Promoted to major general in July, he fought on the Peninsula and at the Second Battle of Bull Run. Kearny was killed at Chantilly, Virginia, on September 1, while reconnoitering Confederate lines. The city of Kearny, New Jersey, is named in his honor.

Bibliography: Werstein, Irving, *Kearny the Magnificent: The Story of General Philip Kearny* (John Day Co., 1962).

Lt. Col. (Ret.) J. W. A. Whitehorne

KEARNY, STEPHEN WATTS (1794–1848)

U.S. military officer, Kearny was born in Newark, New Jersey. He served in the War of 1812 and spent most of the next 30 years on the frontier. He commanded the Army of the West at Fort Leavenworth, Kansas.

In May 1846, at the onset of the Mexican War, Kearny was ordered to lead a military expedition westward from Fort Leavenworth to conquer New Mexico and California. In August, his 1,700-man force captured Santa Fe without a fight and established order, created a legal code for the territory, and incorporated Santa Fe into the territorial system of the United States.

Leaving Alexander Doniphan's 1st Missouri Volunteers in New Mexico, Kearny pushed on to California. Hearing that Lt. Col. John C. Frémont and Comdr. Robert F. Stockton had won control of California, Kearny took only 120 dragoons with him. When he arrived, however, he found the Americans fighting against a Mexican uprising. On Dec. 6, 1846, his troops encountered a Mexican force at San Pasqual and fought an inconclusive engagement. He then joined forces with Stockton in San Diego. Almost immediately, Stockton declared himself governor of California, and while the proclamation carried no legal force, Kearny accepted it to preserve order among the Americans. Kearny led a combined force against the Mexicans at San Gabriel on Jan. 8, 1847, and another at Mesa, outside Los Angeles, the next day. This ended the uprising and brought California under American control.

After this action, Kearny sought to work out the difficulties presented by Stockton and Frémont, both of whom refused to accept his legal position as an army commander. Kearny arrested Frémont for insubordination and took him to Fort Leavenworth for trial. The court-martial proceedings took several months, but Kearny's position prevailed. He then was sent as military commander of Veracruz and

Mexico City. Kearny returned to the United States in September 1848 with malaria and died soon after.

Bibliography: Bauer, K. Jack, *The Mexican War, 1846–1848* (Macmillan Co., 1974); Clarke, Dwight L., *Stephen Watts Kearny: Soldier of the West* (Univ. of Oklahoma Press, 1961).

Roger D. Launius

KEOKUK (c. 1788–1848)

Sac and Fox Indian leader, Keokuk was born near present-day Rock Island, Illinois. While he rose to prominence as a war leader, Keokuk advocated diplomacy when dealing with whites. Impressed with the power of the United States after a trip to Washington, Keokuk, unlike Black Hawk, his chief rival, worked for accommodation rather than confrontation. The government responded by funneling gifts and annuities through Keokuk, further enhancing his position in the tribe. He successfully negotiated the sale of Sac and Fox land in Illinois and the tribes' removal to Iowa in 1829. In 1832, when Black Hawk led his band back into Illinois, sparking the Black Hawk War, Keokuk kept the bulk of his band out of the conflict and minimized the repercussions against it. He subsequently arbitrated his tribe's move to Kansas, where he died in 1848. Keokuk, Iowa, is named in his honor.

Richard F. Kehrberg

LEE, FITZHUGH (1835–1905)

U.S. military officer and Confederate general, Lee was born in Fairfax County, Virginia, and graduated from West Point in 1856, having just barely avoided dismissal. He was wounded in the Indian wars and in 1860 became a cavalry instructor at West Point. Lee resigned his commission in the U.S. Army in 1861 to join the Confederacy.

He fought at the First Battle of Bull Run and rose to lieutenant colonel, 1st Virginia Cavalry. He did well in Gen. Jeb Stuart's ride around Gen. George McClellan and by July 1862 was a brigadier general. He fought at Sharpsburg and Gettysburg and became a major general by 1863. He helped stop Gen. Ulysses S. Grant at Spotsylvania, and later in 1864 he was seriously wounded. After recovering, he commanded the cavalry in the Army of Northern Virginia.

After the war, Lee served as Virginia governor (1886–90). He was consul general to Havana (1896–98) at the outbreak of the Spanish-American War and became military governor of Havana (1899). Lee authored several historical works, the best known being *General Lee* (1894), a biography of his uncle Robert E. Lee.

Lynn L. Sims

LEE, ROBERT EDWARD (1807–1870)

U.S. military leader and commander in chief of the Confederate forces in the Civil War, Lee was born at "Stratford," in Westmoreland County, Virginia, the fifth child of Henry "Light-Horse Harry" Lee. His father was a renowned cavalry officer in the American Revolution. Lee graduated second in the West Point Class of 1829 and was brevetted second lieutenant of engineers. In 1831, he married Mary Ann Randolph Custis, great-granddaughter of Martha Washington. The couple eventually had seven children.

Gen. Robert E. Lee was appointed Confederate general in chief on Feb. 9, 1865. (U.S. Army Military History Institute)

Early Career. Lee's early army career included service at Fort Pulaski, Georgia; as an assistant engineer at Fortress Monroe, Virginia 1831–34); in Washington, D.C., as an assistant in the chief engineer's office (1834–37); as superintending engineer for St. Louis harbor and the upper Mississippi and Missouri rivers (1837–41); and at Fort Hamilton, New York (1841–46). He was promoted to first lieutenant in 1836 and to captain in 1838.

Service in the Mexican War taught Lee numerous crucial military lessons. These included the importance of audacity, of having trained staff officers, of the relationship between detailed and careful reconnaissance and sound strategy, of the value of fortifications in the defense, of the strategic potential of flanking maneuvers, and of the connection between good communications and effective strategy. All of these lessons proved invaluable to him during the Civil War. In Mexico, he won brevet promotions to colonel and was cited for bold reconnaissance, for effectively deploying artillery under heavy enemy fire, and for his accurate reports and well-reasoned recommendations.

At the Battle of Chapultepec, (September 1847), Lee was wounded and sent home.

After the war, he supervised the construction of Fort Carroll in Baltimore (1848–52). In 1852, Lee was appointed superintendent of the Military Academy at West Point. In spite of personal reservations concerning his lack of experience, Lee accepted the position and became an excellent administrator. He tightened discipline and raised academic standards at West Point. An efficient and diligent superintendent, he also devoted much personal attention to the cadets.

In 1855, Lee left the academy to become lieutenant colonel of the 2d Cavalry. Instead of active duty with his command, however, he spent most of the next two years assigned to court-martial duty. Lee obtained leave from the army when his father-in-law died in October 1857. His responsibilities as estate executor and in caring for his ailing wife kept him from military affairs until 1859, when he was recalled to quell John Brown's insurrection at Harpers Ferry.

The Civil War. Lee returned to his regiment in February 1860 and was given command of the Department of Texas. At the outbreak of the Civil War, he was recalled to Washington, and on Apr. 18, 1861, he was offered command of the U.S. Army by Pres. Abraham Lincoln. Lee did not favor secession, but he believed that he owed his primary allegiance to his state of Virginia. Therefore, he resigned from the U.S. forces when Virginia seceded and accepted leadership of the Virginia troops.

A disciplined professional, Lee excelled as a strategist and a topographer but had difficulty in delegating tasks to others. Although a master of fortification and reconnaissance, he had little understanding of logistics and no experience in conducting defensive warfare. Nevertheless, he was appointed general in the Confederate army and became military adviser to Pres. Jefferson Davis. From November 1861 to March 1862, Lee was engaged in organizing the South Atlantic seaboard defenses.

On June 1, 1862, Gen. Joseph E. Johnston was badly wounded at the Battle of Seven Pines in the Peninsular Campaign and was forced to pass to Lee his command of the Confederate Army of the Potomac, which Lee renamed "Army of Northern Virginia." As the Union's Gen. George B. McClellan pressed his numerical advantage, the Confederate forces slowly retreated in the direction of Richmond. In late June to early July, using interior lines and adroit maneuvering, Lee won a succession of battles near Richmond, known as the Seven Days' Battles. As McClellan began to withdraw, Lee turned his attention northward where Gen. John Pope headed a new Union army. In August, Lee met Pope and was victorious in the Second Battle of Bull Run. When Lee divided his army to invade the North in September, however, he was stopped by the Union Army of the Potomac at Sharpsburg, Maryland (Battle of Antietam). However, in December, his well-emplaced troops slaughtered the Union forces of Gen. Ambrose Burnside (who had taken over from McClellan) in their repeated and unsuccessful assaults at Fredericksburg, Virginia.

In May 1863, Lee split his army, attacking and defeating a large Union army under Gen. Joseph Hooker at Chancellorsville, Virginia. The price for victory was high, as Gen. Thomas "Stonewall" Jackson was killed. Trying to follow up on the Chancellorsville victory and to relieve Union pressure elsewhere in the Confederacy, Lee moved his army north again.

Hampered by a lack of cavalry for reconnaissance and with his campaign plans in Union hands, Lee's second invasion of the North was disastrous. He encountered Union forces at Gettysburg, Pennsylvania, on July 1, and the war's best-known battle began. On the third day, it was apparent that the Confederates were beaten, and part of the blame lay with poor decisions by Lee as commander. His decimated forces then returned to Virginia.

Although Lee's army won tactical victories in 1864, numeric, transportation, and logistical deficiencies led it and the Confederacy to defeat. Opposed by Gen. Ulysses S. Grant for the first time, Lee found himself forced into a losing war of attrition. After inflicting heavy Union casualties at the Wilderness, Spotsylvania, and Cold Harbor, Lee still had to retreat toward Richmond. The Petersburg Campaign sapped his forces of their remaining strength. His defensive strategy and tactics during the last year were masterful but ultimately unsuccessful in the face of superior Union troops and supplies. The end came for the Army of Northern Virginia on Apr. 9, 1865, with Lee's surrender at Appomattox Courthouse. After the war, Lee was made president of Washington College (now Washington and Lee University) in Lexington, Virginia, a position he held until his death.

Legacy. Lee gambled many times with his army during the Civil War. Often, his battles were won by the timely arrival of reinforcements at the critical time and point on the battlefield. But he could never call to account any subordinate whose independence, timidity, or disagreement with his concepts altered or destroyed planned operations.

Lee was noted, both in peace and in war, as a thorough gentleman. The esteem with which he has been held, by friend and foe alike, has remained undimmed by the passage of time.

Bibliography: Connelly, Thomas L., *The Marble Man: Robert E. Lee and His Image in American Society* (Knopf, 1977); Davis, Burke, *Gray Fox: Robert E. Lee and the Civil War* (Rinehart, 1956); Freeman, Douglas Southall, *R. E. Lee: A Biography,* 4 vols. (Scribner's, 1934–35); ———, *Lee's Lieutenants: A Study in Command,* 3 vols. (Scribner's, 1950).

Brig. Gen. (Ret.) Uzal W. Ent

LETTERMAN, JONATHAN (1824–1872)

U.S. army surgeon, who organized the medical field service of the Army of the Potomac during the Civil War, Letterman was born in Canonsburg, Pennsylvania. He graduated from the Jefferson Medical College in Philadelphia in 1849 and immediately accepted an appointment as an assistant surgeon in the U.S. Army.

Letterman's prewar service was mostly on the Indian frontier, where he gained firsthand knowledge of the requirements of combat medicine. During the Civil War, he was able to apply the lessons learned to his various posts, culminating with an appointment as medical director of the Army of the Potomac in 1862. Exhibiting tremendous administrative ability, he completely reorganized that army's medical services, emphasizing mobility and speed in the evacuation and treatment of casualties. His improvements were considered so effective that they ultimately were adopted throughout the Union armies. Letterman resigned his commission in December 1864, living in San Francisco for the rest of his life.

Bibliography: Clements, Bennett, *Memoir of Jonathan Letterman* (Putnam's, 1883).

Louise Arnold-Friend

LINCOLN, ABRAHAM (1809–1865)

Sixteenth president of the United States (1861–65), Lincoln was born near Hodgenville, Kentucky. He grew up in Kentucky and Indiana.

Early Career. He moved to Illinois in 1830 and began a career in politics in 1834 as a state representative. He began to practice law in 1836 and served a term in the U.S. Congress (1847–49). He first received national attention in 1854 by opposing the extension of slavery to new territories. By the 1856 election, he was a force in the new Republican party and in 1858 ran for the Senate against Stephen A. Douglas. Although Lincoln lost the election, his impressive performance in the campaign's Lincoln-Douglas debates made him a national figure. He won the Republican nomination for president in 1860 and then took the election over three other candidates. Lincoln's election to the presidency in 1860 precipitated the secession of the South, which led to the Civil War.

The Civil War. By the time he was inaugurated in March 1861, seven states had seceded, and the next month, actual war began with the bombardment of Fort Sumter by the South. While acclaimed for his performance as president, he was uneven in his duties as commander in chief, although he consistently developed during the course of the war.

Lincoln initially believed the war would be short, but after the Union defeat at the First Battle of Bull Run in July 1861, he realized that the conflict would be more protracted. He quickly recognized that the North had overwhelming manpower and advocated a strategy that pressed the Confederates simultaneously on all fronts. Most of his generals did not agree, and Lincoln had to pressure his commanders in the East to take the offensive. In 1862, Lincoln directed the actions of Union forces and contributed to the confused response to Maj. Gen. Thomas "Stonewall" Jackson's Valley Campaign.

Pres. Abraham Lincoln often visited Union commanders at the front during the Civil War. (Library of Congress)

In September 1862, Lincoln took advantage of the North's narrow victory at Antietam to issue the Emancipation Proclamation. Although 1863 brought major successes such as the Union victory at Gettysburg and the capture of Vicksburg, the North was tired of the long war, and Lincoln's political opponents gathered strength. In public, Lincoln stressed the importance of the Union and the Union's obligation to continue the war, as in the Gettysburg Address. Gen. Ulysses S. Grant's success in waging a war of attrition in Virginia and Gen. William T. Sherman's advance across Georgia vastly improved public opinion in the North, and Lincoln was reelected in 1864.

By the time of his second inauguration in March 1865, the Confederacy was collapsing, and Lincoln called for a conciliatory approach toward the South. The euphoria that followed the war's end on April 9 was almost immediately dampened by Lincoln's assassination on April 14 by actor John Wilkes Booth, a Confederate sympathizer.

Analysis. Lincoln was limited by mediocre generals until he selected Grant as general in chief in early 1864. Prior to Grant's appointment, Lincoln was guilty of selecting commanders in chief based on political qualities rather than military effectiveness. While Lincoln tended to allow his commanders to proceed with their own plans, he was known to offer suggestions. Lincoln disliked procrastination and wanted his army to fight. His strategic vision was generally good, but he may have become too involved in the details of wartime operations.

Bibliography: Anderson, Dwight G., *Abraham Lincoln: The Quest for Immortality* (Knopf, 1982); Spiller, Roger J., ed., *Dictionary of American Military Biography,* vol. 2 (Greenwood Press, 1984); Williams, Kenneth P., *Lincoln Finds a General* (reprint Indiana Univ. Press, 1985).

Capt. George B. Eaton

LOGAN, JOHN ALEXANDER (1826–1886)

U.S. military leader, Logan was born in Jackson County, Illinois. An Illinois Democrat and congressman, he was sympathetic to the Union cause at the onset of the Civil War. He recruited and led the 31st Illinois Infantry into battle in late 1861. Logan quickly earned the nickname "Black Jack" for his black eyes and hair. Promoted to brigadier general in March 1862 and major general less than a year later, he led a division in Gen. James B. McPherson's corps at Vicksburg. He then commanded the XV Corps during the Atlanta campaign. When McPherson was killed in front of Atlanta on July 22, 1864, command of the Army of the Tennessee devolved temporarily on Logan. He lost permanent command of the army, however, because he was not a West Pointer. This embittered Logan toward professional soldiers thereafter. After the war he served as a Republican in the U.S. House of Representatives (1867–71) and the Senate (1871–77; 1879–86) and was James Blaine's vice-presidential running mate in 1884.

Bibliography: Jones, John P., *Black Jack: John A. Logan and Southern Illinois in the Civil War Era* (Florida State Univ. Press, 1967).

Daniel T. Bailey

LONGSTREET, JAMES (PETE) (1821–1904)

U.S. soldier and Confederate military leader, Longstreet was born in Edgefield District, South Carolina, and graduated from West Point in 1842. He served in St. Louis and Florida and during the Mexican War participated in Gen. Zachary Taylor's 1846 campaigns and in Gen. Winfield Scott's 1847 campaign to Mexico City. After the war, Longstreet fought Indians on the frontier.

The Civil War. Longstreet resigned from the U.S. Army in June 1861 to join the Confederacy. He was promoted to brigadier general and in July commanded a brigade in the First Battle of Bull Run. Promoted to major general, he led a division during the Peninsular Campaign, and Gen. Robert E. Lee subsequently gave him command of one of the two wings of the Army of Northern Virginia. After

Although he was known as "Lee's Old War Horse," Gen. James Longstreet often disagreed with the war strategies of his superiors. (U.S. Army Military History Institute)

Antietam, Longstreet was promoted to lieutenant general and given command of the newly organized I Corps. During the Battle of Fredericksburg (December 1862), Longstreet's superb defensive positions cost the Union army heavy casualties and established his reputation as a defensive fighter.

In February 1863, he was appointed commander of the Department of North Carolina and Southern Virginia. While there, he conducted operations to resupply the Army of Northern Virginia and offset increasing Union strength in the region. Rejoining the Army of Northern Virginia in late May, Longstreet strongly disagreed with Lee's strategic plan to invade Pennsylvania. Believing that the western situation posed more danger, Longstreet suggested that his I Corps be shipped west to reinforce Gen. Braxton Bragg's Army of Tennessee. He later supported Lee's plan but apparently believed that Lee intended to fight a defensive battle if possible, placing the Army of Northern Virginia astride communications.

I Corps spent July 1 marching toward Gettysburg. Even then, part of the corps did not arrive in the vicinity until after midnight. Longstreet's corps began early on July 2 to move to attack positions against the exposed Union left flank. Faulty reconnaissance by Lee's staff and Longstreet necessitated a countermarch by the I Corps column, and Longstreet did not attack the Union left until 4:00 P.M. By this time, Union troops had been deployed to Little Round Top, thus anchoring the Union flank. The attack failed to break the federal line. The overall Confederate attack, commanded by Lee, failed for a variety of reasons.

Lee placed Longstreet in command of the July 3 attack against the Union center on Cemetery Ridge. Longstreet again disagreed with this order, as he felt that an attack against and to the rear of the Union left would be more successful. After an intense but relatively ineffective artillery bombardment, 15,000 Confederate soldiers attacked across a mile of open ground. The assault, known as "Pickett's Charge," failed miserably, and tremendous casualties were suffered.

Longstreet disagreed with some of Lee's major operational and strategic decisions during this campaign. Although Lee's official report on the campaign did not criticize him directly, Longstreet's performance in this battle became the focal point for Southern apologists and critics who deified Lee after the war. Many accused Longstreet of losing the war at Gettysburg.

A change in Confederate strategy after Gettysburg recognized the deteriorating western situation. Longstreet and two divisions deployed to northern Georgia in early September to reinforce Bragg. On September 19, Bragg attacked the Army of the Cumberland at Chickamauga Creek. Part of Longstreet's corps participated in the fighting that day, although Longstreet did not arrive on the battlefield until later that night. Despite Longstreet's unfamiliarity with the situation, terrain, and his subordinates, Bragg assigned him command of the Confederate left wing for the attack on the following day. Longstreet organized his five divisions of 22,000 men to attack the Union center. The attack poured right through an inadvertent gap in the Union lines. After routing the Union right and center divisions, Longstreet's force pivoted north and ran into the hasty defense erected by Maj. Gen. George Thomas with units from the Union left. After his initial success, Longstreet continued to attack Thomas's defensive line. Eventually the Union army withdrew in the Chattanooga defenses.

The Confederate victory at Chickamauga was obscured by the divisiveness among Bragg's generals. In a tawdry affair, Longstreet and other generals petitioned Pres. Jefferson Davis to remove Bragg from command. Davis did not do so, and this affair ultimately led to Longstreet's second foray at independent command. His corps slipped north to Knoxville to attack and seize the city, hoping to force the Union army to evacuate Chattanooga. Longstreet's generalship reached its lowest point during this campaign, as his offensive operations failed and he quarreled with his subordinate commanders. After a hard winter in barren eastern Tennessee, Longstreet's corps rejoined the Army of Northern Virginia in April 1864.

During the Battle of the Wilderness in May, Longstreet's I Corps used an unfinished railroad cut to approach its attack position and counterattacked the Union left. Longstreet was seriously wounded by his own soldiers in the dense woods during the attack. He returned in October to command I Corps and the left flank of the Confederate defensive positions during the Siege of Petersburg. On Apr. 9, 1865, Longstreet, nicknamed "Lee's Old War Horse," finished the war at Lee's side at the Appomattox Courthouse.

Postwar Career. After the war, Longstreet moved to Louisiana and became active in the Republican party. He served as U.S. minister to Turkey (1880–81), U.S. marshal (1881–84), and U.S. railroad commissioner (1898–1904). In his autobiographical *From Manassas to Appomattox* (1896), Longstreet dispensed criticism of many Confederate figures, particularly Lee.

Although Longstreet was popular with his soldiers, his military reputation suffered for his perceived slowness in certain battles and his postwar criticisms of Lee. Nonetheless, his overall success as a corps commander in both theaters of war illustrated his military skill and great value to the Confederate war effort.

Bibliography: Eckenrode, H. J., and Byran Conrad, *James Longstreet: Lee's War Horse* (Univ. of North Carolina Press, 1936); Foote, Shelby, *The Civil War: A Narrative,* 3 vols. (Random House, 1958–74); Longstreet, James, *From Manassas to Appomattox* (Lippincott, 1896); Piston, William, *Lee's Tarnished Lieutenant: James Longstreet and His Place in Southern History* (Univ. of Georgia Press, 1987); Sanger, Donald, and Thomas Hay, *James Longstreet* (Louisiana Univ. Press, 1952).

Kevin E. McKedy

LORING, WILLIAM WING (1818–1886)

U.S. military officer and Confederate general, Loring was born in Wilmington, North Carolina, but spent most of his early life in Florida. As a teenager, he fought in the Seminole War. Directly commissioned a captain in 1846, he served with the regiment of Mounted Rifles in the Mexican War. Despite the loss of an arm at Chapultepec, he remained on active duty in the West and became colonel of the regiment in 1856.

Resigning his commission on May 20, 1861, Loring was appointed brigadier general in the Confederate army less than a week later. He was promoted to major general in 1862 and commanded Confederate forces in western Virginia. He had a corps command during the Vicksburg Campaign, where he earned the nickname "Old Blizzards" for urging his men to "Give them the blizzards, boys!" He escaped capture at Vicksburg and until the end of the war commanded a division in the Army of Tennessee. After the war, Loring served as a general for the Khedive of Egypt, returning to the United States in 1879.

Bibliography: Wessels, William L., *Born to Be a Soldier: The Military Career of William Wing Loring of St. Augustine, Florida* (Texas Christian Univ. Press, 1971).

Louise Arnold-Friend

LYON, NATHANIEL (1818–1861)

U.S. military leader, Lyon was born in Ashford, Connecticut, and graduated from West Point in 1841. Prior to the Civil War, he served in the Mexican War as well as several Indian wars. In 1861, he was sent to guard the federal arsenal in St. Louis, Missouri, and quickly fell in with that state's Unionists. Acting largely on his own, Lyon armed a pro-Union militia, sent other weapons to Illinois, captured a rebel force assembling near St. Louis, and engineered the replacement of his superior, Gen. William A. Harney. Appointed brigadier general of volunteers in May 1861, Lyon determined to attack rebel forces in southern Missouri. His small federal force met a superior Confederate one near Wilson's Creek on August 10. In the bloody battle that followed, Lyon's federals safely withdrew, although Lyon himself was wounded twice and then killed.

Bibliography: Phillips, Christopher, *Damned Yankee: The Life of General Nathaniel Lyon* (Univ. of Missouri Press, 1990).

Richard F. Kehrberg

MACARTHUR, ARTHUR, JR. (1845–1912)

U.S. military leader, MacArthur was born in Chicopee Falls, Massachusetts, and later moved with his family to Milwaukee, Wisconsin. Only 16 when the Civil War began, MacArthur secured, through his father's political influence, an appointment as first lieutenant in the 24th Wisconsin Infantry in 1862.

MacArthur won considerable fame on the battlefield. At both Perryville and Stones River, his gallant leadership was recognized by senior officers. Grasping the fallen regimental colors at Missionary Ridge on Nov. 25, 1863, MacArthur led the charge that swept the Confederate rebels from the ridge, an action for which he received the Congressional Medal of Honor. Promoted to major and given command of the 24th, MacArthur went on to serve with distinction at Atlanta and Franklin and ended the war a lieutenant colonel.

After the war, he became an officer in the regular army and was stationed primarily in the West, fighting in the Indian campaigns. Posted to the Philippines in the Spanish-American War, MacArthur was promoted to brigadier general and in 1900 was made military governor. As a lieutenant general, he served as army chief of staff from 1906 until his retirement in 1909. Douglas MacArthur was his son.

Bibliography: James, D. Clayton, *The Years of MacArthur; Vol. 1: 1880–1941* (Houghton Mifflin, 1970).

Daniel T. Bailey

MCCALLUM, DANIEL CRAIG (1815–1878)

Civil and railroad engineer and U.S. military officer, McCallum was born in Renfrewshire, Scotland, and moved to the United States at an early age. He developed bridge designs, served as the superintendent of the New York & Erie Railroad, and built railroad bridges in North and Central America.

Called from civilian life in 1862 by Sec. of War Edwin M. Stanton, he was commissioned a colonel and appointed military director and superintendent of railroads. McCallum brought the organizational and managerial skills needed to provide "safe and speedy transport" to the Union army, and, most notably, he organized the strategic deployment of troops by rail from Virginia to Chattanooga. McCallum went to the field himself to manage the effort, organizing the railroads in the west and providing virtually immediate rail support to combat operations. Through the Construction Corps, he maintained or restored lines in the combat zone. Gen. William T. Sherman's success in the Atlanta Campaign was based substantially on the effectiveness of McCallum's railroad operations. McCallum was mustered out in 1866 as a major general of volunteers.

Bibliography: Risch, Erna, *Quartermaster Support of the Army* (Center of Military History, 1989); Weber, Thomas, *The Northern Railroads in the Civil War 1861–1865* (Columbia Univ. Press, 1952).

Thomas W. Sweeney

MCCLELLAN, GEORGE BRINTON (1826–1885)

U.S. military leader in the Civil War, commander of the Army of the Potomac in 1861 and 1862, McClellan was born in Philadelphia to a wealthy and prominent Pennsylvania family. In 1842, he left the University of Pennsylvania for West Point, having secured special permission to enroll at 16, two years under the minimum age. Graduating second in the Class of 1846, he entered the Corps of Engineers, then the plum assignment for Military Academy graduates.

Early Career. A military engineer in the Mexican War on the staff of Gen. Winfield Scott, McClellan was one of that constellation of brilliant junior officers, including Robert E. Lee, Grant, Pierre G. T. Beauregard, James Longstreet, and George C. Meade, that honed their skills in that conflict. Twice brevetted and a promising captain, McClellan emerged from the war to remain in the army. He saw duty as an engineer, as an observer at the Crimean War, and as an instructor at West Point. During this period he designed a military saddle, incorporating the best elements of those of the Prussian and Hungarian cavalries, that remained standard in the army until the end of the cavalry era almost a century later.

Following the lead of many bright young officers disenchanted with the routine of a peacetime army, McClellan resigned in 1857 to seek employment as an engineer in the burgeoning and lucrative railroad business. He soon became chief engineer and vice president of the Illinois Central Railroad and, in 1860, president of the eastern division of the Ohio & Mississippi Railroad.

The Civil War. Ten days after Confederate guns fired on Fort Sumter, Ohio's harried governor, William Dennison, summoned McClellan to Columbus from the latter's home in Cincinnati. Ohio had been tasked by President Lincoln to raise 10,000 volunteers for federal service, but more than twice that number were gathered at Columbus and other mustering grounds throughout the state. The state's blustering adjutant general, Henry B. Carrington, was unable to arm, clothe, feed, or even account for them all. On Apr. 23, 1861, McClellan found himself major general of Ohio Volunteers, charged with organizing 10 regiments of infantry with their attendant supporting forces.

At Dennison's instigation, and with the support of Winfield Scott, senior general of U.S. forces, McClellan was made a federal major general on May 14 and given command of the newly created Department of the Ohio. McClellan was soon under pressure from Dennison to advance into western Virginia and Kentucky to forestall any Confederate threat to the state from those quarters, but he did not share the governor's apprehension and concentrated on the organization and discipline of his troops. Reacting to a call for support from the Wheeling Conference, a group of Unionist western Virginians seeking separation from the state of Virginia, and alarmed at reports of Confederate troops crossing the mountains into Grafton (in northwest Virginia), Dennison forced McClellan's hand on May 24 by sending four regiments of state troops not yet in federal service across the Ohio River into Virginia. Stung into action, McClellan recovered by following with 20,000 men from Ohio, Indiana, and Illinois to lead a short, successful campaign that included victories at Rich Mountain and Corrick's Ford. The expedition secured for the Union what in 1863 became the state of West Virginia and for McClellan a winning reputation at a dark time for the northern cause.

After the debacle of the First Battle of Bull Run in July 1861, Lincoln called McClellan to Washington to take command of the defeated Army of the Potomac. The "Little Napoleon," came to the capital as a hero, reveling in public adulation. His very real talents at organization and discipline once again became evident as he built the Army of the Potomac into a formidable fighting force, clearly the best equipped and best drilled in the nation. But McClellan also possessed a monumental ego that estranged him from Lincoln and Sec. of War Simon Cameron. Even his old mentor Scott was not immune, as McClellan openly campaigned for the old man's removal and succeeded in taking his place.

The McClellan traits of character and leadership that had disappointed Dennison in Ohio now became evident to Lincoln. McClellan was a splendid organizer who saw to the needs of his troops and earned their respect, but he was slow to take the offensive, was a weak strategist, and consistently overestimated the strength of his opposition.

McClellan dawdled near Washington, refusing to take the offensive until directly ordered to do so by Lincoln on Jan. 27, 1862, in the president's General Order No. 1. He then set out at the head of 118,000 Union troops to take Richmond. For several weeks, McClellan's timid advance in the Peninsular Campaign allowed his army to be checked repeatedly by smaller Confederate forces. While victorious at Williamsburg on May 5 and Malvern Hill on July 1, McClellan had been soundly outmaneuvered by July and had been forced to abandon his offensive and retreat to the shelter of naval guns on the James River.

By August, Lincoln had lost confidence in McClellan and shifted most of his troops to the command of Maj. Gen. John Pope, who was subsequently defeated at the Second Battle of Bull Run on Aug. 29–30, 1862. The president turned again to McClellan, who reorganized and reinvigorated the beaten army and set out in September to face Robert E. Lee in the Antietam Campaign. Initially aggressive and daring, McClellan's caution returned as he sparred with Lee. In battle at Antietam on September 17, McClellan was unable to dislodge Lee in a furious and bloody fight, the single most costly day of the war. But during the night, his forces badly depleted, Lee slipped away, leaving the field to his rival.

McClellan paused after the battle, awaiting supplies and reinforcement, much to the exasperation of Lincoln, who criticized the lost opportunity to destroy the main Confederate force in the east. But the president was able to claim Antietam as enough of a victory to provide the occasion for his preliminary Emancipation Proclamation. When McClellan continued to delay and allowed Confederate major general Jeb Stuart to lead his cavalry completely around his position, Lincoln relieved McClellan for good on Nov. 9, 1862. McClellan returned to Trenton, New Jersey, to await orders that never came.

McClellan had never been shy of political affairs while on active service. Convinced of his own prowess and destiny and never in agreement with the free-soil and probusiness policies of the Republican party, McClellan ran for president on the Democratic ticket against Lincoln in 1864. The public was weary of war, and the Democratic platform called for a negotiated peace. While McClellan repudiated that plank in the platform and proclaimed his belief in a fight until victory, he nevertheless drew support from wide Copperhead sentiment in the electorate. Lincoln swept the electoral college 212 to 21, but McClellan lost the popular vote by only 400,000 ballots. Scholars credit Lincoln's reelection to the increase in Union battlefield fortunes in 1864 and the arrangements by the administration for soldiers in the field to vote.

Postwar Career. McClellan resigned from the army on election night and spent the next three years traveling abroad. Upon returning home, he became chief engineer of the New York City Department of Docks (1870–72). In 1877, he ran successfully for governor of New Jersey and served from 1878 to 1881.

Legacy. Years after the war ended, Ulysses S. Grant expressed a view with which many still agree: "McClellan is to me one of the mysteries of the war." Favored by a life of privilege and achievement, McClellan began the war destined for greatness. Before it was over, however, the "Little Napoleon" was "Mac the Unready" and "The Little Corporal of Unsought Fields." Some historians argue that he was perhaps the greatest Union general, denied victory by President Lincoln's impatience and interference. Others maintain that he was temperamentally unfit for high command.

Bibliography: Hassler, Warren W., *General George B. McClellan* (Louisiana State Univ. Press, 1957); McClellan, George B., *McClellan's Own Story* (C. L. Webster, 1887); Sears, Stephen W., *George B. McClellan: The Young Napoleon* (Ticknor and Fields, 1988); Wheeler, Richard, *Sword over Richmond: An Eyewitness History of McClellan's Peninsula Campaign* (Harper & Row, 1986); Williams, T. Harry, *McClellan, Sherman and Grant* (Greenwood Press, 1962).

T. C. Mulligan

McCLERNAND, JOHN ALEXANDER (1812–1890)

U.S. politician and military leader, McClernand was born near Hardinsburg, Kentucky. He practiced law and served in the U.S. House of Representatives (1843–51; 1859–61) before being appointed brigadier general of U.S. volunteers in 1861. McClernand was intelligent and bold, but pompous and ambitious, and was keenly suspicious of all professional soldiers. He fought under Brig. Gen. Ulysses S. Grant at Belmont, Forts Henry and Donelson, and Shiloh. Promoted to major general in 1862, McClernand successfully recruited troops in Illinois, Indiana, and Iowa.

He used his political connections to obtain direct permission from Pres. Abraham Lincoln and Sec. of War Edwin Stanton to lead a campaign against Vicksburg. This put him at odds with Grant, his immediate superior on the Mississippi. Grant prevailed, relegating McClernand to a corps command in the expedition. Following an unsuccessful general assault on Vicksburg on May 22, 1863, McClernand released a press statement claiming that his corps could have captured the city if adequately supported by the rest of the army. Grant, whose own prestige had been enhanced by a brilliant campaign of maneuver behind Vicksburg, reacted by relieving McClernand of his command in June. Returning to his corps briefly in 1864 on the Gulf Coast, McClernand contracted malaria and resigned. He resumed his law practice and political life.

Bibliography: Grant, U. S., *Personal Memoirs of U. S. Grant* (Webster & Co., 1885); McPherson, James M., *Battle Cry of Freedom* (Ballantine Books, 1989); Sherman, W. T., *Memoirs of Gen. W. T. Sherman* (Webster & Co., 1892).

T. C. Mulligan

McDOWELL, IRVIN (1818–1885)

U.S. army officer and Union general during the Civil War. McDowell was born near Columbus, Ohio. He graduated from West Point in 1838 and was assigned to an artillery unit and then to West Point as an instructor in military tactics. During the Mexican-American War, he was brevetted a captain for gallant and meritorious conduct. Coming to the attention of Gen. Winfield Scott, McDowell was soon appointed to the general staff as an assistant adjutant, a post he would hold until the eve of the Civil War.

Despite his lack of experience as a field commander, McDowell was soon appointed to command the first major Union army assembled in the Civil War. Public pressure for a quick victory forced McDowell to engage the Confederates with troops that were not fully trained. On July 21, 1861, the two forces met at the First Battle of Bull Run. McDowell's weaknesses as a commander, untried soldiers, mistakes by his staff and unit commanders, and good performance by the Confederate forces combined to create a Union rout. Following the battle, McDowell was relieved of command and subsequently given command of first a division, and then a corps in the Army of the Potomac, participating in the battles of Cedar Mountain and Second Bull Run in 1862. He finished the war serving in a number of staff assignments in Washington.

Bibliography: Hassler, Warren W., *Commanders of the Army of the Potomac* (Louisiana State Univ. Press, 1962).

Leo J. Daugherty III

MACKENZIE, RANALD SLIDELL (1840–1889)

U.S. military leader, Mackenzie was born in New York, New York. After graduating from West Point in 1862, he accepted a commission in the Corps of Engineers. Over the next two years, he served in various engineering positions in the Army of the Potomac. In 1864, he received the colonelcy of the 2d Connecticut Heavy Artillery and soon was promoted to brigadier general in command of an infantry brigade. He led this unit in the Shenandoah Valley and before Petersburg. In March 1865, he took over a cavalry division and fought at Five Forks. Wounded six times and brevetted for gallantry seven, Mackenzie was referred to by Ulysses S. Grant as "the most promising young officer in the army." After the war, as a colonel, he served on the western frontier during campaigns against the Indians, primarily in Texas, Nebraska, and Wyoming, until his retirement in 1884.

Richard F. Kehrberg

McPHERSON, JAMES BIRDSEYE (1828–1864)

U.S. military leader, McPherson was born near Clyde, Ohio, and graduated first in the West Point Class of 1853. He quickly advanced in the Corps of Engineers, and after completing the fortifications at Alcatraz in California in 1861, he requested combat duty. As chief engineer for Brig. Gen. Ulysses S. Grant's early western campaigns, he earned Grant's trust. At Grant's urging, McPherson, promoted brigadier general in 1862, commanded the 17th Army Corps, leading Grant's army in the Vicksburg Campaign in 1863. Promoted major general and given command of Grant's Army of the Tennessee, McPherson died in the Battle of Atlanta on July 22, 1864. A cautious but able subordinate commander, McPherson was sincerely mourned by both armies. "The nation," Grant claimed, "had more to expect from him than from almost any one living."

Bibliography: Melia, Tamara Moser, "James B. McPherson and the Ideals of the Old Army" (Ph.D. dissertation, Southern Illinois Univ. at Carbondale, 1987).

Tamara Moser Melia

MAGRUDER, JOHN BANKHEAD (1810–1871)

U.S. and Confederate military leader, Magruder was born in Winchester, Virginia, and graduated from West Point in 1830. He earned two brevets in the Mexican War and reached the rank of lieutenant colonel, but is better remembered for his Civil War involvement, particularly his role as foil to Gen. George B. McClellan and his action at Galveston, Texas.

In May 1861 he was commissioned as a colonel in the Confederate forces and by October was a major general. Magruder deceived McClellan on two occasions. In the Peninsular Campaign in 1862, Magruder marched his troops in circles, ostentatiously moved his artillery, and shouted commands to nonexistent units. This caused McClellan to give up his hope of taking Yorktown (May 1862) and later held him in check for Lee's flanking maneuver during the Seven Days' Battles (June 1862). On Jan. 1, 1863, Magruder made a surprise attack on the Union garrison at Galveston, taking the city within four hours.

After the war, Magruder went to Mexico with other disaffected Confederates and became a major general (1866–67) under Emperor Maximilian. He returned to the United States in 1867 and gave lectures about his military career.

Bibliography: McPherson, James M., *Battle Cry of Freedom* (Ballantine Books, 1988); Spencer, James, *Civil War Generals* (Greenwood Press, 1986).

Capt. Karen S. Wilhelm

MAHAN, DENNIS HART (1802–1871)

Commonly regarded as one of the chief architects of the U.S. professional officer corps, Mahan was born in New York, New York, and arrived at West Point as a cadet in 1820. He graduated first in his class and was appointed as instructor of engineering for the next two years. After four years of study in France, he returned to this position. In 1832, he was made full professor, a position he retained until his death.

Mahan, who based much of his military philosophy on the ideas of the Swiss theorist Henri Jomini, had a large part in forming the views and thinking patterns of an entire generation of future Civil War generals. They studied and often carried the text he wrote. His lectures in military theory were the only formal instruction in the subject received by these future leaders, thus his views came to be dominant throughout the army.

The Military Academy was the focus of Mahan's life. He committed suicide on Sept. 16, 1871, when he learned the Academy's Board of Visitors had recommended his mandatory retirement. Students of the U.S. military recognize his lasting influence on the methodology of U.S. military organizations. Mahan was the father of U.S. naval officer and historian Alfred Mahan.

Bibliography: Millet, Allan R., and Peter Maslowski, *For the Common Defense: A Military History of the United States of America* (Free Press, 1984); Weigley, Russell F., *The American Way of War* (Indiana Univ. Press, 1973).

Capt. Karen S. Wilhelm

MARCY, WILLIAM LEARNED (1786–1857)

U.S. statesman, Marcy was born in Sturbridge, Massachusetts, and moved to Troy, New York, as a teenager. Trained as a lawyer, he began a political career that took him to the U.S. Senate (1831–32) and New York's governorship (1833–39).

Marcy, who had been a militia officer during the War of 1812, was appointed secretary of war in 1845 by Pres. James Polk, who wanted to maintain regional balance in the cabinet. War with Mexico soon followed, but Marcy's role was overshadowed by Polk's. Marcy supported the decision to relieve Maj. Gen. Winfield Scott as commander of the field army early in the war but later encouraged the general's reappointment as commander of the Veracruz expedition.

In a highly partisan era, Marcy left office in 1849 with a reputation for fair-mindedness in his dealings with senior army officers. He returned to Washington in 1853 as Pres.

Franklin Pierce's secretary of state, negotiating numerous important treaties. Marcy is remembered for coining the phrase "spoils system," as expressed in a speech (1832) in which he averred that "to the victor belong the spoils of the enemy."

Richard B. Meixsel

MAURY, MATTHEW FONTAINE (1806–1873)

U.S. and Confederate naval officer and oceanographer, Maury was born in Spotsylvania County, Virginia, grew up in Tennessee, and entered the U.S. Navy in 1825. A leg injury in 1839 left him unable to return to sea, but he excelled in the study of naval sciences and by 1842 was director of the Naval Observatory. His work culminated in the publication of *The Physical Geography of the Sea and Its Meteorology* (1855). Maury also played a leading role in efforts to reform the navy's archaic administrative system in the 1840s.

During the Civil War, he joined the forces of the Confederacy and became director of coast, river, and harbor defenses (1861), emphasizing such technological innovations as the electric mine. In 1862, Maury was a special agent in Britain, where he obtained several warships for the Confederacy. He fled to Mexico at war's end but returned to the United States in 1868 and became a professor at the Virginia Military Institute.

Richard B. Meixsel

MEADE, GEORGE GORDON (1815–1872)

U.S. Army leader, Meade was born in Cadiz, Spain, where his father was serving as an agent of the U.S. Navy. He graduated from West Point in 1835 and accepted a commission in the 3d U.S. Artillery.

Early Career. Meade served briefly in Florida in the Seminole Wars until contracting a fever. Upon his recovery, he was assigned ordnance duties at the Watertown (Massachusetts) Arsenal. In 1836, he resigned his commission to pursue a career in civil engineering. As such, he worked for the Alabama, Florida and Georgia Railroad and did surveying work on the borders of Texas and Mississippi. During this time, Meade rejoined the army.

In 1842, he was appointed a second lieutenant in the Corps of Topographical Engineers and engaged in the construction of breakwaters and lighthouses (including that which still stands at Cape May, New Jersey). During the Mexican War, Meade fought at the battles of Palo Alto, Resaca de la Palma, and Monterrey and in Gen. Winfield Scott's Mexico City Campaign. After the war, he resumed military engineering duties.

The Civil War. Shortly after the Civil War commenced, Meade, by then a captain in the engineers, was promoted to brigadier general of volunteers. With no experience as a troop commander, he was given command of a brigade of Pennsylvania troops at the encouragement of that state's governor, Andrew G. Curtin. Meade's command was in the defenses of Washington, D.C., where he supervised the construction of Fort Pennsylvania.

In the summer of 1862, Meade's brigade was transferred to the army of Maj. Gen. George B. McClellan, then launching an offensive on the Confederate capital, Richmond. During the Peninsular Campaign, Meade led troops in the battles of Mechanicsville, Gaines's Mill, and White Oak Swamp (Glendale). At Glendale, he was seriously wounded twice. Barely recovered from those wounds, he returned in time to command his brigade at Second Bull Run. He was in command of a division at South Mountain and Antietam and a two-corps "Grand Division" at Fredericksburg. Shortly after Fredericksburg, he was appointed to command the V Corps, which he led at Chancellorsville.

After Chancellorsville, President Lincoln's search for a successor to Maj. Gen. Joseph Hooker led him to Meade as a possible leader of the Army of the Potomac. His views on the offensive had attracted the president's attention, and the appointment was made on June 28, 1863, while Meade was directing his corps north toward Pennsylvania and the Battle of Gettysburg. Despite having received command in midcampaign, only three days before the beginning of this pivotal battle, Meade commanded the Union forces admirably at Gettysburg. He adopted a defensive posture against Gen. Robert E. Lee's invasion force. He is most often criticized for his failure to pay sufficient attention to his left flank along Cemetery Ridge and at Little Round Top and for his failure to pursue his victory and capture Lee's army as it retreated back to Virginia.

Meade retained command of the Army of the Potomac until the end of the war; however, the appointment of Lt. Gen. Ulysses S. Grant to the position of general-in-chief tended to preempt Meade's leadership. Nevertheless, under Grant's command, he led the army at the battles of the Wilderness, Spotsylvania, Cold Harbor, and Petersburg. In 1864, Meade was promoted to the permanent rank of major general in the regular army.

Postwar Years. After the war, Meade commanded the Division of the Atlantic, headquartered at Philadelphia. In 1867, he was given command of Military District No. 3 (Alabama, Georgia, and Florida). He was dissatisfied with the absence of further promotion and returned to the Division of the Atlantic.

Meade held the distinction of having been the first Union general to have orchestrated a tactical defeat of Lee's Army of Northern Virginia in a major battle, but for much of his postwar life, he was embroiled in a public debate with Daniel E. Sickles over Meade's conduct of the Army of the Potomac at the Battle of Gettysburg. Most modern writers view the feud, waged with speeches and in the public press, as Sickles's attempt to justify his removal of his III Corps from Cemetery Ridge to a second line west of the main Union battle position. It is generally accepted that Sickles moved to a tactically more defensible line, but he was directly disobeying Meade's orders. As a politician with considerable influence, Sickles wielded his power to defend his own actions by tarnishing, in the eyes of many, the abilities and reputation of a fine officer.

Bibliography: Cleaves, Freeman, *Meade of Gettysburg* (Univ. of Oklahoma Press, 1960); Sauers, Richard A., *A Caspian Sea of Ink: The Meade-Sickles Controversy . . .* (Butternut & Blue, 1989).

Louis Arnold-Friend

MEAGHER, THOMAS FRANCIS (1823–1867)

U.S. military leader, Meagher was born in Waterford, Ireland. Banished by the British in 1849 for his activities in behalf of Irish independence, he made his way to the United States and became a leading member of New York City's large Irish-American community.

During the Civil War, Meagher fought at the First Battle of Bull Run, then returned to New York and organized the "Irish Brigade." Appointed brigadier general in 1862, he commanded this brigade in all its actions as part of the Army of the Potomac through Chancellorsville. He resigned his position when prohibited from recruiting Irish replacements for his worn-out unit. He subsequently served with Gen. William T. Sherman's armies until the war's end. Appointed as territorial secretary of Montana, he was acting governor before drowning at Fort Benton in 1867.

Capt. Alan Cate

MEIGS, MONTGOMERY CUNNINGHAM (1816–1892)

U.S. Army leader, Meigs was born in Augusta, Georgia. Upon graduation from West Point in 1836, he had brief duty with the field artillery but transferred to the Corps of Engineers. Meigs began his engineering duties on Mississippi River navigation projects. He also constructed coastal fortifications on the Delaware River south of Philadelphia and served on the board charged with the job of developing all Atlantic coastal defenses. In 1852, he came to Washington, D.C., to survey and construct the city's aqueducts and water supply. His work on the aqueducts and the new Capitol dome brought him into conflict with James Buchanan's secretary of war, John B. Floyd, who "exiled" Meigs to the Dry Tortugas, west of Key West, Florida, to develop fortifications.

The Civil War. With the arrival of the Lincoln administration in 1861, Meigs was back in Washington, where he was appointed brigadier general and named quartermaster general of the army, a position suited to his managerial and organizational skills. He maintained centralized control, required very little staff increase, and strove to support the troops in the field adequately.

Quartermaster general of the Union army, Montgomery Meigs had a talent for management and organization that was an essential factor in Union victories at Gettysburg and Chattanooga. (Library of Congress)

As his predecessor, Thomas Jessup, had done in the Mexican War, Meigs went to the field to supervise personally the critical supply operations. In 1863, his presence at Gettysburg and Chattanooga was essential to Union success; at both sites, he brought railroad men to oversee critical rail operations. Meigs was brevetted a major general in July 1864.

Postwar Years. Meigs remained quartermaster general until his retirement in February 1882. He later served as the architect of the Pension Building in Washington.

Bibliography: Risch, Erna, *Quartermaster Support of the Army* (Center of Military History, 1989); Weigley, Russell, *Quartermaster General of the Union Army: A Biography of M. C. Meigs* (Columbia Univ. Press, 1959).

Thomas W. Sweeney

MILES, NELSON APPLETON (1839–1925)

U.S. military leader, Miles was born in Westminster, Massachusetts. He raised a company for a Massachusetts regiment at the start of the Civil War but saw his first battle as an aide to Gen. Oliver O. Howard at Fair Oaks and Seven Pines (June 1862). Blunt and lacking in tact, Miles was nonetheless an outstanding combat leader and, following Antietam (September 1862) he was given command of the 61st New York Regiment. As a brigadier general of volunteers, he led a brigade at the Wilderness, Spotsylvania, and Cold Harbor and won a promotion to brevet major general (1864).

Miles remained in the army after the war, serving first as Jefferson Davis's jailer and then with the Freedmen's Bureau. After participating in most of the major Indian campaigns, he became commanding general of the army in 1895, the last officer to hold that title. Opposed to the administration's conduct of the war with Spain, Miles led only the expedition to seize Puerto Rico (July–August 1898). He retired in 1903 and died in Washington, D.C.

Richard B. Meixsel

MONROE, JAMES (1758–1831)

Secretary of state, secretary of war, and fifth president of the United States (1817–25), Monroe was born in Westmoreland County, Virginia, and attended the College of William and Mary (1775). During the American Revolution, he fought in numerous battles, ultimately rising to the rank of lieutenant colonel.

He then held various posts in Virginia and the federal government, including U.S. senator (1790–94), minister to France (1794–96), and governor of Virginia (1799–1802). In 1811, Pres. James Madison appointed him secretary of state. In that position until 1814, Monroe struggled unsuccessfully to maintain American neutrality until war with Britain broke out in 1812. After the defeat at Bladensburg and the burning of Washington, Monroe took on the additional responsibilities of secretary of war (1814–15).

When elected to the presidency in 1816, Monroe exhibited a decided capacity for evenhanded administration and compromise that contrasted sharply with his earlier sectional and narrowly partisan stand. He stilled the potential for military confrontation between the United States and Great Britain or Spain over boundary questions.

The Rush-Bagot Agreement with Great Britain signed in 1817 agreed to mutual disarmament on the Great Lakes. The Convention of 1818 established the northwest boundary between the United States and British North America along the 49th parallel from Lake of the Woods to the crest of the Rocky Mountains. Florida was ceded to the United States by Spain in the Adams-Onís Treaty of 1819. Monroe's approval of the 1820 Missouri Compromise (prohibiting the expansion of slavery north of 36°30′) and his signing of the 1824 Survey Act (laying out an elaborate program of internal improvements) served the needs of the entire country.

Monroe rose above sectional preference in his appointments—most notably that of New Englander John Quincy Adams as secretary of state. The president's Monroe Doctrine, which forcefully stated in 1823 that future colonization of the Americas by European powers would be opposed, became a cornerstone of U.S. foreign policy. In 1825, at the end of his second term, Monroe returned to Virginia.

Bibliography: Ammon, Harry, *James Monroe: The Quest for National Security* (McGraw-Hill, 1971).

M. Guy Bishop

MORGAN, JOHN HUNT (1825–1864)

U.S. soldier and Confederate general, Morgan was born in Huntsville, Alabama, and grew up in Lexington, Kentucky. He attended Transylvania College in Lexington but left after two years. He served in the Mexican War as a first lieutenant of Kentucky volunteers and saw action at Buena Vista. After the war, he prospered in the hemp business.

At the outbreak of the Civil War, Morgan joined the Confederate cause and became a popular and able cavalry commander with a knack for unconventional warfare. He excelled at the cavalry raid, disrupting communications, falling on supply points, and causing alarm behind Union lines. Like other successful raiders, his main contribution to the Confederate cause was in drawing large Union forces in his pursuit.

Morgan operated in the western theater, mostly under Maj. Gen. Joseph Wheeler. He commanded at the squadron, regiment, brigade, and division levels, rising to the grade of brigadier general (1862). His raids into Kentucky in July and August 1862 hampered the Union advance on Chattanooga, and other Kentucky raids followed in October and December. On a third sweep north in July 1863, Morgan exceeded his instructions and crossed the Ohio River into Indiana and Ohio, where he caused considerable alarm until he was run down and caught at New Lisbon, Ohio, on July 26.

Confined in the Ohio State Penitentiary, Morgan escaped in November 1862 and made his way back to Confederate lines. On Sept. 4, 1864, he rode into Greeneville, Tennessee, unaware that it had been occupied the night before by Union troops, and was killed in a firefight.

Bibliography: Duke, Basil W., *A History of Morgan's Cavalry* (Indiana Univ. Press, 1960); Ramage, James A., *Rebel Raider* (Univ. of Kentucky Press, 1986); Thomas Edson H., *John Hunt Morgan and His Raiders* (Univ. of Kentucky Press, 1985).

T. C. Mulligan

MYER, ALBERT JAMES (1828–1880)

Founder and director of the U.S. Army Signal Corps, Myer studied medicine at Geneva College and the University of Buffalo. While an assistant surgeon in the Army Medical Corps (appointed 1855), Myer invented a visual communications system called "wigwag." The War Department adopted Myer's system in 1859, and he became, with the rank of major, the first signal officer of the U.S. Army. After the Civil War, Myer created the country's first national weather service within the Signal Corps. In 1880, he received a regular commission as a brigadier general.

Bibliography: Scheips, Paul Joseph, *Albert James Myer, Founder of the Army Signal Corps: A Biographical Study* (University Microfilms, 1966).

Carol E. Stokes

ORD, EDWARD OTHO CRESAP (1818–1883)

U.S. Army general, Ord was born in Cumberland, Maryland. He graduated from West Point in 1839 and served in California during the Mexican War. He participated in the capture of John Brown at Harpers Ferry in 1859. Commissioned a brigadier general of volunteers in 1861, Ord took command of a brigade defending Washington, D.C. His promotion to major general in May 1862 included a transfer to Grant's command in the West. Severely wounded at Corinth, Mississippi, in October 1862, Ord returned to duty in time to lead a corps at Vicksburg. After successful service in Louisiana, he was sent to Petersburg in July 1864 to command the XVIII Corps. He was again seriously wounded but returned in January 1865 to replace Benjamin F. Butler as commander of the Army of the James.

Bibliography: Warner, Ezra, J., *Generals in Blue: Lives of the Union Commanders* (Louisiana State Univ. Press, 1964).

Daniel T. Bailey

OSCEOLA (ca. 1804–1838)

American Indian leader, Osceola was probably born in Georgia. Having achieved prominence among the Seminole due to his presence and personal bravery, he opposed the U.S. government's plan to relocate the Seminole tribes west of the Mississippi. In 1835, Osceola refused to sign the Treaty of Payne's Landing and was arrested on the order of Gen. Wiley Thompson.

Osceola contrived his release but continued to denounce the treaty, a resistance that would come to be known as the Second Seminole War. With more than 2,000 warriors under his command, Osceola overwhelmed several detachments of soldiers, including that of General Thompson, and stymied the subsequent efforts of the regular army to capture or destroy his forces. Osceola was also unwilling to tolerate other Indian leaders who would accept the government's offers and had several of them killed.

After almost two years of resistance, Osceola was deceived into meeting with Gen. Thomas S. Jessup under a flag of truce. While on his way to the meeting, Osceola was seized and removed first to St. Augustine, Florida, and then to Fort Moultrie, South Carolina, where he died. Seminole resistance rapidly collapsed, and, by 1840, the removal of the Seminole tribes to Oklahoma was nearly complete.

2d Lt. R. John Warsinske

PAREDES Y ARRILLAGA, MARIANO (1797–1849)

Mexican military leader, Paredes y Arrillaga was born in Mexico City. He entered the military and advanced rapidly. As commander of the finest military force in Mexico, the Army of the North, Paredes marched on Mexico City in December 1845 and ousted the government, becoming president in his own right on Jan. 4, 1846. Immediately, Paredes announced that he would defend the borders of Mexico as far north as the Sabine River in Texas. His actions during the next six months assured that no diplomatic solution to the Texas question could be found between the United States and Mexico.

Relations between the two nations worsened, and on Mar. 23, 1846, Paredes declared the need for defensive actions against the United States. When fighting began and as the Mexican armies were repeatedly defeated by Gen. Zachary Taylor, the Paredes government's support began to disintegrate.

By early August, the Paredes government had become so unstable that Paredes had to abandon his position in favor of the Mexico City garrison commander, Mariano Salas, who on August 14 turned the government over to Gen. Antonio López de Santa Anna. Paredes died in exile.

Bibliography: Bauer, K. Jack, *The Mexican War, 1846–1848* (Macmillan Co., 1974); Robinson, Fayette, *Mexico and Her Military Chieftains, From the Revolution of Hidalgo to the Present Time* (Silas Andrus & Son, 1848).

Roger D. Launius

PARROTT, ROBERT PARKER (1804–1877)

U.S. inventor and military officer, Parrott was born in Lee, New Hampshire, and graduated from West Point in 1824. He left the army in 1836 to run a foundry and other manufacturing concerns. He studied the developments in military ordnance, and his subsequent experiments led to the design and development of a cast-iron, rifled gun, distinguished by a wrought-iron hoop designed to strengthen the breech of the weapon. The weapons, manufactured in a variety of calibers, became preeminent rifled artillery in the Civil War. Following the war, Parrott resigned his business interest in the artillery works but continued his experiments with projectiles and fuses.

2d Lt. R. John Warsinske

PAULDING, HIRAM (1797–1878)

U.S. naval officer, Paulding was born in Westchester County, New York. As a midshipman, he served on Lake Champlain during the War of 1812; as a lieutenant, he fought West Indies pirates under David D. Porter (1823) and carried dispatches to Simon Bolivar in Peru (1824). Promoted to captain in 1844, Paulding sailed the *Vincennes* to China. As commander of the Home Squadron (1855–58), he arrested filibusterer William Walker in Nicaragua in 1857.

Early in the Civil War, Paulding was responsible for evacuating the Norfolk navy yard. A major supporter of the ironclad *Monitor,* he helped speed its construction. Paulding commanded the Brooklyn Navy Yard from 1862 to 1865. After the war, he served as governor of the Naval Asylum at Philadelphia (1866–69) and as port admiral of Boston (1869–70).

Steve R. Waddell

PEMBERTON, JOHN CLIFFORD (1814–1881)

U.S. soldier and Confederate military leader, Pemberton was born in Philadelphia and graduated from West Point in 1837. An artilleryman, he served in the Seminole War in Florida (1837–39) and on the Canadian border. As a general's aide he saw action in the Mexican War. In September 1850, Pemberton became a captain. He served in Florida, in Kansas, on the Mormon expedition in Utah (1857–58), and in the Northwest.

At the outbreak of the Civil War he joined the Confederate army, supporting his wife's native Virginia. He won promotion to lieutenant general by October 1862, when he commanded the Department of Mississippi, Tennessee, and East Louisiana. Pemberton commanded the defense of Vicksburg in 1863, acting indecisively. After his forces were defeated outside the city, they withdrew to Vicksburg and endured a six-week siege. Pemberton surrendered Vicksburg to Gen. Ulysses S. Grant on July 4. After being exchanged, he resigned his commission in May 1864 and served as colonel and inspector of ordnance. Pemberton farmed in Virginia until 1876, when he returned to Philadelphia.

Robert H. Berlin

PERRY, MATTHEW CALBRAITH (1794–1858)

U.S. naval leader, Perry (brother of naval hero Oliver Hazard Perry) was born in Newport, Rhode Island. He obtained a midshipman's warrant in 1809 and over the next 30 years served in a variety of assignments, culminating in command of the Africa Squadron in 1843. For his earlier efforts while captain of the experimental steamer *Fulton II,* he became known as the "father of the steam navy," an exaggeration, perhaps, but nevertheless indicative of his influential role in convincing the U.S. Navy to adopt steam power.

After assuming command of the Gulf Squadron in 1847, during the Mexican War, Perry conducted a number of successful operations along Mexico's Gulf Coast. By war's end, he had earned a reputation as a courageous combat leader ("Old Bruin") and was afterward much honored for his wartime exploits. Still, it was the expedition he led to Asia in 1852 that secured his place among great U.S. naval leaders. Calling upon all his military and diplomatic skills, in 1854, Perry vastly enhanced the U.S. commercial position in the Pacific by persuading the government of Japan to open its ports to U.S. traders, thereby ending a period of two centuries of Japanese isolation from the outside world. Accorded a hero's welcome upon his return to the United States, Perry devoted 1856 and 1857 to writing his official record of the Asian expedition.

Bibliography: Schroeder, John H., "Matthew Calbraith Perry: Antebellum Precursor of the Steam Navy," *Captains of the Old Steam Navy,* ed. by James C. Bradford (Naval Inst. Press, 1986).

Maj. Grant H. Walker

PICKETT, GEORGE EDWARD (1825–1875)

U.S. and Confederate military leader, Pickett was born in Richmond, Virginia. After graduating last in the West Point class of 1846, he fought in the Mexican War and was brevetted for gallantry at Contreras and Churubusco. Pickett was the first U.S. soldier to mount the parapets at Chapultepec. In 1859, he won plaudits for his defense of U.S. territorial claims to San Juan Island in Puget Sound. Commissioned a colonel in the Confederate army in 1861, he helped to prepare the defenses of the lower Rappahannock River. As a brigadier general, he led his Virginia brigade until wounded severely at Gaines's Mill (June 1862). His promotion to major general preceded his assignment in Fredericksburg (November–December 1862), at which he commanded the Confederate center but saw little action. Pickett is inextricably linked with "Picket's Charge" at Gettysburg on July 3, 1863, even though his division did not lead the attack. At the key crossroads of Five Forks on Apr. 1, 1865, his lines collapsed, forcing the South to abandon the Petersburg defenses eight days before Appomattox.

Carol Reardon

PIERCE, FRANKLIN (1804–1869)

Fourteenth president of the United States (1864–57), Pierce was born in Hillsboro, New Hampshire. He served in the U.S. House of Representatives (1833–37) and the Senate (1837–42). A brigadier general in the Mexican War, he led troops to participate in the attack on Mexico City. Pierce was the compromise Democratic candidate for president in 1852 and was elected, but revival of the slavery issue overwhelmed his presidency. Despite being a Northerner, Pierce never understood Northern public opinion on slavery. He supported certain naval reforms and selected Jefferson Davis as his secretary of war.

Stephen J. Lofgren

PIKE, ALBERT (1809–1891)

U.S. lawyer, newspaperman, and writer, and Confederate general, Pike was born in Boston and by 1833 had settled in Little Rock, Arkansas. He edited the *Arkansas Advocate* and later practiced law. He published *The Arkansas Form Book* (1842), a technical book for lawyers, and won wide recognition for his poetry, notably *Hymns to the Gods* (1834).

Prior to the Civil War, Pike's military experience had been in the Mexican War, when he served as captain of a troop of mounted Arkansas volunteers. His leadership then had been criticized, and his career as a Confederate officer was not much more distinguished. As a brigadier general, Pike organized an Indian partisan force. This unit participated in the Battle of Pea Ridge (Arkansas) on Mar. 7–8, 1862, but was accused of atrocities. After an investigation and political jockeying by all sides, Pike resigned his Confederate commission and sat out the war. Thereafter, Pike moved to Washington, D.C., where he continued practicing law and writing.

Bibliography: Castel, Albert, *General Sterling Price and the Civil War in the West* (Louisiana State Univ., 1968); Johannsen, Robert W., *To the Halls of the Montezumas: The Mexican War in the American Imagination* (Oxford Univ. Press, 1985).

Roger D. Launius

POINSETT, JOEL ROBERTS (1779–1851)

U.S. diplomat and secretary of war, Poinsett was born in Charleston, South Carolina, traveled extensively abroad, and studied law. His political career included service in the U.S. House of Representatives (1821–25) and as the first U.S. minister to Mexico (1825–29). As secretary of war (1837–41), Poinsett became a leading military reformer. To reduce fragmentation and enhance training in the army, he urged the concentration of garrisons. Although the plan failed to gain congressional approval, he concentrated part of the army for training and maneuvers during the summer of 1839. He also organized and equipped the light artillery batteries so essential in the Mexican War. The poinsettia, a native Mexican plant, is named for him because of his work in its cultivated introduction into the United States.

Bibliography: Bell, William Garner, *Secretaries of War and Secretaries of the Army: Portraits and Biographical Sketches* (Center for Military History, U.S. Army, 1982); Rippy, James Fred, *Joel R. Poinsett* (Duke Univ. Press, 1935).

Daniel T. Bailey

POLK, JAMES KNOX (1795–1849)

Eleventh president of the United States (1845–49), Polk was born in Mecklenburg County, North Carolina. He entered national politics in 1825 as a member of the U.S. House of Representatives (1825–39; speaker 1835–39) and left Congress to become governor of Tennessee (1839–41). In the 1844 presidential campaign, Polk was the Democrats' compromise candidate and aggressively advocated territorial expansion, an issue of great interest to a nation that recently had annexed Texas and was engaged in the Oregon border dispute with Great Britain. During Polk's administration, the Oregon question was favorably settled by treaty, but the Texas situation had produced a border dispute with Mexico that by 1846 escalated into the Mexican War. To Polk's satisfaction, the treaty that ended the war (1848) expanded U.S. territory to include the present states of Arizona, New Mexico, California (where gold was discovered in 1848), Nevada, and Utah. Polk declined to run for a second term and died just three months after leaving office.

Christine L. Stevens

POLK, LEONIDAS (1806–1864)

U.S. clergyman and Confederate military leader, Polk was born in Raleigh, North Carolina. An 1827 West Point graduate, he became an Episcopal minister in 1830. Polk was appointed a missionary bishop of the Southwest in 1838 and bishop of Louisiana in 1841. A friend of Confederate president Jefferson Davis, he joined the Confederate army in 1861 with the rank of general.

Polk became the commander of I Corps, Army of the Mississippi, and commanded the Confederate right wing during the Battle of Shiloh (April 1862). Promoted to lieutenant general in October, he served as corps commander in the Army of the Tennessee. Polk's corps fought at Murfreesboro, Tullahoma, and Chickamauga. Following Chickamauga (September 1863), Gen. Braxton Bragg relieved Polk for having disobeyed orders to attack. Davis ignored Bragg's demand of a court-martial and gave Polk command of the Army of the Mississippi.

In May 1864, Polk and three divisions deployed to Georgia to reinforce Gen. Joseph E. Johnston's Army of the Tennessee during the Atlanta Campaign. On June 14, 1864, while on reconnaissance at Pine Mountain, Polk was killed. Respected for his personal courage and known as the "Fighting Bishop," Polk frequently quarreled with senior and subordinate leaders.

Bibliography: Parks, Joseph, *General Leonidas Polk, C.S.A.—The Fighting Bishop* (Louisiana State Univ. Press,

As commander of the Army of the Mississippi, John Pope helped to open the Mississippi River as far as Memphis, but after his defeat at the Second Battle of Bull Run he spent the last two years of the war dealing with Indian uprisings in the Northwest. (U.S. Army Military History Institute)

1962); Polk, William, *Leonidas Polk: Bishop and General* 2 vols. (Longmans, Green, 1915).

Kevin E. McKedy

POPE, JOHN (1822–1892)

U.S. military leader, Pope was born in Louisville, Kentucky, and graduated from West Point in 1842. A topographical engineer, he received two brevets for gallantry in the Mexican War. He was promoted brigadier general June 1861 and commanded a district, then a division, and finally the small Army of the Mississippi. He achieved prominent success at New Madrid and Island No. 10 (March 1862), helping to open the Mississippi River. Pope was promoted to major general and in June was given command of the newly created Army of Virginia. His bombast disenchanted those he led, and he was "outgeneraled" by Robert E. Lee. After the defeat at Second Bull Run, Pope was relieved and assigned to the Department of the Northwest, which embraced Minnesota and the Dakotas and where he showed ability managing the 1864 Sioux uprising. He retired in 1886 as commander of the Division of the Pacific.

Bibliography: Jones, Robert H., *The Civil War in the Northwest* (Univ. of Oklahoma Press (1960).

Lt. Col. (Ret.) J. W. A. Whitehorne

PORTER, DAVID DIXON (1813–1891)

U.S. naval officer, Porter (son of Commodore David Porter) was born in Chester, Pennsylvania. He sailed as a passenger with his father in the West Indies in 1824, and when his father resigned his commission and joined the Mexican navy, the young Porter went with him as a midshipman.

Early Career. Assigned to duty on his cousin's ships *Esmeralda* and *Guerrero,* Porter cruised the West Indies in search of Spanish vessels. Wounded in the severe fight between the *Guerrero* and the Spanish frigate *Lealtad,* he was captured and imprisoned in Havana in 1828. After being paroled, Porter entered the U.S. Navy as a midshipman (1829) and served in the Mediterranean aboard the *Constellation* and the *United States.* Six years' service in the U.S. Coast Survey gave him expertise in channel surveying and piloting.

Promoted to lieutenant in 1841, he sailed aboard the *Congress* to the Mediterranean and South America, then returned to Washington for duty in the Hydrographic Office. Having earned a reputation as a keen observer, he was detached to the State Department in 1846 to investigate secretly the potential for a naval base at Santo Domingo. After a brief period of recruiting duty during the Mexican

Naval hero David Dixon Porter, a veteran of the New Orleans, Vicksburg, and Red River Civil War campaigns, was superintendent of the Naval Academy (1865–69). (U.S. Army Military History Institute)

War, he was assigned as first lieutenant on the steamer *Spitfire* and participated in an unsuccessful naval assault on Veracruz. In recognition of his daring leadership of a landing party of armed sailors who captured the fort at Tabasco, Porter was given command of the *Spitfire*.

After the war, Porter returned to coast survey duty. He also captained steam mail and merchant vessels in the Pacific, including the famous *Golden Age*. He returned to the U.S. Navy in 1855 for special duty commanding the naval store ship *Supply*. Ordered to ferry camels from the Mediterranean to Texas for use as army pack animals, Porter made two successful trips and also took some time to survey war activities in the Crimea. He spent the late 1850s on navy yard and shipbuilding duties, chafing at his inactivity after 20 years' service as a lieutenant.

The Civil War. With the election of Abraham Lincoln and the ensuing secession of southern states, Porter sought more active duty. He convinced Lincoln and Sec. of State William H. Seward to give him command of the *Powhatan* as part of a joint expedition to reinforce Fort Pickens and to recapture Pensacola, Florida. Ignoring later orders to turn back, Porter steamed on to Pensacola, only to find the assigned army forces uncooperative, and the city remained in Confederate hands.

After several months of chasing commerce raiders and sitting on blockade, Porter returned to Washington a commander and assisted in planning the campaign to recapture New Orleans. Convincing the navy and the president that a fleet of small boats with army mortars probably could reduce the city's defensive forts Jackson and St. Philip, allowing the fleet to get within gun range of the city, Porter pressed for the command of the mortar boats and secured the services of his adoptive brother, Capt. David G. Farragut, to command the expedition. When Porter's bombardment failed to demolish the forts, Farragut daringly ran past the batteries and captured New Orleans, leaving Porter to receive the forts' surrender. Porter spent the next four months assisting in fruitless attempts to take Vicksburg, Mississippi, by water.

In October 1862, Lincoln gave Porter, as an acting rear admiral, command of the Mississippi Squadron, the river fleet above Vicksburg, to cooperate with army forces in the capture of that crucial city. After reorganizing his command, Porter cooperated with Maj. Gen William T. Sherman in his disastrous assault on the river's bluffs at Chickasaw Bayou, north of Vicksburg. Their defeat provoked their successful combined assault on Fort Hindman at Arkansas Post (January 1863).

Porter's complete cooperation materially assisted Maj. Gen. Ulysses S. Grant in the 1863 campaign for Vicksburg. After running the Confederate defensive batteries on April 16, Porter assisted Grant's overland campaign by keeping the river open to Union traffic, bombarding the city, and destroying Confederate forts and ships on the rivers. With Grant's capture of Vicksburg on July 4, Porter controlled the Mississippi River from Cairo, Illinois, south to New Orleans, and Lincoln made Porter a permanent rear admiral.

After leading a series of successful raids on inland waterways, Porter was ordered to cooperate with Maj. Gen. Nathaniel P. Banks in a raid up the Red River toward Shreveport, Louisiana. Army delays and defeats and falling water left Porter's ships nearly stranded on the river. Fighting his way downriver, Porter barely managed to extricate his command from disaster.

Sec. of the Navy Gideon Welles then ordered Porter east to command the North Atlantic Blockading Squadron in reducing Fort Fisher, which defended Wilmington, North Carolina, the last remaining Confederate port. In December 1864, Porter and Maj. Gen. Benjamin F. Butler made a disastrous and ill-timed assault on Fort Fisher. Butler was removed from command and replaced with Gen. Alfred H. Terry, with whom Porter successfully took the fort (January 1865). Porter finished the war assisting Grant's army on the James River.

Postwar Career. After the war, Porter became a vice admiral (1866). He was superintendent of the U.S. Naval Academy (1865–69), for which he completely reformed the system of naval education and markedly increased professionalism. His superintendency was interrupted by one unsuccessful diplomatic mission to Santo Domingo, and in 1869, President Grant assigned Porter as a special assistant to the secretary of the navy. After Porter's sweeping reforms caused an uproar throughout the Navy Department, Grant appointed a stronger secretary, who eased Porter from power.

Porter succeeded Farragut as admiral in 1870 and remained the ranking naval officer for the next 21 years. Saddled with peacetime duty in a moribund navy and facing internal political opposition, Porter ultimately had few responsibilities, and his opinions were generally ignored. In 1873, during the *Virginius* crisis, Porter commanded the fleet assembled at Key West, but the affair was settled peacefully, and he never again saw action. He wrote regular advisory reports, sat on inspection boards, and encouraged naval education. His yearly reports to the secretary of the navy went largely unanswered. In later years, with little or no voice in the navy, Porter turned his writing skills to uneven, inaccurate histories and novels. An opinionated, outspoken, courageous, and egotistical naval officer, Porter also proved to be a clever organizer who cooperated well with those who respected his abilities and poorly with those who did not.

Bibliography: Cagle, Malcolm W., "Lieutenant David Dixon Porter and His Camels" (proceedings of the U.S. Naval Inst. 83, Dec. 1957); Lewis, Paul, and Noel B. Gerson, *Yankee Admiral: A Biography of David Dixon Porter* (David McKay, 1968); Melia, Tamara Moser, "David Dixon Porter: Fighting Sailor," *Captains of the Old*

Steam Navy, ed. by James C. Bradford (Naval Inst. Press, 1986); Soley, James Russell, *Admiral Porter* (Appleton, 1903); Still, William N., " 'Porter . . . is the Best Man': This Was Gideon Welles's View of the Man He Chose to Command the Mississippi Squadron," *Civil War Times Illustrated* (May 1977); West, Richard Sedgewick, Jr., *The Second Admiral: A Life of David Dixon Porter, 1813–1891* (Coward and McCann, 1937).

Tamara Moser Melia

PORTER, FITZ-JOHN (1822–1901)

U.S. military leader and Union general who was court-martialed during the Civil War, Porter was born in Portsmouth, New Hampshire, and graduated from West Point in 1845. He fought, was wounded, and earned two brevets in the Mexican War. He was an artillery and cavalry instructor at West Point and on the frontier and later joined the Utah Expedition.

After the outbreak of the Civil War, Porter was promoted to brigadier general and fought in the Shenandoah Valley. He distinguished himself during Gen. George McClellan's 1862 Peninsular Campaign. On Aug. 29, 1862, Porter received orders to attack the right flank of Gen. Thomas "Stonewall" Jackson's forces at the Second Battle of Bull Run. Porter felt that his orders were too vague and had arrived too late for any attack to succeed. An attack was not launched, and Gen. John Pope blamed the Confederate victory on Porter's disobedience.

Porter was relieved of command and court-martialed for disloyalty, disobedience, and misconduct. He was found guilty in January 1863 and forced to leave the army. An 1879 inquiry found Porter's actions were justified. It also determined his actions probably prevented an even greater defeat. In 1886, he was reappointed to active duty but was put on the retired list two days later.

Bibliography: Eisenschiml, Otto, *The Celebrated Case of Fitz-John Porter* (Bobbs-Merrill, 1950).

Capt. Robert K. Angwin

PORTER, JAMES DAVIS (1828–1912)

U.S. attorney and Confederate officer, Porter was born in Paris, Tennessee, and practiced law before becoming active in state politics. In 1861, Porter participated in the legislative session that resulted in Tennessee's secession. He drafted the resolution of Tennessee's pledge to support the South against federal hostilities, and when war broke out, he organized Confederate troops in western Tennessee. For the remainder of the war, he served as Gen. Benjamin F. Cheatham's chief of staff.

At war's end, Porter returned to his Paris law practice and in 1874 was elected governor of Tennessee (1875–79). Later, he served briefly as assistant U.S. secretary of state (1885–87) and as U.S. minister to Chile (1893–94).

Christine L. Stevens

QUANTRILL, WILLIAM CLARKE (1837–1865)

Confederate guerrilla leader, Quantrill (known variously as Billy Quantrill and Charley Hart) was born in Canal Dover, Ohio. A former schoolteacher, he spent most of 1857–67 in eastern Kansas as a gambler and thief. He joined the Confederate forces forming in Missouri at the outbreak of the Civil War but deserted after Gen. Sterling Price's retreat into Arkansas (1861). Thereafter, Quantrill formed a guerrilla band and began raiding Unionist farms and towns. In August 1862, his activities received official Confederate sanction when Price commissioned him a captain. Quantrill and his men attacked settlements in both Missouri and Kansas and quickly gained a reputation for pillage and brutality. In January 1865, however, after the failure of Price's 1864 invasion and under mounting pressure from Union forces, Quantrill left Missouri for Kentucky, where he was surprised and killed by a Union patrol.

Bibliography: Breihan, Carl W., *The Killer Legions of Quantrill* (Hangman Press, 1971).

Richard F. Kehrberg

QUITMAN, JOHN A. (1798–1858)

U.S. politician and military leader, Quitman was born in Rhinebeck, New York. In 1821, Quitman arrived in Natchez, Mississippi, where he became active in state politics. During the 1836 Texas Revolution, Quitman organized a military force but saw no action. In 1846 he became brigadier general of the Mississippi militia and won glory at the battles of Monterrey and Veracruz. On Sept. 13, 1847, his division captured the fortress of Chapultepec, leading to the fall of Mexico City, of which Quitman became governor (1847).

Quitman later continued his political career, serving as Mississippi governor (1850–51) and in the U.S. House of Representatives (1855–58). He also supported filibustering in the Caribbean. Quitman died in Natchez, from food poisoning, two years before Mississippi's secession. An ardent Southern-rights and proslavery advocate, he likely would have applauded the creation of the Confederacy.

Roger D. Launius

REYNOLDS, JOHN FULTON (1820–1863)

U.S. military leader, Reynolds was born in Lancaster, Pennsylvania, and graduated from West Point in 1841. He served with distinction in the Mexican War and won two brevets for gallantry. Commandant of cadets at the Military Academy when the Civil War began, he received a promotion to brigadier general of volunteers.

Captured during the Peninsular Campaign (June 1862) and later exchanged, Reynolds distinguished himself while commanding a division at the Second Battle of Bull Run (August 1862). He was then detached to organize the Pennsylvania militia during the Maryland invasion. Promoted to major general in November, Reynolds commanded the I Corps at Fredericksburg and Chancellorsville. He declined command of the Army of the Potomac after Maj. Gen. Joseph T. Hooker's relief and was killed leading his corps into Gettysburg on the morning of July 1, 1863.

Bibliography: Warner, Ezra J., *Generals in Blue: Lives of the Union Commanders* (Louisiana State Univ. Press, 1964).

Daniel T. Bailey

RINGGOLD, SAMUEL (1796?–1846)

U.S. military officer, Ringgold presumably was born at Fountain Rock, his family's estate near Hagerstown, Maryland. He is best remembered as the "Father of Light Artillery Tactics" and the first U.S. hero of the Mexican War. After graduating from West Point in 1818, Ringgold served in the 2d Artillery as a second lieutenant and in the 3d Artillery as a first lieutenant and captain. In 1836, he saw action in the Seminole War and in 1838 received a brevet promotion to major for conspicuous service in that conflict.

Although the Army Reorganization Act of 1821 called for one company in each of the army's four artillery regiments to be a battery of light artillery, this was not implemented until 1838. Ringgold's Battery C, 3d Artillery, was the first to receive six new field pieces complete with six-horse teams. The following year, he led the battery on maneuvers at a War Department–sponsored "camp of instruction" at Trenton, New Jersey. His performance before numerous government dignitaries was a deciding factor in gaining congressional appropriations for the other three light artillery batteries.

In 1839, Capt. Robert Anderson published *Instruction for Field Artillery, Horse and Foot,* his translation of a French artillery manual. This was officially adopted by the U.S. Army the following year. In 1843, Ringgold presided over the army board that published *Instruction for Field Artillery.* This was basically Anderson's translation, with some modifications suggested by Ringgold, such as the British system for serving the gun. The work of the "Ringgold Board" became the standard for artillery use in the Mexican War and for both sides during the Civil War.

Major Ringgold was able to apply his theories at the Battle of Palo Alto (May 8, 1846), the first battle of the Mexican War. There the U.S. artillery proved decisive, inflicting heavy casualties against a numerically superior Mexican force and saving the day for Gen. Zachary Taylor's army. Ringgold, however, was one of the U.S. casualties, mortally wounded by Mexican counterfire.

Bibliography: Bauer, Jack R., *The Mexican War: 1846–1848* (Macmillan Co., 1974); Peterson, Harold, *Round Shot and Rammers* (Stackpole Books, 1989).

Ted Alexander

RODGERS, JOHN (1812–1882)

U.S. naval leader, Rodgers was born in Havre de Grace, Maryland, son of the distinguished commodore of the same name. He joined the U.S. Navy as an acting midshipman in February 1829, serving early tours on ships commanded by Alexander Wadsworth and Matthew C. Perry, both related by marriage to the Rodgers family. These two men saw to it that Rodgers received the finest education possible aboard ship, although he still had to wait six years before being promoted to lieutenant.

Early Career. From 1840 to 1842, he participated in the Seminole Wars in Florida. Charges that he had administered significantly more lashes to several crew members than were allowed by law were later dismissed by Sec. of the Navy Abel P. Upshur, influenced perhaps by Rodgers's family connections.

After overseeing the construction of the *Allegheny,* an early steam warship, Rodgers spent three years on distant station with the Africa and Mediterranean squadrons before accepting command in 1849 of a hydrographic party charged with surveying the Florida Keys as part of the U.S. Coast Survey. The experience gained there served him in good stead in 1852 when he joined the North Pacific Surveying Expedition, which took him to the East Indies, China, and Japan. Despite the fact that he was once again charged with misconduct (and once again absolved of all wrongdoing), the expedition's success was largely the result of his untiring efforts.

The Civil War. After participating in the abortive Union attempt to destroy the Norfolk navy yard in April 1861, Rodgers was ordered to Cincinnati to oversee the construction of gunboats for future use on the Mississippi River. He served on Adm. Samuel F. Du Pont's staff during the Port Royal operations of late 1861, and from April to November 1862, he commanded the James River Squadron, suffering a major defeat at Fort Darling in May.

Promoted to captain in July 1862, Rodgers next commanded the monitor *Weehawken* in the failed attack on Charleston, South Carolina (Apr. 7, 1863). Two months later, he again sailed the *Weehawken* into battle, this time forcing the surrender of the Confederate ironclad *Atlanta* on June 17. For that he was promoted to commodore, but he saw no more action in the war.

Later Career. Postwar assignments included three years as commandant of the Boston navy yard followed by command of the Asiatic Squadron (1870–72), during which

Rodgers, by then a rear admiral, led a force of five vessels (May 1871) with orders to secure a peaceful treaty with Korea. Fighting broke out between the two sides, however, and despite his best efforts, the mission failed. Rodgers's last years were spent as the superintendent of the Naval Observatory, chairman of the Lighthouse Board, and head of the first Naval Advisory Board.

Bibliography: Clark, Charles E., *My Fifty Years in the Navy* (Little, Brown, 1917) in *Classics of Naval Literature* (Naval Inst. Press, 1984); Johnson, Robert Erwin, "John Rodgers: The Quintessential Nineteenth Century Naval Officer," *Captains of the Old Steam Navy,* ed. by James C. Bradford (Naval Inst. Press, 1986).

Maj. Grant H. Walker

RODMAN, THOMAS JACKSON (1815–1871)

U.S. inventor and military officer, Rodman was born near Salem, Indiana, and graduated from West Point in 1841. Fascinated by the construction of heavy artillery, he experimented with the development of a casting process where the barrel was built of layers of metal cast around a hollow core, which was kept cool by a steady flow of water. This process created a tremendously strong weapon, highly resistant to bore erosion and less likely to burst while being fired.

Although Rodman had developed his techniques for castings around 1845, the Ordnance Department did not approve them for military production until 1859. During the Civil War, he was placed in charge of the Watertown Arsenal and oversaw the production of all calibers of guns, up to the massive 20-inch smoothbore, capable of firing a 1,080-pound shot. After the war, Rodman was responsible for the development of the Rock Island Arsenal in Illinois.

2d Lt. R. John Warsinske

ROSECRANS, WILLIAM STARKE (1819–1898)

U.S. military leader, and Union general during the Civil War, Rosecrans was born in Delaware City, Ohio. He graduated from West Point in 1842 and entered the Corps of Engineers. At the outbreak of the Civil War, he joined Maj. Gen. George B. McClellan, who was organizing Ohio militia troops. Promoted to brigadier general, Rosecrans served in western Virginia, distinguishing himself at the Battle of Rich Mountain (July 1861). He commanded a division at Corinth and the Army of the Mississippi, fighting partially successful battles at Iuka and Corinth in the autumn of 1862. Assuming command of the Army of the Cumberland, he gave battle indecisively at Stones River on December 31.

In a brilliant campaign of maneuver, he forced Confederate general Braxton Bragg out of Chattanooga and into northern Georgia by September 1863. But Bragg rallied and gave battle at Chickamauga, where Rosecrans blundered, allowing a gap in his line. A complete rout was avoided only when Maj. Gen. George H. Thomas made a heroic stand on the right wing. Besieged in Chattanooga, Rosecrans was relieved in October 1863. Popular with the troops but tunable to overcome the Chickamauga and Chattanooga disasters, he resigned in March 1867, having received no assignment for more than two years. Rosecrans then became U.S. minister to Mexico (1868–69), a member of the U.S. House of Representatives (1881–85), and U.S. registrar of the treasury (1885–93).

Bibliography: Lamers, William M., *The Edge of Glory: The Biography of General William S. Rosecrans, U.S.A.* (Harcourt, Brace, 1961).

T. C. Mulligan

SANTA ANNA, ANTONIO LÓPEZ DE (1794–1876)

Mexican military leader and president, Santa Anna was one of the most significant figures of 19th-century Mexico, a general of both outstanding political and military abilities. Born in Jalapa, Veracruz, he became a cadet in the Spanish colonial army in 1810. In 1821, he lent his services to the Mexican Revolution and became a leading officer in the young nation's army. In 1829, he helped overthrow the Mexican president and the next year seized power in his own right.

The Texas Revolution. When the province of Texas revolted and declared its independence in 1836, Santa Anna took personal command of the army and marched north to quash the rebellion. He scored a victory on Mar. 6, 1836, when his 4,000 troops overran an estimated 187 Texans at the Alamo, outside San Antonio, after a 12-day siege. Although it was a Mexican victory, Santa Anna's casualties have been reliably estimated between 1,000 and 1,600, thus seriously hampering his ability to wage a war of attrition. His loss of men, coupled with the length of time required to take the Alamo, hurt Santa Anna's campaign enough to allow the Texans to rally. At San Jacinto on Apr. 21, 1836, Sam Houston surprised the Mexican army and captured Santa Anna, ending the revolution.

Santa Anna returned to Mexico after the Texas Revolution and entered a semiretirement. He returned to action to fight the French occupation forces in Veracruz, where he was wounded and lost a leg. He was regarded as a national hero and again succeeded to the Mexican presidency. After a few years, however, he was exiled to Cuba for malfeasance in office.

The Mexican War. As war arose in August 1846, Santa Anna left his exile and returned to Mexico. By the end of the year, he had formally reascended to the Mexican presidency. He formed an army and, on Feb. 22–23, 1847, fought a pitched battle with Gen. Zachary Taylor's U.S. forces at Buena Vista. In a series of brutal frontal assaults,

Santa Anna was unable to overcome the U.S. positions and was forced to withdraw with his army in disarray.

He returned to Mexico City to reform his army, and when Gen. Winfield Scott began his march from Veracruz on the capital in the summer, Santa Anna moved to oppose him. Fighting a series of delaying actions, Santa Anna had troops fortify both a Franciscan mission and a bridge at Churubusco. When the U.S. force arrived there on August 20, it was surprised by the stiff opposition of the Mexicans, but Scott brought up additional troops and mounted a frontal assault on the bridgehead and the other Mexican fortifications. Although this and other battles on the same day were soon won by the U.S. troops, casualties were high on both sides. Santa Anna lost nearly one-third of his force as either casualties or prisoners of war, setting the stage for the assault of Mexico City and the conclusion of war.

Postwar Years. When Mexico surrendered, Santa Anna entered exile in Jamaica and New Granada, but in 1853, governmental chaos again allowed him an opportunity to take over the Mexican government. He was in power for two years before being overthrown and banished. During the American Civil War, Santa Anna made another bid to take power in Mexico, petitioning the United States for assistance in throwing out Maximilian and the French while offering his services to Maximilian. Neither side supported his overtures. A decade later, Santa Anna was allowed to return to his native land and died a pauper in Mexico City. His military brilliance and charisma had served Mexico well, but his lack of principles, his love of military extravagance, and his penchant for political intrigue had led his country into a series of disasters.

Bibliography: Bauer, K. Jack, *The Mexican War, 1846–1848* (Macmillan Co., 1974); Callcott, Wilfrid Hardy, *Santa Anna: The Story of an Enigma Who Once Was Mexico* (Univ. of Oklahoma Press, 1936); Hanighen, Frank C., *Santa Anna: The Napoleon of the West* (Coward and McCann, 1934); Ramirez, Jose Fernando, *Mexico During the War with the United States* (Univ. of Missouri Press, 1950).

Roger D. Launius

SCHOFIELD, JOHN McALLISTER (1831–1906)

U.S. Army leader, Schofield was born in Gerry, New York, and graduated from West Point in 1853. An instructor at the Military Academy when the Civil War began, he received an appointment as a brigadier general of volunteers. From October 1862 until April 1863, Schofield commanded the Army of the Frontier along the Missouri-Arkansas border. Promoted to major general in May 1863, he took control of the Department of the Missouri. Schofield served under Maj. Gen. William T. Sherman during the Atlanta Campaign as commander of the XXIII Corps. His corps was then dispatched to defend Tennessee. At Franklin, in November 1864, he inflicted a bloody defeat on the Confederate Army of Tennessee. After taking part in the Battle of Nashville (December 1864), Schofield ended the war commanding troops in North Carolina.

Bibliography: McDonough, James L., *Schofield: Union General in the Civil War and Reconstruction* (Florida State Univ. Press, 1972); Warner, Ezra J., *Generals in Blue: Lives of the Union Commanders* (Louisiana State Univ. Press, 1964).

Daniel T. Bailey

SCHURZ, CARL (1829–1906)

U.S. military leader, Schurz was born in Liblar, Prussia, and participated in his homeland's ill-fated 1848–49 revolution. Forced to flee, he eventually arrived in the United States in 1852. He settled in Wisconsin in 1856 and soon became a leader of the German-American community and a radical supporter of the Republican party. President Lincoln appointed him minister to Spain in 1861.

Schurz obtained a brigadier generalship of volunteers in 1862 and commanded the 3d Division of the Union XI Corps at the Second Battle of Bull Run. He remained with the division after promotion to major general and led it in the Chattanooga Campaign in late 1863. Maj. Gen. Joseph Hooker's report of the campaign criticized Schurz's conduct, and, although vindicated by a court of inquiry, Schurz did not again hold an active command.

After the war, Schurz served as a U.S. senator from Missouri (1869–75) and as Pres. Rutherford B. Hayes's secretary of the interior (1877–81). For much of his later life, he was an editor and writer. Among his published works is the two-volume *Life of Henry Clay* (1887).

Richard B. Meixsel

SCOTT, WINFIELD (1786–1866)

U.S. military leader, Scott was born near Petersburg, Virginia, on his family's estate, "Laurel Branch." In 1807, he enlisted in response to the *Chesapeake-Leopard* incident and was advanced to the rank of captain within a year. He later was assigned to New Orleans, where he found himself disappointed in the quality of his fellow officers. Consequently, he was preparing to leave military service when his public speculation regarding General in Chief of the Army James Wilkinson's involvement in the Burr Conspiracy led to his own dismissal.

The War of 1812. At the outbreak of the War of 1812, Scott was offered and accepted the rank of lieutenant colonel. Although captured by the British at the Battle of Queenston Heights (Oct. 13, 1812), he was recognized for his bravery and leadership. After his release, Scott fought and was wounded at Fort George. He was then reassigned under the command of his nemesis, General Wilkinson. Nonetheless, Scott revamped the soldiers' training program, and his efforts were commended by Pres. James

Madison. Scott was promoted to brigadier general in the spring of 1813. Later that year, at the Battle of Chippewa, he demonstrated the effectiveness of his training methods. He fought again at Lundy's Lane, where he was twice unhorsed and wounded and for which he was brevetted a major general.

Post–War of 1812 Years. At the conclusion of the war, Scott requested a leave of absence to observe firsthand Napoleon's return from Elba. When Scott arrived at Liverpool, England, he was met with news of Napoleon's defeat at Waterloo. He spent the remainder of his time in Europe observing the spectacle of the British, Russian, Prussian, and Austrian troops who were then occupying France and interviewing key military leaders. Scott returned to the United States in 1817 and was appointed president of the army's Board of Tactics, which afforded him the opportunity to translate his observations into a revision of the army's tactics manual. Scott thought himself to be the logical choice for promotion to general in chief of the army. When the position was offered to another, Scott, in turn, offered his resignation, which was declined.

The Indian Wars. In 1832, he led troops against the Sac and Fox tribes in the dispute known as the Black Hawk War. Scott contracted cholera; during his recovery, he was ordered to engage Indians in Florida. While fighting the Creek, Scott was accused by Pres. Andrew Jackson of unnecessarily delaying the campaign. Jackson relieved him of command and established a board of inquiry to investigate Scott's conduct. The board not only dismissed the charges but praised Scott's achievements. In 1841, Scott was given command of the U.S. Army.

The Mexican War. In 1846, Gen. Zachary Taylor led U.S. troops into northern Mexico, his objective being to occupy the two northern provinces of Mexico. It was thought that this would convince the Mexican government that continuing the war was futile. When this strategy proved insufficient, Scott was given command of an additional contingent in Mexico. To capture Mexico City, Scott planned and executed the first major amphibious landing in U.S. Army history, on the Gulf Coast at Veracruz.

Scott took Veracruz and executed a daring march through the high country to Mexico City, leaving him with no logistical support and no fallback position. It was here that his reputation as a brilliant strategist was made. His study of Napoleonic warfare expressed itself in his organizational tactic of dividing his army into divisions that independently flanked the enemy. The strength and quality of Scott's command was further demonstrated by his ability to control such an operation.

Scott fought a limited war of maneuver, which avoided costly engagements. He was a strategist who valued the accomplishment of objective by cunning. He also believed in upholding the rights of citizens of invaded territory and therefore maintained strict control over the conduct of his soldiers. His skill as a cunning strategist contrasted with Zachary Taylor's approach to the war, which was more in keeping with the popularized aggressive strategy of the day and which resulted in a high casualty rate. Scott tried to avoid harsh actions that might serve to rally Mexican resolve and prolong the war. In this regard, he did not destroy the Mexican army. Moreover, the inhabitants of Mexico City found daily life almost routine under U.S. occupation. Ironically this left the American public with the false impression that Taylor was the superior leader who faced the more intense combat.

Post–Mexican War Years. At the conclusion of the Mexican War, Scott again came under scrutiny. This time, the issue was his handling of allegations that two of his subordinates had appropriated enemy weapons for personal use. This inquiry was highly politicized, especially among Taylor advocates who feared that Scott could be formidable opposition for the Whig nomination for the presidency in 1848. Congress exonerated Scott of all charges, but by then, Taylor had easily secured his political objective.

In 1852, Scott was promoted to lieutenant general (the first to hold that rank since George Washington) and was nominated for the presidency on the Whigs' 53d ballot. He was soundly defeated by Democrat Franklin Pierce, his subordinate in the Mexican War, and by losing became the last Whig candidate for the U.S. presidency.

At the onset of the Civil War, Scott, although a native Virginian, sided with the North and devised what would come to be known as the Anaconda Plan. The basic tenets of this plan were to secure the Mississippi River and blockade Southern ports. The objective was to constrict the Confederacy logistically and so reduce the demand for Union troops in the South. Gen. Ulysses S. Grant and Pres. Abraham Lincoln embraced a modified version of Scott's plan to include military advances into the South.

Bibliography: Bauer, K. Jack, *The Mexican War, 1846–1848* (Macmillan Co., 1974); Elliott, Charles W. *Winfield Scott: The Soldier and the Man* (Macmillan Co., 1937); Scott, Winfield, *Memoirs of Lieut.-General Scott,* 2 vols. (Sheldon, 1864).

Capt. Ralph P. Millsap, Jr.

SEDGWICK, JOHN (1813–1864)

U.S. military officer and Union general, Sedgwick was born in Cornwall Hollow, Connecticut. After graduation from West Point in 1837, he served in the Seminole War, in the Mexican War, on the Kansas Border, and in the Mormon Expedition, with frontier duty in between each.

A major at the outbreak of the Civil War, Sedgwick was promoted to brigadier general in 1861 and major general in 1862. He commanded a division during the Peninsular and Antietam campaigns, being wounded in each. Following his recuperation, Sedgwick was assigned command of the VI Corps, Army of the Potomac, which he led at the battles of Chancellorsville, Gettysburg, the Wilderness, and Spotsylvania. While personally reconnoitering positions for his artillery at Spotsylvania, he was killed. He was one of the Union Army's most effective field commanders, respected by his troops and fellow officers.

Bibliography: Winslow, Richard, *General John Sedgwick: The Story of a Union Corps Commander* (Presidio, 1981).

Louise Arnold-Friend

SEMMES, RAPHAEL (1809–1877)

Confederate naval officer, Semmes was born in Charles County, Maryland. He entered the U.S. Navy as a midshipman in 1826 and fought in the Mexican War. With the advent of the Civil War, he resigned his commission and became a commander in the Confederate navy. Semmes then proved himself to be the most capable and successful commerce raider in the Civil War. During his tenure as captain of the converted steamer *Sumter* (1861–62), Semmes captured 18 ships. As captain of the *Alabama* (1862–64), he sailed nearly 75,000 miles in search of Union shipping, captured or destroyed 69 vessels, and caused $6.5 million in Union losses. On June 19, 1864, the Union sloop *Kearsarge* sank the *Alabama* off Cherbourg, France. In 1865, Semmes was promoted to rear admiral and given command of the James River squadron. With the South's defeat, Semmes was temporarily imprisoned, after which he practiced law in Mobile, Alabama.

Bibliography: Boykin, E. C., *Ghost Ship of the Confederacy: The Story of the Alabama and Her Captain, Raphael Semmes* (Funk & Wagnalls, 1957).

Maj. Peter Faber

SHAFTER, WILLIAM RUFUS (1835–1906)

U.S. military leader, Shafter was born in Kalamazoo County, Michigan. He enlisted in the 7th Michigan Volunteer Infantry in 1861 and participated in Ball's Bluff and the Peninsular Campaign of 1862. Gallantry during the Battle of Fair Oaks earned him a brevet promotion to lieutenant colonel and later won him the Medal of Honor. Confederate forces captured him at Thompson's Station, Tennessee, in March 1863; he was released during a prisoner exchange after two months in captivity. Shafter became colonel of the 17th U.S. Colored Infantry in April 1864 and led that force during the Battle of Nashville in December. He remained in the army after 1865, eventually leading the expeditionary force to Cuba in 1898.

Matthew Oyos

SHELBY, ISAAC (1750–1826)

U.S. politician and soldier, Shelby was born in Frederick (now Washington) County, Maryland. Considered to be the architect of the colonists' victory at King's Mountain during the American Revolution, he served twice as governor of Kentucky (1792–96, 1812–16). In his second term, during the War of 1812, he appealed to the men of Kentucky to follow him into battle again. Although 63 years old, he personally recruited and led over 3,000 reinforcements north to join Gen. William Henry Harrison in time for the retaking of Detroit. Shelby's men, especially his mounted force commanded by Richard M. Johnson, played a decisive role at the Battle of the Thames in October 1813. In 1817, citing his advanced age, he declined Pres. James Monroe's tender of the post of secretary of war.

Carol Reardon

SHERIDAN, PHILIP HENRY (1831–1888)

U.S. military leader, Sheridan was born in Albany, New York. He graduated from West Point in 1853, after a one-year suspension for misconduct. He was assigned to the 1st Infantry and served in Texas and then with the 4th Infantry in California and the Northwest, where he saw extensive service in campaigns against the Indians.

The Civil War. When the Civil War broke out in 1861, Sheridan was made captain in the 13th Infantry. He served successfully in Corinth, Mississippi, and was promoted to colonel of the 2d Michigan Cavalry (May 1862). In July, he fought well in Boonville, Missouri, and in December was promoted to brigadier general of volunteers.

In January 1863, Sheridan fought at Stones River, Tennessee, amid great slaughter to anchor Gen. George Thomas's line. At a midnight council of war, Sheridan consented to lead the counterattack that eventually brought a Union victory. His later actions at Chattanooga won him the esteem of Gen. Ulysses S. Grant and secured his military future.

Sheridan had shared the humiliation of the Army of the Cumberland when defeated at Chickamauga in September 1863. In November, however, Sheridan's relentless attack upon the Confederate rifle pits at Chattanooga's Missionary Ridge helped win a Union victory. His suicidal advance was intended to take pressure off of Gen. William T. Sherman. After successfully overrunning the rifle pits, Sheridan took the ridge. Following Missionary Ridge, Sheridan's role in the fighting steadily increased. In April 1864, he took command of the Army of the Potomac's cavalry. Throughout the summer, as Grant advanced through Virginia, it was Sheridan who protected the flanks of his army. In August, Grant gave Sheridan command of the Army of the Shenandoah.

Confederate general Jubal Early was sent by Gen. Robert E. Lee to threaten Washington and in hopes of eliminating pressure on Lee's Army of Northern Virginia. In the fall of 1864, Sheridan defeated Early at Winchester (Opequon), Fishers Hill, and Cedar Creek, where his dramatic ride between the opposing lines to encourage and reorganize his troops won a place in national lore. It became one of the

Union general Philip Sheridan commanded the cavalry troops of the Army of the Potomac during the Civil War. (U.S. Military Academy)

best-known episodes of the war and was captured in song, poem, and painting.

Sheridan's victory at Cedar Creek eliminated the Confederate army in the Shenandoah Valley. The victory and the accompanying notoriety won Sheridan a promotion to major general and secured his place among the top echelon of Union generals. Sheridan knew that the war would soon end, and he was eager to have his cavalry "be in at the death." After hurriedly rejoining Grant, Sheridan's men destroyed the right flank of Lee's army. After helping devastate the Army of Northern Virginia, Sheridan blocked Lee's line of retreat, helping to trap Lee at Appomattox.

Postwar Career. At the close of the war, Grant immediately sent Sheridan to Texas. He was told to establish a large force on the Rio Grande, supposedly to force the surrender of Confederate general Kirby Smith. In truth, however, Grant and Sheridan hoped to block the Mexican puppet government of Maximilian from becoming a haven for former Confederates. Sheridan took 52,000 men to Texas to forestall future problems. He also was involved in the reconstruction of Louisiana and Texas, serving as military governor of that district in 1867. His administration was so severe, however, that he was transferred to Missouri. He was promoted to lieutenant general in 1869 and went to Europe (1870–71), where he observed German troops in the field. In 1875, Sheridan was sent to Louisiana to quell political disturbances but was even more harsh in his handling of civic affairs than he had been in 1867. He succeeded Sherman as commander in chief of the U.S. Army in 1883 and became a four-star general in 1888.

Legacy. Sheridan agreed with Sherman's view that war was power. And, like Sherman, he believed in the tactic of ravaging the enemy homeland and quickly learned the effect of terror on a hostile civilian population. During the Civil War, he obtained permission to burn enemy towns, hang captured partisans, and wreak havoc wherever his army went. At the same time, he took great pains to see that his men were well fed and clothed and never willfully wasted lives in battle.

Only 34 years old when the Civil War ended, Sheridan had emerged as the premier Union combat leader. He had developed his cavalry into a powerful fighting force and had utilized the techniques of scouting and spying at a level far in advance of his colleagues. Although cautious and painstaking in planning, on the battlefield, Sheridan was bold and quick to act.

Bibliography: Burr, Frank A., *The Life of Gen. Philip H. Sheridan* (J. A. & R. A. Reid, 1888); Hutton, Paul Andrew, *Phil Sheridan and His Army* (Univ. of Nebraska Press, 1985); McPherson, James M., *The Battle Cry of Freedom: The Civil War Era* (Oxford Univ. Press, 1988).

M. Guy Bishop

SHERMAN, WILLIAM TECUMSEH (1820–1891)

U.S. military leader and renowned Union leader in the Civil War, Sherman was born in Lancaster, Ohio. After the death of his father, a judge, in 1829, he was raised in the home of a family friend, Sen. Thomas Ewing, who won Sherman an appointment to West Point in 1836. Sherman graduated sixth in the Class of 1840 and was commissioned a second lieutenant in the 3d Artillery.

Early Career. His first assignment was to take a company of recruits from New York to Florida. In Florida, he served 18 months, to the end of the Second Seminole War. He then commanded a company at Fort Morgan in Mobile Point, Alabama. In June 1842, he moved his company to Fort Moultrie at Charleston, South Carolina. During the winter of 1844, Sherman was detached for duty with the inspector general in Georgia, where he gained intimate knowledge of the terrain over which he fought in the Civil War.

During the Mexican War, Sherman was stationed in California, where he remained until 1850. In Washington, D.C., Sherman married Senator Ewing's daughter Ellen. Ewing, then secretary of the interior, tried to help his son-in-law's career. Promoted to captain in the Commissary

Corps, Sherman was posted to St. Louis and then served as commissary officer in New Orleans.

Attracted by the prosperity of post–Gold Rush California, Sherman took a six-month leave of absence from the army to try a banking career in San Francisco. Financial rewards came quickly, and he resigned his army commission. In the economic bust that soon followed, Sherman was ruined financially. He depleted his own savings to repay funds he had invested for army friends.

Sherman returned to Ohio in 1857. He next tried to earn a living as a lawyer in Leavenworth, Kansas, but this led nowhere, and he returned to Ohio in 1859. Sherman did better at his next venture, serving as superintendent of a new military school in Louisiana (1859–61). The school, which eventually became Louisiana State University, successfully channeled Sherman's energy and organizational skills. When Louisiana voted to secede from the Union, Sherman was compelled to resign as superintendent. He then volunteered for federal service.

The Civil War. With the support of his father-in-law and his brother John, a U.S. senator, Sherman gained a commission as colonel in June 1861. He led a brigade at the First Battle of Bull Run, where his troops held their own, losing about 300 killed and wounded. On August 3, Sherman was appointed brigadier general.

Assigned to the Department of the Cumberland and charged with the defense of Kentucky, Sherman declared

Gen. William Tecumseh Sherman's brilliant strategic skills were a key factor in Union victory during the Civil War. (U.S. Army Military History Institute)

at a private meeting that 200,000 troops would be essential for any offensive as opposed to the 20,000 present for duty. His comment was publicized out of context and led to public criticism and a feud with the press, who accused him of insanity. In November, he asked to be relieved but then took up a training command in St. Louis under Gen. Henry W. Halleck.

Sherman was assigned next to Paducah, Kentucky, where he supported the supply effort for Gen. Ulysses S. Grant's campaign leading to the capture of Fort Donelson. In March 1862, Sherman took command of the 5th Division of the Army of Tennessee and led it against Confederate railroad communications. In April, he led his forces at the Battle of Shiloh, where he was wounded and fought well, although his forces were surprised. At Shiloh, the growing bond between Grant and Sherman expanded to mutual trust and reliance.

In May, Sherman became a major general of the U.S. volunteers. Following the siege of Corinth, Mississippi, which he supported, Sherman, on July 21, took command of the District of Memphis. In December, he led an expedition of about 30,000 men down the Mississippi River toward Vicksburg. Acting in concert with Grant, who marched his forces overland against the Confederates, Sherman approached the Confederate citadel at Vicksburg. When Grant's first attempt to take Vicksburg was halted by a Confederate cavalry raid on his supply bases, Sherman pressed on. At Chickasaw Bluffs, Sherman's men assaulted nearly impregnable fortifications and were repulsed.

Sherman continued to support Grant's lengthy efforts to capture Vicksburg. He participated along with Gen. John A. McClernand in capturing Arkansas Post, where Sherman lost more than 500 men. Sherman's XV Corps supported Grant's move on Vicksburg by halting a Confederate relief army led by Gen. Joseph E. Johnston. Sherman's efforts were instrumental in the eventually successful operations against Vicksburg, which fell on July 4, 1863.

Sherman then succeeded Grant as commander of the Department of the Tennessee. He participated with Grant in the campaign to relieve Chattanooga and immediately afterward marched his forces to Knoxville to relieve Gen. Ambrose Burnside. Sherman next turned to the South and commanded two divisions on raids against Confederate lines of communication in Mississippi during the Meridian Campaign (January–February 1864). When Grant went east in March to take command of all Union armies, Sherman became commander of the Military Division of the Mississippi and became responsible for Union military activities in the West.

During the last year of the war, Sherman's successes earned him a military standing that rivaled Grant's, while also stamping him with a reputation for ruthlessness. As Sherman's armies pushed eastward across the heart of the South, Grant's forces pressed from the North. Sherman's

Atlanta Campaign lasted six months and involved his command of three armies conducting operations in rugged terrain. Although halted by the battles at Kenesaw Mountain in June, Sherman's initiative and perseverance led his armies to surround Atlanta and capture the city on September 2.

In his next operation, the famous March to the Sea, Sherman marched an army of four corps 300 miles from Atlanta to Savannah in two months. Sherman cut his lines of supply and fed his forces off of the land, cutting a wide swath of destruction through Georgia. In a famous message of Dec. 22, 1864, Sherman presented Savannah to Pres. Abraham Lincoln as a Christmas gift.

Sherman's aggressive leadership continued in the Carolinas Campaign (February-March 1865). Marching north through the Carolinas, Sherman led his army of 60,000 to a junction at Goldsboro, North Carolina, with 30,000 Union troops marching inland from the coast. This powerful force insured the surrender on Apr. 26, 1865, of Johnston's army. Sherman's campaigns through the lower South were instrumental in the Union triumph.

Postwar Career. Sherman was promoted to lieutenant general in July 1866. After the war, he commanded a territorial division in the West and directed campaigns against Indians. He was promoted to full general and made general in chief of the army on Mar. 4, 1869, the day Grant was inaugurated as president. Sherman tried but failed to gain control over the army's bureaus. He became so frustrated over bureaucratic struggles that he moved the army's headquarters temporarily from Washington to St. Louis (1874–76).

As commanding general, Sherman encouraged army reform. He founded the School of Application for Infantry and Cavalry (precursor of the Command and General Staff College) at Fort Leavenworth in 1881. Sherman retired from military service in 1883. By the next year, the Republicans were trying to draft him as a presidential candidate, a maneuver that Sherman halted with his famous statement: "I will not accept if nominated and will not serve if elected."

Bibliography: Lewis, Lloyd, *Sherman: Fighting Prophet* (Harcourt, Brace, 1932); Merrill, James M., *William Tecumseh Sherman* (Rand McNally, 1971); Sherman, William T., *Memoirs of General W. T. Sherman* (1875; reprint, Library of America, 1990).

Robert H. Berlin

SICKLES, DANIEL EDGAR (1819–1914)

U.S. politician and military officer, Sickles was born in New York City. He served in the U.S. House of Representatives (1857–61) prior to his appointment as brigadier general of U.S. Volunteers at the outbreak of the Civil War. He commanded at brigade and division level in the Army of the Potomac before taking command of III Corps in 1863. At Gettysburg, he sparked controversy when, instead of maintaining his assigned position on Cemetery Ridge, he advanced his corps to the Peach Orchard (July 1863), creating a salient that the Confederates overwhelmed. Sickles lost both a leg and his corps in this action, thus ending his combat career.

Gen. Daniel Edgar Sickles (left), *who lost his right leg in the Battle of Gettysburg, confers with General Heintzelman.* (U.S. Military Academy)

After recovering, he performed several political and diplomatic missions and later returned to Congress (1893–95). He was chairman of the New York State Monuments Commission from 1886 until 1912, when he was accused of financial indiscretions. Sickles was largely responsible for New York's acquisition of Central Park and for the national-park status of Gettysburg Battlefield.

Capt. Alan Cate

STANTON, EDWIN McMASTERS (1814–1869)

U.S. attorney general and secretary of war, Stanton was born in Steubenville, Ohio. An impressive legal career led to his selection as U.S. attorney general by Pres. James Buchanan in 1860. A Democrat, but also a strong Unionist, he resigned when Abraham Lincoln took office but returned to the cabinet as secretary of war (1862–68).

Stanton took firm hold of the administration of the army during the Civil War. After Gen. George B. McClellan's relief as commanding general (March 1862), Stanton, with President Lincoln, even assumed direction of the armies in the field for several months. He enforced unpopular draft laws, pushed for the enlistment of blacks, and improved the army's logistical and supply bases. Noted for integrity and efficiency, Stanton was instrumental in organizing the eventual Union victory.

A Radical Reconstructionist by the end of the war, Stanton fell out with Pres. Andrew Johnson but clung to his office long enough to ensure Congress's control of Reconstruction. Pres. Ulysses S. Grant appointed him to the U.S. Supreme Court, but Stanton died in Washington, D.C., before taking office.

Richard B. Meixsel

STEPHENS, ALEXANDER HAMILTON (1812–1883)

U.S. politician and vice president of the Confederacy, Stephens was born near Crawfordville, Georgia. He served in the Georgia state legislature (1836–42) and in the U.S. House of Representatives (1843–59). Although a strong supporter of state sovereignty, he advocated moderation and unsuccessfully argued against Georgia's secession. Once Georgia seceded, Stephens supported his state, and on Feb. 9, 1861, he was elected vice president of the Confederacy. In that role, he frequently criticized Confederate president Jefferson Davis. In January 1865, Stephens met with U.S. president Abraham Lincoln at the failed Hampton Roads Peace Conference. After the war, he spent five months in a Boston prison. Stephens later returned to the House (1873–82) and died soon after his election as governor of Georgia.

Steve R. Waddell

STOCKTON, ROBERT FIELD (1795–1866)

U.S. naval officer, Stockton was born in Princeton, New Jersey. He first saw action at sea as a lieutenant in the War of 1812. He then served in the Mediterranean, off the west coast of Africa, and in the West Indies before taking a leave of absence from the navy for much of the 1820s and 1830s. Recalled to duty and promoted to captain in 1838, he worked closely with Swedish inventor John Ericsson until a bitter feud between the two erupted in 1844 over credit for construction of the revolutionary screw-sloop *Princeton*.

Stockton was ordered to the Pacific in 1845 and was largely responsible for the seizure of California in the Mexican War. After resigning his commission in 1850, he was elected to the U.S. Senate (1851–53), where he championed the abolition of flogging in the navy.

Bibliography: Langley, Harold D., "Robert F. Stockton: Naval Officer and Reformer," *Command Under Sail,* ed. by James C. Bradford (Naval Inst. Press, 1985).

Maj. Grant H. Walker

STONE, CHARLES POMEROY (1824–1887)

U.S. military officer, Stone was born in Greenfield, Massachusetts, and graduated from West Point in 1845. He was twice breveted during the Mexican War. Reentering the army in 1861, he rose to brigadier general of U.S. Volunteers but was disgraced by his defeat at Ball's Bluff (October 1861). Subsequently exonerated from blame, he served until September 1864, when he resigned to work as a civilian mining engineer. In 1870, Stone entered the service of the Khedive of Egypt as his chief of staff, taking the name "Ferik Pasha." He returned to the United States in 1883 and was appointed chief engineer of the Statue of Liberty's pedestal.

Russell A. Hart

STONEMAN, GEORGE (1822–1894)

U.S. politician and military leader, Stoneman was born in Busti, New York, and graduated from West Point in 1846. He fought on the frontier during the Mexican War, and at the beginning of the Civil War he was commander of Fort Brown, Texas. After being forced to surrender the fort in February 1861 to Confederate general David E. Twiggs, Stoneman escaped with several of his men. Later that year, he took command of the Army of the Potomac's cavalry. From July 1862 until February 1863, he led a succession of infantry divisions and, after being made a major general in November 1862, the III Corps. Gen. Joseph Hooker placed Stoneman in charge of the newly created Cavalry Corps, Army of the Potomac, but his poor performance during the Chancellorsville Campaign (April–May 1863) caused him to be relieved. Transferred to the west, Stoneman briefly led the XXIII Corps and then a cavalry division. His abortive raid on Macon, Georgia, during the Atlanta Campaign (July 1864), resulted in his capture with 700 of his men. Released after a few months, Stoneman spent the remainder of the war as a district commander in Ohio and Tennessee.

Richard F. Kehrberg

STUART, JAMES EWELL BROWN (JEB) (1833–1864)

Confederate cavalry leader, Stuart was born in Patrick County, Virginia, and graduated from West Point in 1854. His manner and good looks earned him the nickname "Beaut" from his West Point mates. He served in the West, was wounded in Kansas, and was a captain by 1861. To support the Confederacy in the Civil War, he resigned his commission in May 1861 to enter the 1st Virginia cavalry.

After the First Battle of Bull Run, where he had led a charge that disrupted an artillery unit, he rose to brigadier general. In June 1862, with 1,200 men, he led a spectacular raid against Gen. George B. McClellan. Stuart rode north, crossed the headwaters of the Chickahominy River, went east behind McClellan's lines, and recrossed the Chickahominy far downstream. This "ride around McClellan" found the Union army with an exposed right flank and divided by the Chickahominy.

Confederate Gen. Jeb Stuart became known for his "ride around McClellan" at the Chickahominy River and won fame for his reckless, destructive raids before his death at Yellow Tavern. (U.S. Army Military History Institute)

Stuart earned an unsurpassed reputation as a leader of raids and as a reconnaissance officer, but he sometimes was not where he was needed during an action. He was reckless, impulsive, and loved praise, but had enough military ability to be a competent cavalry commander. He was promoted to major general in July 1862 and commanded all cavalry in Gen. Robert E. Lee's army until his death. Stuart fought brilliantly at the Second Battle of Bull Run, Sharpsburg, and Fredericksburg. In October 1862, after Sharpsburg, he raided north to Chambersburg, Pennsylvania, destroying supply depots and repair shops. He returned with 1,200 horses and 30 government officials, without a man having been killed. Again, he had circled McClellan.

After Gen. Thomas "Stonewall" Jackson fell at Chancellorsville (May 1863), Stuart temporarily assumed command of Jackson's corps and contained a Union army three times the size of his. On June 9, Union cavalry surprised him at Brandy Station, Virginia, but he forced them to withdraw in what was the war's largest purely cavalry action. Later that month, Lee's orders to Stuart were not precise, and Stuart, perhaps to regain some lost prestige at Brandy Station, set out to ride around Union forces. He crossed the Potomac River near Washington and reached Hanover, Pennsylvania, on June 30. He force-marched his fatigued men, finally arriving at Gettysburg late on July 2. Meanwhile, Lee had marched north blindly, without benefit of Stuart's reconnaissance. Stuart's absence hindered the Confederate effort during Lee's advance into the Union.

During Gen. Ulysses S. Grant's 1864 campaign, Gen. Philip Sheridan's cavalry raided deep behind Lee's army to disrupt Confederate supplies. On May 11, Stuart, in an effort to thwart the Union raid, fought a cavalry action at Yellow Tavern, three miles north of Richmond. While meeting a Union charge, he was mortally wounded.

Lynn L. Sims

SUMNER, CHARLES (1811–1874)

U.S. politician and abolitionist, Sumner was born in Boston. As a U.S. senator (1851–74), he gained fame in the 1850s as a leading voice in the antislavery cause. He attacked the Fugitive Slave Law and denounced the Kansas-Nebraska Bill and also helped organize the Republican party. His outspokeness provoked a brutal and incapacitating physical attack on May 22, 1856, from Representative Preston Brooks (South Carolina) on the floor of the Senate, an incident that heightened sectional tensions. During the Civil War, Sumner chaired the Senate Foreign Relations Committee, a position from which he worked for continued peace with Britain. He also established himself as an advocate for emancipation and for the civil rights of ex-slaves. After the war, Sumner pushed for a tough Reconstruction policy and played a prominent part in the impeachment proceedings against Pres. Andrew Johnson.

Matthew Oyos

SYKES, GEORGE (1822–1880)

U.S. military leader, Sykes was born in Dover, Delaware, and graduated from the U.S. Military Academy in 1842. He served in the Seminole and Mexican wars and on the Indian frontier. At the beginning of the Civil War, he held the rank of major, receiving promotions to brigadier general in 1861 and major general in 1862. Nicknamed "Tardy George" early in his career, Sykes was best known for his defensive ability, rarely moving with speed when the initiative was required. He led Union troops in the Peninsular, Bull Run (Manassas), Antietam (Sharpsburg), Chancellorsville, Gettysburg (where his V Corps was instrumental in securing Little Round Top for the Army of the Potomac), and Mine Run campaigns. He was relieved by Maj. Gen. George Meade after this last engagement for excessive caution. He commanded the Department of Kansas until the end of the war, served in the postwar army, and died at Fort Brown (Brownsville), Texas.

Bibliography: Reese, Timothy, *Sykes' Regular Infantry Division, 1861–1864* (McFarland, 1990).

Louise Arnold-Friend

TAYLOR, RICHARD (1826–1879)

Confederate military leader, Taylor was the son of Pres. Zachary Taylor. He was born in Springfield, Kentucky, educated at both Harvard and Yale as well as spending a portion of his education studying in Europe. Unlike most officers during the Civil War, Taylor had no previous military schooling or experience before accepting a commission in the Confederate army as a brigadier general of Louisiana militia. Eventually rising to the rank of lieutenant general in 1864, Taylor became one of the premier generals of the Confederacy. Active primarily in the trans-Mississippi area, he achieved his greatest success during the Red River campaign.

The Union's Maj. Gen. Nathaniel Banks had been tasked by Gen. Ulysses S. Grant with the seizure of the upper part of the Mississippi Valley held by the South, as well as with the capture of Shreveport, Louisiana. Reinforced by Adm. David Porter's fleet of ironclad mortar boats, Banks began moving toward Shreveport in April 1864. Opposite the Union forces were approximately 30,000 Confederate troops commanded by Gen. Kirby Smith. Smith ordered the forces commanded by then-Major General Taylor to launch an offensive designed to stop Banks and regain control over the Red River. Taylor's troops moved swiftly, securing all of the Red River area.

Striking near Mansfield, Louisiana, Taylor's forces completely routed the overconfident Union troops, compelling them to retreat all the way to New Orleans. Taylor could now control all river traffic flowing in a north-south direction, thereby denying the Union army its fire support from Porter's river flotilla. With his army utterly exhausted by its arduous campaign along the Red River, Banks's army was completely useless for months, causing a serious delay in Grant's plans to secure the entire Gulf Coast area.

The ultimate objective of Smith and Taylor was to recapture New Orleans. Assembling a force of nearly 12,000 men, Taylor proceeded to attack Donaldsville but failed to dislodge the Union garrison due primarily to Porter's river monitors. Had Taylor's forces succeeded in taking Donaldsville, Banks would have been cut off from the main Union forces commanded by Grant, thereby allowing Taylor to invest New Orleans. When both Vicksburg and Port Hudson fell to Union troops, however, Taylor was forced to retire from Donaldsville, putting an end to his ambitious plan of retaking New Orleans. Instead, Taylor, promoted to lieutenant general, was ordered to delay the Union forces for as long as possible from entering the port of Mobile Bay, Alabama. Taylor's forces performed a heroic defense against an ever-growing force of Union troops and were the last rebel forces to accept the terms of surrender, holding out until May 1865.

Bibliography: Reed, Rowena, *Combined Operations in the Civil War* (Naval Inst. Press, 1976).

Leo J. Daugherty III

TAYLOR, ZACHARY (1784–1850)

U.S. military leader and 12th president of the United States (1849–50), Taylor was born in Orange County, Virginia. His father commanded the 9th Virginia Regiment during the Revolutionary War and went on to serve in the Virginia constitutional convention and as a member of the state legislature. In 1785, the Taylors moved west into present-day Kentucky and established a small plantation.

Taylor accepted a commission as a first lieutenant in the 7th Infantry in 1808. In 1810, he was promoted to captain and was assigned to Fort Knox. In 1812, he was sent to Fort Harrison, on the Wabash River, where he was brevetted a major, in recognition of his defense against an Indian attack. During the War of 1812, Taylor served on the frontier, recruiting troops from Indiana and Illinois and guarding settlers from Indian attacks. In August 1814, Taylor launched an expedition against Indian encampments at the mouth of the Rock River, with limited success, and subsequently supervised the building of Fort Johnson at Des Moines before returning to Fort Knox.

The end of the War of 1812 resulted in the demobilization of much of the army, and Taylor returned briefly to his family plantation until recalled to active duty by Pres. James Madison in 1816. He served briefly with the 3rd Infantry but spent more than 10 years with the 1st Infantry, first as lieutenant colonel and later as the regimental commander. While in command of the 1st Infantry, Taylor fought in the Black Hawk War and then, in 1837, was ordered to take command of the forces fighting against the Seminole, whom he defeated at Lake Ocheechobee (Dec. 25, 1837). His success resulted in a brevet promotion to brigadier general, and he assumed command of the region in May 1838.

Mexican War. Taylor requested a transfer, was assigned to Baton Rouge, Louisiana, and became commander of the southern division of the western department. In 1845, he received instructions from Sec. of War William L. Marcy that the annexation of Texas was imminent and that he should prepare his command for hostilities. Texas was indeed admitted to the Union in December, and in March 1846, Taylor fortified a position across the Rio Grande from the Mexican town of Matamoros. The Mexican commander, Gen. Mariano Arista, having besieged the works across the river, began deploying his 5,000 men to push Taylor out of the disputed territory, and on May 8, the two armies met while Taylor was returning to the fort with a relief force and supplies.

Taylor had the advantage of superior artillery under the command of Maj. Samuel Ringgold, who advocated quick movement of the guns to take advantage of the tactical situation. At Palo Alto, the artillery, backed by infantry, repulsed the charges of Arista's lancers and forced the Mexicans from the field. The U.S. casualties were light, but Ringgold was mortally wounded. Taylor, ever confident in the ability of his soldiers, hesitated briefly on the morning of May 9 but resumed his advance when his dragoons reported the new location of Arista's men.

Arista had retired to a strong position in a dry riverbed overgrown with chaparral. At Resaca de la Palma, Arista's artillery and infantry were partially sheltered from the long range of the U.S. artillery guns. Outnumbered, Taylor initially attempted to force the Mexicans from the strong position with artillery but found it ineffective. He ordered a squadron of dragoons to rush a key Mexican battery that covered the only road leading up to the Mexican position. In the headlong charge that followed, the dragoons forced the Mexican gunners from their pieces but rode past the guns, which were retaken by the Mexicans. Disgusted, Taylor roared to the commander of the 5th Infantry, "Take those guns, and by God, keep them!" The disputed guns fell to the U.S. Army again, this time for good. The capture of the position turned the tide toward the U.S. forces, and the Mexican lines crumbled, with Arista's troops abandoning all of their supplies and equipment in their headlong rush toward the Rio Grande.

Taylor's victories at Palo Alto and Resaca de la Palma were quickly transmitted to Washington, and Taylor was promoted to major general. Taylor also began receiving reinforcements for his army. Despite a lack of transportation and the untimely expiration of many early enlistments, he was still able to field more than 6,000 men in September to march on Monterrey. Taylor's strategy was simple. He intended to attack only as far south as Monterrey, which he believed to be as far as his supply line would reach. Although orders from Secretary of War Marcy to "prosecute the war with vigor" had been received, Taylor believed it impossible to cross 1,000 miles of near-desert and attack Mexico City. In addition, Taylor was now aware of his public image, and to fail in such an endeavor would ruin his political future.

At Monterrey, Taylor found a rejuvenated Mexican army of more than 7,000, now commanded by Gen. Pedro de Ampudia, occupying a series of strong fortifications. Taylor's attack on the city, beginning on September 21, was marked by a lack of coordination between the separate attacking elements and fierce house-to-house fighting. After three days, the Mexican forces requested a truce. Taylor agreed, and the remaining Mexican forces withdrew within a week, leaving behind most of their artillery and ammunition, but retaining their personal weapons.

Angered by the lenient terms of the truce and frustrated that Taylor had allowed most of the Mexican forces to remain intact, Pres. James Polk ordered Gen. Winfield Scott to prepare for an invasion of Mexico, with the intent of attacking Mexico City. Polk ordered Taylor to assume a defensive position and to release the bulk of his forces from Monterrey and make them available for Scott's expedition. Taylor's weakened force, consisting almost entirely of volunteer militia backed up by a small contingent of regular artillery, appeared to be an easy mark for the Mexicans now commanded by Gen. Antonio López de Santa Anna. Marching his troops north from Mexico City, the two forces met on Feb. 23, 1847, several miles south of Buena Vista. The outnumbered U.S. troops assumed a defensive position. When the Mexican assault began, the artillery held firm, but the volunteer militia fled in confusion. Giving chase, the Mexicans found themselves trapped in a "V" formed by fresh U.S. regiments. The U.S. fire forced a Mexican retreat, but the Mexicans regrouped and charged again. Taylor ordered his artillery under Capt. Braxton Bragg to, "Double-shot your guns and give 'em hell." Three volleys of artillery caused the Mexicans to flee the field permanently.

President. Returning to the United States, he was nominated as the Whig party candidate for president. Defeating Martin Van Buren in the election, he carried 15 states. A soldier all of his adult life, he was unprepared for the realities of politics. The issue of slavery dominated his tenure as president, and while he recommended admission of California as a free state, he was pressured into denying the same status for New Mexico by slaveholding interests. Taylor died just 16 months into his presidency and was succeeded by his vice president, Millard Fillmore.

2d Lt. R. John Warsinske

TERRY, ALFRED HOWE (1827–1890)

U.S. military leader, Terry was born in Hartford, Connecticut, and served as clerk of the New Haven Superior Court. In the Civil War, he fought at the First Battle of Bull Run as a Union militia colonel, then raised a regiment with which he took part in the capture of both Port Royal, South Carolina, and Fort Pulaski, Georgia. He was appointed brigadier general of U.S. Volunteers in April 1862. Terry transferred to the Army of the James and in 1864 led X Corps in operations against Richmond and Petersburg. In January 1865, his forces seized Fort Fisher, sealing off Wilmington, North Carolina, the Confederacy's last port. His corps was subsequently attached to the Army of the Ohio until the war's end.

After the war, Terry commanded campaigns against the Plains Indians. He retired as a major general in 1888 and died in New Haven, Connecticut.

Capt. Alan C. Cate

THAYER, SYLVANUS (1785–1872)

U.S. military leader, known as "Father of the Military Academy," Thayer was born in Braintree, Massachusetts, and graduated from West Point into the Corps of Engineers in 1808. After service in the War of 1812, during which he rose to brevet major, he returned to the military academy as superintendent in 1817. He found the school in disarray, poorly administered, and with its curriculum narrowly circumscribed to meet engineering demands. Thayer, who had attended Dartmouth College and had visited European military schools, added liberal-arts subjects to the syllabus and expanded the cadets' military training beyond military engineering.

Thayer, noted for having instilled a spirit of professionalism into the officer corps of the nation's fledgling army, quarreled with Pres. Andrew Jackson over the disciplining of cadets and resigned his post in 1833. He retired from the army in 1863, having spent most of the interim years on engineering duties in New England.

Richard B. Meixsel

THOMAS, GEORGE HENRY (1816–1870)

U.S. military leader, Thomas was born in Southampton County, Virginia, and graduated from West Point in 1840. He won two brevet promotions for gallantry in the Mexican War and later served in the famed 2d Cavalry. Loyal to the Union at the outbreak of the Civil War, he was appointed a brigadier general of volunteers in 1861 and rapidly earned the respect of his superiors in Kentucky. He received a promotion to major general in April 1862 and soon commanded a corps in the Army of the Cumberland. Thomas earned the nickname "Rock of Chickamauga," on Sept. 20, 1863, for preventing the complete rout of the army. He then commanded the Army of the Cumberland at Chattanooga and Atlanta. Dispatched to Tennessee in late 1864, Thomas virtually destroyed a Confederate army at Nashville in December. After the war, he was given command of the Military Division of the Pacific.

Union Gen. George Thomas's steadfast refusal to be defeated earned him the nickname "Rock of Chickamauga." (National Archives)

Bibliography: McKinney, Francis F., *Education in Violence: The Life of George H. Thomas and the History of the Army of the Cumberland* (Wayne State Univ. Press, 1961); Warner, Ezra J., *Generals in Blue: Lives of the Union Commanders* (Louisiana State Univ. Press, 1964).

Daniel T. Bailey

TRAVIS, WILLIAM BARRET (1809–1836)

U.S. lawyer and soldier, Travis was born in Cambridge, South Carolina. As a young man, he taught school and passed the bar exam at age 20. He had married in 1828 and went to Texas in 1831 after being divorced. Upon his arrival, he became involved in the politics of the Texas independence movement, and after independence was declared, he was ordered to raise a company of cavalry. He was made a lieutenant colonel in December 1835 and was dispatched to San Antonio's stronghold, the Alamo, the following month.

Travis arrived with 30 men. This force was supplemented at various times by other small groups, including those commanded by James Bowie and Davy Crockett, which eventually brought the total to more than 180 men. Reports of impending attack generally were ignored until the Mexican army actually was sighted. The siege began on February 23, and the overwhelming numbers of Mexican troops left no doubt as to the outcome. The final assault crushed the defenders on Mar. 6, 1836. There were no survivors.

Bibliography: Baugh, Virgil E., *Rendezvous at the Alamo: Highlights in the Lives of Bowie, Crockett, and Travis* (Pageant Press, 1960); McDonald, Archie P., *Travis* (Pemberton Press, 1976).

Capt. Karen S. Wilhelm

TRIST, NICHOLAS PHILIP (1800–1874)

U.S. attorney and diplomat, Trist was born in Charlottesville, Virginia. In March 1847, Pres. James K. Polk sent Trist, fluent in Spanish, to Mexico to negotiate for peace in the Mexican War. Trist, who had attended West Point, had been private secretary to Andrew Jackson and had served as consul to Havana. In Mexico, Trist met with Gen. Antonio López de Santa Anna, who said he would negotiate for a million-dollar bribe.

Reconsidering his options and afraid Trist's presence showed the United States overly anxious for peace, Polk recalled Trist in November. Trist, however, was convinced that Mexico wanted peace, and he decided to stay and negotiate. As a result, he signed, without authority, the Treaty of Guadalupe Hidalgo (Feb. 2, 1848). Polk and the Senate approved the treaty, thus ending the Mexican War.

Lynn L. Sims

TWIGGS, DAVID EMANUEL (1790–1862)

U.S. and Confederate military officer, Twiggs was born in Richmond County, Georgia, and is notable for being the only U.S. Army officer actually to commit treason at the start of the Civil War. Twiggs was a brevet major general commanding the Department of Texas during the secession crisis of early 1861. Most officers who opted for Confederate service resigned their commissions and in some cases waited for replacements to arrive before leaving their commands. Twiggs not only did not resign, but actually surrendered his command to Confederate general Ben McCulloch on Feb. 18, 1861.

A veteran of almost 50 years of service, Twiggs was commissioned a major general in Confederate service (May 1861) and appointed to several commands in Louisiana and Alabama. He was, however, too old for active service and retired before the end of the year.

Bibliography: Spencer, James, *Civil War Generals* (Greenwood Press, 1986).

Capt. Karen S. Wilhelm

TYLER, JOHN (1790–1862)

Tenth president of the United States (1841–45), Tyler was born in Greenway, Virginia, and practiced law before entering politics. He served in the U.S. House of Representatives (1817–21), as governor of Virginia (1825–27), and in the U.S. Senate (1827–36). On the Whig ticket with William Henry Harrison, he was elected vice president in 1840. When Harrison became the first president to die in office (Apr. 4, 1841), Tyler set an important precedent by assuming the office in full.

Clashes with Sen. Henry Clay, however, cost Tyler his party's support. His cabinet resigned, except for Sec. of State Daniel Webster. Webster later resigned after negotiating the Webster-Ashburton Treaty with Great Britain (1842), which settled boundary disputes from Maine to Lake-of-the-Woods, with Oregon to be jointly occupied. Tyler also extended the Monroe Doctrine to the Hawaiian Islands, and in 1844, the first bilateral agreement was reached with China, granting the United States most-favored-nation status.

Domestically, Tyler's temperate response to Dorr's Rebellion in Rhode Island, in which rival factions struggled to control the state government, contributed to its peaceful resolution. Tyler also presided over the conclusion of the Second Seminole war, informing Congress in 1842 that "future pursuit of these miserable beings by a large military force seems to be as injudicious as it is unavailing" and authorizing the army commander in Florida to declare the war finished. After the election of James Polk, Tyler achieved the annexation of Texas through a joint resolution of Congress. He presided over the 1861 Virginia Peace Convention but eventually supported secession. Tyler was elected to the Confederate House of Representatives but died before he could be seated.

Bibliography: Peterson, Norma Lois, *The Presidencies of William Henry Harrison & John Tyler* (Univ. Press of Kansas, 1989).

Stephen J. Lofgren

UPTON, EMORY (1839–1881)

U.S. military leader and historian, Upton was born near Batavia, New York. After attending Oberlin College in Ohio (1854–56), he entered West Point, graduating in 1861. A Union artilleryman in the Civil War, Upton rose to command an artillery brigade during the Peninsular Campaign and at Antietam. Although highly regarded by his superiors, he aspired to leave the regular army and in October 1862 obtained the colonelcy of the 121st New York Infantry. By July 1863, he was a brigade commander.

Using new offensive tactics devised by Upton, his men overcame the elaborate Confederate trench works at Spotsylvania on May 10, 1863. Supporting divisions failed to reinforce the breakthrough, however, and Upton's regiments were forced to withdraw after taking nearly 1,000 casualties. Upton received a promotion to brigadier general and went on to fight at Cold Harbor.

Seriously wounded in July 1863 while commanding the 1st Division of the VI Corps, part of Gen. Philip Sheridan's Army of the Shenandoah, Upton returned to duty as a cavalry division commander in the western theater. He finished out the war in the west, participating in the captures of Selma, Alabama, and Columbus, Georgia.

Both disinterested in the army's postwar constabulary duties and convinced by his wartime experiences that U.S. military organization was inadequate, Upton turned his attention to military reform in the years after the Civil War. He authored *A New System of Infantry Tactics* (1867), which was adopted by the U.S. Army, and then served at West Point as commandant of cadets (1870–75).

Union Gen. Emory Upton's experiences in the Civil War prompted him to turn to military reform. The concepts in his books on infantry tactics and operations of foreign armies were adopted by the army after the war. (U.S. Army Military History Institute)

Upton next persuaded the army's commanding general, William T. Sherman, to authorize a tour of foreign armies. Publication of *The Armies of Asia and Europe* (1878) resulted from his travels. The book reflected Upton's high regard for the German army, and he recommended changes for the U.S. Army that drew on his Civil War experiences (especially his dislike of state interference in the selection of officers) and his admiration for Prussian innovations: an efficient, national-based reserve system, a general staff dedicated to war planning, and a war college to train staff officers.

In *The Military Policy of the United States* (completed 1880; published 1904), Upton marshaled the historical data to support the need for military reform. He argued that lack of preparation and the intrusiveness of states' rights had prolonged U.S. wars unnecessarily. His solution was a national, expandable, professional army. Upton committed suicide while in command of the 4th Artillery Regiment at the Presidio, near San Francisco, California.

Bibliography: Ambrose, Stephen, *Upton and the Army* (Louisiana State Univ. Press, 1964).

Richard B. Meixsel

VAN BUREN, MARTIN (1782–1862)

Eighth president of the United States (1837–41), Van Buren was born in Kinderhook, New York. By 1803, he was a lawyer active in New York politics. He was his state's attorney general (1816–19) and a figure central to the building of the Democratic party in New York. Van Buren was a U.S. senator (1821–28) and New York governor (1829), an office from which he resigned to become Pres. Andrew Jackson's secretary of state (1829–31). With Jackson's support, he was made ambassador to Great Britain.

Van Buren was elected Jackson's vice president in 1832; he was elected president in 1836. As president, Van Buren faced an economic collapse. Soundly defeated by William Henry Harrison in the 1840 election, he remained active in politics and was the Free-Soil candidate for president in 1848.

Robert H. Berlin

VAN DORN, EARL (1820–1863)

U.S. military officer and Confederate general, Van Dorn was born near Port Gibson, Mississippi. He graduated from West Point in 1842. After serving in several minor assignments, he saw extensive action during the Mexican-American War and then with the 2d Cavalry along the Texas-Mexico border, against the Commanche. When Mississippi seceded in 1861, Van Dorn resigned his commission and accepted one as a colonel in the Confederate army. Because of his familiarity with Texas, he was assigned to the trans-Mississippi region. After serving only several months as a colonel, Van Dorn was promoted to major general in September 1861 and placed in command of the Trans-Mississippi Department.

While an outstanding small-unit commander, Van Dorn lacked the essential qualities necessary to handle large formations. His leadership came into question after the defeats at Pea Ridge (March 6–7, 1862) and Corinth (October 3–8, 1862). While acquitted on charges of incompetence, Van Dorn was relieved of command and instead placed in command of a troop of cavalry. He regained his reputation as an energetic and aggressive field officer as well as a brilliant tactician in actions at Holly Springs, Mississippi, in December 1862 and at Thompson Station in March 1863.

Undoubtedly, the most brilliantly executed operation of Van Dorn's career was his attack on the Union supply depot at Holly Springs on Dec. 20, 1862. Van Dorn was able to divide his forces and attack the Union force of about 1,500 from all directions, capturing more than 1,000 Union prisoners as well as seizing or destroying an estimated $1.5 million in supplies. Van Dorn's success forced Gen. Ulysses S. Grant to withdraw to Memphis, Tennessee, thereby allowing the Confederates' Gen. John C. Pemberton more time to strengthen the defenses of Vicksburg.

Van Dorn personified the romantic aura that had evolved around cavalrymen, but for him this characteristic would be fatal. On May 8, 1863, while meeting with his staff, Van Dorn was confronted and fatally shot by a man enraged over his wife's involvement with Van Dorn. With the death of Van Dorn, the South lost one of its best cavalry leaders in the trans-Mississippi.

Leo J. Daugherty III

WADDELL, JAMES IREDELL (1824–1886)

U.S. sailor and Confederate naval officer, Waddell was born in Pittsboro, North Carolina. He joined the U.S. Navy as a midshipman in 1841, saw action off Veracruz during the Mexican War, and graduated from Annapolis in 1847. Upon returning from the Far East in 1862, he resigned his commission and joined the Confederate navy. After serving in various posts on the Mississippi and the Atlantic coast, Waddell was ordered to England, where he took command of the Confederate raider *Shenandoah* in October 1864. He set sail for the Pacific, where he succeeded in destroying the Union whaling fleet, much of it after the war had officially ended. The *Shenandoah* was the only vessel to carry the Confederate flag around the world. Waddell concluded his career sailing for private shipping companies.

Steve R. Waddell

WALLACE, LEWIS (LEW) (1827–1905)

A military leader and author, Wallace was born in Brookville, Indiana. Having fought in the Mexican War, he remained active in the militia and was named adjutant general of Indiana at the outbreak of the Civil War. As colonel of the Union's 11th Indiana Regiment, Wallace led his men at Romney and Harpers Ferry. He was commissioned brigadier general in September 1861 and major general in March 1862. He commanded with distinction at Fort Donelson (February 1862) and Shiloh (April 1862). In 1863, Wallace prevented Gen. Kirby Smith's raid on Cincinnati. In July 1864, on the Monocacy River in Maryland, Wallace's troops suffered heavy losses in Gen. Jubal Early's attack, but delayed Early's advance on Washington.

After the war, Wallace served on the court-martial of Lincoln's accused assassins and was president of the court-martial that found Henry Wirz, Confederate commandant of Andersonville Prison, guilty of war crimes. In later years, Wallace's writing brought him fame, principally the publication of *Ben Hur* (1880).

Christine L. Stevens

WARREN, GOUVERNEUR KEMBLE (1830–1882)

U.S. military leader, Warren was born in Cold Spring, New York, and graduated second in his class at West Point (1850). He served in the Corps of Topographical Engineers, surveying much of the Mississippi delta as well as the Dakota and Nebraska territories prior to the Civil War. As part of his duties, Warren, with Capt. Andrew A. Humphreys, made the first examination of possible routes for a transcontinental railroad. Detailed to West Point as an assistant professor of mathematics, Warren accepted a lieutenant-colonelcy with the 5th New York Volunteers at the outbreak of war.

Warren was serving as the chief engineer of the Army of the Potomac in July 1863, and during the second day of the Battle of Gettysburg, he recognized that the extreme left of the Union position at Little Round Top was undefended. Warren's decision to seize this key terrain kept the Union lines from being outflanked by Confederate forces. Following Gettysburg, he was placed in command, first of II Corps, then V Corps, leading with distinction until the Battle of Five Forks (1865), when he was summarily relieved from command.

After the war, Warren was assigned to various topographical and survey projects. However, he repeatedly pressed for an investigation of his relief at Five Forks. In December 1879, a court of inquiry found Warren's conduct during the battle to be beyond reproach and cast aspersions on the actions of Gen. Philip Sheridan, who had relieved him.

2d Lt. R. John Warsinske

WELLES, GIDEON (1802–1878)

U.S. secretary of the navy, Welles was born in Glastonbury, Connecticut, and was an organizer of the Republican party. Prominent in New England's Republican circles, he served as navy secretary (1861–69) to Presidents Lincoln and Johnson. Welles faced the task of mobilizing the U.S. Navy for its Civil War duties of blockading the Confederacy, seizing strategic waterways, and protecting Northern commerce from Southern raiders. He rapidly built up an adequate naval force and ran an efficient department, with the able help of Gustavus Vasa Fox, assistant navy secretary. Welles kept close watch over naval operations and promoted technological developments, including heavy ordnance, steam machinery, and ironclad vessels such as the USS *Monitor*.

Matthew Oyos

WHEELER, JOSEPH (1836–1906)

U.S. military leader and Confederate general, Wheeler was born in Augusta, Georgia, and graduated from West Point in 1859. Commissioned as a second lieutenant of dragoons, he served in the New Mexico Territory, where he earned the nickname "Fightin' Joe." Resigning from the U.S. Army in April 1861, Wheeler acquired a colonelcy with the 19th Alabama Infantry Regiment of the Confederacy. He conducted rearguard actions at Shiloh, Perryville, Murfreesboro, and Chickamauga, earning a reputation as the principal Confederate cavalry commander in the western

Col. "Fightin' Joe" Wheeler's Confederate cavalry gained notoriety for their surprise rearguard attacks during the Civil War. (U.S. Army Military History Institute)

theater. His cavalry provided the only resistance to Gen. William T. Sherman during his March to the Sea and through the Carolinas. Attempting to protect Confederate president Jefferson Davis, Wheeler was taken prisoner near Atlanta in May 1865 but was granted parole two months later.

Bibliography: DuBose, John Witherspoon, *General Joseph Wheeler and the Army of Tennessee* (Neale, 1912); Dyer, John P., *"Fightin' Joe" Wheeler* (Louisiana State Univ. Press, 1941); Horn, Stanley F., *The Army of Tennessee* (Bobbs-Merrill, 1941).

Capt. James Sanders Day

WILKES, CHARLES (1798–1877)

U.S. naval officer, Wilkes was born in New York City. He had been at sea three years when he became a navy midshipman in 1818. His reputation as a naval scientist gained Wilkes the command of the U.S. Exploring Expedition in 1838. He returned in 1842 having circled the globe (in the last expedition to do so entirely by sail) and having brought back both valuable scientific data and a reputation as something of a martinet.

In 1861, while in command of the USS *San Jacinto* in the Caribbean, Wilkes boarded the British mail ship *Trent* and arrested Confederate envoys James Mason and John Slidell. Applauded in the North, Wilkes's action in the *Trent* Affair was nonetheless illegal and worsened relations between Washington and London. Later briefly in command of the James River Flotilla and then again of a squadron in the West Indies, the overly aggressive Wilkes continued to flaunt international law. Recalled in 1863 and court-martialed for insubordination a year later, Wilkes retired in 1866 and died in Washington, D.C.

Richard B. Meixsel

WILKINS, WILLIAM (1779–1865)

U.S. politician and secretary of war, Wilkins was born in Carlisle, Pennsylvania. A lawyer, banker, and judge, he became active in the Democratic party and served in a variety of state and federal positions before gaining a seat in the U.S. Senate (1831–34), where he supported Pres. Andrew Jackson during the nullification crisis. After resigning to become minister to Russia (1834–35), Wilkins returned to Congress as a representative (1843–44). As secretary of war (1844–45) for Pres. John Tyler, Wilkins promoted expansionist policies as he looked for ways to organize and acquire new territories, in particular advocating the annexation of Texas. Wilkins returned to local affairs during the 1850s, became a Pennsylvania state senator in 1855, and served as a major general in the Pennsylvania homeguard in 1862.

Matthew Oyos

WILSON, JAMES HARRISON (1837–1925)

U.S. military leader, Wilson was born near Shawneetown, Illinois. After graduating from West Point in 1860, he received a commission in the topographical engineers. During the first three years (1861–64) of the Civil War, he served the Union as an engineer and an inspector general in the eastern and western theaters.

On the recommendation of his friend Charles A. Dana, assistant secretary of war, Wilson came to Washington in 1864 to reorganize the Cavalry Bureau and its remount system. As a reward for his work in the bureau, he gained command of a cavalry division in the Army of the Potomac and then in Gen. William T. Sherman's cavalry corps. While in the west, Wilson played an important role in the Battle of Nashville and undertook a very successful large-scale raid into central Alabama in the closing weeks of the war. He particularly distinguished himself in the capture of Selma, Alabama. After the war, he oversaw navigation improvements on the Mississippi before resigning in 1870 and entering private business.

Wilson returned to active military duty in the Spanish-American War, where he saw service in both Puerto Rico and Cuba. He was then sent to China as the U.S. second in command during the Boxer Rebellion. After Wilson returned in 1900, he retired as a brigadier general in the regular army, receiving a promotion to major general in 1915.

Bibliography: Longacre, Edward G., *From Union Stars to Top Hat: A Biography of the Extraordinary General James H. Wilson* (Stackpole, 1972).

Richard F. Kehrberg

WOOL, JOHN ELLIS (1784–1869)

U.S. military leader, Wool was born in Newburgh, New York. In 1812, he raised a militia company in Troy, New York. He soon was commissioned a regular captain and fought with distinction at Queenston Heights (1812), where he was badly wounded. His gallantry at the Battle of Plattsburgh (1814) carried further promotion and appointment in 1816 as division inspector general. He later became inspector general of the U.S. Army (1820–41) and in 1836–37 supervised the removal of the Cherokee to Oklahoma. In 1841, Wool was promoted to brigadier general.

In the Mexican War, he led a celebrated 900-mile march from San Antonio, Texas, to support Gen. Zachary Taylor at Buena Vista, where Wool was second in command and for which he was brevetted a major general. At the outbreak of the Civil War, his actions as commander of the Department of the East (1857–61) secured Fortress Monroe and reinforced Washington. Wool was retired on disability in 1863.

Bibliography: Hinton, Harwood P., *"The Military Career of John Ellis Wool, 1812–1863"* (Ph.D. dissertation, Univ. of Wisconsin, 1960).

Lt. Col. (Ret.) J. W. A. Whitehorne

WORTH, WILLIAM JENKINS (1794–1849)

U.S. military leader, Worth was born in Hudson, New York. He began his army career in the War of 1812 and saw action at Chippewa and Lundy's Lane. From 1820 to 1828, he served as commandant of cadets at the U.S. Military Academy, and from 1841 to 1842, he led an expedition against the Seminole, breaking their resistance. During the Mexican War, Worth fought with Gen. Zachary Taylor's army at Monterrey and garrisoned the city of Saltillo. His leadership proved a key to victory at Monterrey and earned him a brevet as major general. He later distinguished himself with Gen. Winfield Scott's army during the campaign to Mexico City. In 1849, while commanding the Department of Texas, Worth died from cholera.

Matthew Oyos

PART III

Battles and Events

ADAMS-ONÍS TREATY (February 22, 1819)

Treaty between the United States and Spain in which Spain relinquished the Oregon Territory and its land east of the Mississippi River and in which the United States withdrew claims to Texas. After the 1803 Louisiana Purchase, the U.S. Pres. James Monroe's desire to obtain Florida from Spain increased, and, as secretary of state (1817–25), John Quincy Adams engaged Spanish minister Don Luis de Onís in a diplomatic duel to acquire the territory. When negotiations bogged down over Florida's western boundary, Maj. Gen. Andrew Jackson forced the issue. Ostensibly chasing Seminole Indians, Jackson and 3,000 men charged into Florida in March 1818 and captured virtually every Spanish post. Eschewing any apology, Adams instead demanded that Spain either properly occupy Florida or immediately cede the "derelict" province to the United States. Spain instructed Onís to abandon Florida for the best possible boundary between Louisiana and Mexico. In the subsequent Adams-Onís Treaty, Adams gave up claims to Texas but, thinking continentally, obtained a western boundary that ran northwest to the 42d parallel and then to the Pacific Ocean.

Bibliography: Bemis, Samuel F., *John Quincy Adams and the Foundations of American Foreign Policy* (1949; reprint, Greenwood Press, 1981); Hickey, Donald, *The War of 1812: A Forgotten Conflict* (Univ. of Illinois Press, 1989); Prucha, Francis P., *The Sword of the Republic: The United States Army on the Frontier, 1783–1846* (Macmillan Co., 1969; reprint, Indiana Univ. Press, 1979).

Stephen J. Lofgren

ALAMO, BATTLE OF THE (February 23–March 6, 1836)

Engagement between Texans and Mexicans, stemming from a December 1835 uprising when a remnant of Texas volunteers forced Mexican troops from San Antonio and occupied the Alamo, a former Catholic mission that had been used after 1801 as a military barracks. Some Texan leaders, especially Sam Houston, counseled the abandonment of the Alamo as indefensible with the small garrison available, but the troops refused to retreat.

After weeks of intelligence about a large army of Mexicans moving north, Gen. Antonio López de Santa Anna arrived in San Antonio on Feb. 23, 1836, with about 4,000 troops. The defenders included an estimated 187 men, many of whom were recent immigrants to Texas from the United States. Led by William B. Travis and Jim Bowie, colonels in the Texas army, as well as Tennessean Davy Crockett, these men held out for 12 days. On March 6, however, the Mexicans were successful in breaching the outer wall of the courtyard and overwhelmed the Texans. Santa Anna had directed that no prisoners be taken, and all of the defenders in the Alamo were killed. Estimates of Mexican casualties have been reliably estimated at 1,000 to 1,600.

The defense of the Alamo has been called the American Thermopylae. Although a defeat, it served the Texas Revolution. The number of Mexican casualties coupled with the length of time required to take the Alamo hurt Santa Anna's campaign enough to allow the Texans to rally. In addition, the defeat at the Alamo crystallized the Texan will to fight. At San Jacinto on Apr. 21, 1836, Houston surprised the Mexican army and captured Santa Anna, bringing an end to the revolution.

Bibliography: Binkley, William C., *The Texas Revolution* (Louisiana State Univ. Press, 1952); Long, Jeff, *Duel of Eagles: The Mexican and U.S. Fight for the Alamo* (Morrow, 1990); Tinkle, Lon, *Thirteen Days to Glory: The Siege of the Alamo* (McGraw-Hill, 1958).

Roger D. Launius

ANACONDA PLAN (1861)

Unrealized strategic plan for the early and total suppression of the Confederacy at the onset of the Civil War. To subdue the newly formed Confederacy, Winfield Scott, general in chief of U.S. forces, advocated a naval blockage of the Southern coast and proposed sending an expedition of 80,000 troops—20,000 by gunboat, 60,000 overland—down the Mississippi River. These combined actions would isolate the Confederacy by cutting off trade with Europe, isolating neutral Mexican ports, and preventing cattle and cereal commerce from Texas, while Union diplomats sought to prevent foreign recognition. Scott, a Virginia Unionist, believed that this political and economic envelopment would smother the rebellious flame, prevent needless bloodshed, and cause Southerners to petition for reinstatement.

Derisively dubbing Scott's strategy the "Anaconda Plan," critics claimed that he overestimated Southern Unionism and that time was too precious. Scott's 42-ship navy would be hard-pressed to shut down 5,000 miles of shoreline, Northern industry needed five months to build gunboats, and the Union army had only 18 companies east of the Mississippi River.

Exploiting the North's advantage in manpower and matériel, Scott's plan emphasized the overall importance of the Mississippi Valley. Nevertheless, when the Confederate capital moved to Richmond, northern Virginia became the primary theater of concern. Cries of "Forward to Richmond" prompted the Union army to advance into Virginia, and the First Battle of Bull Run (July 21, 1861) marked the demise of the Anaconda Plan.

Bibliography: Foote, Shelby, *The Civil War: A Narrative,* vol. 1 (Random House, 1958); Hattaway, Herman, and Archer Jones, *How the North Won* (Univ. of Illinois Press, 1983); McPherson, James M., *Ordeal by Fire* (Knopf,

The horrible conditions and treatment of prisoners at the Confederate prisoner-of-war camp at Andersonville, Georgia, led to the war trial, conviction, and execution of its commander. (National Archives)

1982); ———, *Battle Cry of Freedom* (Oxford Univ. Press, 1988).

Capt. James Sanders Day

ANDERSONVILLE PRISON

Infamous Civil War prison, built and operated by the Confederacy for the last 14 months of the war. The system in force in both the Confederate and Union armies of exchanging or paroling prisoners of war broke down in 1863 when the South began to execute captured black soldiers and also permitted Confederate parolees who had not been properly exchanged to return to duty. The Union responded by refusing to release captured rebels, and the need for prison camps on both sides grew.

In November 1863, the Confederates selected a prison site near Andersonville, in Sumter Country, Georgia, to replace camps nearer Union lines in Virginia. The first prisoners arrived in February 1864, and the 16.5-acre compound—later enlarged to 26.1 acres—was soon overflowing with Union soldiers. By August, the camp (properly named Camp Sumter) held 33,000 prisoners, four times as many men as were held in any other Southern prison and far too many for the prison's confines.

The desperate wartime conditions throughout the South in general made the plight of the prisoners especially dreadful. Little food or medicine, abysmal sanitary conditions, prisoners who preyed on one another, and exposure to the elements combined to make Andersonville among the most horrific of the Civil War's prison camps, with a death rate of 29 percent. (A smaller prison at Salisbury, North Carolina, had a death rate of 34 percent. The worst prison in the North was at Elmira, New York, where 24 percent of the 12,000 inmates died.) At least 13,000 of the 45,000 men (all enlistees) imprisoned at Andersonville died there, making incarceration more deadly than the battlefield for many Union soldiers. Held responsible for Andersonville's particularly inhumane conditions was the camp's commandant, Swiss-born Capt. Henry Wirz (1823–65), who became the only Civil War participant executed for war crimes.

Richard B. Meixsel

ANTIETAM, BATTLE OF
(September 17, 1862)

Civil War engagement that stopped Gen. Robert E. Lee's first invasion of the North; the bloodiest one-day battle in U.S. military history; also known as Sharpsburg. Following the Confederates' withdrawal from the South Mountain passes on the evening of Sept. 14, 1862, Lee concentrated his army on high ground west of Antietam Creek near Sharpsburg, Maryland. On September 16, the 20,000-man command of Lt. Gen. James Longstreet was on the field. The other wing of the Army of Northern Virginia, under Maj. Gen. Thomas "Stonewall" Jackson, also about 20,000, was accepting the federal surrender at Harpers Ferry, 17 miles to the south.

McClellan's Disadvantages. The Union Army of the Potomac under Maj. Gen. George B. McClellan arrived on the east side of Antietam Creek on September 16. McClellan had at his ready approximately 85,000 troops. In addition to the apparent numeric advantage, McClellan knew that Lee's forces were split, since a copy of Special Order No. 191 had fallen into his hands, thus giving McClellan basic knowledge of Confederate troop dispositions. Because the outnumbered Lee had his back to the Potomac River, the Army of the Potomac could be expected to push the Confederates into the river and bring the war to a speedy conclusion.

However, other circumstances conspired against the certainty of Union success. McClellan had an amalgam of commands thrown together to repulse the invasion. Besides the troops from the Washington defenses, he commanded the II, V, and VI Corps of the original Army of the Potomac of the Peninsular Campaign; the I and XII Corps of the Army of Virginia, recently defeated at Second Bull Run; Gen. Ambrose E. Burnside's IX Corps; and the Kanawha Division. Not only had this new army never campaigned together, half of McClellan's corps commanders were new

During the Battle of Antietam, Union general Ambrose Burnside's initial attempts to cross this bridge (now called Burnside's Bridge) over Antietam Creek were met by Confederate fire. (U.S. Army Military History Institute)

to that level of command. The federals also faced natural obstacles. McClellan would have to funnel his army across Antietam Creek at a few sites, some of which would be covered by Confederate fire. Once across, his men would have to maneuver over convoluted terrain, which did, in fact, break up formations and cause other confusion during the battle.

Finally, the Union was faced with the barrier of McClellan himself. He had done an excellent job at pulling together the diverse organizations now under his command and marching them to the front. However, McClellan was not an outstanding field commander. His cautiousness, coupled with his fear that Lee outnumbered him, set the tone for the battle. This was further exacerbated by his failure to inform properly his subordinate commanders as to his plan of battle. Consequently, at Antietam, the Union tactical initiative devolved into a series of piecemeal assaults and was unable to achieve proper concentration of forces at any one point.

Lee's Advantages. Conversely, Lee overcame his handicaps by exploiting several advantages, not the least of which was his army. Although poorly equipped, its morale was high. All summer, the Army of Northern Virginia had been defeating the federals in one battle after another. Organizationally, Lee had a more experienced command structure than his opponent. His army was divided into two wings (later designated as corps) under the able leadership of Generals Longstreet and Jackson. Also, Lee's artillery included a reserve battalion that was unattached and could be called to any part of the field when needed. This was opposed to the Union army, which had an artillery reserve that was basically an administrative entity under the tactical control of brigade and division commanders. This caused the Union to miss a number of opportunities to concentrate their guns and break through the Confederate lines. Lee also had terrain on his side. He held the high ground around Sharpsburg and enjoyed excellent interior lines. The Hagerstown road, which paralleled 75 percent of his lines, enabled him to shift troops quickly to meet the various Union threats.

Battle Preparations. On September 16, Jackson arrived from Harpers Ferry and with the divisions of Lt. Col. John R. Jones and Brig. Gen. Alexander R. Lawton, augmented by those of Brig. Gens. John B. Hood and John G. Walker, took up positions about 1.5 miles north of the town in the West Woods, the Cornfield, and the East Woods. Meanwhile, Maj. Gen. A. P. Hill's "Light Division" remained at Harpers Ferry processing the paroles of the captured Union garrison. Maj. Gen. Daniel H. Hill's division was placed on the high ground to the north of the Boonsboro road. Lee's extreme left flank was guarded by Maj. Gen. Jeb Stuart's horse artillery on Nicodemus Heights, less than 0.5 mile northwest of the West Woods. Jackson's right was equally well bracketed with the artillery reserve battalion under Col. Stephen D. Lee, positioned on a rise of ground east of the Dunkard Church. Elements of Longstreet's command were placed east and south of Sharpsburg facing Antietam Creek. Meanwhile, the divisions of Maj. Gens. Richard H. Anderson and Lafayette McLaws prepared to march from Harpers Ferry to Sharpsburg. That evening, McClellan directed Maj. Gen. Joseph Hooker's I Corps and Maj. Gen. Joseph K. F. Mansfield's XII Corps to cross Antietam Creek via the Upper Bridge, with intentions of striking the Confederate left the next morning. Elements of the I Corps skirmished with Hood's division until dark; then both sides rested and prepared for the next day.

Numerous actions took place on various parts of the field throughout September 17, but the Battle of Antietam generally is considered in three basic phases: the morning phase, on the northern end of the battlefield; the midday phase at Sunken Road and Piper Farm; and the afternoon phase at the Lower Bridge and south of Sharpsburg.

Morning. The action began around 8:00 A.M. on the Confederate left. There, the I Corps struck the Confederates in the Cornfield and East Woods. Jackson struck back with numerous counterattacks, and Hooker's artillery caused horrendous casualties by concentrating direct fire on the Confederates in the Cornfield. When the XII Corps arrived on the field, the I Corps attacks were beginning to peter out and Hooker had been wounded. XII Corps commander Mansfield was mortally wounded when he rode toward a Confederate skirmish line he mistook for friendly troops. Although the XII Corps was able to drive the Confederates across the Hagerstown pike, it was too small to continue the advance.

After a lull in the fighting, Maj. Gen. Edwin V. Sumner's II Corps came on the field at approximately 9:00 A.M. In the smoke and confusion, this command was split. Sumner himself led the division of Maj. Gen. John Sedgwick toward the West Woods. The divisions of Brig. Gens. William H. French and Israel B. Richardson moved through Mumma and Roulette farms toward Sunken Road. Meanwhile, the Confederates reorganized in the West Woods. Stuart's artillery moved to a ridge behind the woods, and McLaws's division, fresh from Harpers Ferry, moved north on the Hagerstown road on a collision course with Sedgwick's left. What followed has been called the "West Woods Massacre." The Union left was completely enveloped by McLaws. Simultaneously, the Union front was hit by heavy fire. Those federal units able to clear the woods were met with plunging fire from Stuart's guns. In about 20 minutes, 40 percent of Sedgwick's division were casualties. The remnants fled the field. Thus ended the morning phase. In less than 4 hours, more than 12,000 men had become casualties.

Midday. The battle now shifted to the Confederate center at Sunken Road. Earlier that morning, D. H. Hill's division had moved into this old eroded farm lane that served as a natural trench. Behind them in support was the division of Brig. Gen. George B. Anderson and several Confederate batteries. Hill had fewer than 5,000 men to oppose nearly 10,000 federals. The remaining two divisions of the II Corps attacked separately. French's division struck first. This division was formed on the march to Antietam and included one brigade of new recruits. After several attempts to take the lane, French's men fell back and exchanged volleys with the Confederates. However, heavy casualties and low ammunition caused the attack to lose momentum.

By now, Richardson's division was striking Hill's right. The Confederates may have been able to hold the lane had it not been for a misunderstood order. Hill directed one of his regiments to move out of the land to help cover his right from the Union enfilade. In the confusion, other units followed suit, and soon the entire line was withdrawing from the lane. A rout ensued, and the Confederates dissolved back to Piper Farm. The battle might have ended here in a Union victory, but when Richardson was seeking reinforcements, he was mortally wounded. His absence left a field of exhausted federals sorely in need of his aggressive command. The casualties at Sunken Road were nearly 3,000 suffered by the North and more than 1,500 by the South, including Anderson, who died one month later. As grim testimony to the carnage, the battle site has since been known as "Bloody Lane."

Afternoon. Meanwhile, on the southern end of the field, Burnside's IX Corps had spent the morning attempting to cross Antietam Creek and turn the Confederate right. These efforts were hampered by about 400 Confederate sharpshooters on the opposite shore supported by 2 batteries. Burnside has been criticized for becoming fixated on the Lower Bridge, the stone structure that crossed the Antietam in this sector; however, the steep creek banks would have made the crossing of men burdened with arms and equipment and under hostile fire very costly. Therefore, the bridge became his primary goal.

The federals got across about 1:00 P.M. By then, the Georgians were running out of ammunition, and part of the IX Corps, having crossed downstream at Snavely's Ford, were threatening their flank. The Confederates fell back toward the town. The IX Corps numbered around 12,000 and could have easily crushed Lee's frayed right, but Burnside's advance delayed for two hours to replenish ammunition and bring up fresh reinforcements. The attack resumed at around 3:00 P.M., but in a timely action, A. P. Hill's division, Lee's final reinforcements, arrived from Harpers Ferry, driving the federals back to the creek. By around 5:30 P.M., the battle ended a tactical draw. Union losses were 2,010 killed, 9,416 wounded, and 1,043 captured or missing. Confederate losses have been estimated at 1,587 killed, 8,725 wounded, and 2,000 captured or missing.

Consequences of Battle. Lee had lost more than 25 percent of his force, leaving him with fewer than 25,000 men available for combat, as opposed to McClellan's available strength of almost 50,000 including nearly 25,000 fresh troops of the V and VI Corps, most of whom had been held in reserve. Despite this advantage, McClellan did not attack on September 18. Late that night, the Confederates withdrew across the Potomac. McClellan did not

At Antietam, the bloodiest battle of the Civil War with no clear victory for either side, more than 3,500 men were killed. (Library of Congress)

pursue. A disgusted President Lincoln relieved him of command less than two months later. Lee's retreat from Maryland, however, gave Lincoln the impetus he needed to issue the Emancipation Proclamation (September 22). Many historians feel it also dashed any Southern hopes for European recognition.

Bibliography: Luvass, Jay, and Harold W. Nelson, eds., *The U.S. Army War College Guide to the Battle of Antietam: The Maryland Campaign of 1862* (South Mountain Press, 1987); Murfin, James V., *The Gleam of Bayonets: The Battle of Antietam and Lee's Maryland Campaign, September 1862* (A. S. Barnes, 1965); Sears, Stephen W., *Landscape Turned Red: The Battle of Antietam* (Ticknor and Fields, 1983); U.S. War Department, *War of the Rebellion: A Compilation of the Official Records of the Union and Confederates Armies,* series 1, vol. 19, parts 1 & 2 (1880–1901).

Ted Alexander

APPOMATTOX CAMPAIGN
(March 29–April 9, 1865)

Civil War operation that culminated in the Confederate surrender that ended the war. Although Richmond, Virginia, had been redeemed through the winter of 1864–65 by the stout defenses around Petersburg, it became clear as spring arrived that Gen. Robert E. Lee would have few advantages when the fighting resumed. Short of supplies and outnumbered almost two to one, Lee became convinced that the best chance to achieve a decisive victory would be to break out of Petersburg with the bulk of his army and join up with Gen. Joseph E. Johnston's troops in the Carolinas. There, the combined armies would confront Gen. William T. Sherman, then cutting his way up the coast from Savannah, and, presuming victory, would return to Virginia and deal with Gen. Ulysses S. Grant.

Fort Stedman. To execute Lee's plan required a breakout from the Petersburg trenches. Lee called upon Maj. Gen. John B. Gordon to select the point of assault. The young general chose Fort Stedman and several outlying Union batteries as the target of the assault, with barely 150 yards of no man's land separating them from the nearest Confederate positions. If successful, Lee would be able to push his army to sever the rail line that provided for the remainder of the Union line south of Petersburg. Planning was performed in the greatest detail. Handpicked detachments of axmen were assigned to cut down the wooden obstacles between the lines. Other groups were advanced solely to employ captured artillery against the Union forces. The bulk of the remaining forces, almost half of Lee's strength at Petersburg, were to exploit any breakthrough in the lines, with the intent of rolling up the Union flank.

The attack began before sunlight on Mar. 25, 1865. Quickly, and with little notice, the attackers forced their way past the surprised Union sentries and overwhelmed Stedman's garrison. Part of the attacking column moved south, and took two smaller positions, which had been garrisoned by Massachusetts and New York regiments. Flush with victory, the Confederates attempted to push north but found that the Union retreat had been halted and the blue lines bolstered by fresh troops from adjoining regiments. The sounds of battle alerted the Union troops occupying Fort Haskell, some 2,500 yards south of Fort Stedman, and they quickly responded with heavy artillery fire into the positions now occupied by the Confederates. Slowly, the Union forces sealed off the salient and began to retake the lost positions. By 8:00 A.M. it was clear that despite the extensive preparations, the attack had failed, and the retreat was sounded. Lee had lost more than 2,500 men and had nothing to show for it. On March 26, he notified Confederate president Jefferson Davis that Richmond could no longer be defended. The end of the Confederacy was at hand.

Five Forks. To bring the war to a conclusion, Grant sought to capitalize on the mobility of Gen. Philip H. Sheridan's cavalry divisions. By attempting to flank the Confederate defenses to the southwest of Petersburg, Grant hoped to draw the rebels into a fight where the numerical advantage of the Union troops would be decisive. Both sides were hampered by heavy rains on March 29, but the Union troops continued to grope their way forward. Sharp clashes between the lead Union brigade commanded by Brig. Gen. Joshua L. Chamberlain and Confederate troops under Maj. Gen. Bushrod R. Johnson marked the advance of the armies. Chamberlain, who had led the 20th Maine at Gettysburg, was seriously wounded during the fighting but rallied his troops to hold the Union lines to the southeast of Five Forks just short of the Boydton Road.

Grant ordered the Union commanders to close with the enemy infantry. On March 30, the heavy rains continued, and the Union offensive was limited to reconnaissance toward Five Forks, which disclosed the location of the main body of Gen. George E. Pickett's troops. Ordered to attack by Lee, Pickett managed to maneuver his cavalry under Maj. Gen. Rooney Lee to the west of the Union lines, and they drove Sheridan's troopers back to the town of Dinwiddie, where fresh troops under Gen. George A. Custer finally repelled the enemy attacks.

Pickett's men also battled against Gen. Gouverneur K. Warren's V Corps across the Boydton Road. The battle seesawed during the day, but Confederate gains were merely temporary, as once again the redoubtable Chamberlain was called upon to lead his troops into combat. His small brigade regained the lost ground and, after fierce fighting, took up positions slightly in advance of where the Union troops had stopped the previous day. Grant called for an immediate attack by Warren's corps at daybreak. Unfortunately, the combination of Warren's exhausted men and the poor terrain were not anticipated. As the morning of

April 1 dawned, Warren's men were just beginning to move toward their assigned attack positions, while at the same time Pickett's men were withdrawing toward their entrenchments around Five Forks. There, the Confederate lines formed a rough "L," with the long leg running west-east along the White Oak Road, then turning north and continuing toward Hatcher's Run.

As the opportunity for a successful engagement slipped away, Sheridan directed Warren to strike at the point of left flank of the Confederate line, while Sheridan's cavalry would pin down the Confederate center and right. To execute the complicated plan required quick movement of troops and excellent coordination of effort. By late afternoon, as the movement progressed, the bulk of the Union troops unintentionally maneuvered too far north and missed the intended target. Sheridan, livid with rage, charged his horse ahead of the Union lines, waving his personal standard to rally the troops. Farther north, Warren was also in the lead of his troops, urging them on to the attack. Sheridan's cavalrymen to the south and west executed their tasks flawlessly, and the error in disposition soon turned to advantage as the Confederates found themselves being attacked from three sides. Quickly, the Confederates fell back in disarray, with more than half of Pickett's men either prisoners or casualties. Although the battle was a clear Union victory, Sheridan blamed Warren for the miscoordination. Warren was relieved from command of V Corps and reassigned. (After the war, a court of inquiry found his actions to be beyond reproach, but by then Warren's career had been ruined.)

The Final Offensive. The lines around Petersburg were active on April 1 as well. Union troops were prepared for another assault on the Confederate lines to the south and west of the city. On April 2, the Union forces under Gen. George G. Meade cracked the western line of trenches and strongholds and advanced against the city. Lee recognized his position as untenable and by noon was planning for a complete withdrawal of his troops from around Petersburg and Richmond. He planned to assemble his scattered command at Amelia Courthouse, some 35 miles to the west. In Richmond, the government hastily evacuated what it could from the treasury and other key offices. What could not be moved was burned, and the ensuing conflagration almost completely destroyed the town. Lee's forces withdrew west, followed by two armies—Grant's and the legion of noncombatants fleeing Richmond.

Upon his arrival at Amelia Courthouse, Lee found that the rations so carefully stockpiled in Richmond had not been moved west. Foragers from the regiments turned up little, and the Army of Northern Virginia continued its westward march. Sheridan's cavalrymen kept a constant pressure on the flanks of Lee's column, and Grant's infantry followed in close pursuit. At Sayler's Creek, Sheridan's troops cornered Lee's rear guard, and more than 6,000 Confederates were taken prisoner, including Lt. Gen. Richard S. Ewell and Lee's eldest son, Maj. Gen. George W. C. Lee.

Lee's Surrender. On April 7, Grant sent a demand for surrender to Lee, but the Confederate general had one last chance. If he could reach Appomattox Station, where provisions were waiting for his army, he might still manage to escape with the bulk of his forces. However, Sheridan's men led by Custer reached the railhead on the following morning, and Lee drew up the remnants of his command around the village of Appomattox Courthouse, a few miles to the north of Appomattox Station. On April 9, Lee found himself cut off to the south by Sheridan and from the north by the federal II and VI Corps. With no options left, a truce was called and Lee sought terms of surrender from Grant. The two generals met that afternoon, and Lee surrendered the Army of Northern Virginia. The remaining Confederate troops were to be paroled and allowed to return home with, as Lee and Grant had agreed, their mules and horses. On the morning of April 12, the Confederate regiments formed up and marched down the road toward Appomattox. Lining the route were the men of Chamberlain's brigade. As the Confederates drew up, Chamberlain ordered his men to shoulder their arms. Recognizing Chamberlain's action as an honor, Gordon returned the gesture by raising his sword then touching the tip of the weapon to his toe. Gordon called out a command, and his men shouldered their weapons as well. The Confederates then stacked their arms, folded their battle flags, and, no longer soldiers, made their way back to their homes across the South.

Bibliography: Nine, William G., and Ronald G. Wilson, *The Appomattox Paroles April 9–15, 1865* (H. E. Howard, Inc., 1984); Rodick, Burleigh C., *Appomattox: The Last Campaign* (1965; reprint, Olde Soldier Books, 1988).

2d Lt. R. John Warsinske

ATLANTA CAMPAIGN
(May 1–September 8, 1864)

Civil War campaign during which the Union's Gen. William T. Sherman advanced west-to-east across Georgia to split the Confederacy. Sherman entered Georgia in May 1864 with more than 100,000 Union troops. His command consisted of the Army of the Tennessee under Maj. Gen. James McPherson, the Army of the Cumberland commanded by Maj. Gen. George Thomas, and Maj. Gen. John Schofield's Army of the Ohio. On May 4, Sherman launched an attack against Gen. Joseph Johnston's Army of Tennessee, hoping to destroy the Confederate army at Dalton, Georgia, with a flanking movement through Snake Creek Gap.

Johnston, who had replaced the martinet Braxton Bragg, brought fresh life to his command of 45,000. The improved morale and Johnston's ability to take advantage of prepared defenses and rough terrain blunted all Union frontal assaults. McPherson's attack on Resaca through Snake Creek Gap, however, caused Johnston enough concern that he fell back into entrenchments around the town.

Resaca. Maj. Gen. Leonidas Polk's Army of Mississippi reinforced Johnston's contingent at Resaca, raising Confederate manpower to nearly 60,000. Sherman realized Confederate ranks would continue to swell as they moved back toward Atlanta. He also saw his own army dwindling as he left units behind to protect extended supply lines. Sherman opted for a major attack on Resaca, hoping to destroy Johnston once and for all. For three days (May 13–15) the federals pounded Confederate lines in a game of push and shove. Even though Johnston repulsed Sherman's main force, he was again forced to retreat; McPherson's army was behind him, threatening to cut off the rail lifeline to Atlanta.

Kingston. At Kingston, Sherman tried to pin Johnston down with McPherson's and Thomas's forces while wheeling Schofield's smaller army around the Confederate right. Johnston saw this as his opportunity to hit the isolated Army of the Ohio. Both Polk and Gen. John Bell Hood argued against any offensive action, however, believing it to be too risky. Johnston acquiesced and followed their advice to pull back yet again.

New Hope Church. As Johnston withdrew, Sherman again tried to run his flank by launching an assault at Dallas, Georgia. Johnston, ever the defensive tactician, cut him off in a three-day running battle at Dallas and New Hope Church. Gaining no advantage in the battles, Sherman saw little hope of moving his armies along the small country roads west of Atlanta. He swung McPherson and Thomas back to the east as Schofield held the corner. Johnston just as adeptly pulled his forces back to the railroad. He anchored his defenses on Kennesaw Mountain, just outside Marietta.

Kennesaw Mountain. Three weeks of rain (which began with a spectacular thunderstorm during the last day of fighting around New Hope Church) had turned the countryside to mud. Union soldiers grumbled about marching too much during this war of maneuver and complained even more about marching in the heavy mud. Sherman saw little chance of continuing rapid movement in quagmiry roads and fields. By June 25, his lines were thin trying to cover the Confederate front, and he expected Johnston's to be even thinner. Sherman felt the time had come for an all-out assault. Because the Kennesaw Mountain fortifications were extensive, he assumed they would be lightly held in order to put more manpower on the Confederates' weaker left. He was wrong.

On June 27, Thomas's Army of the Cumberland climbed the mountain under the intense Georgia sun and even more intense rebel fire. According to one Southerner, "They seemed to walk up and take death as coolly as if they were automatic or wooden men." The frontal attack resulted in more than 3,000 Union casualties. Johnston lost about 500. Sherman once more reverted to flanking his enemy, and his soldiers no longer grumbled about marching.

Johnston was frustrated at constantly being flanked and decided to pull back into prepared entrenchments along the west bank of the Chattahoochee River. Sherman sent Schofield's army (now on the Union left) upstream to find a crossing for another end run. As they forded the river, they surprised a cavalry security force detached to guard the crossing. The fighting once again forced Johnston to pull back.

As Johnston's army retired to the Atlanta fortifications, Sherman rested and prepared his forces for an assault on the city. The battle of wits between these two men finally ended on July 17, when Confederate president Jefferson Davis replaced Johnston with Hood, a change of command that pleased Sherman. Grant had given Sherman the task of destroying the Army of Tennessee three months before, but Johnston had never given him an opportunity. Hood was more aggressive, if not reckless.

Peach Tree Creek. As Thomas's 20,000 men crossed Peach Tree Creek on July 20, Hood perceived an opening between Union armies and sent Gen. William Hardee's 20,000 rebels to meet them. During an intense two-hour onslaught, Thomas continued to rally his men and quickly filled gaps as they appeared. He lost 1,600 men in the battle but sent the Confederates back to their lines with 2,500 casualties of their own. Unmoved by this loss (in fact, Hood claimed Hardee lacked aggressiveness in the battle), Hood pulled the same unit out of the line and moved them south out of Atlanta, then turned them east to strike McPherson's left flank. On the morning of July 22, Hardee's weary corps began the Battle of Atlanta.

Battle of Atlanta. Looking into the city, Sherman viewed the lack of activity as an indication Hood had evacuated. The sound of cannon and musket fire from the east broke the spell as he realized the Confederates were hitting his extended left flank. Sherman could do nothing but wait for word from McPherson, who was killed early in the battle. As Hardee's troops pressed attack after attack, the federals had to scramble from one side of their earthworks to the other for protection from waves of Confederates coming from every direction. Gen. John Logan managed to rally the Union soldiers by riding along the line shouting, "Will you hold this line for me? Will you hold this line?" With reinforcements, the men responded with an intensity that blunted Hardee's attack and caused Hood to call for a withdrawal. The battle cost Hood 8,000 men. Again, Sherman sent the Army of the Tennessee on another of its long marches, drawing them around to the west behind his other

Although Union losses were far greater than Confederate losses at Kennesaw Mountain, the Confederates were forced to retreat. Shortly thereafter, Confederate Pres. Jefferson Davis replaced Johnston with Gen. John Bell Hood. (U.S. Army Military History Institute)

two armies. As they pulled into position on July 28, Hood struck once more. He hit the lines hard at Ezra Church, but was once again repulsed with a loss of 5,000 men.

Jonesboro. As Sherman continued his wheeling movement to the west, Hood sent forces to prevent his reaching the tracks of the Macon railroad at Jonesboro. Hood's army attacked on August 31 but were repulsed. Schofield and Thomas took the town, isolating the Southern army from the rest of the Confederacy, and Hood was forced to evacuate Atlanta the next day.

For almost four months, Sherman had driven first Johnston then Hood from Tennessee nearly to Macon. Although he finally captured Atlanta, he never completed his mission of destroying the Army of Tennessee. Hood would soon swing west and begin his own campaign to drive Union troops back out of Tennessee as Sherman made his march to the sea.

See also Sherman's March to the Sea.

Bibliography: Catton, Bruce, *This Hallowed Ground* (Doubleday, 1956); ———, *Never Call Retreat* (Doubleday, 1965); Johnson, Robert U., and Clarence C. Buel, eds., *The Way to Appomattox, Battles and Leaders of the Civil War,* vol. 4 (Yoseloff, 1956); Johnston, Joseph E., *Narrative of Military Operations* (Indiana Univ. Press, 1959); Sherman, William T., *Memoirs of Gen. W. T. Sherman* (Webster & Co., 1891).

Capt. Michael J. Reed

BALL'S BLUFF, BATTLE OF (October 21, 1861)

Relatively minor but much-publicized Civil War engagement in the vicinity of a precipice in the northeast tip of Virginia, on the Potomac River. In October 1861, Union general George B. McClellan dispatched Gen. Charles P. Stone to Poolesville, Maryland, to command a Potomac crossing. On October 21, one of Stone's subordinates, Col. Edward D. Baker, crossed the Potomac in force without previous reconnaissance nor with sufficient ferrying capacity. To cover this precarious crossing, Stone dispatched an

Railroad tracks in battle-torn Atlanta after being destroyed by Union artillery in 1864. (U.S. Army Military History Institute)

additional brigade across at Edwards Ferry in a feint to draw enemy attention.

The Confederate commander, Gen. Nathan G. Evans, undeceived by Stone's ruse, moved to engage Baker's disembarking troops, and battle ensued at 12:30 P.M. On poor defensive ground, the Union flanks were steadily pushed back and outflanked, trapping the Union brigade with their backs against the 100-foot-high bluff. Baker was killed during the late afternoon fighting, and a desperate breakout bid to Edwards Ferry was crushed. By 6:00 P.M., the Union troops had been pushed back to the riverbank, where evacuation began. The final Confederate assault overran the last defense line, and many Union soldiers drowned swimming to the Maryland shore. Organized resistance had ceased by 7:00 P.M. Total Union losses were 921 (49 killed, 158 wounded, and 714 missing or captured), well over half the brigade strength. Confederate losses totaled 149 (33 killed, 115 wounded, and 1 missing), about 9 percent of those engaged.

Bibliography: Patch, Joseph D., *The Battle of Ball's Bluff* (Potomac Press, 1958).

Russell A. Hart

BENTONVILLE, BATTLE OF (March 19–21, 1865)

Indecisive Civil War engagement fought two miles south of Bentonville, North Carolina. Confederate general Joseph E. Johnston, commanding the Army of Tennessee, found the isolated left wing of Gen. William T. Sherman's Union Army of Georgia. Johnston attacked the federal forces in an attempt to prevent the juncture of Sherman's and Gen. Ulysses S. Grant's armies. On Mar. 19, 1865, after skirmishes the previous day, federal units under Maj. Gen. Henry W. Slocum attacked the Confederate forces. The Confederates counterattacked and pushed the 14th Army Corps back onto the entrenched 20th Army Corps. The Confederate attack faltered in dense woods. Skirmishes occurred on March 20, and on the following day, united federal forces attacked. A Confederate counterattack stabilized the line, allowing Johnston's forces to slip away toward Raleigh, North Carolina.

Capt. George B. Eaton

BIG BETHEL, BATTLE OF (June 10, 1861)

First land battle of the Civil War and part of the operations around Fort Monroe, Virginia. On June 10, 1861, federal forces under Brig. Gen. E. W. Pierce attacked Confederate positions at Big Bethel. Confusion marked the federal attack. Not knowing the password, the 7th New York, under Col. John E. Bendix, fired on the 3d New York in the predawn dark. The situation was further confused as some federal troops wore gray, the color of the Confederate uniforms. The gunfire led forward federal troops to believe the enemy was in their rear while simultaneously alerting the Confederates. Fighting behind field fortifications, the Confederates, under the command of Col. John B. Magruder, lost 11 of their 1,408 soldiers while inflicting 76 casualties on the approximately 4,400 federals. The battle itself had little military significance, but Magruder won immediate renown throughout the South, and the Confederate victory was particularly inspirational at this early stage of the war.

Capt. George B. Eaton

BLACK HAWK WAR (April–July 1832)

Armed hostility between the United States and the Sac and Fox Indians. Increasing white settlement in the 1820s resulted in the removal of the Sac and Fox into Iowa. Disillusioned with conditions in Iowa, Sac chieftain Black Hawk was eager to believe suggestions that other tribes and even the British would support his reoccupation of northwestern Illinois. In April 1832, he recrossed the Mississippi River with 1,800 followers. U.S. troops immediately converged on the band. With no Indian or British support forthcoming, Black Hawk attempted to flee and then surrender. Nervous militiamen fired on the band sparking an Indian retreat into Wisconsin. After a series of rearguard actions, Black Hawk's band reached the Mississippi near the mouth of the Bad Axe River. Here, in late July, Gen. Henry Atkinson's troops intercepted their attempt to cross the river. After a brief, bloody battle, Black Hawk's forces were suppressed and the war was ended.

Bibliography: Eby, Cecial, *"That Disgraceful Affair," the Black Hawk War* (Norton, 1973).

Richard F. Kehrberg

BRANDY STATION, BATTLE OF (June 9, 1863)

By most accounts, the first significant, as well as the largest, cavalry battle of the Civil War, fought between the Union Army of the Potomac's Cavalry Corps (under Brig. Gen. Alfred Pleasonton) and the Confederate Army of Northern Virginia's cavalry (under Maj. Gen. Jeb Stuart) at Brandy Station, Virginia. In late spring 1863, the Confederate cavalry was concentrated at Brandy Station in the interim between the Chancellorsville and Gettysburg campaigns. The Union commander, Maj. Gen. Joseph Hooker, correctly anticipated a major cavalry raid by Stuart and sent Pleasonton, supported by 3,000 infantry, to disperse Stuart's forces. Having conducted a cavalry review on June 8, Stuart was surprised by Pleasonton on the following morning. The resulting clash was essentially a draw, with the Confederates suffering at least 485 casualties and the Union 866.

Bibliography: U.S. War Department, *The War of the Rebellion: A Compilation of the Official Records of the Union and Confederate Armies,* series 1, vol. 27, pt. I (U.S. Govt. Printing Office, 1889).

Jonathan M. House

BUENA VISTA, BATTLE OF (February 22–23, 1847)

Mexican War battle that ended Mexican threats against the lower Rio Grande. While a Mexican victory probably would not have changed the final outcome of the war, the U.S. victory at Buena Vista in northeastern Mexico left the Mexicans with no military options in the area except for guerrilla operations.

When the military actions of 1846 did not force the Mexican government to the peace table, U.S. president James Polk determined to launch an expedition under the command of Maj. Gen. Winfield Scott to capture Mexico City. Maj. Gen. Zachary Taylor's northern theater was deemphasized, and he was ordered to assume the defensive. Scott pulled almost half of Taylor's force from him, leaving Taylor with approximately 5,000 men, almost all of whom were unblooded volunteers.

Santa Anna's Strategy. On Jan. 13, 1847, a U.S. courier was ambushed and killed, and Mexican general Antonio López de Santa Anna learned of Taylor's weakness. He decided to attack at Saltillo, 8 miles north of Buena Vista. Santa Anna marched his force north from San Luis Potosí across more than 200 miles of arid wasteland. A total of 21,553 men plus 21 artillery pieces departed San Luis Potosí between January 27 and February 2. Almost all were green troops, except one regiment of crack hussars and the elite Regiment of Engineers. Santa Anna intended to conduct the main battle at a time and place where the Mexican advantage in numbers would be decisive, drive the U.S. forces back across the Rio Grande, and then turn south to deal with Scott's invasion. With this thinking, he failed to recognize that the U.S. forces would choose the battleground as long as they remained on the defensive.

Taylor's Strategy. Taylor, ignorant of Santa Anna's plans, moved his forces 17 miles south of Saltillo through Buena Vista to Agua Nueva, which offered a better campsite. On February 16, Santa Anna's advance screen met a U.S. patrol in the vicinity of Encarnación. His main body of more than 15,000 arrived at Encarnación on February 18–19. Within another day, they were discovered and thoroughly scouted, after which Taylor elected to withdraw to a position at Angostura.

Angostura, five miles south of Saltillo and just over one mile south of Buena Vista, held excellent defensive possibilities. Taylor allowed Brig. Gen. John E. Wool to make the dispositions since Taylor was unfamiliar with the ground. Wool took advantage of the terrain. He stationed artillery, supported by infantry on two nearby hills, at the narrowest portion of a plateau. A second line formed along a ridge to the rear of the first. Cavalry covered the gap from the left of the line to the mountains, and Wool held two squadrons of regular dragoons and one company of Texans in reserve.

The Battle. On February 22, Santa Anna deployed his forces for battle. He placed his strength in the center. On his right, he deployed his light infantry, a cavalry brigade, and two batteries on high ground that enfiladed most of the U.S. line. His left was covered by the Regiment of Engineers with three 16-pounders, and he had one infantry division in reserve. The placement of his artillery batteries was of particular importance since their mobility was extremely limited.

The attack began at approximately 3:30 P.M. with a series of skirmishes as Mexican light infantry under Gen. Pedro de Ampudia advanced along the slopes of the mountains. Dismounted U.S. cavalry units extended to keep pace with the Mexicans, and after an afternoon of fighting, both sides rested in place with neither having gained an advantage.

Santa Anna reinforced his right during the night and renewed the attack at dawn on February 23. Wool reinforced his own left as well, but the weight of the Mexican assault gradually forced the U.S. troops back. A concurrent assault on the U.S. right was broken up by concentrated artillery fire. Santa Anna then launched his main attack at the U.S. center. The U.S. units broke and ran, exposing their supporting artillery, which lost a four-pounder in the subsequent retreat.

The steady Mexican pressure continued on the U.S. center. A magnificent slow withdrawal exposed the cavalry units on the mountain slopes, who also had to withdraw. These withdrawals allowed Mexican cavalry to turn the flank and threaten the weakly held supply point at the

Buena Vista hacienda. While Taylor merely observed, Wool fought to reestablish control of his men and the battlefield. The U.S. position appeared critical, but Wool's new line was actually still fairly strong.

The Mexican cavalry attack at the hacienda was broken up by a few stalwart volunteers aided by more devastating artillery fire. On the main battlefield, Santa Anna reorganized his forces and pushed forward onto the plateau. In fierce fighting, the Mexican advance was inexorable. Two more U.S. guns were lost, and at this critical juncture, Capt. Braxton Bragg arrived with his battery, having moved from the U.S. right. As the Mexicans bore down on his guns, Taylor ordered, "Double-shot your guns and give 'em hell, Bragg." Bragg's volleys broke the Mexican advance for the last time and to all intents ended the fighting. While Santa Anna retained a superiority in numbers, he and his men had lost the will to fight. Of the 4,594 men with Taylor, 264 were killed, 450 wounded, and 26 were reported missing. Mexican losses were much higher: 591 killed, 1,048 wounded, and 1,894 missing. Taylor chose not to counterattack, believing such an action beyond the capability of his volunteers.

Analysis. The Battle of Buena Vista was a series of disjointed actions under only nominal control of either commander. Most historians agree the decisive factor was the steadfastness, expertise, and unparalleled mobility of the U.S. artillery. While Santa Anna's plan was strategically sound, his battlefield execution left much to be desired. Taylor's shortcomings as a commander were almost as great, but he relied upon the expertise of his subordinate commanders. While his deficiencies in the art of war were apparent, his ability to inspire his men was his strongest attribute. His steadfast physical and mental courage gave them a rallying point that cannot be overlooked in its importance. A more skillful commander might have achieved a greater triumph. In the final analysis, however, a more decisive U.S. victory would not have obviated Scott's campaign nor changed the course of the rest of the war.

Bibliography: Bauer, K. Jack, *The Mexican War: 1846–1848* (Macmillan Co., 1974); Esposito, Vincent J., ed., *The West Point Atlas of American Wars; Vol. 1: 1689–1900* (Praeger, 1978).

Capt. Karen S. Wilhelm

BULL RUN, FIRST BATTLE OF (FIRST MANASSAS) (July 21, 1861)

First serious engagement of the Civil War, a decisive victory for the South and a demoralizing defeat for the North. Public opinion in the North expected a quick resolution to the secession crisis, epitomized by the popular cry, "On to Richmond" (the Confederate capital). The Union commander, Gen. Irvin McDowell, pressed by Pres. Abraham Lincoln, sent 28,000 men toward Manassas, Virginia, about 25 miles southwest of Washington, where the Confederate general P. G. T. Beauregard blocked the sole railroad from Washington to Richmond. Most of McDowell's troops were 90-day volunteers whose enlistments would soon expire. Civilians, including congressmen and their families, followed the Union army to Manassas in a holiday atmosphere.

The Confederate forces of 32,000 waited behind Bull Run, a tributary of the Potomac River. The federals arrived on June 18 but were too undisciplined for battle, so McDowell trained them for three days.

The rival commanders had been classmates at West Point, so it was not surprising that they planned the same tactics—feint at the enemy's right and move the main attack around his left. On July 21, the Union forces attacked. The Confederates spotted them from Signal Hill but were late beginning their own attack, so the fight developed on the Confederate left, Union right.

The attack hit the Stone Bridge, and the Confederate troops retreated to the Henry House, where Gen. Thomas Jackson stood firm before an apparent Union victory and earned the nickname "Stonewall." Shortly, Gen. Kirby Smith's fresh rebel brigade arrived and hit the Union's vulnerable right flank. This, coupled with a general push along the front, caused the Yankees to fall back. Exploding Confederate artillery shells along the line of retreat, and anticipation of rebel cavalry, turned soldiers and spectators into a frightened mob rushing back to Washington. The Union army lost 2,645, the rebels 1,981. For two days, stragglers limped into Washington.

Bull Run was the first of many examples on both sides of failing to exploit an advantage; in this case, the Confederates were too disorganized to follow up. Confederate president Jefferson Davis arrived in the afternoon but would not authorize an advance on Washington because he planned a defensive war. Some feel that Bull Run was a turning point of the war because it was the last time the South could have captured something valuable—Washington—and exchanged it for recognition of independence.

Few military historians study this battle, one of the most important in U.S. history, because it was a meeting of mobs. The outcome had broad and pivotal effects: The North woke up to the reality that this war would not be won quickly, nor with volunteers. The South received some aid from Europe, but the victory at Bull Run reinforced the Southern notion that "one rebel could whip four Yankees," which led to overconfidence. McDowell lost his command as a result of the defeat. Lincoln, deeply humiliated, resolved to lift himself and the Union out of defeat.

Lynn L. Sims

BULL RUN, SECOND BATTLE OF (SECOND MANASSAS) (August 29–30, 1862)

Third of four battles fought in the Second Bull Run Campaign of the Civil War. By early August 1862, Confederate forces had successfully driven Maj. Gen. George B.

Confederate troops under Gen. P. G. T. Beauregard decisively defeated Union troops commanded by Gen. Irvin McDowell at the First Battle of Bull Run in July 1861. Initial action took place at the Stone Bridge. (U.S Army Military History Institute)

McClellan's army from the Peninsula in front of Richmond, Virginia, but Gen. Robert E. Lee had failed to destroy his enemy. Other Union armies under Gens. Irvin McDowell, Nathaniel P. Banks, and John C. Frémont had been likewise unsuccessful in clearing the Shenandoah Valley of Confederates under Maj. Gen. Thomas "Stonewall" Jackson. The federal war department consolidated these forces as the "Army of Virginia" and to command it brought from the western theater Maj. Gen. John Pope, the recent commander of the Army of the Mississippi at Island No. 10.

Pope's primary mission was to relieve pressure on McClellan by covering Washington and disrupting Confederate lines of communication, thus permitting McClellan's army to capture Richmond. McClellan, however, met with a series of reverses serious enough to force his withdrawal from the Peninsula in early August. He then assumed command of the defenses of Washington.

In mid-July, General Lee, fresh from his Peninsular victories, had sent Jackson to protect the railroad at Gordonsville in north-central Virginia. Pope also moved, and Jackson, threatened by federal cavalry, continued northward and forced a battle at Cedar Mountain on August 9. In late August, Lee settled on a plan that would eradicate a now-consolidated Union force—Pope with 75,000 men north of the Rappahannock River. Lee split his 54,000-man army, sending Jackson with half the force on a flanking march around Pope's right. He attacked the Union supply depot at Manassas Junction, about 60 miles northeast of Gordonsville, forcing Pope to meet the impending threat in his rear. Pope's position was discovered at the August 28 engagement at Groveton (Brawner's Farm). Following this battle, he ordered the Army of Virginia to concentrate at Bull Run, a battlefield of the previous summer.

First Day. Pope moved the army on Jackson, who had 18,000 men and 40 guns behind an abandoned railroad embankment south of Sudley Springs. The Army of Virginia was committed piecemeal, one division at a time. Gens. Franz Sigel, Robert H. Milroy, and John F. Reynolds were ordered to attack at dawn on August 29. Pope anticipated crushing Jackson before the arrival of Lee, then falling back to Centreville, just northeast of Manassas, to await the remainder of the Confederate army. The morning attacks and three more throughout the day failed, leaving the Union left flank weakened and vulnerable.

Pope, with reinforcements due, ordered Maj. Gen. Fitz-John Porter on the Union far left to move on the Confederate right flank. Unbeknown to the federal commander, Lee and Gen. James Longstreet, with 30,000 men, had arrived near midday and extended the Confederate right. Porter moved as far as Dawson's Branch, encountered

Longstreet, deployed, and informed an unbelieving Pope that the new enemy troops had arrived. Pope, thinking Porter had reached Gainesville and possessed a clear approach to Jackson, renewed his order to attack, an order that Porter received at 6:30 P.M. Porter commenced an advance but never carried out the attack because of approaching darkness.

Second Day. Overnight, the Confederates abandoned the advance lines they had taken during the day and took the original railroad embankment positions. As dawn broke on August 30, Pope, not seeing the enemy in their original line, assumed they had retreated and wired that information to Washington. At noon, he ordered a vigorous pursuit to be spearheaded by Porter's corps.

Porter, followed by Reynolds, moved down the Warrenton Turnpike; Gens. James B. Ricketts and Samuel P. Heintzelman were to move in concert via the Sudley Springs (Haymarket) Road. The force had not far advanced when they discovered that Pope had seriously miscalculated the enemy's location. The Confederate line, some four miles long and reinforced by artillery, overlapped Pope's, which extended for only three miles. Longstreet on the Confederate right overlapped Pope's left, and Porter attacked the enemy's right. Confederates responded with galling rifle fire against three separate Union attacks, the last time resorting to rock throwing when they ran out of ammunition. Pope began to withdraw troops from his left to reinforce Porter on the right, which paved the way for a successful assault by Longstreet, whose men captured Bald Hill, on which the federal left rested.

Failing to retake Bald Hill, Pope ordered Henry House Hill on his right center reinforced. At 4:00 P.M., Lee ordered a general advance on the seemingly impenetrable Henry House Hill, and Pope began reinforcing his left flank from the right, weakening the right so much that Jackson was able to rush forward and crush it. The Confederate attacks were, however, only partially successful largely because Jackson's men were worn down from hard marching prior to the battle and could not keep pace with Longstreet's more rested troops. Darkness and heavy rain brought an end to the battle, and Pope began a confused retreat back to Centreville. Troops from McClellan's command arrived from Washington, but they were too late to provide any reinforcement.

Lee next ordered Jackson to exploit the weakened federal right with a move on Chantilly, just northeast of Centreville. Here on September 1, Jackson advanced and attacked, the results being a draw more than a clear-cut victory. The Battle of Chantilly did, however, bring to a conclusion the Second Bull Run Campaign, a campaign that cost Pope his command and cleared the way for Lee to move north toward Pennsylvania. Lee's conduct of his army at Second Bull Run (better known to the Confederacy as "Second Manassas") broke all accepted principles of warfare of the day. Leaving his capital defended by a sparse force, he split his outnumbered army in the face of the enemy and won with a much lower casualty rate than that of his opponent. He was, however, unable to exploit fully his victory. For the North, Second Bull Run became yet another costly lesson of the war. Pope enjoyed some small successes during the campaign and battle but was unable to overcome the effects of a weak command structure.

Bibliography: Hennessy, John, *Historical Report on the Troop Movements for the Second Battle of Manassas* (Nat. Park Serv., 1985); Stackpole, Edward J., *From Cedar Mountain to Antietam, August–September, 1862* (Stackpole Books, 1959).

Louise Arnold-Friend

CARNIFEX FERRY, BATTLE OF (September 10, 1861)

Early Civil War engagement in what is now West Viginia. The Union forces of Maj. Gen. George B. McClellan established a firm foothold in Virginia's northwestern counties by midsummer 1861. While his green recruits no doubt received assistance from the largely pro-Union inhabitants of the area, their occupation was eased greatly by a lack of cohesion of Confederate forces in the region.

Brig. Gens. John B. Floyd and Henry A. Wise were subordinate to Gen. Robert E. Lee by August, but they functioned virtually independent of him and of each other. During August, Floyd moved his 2,600-man command up the Kanawha River Valley toward Union forces who were, by then, commanded by Brig. Gen. William S. Rosecrans. The Union officer attacked Floyd on September 10 at Carnifex Ferry on the Kanawha. Nightfall, compounded by the exhaustion of Rosecrans's troops, halted the federal advance. Floyd, outnumbered almost three to one, used the darkness to evacuate his troops across the ferry, which he then destroyed.

Bibliography: Lowry, Terry, *September Blood: The Battle of Carnifex Ferry* (Pictorial Histories, 1985).

Louise Arnold-Friend

CARTHAGE, BATTLE OF (July 5, 1861)

Early Civil War conflict in southwestern Missouri, 148 miles south of Kansas City, in which 4,000 Confederate troops under Gen. James E. Rains and Mosby M. Parsons, accompanied by Gov. Claiborne F. Jackson, indecisively skirmished with 1,500 Union troops under Col. Franz Sigel. Sigel, in an attempt to block the southward retreat of Governor Jackson, advanced on the morning of July 5, 1861, to Coon Creek Ridge in an attempt to take the enemy by surprise. Rapidly in danger of being outflanked by the numerically superior enemy, Sigel retired in good order across the creek and then across the Spring River into Carthage.

Bibliography: Snead, Thomas L., *The Flight for Missouri* (Scribner's, 1886).

Russell A. Hart

CEDAR MOUNTAIN, BATTLE OF
(August 9, 1862)

Civil War engagement fought at the base of Cedar Mountain, Virginia, during the Second Bull Run Campaign, in which Maj. Gen. Thomas "Stonewall" Jackson defeated a Union force under the command of Maj. Gen. Nathaniel P. Banks. On July 13, 1862, Jackson began a march from Mechanicsville, Virginia, in an attempt to stop Maj. Gen. John Pope's move south to the Rapidan River. Finding himself outnumbered, Jackson waited until reinforced by Maj. Gen. A. P. Hill. Jackson then decided to attack Banks's forces before they could be reinforced by Pope. Jackson was surprised by a determined attack by the smaller Union force.

The battle opened with an artillery duel. Jackson became overly involved in the artillery battle and failed to place his forces correctly. A federal attack led by Brig. Gen. Samuel W. Crawford struck a seam in the Confederate line and threatened to roll up Jackson's entire left flank. The Confederate position was saved only after Jackson personally drew his sword and led a charge supported by Hill's forces.

The Confederates lost 241 killed and 1,120 wounded of over 22,000 effectives. The federals lost 314 killed, 1,445 wounded, and 622 missing of approximately 12,000. Crawford's brigade of 1,767 alone lost 494 killed and wounded and 373 missing.

Capt. George B. Eaton

CERRO GORDO, BATTLE OF
(April 18, 1847)

Mexican War battle fought on the site of a mountain pass in eastern Mexico, between Veracruz and Jalapa. In April 1847, after landing his expeditionary force in Mexico, Gen. Winfield Scott brought forces inland to confront Mexican leader Antonio López de Santa Anna. Santa Anna had established extensive fortifications, manned by several thousand men and 19 cannon, overlooking Cerro Gordo, a deep ravine through which passed the National Road to Mexico City. After a reconnoiter of the area, on April 17, Scott sent a force around the fortifications to cut the Mexican supply line. Unsuccessful in this action, on April 18, Scott ordered another attack using flanking movements to overcome the opposition. The Battle of Cerro Gordo lasted about three hours, after which the Mexican defense began to crumble and troops began to flee the battlefield. About 3,000 Mexicans were captured, but casualty figures are unknown. The United States suffered 431 casualties out of 8,500 engaged.

Bibliography: Bauer, K. Jack, *The Mexican War, 1846–1848* (Macmillan Co., 1974).

Roger D. Launius

CHANCELLORSVILLE CAMPAIGN
(April–May 1863)

Civil War operation that culminated in a two-day battle that effected a Confederate victory but resulted in the subsequent death of Lt. Gen. Thomas "Stonewall" Jackson. Maj. Gen. Joseph Hooker assumed command of the Union's demoralized Army of the Potomac on Jan. 26, 1863. Hooker immediately began to revitalize and reorganize the army. Gen. Robert E. Lee's 60,000 men in the Confederacy's Army of Northern Virginia (ANV) occupied fortified positions in the vicinity of Fredericksburg, a northeastern Virginia city on the Rappahannock River.

Hooker's Campaign Plan. Hooker developed a plan to force the ANV to withdraw and provide the 130,000-man Union army the opportunity to threaten Richmond, the Confederate capital, 50 miles south of Fredericksburg. Hooker planned for three corps to march upriver from their encampment near Falmouth (less than 2 miles northeast of Fredericksburg), turn southeast, and cross the Rappahannock and Rapidan Rivers. This Union turning movement would envelop Lee's Fredericksburg position. To divert Confederate attention, Hooker planned for Maj. Gen. John Sedgwick and two corps to demonstrate against Confederate positions at Fredericksburg. Hooker hoped to deceive the enemy further by leaving another force encamped near Falmouth within sight of Confederate pickets. He assigned his cavalry corps the mission of attacking deep behind Lee's front. The plan, if properly executed, promised great results. It would place Lee's army, outnumbered two to one, between two converging forces, forcing Lee either to withdraw or fight a difficult battle.

Initial Union Success. The march upriver began on April 27. Sedgwick's demonstration started on April 28, and the Union plan initially worked well. By noon on April 30, the three Union corps had crossed the river and converged just west of Fredericksburg, on the nondescript crossroads known as Chancellorsville. Instead of pressing on through the heavily forested area known as the Wilderness, Hooker ordered his army to concentrate and occupy defensive positions. Hooker thereby surrendered the temporary advantage gained from the Union turning movement. In addition, occupying defensive positions in the Wilderness forfeited Union superiority in manpower and firepower.

Despite being heavily outnumbered and flanked, Lee did not withdraw. His army retained an advantageous central position between the two wings of Hooker's army. In addition, Lee's cavalry consistently provided Lee key intelligence information as to Union positions. On April 29, Lee had sent one division west toward Chancellorsville in order to establish contact with and observe the Union positions.

Hooker ordered the Union advance to continue about midday on May 1. By this time, however, Lee had decided that Sedgwick's demonstrations were part of Hooker's deception effort, and Lee ordered Jackson's corps to reinforce the Confederate position near Chancellorsville. Jackson left a reinforced division of 10,000 men to defend the Confederate positions at Marye's Heights near Fredericksburg. Hooker's advancing troops met heavy resistance in the woods, and Hooker ordered a withdrawal back to Chancellorsville. That evening, the five Union corps occupied a strong defensive position. The right flank, anchored on no terrain features, lay open to attack.

Jackson's Flank March. Lee decided to attack Hooker's right flank with Jackson's corps. This entailed great risk for Lee, however, as it meant dividing his command of about 45,000 men in the presence of a larger force. Early on May 2, Jackson's force of 26,000 men began a 12-mile road march to attack the open Union right flank. Lee remained with 17,000 men to hold Hooker in place.

Hooker had decided to allow Lee to attack the Union army behind its growing breastworks. Nonetheless, the Union army did not sit idly by as Jackson's corps marched across its front. Reports of the movement led Hooker to believe initially that Lee's force was moving against the Union right. Hooker authorized a minor attack by Maj. Gen. Daniel E. Sickles's III Corps, which harassed the rear guard of Jackson's column. Hooker also sent orders to Sedgwick to attack and seize Fredericksburg. Nonetheless, the Union right flank still remained relatively unprepared to defend against a major attack. Despite Hooker's earlier warning, little preparation had occurred, and Hooker never inspected the defenses.

Jackson's Attack. The road march and attack deployment against the Union right took the entire day. Jackson's attack began about 5:00 P.M. and routed the forward federal units. The Confederate attack stalled as darkness fell, and Union defenses stiffened amidst the thick foliage. In the darkness, Confederate troops fired on Jackson and his reconnaissance party. Jackson was hit three times and eventually lost his left arm. Command of his corps passed to Maj. Gen. Jeb Stuart, Lee's cavalry commander.

The federal units reorganized that night. On May 3, Hooker still had the tactical advantage. His main force at Chancellorsville faced an enemy army divided into three parts, none of which were mutually supporting. Hooker, however, had by this time lost his aggressiveness. Hooker ordered Sickles to fall back from his positions on the dominant terrain at Hazel Grove. The Confederate artillery moved onto Hazel Grove and then supported the subsequent attack by Stuart's (Jackson's) corps and the two divisions controlled by Lee. About 11:00 A.M., Hooker ordered a Union withdrawal, and this withdrawal allowed Stuart's and Lee's forces to link up.

Sedgwick's Defeat. Meanwhile, Sedgwick attacked and seized Fredericksburg. He continued the attack west toward Chancellorsville, about 12 miles away. After Hooker withdrew northward into a well-entrenched defensive position, Lee decided to divide his army once again in order to attack Sedgwick. He left Stuart with 25,000 troops to contain Hooker's 75,000. Lee attacked Sedgwick's force late on May 4 while Hooker sat passively. Sedgwick's units withdrew across the Rappahannock that night. During the evening of May 5, Hooker's force withdrew across the river, thus ending the campaign.

Results. The Army of the Potomac suffered more than 17,000 casualties, the Army of Northern Virginia almost 13,000. Lee's losses, however, were tougher to replace. Jackson died of pneumonia on May 10.

This battle has become known as "Lee's greatest victory." Lee beat an army twice the size of the ANV through the bold use of maneuver and surprise. Lee maintained the initiative as opposed to the hesitant and vacillating Hooker. Hooker's failure to capitalize on his initial success and numerical superiority cost the Union army dearly.

Bibliography: Adams, Michael, *Our Masters the Rebels: A Speculation on Union Military Failure in the East, 1861–1865* (Harvard Univ. Press, 1978); Bigelow, John, Jr., *The Campaign of Chancellorsville* (Yale Univ. Press, 1910); Catton, Bruce, *The Army of the Potomac* (Doubleday, 1951–53); Douglas, Henry Kyd, *I Rode with Stonewall* (Univ. of North Carolina Press, 1940); Freeman, Douglas S., *Lee's Lieutenants: A Study in Command,* 3 vols. (Scribner's, 1942–44); Stackpole, Edward, *Chancellorsville: Lee's Greatest Battle* (Stackpole Books, 1958); Vandiver, Frank, *Mighty Stonewall* (McGraw-Hill, 1957).

Kevin E. McKedy

CHAPULTEPEC, BATTLE OF
(September 12–13, 1847)

U.S. assault on the 18th-century castle of Chapultepec, a Mexican stronghold three miles southwest of Mexico City, during the Mexican War. Having failed to achieve a negotiated settlement of the war following the August 1847 victories at Contreras and Churubusco, Gen. Winfield Scott took the offensive and resumed his advance on Mexico City. While it was clear that the U.S. Army was a more capable military force than that of the Mexicans, the terrain clearly favored the defenders. The approaches to the city consisted of a series of straight causeways crossing marshy plains. The causeways fed into several squares, or *garitas,* and these were defended by artillery and infantry behind walls and breastworks.

Some of Scott's engineers, including Capt. Robert E. Lee, found the southern approaches to the city to be most advantageous. Others, such as Lt. P. G. T. Beauregard, had surveyed the ground around the city in preparation for an assault; they felt that the western approaches to the city held the best opportunity for the attack, due in part to the Mexican general Antonio López de Santa Anna's decision to focus his defense along the southern approaches, which lay astride the most direct routes for the approaching U.S. troops. In a council of war on the morning of September 11, Scott weighed the advice from his staff and the key commanders and decided to attack from the southwest, take Chapultepec, and drive into the city along the western and southwestern approaches.

Chapultepec dominated the southwestern skyline. The 200-foot summit was crowned by the buildings of the Colegio Militar. With high walls and a commanding position, the fortress appeared impregnable. The approaches had been mined, and several artillery pieces had been emplaced. However, the position was undermanned, the walls had not been sufficiently reinforced to withstand bombardment, and the ramparts were not complete. To the west of Chapultepec stood Molino del Rey, scene of bitter, yet inconclusive fighting on September 8. Although U.S. soldiers had forced the Mexicans from the position, the attackers had lost almost 800 men and were ordered to withdraw from the advanced position by Scott. The fight at Molino del Rey set the tone for what was to come, as stories quickly spread among U.S. troops that the Mexicans had murdered defenseless prisoners.

The offense was scheduled to begin on the morning of September 13. To disguise his intentions, Scott ordered Gen. John A. Quitman's division to take up a position directly opposite Santa Anna's strong southern defenses but withdrew them during the night of September 12, to take up attack positions near Chapultepec. Scott had also ordered a preparatory bombardment of the castle that lasted that entire day. The barrage halted at nightfall but was resumed on the morning of September 13. At 8:00 A.M., the U.S. guns again ceased firing, as troops under Maj. Gen. Gideon J. Pillow attacked the west side of Chapultepec. Supported by a section of artillery under Lt. Thomas J. Jackson, the 11th and 14th infantry regiments moved to positions west of the castle and covered the advances of the 9th and 15th infantries as they made their way through swamps to the base of the castle. Inexplicably, the scaling ladders had not yet arrived, and the U.S. infantrymen traded musket fire with the castle's defenders until the arrival of the storming parties from Quitman's Pennsylvania and New York volunteer regiments.

As the storming parties assaulted the walls, the U.S. troops kept up a steady musket fire against the defenders. Slowly, the men on the ladders began to make headway against the defense, but casualties among the first wave were high. Still, the troops advanced, and the trickle of men became a flood. Inside the fort, the defenders were becoming desperate. Some of the Mexican troops broke and ran, but many stayed to the end. A handful of the cadets at the Colegio Militar, boys as young as 13, ignored the order for their withdrawal from the hill and fought to their deaths atop the hill. Santa Anna, now aware that the assault was not a feint but actually the main effort, was unable to reinforce the beleagured garrison. Quitman's soldiers tried to close the Mexican route of retreat into Mexico City, and while some defenders were able to escape, others chose to leap from the castle walls rather than face the U.S. troops, who, following the slaughter at Molino del Rey, were not inclined to grant quarter.

Little more than an hour passed from the first charge until the time the U.S. flag flew above Chapultepec. Although the way to Mexico City was open, the U.S. Army was still in for a hard fight. Mexican artillery pounded the U.S. columns as Quitman's troops pushed up the road toward the Garita de Belen. Other troops under Gen. William T. Worth pressed north until they reached Santo Tomas, then turned east and seized the Garita de San Cosme. By nightfall, Santa Anna's position was untenable, and he withdrew the remnants of his army from Mexico City, which was formally occupied by Scott on the morning of Sept. 14, 1847.

2d Lt. R. John Warsinske

CHARLESTON

City in southeastern South Carolina. An important Confederate seaport during the Civil War, Charleston was evacuated by the Confederacy after two years of siege. The task of seizing Charleston initially fell to Rear Adm. Samuel F. Du Pont. His earlier success in capturing nearby Port Royal (November 1861) convinced Union leaders in Washington that Charleston, too, could be taken by a strong naval force. Du Pont, however, harbored no illusions about the difficulties confronting him. When he reluctantly launched an attack on the morning of Apr. 7, 1863, the city's stout defenses poured such a barrage of fire into his nine ironclad steamers that at dusk he was forced to order their withdrawal. The next day, he called off the attack altogether; shortly thereafter, he was relieved of command.

Du Pont was replaced by Rear Adm. John A. Dahlgren. Unlike his predecessor, Dahlgren was supported by the army forces of Brig. Gen. Quincy A. Gillmore. Their first objective was Fort Wagner, an earthwork fortress that guarded the outer harbor's western entrance. Two assaults in July failed outright, but after two months of further bombardment, the defending garrison abandoned the fort on Sept. 7, 1863. The next day, Dahlgren and Gillmore launched badly coordinated assaults against Fort Sumter, but again the defenders held on, taking a heavy toll of Union soldiers and marines.

After that, the attack settled down into a protracted siege. For more than a year "Brave Charleston" held out, at last surrendering on Feb. 18, 1865, only when the overwhelming forces of Gen. William T. Sherman approached the city after their "March to the Sea."

Bibliography: Potter, E. B., ed., *Sea Power: A Naval Victory* (Naval Inst. Press, 1981).

Maj. Grant H. Walker

CHATTANOOGA CAMPAIGN
(October–November 1863)

Civil War campaign in Chattanooga, Tennessee, a key center of railroad operations and a vital link to the Union's westward progression to the Mississippi River. By securing Chattanooga, after a prolonged siege, Union forces opened a route to Georgia.

The Cracker Line. Maj. Gen. Ulysses S. Grant arrived in Chattanooga on Oct. 23, 1863, to replace Maj. Gen. William S. Rosecrans after his Army of Cumberland was defeated at nearby Chickamauga in September. The Union troops at Chattanooga were in dire straits due to lack of supplies. The men were on quarter rations and did not have enough ammunition for one day of fighting. Grant realized that a new Union supply line was needed, and, from a conference, Brig. Gen. William F. Smith emerged with a plan.

Smith's plan called for Brig. Gen. Joseph Hooker to cross the Tennessee River at Bridgeport (in the northeast corner of Alabama, three miles south of the Tennessee border), march northward, and take Brown's Ferry from the rear. Concurrently, Brig. Gen. George H. Thomas's troops would march toward the same point and join Hooker's forces to secure Brown's Ferry. The combined forces would then open Cumming's Gap, secure Kelley's Ferry, and take control of Raccoon Mountain. Grant ordered implementation of the plan with only one change: Smith, because of his familiarity with the plan, would lead Thomas's troops. The plan worked, and on October 27, the "Cracker Line" was opened and supplies started getting through.

By November 20, Grant's army was further reinforced when Maj. Gen. William T. Sherman's Army of the Tennessee arrived at Brown's Ferry. Grant wanted to start offensive operations immediately, but bad weather delayed him.

Bad weather turned into Grant's good fortune when, on November 22, a Confederate deserter came to Grant's camp and informed him that Confederate general Braxton Bragg had dispatched a division to Knoxville (115 miles northeast of Chattanooga) and was planning to withdraw from Chat-

Union transport boats are anchored on the Tennessee River at Chattanooga. (U.S. Army Military History Institute)

Union troops charged Missionary Ridge despite Confederate artillery fire from above; they reached the top only to find that the Confederate troops were breaking up and fleeing the attack. (U.S. Army Military History Institute)

tanooga and move his whole army there. Grant was skeptical but was reassured when, on the next day, Bragg dispatched both Maj. Gens. Simon B. Buckner's and Patrick R. Cleburne's divisions to Knoxville. Grant now realized that by immediately taking the offensive he would not only secure Chattanooga but would also relieve Maj. Gen. Ambrose E. Burnside.

Orchard and Bushy Knobs. On November 23, Grant ordered a probing attack against an outpost line just forward of Missionary Ridge. At approximately 1:30 P.M., Thomas's two divisions, from what appeared to the Confederates to be a pass-in-review, made a sudden dash across an open field and assaulted the surprised rebels. Thomas's troops took the outposts at both Orchard Knob and Bushy Knob and moved the Union cause one mile closer to Missionary Ridge. That night, Sherman's troops started moving across the Tennessee River to assume positions at the mouth of Chickamauga Creek.

Grant wanted the main attack to commence on November 24. He had Sherman's three divisions to the north, Thomas's two divisions in the center, and Hooker's three divisions on the south. By 1:00 P.M. on November 24, all of Sherman's forces had crossed the Tennessee and were ready to attack Cleburne's recalled forces on the north of Missionary Ridge.

Lookout Mountain. On the misty afternoon of November 24, Hooker's three divisions attacked Maj. Gen. Carter L. Stevenson's heavily outnumbered Confederate troops on Lookout Mountain. The rebels poured heavy fire down onto the attacking federals, but Stevenson was under orders to withdraw to Missionary Ridge if attacked. The federals eventually charged above cloud level to find the defender's retreating. During the night and the early hours of the next day, the rebels completed their withdrawal. By sunrise, the Union had won "The Battle above the Clouds."

Missionary Ridge. Grant's plan on November 25 was for Sherman to attack Bragg's right flank, forcing Bragg to reinforce the right, while Hooker attacked Bragg's left flank, forcing Bragg to reinforce the left. Thomas would be held in reserve to later attack the weakened center. On the northern flank, Sherman's infantry launched several fierce, but unsuccessful, attacks against Cleburne's division on Missionary Ridge. In more than eight hours of fighting, his troops made no appreciable gain.

Hooker was unable to put any pressure on Bragg's southern flank, as he was delayed getting across Chattanooga Creek, for the rebels had burned the only bridge crossing it during their retreat. At 3:30 P.M., Grant made a critical decision for Thomas to attack the center to take the pressure off Sherman's troops. The plan called for them to attack the Confederate fortifications at the base of Missionary Ridge, stop, regroup, and then attack the hill. Instead of obeying their orders, Thomas's divisions broke their ranks when the 112 Confederate artillery pieces rained down on them. They rushed headlong into the heart of the Confederate positions yelling "Chickamauga!" They completely overran the Confederate positions and kept running up Missionary Ridge. Grant and his staff watched from afar, waiting and hoping for the best.

By 4:30 P.M., Bragg lost control of his troops, and the Confederate lines retreated. Only nightfall saved the rebels from a more crushing defeat. Bragg offered no excuse for the poor performance of his troops and, on December 2, asked to be relieved of his command. The road into the heartland of the South was now open, defended only by the troops that were fleeing Missionary Ridge.

Analysis. The critical mistake that cost the Confederates this campaign was their misplaced breastworks. Instead of being placed on the military crest, they were placed on the highest elevation. By doing this, the rebels were unable to depress their fire enough to suppress the attacking Union army. This also rendered the Confederate infantrymen unable to fire their muskets without unduly exposing themselves to Union fire. Grant's only mistake was not pursuing the fleeing Confederates.

Of the 64,000 Confederate soldiers at Chattanooga, 361 were killed, 2,160 were wounded, and 4,146 were missing or captured. The Union's 56,000 soldiers suffered 753 dead, 4,722 wounded, and 349 missing or captured.

Bibliography: Esposito, Vincent J., ed., *The West Point Atlas of American Wars* (Praeger, 1978); Foote, Shelby, *The Civil War, a Narrative, Fredericksburg to Meridian* (Random House, 1963; reprint, Vintage, 1986); MacDonald, John, *Great Battles of the Civil War* (Macmillan Co., 1988).

Capt. Jeffrey S. Cohen

CHEROKEE, REMOVAL OF (1838)

U.S. government's westward displacement of thousands of Indians from Appalachia that resulted in a tragic attrition of the Cherokee nation. The discovery of gold in the north Georgia mountains and the white settlers' thirst for land led to demands for the relocation of Cherokee Indians from Georgia, Tennessee, Alabama, and North Carolina to federal territory in the West. Under the Treaty of New Echota (Georgia), signed in December 1835, the Cherokee agreed to leave within two years in return for $5,000,000 and other benefits.

Most of the tribe had not supported the treaty, and although a few hundred Indians departed voluntarily, thousands remained east of the Mississippi River. Pres. Andrew Jackson and his successor, Martin Van Buren, were neither sympathetic to the Indians' plight nor willing to antagonize state officials who demanded the Cherokee's departure.

Brig. Gen. Winfield Scott arrived in Georgia in the spring of 1838 to oversee the removal of 15,000 Indians. Seven thousand regular and militia soldiers joined him to round up the Cherokee, and while Scott was personally solicitous of the Indians' welfare, some soldiers and would-be settlers were less so. Many Indians lost their possessions and arrived destitute in detention camps.

The forced relocation of the Indians (to the present-day state of Oklahoma) began in June 1838 but was then delayed by drought and the difficulty of making the journey via the Tennessee River. Emigration resumed overland during the harsh winter of 1838–39. Many of the Indians had fallen ill in camp before leaving, and, with little food and insufficient clothing provided, roughly 4,000 died on the four-month trek westward—known to history as "The Trail of Tears."

Richard B. Meixsel

CHICKAMAUGA, BATTLE OF (September 19–20, 1863)

Civil War engagement in the northwest corner of Georgia, on a Tennessee River tributary, in which Union forces under the command of Maj. Gen. William Rosecrans were defeated by the Confederates under Gen. Braxton Bragg; the conclusive action of the Chickamauga Campaign, prelude to the Union's successful campaign for Chattanooga, Tennessee. On Sept. 18, 1863, Bragg was positioned east of Chickamauga Creek as Lt. Gen. James Longstreet's leading three Confederate brigades arrived. With these reinforcements in place, Bragg moved across the creek. However, Rosecrans's two corps of Unionists defended the banks of the Chickamauga so effectively that only a small number of Confederate troops successfully crossed. During the night, more Confederates quietly crossed over, and by the next morning, approximately three-fourths of Bragg's forces stood on the west bank of Chickamauga Creek.

Fighting ensued and lasted most of the day, but by sunset, the Union forces still controlled the roads to Chattanooga, just 15 miles north of Chickamauga. On the evening of August 19, Longstreet himself arrived with two more brigades. That evening, as Longstreet wandered through the woods looking for Bragg, Rosecrans dug in.

On the following morning, at approximately 9:00 A.M., Bragg attacked again. The Union forces held firm until Rosecrans received an erroneous report that indicated that one of his units was fighting unsupported. Consequently, he ordered other Union forces to reposition in support of the failing unit. Rosecrans's orders became confused in transmittal, and a unit engaged in combat was removed from the front lines. As this unit abandoned its position, it left in the Union line a gap that was readily recognized and filled by the attacking Longstreet. Most of the Union right flank dissipated and retreated toward Chattanooga. As

Rosecrans retreated to Chattanooga to organize for the defense of the city, approximately two-thirds of his army remained at Chickamauga under the command of Maj. Gen. George H. Thomas to repeal the attacks by the Confederate forces. As a result, Thomas and his unit, the U.S. 19th Infantry, would come to be known as the "Rock of Chickamauga."

Bragg would later conclude that a decision was not possible that day as his subordinates attempted to persuade him to pursue the retreating federals and recapture Chattanooga. However, the numbers of casualties absorbed by the Confederate forces (18,000) had taken its emotional toll on Bragg, and he allowed Thomas to retreat with no interference to a position from Missionary Ridge to Lookout Mountain. The following day, Thomas also retired to Chattanooga. Bragg received severe criticism from his subordinates for his failure to capitalize on the vulnerability of the retreating Rosecrans; nevertheless, the Confederates had indeed won a great victory.

Bibliography: Esposito, Vincent, ed., *The West Point Atlas of American Wars,* vol. 1 (Praeger, 1959); Matloff, Maurice, ed., *American Military History,* (Office of the Chief of Military History, U.S. Army, 1973).

Capt. Ralph P. Millsap, Jr.

CHURUBUSCO, BATTLE OF
(August 20, 1847)

Mexican War battle just outside Mexico City. During the drive of Gen. Winfield Scott's expeditionary force for Mexico City in August 1847, Churubusco represented the last significant engagement prior to the attack on Mexico City. Fighting a series of delaying actions, Mexican general Antonio López de Santa Anna had troops fortify both a Franciscan mission at Churubusco and the bridge over the Churubusco River. When the U.S. force arrived at Churubusco on August 20 tired from numerous skirmishes, high cornfields obscured the strength of the Mexican po-

The American offensive at the bridge over the Churubusco River was one of the last battles before the taking of Mexico City during the Mexican War. (U.S. Marine Corps)

sitions. Scott's troops were surprised by the stiff opposition of the Mexicans, but he brought up additional troops and mounted a frontal assault on both the bridgehead and the other Mexican fortifications.

Although the battle was soon lost by the Mexicans, it was one of their most persistent engagements of the war, and casualties were high on both sides. Santa Anna lost nearly a third of his force as either casualties or prisoners of war, and Scott suffered nearly 1,000 casualties. The Battle of Churubusco set the stage for the assault of Mexico City and the ending of the war.

Bibliography: Bauer, K. Jack, *The Mexican War, 1846–1848* (Macmillan, 1974); Ramirez, Jose Fernando, *Mexico During the War with the United States* (Univ. of Missouri Press, 1950).

Roger D. Launius

COLD HARBOR, (SECOND) BATTLE OF (June 3, 1864)

Brief and bloody Civil War conflict fought during a two-week military operation in Cold Harbor, Virginia. Cold Harbor was a vital road junction just northeast of Richmond. The armies of Gens. Robert E. Lee and Ulysses S. Grant, maneuvering against each other in May and June 1864, clashed at Cold Harbor on June 3. The Union's Army of the Potomac, numbering 108,000, confronted Lee's Confederate force of 59,000. The main federal assault began with three corps early in the morning. The frontal assault met heavy fire in front and on the flanks and, in a matter of minutes, was repulsed with the loss of 7,000 federals, compared to 1,500 Confederate casualties. The Union forces continued a costly offensive (against constant counterattack) for several days and then withdrew. (A previous battle at Cold Harbor took place in June 1862 and is better known as the Battle of Gaines's Mill, the third of the Seven Days' Battles.)

Robert H. Berlin

CONTRERAS, BATTLE OF (August 19, 1847)

Brief Mexican War engagement 14 miles southwest of Mexico City, in which U.S. forces under Gen. Winfield Scott prevailed. Scott's forces marched toward Mexico City in August 1847. Not far south of their goal they were unknowingly caught between the Mexican armies of Gens. Antonio López de Santa Anna and Gabriel Valencia. On the night of August 18, a violent storm raged, causing Santa Anna to retreat for cover at nearby San Angel. Despite orders to the contrary, Valencia chose to remain and quash the supposedly defeated Americans. At 3:00 A.M., Scott's men slipped out of their camp and fell upon the unexpecting Valencia at Contreras. In 17 minutes, the Battle of Contreras was over, with the U.S. force victorious, and the road to the Mexican capital was now open to Scott's advancing army.

M. Guy Bishop

CORINTH, BATTLE OF (October 3–4, 1862)

Civil War battle in the northeast corner of Mississippi, in which Gen. William S. Rosecrans's Union forces repulsed the Confederates under Gen. Earl Van Dorn. Situated 90 miles southeast of Memphis, Tennessee, Corinth, Mississippi, played an important part in the western campaigns of the war. On Oct. 3, 1862, 22,000 Confederate troops under Gen. Sterling "Pap" Price, returning from the Battle of Iuka (September 19), and his superior Van Dorn, clashed with the Union forces of Rosecrans outside Corinth. By 6:00 P.M., the Union troops had been pushed back in disarray to their rearward defense line. Van Dorn, though, elected to wait until morning to assault this strongly fortified line.

Although Confederate troops stormed both Forts Robinette and Powell and broke into the city in confused fighting the next day, Union reserves energeticallly counterattacked and routed the Confederate van, forcing a full Confederate retreat. Van Dorn was court-martialed for this failure but was acquitted by the court of inquiry.

Bibliography: Cockrell, Monroe F., ed., *The Lost Account of the Battle of Corinth and the Court Martial of Gen. Van Dorn* (McCowat-Mercer Press, 1955).

Russell A. Hart

DADE MASSACRE (December 28, 1835)

Tragic event that precipitated the Second Seminole War (1835–42). After receiving a series of U.S. government ultimatums to vacate their central Florida reservation, aggrieved Seminole Indians massacred a column of 108 U.S. soldiers led by Maj. Francis Dade. The December 28 attack occurred as Dade's column marched through the wilderness to reinforce the undermanned garrison at Fort King, an outpost 106 miles northeast of military facilities at Tampa Bay. Because his troops were in open country, Dade did not employ flanking parties, and because of an early morning rain, the soldiers had buttoned their overcoats over their guns and cartridge boxes. As a result, a salvo of at least 180 Indian guns, fired from a nearby stand of palmettos, instantly killed half of Dade's men. Only 4 soldiers survived the ensuing carnage.

Bibliography: Laumer, Frank, *Massacre!* (Univ. of Florida Press, 1968).

Maj. Peter R. Faber

DRAFT RIOTS, NEW YORK CITY (July 13–16, 1863)

Most spectacular draft protest of the Civil War. Opposition to the Union draft was common in the North. In New York

City, the poor and the foreign-born were angry over inflation and being forced to fight a war to free the slaves. These fears were aroused by Democratic newspapers and politicians, stimulating a violent response to the first draft call and prompting a combination draft and race riot. In mid-July 1863, mobs of Irish working men burned the draft office, homes of Republican leaders, and other buildings. The mob, numbering in the tens of thousands, attacked blacks in the city and burned down the black orphanage. The riot lasted four days until Union soldiers brought from Gettysburg halted it. Although inflated casualty figures are often cited, the death toll was likely about 120.

Robert H. Berlin

EARLY'S RAID (July 1864)

Diversionary attack on Washington, D.C., by Maj. Gen. Jubal Early, on behalf of the Confederacy during the Civil War. The successful advance of Union general David Hunter deep into the Shenandoah Valley to Lynchburg, Virginia (June 1864), led Confederate general Robert E. Lee to dispatch Early's II Corps to defend the city. Early's arrival persuaded Hunter to withdraw across West Virginia to the Kanawha Valley, taking his force out of the theater. This gave Early the chance to move against Washington, D.C., in the hopes of luring away some of the federal forces engaging Lee around Richmond.

Moving down the valley, Early thrust aside federal defenders at Winchester and Harpers Ferry, Virginia, and reached Frederick, Maryland. On July 9, just to the east of Frederick, the Union's Maj. Gen. Lew Wallace fought at Monocacy, a doomed delaying action that resulted in 1,880 federal and 700 Confederate casualties. Early pressed on to arrive at Silver Spring, Maryland, on July 11. His advance had created the desired effect, and federal reinforcements from Gen. Ulysses S. Grant's command could be seen entering Fort Stevens opposite the Confederates. After a brief skirmish, witnessed by Pres. Abraham Lincoln, Early withdrew across the Potomac River into Loudoun County, Virginia, then back to the Shenandoah Valley. He halted federal pursuit at the sharply fought Battle of Cool Spring on July 18. The strategic diversion had worked, luring at least two federal corps away from Grant's main effort.

Bibliography: Cooling, Benjamin F., *Jubal Early's Raid on Washington, 1864* (Nautical and Aviation, 1989).

Lt. Col. (Ret.) J. W. A. Whitehorne

EMANCIPATION PROCLAMATION

Declaration made by Pres. Abraham Lincoln during the Civil War that proclaimed the unconditional freedom of all slaves in seceded states. By the summer of 1862, Lincoln was beginning to realize that new steps would have to be taken in order to defeat the Confederacy. Lincoln and other Northern leaders had come to see slavery as a major bulwark of the Southern military effort. Slaves dug trenches and performed other duties that freed Southern white males for combat.

Although the president was personally opposed to slavery, he knew he would have to move prudently lest he offend the border states as well as most Northern whites. In March 1862, he proposed a plan for compensated emancipation that was strongly rejected by Congress. On July 22, 1862, he presented a preliminary emancipation proclamation to his cabinet that called for total uncompensated emancipation in those states still in rebellion. Sec. of State William Seward advised Lincoln to wait for a Union victory before announcing emancipation to the public; otherwise it would appear as an act of desperation by a Union government.

The nominal Union victory at Antietam (Sept. 17, 1862) gave Lincoln the impetus he needed to issue the proclamation. Conservative Republicans pleaded with him not to issue it. This was understandable since the preliminary proclamation caused a Republican defeat at the polls during that fall's elections. However, Lincoln signed the proclamation on Jan. 1, 1863, saying, "If my name ever goes into history, it will be for this act."

Since the Emancipation Proclamation freed only those slaves in states still in rebellion, Lincoln critics cite it as a purely pragmatic move by a shrewd politician. Admirers of the president say that it shows Lincoln's "growth" regarding the slavery issue. Partisan opinions aside, the Emancipation Proclamation changed the whole nature of the Union war effort from one of fighting just to preserve the Union to fighting to end slavery as well. It also influenced England to shy away from any attempt to recognize the Confederacy and opened the way for black enlistments in the Union army. Ultimately, it represented the first federally sanctioned step toward the abolition of slavery in the United States.

Bibliography: Oates, Stephen B., *Abraham Lincoln: The Man Behind the Myths* (Harper & Row, 1984).

Ted Alexander

FORREST'S TENNESSEE RAIDS (1862–1863)

Series of cavalry forays led by Confederate general Nathan Bedford Forrest during the Civil War. In February 1862, Forrest and his men escaped capture when the Union forces of Brig. Gen. Ulysses S. Grant beat the rebels at Fort Donelson in northwestern Tennessee. The following April, Forrest's battalion fought at Shiloh in southwestern Tennessee. His scouts reported boatloads of Gen. Don Carlos Buell's U.S. forces ferrying across the Tennessee River at Pittsburg Landing (Shiloh). Forrest tried unsuccessfully to warn Confederate general P. G. T. Beauregard. When he did not convince other Southern generals of the danger,

The Emancipation Proclamation, issued by Pres. Abraham Lincoln at the beginning of 1863, was considered by some just another strategy of war, because it said nothing about the slavery that existed in southern and border states that were still part of the Union. (U.S. Army Military History Institute)

Forrest predicted, "We'll be whipped like hell" in the morning.

In July 1862, Forrest's cavalry struck the Union army at Murfreesboro, Tennessee. It captured the garrison, wrecked the rail lines that supplied Buell, then swiftly escaped. As repair crews finished mending the damage, Forrest struck again. His unrelenting attacks stalled Buell's advance.

Beginning in December 1862, Forrest launched a second series of raids aimed at disrupting Grant's communications and supply lines between his primary base in Kentucky and his field operations in northern Mississippi. Although he inflicted some damage on the Mobile & Ohio Railroad and captured many prisoners, Forrest ultimately had to break off contact.

In September 1863, Forrest's cavalry supported Gen. James Longstreet at Chickamauga and Chattanooga. While Longstreet and Forrest urged pressing ahead with the battle at Chickamauga, Confederate commander Braxton Bragg moved cautiously. By November, the Southern forces yielded to Grant's constant pressure, and Tennessee fell.

Bibliography: Wyeth, John A., *That Devil Forrest* (Louisiana State Univ. Press, 1989).

M. Guy Bishop

FORT DELAWARE

Federally operated prisoner-of-war facility during the Civil War. Built as an earthen fortification on Pea Patch Island (in the Delaware River halfway between New Jersey and Delaware) during the War of 1812, Fort Delaware was gradually modernized to a six-acre masonry fort completed in 1859. Garrisoned throughout the Civil War, the fort was used to incarcerate Confederate military and "political" prisoners.

In late July 1861, 8 Southern soldiers, captured during the West Virginia Campaign, arrived at Fort Delaware. Over the next four years, more than 30,000 inmates would pass through the facility. The prison population generally hovered around 6,000, with occasional influxes; Confederates captured at the Battle of Gettysburg increased the numbers to 12,500. Overcrowding led to disease, resulting in nearly 3,000 deaths during the course of the war.

Bibliography: Brown, Ann L. B., "Fort Delaware: The Most Dreaded Northern Prison," *Civil War Quarterly,* vol. 10; Graham, Martin G., "The Immortal Six Hundred: Their Long Journey to Freedom," *Civil War Quarterly,* vol. 10.

Louise Arnold-Friend

FORT FISHER, SIEGE OF
(January 12–15, 1865)

Taking of a strategically situated Confederate stronghold by a Union naval force during the Civil War; also known as Terry's Expedition (in contrast to Maj. Gen. Benjamin F. Butler's failed assault on the fort the previous month). On Jan. 4, 1865, federal troops under Maj. Gen. Alfred H. Terry sailed for Fort Fisher at the mouth of the Cape Fear River in Wilmington, North Carolina. Adm. David D. Porter's fleet and Terry's force assembled 60 ships, but storms held them up until January 12.

On January 13, they opened fire and, in three days, fired 20,000 rounds. Unopposed, 8,000 Union troops landed above Fort Fisher and dug in facing Gen. Braxton Bragg's Confederate force in Wilmington. Maj. Gen. William H. C. Whiting, the Confederate district commander, reinforced the fort with 700 men, while Col. William Lamb, the fort commander, pleaded in vain for Bragg to attack the federals. On January 15, after more than 12 hours of naval bombardment and ground combat, the fort and 1,900 defenders were taken. About 500 Confederates had been lost, and the Union had sustained 1,300 casualties. Confederate troops destroyed nearby forts, by then untenable, and the last blockade-runner port closed.

Lynn L. Sims

FORT LEAVENWORTH

U.S. military post, comprising 8,000 acres in eastern Kansas. Established in the spring of 1827 on the bluffs above the west bank of the Missouri River, Fort Leavenworth is named for its founder, Col. Henry Leavenworth. The fort's original purpose was to protect traders and preserve peace with Indian tribes. The fort served as the starting place for Stephen W. Kearny's and Alexander W. Doniphan's expeditions during the Mexican War, as well as being a supply and replacement depot. The fort remained important owing to its location on both the Santa Fe and Oregon trails.

Fort Leavenworth was a garrison site during the Civil War. Following the war, the fort was headquarters for the Department of the Missouri, a supply depot, and home of the military prison established in 1875. In 1881, the U.S. Army created the School of Application for Infantry and Cavalry, the forerunner of the Command and General Staff College, at Fort Leavenworth.

Robert H. Berlin

FORT PILLOW "MASSACRE"
(April 12, 1864)

Reportedly brutal routing by Confederate soldiers of a Union navigation-defense post during the Civil War. In April 1864, Maj. Gen. Nathan Forrest, leading a Confederate cavalry raid, appeared before Fort Pillow, a fort on the Mississippi River 40 miles north of Memphis, Tennessee. Forrest, with 1,500 troops, demanded the surrender of the 557 Tennessee Unionists and black artillerists under Maj. Lionel F. Booth. Booth spurned surrender, and Forrest successfully attacked the fort. Once Fort Pillow was taken, Confederate troops continued to shoot Union soldiers, including many who tried to surrender. Federal casualties totaled 557, while the Confederates lost 100. The battle is still controversial, but it seems clear that Confederates shot a number of defenseless black soldiers. Forrest's part in this action remains unknown. The incident at Fort Pillow was widely publicized during the war.

Mark Pitcavage

FORT SUMTER, BATTLE OF
(April 12–13, 1861)

Initial military engagement of the Civil War. In December 1860, Maj. Robert Anderson, commander of Union forts in South Carolina's Charleston harbor, made a covert withdrawal of his garrison from Fort Moultrie to Fort Sumter, a five-sided brick fortress in the harbor's main channel. Confederate batteries were built up near Sumter, and on Apr. 10, 1861, Gen. P. G. T. Beauregard demanded the immediate evacuation of the fort. When Anderson declared that he would evacuate by midday April 15 (unless attacked or under new orders), Beauregard replied that he would open fire on April 12.

At 4:30 A.M., April 12, the Confederates fired their first shot. The first Union response was fired at 7:30 A.M., by Capt. Abner Doubleday; by afternoon, only six Union guns had been fired. In contrast, the Confederate bombardment was heavy—some 4,000 shells in 34 hours—and by the following afternoon, much of Fort Sumter was ablaze. When Anderson surrendered on April 13, his only casualties were two wounded. On April 14, the Union garrison evacuated to New York by ship.

Christine L. Stevens

FORTS HENRY AND DONELSON CAMPAIGN (February 1862)

Strategic Civil War operation in which the Union commenced its fission of the Confederacy's geographical seam. The close of 1861 found a beleagured Union government;

the public appeal for decisive action against the Confederacy evoked criticism of seemingly inactive federal field commanders. Officers such as Brig. Gen. Ulysses S. Grant complained of inferior arms, equipment, and support services, while their political and military superiors argued over the best way to conduct offensive operations against the insurgent South. Late in January 1862, Maj. Gen. Henry W. Halleck reluctantly approved a joint land and naval attack on two key Confederate fortifications in northwestern Tennessee, at the Kentucky border.

Fort Henry (on the Tennessee River) and Fort Donelson (on the Cumberland River) were located in the middle of a line defending the heartland of the Confederacy. Loss of these forts would open Union invasion routes into Kentucky and western Tennessee and points to the west and the south. Land forces under Grant and a naval flotilla under Adm. Andrew H. Foote were selected to move on the forts. On February 4, Foote's gunboats reached Fort Henry, and the two officers planned their strategy.

Confederate brigadier general Lloyd Tilghman had a scant 3,400 poorly trained troops to protect the unfinished, low-lying Fort Henry, as well as the nearby Fort Heiman, set on high ground but also unfinished. While Foote's gunboats bombarded the forts, Grant's soldiers approached via roads turned to mud by heavy rains. By the time Grant arrived, Tilghman had partially abandoned Fort Henry and had surrendered to Foote. Grant then turned his attention to Donelson.

After learning of the loss of Fort Henry, Gen. Albert Sidney Johnston sent close to half of his Confederate forces defending the region to Fort Donelson. Brig. Gen. John B. Floyd was to command the installation with nearly 20,000, assisted by Maj. Gen. Gideon J. Pillow and Brig. Gen. Simon B. Buckner. Grant's force of 15,000 arrived at the fort on February 12, and Foote steamed up the Cumberland with six gunboats two days later. Unlike at Fort Henry, Confederate guns at Donelson were on high ground, and their fire forced Foote to withdraw.

Despite the retreat of Union gunboats, Floyd determined that his troops could not hold the fort and that he could take the initiative. On February 15, his troops attacked and pushed Grant's lines back, opening an escape route toward Nashville. The triad command structure of the Confederate force at Donelson led to its downfall. Floyd refused to follow up his victory and would not begin a withdrawal. Grant took advantage of Confederate inaction and counterattacked, regaining most of his lost ground. That night, Floyd and Pillow decided to surrender but left command of the fort and all arrangements to Buckner. Some Confederate troops, including Floyd and Pillow, escaped across the river, while the hapless Buckner requested terms of surrender from Grant, who responded with his famous demand for "unconditional surrender."

The capture of Forts Henry and Donelson won Grant national attention and opened Kentucky and western Tennessee for Union occupation. Nashville fell on February 23. The path was now open for Union forces to split the Confederacy in two.

Bibliography: Cooling, B. Franklin, *Forts Henry and Donelson: The Key to the Confederate Heartland* (Univ. of Tennessee Press, 1987); Hamilton, James, *The Battle of Fort Donelson* (Yoseloff, 1968).

Louise Arnold-Friend

FORTRESS MONROE

U.S. stronghold situated at the tip of the Virginia Peninsula between the York and James rivers. Only 70 miles from Richmond (the Confederate capital during the Civil War), the post helped control Hampton Roads, the James River, Newport News, and the approaches to Richmond. Fortress Monroe was built in the 1820s in the mortar and brick design and had been the home of the U.S. Army's Artillery School until 1860. Considered an extremely strong position, it remained in federal hands throughout the war despite its location within the Confederacy. The fort served as a base of operations for the Peninsular Campaign (March–July 1862) and overlooked the site of the naval battle between the *Monitor* and the *Merrimac* (Mar. 9, 1862). Confederate president Jefferson Davis was imprisoned in Fortress Monroe on May 22, 1865.

Capt. George B. Eaton

FRANKLIN, BATTLE OF
(November 30, 1864)

Civil War engagement during Lt. Gen. John B. Hood's Tennessee invasion. The five-hour conflict was among the war's bloodiest battles: some 7,200 Confederate casualties were sustained, including the loss of six generals; Union forces suffered nearly 2,400 casualties.

Hood commanded the Confederate Army of Tennessee in November 1864. Deciding to ignore the Union advance of Maj. Gen. William T. Sherman across Georgia, Hood instead embarked on an invasion of Tennessee, with only 40,000 men. Sherman had foreseen such a threat and dispatched Maj. Gen. George H. Thomas to Nashville to defend the state.

Reinforcements under the command of Maj. Gen. John M. Schofield were sent to join Thomas from southern Tennessee and included Schofield's XXIII Corps and Maj. Gen. David S. Stanley's IV Corps. Ordered to delay Hood's advance, Schofield skirmished with the rebels on several occasions and was nearly trapped at Spring Hill on November 29. After an all-night march to Franklin, 15 miles south of Nashville, he put his 30,000 troops behind entrenchments on the morning of November 30.

Hood arrived that afternoon and ordered a frontal assault to begin at 3:00 P.M. Although he held a slight numerical advantage, part of his infantry and most of his artillery were still on the road to Franklin when the attack began. Wave after wave of rebel soldiers hit the Union entrenchments, but each attempt to overrun them failed. Darkness finally intervened and halted the fighting. Schofield withdrew to Nashville that night having successfully delayed Hood. The battered Confederate army followed the next day.

Bibliography: McDonough, James Lee, and Thomas L. Connelly, *Five Tragic Hours: The Battle of Franklin* (Univ. of Tennessee Press, 1983).

Daniel T. Bailey

FREDERICKSBURG, BATTLE OF (December 11–13, 1862)

Civil War engagement in northeastern Virginia in which the strategic weakness of the Union command resulted in a costly defeat for the U.S. Army of the Potomac. On Nov. 7, 1862, Pres. Abraham Lincoln relieved Maj. Gen. George C. McClellan as commander of the Army of the Potomac and replaced him with the likeable but uncertain Maj. Gen. Ambrose E. Burnside. Burnside quickly formulated an aggressive plan that called for the army to march from its position near Warrenton, Virginia, southeast to Falmouth, Virginia, a small town on the Rappahannock River opposite Fredericksburg. The concentrated Union army would then cross the river, seize Fredericksburg, a town nearly equidistant between Richmond and Washington, D.C., and march on Richmond. Despite his misgivings, Lincoln acquiesced in the new commander's plan. By adopting this plan, Burnside neglected the opportunity presented by the dispersed deployment of the Army of Northern Virginia (ANV) to defeat it in detail.

Union Initiatives and Delays. Burnside reorganized the Army of the Potomac into three grand divisions commanded by Maj. Gens. William B. Franklin, Joseph Hooker, and Edwin V. Sumner. On November 15, Sumner's Right Grand Division marched rapidly to Falmouth, occupying it on November 17. Only a small force of Confederate troops occupied Fredericksburg. By moving quickly, the Army of the Potomac had caught the ANV strung out between Culpeper, Virginia, and the Shenandoah Valley.

Sumner failed to cross the river, fordable at several points, and establish a bridgehead. Lt. Gen. James Longstreet's I Corps of the ANV arrived two days later and occupied Fredericksburg, negating any Union advantage. The Union attack was further delayed by poor staff work, which caused the late delivery of the pontoon bridges necessary to conduct a major river crossing.

Burnside's Unclear Plan of Attack. Fredericksburg itself lay on the west bank of the river. Marye's Heights, high ground to the west of the town, afforded good defensive positions for the Confederates, and Stafford Heights, to the east, provided good artillery positions for the attacking federals. Most of the Union artillery, however, could not range on the summit of Marye's Heights. The terrain below Marye's Heights and between the town and Hamilton's Crossing possessed little maneuver space and was broken by numerous small ravines and a canal.

Burnside's army numbered more than 120,000 men and 312 guns. Despite the loss of tactical and strategic surprise, Burnside proceeded with a plan to cross the Rappahannock at three points and launch a two-pronged attack against the strong Confederate defenses on the high ground west of Fredericksburg. Burnside's rambling attack order, issued orally on December 10, lacked clarity as to his objectives and scheme of maneuver. Apparently, he intended Franklin's Left Grand Division (six divisions, 46,000 men) to launch the main effort and dislodge the right flank of Gen. Robert E. Lee's position in the vicinity of Hamilton's Crossing. Sumner's Right Grand Division (26,000 men) would fix the Confederate defenders on Marye's Heights. Hooker's Centre Grand Division (27,000 men) would remain in reserve. Written orders were not issued until the morning of December 11.

During the initial bridging attempt that day, intense federal artillery fire destroyed Fredericksburg. Despite establishing bridgeheads at three crossing points by nightfall, the Union army did not begin a major assault until December 13.

In the meantime, the last two Confederate divisions occupied their defensive positions. Lee's army—consisting of Longstreet's I Corps, Maj. Gen. Thomas "Stonewall" Jackson's II Corps, and Maj. Gen. Jeb Stuart's cavalry—now numbered about 79,000 soldiers and 275 guns, most of them emplaced to take full advantage of the open fields of fire below their positions. Union delays had allowed the ANV to concentrate fully and to occupy prepared defensive positions.

The Main Offensive. A cold, dense fog blanketed Fredericksburg as Union attacks started about 8:30 A.M. on December 13. Beginning the piecemeal effort that would characterize Union attacks all day, one corps of Franklin's grand division attacked with only one division, supported by a second division, across the open ground toward the woods north of Hamilton's Crossing. The rest of the Left Grand Division remained inactive. Despite a temporary penetration of Jackson's line and initial success, Franklin failed to continue the attack with the remaining divisions. Franklin's troops withdrew to the river line later that afternoon. Lee's right flank had held.

Sumner's grand division, deployed in Fredericksburg, awaited information on Franklin's attack. At 11:00 A.M., Sumner's lead corps finally began its attack through the

A Confederate caisson and eight dead horses are found at Marye's Heights near Fredericksburg. (National Archives)

town. The moment the Union soldiers cleared the town, Longstreet's troops on Marye's Heights took them under fire. Still under fire as they crossed the ditch west of town, the Union troops reformed and attacked across the open ground toward Marye's Heights. Union attacks focused on a Confederate position behind a stone wall in a sunken road. This superb position, manned by two lines of infantrymen, repulsed 14 successive piecemeal attacks. The Union forces suffered 6,300 casualties in the attacks against Marye's Heights. Franklin's failure to continue his attacks against the Confederate right flank allowed Lee the chance to shift forces to his now threatened left. Through it all, Burnside remained on the opposite bank of the river, out of touch with the battle. Hooker, on the western side of the river, suspended all attacks as darkness fell.

Aftermath. After a cold night, Burnside thought of renewing the attack December 14, possibly in person. His subordinates dissuaded him. The Army of the Potomac conducted a masterful withdrawal across the river on the following evening, a feat the Confederate army failed to detect.

Burnside's lack of flexibility and poor planning had doomed the Union attack. Improper reconnaissance and uncoordinated attacks against entrenched defensive positions also contributed to the Union disaster. Using fewer than half his committed brigades, Lee inflicted nearly 13,000 casualties while suffering about 5,300. The demoralized Army of the Potomac withdrew to encampments near Falmouth as the ANV, maintaining its position, continued to fortify and bivouac in winter quarters. Lincoln replaced Burnside with Hooker on Jan. 15, 1863.

Bibliography: Esposito, Vincent J., ed., *The West Point Atlas of American Wars,* vol. 1 (Praeger, 1959); Hassler, Warren, *Commanders of the Army of the Potomac* (Louisiana State Univ. Press, 1962); McMurry, Richard, *Two Great Rebel Armies* (Univ. of North Carolina Press, 1989); Stackpole, Edward, *The Fredericksburg Campaign: Drama on the Rappahannock* (Stackpole Books, 1957); Whan,

Vorin, Jr., *Fiasco at Fredericksburg* (Pennsylvania State Univ. Press, 1961).

Kevin E. McKedy

FRONTERA, SIEGE OF (October 23, 1846)

Naval blockade of a southeastern Mexican port by the United States during the Mexican War. As U.S. forces made plans to capture Tampico, the central port on Mexico's east coast, it became necessary that Frontera, 500 miles southeast, on the Bay of Campeche, be under U.S. control as well. In the fall of 1846, U.S. naval commodore David Conner sent an expedition under Capt. Matthew C. Perry, with eight small craft, to sweep the Gulf Coast along the Isthmus of Tehuantepec, from the Coatzacoalcos River east to Carmen. On October 23, Perry seized Frontera, a vital Mexican supply depot, 55 miles west of Carmen, at the mouth of the Grijalva (or Tabasco) River. He then sent men 72 miles upriver to attack San Juan Bautista, the capital of the state of Tabasco.

M. Guy Bishop

GALVESTON, BATTLE OF (January 1, 1863)

Naval conflict during the Civil War. Confederate major general John B. Magruder was determined to oust Union forces consisting of five gunboats and three infantry companies from Galveston, Texas. He converted two riverboats to warships, and, with approximately 500 men, he attacked on Jan. 1, 1863. The decisive action took place in the harbor.

One U.S. gunboat ran aground and was blown up. A second gunboat surrendered. The remaining boats beat a hasty retreat. Observing the action in the harbor, the Union land forces surrendered en masse. Confederate casualties were 143 killed and wounded, while the Union lost approximately 600 killed, wounded, and captured. While typifying the outcome of many such encounters, the battle was insignificant. The possession of the town was irrelevant, and the blockade was merely resumed from outside the harbor.

Bibliography: Foote, Shelby, *The Civil War, A Narrative: Fredericksburg to Meridian* (Random House, 1958); Long, E. B., *The Civil War Day by Day* (Doubleday, 1971).

Capt. Karen S. Wilhelm

GETTYSBURG, BATTLE OF (July 1–3, 1863)

Major Civil War engagement that crushed the Confederacy's intention to defeat Union forces on Northern soil. Confederate objectives in invading the North in 1863 included (1) capturing Harrisburg, the capital of Pennsylvania; (2) threatening Baltimore, Philadelphia, and Washington (from the north); (3) increasing support from Europe (specifically, England) by one great victory; (4) drawing Union troops away from Vicksburg, Mississippi; and (5) further discouraging the North's will to continue the war.

The move north began June 3. To confound the enemy, Maj. Gen. Jeb Stuart took five brigades of Confederate cavalry through the rear of the Union army. The resulting loss of contact with his cavalry deprived Gen. Robert E. Lee of vital information about his opponent. By June 28, one Southern infantry division was at Wrightsville, Pennsylvania, and another at Carlisle, threatening Harrisburg. The remainder of both armies were south and west of Gettysburg, a southern Pennsylvania village of about 2,500 people. On June 30, James J. Pettigrew's Confederate brigade (part of Lt. Gen. Ambrose P. Hill's corps) discovered Union cavalry at Gettysburg. Two Union brigades, commanded by Brig. Gen. John Buford, were deployed north and west of the town.

The First Day. Early on July 1, the Confederate brigades of Brig. Gens. James J. Archer and Joseph R. Davis (Maj. Gen. Henry Heth's division of Hill's corps) attacked Buford from the west. Buford's men, many armed with Spencer repeating carbines, held out until 10:00 A.M., when they were relieved by the arrival of Maj. Gen. John F. Reynolds's I Corps. Reynolds was soon killed.

Maj. Gen. Robert E. Rodes's division (from Lt. Gen. Richard S. Ewell's corps), hurrying from Carlisle, attacked the northern (right) flank of the Union I Corps, now led by Maj. Gen. Abner Doubleday. Doubleday shifted troops and halted the attack. Two divisions of Maj. Gen. Oliver O. Howard's XI Corps reinforced and extended Doubleday's line north of Gettysburg. Then the Confederate division of Maj. Gen. Jubal A. Early assaulted Howard's men, driving the whole force through Gettysburg.

West of town, Maj. Gen. William D. Pender's division relieved Heth and drove Doubleday back through Gettysburg. By 5:00 P.M., the remnants of the Union force were driven onto Cemetery and Culp's hills, south of the village.

That night, the federal III Corps of Maj. Gen. Daniel Sickles and the XII Corps of Maj. Gen. Henry W. Slocum reinforced Culp's Hill and extended the line south along Cemetery Ridge to Little Round Top. The Union line now resembled a fishhook three miles long south of Gettysburg. The Confederates occupied a six-mile line on low ground opposite Culp's Hill, west through the town, and south along Seminary Ridge, paralleling the Union position.

The Second Day. Lee decided to attack, against the advice of Lt. Gen. James Longstreet (I Corps). That afternoon, Lee sent Longstreet against the Union left flank. Longstreet attacked Sickles's division, which had moved forward to occupy a peach orchard, a wheat field, and the north-south Emmitsburg Road, a very exposed position. Longstreet also sent the brigades of Brig. Gens. Evander

M. Law and Jerome B. Robertson to seize unoccupied Little Round Top.

Maj. Gen. Gouverneur K. Warren, chief of engineers under George G. Meade (commander of the Union's Army of the Potomac), discovering that Little Round Top was unoccupied, except for a signal station, diverted the brigades of Col. Strong Vincent and Brig. Gen. Stephen H. Week, advance elements of Maj. Gen. George Sykes's V Corps. A desperate battle ensued for the hill. The federals prevailed there but lost the peach orchard and wheat field. Longstreet also occupied (Big) Round Top, south of Little Round Top and Devil's Den, an imposing collection of huge rocks at the foot of the Round Tops.

Early attacked at dusk, gaining the crest of East Cemetery Hill, but Rodes's division failed to attack from the west, and Early was repulsed. The frontal assault on Culp's Hill by Maj. Gen. Edward Johnson's Confederate division was thwarted, so he attacked the southern slope, taking some unoccupied Union entrenchments. There he halted for the night, only a few hundred yards from the federal supply trains.

The Third Day. Meade decided to defend in place, concluding that Lee, having tested his flanks on July 2, would concentrate on the Union center the following day. At daybreak, the federal troops returned to their entrenchments on Culp's Hill and drove Johnson out. The II and XII Corps and elements of the I and XI Corps were disposed along Culp's Hill and Cemetery Ridge. The V Corps extended the line to Round Top. Brigades of the VI Corps were used as local reserves, and the III Corps was positioned behind the center as a general reserve. The Confederate I Corps was facing generally south opposite Culp's Hill and a portion of Cemetery Hill. The II and III Corps occupied Seminary Ridge, facing east toward the federal line.

Both sides brought up artillery and repositioned troops. Some 150 guns were arrayed by Lee to support a massive attack by 15,000 infantrymen against Meade's center. Meade posted about 118 guns to meet the expected charge. Stuart had arrived with his cavalry late on the night of July 2. Lee sent him to the left flank to attack the Union rear when the infantry assaulted their center.

Confederate artillery opened fire at 1:00 P.M. The artillery dueled hotly for almost two hours, when the federals ceased fire to replace batteries running out of ammunition or disabled by enemy fire. At 3:00 P.M., two brigades from Anderson's division, all of Heth's division, two brigades of Pender's division (all from Hill's corps), and the three brigades of Maj. Gen. George E. Pickett's division (Longstreet's corps)—11 brigades in all—began their charge. Pickett was in overall command.

Union artillery, from Cemetery Hill to Little Round Top tore great gaps in the advancing ranks. As the host drew closer, canister and infantry fire cut down thousands. As they approached Cemetery Ridge, Brig. Gen. George J. Stannard's Vermont Brigade executed turning movements from its position and fired into the flanks of two different bodies of charging Confederates. Only 150 men entered the federal lines. All were killed or captured. Remnants of the charging brigades streamed back to their lines.

Early in the afternoon, Stuart's cavalry was detected by Brig. Gen. David M. Gregg's Union horsemen, making their way down the valley of Cress Run, three miles east of Gettysburg. The two cavalry forces soon engaged in a series of charges and countercharges. The coordinated thrusts by the Union horsemen halted Stuart's men after three hours of heavy fighting. Lee had been repulsed, but Meade did not counterattack. The Battle of Gettysburg ended. Lee withdrew late on July 4 and returned to Virginia. Meade was severely criticized for allowing him to escape.

Outcome. Gettysburg cost the North more than 23,000 men of some 85,000 engaged. The South lost nearly 21,000 of about 75,000. Close to 10,000 men were killed and more than 20,000 wounded. After the defeat at Gettysburg and the subsequent fall of Vicksburg (July 4), the South lost the initiative, never to regain it during the remainder of the war.

Bibliography: Coddington, Edwin B., *The Battle of Gettysburg: A Study in Command* (Morningside Press, 1979); Hoke, Jacob, *The Great Invasion of 1863; or, General Lee in Pennsylvania* (Yoseloff, 1959); Nye, Wilbur S., *Here Come the Rebels!* (Louisiana State Univ. Press, 1965); Stackpole, Edward J., *They Met at Gettysburg* (Telegraph Press, 1956).

Brig. Gen. (Ret.) Uzal W. Ent

GRIERSON'S RAID (April 17–May 2, 1863)

Diversionary operation during the Civil War's Vicksburg Campaign in which Union horsemen successfully confounded Confederate troops. As part of his plan for the capture of Vicksburg, Mississippi, Union general Ulysses S. Grant dispatched Col. Benjamin H. Grierson in April 1863 with 1,700 cavalrymen to raid eastern Mississippi and thereby distract the Confederates from Grant's real intention of crossing the Mississippi River south of Vicksburg. Grierson's command left La Grange, Tennessee, on April 17. Twice he detached troops to return to Tennessee and distract his pursuers. The baffled Confederates shuffled their troops about the state attempting to trap the Union column. Grierson's men, however, avoided contact and destroyed rail lines and military stores around the eastern Mississippi towns of Newton, Starkville, Macon, and Enterprise. The Confederates finally closed in, and the Union force made a dash for Baton Rouge, Louisiana, which it reached on May 2.

Bibliography: Brown, D. Alexander, *Grierson's Raid* (Univ. of Illinois Press, 1954).

Richard F. Kehrberg

GUADALUPE-HIDALGO, TREATY OF (February 2, 1848)

Treaty signed by Mexican representatives and Nicholas P. Trist, chief clerk of the U.S. Department of State, that concluded the Mexican War (1846–48). In its provisions, Mexico recognized the Rio Grande as its border with Texas, and it ceded to the United States the territory that now comprises California, Nevada, Utah, most of Arizona and New Mexico, and parts of Colorado and Wyoming. The treaty also gave the United States the right to transit the Isthmus of Tehuantepec, contingent on its building an interocean canal. The U.S. government, in turn, paid Mexico $15,000,000 and assumed responsibility for $3,250,000 in damage claims submitted by U.S. citizens against the Mexican government.

Bibliography: Bauer, K. Jack, *The Mexican War* (Macmillan Co., 1974); Smith, Justin H., *The War with Mexico* (Macmillan Co., 1919).

Maj. Peter Faber

HAMPTON ROADS, BATTLE OF

See Monitor and Merrimac.

HARPERS FERRY, CAPTURE OF (September 15, 1862)

Civil War engagement during the Antietam Campaign that resulted in the largest surrender of Union forces in the war. Situated at the confluence of the Potomac and Shenandoah rivers in West Virginia, Harpers Ferry was an important communications center that was seized by Virginia secessionists on Apr. 18, 1861, the day after secession. It was reoccupied by Union forces on June 15, 1861.

During Confederate general Robert E. Lee's first invasion of the North in September 1862, Gen. in Chief Henry W. Halleck refused to withdraw the outnumbered Union garrison at Harpers Ferry, consisting of 10,800 men under the command of Col. Dixon S. Miles. The Union defense was anchored on two commanding hilltops, the Bolivar and Maryland heights. On September 13, Maj. Gen. Lafayette McLaws carried Maryland Heights, and two days later, as Maj. Gen. Thomas "Stonewall" Jackson readied to assault Bolivar Heights, the heavily outnumbered Union garrison surrendered.

Federal losses were 44 killed, including Miles, and 12,520 captured. The rapid fall of Harpers Ferry allowed Jackson to rejoin Lee on the following day and participate in the Battle of Antietam. Responsibility for this major reverse appears to have been Halleck's, although Miles was officially blamed at the time.

Russell A. Hart

HARPERS FERRY, JOHN BROWN'S RAID ON (October 16–18, 1859)

Attack on a federal arsenal by abolitionist John Brown. Brown was one of the most effective, and controversial, of the antebellum American demagogues. During the mid-1850s, he was active in the Underground Railroad and the often bloody struggle to keep slavery out of Kansas. By 1857, he was planning an armed assault on the slaveholding South.

With financial backing from abolitionists, Brown began to put his plan into action. He envisioned slaves from Virginia farms joining his small band of devoted followers and rising in armed rebellion. His first target was the federal arsenal at Harpers Ferry, Virginia (now West Virginia). In the summer of 1859, he rented an isolated Maryland farm near the facility. On October 16, he and fewer than 25 men gained control of the arsenal and took civilian hostages.

Local response was quick from militia and private citizens, always edgy at the prospect of armed slaves incited to insurrection. The next day, they drove Brown's force from structures on the arsenal grounds into the firehouse. Official reaction was equally swift. By October 19, a detachment of marines led by Lt. Col. Robert E. Lee arrived from Washington. When Brown refused to surrender, Lee ordered the firehouse stormed. During the assault (led by Lt. Jeb Stuart), Brown was wounded and captured. Following a much-publicized treason trial at nearby Charles Town, during which Brown passionately defended his actions, he was hanged on December 2.

Brown's raid and subsequent punishment was a catalyst to public opinion in both the North and the South. He became a martyr to many northern abolitionists and a symbol of warning to Southerners that if antislavery politicians gained more of a foothold in national life, these slave revolts, encouraged by Northerners, would become commonplace, and secession would be the South's only salvation.

Bibliography: Nalty, Bernard C., *The United States Marines at Harpers Ferry* (U.S. Marine Corps, 1966).

Louise Arnold-Friend

HATTERAS INLET (FORTS HATTERAS AND CLARK), SIEGE OF (August 28–29, 1861)

Federal occupation of two Confederate strongholds in eastern North Carolina at the beginning of the Civil War. Acting on the orders of Maj. Gen. Benjamin F. Butler, a Union navy squadron with army transports commanded, respectively, by Adm. Silas H. Stringham and Col. Rush C. Hawkins bombarded Forts Hatteras and Clark on Aug. 28–29, 1961. The forts protected North Carolina's Hatteras Inlet, an important strait from the Atlantic into Pamlico Sound and thus called the "back door" to the Confederacy.

The Kearsarge, *a Union sloop of war, and the* Alabama, *a Confederate commerce raider, battle outside of France's Cherbourg harbor in June 1864.* (Americana Image Gallery, Gettysburg, Pennsylvania)

After the bombardment by Dahlgren guns, which outdistanced the Confederates's smoothbores, a force of 800 Union troops landed and demanded full capitulation. The Confederate surrender, at midday August 29, yielded 730 prisoners and 35 guns and brought U.S. Sec. of the Navy Gideon Welles his first national attention. Federal troops garrisoned the forts to stop blockade-runners and Confederate raiders but never exploited the access to the mainland. The Confederates fell back and occupied Roanoke Island, 50 miles north.

Lynn L. Sims

IUKA, BATTLE OF (September 19, 1862)

Civil War engagement in which Union forces under Maj. Gen. William S. Rosecrans attacked the Confederate troops of Maj. Gen. Sterling Price at Iuka, Mississippi, a town 25 miles southeast of Corinth and 8 miles south of the Tennessee River. Iuka was occupied on Sept. 14, 1862, by Price's Confederate force of 16,800 men, which drove out the small Union garrison of 1,500 men. On September 19, a partial engagement took place between Price's two brigades, totaling 3,179 men, and Rosecrans's column of 9,000 men. Outnumbered, Price fought a skillful defense. However, the imminent arrival in his rear of Union forces under Maj. Gen. Ulysses S. Grant compelled Price to retire in good order from Iuka on the following day. Union casualties at Iuka were 782 killed, wounded, and missing; Confederate losses totaled 1,516.

Bibliography: Gunn, Jack W., "The Battle of Iuka," *Journal of Mississippi History* (July 1962).

Russell A. Hart

KEARSARGE VS. ALABAMA (June 19, 1864)

Civil War battle between a Confederate commerce raider (the *Alabama*) and a Union sloop of war (the *Kearsarge*); one of the most famous ship-to-ship duels in U.S. naval lore. The engagement took place on June 19, 1864, in the neutral waters outside the harbor at Cherbourg, France, where the *Alabama*'s captain, Raphael Semmes, had come in search of docking facilities for his ship and crew after a remarkable 22-month voyage highlighted by the capture of 64 Union prizes. Upon spotting the elusive Confederate cruiser, the U.S. consul in Cherbourg quickly telegraphed news of the *Alabama*'s position to Capt. John A. Winslow of the U.S. screw sloop *Kearsarge,* located only a few hundred miles north at Calais. Winslow weighed anchor immediately and steamed south, arriving at Cherbourg three days later. Semmes was trapped. Refusing to accept internment in the French port, he chose instead to fight his way out, issuing a challenge for a naval duel with his pursuer. Winslow eagerly accepted, and on the morning of June 19, the *Alabama* steamed out of port.

The battle, viewed by thousands of spectators on shore, proved to be very one-sided: the *Alabama* was badly in need of repair after her 75,000-mile voyage, and the *Kearsarge* was newly refitted and battle ready. Within an hour, Semmes was forced to strike his colors; as his ship sank, however, he and 40 of his crew swam to a nearby English yacht and escaped to England.

Bibliography: Spencer, Warren F., "Raphael Semmes: Confederate Raider," *Captains of the Old Steam Navy,* ed. by James C. Bradford (Naval Inst. Press, 1986).

Maj. Grant H. Walker

KENTUCKY CAMPAIGN
(August–October 1862)

Confederate offensive in the second year of the Civil War. After the setbacks of early 1862, the Confederate forces in the western theater launched this campaign to regain control of Tennessee and recruit further strength from Kentucky. Although the Confederates won several tactical victories, their lack of numbers and the failure of Kentucky to rally to them forced their withdrawal.

From the first, a division in the Confederate command structure made coordination difficult. Gen. Braxton Bragg controlled approximately 56,000 troops, primarily Maj. Gen. Leonidas Polk's Army of Mississippi, while Lt. Gen. E. Kirby Smith commanded 13,000 others in eastern Tennessee. Bragg and Smith never concentrated their forces at one point. By contrast, Gen. Henry W. Halleck controlled at least 108,000 federal troops in the theater of war, of which Maj. Gen. Don Carlos Buell's Army of the Ohio was directly opposed to the Confederate invasion.

Richmond. Smith marched north from Knoxville, Tennessee, into central Kentucky on Aug. 14, 1862. On August 30, he overwhelmed the 6,500 raw Union troops of Maj. Gen. William Nelson at Richmond, Kentucky, although the Northern forces fought stubbornly in an attempt to outflank the Confederate left.

Munfordville. At the same time, Bragg advanced north from Chattanooga, Tennessee, toward Louisville, Kentucky. Confederate cavalry raids by Col. Joseph Wheeler, plus the need to defend Nashville, Tennessee, made Buell slow to follow Bragg. Upon learning of the defeat at Richmond, Buell entrusted the defense of Nashville to Maj. Gen. George H. Thomas on September 7 and hastened north, using the railroads to Bowling Green, Kentucky, to keep him parallel to Bragg. Both sides lost considerable strength during these rapid moves, dropping stragglers all along the route. Bragg's advanced guard was repulsed by the 4,000-man garrison at Munfordville, Kentucky, on September 14, but Bragg forced that garrison to surrender three days later.

When Buell arrived at Munfordville on September 18, he found Bragg entrenched south of the town, using the former Union fort as part of his defenses. Neither side had enough forces to attack nor enough supplies to remain indefinitely. On September 20, Thomas arrived with additional Union troops, and this prompted Bragg to break contact, hurrying northeast to Bardstown, Kentucky. Buell was able to reinforce Louisville and forestall the Confederates there.

A second stalemate ensued for the remainder of September. The Confederates recruited a few hundred Kentucky volunteers and prepared to install their own state government in Frankfort. They held virtually all of Kentucky east of Louisville, with Polk in Bardstown to observe the federal army and Smith in Lexington, southeast of Frankfort.

On September 29, the Union command structure suffered two severe shocks. First, the talented corps commander Nelson was murdered in a quarrel with another volunteer general; Nelson was succeeded by Maj. Gen. Charles C. Gilbert, who until recently had been a captain in the regular army. Next, Pres. Abraham Lincoln and Halleck, exasperated by Buell's frequent failures, decided to relieve Buell of his command and replace him with Thomas. Thomas declined the appointment, however, arguing that Buell was on the verge of launching an offensive.

This offensive began two days later and initially had great success. Buell deceived Bragg as to his main effort, sending two divisions under Brig. Gen. Joshua W. Sill due east toward Frankfort, while the majority of his troops moved southeast, seeking to cut the Confederate line of communications and retreat. On October 3, Polk retreated toward Perryville, Kentucky, ignoring Bragg's orders to concentrate with Smith at Lexington. The next day, the sound of Sill's cannon fire brought the Confederate governor's inauguration in Frankfort to a hasty conclusion.

Perryville. Despite rear-guard actions by Confederate cavalry, Buell pressed forward so hard that, on October 7, Polk felt compelled to make a stand at Perryville. On the following morning, the federal III Corps under Gilbert attacked Polk on the open slopes west of Perryville; Brig.

Gen. Philip H. Sheridan achieved control of water holes in the area, but the inexperienced Gilbert would not allow him to press the attack. When Bragg arrived on the field at 10:00 A.M., he ordered Polk to withdraw his 14,000 men through the town, then turn them north onto a sunken road and streambed. This led the Confederate forces on a concealed route to the Union left flank, where they arrived about 2:00 P.M. In the interim, the other two Union corps had arrived, one on each flank of Gilbert. On the left, Maj. Gen. Alexander M. McCook's I Corps was unaware of the enemy until a sudden attack shattered the raw troops. Polk pressed westward for about 1,000 yards until checked by a Union brigade on the next high ground.

Because of a hollow in the ground, the sound of this fighting did not reach Buell's headquarters only two miles away, so that Union reinforcements were slow to arrive. The heat and exertion, as much as any Union resistance, halted the Confederates short of victory. Total casualties included 3,396 Confederate and 5,348 Union troops.

For two days, the contending armies remained motionless, but ultimately, Bragg's lack of numbers forced him to retreat, taking with him large supply trains but few recruits. Buell was relieved and investigated for his failure to use his great numerical superiority, while Southerners were equally critical of Bragg for losing several opportunities to crush parts of the Union army. Kentucky remained in the Union.

Bibliography: Johnson, Robert U., and Clarence C. Buel, eds., *Battles and Leaders of the Civil War,* vol. 3, part 1 (Century, 1914); McWhiney, Grady, *Braxton Bragg and Confederate Defeat; Vol. 1: Field Command* (Columbia Univ. Press, 1969); U.S. War Department, *The War of the Rebellion: A Compilation of the Official Records of the Union and Confederate Armies,* series 1, vol. 16, parts 1 & 2 (U.S. Govt. Printing Office, 1886).

Jonathan M. House

KNOXVILLE CAMPAIGN (November–December 1863)

Civil War campaign in eastern Tennessee, on the Tennessee River. While besieging the Union forces at Chattanooga, Tennessee, in November 1863, Gen. Braxton Bragg (with the concurrence of Confederate president Jefferson Davis) sent Lt. Gen. James Longstreet and 20,000 Confederates to attack the Union troops in eastern Tennessee under Maj. Gen. Ambrose E. Burnside. Longstreet's thrust was frustrated by the skillful delaying action of Burnside, who, with 12,000 troops, slowed Longstreet enough to finish fortifications around Knoxville, 105 miles northeast of Chattanooga. Longstreet attacked Knoxville on November 29 but was repulsed. The combatants, both at the ends of tenuous supply lines, settled into a loose siege until after the Battle of Chattanooga, when Maj. Gen. William T. Sherman arrived with aid for Burnside. Bragg lost that battle in large part by sending Longstreet away.

Mark Pitcavage

LAGUNA, SIEGE OF (December 21, 1846)

Taking of a Mexican port by the U.S. Navy during the Mexican War. It was part of U.S. naval strategy during the war to attempt to severely limit Mexico's outlets to the sea. With this goal in mind, on Dec. 21, 1846, Commodore Matthew C. Perry captured the Mexican garrison at Laguna on El Carmen Island off of the eastern shore of Yucatan. The site controlled a river outlet into the Caribbean. Perry seized two small forts in the area, disabled their guns, and maintained U.S. occupation of Laguna and El Carmen Island for the remainder of the war. He appointed a U.S. naval officer as governor, attempted to control all commercial trade through Laguna, and curtailed all contraband traffic. The U.S. presence at Laguna helped to minimize Mexican commerce throughout the Carribean area.

M. Guy Bishop

MEMPHIS, BATTLE OF (June 6, 1862)

Civil War naval confrontation on the Mississippi River just north of Memphis, Tennessee. By 1860, Memphis had become one of the busiest U.S. ports, and at the outbreak of the Civil War, it became a vital Confederate center. At daybreak on June 6, 1862, five Union gunboats under Flag Officer Charles H. Davis were attacked by Capt. J. E. Montgomery's Confederate River Defense Fleet. Three of Col. Charles Ellet's unarmed Union rams broke Montgomery's double line of eight armed rams. Davis's gunboats then attacked with relentless fire, and in little over an hour, three of the Confederate boats had been sunk, four were captured, and one escaped. Davis accepted the surrender of Memphis, and this key port remained under Union control throughout the war.

Christine L. Stevens

MERIDIAN CAMPAIGN (February 3–March 5, 1864)

Civil War expedition into central and eastern Mississippi, led by Union general William T. Sherman. In early 1864, Sherman was to support Gen. Nathaniel P. Banks in the Red River Campaign but first opted to strengthen the Union hold on Vicksburg, in western Mississippi, by destroying central Mississippi's resources and railroads. To that end, he set out from Vicksburg for Meridian, in eastern Mississippi, on February 3, with a force of 25,000. As Sherman advanced, two of four 5,000-man Confederate units moved into Alabama and one went north.

Sherman arrived in Meridian on February 14 and ravaged it for five days, while waiting for Gen. W. Sooy Smith, who was to lead 7,000 Union cavalrymen from Memphis to disperse Gen. Nathan B. Forrest's smaller Confederate cavalry. Smith delayed, however, and on February 21 was routed by Forrest at West Point, Mississippi. Sherman, meanwhile, had moved back into central Mississippi and on March 3 returned to Vicksburg. Union casualties during the Meridian Campaign, according to Sherman, were 89 killed and wounded and 81 missing. Confederate losses were reported as 400 killed and wounded and 200 captured.

Christine L. Stevens

MILL SPRINGS (LOGAN CROSS ROADS), BATTLE OF (January 19, 1862)

Civil War engagement in which an outnumbered Union force soundly defeated a Confederate attack. In early January 1862, Don Carlos Buell, commanding the Union's Army of the Cumberland, sent George H. Thomas's division into southeastern Kentucky to remove a Confederate threat from that direction. Opposing Thomas's 4,000 men were 6,250 troops under Confederate generals George B. Crittenden and Felix K. Zollicoffer, who launched a surprise attack on Thomas at Mill Springs. The Union troops resisted stoutly, routing green Confederate units and fatally wounding Zollicoffer. Thomas quickly initiated a counterattack, which drove the Confederates from the field. The Union suffered 237 casualties, while the Confederates lost 658. Accompanied as it was shortly thereafter by Brig. Gen. Ulysses S. Grant's Union victories at Forts Henry and Donelson, Mill Springs helped to influence Confederate commander Joseph E. Johnston to abandon Kentucky.

Mark Pitcavage

MOBILE, SIEGE OF (March–April 1865)

Civil War engagement in southwestern Alabama at the head of Mobile Bay. Mobile, Alabama, had been blockaded by the Union from May 1861 until the naval battle of Aug. 5, 1864, when Union troops occupied Mobile Point and Dauphin Island. In the spring of 1865, Maj. Gen. Edward R. S. Canby advanced from Pensacola, Florida, with a federal force of 45,000 men and laid siege to Fort Blakely and Spanish Fort on the east side of the bay opposite Mobile itself.

Mobile was defended by Gen. Randall L. Gibson with about 5,000 men. Gibson held Spanish Fort for 13 days (March 27–April 8) until prized out by the threat of encirclement. On April 9, Fort Blakely was stormed, rendering the city defenseless. Gibson evacuated Mobile on April 11, and Union troops occupied it the following day.

Bibliography: Hamilton, P. J., *Mobile of the Five Flags* (Gill Printing Co., 1913).

Russel A. Hart

MOBILE BAY, BATTLE OF (August 5, 1864)

Civil War naval action that resulted in the Confederates' loss of a major Southern port. By July 1864, Union admiral David G. Farragut had assembled a powerful force of 4 ironclad monitors and 14 wooden screw sloops to attack Mobile, Alabama. Opposing him was Adm. Franklin Buchanan, commanding only the ironclad ram *Tennessee* and 3 small gunboats. But Buchanan could count as well on the guns of Forts Gaines and Morgan, which flanked the entrance to Mobile Bay; moreover, between the forts he had placed a row of submerged pilings and mines (then called torpedoes), blocking the entire mouth of the bay except for a narrow channel left open for blockade-runners.

Into that channel, Farragut sent his ships, arrayed in a column with the monitors leading, on the morning of August 5. But when one of the monitors veered out of the channel and hit a mine, the lead sloop, *Brooklyn,* halted, threatening to throw the rest of the oncoming Northern ships into chaos. It was then that Farragut shouted, "Damn the torpedoes, full steam ahead," sailing his flagship, the sloop *Hartford,* past the stalled *Brooklyn* and through the minefield. The other sloops followed unscathed, and within a few hours, only the *Tennessee* remained to contest Union control of the inner bay.

Despite the odds, and much to Farragut's surprise, Buchanan at that point chose not to hide under the guns of Fort Morgan but instead sailed the *Tennessee* right into the middle of Farragut's remaining 17 ships, bringing on a wild melee, which ended inevitably with the surrender of the Confederate ship. By the end of August, both forts, too, had surrendered, leaving Mobile Bay securely in Union hands.

Bibliography: Todorich, Charles M., "Franklin Buchanan: Symbol of Two Navies," *Captains of the Old Steam Navy,* ed. by James C. Bradford (Naval Inst. Press, 1986).

Maj. Grant H. Walker

MOLINO DEL REY, BATTLE OF (September 8, 1847)

Mexican War battle southwest of Mexico City, in which the superior forces of Mexican general Antonio López de Santa Anna were defeated by U.S. troops. On the afternoon of Sept. 7, 1847, U.S. general Winfield Scott, then encamped at Tacubaya, received word that a large body of Mexican troops were gathering at nearby Molino del Rey. Feeling his forces unprepared for a major battle, Scott decided to take a delaying action. Brig. Gen. William J. Worth's division, augmented by Brig. Gen. George Cadwalader's brigade and 270 dragoons under Maj. Edwin V. Sumner, marched on Molino del Rey the following day. Although Mexican artillery defended Molino, Worth employed his division admirably. After neutralizing the artillery, Worth stormed the enemy positions and carried the day in a bloody battle resulting in 116 U.S. soldiers killed and nearly 700 wounded. Mexican casualties were even higher.

M. Guy Bishop

The USS Monitor (right), *with only its gun-carrying turret and forward pilothouse above water, attacks the CSS* Virginia (*formerly the USS* Merrimac) *off Hampton Roads, Virginia.* (U.S. Army Military History Institute)

MONITOR AND MERRIMAC
(March 8–9, 1862)

Civil War naval battle at Hampton Roads, Virginia, famous as the first duel between ironclad warships (the *Monitor* and the *Merrimac*), although the outcome was indecisive and had little impact on the course of the war. The Confederate ironclad *Virginia* was fashioned from the wreck of the Union steam frigate *Merrimac* (by which name it is more commonly known), which was scuttled when the Union abandoned the Norfolk navy yards in southeast Virginia on Apr. 20–21, 1861. The Confederates constructed an armored casemate housing six 9-inch and four 6- and 7-inch guns upon the original hull, adding a 2-foot iron ram. Renamed *Virginia,* the vessel's conversion was completed on Mar. 5, 1862. Although heavily armed, it lacked speed and maneuverability.

The Union began construction of its ironclad *Monitor* in October 1861 at Greenpoint, Long Island. In its design, emphasis was laid on speed and a minimal freeboard and draft, so that when at speed, only its revolving turret (housing two 11-inch guns) and its forward pilothouse would remain above water. The *Monitor* was launched on Jan. 30, 1862, and became operational on February 19.

At 1:00 P.M. on March 8, the *Virginia,* commanded by Commodore Franklin Buchanan, and two 1-gun gunboats steamed out of the Elizabeth (a Norfolk-county river that empties into the channel of Hampton Roads) to engage two wooden Union sailing ships—the frigate *Congress* (50 guns) and the sloop *Cumberland* (30 guns)—anchored off nearby Newport News. The *Virginia* rammed the *Cumberland,* while the *Congress* ran aground fleeing its withering fire. At 3:30 P.M., the *Cumberland* went down still firing. By 4:30 P.M., the *Congress* had struck its colors, but not before Buchanan was badly wounded. The Union steam frigates *Minnesota, Roanoke,* and *St. Lawrence,* coming to join the fray, grounded as the tide ebbed. The *Virginia* anchored off Sewell's Point to await the next day's high tide to continue the attack.

During the night, however, the shallow-drafted *Monitor* arrived and anchored to protect the grounded frigates. From 9:00 A.M. on March 9, the two ironclads clashed ineffectually until 11:30 A.M., when a shell splinter blinded the *Monitor*'s commander, Lt. John L. Worden, forcing the ship to withdraw. The *Virginia* returned to Norfolk that day, only to be scuttled two days later when the Confederates abandoned Norfolk. The battle had been indecisive but the *Monitor,* by defending the Union blockade, was seen as the psychological victor in that its successful resistance alleviated Northern fears caused by the *Virginia*'s initial successes.

Bibliography: Soley, James R., *The Blockade and the Cruisers* (Scribner's, 1883); Swinton, William, *Twelve Decision Battles of the Civil War* (Dick and Fitzgerald, 1867).

Russell A. Hart

MONTERREY, BATTLE OF
(September 21–25, 1846)

One of a series of Mexican War battles fought and won by U.S. forces under the command of Brig. Gen. Zachary Taylor. In September 1846, Taylor and his forces landed on the eastern coast of Mexico and proceeded inland to an advance base at Camargo. They arrived outside the city of Monterrey on September 19.

Monterrey was located on terrain well-suited to defense and had the benefit of natural and man-made fortifications. The city stood on high ground on the north bank of the Rio Santa Catarina. There were two fortified hills to the west and two small forts in the east. An uncompleted cathedral served as a citadel and guarded the north. The well-built stone houses would require direct assault, and the straight streets provided open fields of fire. The city was garrisoned by a force of approximately 7,500 under the command of Gen. Pedro de Ampudia, who also had 42 artillery pieces. Taylor, in contrast, had 6,220 men in his force, with very few siege guns. In Taylor's favor, however, was the fact that Ampudia's line of communication to the rear (Saltillo) was poorly protected.

Taylor divided his force in the face of a superior enemy. He sent Brig. Gen. William J. Worth's division from the north around to the west to cut Ampudia's avenue of retreat and attack from the west and south. His remaining divisions under Gen. David E. Twiggs and William O. Butler attacked from the north and east. Ampudia did not take advantage of the opportunity to defeat Taylor's forces in detail. Taylor's men fought their way into the city over a period of four days. Ampudia was trapped in the city center and surrendered. Taylor agreed to an eight-week armistice, which allowed Ampudia's force to leave intact, and the U.S. troops occupied the city without further fighting.

Taylor's attack was poorly executed. His orders were ambiguous, he committed his troops piecemeal without coordination, he sent unsupported infantry against artillery, and he exposed large numbers of troops to fire from Mexican forts. Only a similar degree of incompetence on the part of Ampudia allowed him to win. Upon learning of the armistice, Pres. James Polk castigated Taylor for not capturing Ampudia's army and pushing further into Mexico, thus ending the war. Polk abrogated the armistice, whereupon Taylor notified the Mexicans and advanced further south to occupy Saltillo and Victoria.

Polk showed no appreciation of Taylor's position, but with the benefit of hindsight, Taylor is proven to have been correct. To capture the city and Ampudia's army, Taylor's men would have had to continue house-to-house fighting with the attendant casualties. Taylor had already lost more than 500 men (120 killed, 368 wounded, 43 missing) and was short of supplies. The Mexicans had suffered 367 killed and wounded. The armistice was a mistake, however, because the civilian authorities already had been pressuring Ampudia to end the fighting. The destruction of the city would not have been necessary, and Taylor would not have had to give such generous terms.

Bibliography: Bauer, K. Jack, *The Mexican War: 1846–1848* (Macmillan Co., 1974); Millet, Alan R., and Peter Maslowski, *For the Common Defense: A Military History of the United States of America* (Free Press, 1984).

Capt. Karen S. Wilhelm

MORGAN'S KENTUCKY RAIDS
(October 1862–January 1863)

Strategically significant Confederate cavalry raids against Union supply lines during the Civil War. In early October 1862, Col. John Hunt Morgan was leading a brigade of Confederate cavalry in Lt. Gen. E. Kirby Smith's retreat from Kentucky. After persuading Smith to turn him loose on a raid behind enemy lines in an effort to slow the Union advance, Morgan set off from near Richmond on October 17. He rode through several Kentucky towns, crossed the Green and Muddy rivers, and, on October 25, reached Hopkinsville, where his troops were welcomed by sympathetic Kentucky citizens. The Union pursuit was so disorganized that Morgan was able to call a three-day halt to rest his horses.

By November 1, Morgan's men had crossed into Tennessee at Springfield and ridden through Gallatin on their way back to Confederate lines. They damaged railroads in Union territory, destroyed bridges, captured and paroled several prisoners, and suffered few losses. The successful raid enhanced Morgan's reputation and caused minor disruption to Union forces in Kentucky.

Promoted to brigadier general on December 11, and gathering more than 3,000 horsemen into a division of cavalry, Morgan received orders from Gen. Braxton Bragg to make another raid into Kentucky. The Union's Maj. Gen. William S. Rosecrans was conducting a spirited campaign against Bragg, but the latter intended to counterattack. Rosecrans's exposed supply line from Louisville seemed a lucrative target.

Morgan set out on December 22, crossed the Cumberland River, and destroyed two key trestles on the Louisville & Nashville Railroad, Rosecrans's main supply route. He went on to capture Elizabethtown on December 27 and once again was astride the Union supply line. Union troops closed on him there, and, in a dashing evasion, Morgan led his horsemen back over the Cumberland on Jan. 2, 1863.

Along with the two trestles, Morgan destroyed three rail depots, three water stations, and several sections of the rail line itself. He burned large stores of Union supplies, took more than 1,800 prisoners (paroling most of them), and caused more than 20,000 Union troops to chase him at one time or another during the raid. Morgan's own losses were 2 killed and less than 100 missing and wounded.

Confederate cavalry raids such as Morgan's were quickly popularized throughout the South and aided the Confederate cause, particularly in the early stages of the war, before Union forces became overwhelming. Fighting on their own territory, often among sympathetic citizens who supplied food, fodder, and, most important, intelligence, Confederate cavalrymen could outwit clumsy Union pursuit and cause much destruction. Disruption of Union supply lines and diversion of troops were their most important contributions. As the war dragged on, however, Morgan allowed pillage and plunder to occur, as did other commanders on both sides, adding to the legacy of bitterness of this tragic time in U.S. history.

Bibliography: Duke, Basil W., *A History of Morgan's Cavalry* (Indiana Univ. Press, 1960); Ramage, James A., *Rebel Raider* (Univ. of Kentucky Press, 1986); Thomas, Edson H., *John Hunt Morgan and His Raiders* (Univ. of Kentucky Press, 1985).

T. C. Mulligan

MORGAN'S OHIO RAID (July 1–26, 1863)

Fourth of Brig. Gen. John H. Morgan's famous Confederate cavalry raids during the Civil War. In June 1863, Gen. Braxton Bragg had directed Morgan to operate behind Union lines in Kentucky, but Morgan disregarded his instructions, crossed the Ohio River in July, and galloped a wide sweep around Cincinnati and into southern Ohio from west to east.

No doubt, Morgan intended to cause panic and confusion in Yankee territory and to draw Union troops from Kentucky (which he accomplished), but it is also likely that he expected to rally Confederate sympathizers in Ohio. Capt. Thomas C. Hines, a Morgan scout who later tried to organize anti-Union operations in Canada, was one of many Southerners who reported to Confederate president Jefferson Davis about opposition to the war in Ohio. Ohio Copperheads were affiliated with antiwar and states-rights politician Clement L. Vallandigham and his Sons of Liberty movement, among other groups. If it was Morgan's intent to foment a Copperhead rising, his tactics alone (extortion, burning of commercial buildings, and wholesale looting) insured that he would fail in that regard. But Morgan, like other Confederates, also misread Vallandigham and the Copperheads, mistaking their antiwar and states-rights convictions for pro-Southern sentiment. In addition to fear and panic, this raid sowed anger and disgust in southern Ohio and in much of the Union.

Morgan then crossed the Ohio at Brandenburg and covered 90 miles in 35 hours in his ride around Cincinnati. By July 18, he was in Pomeroy, three-quarters of the way across Ohio. On July 12, Ohio governor David Tod had called out the common militia in the southern counties for the only time in the war. Thousands of farm boys, merchants, and mechanics, with their squirrel guns and fouling pieces, mustered in mostly company-size formations in town squares and at courthouses. They scored no spectacular successes, but they did hide horses and build roadblocks that kept Morgan moving as his men and horses played out. For reasons of design, lack of remounts, or simply poor discipline, hundreds of rebels fell out of Morgan's columns, extending the panic and confusion by looting and pillaging. Morgan cut railroads at over 60 locations, destroyed 34 bridges, diverted more than 14,000 Union troops, caused at least 100,000 militiamen to muster in Indiana and Ohio, and inflicted hundreds of thousands of dollars of damage to public and private property. In 25 days, he covered more than 700 miles and fought countless skirmishes, the longest cavalry raid of the war.

Brig. Gen. Edward H. Hobson pursued Morgan as he tried to recross the Ohio at Buffington Island on July 19 and dealt him a stinging defeat. Morgan himself and what was left of his command were run down and captured at New Lisbon on July 26. Incarcerated as common criminals in the Ohio Penitentiary, Morgan and some of his men escaped in November and made their way back to Confederate lines.

Bibliography: Duke, Basil W., *A History of Morgan's Cavalry* (Indiana Univ Press, 1960); Ramage, James A., *Rebel Raider* (Univ. of Kentucky Press, 1986); Reid, Whitelaw, *Ohio in the War,* vol. 1 (Robert Clarke Co., 1895); Thomas, Edson H., *John Hunt Morgan and His Raiders* (Univ. of Kentucky Press, 1985).

T. C. Mulligan

MURFREESBORO, BATTLE OF

See Stones River, Battle of.

NASHVILLE, BATTLE OF (December 15–16, 1864)

Civil War battle during the Franklin and Nashville Campaign in which greatly outnumbered Confederate troops suffered a decisive defeat. As Maj. Gen. William T. Sherman prepared for his sweep through Georgia in November 1864, he anticipated the likelihood of a Confederate thrust into Tennessee by Lt. Gen. John Bell Hood. Sherman, therefore, ordered Maj. Gen. George H. Thomas to Nashville to counter such a threat. Besides the Union garrisons in the state, Thomas received substantial reinforcements, including Maj. Gen. John M. Schofield's XXIII Corps and Maj. Gen. David S. Stanley's IV Corps. In addition, Maj. Gen. Andrew J. Smith commanded three divisions coming from Missouri. Nearly 60,000 Union troops would be in Nashville by early December.

In mid-November, Hood began to move the 40,000 men of the Army of Tennessee north. Needing time to concentrate his forces, Thomas ordered Schofield to delay Hood's advance in southern Tennessee. After some skirmishing, the two clashed 15 miles south of Nashville at Franklin on Nov. 30, 1864. It was a bloody encounter that severely weakened Hood's army but did not stop it. The rebels continued to advance on Nashville.

The heavy losses at Franklin and desertions lowered the effective strength of the Army of Tennessee to fewer than 30,000 men. Lacking the manpower to take the heavily fortified city, Hood simply took up positions outside Nashville and waited. Thomas did the same and spent the next two weeks meticulously preparing his forces. Repeated requests by the U.S. War Department to take action fell on deaf ears. Maj. Gen. Ulysses S. Grant became so exasperated with the delay that he pondered going to Nashville himself. Instead, he ordered Thomas relieved by Maj. Gen. John A. Logan. Fortunately for Thomas, Logan failed to arrive in time to carry out the order.

Despite the concern of his superiors, Thomas had everything under control. His hastily organized command required time to rest and deploy itself. And a sleet storm on December 9 prevented action for several days. Finally, on December 15, the well-planned Union assault began. Pinning the Confederate right flank with James B. Steedman's division, which included a number of black regiments, Thomas sent Smith's three divisions and a large body of cavalry on a wide swing around Hood's left flank. The IV Corps held the Union center and pressured the main rebel line, while Schofield's corps was held in reserve. Heavily outnumbered and eventually outflanked, the Army of Tennessee made a gallant stand for most of the day. But late in the afternoon, Thomas ordered Schofield to join the attack; by nightfall, the Confederates began to withdraw.

Despite heavy losses, the tenacious Hood fell back just a few miles and organized a new defense line. The next day, Thomas repeated his tactics. Union infantry and cavalry flanked Hood, while a frontal assault sent the Army of Tennessee fleeing to the rear in disorder. It soon ceased to exist as an effective combat force, and Hood resigned his commission within a month. Nashville brought a decisive end to any Southern hopes for victory in the West.

Bibliography: Horn, Stanley F., *The Decisive Battle of Nashville* (Louisiana State Univ. Press, 1956); McKinney, F. Francis, *Education in Violence: The Life of George H. Thomas and the History of the Army of the Cumberland* (Wayne State Univ. Press, 1961).

Daniel T. Bailey

NEW MADRID AND ISLAND NO. 10
(March–April 1862)

Two Mississippi River positions in southeastern Missouri that, from the onset of the Civil War (April 1861), were held by Confederate forces to block federal passage but which, one year later, were bypassed by Union vessels. Following the loss of Fort Donelson in February 1862, Confederate forces withdrew to a site near New Madrid, Missouri, where the Mississippi makes two 180-degree turns, much like a sideways, inverted "S." Occupying Island No. 10 in the easternmost bend in the river and the high ground encompassed by the western bend, 7,000 rebel soldiers with 130 guns awaited the Union forces of Brig. Gen. John Pope.

Stymied by the seemingly impassable Southern positions, Pope turned to his supporting gunboats to run the gauntlet of enemy gunfire. During wild thunderstorms on the nights of April 4 and 6, two Union gunboats successfully steamed past Island No. 10, thereafter supporting Pope's successful thrust west below the Confederate forces, blocking their retreat and forcing their surrender the next day.

Bibliography: Potter, E. B., ed., *Sea Power: A Naval History* (Naval Inst. Press, 1981).

Maj. Grant H. Walker

NEW ORLEANS, SIEGE OF
(April–May 1862)

Civil War engagement in which a vital Southern port was captured by Union forces in a joint army-navy operation. Strategically situated between the Mississippi River and Lake Ponchartrain, New Orleans, Louisiana, was guarded by Forts Jackson and St. Philip (75 miles downriver), supplemented by gunboats and fire rafts. The Confederate commander, Maj. Gen. Mansfield Lovell, had only 3,000 militia men to insure the defense of the city in April 1862.

The Union commander, David G. Farragut, had 18 warships and 20 mortar schooners plus 18,000 troops. A six-day bombardment of the forts was ineffective, and Farragut determined to run the gauntlet. He broke through after fierce fighting on April 24 and arrived outside New Orleans the next day. Lovell left the city open, and the federal troops moved in May 1.

The South lost control of the lower Mississippi in addition to the factories, ordnance facilities, and shipbuilding complex of New Orleans. Baton Rouge, Louisiana, and Natchez, Mississippi, surrendered, but Vicksburg, Mississippi, refused, and it was a year before the entire river was opened.

Bibliography: Foote, Shelby, *The Civil War, A Narrative: Fort Sumter to Perryville* (Random House, 1958); Millett, Allan R., and Peter Maslowski, *For the Common Defense: A Military History of the United States of America* (Free Press, 1984).

Capt. Karen S. Wilhelm

OKEECHOBEE SWAMP, BATTLE OF (December 25, 1837)

Largest pitched battle of the Second Seminole War (1835–1842), fought on the shore of Lake Okeechobee in south-central Florida on Christmas Day 1837. A force of infantry and artillery under Col. Zachary Taylor soundly defeated the Seminole, who, encouraged by a strong defensive position, made the mistake of trying to stand against a bayonet charge by well-drilled U.S. regulars. Although the battle, fought in waist-deep swamp and five-foot-high swamp grass, was clearly a victory for Taylor, it was indecisive. The surviving Seminole took covert refuge throughout the swamp, and four more years of guerrilla warfare ensued.

Bibliography: Dupuy, R. Ernest, *The Compact History of the United States Army,* rev. ed. (Hawthorn Books, 1961); Weigley, Russell R., *The American Way of War: A History of United States Military Strategy and Policy* (Macmillan Co., 1973).

Lt. Col. (Ret.) Charles R. Shrader

PALO ALTO, BATTLE OF (May 8, 1846)

Initial battle of the Mexican War. In May 1846, Gen. Zachary Taylor led U.S. forces toward Matamoros, Mexico, near the mouth of the Rio Grande, across from Brownsville, Texas. On May 5, Taylor's troops found the Mexican army of Mariano Arista blocking their advance near Palo Alto (12 miles northeast of Brownsville). Arista chose his position well, but, despite his numerical superiority, he was content simply to defend the approach to Matamoros, waiting for Taylor to make a move. On May 8, as Taylor began to deploy a line of skirmishers, Arista opened up with his artillery. Lacking high-explosive shells, however, the Mexican bombardment fell short. Taylor's men soon commenced a return fire, crushing Mexican morale. The following morning, Arista, who had suffered heavy casualties (nearly 400 lost, compared to 9 U.S. soldiers killed) withdrew to a better defensive position at Resaca de la Palma (just north of Brownsville).

M. Guy Bishop

PEA RIDGE (ELKHORN TAVERN), BATTLE OF (March 7–8, 1862)

Civil War engagement that ended any serious Confederate threat to Missouri. Launched in a blizzard on Mar. 4, 1862, an attempted invasion of southwestern Missouri by 16,500 Confederate troops under Maj. Gen. Earl Van Dorn was opposed by 10,250 Union troops under Brig. Gen. Samuel R. Curtis, who established defensive positions near Elkhorn Tavern, three miles south of Pea Ridge, Arkansas. On the night of March 6–7, Van Dorn enveloped the Union forces. Attacked from the rear the following morning, Curtis skillfully faced his troops about and counterattacked. Brig. Gen. Benjamin McCulloch's Confederate division was met one mile north of Leetown by two Union divisions, which killed both McCulloch and his successor and drove the Confederates back. Meanwhile, heavier fighting took place near Elkhorn Tavern, where rebel forces under Van Dorn and Brig. Gen. Sterling Price encountered Curtis's 4th Division, commanded by Col. Eugene C. Carr. Attacking from a deep valley, the Confederates pushed Carr's troops back a mile by nightfall. Curtis then reformed his forces and attacked at dawn on March 8. Exhausted, hungry, and short of artillery ammunition, Van Dorn's troops near Elkhorn Tavern were routed but managed to withdraw without pursuit. Confederate losses were about 1,500, and Union casualties numbered 1,384.

Bibliography: Hattaway, Herman, and Archer Jones, *How the North Won: A Military History of the Civil War* (Univ. of Illinois Press, 1983); McWhiney, Grady, and Perry D. Jamieson, *Attack and Die: Civil Military Tactics and the Southern Heritage* (Univ. of Alabama Press, 1982); Shea, William L., and Earl J. Hess, "Pea Ridge, 7–8 March 1862," *The Civil War Battlefield Guide—The Conservation Fund,* ed. by Frances H. Kennedy (Houghton Mifflin, 1990).

Lt. Col. (Ret.) Charles R. Shrader

PENINSULAR CAMPAIGN (March–July 1862)

Civil War's first major military campaign in the eastern theater. On Mar. 16, 1862, Maj. Gen. George B. McClellan, recently relieved by Pres. Abraham Lincoln as commander in chief of the federal armies but still commander of the Department and Army of the Potomac, agreed to take command of a campaign against Richmond, Virginia, the Confederate capital. As early as November 1861, he had had an ill-conceived plan of embarking his army to Fortress Monroe, Virginia, at the tip of the peninsula between the James and York rivers, to begin the Peninsular Campaign.

After the famous *Monitor* and *Merrimac* naval battle (Mar. 9, 1862) cleared the way, McClellan used more than 400 ships of various types to move more than 75,000 men plus all necessary equipment, without incident, down the Potomac River through the Chesapeake Bay to Fortress Monroe by April. He left troops in the Shenandoah Valley to protect Washington, D.C., from Maj. Gen. Thomas "Stonewall" Jackson, but on March 31, Lincoln, fearing McClellan had left too few, recalled 40,000 men. On April 3, McClellan discovered that Lincoln had withheld Maj. Gen. Irvin McDowell's I Corps and protested he needed more men, even though by now he had more than 100,000 troops. Lincoln's interference in military matters demoralized McClellan and lessened his chances for success.

Advance on Yorktown. From his base at Fortress Monroe, McClellan, with troops still arriving, prepared to assault the weak Confederate line (fewer than 15,000 troops) stretched across the Peninsula near Yorktown, Virginia. On April 4, armed with the greatly exaggerated belief that the Confederates had 120,000 troops on the Peninsula (the estimate of secret-service man Allan Pinkerton), he began moving his army northwest toward the undermanned Confederate entrenchments known as the "Magruder Line" held by Maj. Gen. John B. Magruder. The line protected Yorktown and the artillery positions, which prevented the Union navy from sailing up the York River and flanking the Confederates, which would have forced them to abandon their trenches.

The Peninsular roads were dirt tracks through heavy, low-lying woods. The Confederates turned the land into a swamp by damming small rivers, and this helped to bring the Union march to a halt. McClellan used a hydrogen observation balloon and erroneously determined that the Confederates were strongly entrenched enough to warrant immediate plans for siege operations.

McClellan surprised everyone when he decided to lay siege instead of overrunning the positions. His excessive caution and habit of overestimating his enemy's power nullified his great organizational and strategic abilities. In the month that it took him to prepare to take Yorktown by siege, the Confederates rushed reinforcements to Magruder. Meanwhile, McDowell's corps marched to Fredericksburg (50 miles north of Richmond) on April 18 and became a second threat to the capital.

On May 4, the Confederates, now commanded by Gen. Joseph E. Johnston, abandoned Yorktown and moved back toward trenches around Richmond. On their retreat, they tore up the roads, felled trees, ruined fords, and left behind land mines ("torpedoes") after a heated debate as to the morality of such mines in war. Confederate strength on the Peninsula and in front of Richmond was 55,000, or half that of the Union army. Hard fighting broke out on May 5 near Williamsburg, but the Confederates continued to retreat because McClellan, by using his navy, could make a waterborne turning movement and entrap Magruder's entire force.

Battle of Seven Pines. On May 6, Lincoln arrived at Fortress Monroe and tried to hurry McClellan in capturing Richmond before the Confederates improved their positions. On May 9, the Confederates evacuated Norfolk (south of the James River), burned some naval stores, and blew up their ironclad *Virginia (Merrimac),* all of which inflicted a killing blow to any chance the South had of controlling the water. The James and York rivers were now open to the Union. On May 15, Union ships on the James dueled with Confederate land batteries seven miles from Richmond at Drewry's Bluff, or Fort Darling. The fort's guns covered obstacles the Confederates had placed in the river.

Johnston's army fell back slowly, and McClellan followed more slowly, hampered by bad roads, no maps, and lots of rain. Johnston occupied strong positions behind the swampy Chickahominy River, some placed only three miles from Richmond, the Union's objective.

After fighting his way through 13 lines of thinly manned fortifications, McClellan established headquarters and a supply base at White House, 22 miles east of Richmond, where the Richmond & York River Railroad crossed the Pamunkey River, one of two rivers forming the York. Skirmishes took place all across the front. Still, McClellan blamed Lincoln's administration for his lack of troops, believing he had too few men to attack. On May 25, the president wired McClellan to attack or return to Washington. McClellan still did not take any offensive action. Instead, he split his force, with three corps on the northeast side of the Chickahominy and two on the south side.

The situation in Richmond seemed tenuous, and the government prepared to ship out its vital papers. Then on the night of May 30, there was a violent rainstorm, which began to sweep away bridges. Johnston realized the Union army was divided by a flooding Chickahominy River and, on May 31, quickly drew up imperfect plans to attack the corps of Erasmus D. Keyes and Samuel P. Heintzelman at the crossroads of Seven Pines (Fair Oaks), south of the river. McClellan and his other three corps (under Brig. Gens. Fitz-John Porter, William B. Franklin, and Edwin V. Sumner) were north of the river.

The Confederates moved by several roads to an attack position to strike the two corps south of the river, but Maj. Gen. James Longstreet put his division on the wrong road, and the march was confused and late. The Union army did have time, however, to get Sumner's corps south of the river as reinforcements. The Confederates attacked piecemeal, including a series of bloody engagements spearheaded by Maj. Gen. Daniel H. Hill's men. The Union line, often fighting in knee-deep water where the wounded had to be propped up to keep them from drowning, fell back twice but managed to hold its third position.

The two-day action at Fair Oaks was indecisive. Both armies fought much better than at Bull Run the previous year. The battle was a test of the men, as there were few orders from the commanding generals. Confederate commander Johnston failed to rout or destroy two isolated enemy corps. Late in the battle, he was badly wounded, one of more than 6,100 Confederate casualties, while the Union lost 5,000 of 42,000 engaged. Most of McClellan's troops saw no action.

On June 1, Pres. Jefferson Davis replaced Johnston with Gen. Robert E. Lee as commander of the Confederate army, soon to be known as the Army of Northern Virginia. The Union army went on the defense, strengthening its position within view of Richmond.

Union Withdrawal. McClellan had been greatly unnerved at the sight of "mangled corpses" and turned his energies to the defense and making contact with the Union navy on the James River to evacuate his wounded. McClellan had been stopped. Heavy rains started on June 5, causing movement across streams to be hazardous and difficult. By June 8, there was skirmishing along the Chickahominy River, and McDowell, now 50 miles north of Richmond, received orders to face his army toward Richmond. It was time for Lee to seize the offensive in what became known as the Seven Days' Battles.

Bibliography: Cullen, Joseph P., *The Peninsular Campaign* (Stackpole, 1973).

Lynn L. Sims

PETERSBURG CAMPAIGN (June 1864–April 1865)

Civil War campaign focused on Petersburg, Virginia, the hub of five converging railroads and many wagon roads, which made it the logistics center and lifeline for Richmond (the Confederate capital), some 20 miles to the north; one of the war's final operations. During May and June 1864, Gen. Ulysses S. Grant, in response to Gen. Robert E. Lee's refusal to leave the trench lines to fight, moved his Union forces around the Confederate right flank. The crossing of the James River was such a movement. Grant, a former quartermaster, built a 2,000-foot pontoon bridge over the James, while Lee, trained as an engineer, grappled with supplies and logistic matters.

Trench Warfare. As early as May, Maj. Gen. Benjamin F. Butler controlled the land called Bermuda Hundred between the James and Appomattox rivers and only threatened the rail connection between Richmond and Petersburg. Petersburg was held by Brig. Gen. Henry A. Wise and a small Confederate garrison manning a long trench system called the Dimmock Line, built two years earlier. They checked Butler's June 9 advance on Petersburg.

By June 15, Grant had crossed his XVIII Corps (under Maj. Gen. William F. Smith) and attacked the Dimmock Line, which forced the Confederates, now under Gen. P. G. T. Beauregard, to give up more than a mile of ground and quickly dig new trenches. It was not until June 18 that Lee, in Richmond, believed Grant's army had crossed the James and only then sent reinforcements from the Richmond defenses.

In the first few days around Petersburg, Grant lost about 8,000 men attacking prepared Confederate positions. On June 22, Grant's army was stopped at the Weldon Railroad. On June 29, the Union cavalry was beaten at Reams' Station. Grant, recognizing his troops were fatigued from seven weeks of constant fighting, extended his trench line to the south and settled down in front of the entrenched Confederates east and south of Petersburg. Grant stopped trying to maneuver his troops around Lee's right flank, and the siege of Petersburg began. This siege would decide the fate of Petersburg, Richmond, Lee's Army of Northern Virginia, and the Confederacy itself.

By pushing his trench line south and west, Grant forced Lee to stretch his already thinly spread troops to the danger point. For nearly 10 months, the siege continued with sporadic battles. In their bombardments of Petersburg, the federals used a dictator-class mortar that could hurl a 220-pound exploding ball over 2 miles, but there was no possibility of aiming it accurately. Its value was the psychological impact on residents of the city caused by the screaming shells and random air bursts. During the siege, there were also long periods of quiet during which Northern quartermasters gathered the overwhelming supplies that were to decide the war's outcome. On the Appomattox River at City Point, Grant built the largest supply depot the world had seen, only 15 miles from the siege line.

The Union army did not completely surround the Confederates or Petersburg. Nor did Grant conduct a siege in the usual military manner by battering down the enemy ramparts and digging closer parallel trenches. Grant knew Petersburg was the key to Richmond's existence, and if he could cut that connection, Richmond would die without a pitched battle. From City Point, Grant built a U.S. military railroad that literally ran from the docks to within a few yards of the Union trenches, bringing the North's agricultural and industrial resources to the very point of conflict.

On July 27 and again on August 14, Grant sent large elements of his army north of Petersburg to cut the rail line to Richmond. Both attempts were unsuccessful, but on August 18, the Union army attacked the Confederate line at Globe Tavern south of Petersburg, which had been weakened to meet the August 14 Union advance, and captured the Weldon Railroad. On October 27, the federals struck both Confederate flanks at the same time. The North was beaten back quickly in the north; however, the southern battle was closer but with the same results. This two-pronged failure caused Grant to concentrate his forces on the south, or Union left flank, where the Confederate line would eventually break.

Lee defended the railroads coming in from rich southern farmlands. Grant did not use his trench line, in some cases only a few hundred yards from the Southern trenches, to launch frontal attacks by his larger army. Rather, he held his ground and sent out forces to cut the wagon roads and Southside Railroad running into Petersburg. Those raids dominated the rest of the campaign.

From the time Grant dug trenches, there were few battles. There was one unusual Union frontal attack called the "Crater." In July, a Pennsylvania regiment tunneled more than 500 feet under a salient of the Confederate line, packed the end with 8,000 pounds of powder, and exploded it. The result was a large crater where the Southern artillery battery had stood. The Union army was slow to charge through the gap to exploit the temporary advantage. At the last moment, black troops trained for that specific mission were replaced by untrained white units that charged into the gigantic pit instead of around it. The Confederates quickly sent reinforcements who slaughtered the Union soldiers in the crater. The affair, which cost the lives of

4,000 Union and 1,500 Confederate soldiers, had little military significance. A few weeks later, Confederate agents planted a time bomb on a Union barge loaded with 80,000 pounds of powder at the City Point wharf. The explosion wrecked part of the dock but did not cripple the North's operation.

Final Stages. The Confederate supply systems were as poor as the Union's were good. Maj. Gen. William T. Sherman and other Union commanders created havoc deep in the Confederacy, preventing supplies from reaching Lee. Sherman's campaign through Georgia and the Carolinas, aimed at the Confederate logistics, was a key part of the North's strategy to isolate Lee's army. The Confederate supply system, at its best never more than local and barely adequate, now collapsed. On one Confederate raid behind Union lines, rebels captured about 2,000 head of cattle, which only briefly raised Southern morale. The overwhelming reelection of Pres. Abraham Lincoln, which promised more war, and the fact the Southern soldiers at Petersburg knew their families were suffering from Union occupation, added to the hopelessness of the Southern cause. When spring 1865 signaled the beginning of another fighting season, most Confederate soldiers could see that the end was near.

Lee had struggled against long odds for four years. In the last year of the war, he had fought from trenches to negate the North's numerical superiority. On March 25, as the Petersburg Campaign merged into the Appomattox Campaign, Maj. Gen. John B. Gordon led rebel units on a daring strike against Fort Stedman, which was at the closest point to Confederate lines. His initial breakthrough could not be supported, and the Southerners retreated with heavy losses. Lee could not dislodge the federals in front of Petersburg, just contain them, and that for only a short time before the North won everything. Northern units overwhelmed the Southerners at Five Forks, Virginia, on April 1. The last wagon road and railroad were gone, and there was no more military justification for Lee to defend Petersburg. On April 2–3, both Petersburg and Richmond were abandoned. One week later, the war would end at nearby Appomattox.

Lynn L. Sims

PORT HUDSON, SIEGE OF (May 27–July 9, 1863)

Civil War operation in which an important Confederate strongpoint was captured by Union forces. Port Hudson, Louisiana, was vital to the Confederacy primarily because

Wood and earthen shelters housed and protected Union soldiers during the nine-month siege of Petersburg. (U.S. Army Military History Institute)

it controlled the South's last east-west line of communications via the Red River, a conduit for meat and grain shipped from Texas. In the summer of 1863, as federal forces besieged Vicksburg, Mississippi, 150 miles to the north, Rear Adm. David G. Farragut's mixed fleet of Union screw sloops and gunboats supported the efforts of Maj. Gen. Nathaniel P. Banks to seize Port Hudson. After an assault on May 27 failed, the Union offensive settled down into a classic siege. News of the fall of Vicksburg on July 4 convinced the defending garrison that further resistance was futile, and five days later, Port Hudson—the last Confederate stronghold on the Mississippi River—surrendered.

Bibliography: Potter, E. B., ed., *Sea Power: A Naval History* (Naval Inst. Press, 1981).

Maj. Grant H. Walker

PORT ROYAL (FORTS BEAUREGARD AND WALKER), SIEGE OF (November 7, 1861)

Early Civil War naval operation. Seeking a local base for the growing fleet of Union steamers on blockade duty off the South's Atlantic seaboard, Sec. of the Navy Gideon Welles determined in mid-1861 to seize control of Port Royal, South Carolina, an ideal site owing to its deep harbor and proximity to both Charleston, South Carolina, and Savannah, Georgia.

On November 7, the commander of the Union expedition, Capt. Samuel F. Du Pont, led 14 warships past the two forts that guarded the entrance to Port Royal Sound. Circling repeatedly and firing at point-blank range, Du Pont at length forced the two outgunned Confederate forts to capitulate, thereby securing the first significant supply depot on the south Atlantic coast for use by Northern blockaders.

Bibliography: Bauer, K. Jack, "Samuel Francis Du Pont: Aristocratic Professional," *Captains of the Old Steam Navy,* ed. by James C. Bradford (Naval Inst. Press, 1986).

Maj. Grant H. Walker

PRAIRIE GROVE, BATTLE OF (December 7, 1862)

Civil War battle 10 miles south of Fayetteville, Arkansas. Knowing that Brig. Gen. James G. Blunt's Union division was alone near Fayetteville in December 1862, Confederate major general Thomas C. Hindman decided to strike. Blunt detected Hindman's advance and warned his superiors, who dispatched Maj. Gen. Francis J. Herron with two divisions to his aid. As Hindman closed in on Blunt, he discovered Herron's approach and, leaving a small force to contain Blunt, moved to attack Herron. On making contact, however, Hindman inexplicably took up defensive positions on Prairie Grove Ridge. Thereafter, on December 7, Herron launched three unsuccessful attacks on the Confederate lines. Blunt, hearing the sound of gunfire, marched to the battlefield and arrived on Hindman's left flank in the afternoon. The hard-pressed rebels held on until dark and then withdrew, ending their control of northwest Arkansas.

Bibliography: Monaghan, Jay, *Civil War on the Western Border, 1854–1865* (Little, Brown, 1955).

Richard F. Kehrberg

QUANTRILL'S RAID (August 21, 1863)

Act of massacre and plunder committed by Confederate raiders during the Civil War. In the summer of 1863, Col. William C. Quantrill's Confederate guerrillas determined to attack Lawrence, Kansas, the center of Kansas abolitionism. After a two-day ride from Missouri, Quantrill and his 450 followers approached Lawrence on the morning of August 21. Splitting his column into squadrons of 45 men each, Quantrill instructed them to "Kill every man big enough to carry a gun." At dawn, the guerrillas poured into town armed with lists of those to be executed and houses to burn. Especially singled out for destruction were the recruiting camps of the 14th Kansas Cavalry and 2d Kansas Colored Regiment. The raid quickly degenerated into a series of individual lootings and murders. At 9:00 A.M., the raiders packed up their booty and abandoned the town, leaving more than 150 dead men and boys and 185 burned buildings.

Bibliography: Brownlee, Richard S., *Gray Ghosts of the Confederacy: Guerrilla Warfare in the West, 1861–1865* (Louisiana State Univ. Press, 1958).

Richard F. Kehrberg

RED RIVER CAMPAIGN (March 10–May 22, 1864)

Failed Union offensive during the Civil War. In the spring of 1864, Pres. Abraham Lincoln directed that the Union army should seize east Texas. He hoped such a move would impress the French, then in Mexico, not to aid the Confederacy. In New Orleans, Union major general Nathaniel P. Banks, after several unsuccessful operations on the Texas coast, decided the best route into Texas lay up the Red River and through Shreveport, Louisiana. Banks planned to move 17,000 of his troops to Alexandria, Louisiana, there to be joined by 10,000 men from Maj. Gen. William T. Sherman's army, and then advance up the Red River. Simultaneously, 15,000 Union soldiers were to move south from Arkansas. Opposing the federal advance were 30,000 Confederates under Gen. E. Kirby Smith.

In mid-March, Banks joined up with the detachment from Sherman and a Union fleet, and began a fighting advance up the Red River. On April 8, at Sabine Cross Roads, however, the skirmishing escalated, and the rebels routed the Union advance guard. Banks fell back and fought off a rebel attack at Pleasant Hill the following day. Thereafter, he initiated a general withdrawal. Noting this, Smith divided his command, leaving a small force to harass

Banks, and then marched north and checked the Union force moving in from Arkansas. Low water and constant pressure from the Confederates turned Banks's retreat into a painful ordeal. The expedition cost the Union some 8,000 men, 9 ships, and 57 guns. The rebels lost 4,000 men but kept the Red River country for the remainder of the war.

Bibliography: Johnson, Ludwell H., *Red River Campaign* (Johns Hopkins Univ. Press, 1958).

Richard F. Kehrberg

RESACA DE LA PALMA, BATTLE OF (May 9, 1846)

First major battle (together with its prelude at Palo Alto the previous day) of the Mexican War; a flawed U.S. victory by Brig. Gen. Zachary Taylor over the Mexican general de division Mariano Arista. As hostilities approached in March 1846, Taylor moved his small army of 3,000 regulars into disputed Texas territory and built Fort Texas just across the Rio Grande from Matamoros, Mexico. Beginning on April 24, Arista crossed the river east of Matamoros, ambushed several U.S. detachments, and besieged Fort Texas. In reply, Taylor moved a large supply train from his supply base at Point Isabel southwest to relieve Fort Texas, but this movement was blocked by the Mexicans at Palo Alto. Taylor used his extremely mobile horse artillery batteries to goad the thin Mexican line into a series of attacks that resulted in 257 Mexican and 55 U.S. casualties.

During the night of May 8–9, Arista pulled back five miles to the Resaca de la Palma, a strong defensive position with numerous ponds and depressions to impede attacks on the Mexican line. Reinforced by troops from the siege of Fort Texas, Arista had approximately 3,700 men, compared to fewer than 2,000 U.S. soldiers who actually fought. Despite these advantages, the Mexican defenders were tired and hungry and lacked confidence in their commander.

Taylor devoted the morning of May 9 to construction of an elaborate breastwork, reinforced by his heavier artillery, to protect the supply train that had previously encumbered his movements. At 2:00 P.M., Taylor pushed forward along the road leading into the left center of the Mexican position. Units on both sides were broken up by the terrain and dense vegetation, but several companies of the U.S. 4th Infantry Regiment found their way around the thinly held Mexican left (west) flank, capturing Arista's headquarters by surprise.

Unaware of this, Taylor concentrated on breaking through along the road. After repeated charges by U.S. dragoons overran but could not hold the defending Mexican artillery, Taylor sent the 5th and 8th infantry regiments forward into a desperate, hand-to-hand combat that completed the destruction of the Mexican army. Arista led his cavalry in a rearguard charge that failed to stop the U.S. Army or halt the rout of his own troops. Fortunately for the Mexicans,

Mexican Gen. La Vega was captured at the Battle of Resaca de la Palma, one of the first engagements of the Mexican War. (U.S. Army Signal Corps)

Taylor missed the opportunity to pursue a foe who was fleeing across the Rio Grande.

Resaca de la Palma cost the Mexican army 515 casualties, as compared to 132 U.S. losses. Apart from an incomplete victory, the U.S. Army derived exaggerated ideas about the efficacy of mobile guns and advancing infantry at close quarters with the enemy, ideas that resulted in far greater casualties during the Civil War.

Bibliography: Bauer, K. Jack, *The Mexican War 1846–1848* (Macmillan Co., 1974); Heller, Charles E., and William A. Stofft, eds., *America's First Battles: 1776–1965* (Univ. of Kansas Press, 1986).

Jonathan M. House

SABINE CROSS ROADS, BATTLE OF (April 8, 1864)

Battle fought in the Red River Campaign of the Civil War in which a superior Union force suffered a costly defeat. Following the capture of Vicksburg, Mississippi, in July 1863, Union attention turned toward Louisiana. Pres. Abraham Lincoln hoped to subdue the Confederate forces there and then establish a Union presence in Texas as a warning to France, which was in the process of raising a puppet government in Mexico. The Confederates had 30,000 troops scattered throughout the trans-Mississippi region, mainly in Louisiana. Maj. Gen. Nathaniel P. Banks was ordered to subdue the rebels in Louisiana, occupy Shreveport, and then send most of his army on to New Orleans. But Banks ran a poor campaign. His effort collapsed on Apr. 8, 1864, when Confederate forces under Maj. Gen. Richard Taylor, son of former U.S. president Zachary Taylor, routed his advance divisions at Sabine Cross Roads 40 miles south of Shreveport. Due to this failure, the Confederacy continued to hold Texas, northern Louisiana, and southern Arkansas.

M. Guy Bishop

SALTVILLE MASSACRE (October 2, 1864)

Ill-fated Union raid into Virginia during the Civil War, designed to damage Confederate slate and lead production. Distinguishing itself in the assault was the new 5th U.S. Colored Cavalry, which charged and captured the Confederate works but met with formidable opposition in the hastily raised Confederate troops formerly of John Hunt Morgan's command at Saltville, Virginia. The 5th held the position for several hours but was ordered to withdraw because no support was available. Confederates executed numerous black prisoners during the battle, and during the next two days raided hospitals, killing seven more black soldiers lying in their beds. The Saltville Massacre highlighted the additional dangers faced by black soldiers who fought in the Civil War.

Mark Pitcavage

SAN JACINTO, BATTLE OF (April 21, 1836)

Decisive battle that won Texas its independence from Mexico. In February–March 1836, the Mexican military dictator Antonio López de Santa Anna quickly overran and massacred the Texan outposts of San Patricio, Goliad, and the Alamo. He then pursued Sam Houston (commander in chief of the Texan forces) across eastern Texas, in the process allowing his troops to become dispersed. Santa Anna apparently considered the campaign over and was not prepared for a counterattack. As a result, only 1,200 Mexicans were actually with Santa Anna when Houston surprised him at the ferry over the San Jacinto River on the afternoon of April 21. In a sudden charge, the 750 Texans shattered their opponents, at a cost of 2 Texans killed and 23 wounded.

Bibliography: Stephenson, Nathaniel W., *Texas and the Mexican War: A Chronicle of the Winning of the Southwest* (Yale Univ. Press, 1921).

Jonathan M. House

SANTA FE

Western terminus of the Santa Fe Trail; a city occupied by U.S. forces during the Mexican War. The outbreak of hostilities between Mexico and the United States in 1846 made Santa Fe, New Mexico, important to U.S. military strategy. The sleepy village had been penetrated years earlier by U.S. traders and fur trappers. It was rumored that the people of New Mexico were discontented with Mexican rule. The U.S. government believed Santa Fe could be captured without a fight. Col. Stephen W. Kearny, commanding the 1st Dragoons at Fort Leavenworth, Kansas, received orders to seize New Mexico. In August 1846, Kearny entered Santa Fe. After consolidating his forces, now bolstered by volunteers from Missouri and a battalion of Mormons recruited in Iowa and Nebraska, Kearny's army marched on to California.

M. Guy Bishop

SEMINOLE WARS

Two series of conflicts between the United States and the Seminole Indians in Florida.

First Seminole War: 1817–1819. Although Georgia began an almost programmatic attempt to take Florida away from Spain in 1811, the immediate rationale for war was the perceived need by expansionist settlers in southern Alabama and Georgia to pacify "centers of border anarchy." The settlers saw cross-border Indian attacks and the continuous departure of runaway slaves, who either found freedom or benign bondage with the Indians in Spanish territory, as major challenges to the U.S. doctrine of Manifest Destiny and the institution of slavery. As a result, when Neamathla, a Mikasuki chief, warned Gen. Edmund P. Gaines to stay north of the Flint River, Gaines took the opportunity to initiate hostilities on Nov. 21, 1817. Maj. Gen. Andrew Jackson subsequently worked his way down the Apalachicola River; by April 1818, he had broken Seminole power in northern Florida. By successfully attacking such Spanish cities as Pensacola and St. Marks, Jackson convinced the Spanish they were powerless to defend their Florida territory. The First Seminole War concluded with the 1819 Adams-Onís Treaty, which formally ceded Spanish Florida to the United States.

Second Seminole War: 1835–1842. Throughout this war, which is remembered as the longest, costliest, and bloodiest Indian conflict in U.S. history, 10,000 U.S. Army regulars and 30,000 volunteers fought. They primarily opposed a total of 5,000 Seminole, 1,200 of whom were lightly armed warriors. Despite their overwhelming numerical superiority, the U.S. forces were unable to fulfill their primary objectives: the cessation of Indian attacks against land-hungry settlers and the complete removal of the Seminole from their 2,000,000-acre central Florida reservation.

The Indians did not have a permanent infrastructure that the U.S. troops could attack. What the latter did face, beginning with the Dade Massacre of 1835, was an enemy that waged guerrilla warfare. The Indians struck quickly and then faded back into the wilderness. Such tactics—along with the malarial terrain, brutal weather, and runaway slaves who also fought against U.S. forces—proved too much for the eight commanders who successively tried to suppress native resistance.

Some commanders, however, did make progress. Col. Zachary Taylor, for example, forever broke organized Seminole resistance at the 1837 Battle of Lake Okeechobee, one of the few instances where the Seminole directly confronted their foes. Maj. Gen. Thomas Jesup, in turn, violated tradition and arrested Indian leaders involved in truce talks. The detention of individuals such as Osceola caused a serious void in Seminole leadership. Jesup also implemented a policy designed to starve the Seminole into submission by destroying their villages and crops.

Col. William Worth used the latter tactic in 1841, when he conducted the first summer campaign of the war. Because Worth interrupted the raising and harvesting of crops, he starved the Seminole into inactivity. With only 250 Seminole left, the U.S. government announced that the war was over in August 1842. But, despite the deaths of an estimated 1,500–2,000 U.S. soldiers and a cost of nearly $30,000,000, native Americans remained in Florida. It would take another war (1855–58) to force the Seminole remnant westward.

Bibliography: Mahon, John K., *History of the Second Seminole War* (Univ. of Florida Press, 1967); Sprauge, John T., *The Origin, Progress, and Conclusion of the Florida War* (Univ. of Florida Press, 1964).

Maj. Peter R. Faber

SEVEN DAYS' BATTLES (June 25–July 1, 1862)

Series of Civil War battles that ended the Peninsular Campaign. On June 12, 1862, in an effort to find the extent of the Union army of well over 100,000 men now in defensive positions east of Richmond, Brig. Gen. Jeb Stuart began a ride with 1,200 cavalrymen that would encircle Maj. Gen. George B. McClellan's Union army. Stuart's ride was an embarrassment to McClellan.

At the same time, Gen. Robert E. Lee sent reinforcements from his 55,000 Confederates in trenches around Richmond, 100 miles west to Maj. Gen. Thomas "Stonewall" Jackson in the Shenandoah Valley to give the impression that a reinforced Jackson would make a major thrust toward Washington, the Union's center of gravity. On June 16, Lee's reinforcements to Jackson, plus Jackson's army, left the valley and headed not toward Washington but to the northern flank of Lee's army east of Richmond. The Union army did not detect the movement.

On June 25, the Seven Days' Battle east of Richmond began with skirmishing as the Confederates blunted probing Union attacks. By now, Union forces numbered more than 156,000 and Confederate forces more than 75,000. Lee believed he could not stand still before such a powerful enemy, because eventually McClellan's tactics of siege warfare would wear down the South. On June 26, Lee and his generals decided to attack the Union army's right flank of about 30,000 troops to cut its overland rail connection with the north. Richmond could not stand a siege. This was Lee's first major operation as a field commander, and he left only 25,000 men in the trenches defending Richmond from about three times that many Union troops. Lee was not merely trying to make McClellan retreat, he wanted to destroy his army. If McClellan caught on, he could drive through the weak defensive positions and capture the capital. Lee's plan was a gamble that could win or lose the war.

Stuart's ride showed Lee, as well as McClellan, that the Union supply base on the Pamunkey River could be destroyed. McClellan began to move his supplies from White House south, overland across the peninsula to Harrison's Landing on the safe James River. However, once he lost the Richmond & York River Railroad, he could never bring up his heavy siege guns through the swamps, over narrow bridges and thick woods, and therefore could not lay siege to Richmond. McClellan could only win a siege battle. This move away from White House sealed his defeat.

On June 26, three Confederate divisions were poised to attack Brig. Gen. Fitz-John Porter's Corps on the extreme right flank of McClellan's army, but Jackson had not yet brought his reinforced corps on line. At 3:00 P.M., Maj. Gen. A. P. Hill, impatient of waiting, attacked without Jackson. Hill's men swept through Mechanicsville but faltered at Ellerson's Mill on Beaver Dam Creek. The Union position on the east side of the steep-sided creek was strong, and the South lost several thousand men with no apparent success. Except for Malvern Hill, the sacrifice at Beaver Dam Creek was not equaled during this summer.

Jackson, for no known reason, arrived 12 hours late and began to flank the strong Union position. After nightfall, the federals evacuated their strong position, throwing away a great advantage, and fell back to prepared positions.

The next day, Lee struck the Union army dug in behind Boatswain Swamp to cover the Union withdrawal through Gaines's Mill. After a long and indecisive day of fighting, during which Jackson was late again, the Confederates, at 7:00 P.M., attacked through a tangled undergrowth and swampy bottom. The Confederate charge was only about 500 yards, but the terrain was most difficult. The South lost 8,750 killed at Gaines's Mill but captured thousands of rifles and 52 artillery pieces. The federals pulled back again, but the retreat remained orderly at the expense of 6,840 killed. So far, McClellan had had only one corps fully engaged, and it had done well. Confederate determination at Beaver Dam Creek and again at Gaines's Mill had unnerved McClellan, and he was moving his whole army parallel to the battle lines (not a good tactic), crossing the Chickahominy River to gather at the James River for evacuation.

June 28–July 1. On June 28, Lee was trying to understand what McClellan was doing. As it turned out, this was the quietest day of the seven, with the last Union supply elements leaving White House. McClellan's army destroyed a vast amount of supplies they could not carry and joined the long line of troops moving across the peninsula behind the front lines. The Union navy began moving transport ships up the James.

On June 29, Confederate forces pressed the retreating Union army, forcing it to fight many small rearguard actions. The federals, in their hurry, purposely left 2,500 wounded at Savage Station, a stop on the rail line, as they quickly kept moving south. The Confederate army once again moved too slowly to surround the Union army, and there was hardly a battle.

On June 30, the armies fought a confused but bloody action at Frayser's Farm. Lee pressed from the north and west across White Oak Swamp. The Confederates were not coordinated in their attack, and the fighting was done by small groups, ambushes, and hand-to-hand struggles. This action allowed the Union retreat to continue in an orderly fashion. By nightfall, McClellan had drawn in his lines around Malvern Hill, close to Harrison's Landing. Lee had lost any chance to maneuver his army in a position to destroy the Union army while it was on the move.

On July 1, the Seven Days' Battles came to a bloody end for the Confederates as Lee, trying one last time to cut off McClellan from the river, launched a series of disjointed attacks against the Union's strong defensive position bolstered by well-manned artillery on Malvern Hill (a gently sloping hill about 150 feet in elevation but accessible only on one side because of swamps and deep ravines). The Confederates charged up this slope against sweeping artillery fire. The Union's position on the crest was so strong that McClellan's men stood in parade-ground order rather than dig trenches.

In retrospect, Lee's attack order seems suicidal, but the Union army had been getting beaten and retreating day after day and was developing a defeatist attitude. Lee hoped that one more battle would break the Union troops, but that did not happen. It was a tactical defeat for the Confederates and one of the few battles where most of the casualties came from artillery. The Seven Days' Campaign was a strategic victory for the South.

McClellan refused to consider a counterattack, and, under a heavy downpour, the Union army made its way 10 miles from Malvern Hill to the boats. Lee was in no position to follow. McClellan had failed to take Richmond, and Lee had failed to destroy McClellan. On July 14, a Union army under Maj. Gen. John Pope moved toward Richmond from Washington, which shifted Lee's attention away from McClellan, who evacuated his army down the James.

For the whole campaign, a week of sustained and furious fighting, Lee lost 20,000 men and the Union 16,000. The aggressive strategy of Lee that saved Richmond would be too costly in terms of human life for it to be used regularly. Lee's casualties were almost one-fourth of his entire command. This was the last time Lee had a chance to destroy an entire Union army. A quick end to the war seemed out of reach, as the war was growing more violent, demanding greater numbers of men. Some historians see these seven days as the turning point of the entire war.

Bibliography: Ketchum, Hiram, *General McClellan's Peninsular Campaign,* ed. by George R. Stewart (Birmingham Public Library, 1990); Sears, Stephen W., *The Civil War Papers of George B. McClellan: Selected Correspondence, 1860–1865* (Ticknor & Fields, 1989).

Lynn L. Sims

SHENANDOAH VALLEY CAMPAIGN OF JACKSON (May–June 1862)

Confederate major general Thomas "Stonewall" Jackson's 1862 Civil War campaign that always will be cited as a masterpiece of strategic diversion. In November 1861, Jackson assumed command of the Confederate Valley District with headquarters at Winchester, Virginia. There, he trained his 4,500-man force and led a series of aggressive winter raids on federal facilities to the north. He established a reputation as an ascetic, hard-driving disciplinarian in the process.

A 38,000-man federal force under Maj. Gen. Nathaniel P. Banks began entering the valley on Feb. 26, 1862. Banks's command was moving in support of the main federal effort devised by Maj. Gen. George B. McClellan. While the various approaches to Washington such as the valley were being secured, McClellan planned to take the Army of the Potomac by water to attack Richmond, Virginia, from Fortress Monroe along the Virginia Peninsula. A direct supporting force under Maj. Gen. Irvin McDowell was to be formed at Fredericksburg, Virginia, prepared to advance on Richmond overland from the north.

Banks's approach forced Jackson to evacuate Winchester on March 11. He withdrew to Rude's Hill above Mount Jackson in the hopes of luring the federals after him. Banks was not enticed, placing Brig. Gen. James Shields's division no further south than Strasburg. Assuming Jackson was successfully out of the way, Banks began sending his other two divisions east to join McDowell in the move against Richmond.

By March 20, Shields's division had pulled back into Winchester, and Jackson immediately advanced, presuming Shields was leaving also. On March 23, he attacked what he thought was a rear guard at Kernstown, but it was Shields's entire force deployed to lure Jackson into such an assumption. This first battle of Kernstown was not well fought by the Confederates, in part because Jackson's subordinates did not have a clear concept of his intent. Thus, when Brig. Gen. Richard B. Garnett withdrew his brigade for what he thought was good reason, Jackson was furious, but there was no reforming of the Confederate line, and the Confederates were forced to withdraw. Jackson suffered 718 casualties against 568 federal losses. His audacity had the desired effect, however. The Lincoln

The Union position on Malvern Hill, the last engagement of the Seven Days' Battles, was so strong that the troops did not need entrenchment to withstand the Confederate attack. (U.S. Army Military History Institute)

government was convinced that Jackson was a greater threat to Washington than hitherto presumed, and numerous forces were redirected away from the main effort at Richmond. Shields's division was retained in the valley, and corps commander Banks was returned with a second division, first pursuing Jackson southward and eventually setting up at Strasburg.

Jackson reorganized his force while based at Swift Run Gap. He was given command over Maj. Gen. Richard S. Ewell's division, then at Stannardsville, as well as Brig. Gen. Edward Johnson's forces defending to the west of Staunton. These additions raised the strength of his command to 17,000 men. The federal force building at Fredericksburg was posing such a threat to Richmond that Jackson was directed by Robert E. Lee, then on Pres. Jefferson Davis's staff, to continue whatever operations he could to keep the Union commands separate and as many as possible diverted from Richmond.

Accordingly, Jackson ordered Ewell into the valley, while on May 1 he marched his own division into Albermarle County, placed it on trains and ran it back into the valley at Staunton, where he linked with Johnson's division. The move fooled the federals into thinking an ordinary unit replacement had occurred. Instead, Jackson then advanced against the vanguard of Maj. Gen. John C. Frémont's division set up at McDowell under Brig. Gen. Robert H. Milroy. There, on May 8, the outnumbered federals fought gallantly but were forced to retreat. After pressing them to Franklin, thus neutralizing Frémont for the time being, Jackson moved back to the valley, joining his and Johnson's divisions with Ewell's on May 20.

Instead of moving down the main valley against the well-entrenched Banks at Strasburg, Jackson used the more easterly Luray Valley, moving into it through New Market Gap on May 21. This brought his force unnoticed to Front Royal east of Banks's main body. There, on May 23, Jackson sent cavalry to Buckton in the direction of Strasburg to block any federal approach and then attacked the small federal garrison. The outnumbered Union soldiers held for several hours before being pressed northward out of Front Royal to Cedarville, where they were overwhelmed by a vicious cavalry charge with 792 losses to Jackson's 35. Jackson had learned of the federal dispositions thanks to the spy Belle Boyd; curiously, the main units engaged on both sides were the 1st Maryland infantry regiments.

Banks reluctantly withdrew to Winchester, his trains fighting off Jackson's vanguard in an action at Middletown. Meanwhile, Ewell's division advanced down the Front Royal Road, pressing the federals back to the east side of Winchester. Jackson took the remainder of his force down the Valley Pike to threaten Winchester from the south. Early on May 25, each element attacked the federals, who were established on high ground at both points. Ewell's men on the east made little headway attacking in the early morning fog, and neither did Jackson's until the Louisiana Brigade made its famous charge against Banks's west flank. This forced the federals to withdraw. Banks soon lost control as his men retreated through Winchester, but Jackson's cavalry was not available to exploit the confusion. Jackson suffered 400 casualties for about 2,000 federal losses. Jackson immediately sent one brigade to Harpers Ferry, forcing all federals out of the lower valley.

June Events. Lincoln, deviating from McClellan's plan, reacted by sending McDowell's corps from Fredericksburg to the valley and directing Frémont to advance from West Virginia. The idea was for the two federal forces to close a trap at Strasburg, cutting off Jackson's line of retreat from Winchester. But they were too slow, and Jackson was too fast. By June 1, Jackson was south of the federals, heading for Port Republic, which he reached on June 7. Frémont pursued up the main valley, his advance killing Brig. Gen. Turner Ashby in a skirmish at Harrisonburg on June 6. McDowell's lead division under Shields struggled up the Luray Valley, delayed by downed bridges and rough terrain.

The position Jackson selected allowed him to use the South Fork of the Shenandoah River and the Massanutten Mountain to separate the advancing federal force. He dealt with Frémont first at the Battle of Cross Keys (June 8). The hesitant Frémont committed only a fraction of his force against Ewell's position then was stymied and rendered inactive by a powerful counterattack. There were 684 federal and 288 Confederate casualties in this short fight.

Meanwhile, Shields's vanguard led by Brig. Gen. Erastus B. Tyler took up a position on the opposite side of the river, two miles north of Port Republic, after probing the village itself. On the morning of June 9, Jackson's frontal attack against him failed. Jackson then directed the Louisiana Brigade to make another flank attack, which ultimately was successful after some of the hardest fighting of the campaign. A federal battery position was won and lost three times. Frémont could provide little support from west of the river. The Confederates lost 804 men to the federals' 1,018, and the Union troops were forced to withdraw. The federals pulled northward, content to protect the lower valley. Jackson rested his men at Weyer's Cave until June 18, when he led them out of the valley to the battles around Richmond.

Jackson's 17,000 men had lured 60,000 federals away from their main objective. Beginning on March 22, and ending the day they reached Richmond (June 25), Jackson's foot cavalry covered 676 miles. They had fought six battles and at least four major skirmishes, completely upsetting federal strategy. There were no tactical masterpieces, but the overall result gave Jackson and his men immortality for brilliant daring and endurance. Their achievement contributed to the Southern victory at Richmond and gave the Confederacy new life.

Bibliography: Cohn, Douglas A., *Jackson's Valley Campaign* (Amer. Publ. Co., 1986); Henderson, G. F. R., *Stonewall Jackson and the American Civil War* (Longmans, Green, 1919); Robertson, James I., Jr., The Stonewall Brigade (Louisiana State Univ. Press, 1963); Tanner, Robert G., *Stonewall in the Valley: Thomas J. "Stonewall" Jackson's Shenandoah Valley Campaign Spring 1862* (Doubleday, 1976).

Lt. Col. (Ret.) J. W. A. Whitehorne

SHENANDOAH VALLEY CAMPAIGN OF SHERIDAN (August 1864–March 1865)

Civil War campaign in northern Virginia in which Maj. Gen. Philip H. Sheridan turned a would-be Union defeat into a long-awaited victory. Following his withdrawal on July 11, 1864, from the Washington, D.C., area, Maj. Gen. Jubal A. Early continued to tie down federal troops in the Shenandoah Valley. He defeated Maj. Gen. George Crook's VIII Corps at the Second Battle of Kernstown on July 23 and sent raiding parties to Martinsburg, West Virginia, and Chambersburg, Pennsylvania. As a result, Lt. Gen. Ulysses S. Grant (general in chief of all Union armies) assigned Sheridan to command a reorganized Union military district and added two infantry and one cavalry corps to the forces in the region. Grant instructed Sheridan to destroy Early's military capabilities as well as the economic assets of the Shenandoah Valley, but to avoid any further embarrassments. The two forces sparred warily with each other across the lower valley for nearly a month.

Then, Early made a mistake by spreading his forces beyond supporting distance of each other in the vicinity of Winchester, Virginia. Sheridan immediately reacted on September 19, attacking Maj. Gen. Stephen D. Ramseur's division west of the town. The federals were delayed by the terrain sufficiently to allow Early to gather the remainder of his forces around Winchester where they fought most of the day until their lines were broken by a massed cavalry charge, one of Sheridan's trademarks. Casualties in this third battle of Winchester were about 5,018 federals and 3,921 Confederates.

Early retreated 20 miles southwest to a strong position at Fishers Hill, two miles from Strasburg, where the valley narrows to about 5 miles. Early did not have sufficient forces to man his entire line in strength, and he chose to put the bulk of his force on his east side. Sheridan noticed this and sent cavalry further to the east to interdict Early's line of retreat. He then deployed two corps against Early's line with orders to act as if they were about to attack. In the meantime, Crook's VIII Corps moved stealthily around Early's western flank, attacking the surprised Early in the afternoon of September 22. Another rout ensued, aided by federal cavalry attacks. (Federal losses were 528, while Confederate were 1,235.) The eastern federal cavalry thrust was stopped at Overall south of Front Royal. Early, thus, was able to withdraw his battered forces first to New Market then back to Rockfish Gap near Waynesboro. Although his force was largely intact, he had lost large amounts of equipment and men. Sheridan assumed that Early no longer was a factor, and he turned his attention to the economic destruction of the valley. His forces slowly pulled northward from the Staunton area, burning or carrying off vast amounts of matériel and foodstuffs. Early was reinforced from Richmond and aggressively followed the federals. Sheridan ordered his cavalry to counter this threat at the Battle of Tom's Brook on October 9, in which the Confederate cavalry was mauled.

Cedar Creek. The federals camped on October 10 on the north bank of Cedar Creek, midway between Strasburg and Middletown. Generals Grant and Sheridan planned the redeployment of Sheridan's forces, and one corps began to move east. Early's aggressiveness led to some changes in which one infantry corps and the cavalry corps were moved out of their original positions, weakening the federal dispositions. By the morning of October 13, Early was in position on Fishers Hill, probing the federal lines for weakness. A sharp engagement was fought at Hupps Hill that day with 200 federal and 75 Confederate casualties.

Nevertheless, the federals felt secure, assuming Early was too numerically inferior to be a serious menace. Sheridan left for a conference in Washington, placing Maj. Gen. Horatio G. Wright in command. By October 17, Early had reached a point where he had to attack or retreat because of the effects of earlier federal devastation of his supplies. Maj. Gen. John B. Gordon observed from a vantage point that Crook's VIII Corps on the federal east flank seemed to be relying on rough terrain alone for security. Accordingly, he proposed a daring plan to Early that would take the federal units in echelon, offsetting Confederate numerical inferiority. Early approved what was in essence a three-column converging night attack with cavalry support on each flank.

Gordon led three divisions over a ridge to fords across the Shenandoah River, along a route that placed his force on Crook's flank. Another division moved against Crook's front, while yet another advanced against the center of the federal position. Confederate cavalry operated with what was to be no effect on both flanks of the attacking infantry. Gordon's force smashed into Col. Rutherford B. Hayes's division under cover of a heavy ground fog early on October 19. Crook's other division was dispersed rapidly by the division attacking frontally, and the entire VIII Corps was dashed northwestward into the camps of the XIX Corps, next in the federal line. Confused, this unit hesitated in its trenches then tried to realign to confront the threat to its eastern flank. Twice, desperate resistance from XIX brigades briefly impeded the Confederate juggernaut as it swirled around the federal headquarters at Belle Grove Mansion.

This defense gave the three divisions of the U.S. VI Corps sufficient time to organize a hasty defense west of the mansion. Aided by the terrain, which squeezed out one of the attacking Confederate divisions, the federals held until the fog burned off. Two divisions then withdrew, while one fought an epic defense on a hill west of Middletown, thus ending the Confederate momentum. Early felt at this point that he had won and called a halt to form a defensive line, much to the ire of several of his generals, who felt it better to keep the pressure on the retreating federals.

Wright therefore gained the time to reform his battered force in a firm line about two miles north of the Confederates. About 10:30 A.M., Sheridan rejoined his command from his Washington conference, arriving after a legendary ride from Winchester. He quickly completed the reorganization begun by Wright, galvanizing morale in the process. He placed a cavalry division on each flank with the VI and XIX Corps in line and the remnants of the VIII in reserve. The federal counterattack began in the late afternoon, and Confederate resistance north of Middletown was fierce for about an hour. Then Brig. Gen. George A. Custer's cavalry on the west flank punched through the thinning Confederate line and charged en masse for the Confederate rear. This panicked the whole Confederate line, which quickly collapsed in a rearward stampede. Early soon lost control as his forces dissolved in an effort to escape the federal pursuit. Lost in the battle were 2,910 Confederates and 5,672 federals.

Last Stages. The disaster escalated when a bridge broke on Valley Pike, southwest of Strasburg. This caused a jam that stopped any rolling stock from moving further south. Thus, most of the guns and wagons captured in the morning, plus nearly all those belonging to Early's forces, had to be abandoned to the rampaging federal cavalry. Early's shattered force gathered at Fishers Hill and before dawn the next day withdrew southward to New Market. From there, Early launched a few probes northward, then both armies went into winter camp.

The cavalry continued to ignore the increasingly grim winter weather. On December 19, two federal divisions made an unsuccessful foray towards Gordonsville. Custer's division, which had been sent up the valley as a diversion, was surprised at Lacy's Springs by Brig. Gen. Lunsford L. Lomax. The federals quickly pulled back to join the rest of the army in winter camps around Winchester. Most of Sheridan's infantry was sent to other theaters during the winter, leaving him only two cavalry divisions as a mobile force.

These were sufficient to confront Early's rapidly dwindling force based between Staunton and Waynesboro. Supply problems had forced him to disperse his cavalry over a wide area, and most of his infantry was siphoned off to the defenses of Petersburg. Thus, it was no contest when

Sheridan's sleek force emerged from Winchester. On Mar. 2, 1865, at Waynesboro, Custer demolished Gabriel C. Wharton's small division, the last sizeable Confederate force in the valley.

Sheridan went on with his force to participate in the Appomattox Campaign. He had achieved total destruction of Confederate military power and control in the valley. He had completed the task conceived nearly a year earlier by Grant but delayed so well and so long by Early.

Bibliography: Brice, Marshall M., *Conquest of a Valley* (McClure Press, 1974); Lewis, Thomas A., *The Guns of Cedar Creek* (Harper & Row, 1988); Stackpole, Edward J., *Sheridan in the Shenandoah: Jubal Early's Nemesis* (Stackpole Co., 1961); Wert, Jeffrey D., *From Winchester to Cedar Creek: The Shenandoah Campaign of 1864* (South Mountain Press, 1987); Whitehorne, Joseph W. A., *Battle of Cedar Creek* (Wayside, 1987).

Lt. Col. (Ret.) J. W. A. Whitehorne

SHENANDOAH VALLEY, OPERATIONS IN (1863–1864)

After Maj. Gen. Thomas "Stonewall" Jackson's 1862 Shenandoah Valley Campaign, the lower valley twice more found itself involved as part of larger strategic operations. The second time came as a prelude to Gettysburg. The federal garrison in Winchester, Virginia, under Brig. Gen. Robert H. Milroy, had to be eliminated to allow the Confederates secure mobility for the invasion of Pennsylvania. The rebel vanguard consisting of Maj. Gen. Richard H. Ewell's Corps marched through Chester Gap south of Front Royal on June 12, 1863, and camped around Cedarville. Ewell then sent Maj. Gen. Robert E. Rodes's division east to try to capture the federal garrison at Berryville. Maj. Gen. Jubal A. Early's division was ordered northwest through Ninevah and Newtown to the Valley Pike, where it was to approach Winchester from the south. Maj. Gen. Edward Johnson's division was ordered down the Front Royal Road to reach Winchester on its southeastern edge.

Cavalry skirmishes fought at Vaucluse and Ninevah did not alert the complacent federal garrison. Confederate forces began contact in earnest south of Winchester on the morning of June 13. Johnson pressed a fiercely resisting group of federals onto the high ground southeast of the city. Early encountered similar hard going around Kernstown, eventually pressing the federals northward to Bower's Hill. Meanwhile, the federal garrison at Berryville eluded Rodes and eventually rejoined its main force in Winchester.

The heart of the federal defense was a series of forts north and west of the city located on two parallel ridges. These, in turn, were dominated by an even higher ridge further west. Milroy pulled his men back into the forts on the night of June 13–14, assuming their strength might lead the Confederates to bypass him. Early recommended that he move the bulk of his division around to the dominant ground on the west while other Confederate units on Bower's Hill and to the east attracted federal attention. Thus, while spirited skirmishing transpired in the latter two places, Early executed his shift and late on June 14 attacked the westernmost federal fort from the higher ground with devastating effect.

Milroy decided he was about to be surrounded and ordered a night withdrawal. Ewell sensed this was underway and directed Johnson to break contact east of Winchester, move cross-country in the darkness, and interdict the federal line of retreat north on the Valley Pike. The two forces collided in a confusing and brutal night meeting engagement at Stephenson's Depot. Milroy called it off just as his men were prevailing and lost control of his force. An utter rout ensued. There were about 4,443 federal and 269 Confederate losses in this series of engagements.

The Confederates pressed on to defeat at Gettysburg, and relative peace returned to the valley until early 1864 when again a large federal force (under Maj. Gen. Franz Sigel) appeared, this time as part of Lt. Gen. Ulysses S. Grant's new strategy. His plan called for a force in the valley to protect Maj. Gen. George G. Meade's strategic flank during his Overland Campaign against Gen. Robert E. Lee and Richmond. Sigel moved slowly southward against a scratch force led by Maj. Gen. John C. Breckinridge. The Southern force included the Corps of Cadets from Virginia Military Institute, so critical was Sigel's threat.

The Confederates were massed in Staunton by May 12, while Sigel had let his units become badly strung out between New Market and Woodstock. Contact began on May 13 at the Mount Jackson Bridge. Growing federal forces fought the rebel cavalry screen 8 miles southward to New Market by the night of May 14. The federals set up a line on the north side of the village and on the high ground to its west. Breckinridge, by now in camp 12 miles south at Lacy's Springs, immediately decided to attack. He had his force deployed on Shirley's Hill a mile south of New Market by dawn on a rainy May 15. An artillery duel ensued while more federal infantry arrived. Confusion and excessive dispersion among the federals led Sigel to direct formation of a new line north of Bushong's Farm, 2 miles below the village.

Meanwhile, the federal passivity had led Breckinridge to order an attack at about 11:00 A.M. The Confederates cleared the village by 12:30 P.M. and forced the federal western flank northward. All but the cadets participated, the terrain protecting a few other units from the effect of the federal fire. The federal line just north of Bushong's Farm consisted of three batteries west on the bluffs above the Shenandoah River, extended eastward by three infantry regiments and a cavalry screen to Smith's Creek, a tributary.

By the time the rebel advance had reached the line of Bushong's Farm, many units had suffered all they could take. The cadets were committed to stiffen the line. Sigel noticed this wavering and tried to direct a charge to exploit it. This was poorly executed and soon sputtered to a halt. Breckinridge saw his chance in the federal faltering and directed a countercharge. The federal artillery was forced to withdraw, and the doomed federal infantry soon was forced back in disorder. The rebels swept on until confronted by another federal battery, which caused Breckinridge to order a halt. Sigel then pulled all his survivors north of the Shenandoah and, at 7:00 P.M., destroyed the Mount Jackson Bridge, preventing close pursuit. The federals were back at Belle Grove the night of May 16. The Southern victory unhinged Grant's plans, preserving valley resources longer for the South and securing Lee's strategic flank as he struggled against Meade and Grant.

Bibliography: Davis, William C., *The Battle of New Market* (Doubleday, 1975); Hale, Laura H., *Four Valiant Years in the Shenandoah Valley 1861–1865* (Hathaway, 1986); Nye, Wilber S., *Here Come the Rebels!* (Louisiana State Univ. Press, 1965); Whitehorne, Joseph W. A., *The Battle of New Market* (Center of Military History, 1988).

Lt. Col. (Ret.) J. W. A. Whitehorne

SHERIDAN'S RICHMOND RAID (May 9–24, 1864)

Civil War cavalry raid against the Confederate capital. At Fredericksburg, Virginia, Lt. Gen. Ulysses S. Grant verbally directed his new cavalry commander, Maj. Gen. Philip Sheridan, to draw off the Confederate cavalry, thereby depriving Gen. Robert E. Lee of his "eyes and ears." Sheridan passed west around Lee's army, cutting rail and telegraph lines, destroying supplies, freeing prisoners and taking others.

With the Confederate cavalry chasing Sheridan, the Union flanks and rear were safe for more than two weeks, as Grant's supply base was Fredericksburg and his army was moving away farther south. Sheridan engaged in numerous fights on his flanks and rear guard and won all four frontal engagements (Beaverdam, Ashland, Yellow Tavern, and Meadow Bridge). Confederate cavalrymen tried to stay between Sheridan and Richmond; their commander, Maj. Gen. Jeb Stuart, was killed at Yellow Tavern. Sheridan rode around Lee's army and pierced the outer defense of Richmond, causing the city to mobilize its home guard.

Heavy rains and the swampy Chickahominy area north of Richmond made movement difficult. A Confederate force was present, so Sheridan rode east without trying to enter the city and met Maj. Gen. Benjamin F. Butler on the James River, where he was resupplied. On May 21, Sheridan rode north, rejoining Grant four days later. His raid, during which he sustained 625 casualties among his 10,000 men, raised the morale of the Union cavalry and army.

Lynn L. Sims

SHERMAN'S MARCH TO THE SEA (November 15–December 21, 1864)

Maj. Gen. William T. Sherman's famous Civil War march through Georgia. On Nov. 16, 1864, Sherman departed the torched city of Atlanta, Georgia, on his "March to the Sea" and into history. Determined to break the logistical back of the South, Sherman conducted a form of warfare never before experienced. Having accomplished the destruction of Atlanta, the South's major source of war supplies, he turned his attention to the morale of the fragile Confederacy. By destroying cotton mills, agriculture, and rail lines, he hoped to convince the Southerners that their cause was lost.

Sherman divided his forces, approximately 62,000 strong, into two main columns. The southern wing was commanded by Gen. Oliver O. Howard and the northern by Gen. Henry W. Slocum. Howard was to feint in the direction of Macon and Slocum toward Augusta. The real targets, however, were Milledgeville (then the capital of Georgia) and Savannah.

In his request to Lt. Gen. Ulysses S. Grant for approval for the march, Sherman's major concern was food supply. His solution to the problem was to have his army live off the land. Foraging teams would be established for authorized commandeering of food supplies and farm animals. Sherman studied the land between Atlanta and Savannah and determined which paths would provide the best resources for his men. Logistics proved not to be as big a problem as he had feared. Southern Georgia was one of the richest agricultural areas left in the ailing Confederacy. Sherman's men would feast well until reaching the swampy lowlands just west of Savannah.

On his March to the Sea, Sherman encountered little rebel resistance. During his feint toward Augusta, Gen. Hugh J. Kilpatrick, Sherman's cavalry commander, encountered Gen. "Fightin' Joe" Wheeler's cavalry near the town of Waynesboro. After three days of almost constant fighting, Kilpatrick was aided by federal infantry and took Waynesboro, forcing Wheeler's retreat. This was to be the only major confrontation during the march, and even this rebel show of force was in defense of the wrong target. Kilpatrick never intended to press on to Augusta.

"Making Georgia Howl." Sherman became famous for the conduct of his men as they scoured southern Georgia for food, supplies, and booty, not for his military prowess in conducting the march. Stories abound of ill-treatment of women and slaves and of the almost total disregard for private property. Diaries of participants of both sides tell of Yankee soldiers taking mirrors and silver only to later abandon some of their plunder along the way. Reporters from Northern papers wrote of the indiscriminate ransacking of innocent Southerners. Officers not responsible for the foraging but witnesses to it wrote in their diaries and letters home of the outrages they had seen. Farmers and plantation owners, rumored to have large caches of gold and silver, were ordered at knife- or gunpoint to reveal the hiding places of their treasures. Some of those claiming not to have any gold, whether true or not, were either killed or had everything they owned burned or destroyed. While Sherman gave strict orders as to how his men should conduct themselves, rarely did anyone try to enforce them. Some witnesses (on both sides) attest that Sherman was aware of some of his men's behavior and did nothing to correct the situation. In fairness to the federal soldiers, it should be noted that there were good deeds done for the Southern women and children as well. One instance was the discovery of two small girls abandoned in a farmhouse. Clothed only in sacks, the children were taken by the soldiers, fed, provided with clothes, and taken care of until a family could be found to care for them.

The slaves of southern Georgia viewed Sherman as the arrival of the long-anticipated "Jubilo." Expecting Sherman to shelter them and take them north with him to freedom, slaves escaped from their masters whenever Sherman was near and followed their redeemer. However, Sherman's purpose was not the freeing of slaves, and they were usually tolerated at a distance and, in some instances, abandoned. While attempting to cross Ebeneezer Creek, Brig. Gen. Jefferson C. Davis (no relation to the Confederate president) ordered the removal of a pontoon bridge once his men had crossed. This caused hundreds of slaves that had been following Davis to be stranded on the other side. Many panicked for fear of rebel cavalry and tried to cross even though most could not swim. Several drowned, including women with babies, and the incident caused an uproar in the North. This, however, was an extreme example. Other than using the slaves for intelligence on rebel activities, Sherman's troops for the most part ignored them.

Savannah. Sherman's ultimate goal during this phase of his march was to take Savannah, a key Confederate port. As he was approaching Fort McAllister to the south of Savannah, Gen. William J. Hardee was preparing his 9,000 Confederate troops within Savannah. However, Hardee's preparations were not for defense, but escape. He had been ordered by Gen. P. G. T. Beauregard, headquartered in Charleston, South Carolina, to withdraw his troops to prevent their capture. Hardee directed that a pontoon bridge be built over the Savannah River in order that he make his escape into South Carolina. During the night of December 20, Hardee and his troops and their supplies made their way across the temporary bridge into South Carolina.

Having captured Fort McAllister in only 15 minutes on December 13, Sherman's troops' way was now clear into Savannah. Upon learning of the Confederates' departure during the night, the federal army walked into and occupied Savannah on the morning of December 21. Ironically, Sherman missed the climax of his March to the Sea. Federal general John L. Foster had landed a division near Hilton Head, South Carolina, and Sherman had gone to convince him to move south and cut off Hardee's escape route. During his return on December 21, Sherman's boat was intercepted, and he was informed that his troops had occupied Savannah.

Sherman's march through Georgia was the first serious military engagement aimed at destroying the enemy's will and logistical capability to wage war. Although it had a serious impact on Southern morale, its results were tarnished by the conduct of his army toward the civilian populous.

Bibliography: Davis, Burke, *Sherman's March* (Random House, 1980); Foote, Shelby, *The Civil War: A Narrative, Red River to Appomattox* (Vintage, 1974); Gibson, John M., *Those 163 Days* (Coward-McCann, 1961); Key, William, *The Battle of Atlanta and the Georgia Campaign* (Twayne, 1958).

Capt. Edward B. Martin

SHERMAN'S MARCH (February–April 1865)

The Union operation of Maj. Gen. William T. Sherman during the Carolinas Campaign of the Civil War. After his successful capture of Atlanta (May–September 1864) and before the end of the March to the Sea (Nov. 15–Dec. 21, 1864), Lt. Gen. Ulysses S. Grant (general in chief of all Union armies) considered having Sherman bypass the city of Savannah and join the forces of Maj. Gen. George G. Meade and Benjamin F. Butler to crush Gen. Robert E. Lee's Confederate Army of Northern Virginia. As Sherman approached, then occupied, Savannah, however, Grant reconsidered and allowed his field commander to select his own route northward. Sherman elected to advance through the Carolinas on an inland route, enabling him to split the states on a north-south axis.

To enhance Sherman's plan and to relieve expected logistical shortfalls, Grant ordered the reduction of Fort Fisher (coastal North Carolina). After Butler's failed attempt in December, a combined Union land and naval force under Brig. Gen. Alfred H. Terry captured the Confederate stronghold on Jan. 15, 1865.

Inclement weather postponed Sherman's advance until February 1, when he moved north from Savannah with more than 60,000 troops. His three infantry corps, two cavalry brigades, and one artillery brigade overmatched the beleagured Confederates along his chosen path. By February 17, the van of his army reached Columbia, South Carolina, where the greatest of the devastation of the march occurred. Although Sherman's troops are famed for their wanton destruction throughout the South, local citizens

Union Gen. William T. Sherman's army left the city of Atlanta, Georgia, in ruins as it began its march through Georgia to the sea. (Library of Congress)

were responsible for burning the state capital, having set fire to cotton bales in the city streets even before Union troops arrived.

Continuing north, Sherman occupied Fayetteville, North Carolina, on March 11. By then, Confederate general Joseph E. Johnston had assembled a 20,000-man force, with which he unsuccessfully attempted to delay Sherman at the Battle of Bentonville (March 19–21). The failure to halt Sherman allowed him to link forces with Terry, who had moved in from the east. By April 26, Confederate resistance ceased with Johnston's surrender to Sherman near Raleigh, North Carolina.

Bibliography: Glatthaar, Joseph T., *The March to the Sea and Beyond: Sherman's Troops in the Savannah and Carolinas Campaigns* (New York Univ. Press, 1985); Harwell, Richard, and Philip N. Racine, eds., *The Fiery Trail: A Union Officer's Account of Sherman's Last Campaigns* (Univ. of Tennessee Press, 1986).

Louise Arnold-Friend

SHILOH (PITTSBURG LANDING), BATTLE OF (April 6–7, 1862)

High-casualty Civil War battle fought in southwestern Tennessee during the Shiloh Campaign (so named for the nearby Shiloh Church). In early March 1862, the Union forces in the western theater commanded by Maj. Gen. Henry W. Halleck prepared to advance farther south along the Tennessee River. Maj. Gen. Ulysses S. Grant's 42,000-man army bivouacked at Pittsburg Landing and awaited the arrival of Maj. Gen. Don Carlos Buell's 50,000 men from Nashville. After linking up, they planned to attack the Confederate forces of Gen. Albert S. Johnston and seize crucial rail centers.

Confederate Reactions. Johnston began concentrating units in the vicinity of Corinth, Mississippi, in mid-March and decided to attack Grant's position at Pittsburg Landing before Buell reinforced Grant. Johnston approved Gen. P. G. T. Beauregard's initial battle plan, which organized the 40,000-man force into four corps. The operational plan seems to have called for an early-morning frontal attack that would pin the Union right and center and envelop the Union left, destroying the Union force against the Tennessee River. Two corps, commanded by Maj. Gens. William J. Hardee and Braxton Bragg, would attack in a formation of corps in column with divisions on line, in effect creating three successive skirmish lines, with the corps commanded by Maj. Gens. Leonidas Polk and John C. Breckinridge in reserve. The complicated plan failed to take the inexperience of the Confederate forces into account and neglected unit cohesion and the ability to concentrate combat power at crucial points.

Union Situation. The bivouac site at Pittsburg Landing occupied a good defensive position along the Tennessee River. The parallelogram-shaped plateau, with high bluffs along the river, was protected by the Owl and Snake creeks in the north and the Lick Creek about five miles to the south. Numerous roads and trails pervaded the site. Heavy

At the Battle of Shiloh, Confederate general Albert Sidney Johnston was killed during fighting at the "Hornet's Nest," an area of sunken road, split-rail fences, and open fields. (U.S. Army Military History Institute)

forest and brush restricted observation, fields of fire, and command and control. The federals failed to establish a strong defense, the commanders discounting the possibility of a Confederate attack. No fortifications were prepared, and Union troops conducted few patrols to the front of their positions.

Grant's army was organized into six divisions. Two divisions, both green, under Brig. Gens. William T. Sherman and Benjamin M. Prentiss, occupied the easternmost positions. Between them and the river bivouacked three divisions under Brig. Gens. John A. McClernand, Stephen A. Hurlbut, and William H. L. Wallace. Maj. Gen. Lew Wallace's division occupied a position six miles to the north at Crump's Landing. Grant remained at his headquarters near Savannah, nine miles north.

Initial Confederate Attacks. The Confederate army began to march on April 3, planning to attack early the following morning. Confederate inexperience and poor march discipline prompted Johnston to postpone the attack until April 6. Achieving almost complete surprise, the Confederates' early-morning assault pushed the encamped Union divisions back. The federal units formed new defensive lines about two miles to the rear, with the ragged line running between the swamps of Owl Creek southeast to Lick Creek.

The heavy brush, ravines, Union resistance, and Confederate looting slowed the rate of advance and caused the three assault waves to become intermingled. The battle deteriorated into numerous small fights that few commanders could directly control.

About 7:30 A.M., Beauregard deployed the Confederate reserves, sending Breckinridge's corps to the right and Polk's to the left. Despite extending both flanks, the Confederates no longer possessed a reserve with which to exploit Confederate success.

Grant arrived on the battlefield about 8:30 A.M. He visited his line, ordered stragglers assembled near the landing, and sent word for Buell's divisions to move quickly to Pittsburg Landing.

Hornets' Nest—Defense of the Union Center. Despite hard fighting, Union withdrawals continued throughout the morning, and Grant ordered Prentiss's division to hold a position along a sunken road. The importance of this position, later known as the "Hornets' Nest," stemmed from its defensible central location relative to the rest of the Union line.

Despite the tenacious defense of the Union center, Union forces continued to withdraw; at about 3:00 P.M., Bragg's and Breckinridge's troops on the right broke the Union left flank. The Confederates could not exploit this situation due to their exhausted condition and the lack of a reserve. To further complicate the Confederate situation, Johnston had been mortally wounded about 2:30 P.M. Beauregard assumed command.

During the late afternoon, the Confederates massed 62 guns against the Hornets' Nest and slowly encircled it. Prentiss finally surrendered the Union position about 5:30 P.M. The Union defense had attracted Confederate units and firepower better used elsewhere.

In response to Confederate pressure, Union officers assembled a 50-gun battery, some reorganized units, and support from 2 gunboats to protect the Union left flank just south of Pittsburg Landing. This force defeated the last Confederate assaults on the Union left shortly after Beauregard decided to suspend Confederate attacks until the next day.

Union Reinforcements. During the wet night of April 6–7, both sides reorganized. By morning, nearly three of Buell's fresh divisions and Maj. Gen. Lew Wallace's division were on the battlefield. These new troops meant that the Confederates would face a numerically superior force.

The federals' main counterattack began about 5:00 A.M. Due to poor coordination between Grant and Buell, not until 10:00 A.M. did all Union units begin attacking. The federals gradually pushed the exhausted Confederates back, and Beauregard finally issued the retreat order about 2:30 P.M. The Confederate retreat toward Corinth began about 4:00 P.M. Union forces failed to pursue aggressively the retreating Confederates, waiting until April 8 to attempt a cursory effort, which was roughly repulsed by Confederate cavalry.

Results. Union casualties totaled nearly 14,000, to include 1,800 killed in action. Confederate casualties numbered 10,700. The battle was hailed as a Union victory, although Grant suffered severe but justifiable criticism for allowing his army to be surprised.

Union success at Shiloh forced the Confederates to evacuate most of eastern Tennessee, solidified the Union penetration of the Confederacy's defensive perimeter, and precipitated further Union advances along the Mississippi River.

Bibliography: Catton, Bruce, *Grant Moves South* (Little, Brown, 1960); Connelly, Thomas, *Army of the Heartland: The Army of Tennessee, 1861–1865* (Louisiana State Univ. Press, 1967); Foote, Shelby, *The Civil War, A Narrative; Vol. 1: Fort Sumter to Perryville* (Random House, 1958); McDonough, James Lee, *Shiloh—In Hell before Night* (Univ. of Tennessee Press, 1977); Roland, Charles, *Albert Sidney Johnston: Soldier of Three Republics* (Univ. of Texas Press, 1964); Sword, Wiley, Shiloh: *Bloody April* (Morrow, 1974); Williams, T. Harry, *Beauregard, Napoleon in Gray* (Louisiana State Univ. Press, 1955).

Kevin E. McKedy

SIBLEY'S NEW MEXICO CAMPAIGN (November 1861–May 1862)

Essentially inconsequential Civil War operation initiated by the Confederacy. Following secession, the Confederacy sought to win the allegiance of the territories of New Mexico and Arizona. Brig. Gen. Henry Hopkins Sibley received the assignment to subjugate New Mexico. In mid-December 1861, Sibley established his command at Fort Bliss, Texas. In January 1862, Sibley advanced up the Rio Grande. His plan was to march upon Fort Union northeast of Santa Fe. Lt. Col. William R. Scurry, commanding Sibley's 4th Regiment, led the advance toward Fort Union. On the morning of March 28, Scurry contacted the federal forces under Col. John P. Slough at Glorieta Pass. The ensuing battle lasted for six hours. Finally, the Southerners drove the federals from the field. The victory proved meaningless, however, as lack of manpower and logistical problems soon forced the Confederacy to abandon New Mexico.

M. Guy Bishop

SOUTH MOUNTAIN, BATTLE OF (September 14, 1862)

Name given collectively to three Civil War actions fought on a seven-mile front along the South Mountain range of western Maryland. It was the first major action of the Antietam Campaign of 1862 and ranks as the second largest Civil War battle fought in Maryland. On September 4, 1862, Gen. Robert E. Lee led his Army of Northern Virginia across the Potomac in the first major Confederate incursion north of the river. At Frederick, Maryland, he split his army, sending half with Gen. Thomas "Stonewall" Jackson to capture the Union garrison at Harpers Ferry. The command of Gen. James Longstreet was sent north to Hagerstown, Maryland, in preparation for a movement into Pennsylvania.

Although dividing an army, particularly in enemy territory, was a bold move, Lee felt confident that he would be deep into Pennsylvania before his cautious opponent, Gen. George B. McClellan, realized what had happened. Therefore he left only part of the division of Gen. Daniel H. Hill (fewer than 5,000 men) to guard Lee's rear at Boonsboro and the South Mountain passes of Turner's Gap and Fox's Gap. Farther down the mountain range, elements of Gen. Lafayette McLaw's division and Gen. Jeb Stuart's cavalry guarded Crampton's Gap.

Unbeknown to Lee, a copy of his operational plan (wrapped in three cigars), detailing the splitting of his army, had been discovered by the federals in an abandoned Confederate camp near Frederick. McClellan, confident he could destroy the Army of Northern Virginia, put his forces in motion to do just that. However, thinking that Lee outnumbered him, McClellan moved slowly and cautiously.

On September 14, three of his corps moved toward the Confederate positions on South Mountain.

Fox's Gap. The battle began around 9:00 A.M. as Gen. Jacob D. Cox's division of the IX Corps struck the Confederate brigade of Gen. Samuel Garland at Fox's Gap. The Confederates were outnumbered three to one, and Garland was mortally wounded. His brigade was decimated and withdrew from the gap. However, the Union assault had lost momentum, and Cox did not pursue. Later in the day, the rest of the IX Corps came up and attacked the now-reinforced Confederates, in concert with I Corps attacks on Turner's Pass. Fighting continued there until late evening, and IX Corps commander Gen. Jesse L. Reno was killed.

Crampton's Gap. A few miles to the south, Union general William B. Franklin's VI Corps was moving toward the thin Confederate line at Crampton's Gap. Not realizing that his more than 12,000 men were facing only about 1,000 Confederates, Franklin waited until the afternoon to attack. By dusk he had driven the Confederates off the mountain. If he had pushed on, he would have raised the siege of Harpers Ferry.

Turner's Gap. This was the main Union objective. About 4:00 P.M., the Union I Corps attacked in concert with the federal assault on Fox's Gap. Hill, reinforced by Longstreet, held out until late in the evening. Realizing his position to be untenable, Lee ordered Hill to withdraw to Boonsboro before the morning of September 15.

Conclusion. Union losses for the day were 436 killed and 1,908 wounded. Total Confederate casualties were around 2,000. McClellan now held all three South Mountain passes. If he had pursued aggressively, he might have beaten the separated commands of Lee's divided army. Instead, the ever-cautious Union commander paused, giving Lee time to regroup his forces along Antietam Creek, near Sharpsburg. The stage was now set for the Battle of Antietam (September 17).

Bibliography: Luvass, Jay, and Harold W. Nelson, eds., *The U.S. Army War College Guide to the Battle of Antietam: The Maryland Campaign of 1862* (South Mountain Press, 1987); Murfin, James V., *The Gleam of Bayonets: The Battle of Antietam and Lee's Maryland Campaign, September 1862* (A. S. Barnes, 1965); Sears, Stephen W., *Landscape Turned Red: The Battle of Antietam* (Ticknor and Fields, 1983); U.S. War Department, *War of the Rebellion: A Compilation of the Official Records of the Union and Confederate Armies,* series 1, vol. 19, parts 1 & 2 (1880–1901).

Ted Alexander

SPOTSYLVANIA CAMPAIGN (May 7–20, 1864)

Technically indecisive series of Civil War battles fought in northeastern Virginia. After the Battle of the Wilderness (May 5–7, 1864), Lt. Gen. Ulysses S. Grant attempted to again outflank the Confederacy's Army of Northern Virginia. Having fought for three days in the tangled brush (May 5–7), the Union's Army of the Potomac withdrew late on May 7 and marched to envelop the Confederate army in the vicinity of Spotsylvania Courthouse, a crucial crossroads 11 miles southwest of Fredericksburg and 12 miles southeast of the Wilderness.

Correctly discerning that Grant was redeploying to Spotsylvania, Gen. Robert E. Lee ordered his Confederate army to occupy blocking positions in that vicinity. The I Corps, led by Maj. Gen. Richard H. Anderson, barely won the race to Spotsylvania. I Corps arrived just after dawn on May 8 to reinforce Confederate cavalrymen about two miles north of Spotsylvania Courthouse, barely beating the Union advance elements of Maj. Gen. Gouverneur K. Warren's V Corps. The Union columns had been slowed by Confederate cavalry and Union confusion. The Confederates hastily reinforced their line and built entrenchments that stymied Union attacks the remainder of May 8.

On May 9, Grant ordered an attack against the Confederate left flank by Maj. Gen. Winfield S. Hancock's II Corps. The attack never fully developed, and the Confederates nearly flanked II Corps. Other Union attacks also failed. By late on May 9, the Confederate line resembled a ragged inverted "V" and presented a formidable fortified position.

Union forces attacked the Confederate line on May 10. The most successful attack occurred about 6:00 P.M., when a VI Corps brigade commanded by Col. Emory Upton used innovative tactics to penetrate Confederate lines on the western edge of the salient known as the "Mule Shoe." The failure of a neighboring division to support Upton's initial penetration and the late hour negated the Union effort.

Encouraged by Upton's success, Grant ordered massive Union attacks to begin on May 12, allowing May 11 for the troop redeployment. The Union attack began at 4:30 A.M., May 12, with II Corps conducting the main attack directly against the Mule Shoe salient. The Union forces successfully occupied the salient, greatly weakened by the overnight withdrawal of most of the Confederate artillery (Lee had ordered the withdrawal due to his belief that the lack of action on May 11 signaled another Union attempt to envelop his army). Hasty reinforcement and great bravery on the part of Confederate units pushed Union units back after desperate hand-to-hand fighting.

The Confederates evacuated the corpse-strewn salient on the evening of May 12. Union attempts to redeploy to the east for further attacks were hampered by heavy rains. A Union attack by the II and VI Corps on May 18 again failed.

Lee attacked the Union right on May 19 with Lt. Gen. Richard S. Ewell's II Corps. New Union formations blunted

Fighting at the Spotsylvania Courthouse crossroads was so fierce that the Union and Confederate troops often resorted to hand-to-hand combat. (U.S. Army Military History Institute)

this assault, which signaled the end of the major fighting in the vicinity of Spotsylvania Courthouse. Grant quickly continued his attempts to outflank Lee, marching his army away from Spotsylvania.

The successive battles in the Wilderness and at Spotsylvania severely weakened the Army of the Potomac. Between May 5 and May 20, the Union forces suffered more than 36,000 casualties. The Confederates lost about 17,000 in these two battles, including some 10,000 at Spotsylvania.

Bibliography: Catton, Bruce, *A Stillness at Appomattox* (Doubleday, 1953); Foote, Shelby, *The Civil War, A Narrative; Vol. 3: Red River to Appomattox* (Random House, 1974); Frassanito, William, *Grant and Lee, the Virginia Campaigns: 1864–1865* (Scribner's, 1983); Grant, Ulysses S., *Personal Memoirs of U. S. Grant* (1894; reprint, Da Capo Press, 1982); Matter, William, *If It Takes All Summer: The Battle of Spotsylvania* (Univ. of North Carolina Press, 1988).

Kevin E. McKedy

STONES RIVER (MURFREESBORO), BATTLE OF (December 31, 1862–January 2, 1863)

Militarily indecisive, yet bloody, Civil War battle in which two newly-created armies (the Union's Army of the Cumberland and the Confederacy's Army of Tennessee) opposed one another in central Tennessee. Following the Battle of Perryville (October 1862), in central Kentucky, Confederate general Braxton Bragg withdrew his troops 150 miles southwest, to the area around Murfreesboro, Tennessee. From there he reorganized his forces into the Army of Tennessee and dispatched his cavalry to raid central Kentucky and western Tennessee. Maj. Gen. William S. Rosecrans assumed command of the Army of the Cumberland at Nashville, Tennessee, in late October and began preparing for a campaign. In December, he noted the absence of Bragg's cavalry and decided to attack. Bragg's intelligence service, however, detected the Union advance, and Bragg hurriedly concentrated his army.

During the late afternoon of December 29, the Union's leading corps approached Murfreesboro. Believing that the Confederates were retreating, the corps commander, Maj. Gen. Thomas L. Crittenden, attacked Bragg's line, only to be rebuffed. The following day, both stayed idle as the remainder of Rosecrans's army moved in. On December 31, the two armies sat opposite one another just west of Stones River. Curiously, each commander had decided on the same plan of attack: hold his right and attack with his left.

The Confederates delivered the first blow when, at dawn, Gen. William J. Hardee's corps struck the far right end of the federal line. Although at least one brigade was caught by surprise, the Union troops held their ground through two assaults. A third attack, however, cracked the Union line. Only the timely counterattack of Gen. Philip H. Sheridan's division allowed the battered federals to withdraw to a new position along the Nashville Pike, perpendicular to their original line. Rosecrans immediately ordered two divisions from his attack force to move and bolster the right flank, but before they could arrive, Confederate attacks pushed the remainder of the Union right and center back along the Nashville Pike. By noon, the Union line had come to resemble a large "L," with its long stem along the pike.

Bragg moved in for what he hoped would be the knockout blow. Withdrawing units from his inactive right, he ordered several assaults in the afternoon. All were bloodily repulsed. Nevertheless, he telegraphed Richmond (the Confederate capital) that he had won an important victory.

Rosecrans remained on the field throughout the night, and the first day of the new year passed quietly. On January 2, the fighting began anew when Bragg ordered an attack on the high ground northeast of the Nashville Pike. The Union defenders were driven off, but the exuberant rebels pursued them down the reverse side of the hill and into the massed fire of 58 Union cannon. The deadly fire stunned the Confederates, who were then driven back by a Union counterattack. The two exhausted armies were inactive the following day. During the night of January 3, Bragg withdrew his army and marched south.

Murfreesboro had been a costly battle. Bragg lost 9,239 killed and wounded of his 34,732-man army. Rosecrans also had lost heavily: 9,532 killed and wounded of his 41,400 men. Militarily, each side had gained little of importance. Bragg, although largely regarded the tactical victor, had not destroyed Rosecrans, and Rosecrans had been too badly weakened to pursue Bragg. Because of Bragg's retreat, however, the Union accepted the Murfreesboro action as Rosecrans's victory, at least strategically.

Bibliography: Cozzens, Peter, *No Better Place to Die: The Battle of Stones River* (Univ. of Illinois Press, 1990); McDonough, James Lee, *Stones River: Bloody Winter in Tennessee* (Univ. of Tennessee Press, 1980).

Richard F. Kehrberg

TABASCO, BATTLE OF (October 26, 1846)

U.S. naval assault upon a Mexican garrison during the Mexican War. Throughout the war, the U.S. Navy bore the responsibility of maintaining a blockade of Mexico's east coast. U.S. vessels were active during 1846 in the vicinity of Alvarado and Tampico along the shores of the Gulf of Mexico. With seven small naval craft and a landing force of 253 men, Commodore Matthew C. Perry approached Tampico on Oct. 23, 1846. A detachment was landed that afternoon. But Perry, not knowing the Mexican strength, was forced to recall them before dark. On the morning of October 26, Mexican batteries opened fire on the U.S. vessels offshore. Later that day, Perry assumed a truce had been reached. Then, unexpectedly, the Mexicans again opened fire. Perry ordered a devastating retaliatory fire. Having made his point, Perry departed from Tabasco on the morning of October 27. Four Americans and nine Mexicans died as a result of this brief battle.

M. Guy Bishop

TAMPICO, SIEGE OF (September–October 1846)

Uncontested capture of a Mexican port by U.S. army and naval forces during the Mexican War. On May 14, 1846, U.S. naval commander David Conner issued orders placing the Mexican ports of Veracruz, Alvarado, Matamoros, and Tampico under blockade. Other Mexican ports escaped this quarantine only because the U.S. Navy lacked the necessary ships to enforce the policy more broadly. Tampico, an important coastal city separated from Matamoros at the mouth of the Rio Grande only by the eastern chain of the Sierra Madre, had great strategic importance. Conner planned to seize the city and thus control the Gulf of Mexico. A naval assault upon Tampico presented a complex problem, however. The waters at the mouth of the Pánuco River were difficult, and ships anchored offshore were vulnerable to the storms that raged in the region. In September 1846, 3,000 men from Gen. Zachary Taylor's army were sent to assist Conner. By October, the increased U.S. presence near Tampico led to the withdrawal of the Mexican troops. Thus Tampico was taken without the anticipated struggle.

M. Guy Bishop

TULLAHOMA CAMPAIGN (June 23–July 2, 1863)

Civil War campaign against a Confederate advance within Tennessee. After months of intense pressure from the Lincoln administration, Maj. Gen. William S. Rosecrans, commander of the Union's Army of the Cumberland, decided to go on the offensive in June 1863. His objective was to force the Confederate's out of middle Tennessee and back to their base at Chattanooga in southeastern Tennessee. His opponent, Gen. Braxton Bragg (Army of Tennessee), occupied a strong defensive position just south of Murfreesboro (a central Tennessee city nearly 80 miles northwest of Chattanooga).

Beginning his brilliantly planned maneuver on June 23, Rosecrans confused Bragg by feinting at the rebel left flank. He then pushed the bulk of his troops through the gaps in the Cumberland foothills southeast of Murfreesboro. This put the Union army behind the Confederate right flank. The Union XXI Corps, under Maj. Gen. George H. Thomas, led the advance with a brigade of mounted infantry. Although slowed by hard rains and deep mud, Thomas's corps came pouring from the Hoover Gap to take the town of Manchester on June 27.

By June 29, Thomas was moving on the rail center at Tullahoma and the Confederate rear. The city sat astride the important Nashville & Chattanooga Railroad and was the main rebel base of operations north of the Tennessee River. Forced to abandon Tullahoma or risk being trapped there, Bragg ordered his army to withdraw. Rosecrans carried the pursuit to the Elk River but halted there on July 2 due to high water. The Confederate withdrawal, however, did not stop there; Bragg pulled the Army of Tennessee all the way back to Chattanooga. Rosecrans had achieved a fine strategic victory.

Bibliography: McKinney, Francis F., *Education in Violence: The Life of George H. Thomas and the History of the Army of the Cumberland* (Wayne State Univ. Press, 1961).

Daniel T. Bailey

UTAH EXPEDITION ('MORMON WARS') (1857–1858)

Action taken by the U.S. government in response to a growing conflict between Utah Mormons and federal authorities. In 1857, Pres. James Buchanan named new officials to Utah Territory, the Mormon stronghold in the Great Basin, replacing, among others, territorial governor Brigham Young, also president of the Mormon church. Opposition from the Mormons resulted, and reports from U.S. officials in Utah declared the Mormons in rebellion against the government. To counter the situation, Buchanan sent a military expedition to Utah to quell the Mormons and install the newly appointed territorial governor, Alfred Cumming.

The Expedition. On May 25, 1857, orders were issued for 2,500 troops to march from Fort Leavenworth, Kansas, to Utah, under the command of Gen. William S. Harney. The first contingents began the trek on July 18, but the slavery controversy in Kansas prompted Harney's retention in the territory, and late in August, Albert Sidney Johnston was named his replacement. Since his force was well ahead of him, Johnston did not join his command until early November.

Meanwhile, word reached Utah that the federal government was sending an army to subdue the Mormons. Believing that this was a continuation of the Missouri massacres of the 1830s, Young, on September 15, issued a proclamation forbidding the entry of armed forces into Utah, declaring marital law and mobilizing the militia.

As U.S. troops drew nearer, conflict grew more likely. Although negotiations between the two groups was continued, on October 5, Lot Smith and a band of Mormon militia captured and burned 2 army supply trains and 52 wagons and ran off cattle and other animals east of Green River. With winter approaching, troops scattered in columns across the plains. Johnston, low in supplies, decided to winter at Fort Bridger, in present-day Wyoming.

Resolution. The winter also allowed time to negotiate a settlement. Thomas L. Kane, a Philadelphian who knew Young and was respected by him, offered to mediate. With Buchanan's approval, Kane reached Salt Lake City in February 1858 and met with Young. He then went to Fort Bridger and persuaded Cumming to return to Salt Lake City with him and talk to Young. When he arrived, Cumming was properly recognized as the new territorial governor and, with his diplomatic skills, soon won Mormon support.

With this issue settled, it was now possible to avoid military action. Although he promised a "scorched earth" policy if U.S. troops took any action against Mormons, Young agreed to allow them to enter the territory. Finally, on June 26, Johnston's army marched through Salt Lake City and set up Camp Floyd 35 miles from the city. The affair thus ended.

Bibliography: Furniss, Norman F., *The Mormon Conflict, 1850–1858* (Yale Univ. Press, 1960); Hafen, LeRoy R., and Ann W. Hafen, *The Utah Expedition, 1857–1858* (Arthur H. Clark, 1958).

Roger D. Launius

VERACRUZ, SIEGE OF (March 9–29, 1847)

U.S. military action against a key Mexican port during the Mexican War. During the fall of 1846, it became obvious to senior U.S. officials that to conclude the war with Mexico, the capture of Mexico City would be required. Pres. James K. Polk suggested landing a force at Veracruz, Mexico's chief port, as a reasonable departure point for an offensive against Mexico City. Gen. Winfield Scott developed a detailed plan for an amphibious operation against Veracruz and was eventually chosen as its commander.

During the winter of 1846–47, Scott assembled troops, ships, and supplies at the island of Lobos, about 65 miles southeast of Tampico, as the point of origin for the operation. There he brought together about 15,000 men and numerous assault boats.

Scott's men first landed on March 9, about two miles south of Veracruz, and proceeded to encircle the city. The amphibious landing was the largest in U.S. military history up to that time, and it was an efficient and impressive operation. The U.S. Navy also blockaded Veracruz from the sea.

For nearly three weeks, the siege continued. There were numerous clashes between U.S. and Mexican forces, all of which were inconclusive. On March 22, Scott issued a formal call for the surrender of Veracruz, but the Mexican commander refused. Scott then had his artillery open up on the city. The barrage continued intermittently for several days, in the process firing about 6,700 rounds into the city and devastating the Mexican defenses. On March 26, the Mexicans opened negotiations, and formal surrender ceremonies took place three days later.

Bibliography: Bauer, K. Jack, *The Mexican War, 1846–1848* (Macmillan Co., 1974); Ramirez, Jose Fernando, *Mexico During the War with the United States* (Univ. of Missouri Press, 1950).

Roger D. Launius

VICKSBURG CAMPAIGN (November 1862–July 1863)

Civil War campaign that eventually devastated Confederate defenses and secured federal access to the Mississippi River. Gen. George G. Meade's Union victory at Gettysburg, Pennsylvania (July 3, 1863), and the Confederacy's surrender of Vicksburg, Mississippi (July 4, 1863), together comprise what are perhaps the most significant events of the Civil War.

Preliminaries. Gen. Ulysses S. Grant left Grand Junction, Tennessee, for Vicksburg on Nov. 13, 1862. Confederate forces in the area were commanded by Gen. John C. Pemberton, who slowly retreated in the face of Grant's advance. The Union advance was also slowed by harassment from Confederate cavalry and the capture of the Holly Springs supply depot. Grant sent Gen. William T. Sherman's corps (40,000 men) down the Mississippi River in an amphibious operation against Chickasaw Bluffs, a defensive strongpoint north of Vicksburg manned by 13,800 Confederate veterans. Sherman's three-day assault (December 27–29) proved fruitless as he sustained casualties eight times those of the rebels. The year ended with Sherman's retreat to the mouth of the Yazoo River and Grant's continued slow progress.

After Holly Springs, Grant decided that an advance down the west bank of the Mississippi would be more conducive to maintaining his supply lines. He crossed the river at Memphis, marched south, and established a position opposite Vicksburg on the west bank. January through March 1863 were consumed in probing through the bayous, swamps, creeks, and rivers of the area in a futile effort to find the elusive "back door" to Vicksburg. Grant was defeated in seven separate operations, mostly by the terrain and the worst flooding experienced in the area in decades.

By April, Grant had decided on a course of action. Leaving Sherman's corps above Vicksburg, he moved the remainder of his 50,000 men below the city to Hard Times, opposite Grand Gulf. To add to Confederate confusion, Grant sent three cavalry regiments under the command of Col. Benjamin H. Grierson on a spectacular raid through the heart of Mississippi from La Grange, Tennessee, to Baton Rouge, Louisiana. They cut Pemberton's supply line between Jackson and Meridian (two important depot cities on the Southern Mississippi Railroad), continued for a total of 600 miles, and lost about 25 men from a force of 1,700. Grant learned a valuable lesson from this expedition. He remarked, "It was Grierson who first set the example of what might be done in the interior of the enemy's country without any base from which to draw supplies."

Grant confronted a rebel force of about 50,000 defending Vicksburg from Haines's Bluff 10 miles north, to Grand Gulf 40 miles south of the city. After the U.S. Navy was rebuffed in a direct attempt on Grand Gulf, Grant ordered Sherman to stage a demonstration up the Yazoo; on April 30, Sherman ferried the remainder of his force across the river at Bruinsburg, 10 miles below Grand Gulf.

Brig. Gen. John S. Bowen commanded a Confederate force of fewer than 5,000 at Grand Gulf. Upon learning of Grant's crossing, he left the town and took up a position four miles west of Port Gibson on a wooded ridge astride the road. Gen. John A. McClernand (one of Grant's corps commanders—the other two being Sherman and Gen. James B. McPherson) attacked this position May 1, and after an all-day fight in which the federal weight of numbers was the deciding factor, Bowen had to pull back to the outskirts of Port Gibson. That night, he retreated across Bayou Pierre and destroyed the bridge behind him. The next day, Grant flanked him by building a bridge farther upstream. As a consequence, Bowen had to abandon Grand Gulf, and then Grant embarked on what has been called "the most brilliant campaign ever fought on American soil."

Big Black River Campaign. In addition to Pemberton's men, Grant also had to deal with a force of 9,000 commanded by Gen. Joseph E. Johnston at Jackson, 45 miles east of Vicksburg. He chose to advance on Jackson first. Pemberton, of course, recognized the danger presented by Grant's river crossing.

The key to Grant's success in this entire campaign was his decision to abandon his supply lines and live off the land. This completely befuddled Pemberton, who probed ineffectually again and again for those supposedly vital lines of communication.

Grant chose to mount a two-pronged approach to breaking the link between Jackson and Vicksburg. This phase began on May 12, and in a brilliant series of improvisations, Grant changed his objective, changed the line of march of all three corps on two separate occasions, and drove all rebel resistance to the outskirts of Jackson.

On May 14, after overcoming minimal opposition, Sherman and McPherson drove Johnston out of Jackson. Grant then turned to the west, while Johnston retreated unpursued. Johnston and Pemberton discussed the possibility of uniting their forces at some point between Vicksburg and Jackson, but McClernand's corps threatened the flank of any such operation. In any event, Grant had no intention of allowing his enemy to seize the initiative.

Pemberton did sortie from the fortress with a fairly large force, but Grant learned of the move almost immediately. On May 16, the Union forces encountered the rebels in a strong defensive position at Baker's Creek. The Confederate troops were drawn up on Champion's Hill and a heavily wooded ridge adjoining it. A Union frontal assault resulted in heavy fighting and numerous casualties for both sides, but the rebels were driven off, burning the bridge behind them.

Grant crossed the creek at this point, and Sherman crossed farther north. Pemberton assumed another strong defensive position at the Big Black River crossing. Grant intended merely to fix him in place while Sherman flanked the position. McClernand, however, decided to launch another frontal attack. In what a reporter described as "the most perilous and ludicrous charge I witnessed during the war," McClernand's men "charged" through a shoulder-high bayou into the teeth of the rebel guns. The rebels broke and ran.

Pemberton retreated yet again, this time to a position on the west bank of the Big Black. But he then learned of Sherman's flanking movement and consequently had to continue into the Vicksburg fortifications, driving cattle, sheep, and pigs before him and picking corn all the way.

The brilliance of the campaign rested upon Grant's willingness to take risks, his aggressiveness in keeping his enemy off balance, and his adaptability in a constantly changing environment. He had marched 180 miles in 20 days; decisively defeated his enemy at Port Gibson, Raymond, Jackson, Champion Hill, Big Black River, and numerous other skirmishes; and bottled up 30,000 men in Vicksburg, all while inflicting almost twice as many ca-

The USS Queen of the West (right) *engages the CSS* City of Vicksburg *in February 1863 during the Union campaign against Vicksburg.* (Harper's Weekly)

Confederate artillery is fired at the Union's ironclad Indianola *as it runs the blockade at Vicksburg.* (Library of Congress)

sualties as his own 4,400. After this series of events, the outcome of the siege was never in doubt.

Siege and Surrender. Pemberton's position was a formidable one, even after he abandoned the Haines's Bluff fortifications. He began the siege with 20,000 effectives dug into the high bluffs surrounding the city.

Grant began with two unsuccessful frontal assaults on the defenses (May 19 and 22). Furious fire from almost unseen defenders cut down his men almost before they got started. Grant took more casualties in these three days than he had in the previous three weeks. These two exercises in futility at least served the purpose of convincing his men they should be diligent in their spade work. Reinforced to a total of 71,000 men, and establishing two lines back to back, one facing Vicksburg and the other facing Jackson, he at last settled down to classic siege work—digging approach trenches and parallels, and moving ever closer to the point of final assault.

Federal artillery (220 guns) and Adm. David Porter's gunboats maintained a continuous bombardment, while Vicksburg's inhabitants (both military and civilian) burrowed caves into the bluffs to escape its effects. By mid-June, the defenders were reduced to eating their mules and bread made from equal parts of ground corn and peas. On June 28, Pemberton received a letter signed "many soldiers," warning of the possibility of mutiny caused by the lack of food. Threatened with starvation, having no hope of relief, and learning that Grant's preparations for the final assault were complete, Pemberton chose to give up the valiant fight. He surrendered on July 4. Grant immediately supplied the people with rations and occupied the city.

The implications of Grant's triumph were vast indeed. Confederate president Jefferson Davis had astutely called Vicksburg "the nailhead that held the South's two halves together." Certainly the Union victory here would prove his sentiments. Not only was the Confederacy completely split in two, the Mississippi was now open for Union commerce.

Bibliography: Esposito, Vincent J., ed., *The West Point Atlas of American Wars; Vol. 1: 1689–1900* (Praeger, 1978); Foote, Shelby, *The Civil War, A Narrative: Fredericksburg to Meridian* (Random House, 1958); Grant, Ulysses S., *Memoirs and Selected Letters* (Library of America, 1900); McPherson, James M., *Battle Cry of Freedom* (Oxford, 1988).

Capt. Karen S. Wilhelm

WAYNESBORO, BATTLE OF (March 2, 1865)

Late Civil War battle, fought in southern Tennessee during the Shenandoah Valley Campaign of Maj. Gen. Philip H. Sheridan. On Feb. 28, 1865, Sheridan led the cavalry divisions of Brig. Gens. George A. Custer and Wesley Merritt southward in foul winter weather from Winchester, Virginia. Custer's division captured the Mount Crawford Bridge from Brig. Gen. Thomas L. Rosser's defenders in a dramatic thrust on March 1. The federal column reached Staunton the next day, and Custer headed toward Waynesboro, where Maj. Gen. Jubal A. Early had gathered the remnants of Brig. Gen. Gabriel C. Wharton's Confederate division on a ridge west of town with their backs to the South River. The superior federal force smashed its opponents so swiftly that defeat was total and nearly every rebel was captured. Only Early and his staff were able to escape. Union accounts claimed 1,600 Confederates were captured to the loss of 9 federals.

Lt. Col. (Ret.) J. W. A. Whitehorne

WESTERN VIRGINIA, OPERATIONS IN (1861)

Civil War actions within western Virginia, an area torn by the respective interests of the Union and the Confederacy. From the outbreak of hostilities, Union and Confederate forces wrestled for political and military control of the area of western Virginia that now comprises the state of West Virginia. Virginia's secession vote on Apr. 17, 1861, created great public dissent and unrest in the state's largely pro-Union counties west of the Allegheny Mountains. Longstanding cultural and political differences between the inhabitants of the mountainous west and affluent eastern Virginians who had long controlled the state's politics intensified as the region became a battleground for the Ohio River and the Baltimore & Ohio Railroad. On June 11, Unionist leaders convened at Wheeling to commence the creation of a new state. Meanwhile, open hostilities had already begun for control of the region.

Philippi (June 3). Maj. Gen. George B. McClellan, as commander of the Union's Department of the Ohio, sent Brig. Gen. Thomas A. Morris's brigade of Indiana troops to drive Confederates (Virginia troops) commanded by Col. George A. Porterfield from Philippi. Morris had feigned a movement toward Harpers Ferry and caught Porterfield's estimated 1,000 men by surprise. Although hardly a major engagement, this encounter is sometimes called the first battle of the Civil War.

Rich Mountain (July 11). Some 5,000 Confederates under Brig. Gen. Robert S. Garnett were posted throughout northwestern Virginia to oppose the almost 20,000 federals under McClellan. Garnett held almost half his force at Laurel Hill, with two regiments under Lt. Col. John Pegram at Rich Mountain. After his victory at Philippi, McClellan moved on both, Pegram's position being surrounded by three brigades under Brig. Gen. William S. Rosecrans. Pegram retreated to Laurel Hill, then to Beverly, where he surrendered to McClellan. Garnett was killed on July 13 while supervising the retreat of the remainder of the Confederate force across the Cheat River at Carrick's Ford.

Cheat Mountain (September 11–13). To regain its lost territory, the Confederate War Department appointed Gen. Robert E. Lee to command the forces in western Virginia. His first major offensive action was an advance on the key federal position at Cheat Mountain, a position that guarded several mountain passes. Inclement weather and rugged terrain contributed to Lee's defeat, which, in turn, resulted in Pres. Jefferson Davis's reassigning Lee to the defenses of Charleston, South Carolina.

Greenbriar River (October 3). Heavy rains that had so stymied Lee's attempt at Cheat Mountain persisted for two weeks. Brig. Gen. Joseph J. Reynolds, retaining Union control of Cheat Mountain, decided to advance upon the enemy as the rains subsided. With a force of 5,000, he moved off the mountain at midnight on October 2. The next day, he encountered Confederate brigadier general Henry R. Jackson at Camp Bartow on the Greenbriar River. Through the course of the day, federals attacked twice, only to be repulsed both times by Jackson's 1,800 men. Reynolds then retreated back to Cheat Mountain.

The repulse of the federals from Greenbriar River brought to a close an inconclusive but important campaign. Indecision on the battlefield had long-range implications on a national scale. McClellan's early victories brought him to the national limelight, and, on July 27, Pres. Abraham Lincoln moved him to command what would become the Army of the Potomac. Conversely, Lee's defeat in his first combat situation made him the target of much official and popular derision, perhaps shaping some of his tenacity during his command of the Army of Northern Virginia.

The absence of a clear-cut victory in western Virginia in 1861 left fertile ground for that state's "war within a war." Like so many other states whose loyalties were sharply divided, Virginia became fertile ground for irregular warfare, and the bitterness left by the contest for control of western Virginia would not subside when the war reached its conclusion four years later.

Bibliography: Cohen, Stan, *The Civil War in West Virginia: A Pictorial History* (Pictorial Histories, 1982); Hall, Granville D., *Lee's Invasion of Northwest Virginia in 1861* (Mayer & Miller, 1911); Stutler, Boyd B., *West Virginia in the Civil War* (Education Foundation, 1963).

Louise Arnold-Friend

WILDERNESS, BATTLE OF THE (May 5–7, 1864)

A bloody and indecisive Civil War battle between the Union's Army of the Potomac and the Confederacy's Army of Northern Virginia in the forested area south of the Rapidan River (in northern Virginia) known as "the Wilderness." The battle initiated Lt. Gen. Ulysses S. Grant's new strategy for 1864.

Grant's Campaign Strategy. On May 4, 1864, the Army of the Potomac attempted to move quickly through the Wilderness before the Army of Northern Virginia, deployed to the west and commanded by Gen. Robert E. Lee, could respond. Grant and Maj. Gen. George G. Meade, commander of the Army of the Potomac, hoped, by threatening Richmond and the Confederate lines of communication, to force the Confederate army into open battle.

The Army of the Potomac, consisting of the II, V, and VI Corps, along with the independent IX Corps, began crossing the Rapidan on May 4. The supply trains' slow rate of march forced the Union army to bivouac that night in the Wilderness. This delay allowed the Confederates time to approach from the west with two corps: Lt. Gen. Richard S. Ewell's II Corps along Orange Turnpike and Lt. Gen. A. P. Hill's III Corps along the Plank Road. The remaining corps, the I Corps commanded by Lt. Gen. James Longstreet, was farther west and would not arrive until early May 6.

Initial Battles. About noon on May 5, the Union V Corps of Maj. Gen. Gouverneur K. Warren attacked part of Ewell's II Corps on the Orange Turnpike. To the south, along the Orange Plank Road, Maj. Gen. Winfield S. Hancock's II Corps attacked west against Hill's III Corps. The dense forest negated Union superiority in manpower and firepower, allowing the greatly outnumbered Confederates to stop the Union attacks.

Meade resumed the attack early on May 6. Initial Union success against Hill's III Corps on Orange Plank Road ended with the 9:00 A.M. arrival of Longstreet's I Corps in the vicinity of Tapp Farm. Longstreet pushed the disorganized enemy back and, at about 11:00 A.M., attacked Hancock's left flank using an unfinished railroad cut south of the Plank Road. Confederate success turned to confusion after Longstreet was wounded by Confederate soldiers on the Plank Road. Further Confederate attacks later in the afternoon made no substantial gain.

Union attacks in the north along the Orange Turnpike by Maj. Gen. John Sedgwick's VI Corps and Warren's V Corps failed to dislodge Ewell's II Corps. Late-afternoon attacks by a reinforced Confederate brigade against the exposed right flank of VI Corps initially caused some Union panic, but the attack petered out with the onset of darkness. Neither side renewed the attack on May 7, and that evening the Army of the Potomac withdrew and marched southeast, attempting another turning movement, which resulted in battle near Spotsylvania (May 7–20).

Conclusion. The Wilderness was an indecisive engagement. Union superiority in numbers and firepower mattered little in the tangled brush. The Union army suffered about 18,000 casualties, the Confederates about 8,000.

Bibliography: Foote, Shelby, *The Civil War, A Narrative; Vol. 3: Red River to Appomattox* (Random House, 1974); Frassanito, William, *Grant and Lee, the Virginia Campaigns: 1864–1865* (Scribner's, 1983); Grant, Ulysses S., *Personal Memoirs of U. S. Grant* (1894; reprint, Da Capo Press, 1982); Matter, William, *If It Takes All Summer: The Battle of Spotsylvania* (Univ. of North Carolina Press, 1988); Piston, William Garret, *Lee's Tarnished Lieutenant: James Longstreet and His Place in Southern History* (Univ. of Georgia, 1987); Scott, Robert Garth, *Into the Wilderness with the Army of the Potomac* (Indiana Univ. Press, 1985).

Kevin E. McKedy

WILSON'S CREEK, BATTLE OF (August 10, 1861)

Unsuccessful Union counteroffensive against a Confederate advance into Missouri during the Civil War. In early August 1861, Confederate troops moved into southwest Missouri in the opening stages of a campaign designed to gain control of that state. Union general Nathaniel Lyon determined to drive the rebels out of the state and marched against the Confederate forces encamped at Wilson's Creek, southwest of Springfield. Although heavily outnumbered, Lyon split his command in the hope of hitting the Confederate front and rear simultaneously. While the Union troops were initially successful, Confederate counterattacks routed the Union force in its rear and pushed Lyon's main body back to a small hill. There the Union troops repulsed four Confederate charges before both sides, heavily bloodied in the seven-hour battle, withdrew. The Union troops then moved north, leaving southwest Missouri to the rebels.

Bibliography: Monaghan, Jay, *Civil War on the Western Border, 1854–1865* (Little, Brown, 1955).

Richard F. Kehrberg

YELLOW TAVERN, BATTLE OF (May 11, 1864)

Civil War battle sparked by Gen. Philip H. Sheridan's Richmond raid. During the Virginia operations of 1864, while the Battle of the Wilderness was in progress, Gen. Ulysses S. Grant gave Sheridan permission to conduct a cavalry raid around the Confederate army. When Sheridan advanced toward Richmond, Virginia, the Confederate cavalry, led by Gen. Jeb Stuart, pursued to stop them. The two forces met on May 11 at Yellow Tavern (directly north of Richmond), where Stuart had established a blocking position. The Confederates were defeated in a fierce and closely fought battle in which Stuart, the famed "Cavalier of Dixie," was mortally wounded. The battle gave the Confederates more time to strengthen Richmond's defenses.

Robert H. Berlin

Bibliography

1. The Organization of Military Forces: 1815–1865

Armed Forces Information School, *The Army Almanac* (U.S. Govt. Printing Office, 1950).
Coletta, Paolo E., *The American Naval Heritage in Brief* (Univ. Press of America, 1978).
Department of the Army, *The Army* (1978).
———, *Army Heritage,* pamphlet 355–27 (1963).
Dupuy, R. Ernest, *The Compact History of the United States Army,* rev. ed. (Hawthorn Books, 1961).
Faust, Patricia L., ed., *Historical Times Illustrated Encyclopedia of the Civil War* (Harper & Row, 1986).
Goldich, Robert L., "Historical Continuity in the U.S. Military Reserve System," *Armed Forces and Society* (fall 1980).
Matloff, Maurice, ed., *American Military History* (Office of the Chief of Military History, U.S. Army, 1969).
Military History Team, Department of Unified and Combined Operations, U.S. Army Command and General Staff College, *Evolution of the Division Span of Control, Equipment, and Tactical Doctrine,* chart: fig. 1 (1978).
Millett, Allan R., *Semper Fidelis: The History of the United States Marine Corps* (Macmillan, 1980).
Moore, Jamie W., "Evolution of U.S. Coastal Fortifications," 8 pages of tables (1982 annual meeting of the Amer. Military Inst.).
Parker, William D., *A Concise History of the United States Marine Corps, 1775–1969* (Historical Div., U.S. Marine Corps Hdqrs., 1970).
Paullin, Charles Oscar, *Paullin's History of Naval Administration, 1775–1911* (Naval Inst. Press, 1968).
Weigley, Russell F., *The American Way of War: A History of United States Military Strategy and Policy* (Macmillan, 1973).
———, *History of the United States Army* (Macmillan, 1967).
Williams, T. Harry, *The History of American Wars: From 1745–1918* (Knopf, 1981).

2. National Consolidation: 1815–1835

Beers, Henry P., *The Western Military Frontier, 1815–1846* (Univ. of Pennsylvania Press, 1935).
Bernardo, C. Joseph, and Eugene H. Bacon, *American Military Policy: Its Development Since 1775* (Stackpole Co., 1957).
Chapelle, Howard I., *The History of the American Sailing Navy: The Ships and Their Development* (Bonanza, 1949).
Clarke, Dwight L., *Stephen Watts Kearny: Soldier of the West* (Univ. of Oklahoma Press, 1961).
Goetzmann, William H., *Army Exploration in the American West* (Yale Univ. Press, 1959).
Hill, Forest C., *Roads, Rails and Waterways: The Army Engineers and Early Transportation* (Univ. of Oklahoma Press, 1957).
Mahon, John K., *History of the Second Seminole War* (Univ. of Florida Press, 1967).
Millett, Allan R., and Peter Maslowski, *For the Common Defense: A Military History of the United States of America* (Free Press, 1984).

Morrison, James L., *"The Best School in the World": West Point, the Pre–Civil War Years, 1833–1866* (Kent State Univ. Press, 1986).
Nevins, Allan, *Frémont: Pathmaker of the West* (Appleton-Century, 1939).
Oliva, Leo, *Soldiers on the Santa Fe Trail* (Univ. of Oklahoma Press, 1967).
Prucha, Francis P., *Broadax and Bayonet: The Role of the United States Army in the Development of the Northwest, 1815–1860* (State Hist. Soc. of Wisconsin, 1953).
———, *The Sword of the Republic: The United States Army on the Frontier, 1783–1846* (Macmillan, 1969).
Weigley, Russell F., *History of the United States Army* (Macmillan, 1967).
Wesley, Edgar B., *Guarding the Frontier: A Study of Frontier Defense from 1815–1825* (Univ. of Minnesota Press, 1935).
Wood, R. G., *Stephen Harriman Long, 1784–1864* (Arthur H. Clark, 1966).

3. Expansion and Reform: 1815–1846

Beers, Henry P., *The Western Military Frontier, 1815–1846* (Univ. of Pennsylvania Press, 1935).
Bernardo, C. Joseph, and Eugene H. Bacon, *American Military Policy: Its Development Since 1775* (Stackpole Co., 1957).
Chapelle, Howard I., *The History of the American Sailing Navy: The Ships and Their Development* (Bonanza, 1949).
Clarke, Dwight L., *Stephen Watts Kearny: Soldier of the West* (Univ. of Oklahoma Press, 1961).
Coffman, Edward M., *The Old Army: A Portrait of the American Army in Peacetime, 1784–1898* (Oxford Univ. Press, 1986).
Cunliffe, Marcus, *Soldiers and Civilians: The Martial Spirit in America 1775–1865* (Little, Brown, 1968).
Goetzmann, William H., *Army Exploration in the American West* (Yale Univ. Press, 1959).
Hagan, Kenneth J., *This People's Navy: The Making of American Sea Power* (Free Press, 1991).
Hill, Forest C., *Roads, Rails and Waterways: The Army Engineers and Early Transportation* (Univ. of Oklahoma Press, 1957).
Langley, Harold D., *Social Reform in the United States Navy, 1798–1862* (Univ. of Illinois Press, 1967).
Millett, Allan R., and Peter Maslowski, *For the Common Defense: A Military History of the United States of America* (Free Press, 1984).
Morrison, James L., *"The Best School in the World": West Point, the Pre–Civil War Years, 1833–1866* (Kent State Univ. Press, 1986).
Nevins, Allan, *Frémont: Pathmaker of the West* (Appleton-Century, 1939).
Oliva, Leo, *Soldiers on the Santa Fe Trail* (Univ. of Oklahoma Press, 1967).
Prucha, Francis P., *Broadax and Bayonet: The Role of the United States Army in the Development of the Northwest, 1815–1860* (State Hist. Soc. of Wisconsin, 1953).
———, *The Sword of the Republic: The United States Army on the Frontier, 1783–1846* (Macmillan, 1969).
Sprout, Harold, and Margaret Sprout, *The Rise of American Naval Power, 1776–1918* (Princeton Univ. Press, 1967).
Weigley, Russell F., *History of the United States Army* (Macmillan, 1967).
Wood, R. G., *Stephen Harriman Long, 1784–1864* (Arthur H. Clark, 1966).

4. The Mexican War: 1846–1848

Bauer, K. Jack, *The Mexican War, 1846–1848* (Macmillan, 1974).
———, *Surfboats and Horse Marines: U.S. Naval Operations in the Mexican War* (Naval Inst. Press, 1969).
Clarke, Dwight L., *Stephen Watts Kearny: Soldier of the West* (Univ. of Oklahoma Press, 1961).
Cunliffe, Marcus, *Soldiers and Civilians: The Martial Spirit in America 1775–1865* (Little, Brown, 1968).
Dyer, Brainerd, *Zachary Taylor* (Louisiana State Univ. Press, 1946).
Elliott, Charles Wilson, *Winfield Scott, The Soldier and the Man* (Macmillan, 1937).
Hamilton, Holman, *Zachary Taylor, Soldier of the Republic* (Bobbs-Merrill, 1941).
Heinl, Robert Debs, Jr., *Soldiers of the Sea: The United States Marine Corps, 1775–1962* (Naval Inst. Press, 1962).
Henry, Robert Selph, *The Story of the Mexican War* (Bobbs-Merrill, 1950).
Kreidberg, Marvin A., and Merton G. Henry, *History of Military Mobilization in the United States Army, 1775–1945* (Department of the Army, 1955).
Morison, Samuel Eliot, *"Old Bruin" Commodore Matthew Calbraith Perry* (Little, Brown, 1967).

Nevins, Allan, *Frémont: Pathmaker of the West* (Appleton-Century, 1939).
Prucha, Francis P., *The Sword of the Republic: The United States Army on the Frontier, 1783–1846* (Macmillan, 1969).
Singletary, Otis A., *The Mexican War* (Univ. of Chicago Press, 1960).
Sprout, Harold, and Margaret Sprout, *The Rise of American Naval Power, 1776–1918* (Princeton Univ. Press, 1967).
Weigley, Russell F., *History of the United States Army* (Macmillan, 1967).

5. From the Mexican War to the Civil War: 1848–1861

Battles and Leaders of the Civil War, vol. 1 (Century, 1884–87).
Billington, Ray A., *Westward Expansion,* 3d ed. (Macmillan, 1967).
Carley, Kenneth, *The Sioux Uprising of 1862,* rev. ed. (Minnesota Hist. Soc., 1976).
Donald, David H., *Charles Sumner and the Coming of the Civil War* (Knopf, 1960).
Eaton, Clement, *Henry Clay and the Art of American Politics* (Little, Brown, 1957).
Franklin, John H., *From Slavery to Freedom,* 4th ed. (Knopf, 1974).
Huston, James, L., *The Panic of 1857 and the Coming of the Civil War* (Louisiana State Univ. Press, 1982).
McPherson, James, *Ordeal by Fire; Vol. 1: The Coming of War* (Knopf, 1982).
Nevins, Allan, *The Emergence of Lincoln* (Scribner's, 1950).
Peters, Joseph P., compiled by, *Indian Battles and Skirmishes on the American Frontier 1790–1898* (Ayer Company, 1966).
Potter, David M., *The South and the Sectional Conflict* (Louisiana State Univ. Press, 1968).
Wellman, Paul I., *Death in the Desert: The Fifty Years' War for the Great Southwest* (Univ. of Nebraska Press, 1987).
———, *Death on the Prairie: The Thirty Years' Struggle for the Western Plains* (Univ. of Nebraska Press, 1987).

6. & 7. The Civil War: 1862–1865

Battles and Leaders of the Civil War, 4 vols. (Century, 1884–88).
Boatner, Mark M., III, *The Civil War Dictionary,* rev. ed. (Random House, 1988).
Catton, Bruce, *A Stillness at Appomattox* (Doubleday, 1953).
———, *This Hallowed Ground: The Story of the Union Side of the Civil War* (Doubleday, 1956).
Commanger, Henry Steele, ed., *The Blue and the Gray: The Story of the Civil War as Told by Participants,* 2 vols. (Bobbs-Merrill, 1950).
Donald, David, *Lincoln Reconsidered* (Knopf, 1947).
———, ed., *Why the North Won the Civil War* (Macmillan, 1962).
Foner, Eric, and Olivia Mahoney, *A House Divided: America in the Age of Lincoln* (Norton, 1990).
Foote, Shelby, *The Civil War: A Narrative,* 3 vols. (Random House, 1986).
Hagerman, Edward, *The American Civil War and the Origins of Modern Warfare: Ideas, Organization, and Field Command* (Indiana Univ. Press, 1988).
Hattaway, Herman, *How the North Won: A Military History of the Civil War* (Univ. of Illinois Press, 1983).
Josephy, Alvin M., Jr., *The Civil War in the American West* (Knopf, 1992).
Leckie, Robert, *None Died in Vain: The Saga of the American Civil War* (HarperCollins, 1990).
McFeely, William S., *Grant: A Biography* (Norton, 1981).
McPherson, James, *Battle Cry of Freedom: The Era of the Civil War* (Oxford Univ. Press, 1988).
———, *Ordeal by Fire,* 3 vols. (Knopf, 1982).
McWhitney, Grady, *Attack and Die, Civil War Military Tactics* (Univ. of Alabama Press, 1982).
Nevins, Allan, *The War for the Union,* 4 vols. (Scribner's, 1971).
Randall, James J., and David H. Donald, *The Civil War and Reconstruction,* 2d ed. (Heath, 1969).
Roland, Charles P., *The Confederacy* (Univ. of Chicago Press, 1960).
Smith, Page, *Trial by Fire: A People's History of the Civil War and Reconstruction,* vol. 5 (McGraw-Hill, 1982).
Stampp, Kenneth M., *The Peculiar Institution* (Knopf, 1958).
Symonds, Craig L., *A Battlefield Atlas of the Civil War* (Nautical and Aviation, 1983).
Ward, Geoffrey C., et al, *The Civil War: An Illustrated History* (Knopf, 1990).
Williams, T. Harry, *Lincoln and His Generals* (Knopf, 1952).

Index

Bold face numbers indicate main essays; italic numbers indicate illustrations.

G

H

T

U

V

W

Y

Z